The initial surprise assault that so nearly broke through to the river Meuse, the unexpectedly stiff and gallant assistance of the untried troops manning the American front line, the siege of the key town of Bastogne, the part played by the British under Field-Marshal Montgomery in stabilizing the front—these and other aspects of one of the bloodiest battles of World War II are garnished by the author with many descriptions of acts of individual heroism and many errors of judgment.

Logistics were against Hitler—he could never have reached his objective, the port of Antwerp. The German tanks ran out of gas, and Hitler hopelessly underestimated the resolution of the Allies. Paradoxically all he ensured was that the Russians should get to Berlin first.

Also by Peter Elstob

BASTOGNE: The Road Block
BATTLE OF THE REICHSWALD

Published by Ballantine Books

HITLER'S LAST OFFENSIVE

The Full Story of the Battle of the Ardennes

Peter Elstob

BALLANTINE BOOKS • NEW YORK

Library of Congress Catalog Card Number: 71-134879

SBN 345-03259-4-165

This edition published by arrangement with
The Macmillan Company

First Printing: December, 1973

Printed in the United States of America

Cover photo: courtesy of Authenticated News

BALLANTINE BOOKS, INC.
201 East 50th Street, New York, N.Y. 10022

To
BARRIE PITT

CONTENTS

Part Three

THE RÔLES ARE REVERSED

DIAGRAMS AND MAPS

The courage of your enemy honours you.
Sun Tzu, *The Chinese Book of War*, 500 BC

FOREWORD

The objective historian sets out to 'tell it as it was'. It is a simple, straightforward aim and yet impossible to achieve for no man knew the whole truth. The memory of eye-witnesses is fallible and increasingly selective and dusty records bear about the same relation to reality that our pinned and labelled butterfly does to the darting bit of beauty that flashed across our vision on a summer's afternoon.

If all history falls short of the ideal the history of war is particularly suspect for its necessarily imperfect sources are further sullied by suppressions, distortions and downright lies. Some of the motives for this assault on truth are even to be admired: patriotism, loyalty to comrades in arms, respect for the dead, an unwillingness to hurt the living and the need to justify acts committed in the fears and passion of battle. Other motives though less admirable are still wholly understandable; the temptation to be wise after the event, the settling of old scores, the desire of professional soldiers to demonstrate their competence or to find excuses for their failures or to lessen the victories of their enemies or simply to embellish the record of a particular formation.

The military historian's raw material is this mass of evidence much of which is contradictory and almost all of which falls short of the objective truth in some degree. If he happened to have taken part himself, as is often the case, he is soon compelled to distrust his own recollections. Even his diaries and contemporary letters are often found to be mistaken because of the limitations of any single viewpoint on so complex a picture as a great battle.

He has to pick his way with care through conflicting accounts guided by certain general rules and by a slowly developed instinct which leads him to give more weight to one, less to another and to distrust a third completely. He must always keep in mind that particularly in modern mobile warfare the comparatively few men actively engaged in trying to kill one another knew one kind of truth while the men who were directing them knew another and the higher up the command structure he goes the greater the difference between these truths becomes.

He must strictly separate moral judgment from military assessment and he must keep a keen ear for the sound of axes being ground. He must avoid the trap set by generals in their

13

memoirs which suggests that their battle was fought to a master plan, rather as an orchestra performs a symphony with every player coming in at the exact moment, the whole always under the unwavering control of the great conductor.

Finally he must set it down exactly as he has come to believe it happened, not faltering if he has been led to unpopular conclusions or to destroy fiercely-believed myths. He will have offended many and even outraged some for old men do not know they forget and myths die hard. Although he will not have succeeded in telling the truth, the whole truth and nothing but the truth he will have to be content with coming as near that unattainable ideal as he is able.

The outcome of the great German gamble of December 1944 was decided in the first three days. After that it was not a question of whether it would succeed, only of the extent of its failure. But it is precisely the happenings of this critical period about which least is known for in the confused fighting many American records were destroyed while the final complete collapse of Germany, some four months later, resulted in most of their records, particularly at divisional level and below, being scattered and destroyed.

For this reason most of the accounts of the Ardennes Offensive, or the Battle of the Bulge as it is popularly called, begin in detail with the third or fourth day when the front had more or less been stabilized, plans were made for dealing with the breakthrough and from when records are fairly complete. It is said or implied that the Americans holding the front line positions were quickly overwhelmed and for the first two or three days the Germans, with the sole exception of the St Vith sector, were allowed to advance almost unhindered.

Had this been the case the German offensive would have accomplished a great deal more than it did. That the panzer columns did not even reach the Meuse was due to many things not the least of which was the stout resistance of some of the forward American units which seriously upset the German time-table. Many of these units were practically destroyed and it has been most difficult to reconstruct what happened but a careful reading of After Action Reports, Unit Journals, Signal Logs, conversations with civilians who were in the areas, interviews with soldiers on both sides and examinations of the actual ground has made it possible, I think, to reconstruct much of what happened in the beautiful country between Monschau and Echternach when Adolf Hitler flung a mighty force of infantry and armour against the lightest-held sector of the Allied line in a last, desperate attempt to avoid complete

14

disaster.

It is a story of courage and cowardice, or self-sacrifice and self-interest, of command at its best and command at its worst, of great luck and great misfortune and all these things, old soldiers will not be surprised to learn, were about evenly divided between the two sides.

Many people have helped me during the four years it has taken to gather the information and to write this account: American and German commanders, front-line soldiers of all ranks and both sides, civilians in whose villages and farms so much of the fighting took place, members of the resistance, researchers, fellow-historians and librarians. Almost without exception they have given me their time and have often supplied bits of information which enabled me to fit in missing pieces of the puzzle. I have been taken along back roads and forest tracks, past stumps of trees felled to slow down the armour, past the rusting hulks of panzers to the site of the last stand of a small group of American or German soldiers who bought valuable time for their comrades. In some cases I was able to confirm the information from my own experience. One famous resistance leader for instance took me to the exact location of my own tank north of Foy Notre Dame, the point of furthest German penetration. Away from the battlefield I have been shown documents, diaries, letters and interviews in the records held in Germany, Belgium, England and the United States. To all these people I owe a great deal but the list runs into hundreds and I cannot name them all—some indeed have asked that I do not.

Among the soldiers I should like to thank: Major-General R. H. Barry, Brigadier A. W. Brown, Major-General N. W. Duncan, the late Captain Sir Basil Liddell Hart, Brigadier-General C. B. C. Harvey, Lt-General Sir Brian Horrocks, Major-General Sir Francis de Guingand, and Major-General G. P. B. Roberts.

In Belgium I was given much assistance at l'Ecole Royale Militaire and I should like to thank Professor Henri Bernard, Professor Jean-Léon Charles and M. Bargibant. Baron Jacques de Villenfagne de Sorinne took me over a portion of the battlefield and was able to point out every German position from maps made at the time. M. Maurice Delaval of Vielsalm allowed me free access to his extensive collection of original material on the battle both published and unpublished and including letters from many of the commanders who have since died.

In the United States both at the Office of the Chief of Military History in Washington and at the Office of Military Archives in Alexandria, Virginia, I was accorded every facility to examine and have microfilmed almost any document I required from the comprehensive American files or the captured German records. Practically every phase and aspect of the Ardennes Offensive has been the subject of detailed study and among the most useful of the unpublished material are those of Magna E. Bauer, Charles V. P. von Luttichau, Royce L. Thompson and Major Percy E. Schramm. For help in finding my way around the massive archives at Fort McNair and for their patience in answering my questions I would like to thank Colonel Raymond C. Ball, Lt-Colonel E. B. Scovill, John W. Wike and Hannah M. Zeidlik. At the National Archives in Alexandria I was helped by Mr Avery, Mr Finch, Mr Holman and Mr Nye. Lt-Colonel Robert Webb of the Office of the Assistant Secretary of Defence allowed me to examine many photographs taken at the time and Colonel John Eisenhower, who was researching his book, *The Bitter Woods*, at the Office of the Chief of Military History at the same time as I was there could not have been more generous in pointing out material to me and generally smoothing my passage in official circles.

I was particularly anxious for German participation in the battle to be described as completely and as objectively as possible. Even at that late stage of the war and after gigantic losses most German soldiers fought with skill and courage, maintaining a high standard of soldierly conduct. The excesses and atrocities of the SS were condemned at the time by the majority of the front-line Wehrmacht.

I have talked with many Germans who took part in the battle from privates to generals and have read the interrogations, interviews and reports of many more. Information given by the following has been of the greatest help in understanding the German side: Lt-General Fritz Bayerlein, General Erich Brandenberger, Major Herbert Buechs, Major-General Hugo Dempwolff, Major-General Walter Denkert, General Sepp Dietrich, Lt-General Gerhard Engel, Major-General Rudolf von Gersdorf, General Paul Hauser, Major-General Ludwig Heilmann, Baron Friedrich von der Heydte, General Otto Hitzfeld, General Alfred Jodl, Major-General Erwin Kaschner, General Baptist Kneiss, Major-General Heinz Kokott, Major-General Fritz Kraemer, Colonel Meinrad von Lauchert, Major-General Rudolf Langhaeuser, General Walter Lucht, General Heinrich von Luettwitz, General Hasso von Manteuffel, Colonel Wolfgang Maucke, Lt-Colonel Jochen Peiper, Lt-General Hermann Priess, Major-General Helmuth Reinhardt, Colonel Otto Remer, Rittmeister Dr Wilhelm Scheidt, Lt-General Franz

Sensfuss, Major-General Siegrfried von Waldenburg and General Walter Warlimont.

I should like to thank the staff of the Imperial War Museum, the War Office Library and the U.S. Armored School at Fort Knox for the source material supplied to me. Among others who have given me valuable information are Anthony Brett-James, Constantine FitzGibbon, Blake Nevius, Kenneth Pendar, Arthur Swinson, Professor Hugh Trevor-Roper and Dr Heinz Wolff.

Julian Bach, Barbara Elstob, Cecil Scott, Anthony Sheil and David Farrer read the book in typescript and I have adopted many of their suggestions and have even admitted the justice of some of their criticisms. Finally I should like to thank Mrs D. L. Mackay who typed the whole thing at least twice and Richard Natkiel the cartographer who was able to make such good sense out of my own rough and messy maps.

PART ONE

BACKGROUND AND PREPARATIONS

A swift and vigorous assumption of the offensive—the flashing sword of vengeance—is the most brilliant point in the defensive.

VON CLAUSEWITZ

1

IN HITLER'S DARK FOREST

*The offensive is the straight way to the goal; the
defensive is the long way round.*

VON MOLTKE

By December 1944, just six months after the Normandy landings, the total defeat of Germany seemed inevitable. All her
earlier conquests had been lost and on both Eastern and
Western Fronts foreign troops were on German soil. Casualties were in millions—a million German soldiers had been lost
since D-day in France alone. Her sources of fuels were lost,
her transport system wrecked and her great cities had been
bombed so often that it seemed new explosives only redistri-
buted the rubble. The dragon which had rampaged over
Europe, Africa and the Middle East was surely in its death
throes.

Professional soldiers of both sides dispassionately weighed
all the factors and decided that it only remained for the Allies
to play their cards correctly for 'unconditional surrender' to be
accepted. They were all agreed that there was now nothing
that Germany could do to avoid it.

That is, almost everyone was agreed, but there were excep-
tions; among these were the Prime Minister of Great Britain
and the Supreme Commander of the German Armed Forces—
but then neither of them was a professional soldier.

Thinking globally as always, Winston Churchill saw that if
Hitler behaved logically—by which he meant acting as
Churchill would himself—he would now bring back inside
Germany his considerable forces from Italy, the Balkans and
the Scandinavian countries to form a tight defence in depth,
thus becoming difficult and costly to defeat.

The Prime Minister was very worried and on December 6,
1944, he wrote one of his many letters to President Roosevelt
pointing out some harsh truths about the situation on the
Western Front. He contrasted 'these realities with the rosy
expectations of our peoples' and asked if, as soon as practicable, the American Chiefs of Staff could be sent to Europe to
be close to their main armies and to General Eisenhower and
where 'the whole stormy scene can be calmly and patiently
studied'. President Roosevelt delivered a gentle snub, replying
that broad strategy was proceeding according to plan and re-

minding the Prime Minister that the prosecution and outcome of battles lay with the Field Commanders—in whom he had every confidence. As Churchill had written to Smuts: '... our armies are only about one-half the size of the American and will soon be little more than one-third. It is not so easy as it used to be for me to get things done.'

But the Supreme Commander of the Armed Forces in Germany, Adolf Hitler, had no such troubles. The officers' failure to kill him in the July 20 bomb plot had strengthened his grip on the Army: field marshals and generals had trodden on each other's toes in their eagerness to convince him not only of their loyalty to him personally but of their high regard for the Nazi party and the SS. They had even asked that the Nazi salute replace the military and some generals had requested SS aides-de-camp. Hitler accepted all this without comment, but in August he proclaimed that the sole responsibility of all commanders, even the most senior, was simply to carry out his orders unconditionally and to the letter. So, if he had reasoned as Churchill guessed, he could have saved most of his armour, got out of France and withdrawn behind the Siegfried Line in August 1944.

Instead, modelling himself on Frederick the Great, who when faced with a similar situation had boldly attacked superior forces and caused the alliance against him to split, Hitler gave orders as early as August 19: 'Prepare to take the offensive in November when the enemy air force can not operate. Some twenty-five divisions must be moved to the Western Front in the next one to two months.'

This apparently unreal order was given on the actual day that almost all the German armour in the west was destroyed in the Falaise pocket and only a few days after the Commander-in-Chief West, Field Marshal von Kluge, had committed suicide. Furthermore the Allies had landed in strength on the Mediterranean shore of France four days before and it was already apparent that there was no chance of containing them. By November, Hitler's amazed generals thought, there was unlikely to be any Western Front from which to launch a counter-attack. But no one dared to voice these opinions to the Führer himself.

This bold decision was taken, like so many others, in the underground bunker, in an East Prussian forest, known as the 'Wolfsschanze'*—the Wolf's Lair. The name had been chosen

---

* Literally 'Fort Wolf' but usually, in English, called 'The Wolf's Lair'. 'Wolf' was Hitler's undercover name in the years before he got power.

by Hitler himself in 1941 when HQ Area No 1 was set up there to direct the invasion of Russia.

Apparently in those far-off days of heady success it had been quite a cheerful place with built-in cupboards, electrical gadgets galore and the harsh concrete walls covered by brightly coloured panels. Hitler's own hut, with all windows facing north because he disliked the sun, was off in a corner apart from the others.

Here in the middle of the forest of Gorlitz, where the trees grew so closely together it was rare for the sun to penetrate at all, Hitler spent most of the war. Inside HQ Area 1 was Security Zone 1 where he and his closest associates lived. Permanent passes to enter this zone were not given even to the most trusted members of the General Staff. All approaches to HQ Area No 1 were closely guarded with barbed wire, and electric fencing totally enclosed it. Except for a daily short stroll near his quarters with his Alsatian bitch Blondi, Hitler hardly ever left his rooms. As one of his generals has said, 'He was in a little corner sheltered from the blast; neither he nor his immediate entourage got any direct impression either of the severity of the struggle on the main fronts on one hand or of the blazing effects of the air war on German cities on the other.'*

In 1944, as soon as it had become obvious that a cross-Channel invasion was coming, Field Headquarters had moved from East Prussia to Berchtesgaden, but within a month of the Normandy landings Hitler moved back to his dark forest. In the interval it had been completely transformed. The wooden huts and bunkers above ground had been replaced by enormous concrete forts and bomb-proof underground steel-and-concrete shelters with walls twenty feet thick. Hitler had a suite of three rooms but now the atmosphere was Spartan—the concrete walls were left undecorated and the furniture was of the simplest wooden kind. 'A mixture of cloister and concentration camp.'† A rigid régime built round the Führer's pattern of life now prevailed. He seldom went to bed before five or six in the morning or rose before eleven. He breakfasted late, alone, and saw first his Chief of Operations Staff, General Jodl, who had ready for him a briefing of the situation on all fronts. Field Commanders' reports had to be at FHO early every morning. Hitler would, in almost all cases, make his daily tactical decisions at this time.

Later, about one o'clock, the daily 'Führer Conference'

* General Warlimont, *Inside Hitler's Headquarters*, p. 177.
† General Jodl at his Nuremberg trial.

would begin at which certain officers were always present: Field Marshal Keitel, the Chief of the High Command of the Armed Forces (OKH), Colonel-General Jodl, Chief of Operations Staff (OKW), and his deputy General Warlimont. These titles sounded more powerful than they were—particularly in the last year of the war. Hitler had by then gathered the strings into his hands—all other commanders were puppets.

As well as President, Chancellor and Führer, Hitler was Minister of War, Supreme Commander of all the Armed Forces and Commander-in-Chief of the Army. Goering was Commander-in-Chief of the Air Force and Dönitz of the Navy, but as Supreme Commander Hitler also completely controlled them.

The nominal Chief of the High Command, Field Marshal Keitel, seems to have been a poor creature, hated and ridiculed by his fellow generals and held in contempt by Hitler himself who had chosen him for high office because he could utterly dominate him. Keitel had been recommended to Hitler by von Blomberg, a former War Minister, who had said no more than that Keitel would make a good 'chef de bureau'. He was a loyal Nazi—indeed loyalty to Hitler would appear to be his only virtue—who never once questioned any of his Führer's orders or decisions. In return Hitler despised him, treating him at times little better than a lackey (Berliners called him 'Lackaitel') and saying of him once, when it was suggested he be sent for and his advice on a military matter asked, that the opinion of a man with the brains of a cinema attendant wouldn't be of much use. Keitel was under no illusions about Hitler's regard for him: when asked how matters stood between the High Command and Hitler he replied, 'I don't know; the Führer tells me nothing—he only spits at me.'

As head of the Armed Forces Field Marshal Keitel gave orders to generals in the field but they knew that not only did these come from Hitler but that Keitel's advice was never sought nor did he ever dare to criticize anything, confining himself to crude flattery and unquestionable acquiescence—another of his nicknames was 'Knick-Keitel' because of his habit of continually nodding agreement while Hitler was talking—and they much resented his authority. He did not belong to one of the traditional Prussian military families and had been made Chief of Staff when his son married the Minister of War's daughter; his battle experience in World War I had been slight and he had never commanded a large formation: he tried his best to look and behave like a traditional Junker General but he deceived no one. In less terrible circumstances than the centre of a holocaust he might have been a comic figure; instead, by cravenly eschewing his responsibility to the soldiers whose lives Hitler was throwing away, by stifling his conscience and hearkening only to the voice of ambition, he brought about his own tragic end. He was to see his Führer commit suicide amid the ruins of his capital; he was to sign the unconditional surrender; he was to stand in the dock and hear his crimes publicly declared and he was to end his shabby life on the gallows.

The other man close to Hitler—probably closer than anyone else—was Keitel's Chief of Operations Staff, Colonel-General Jodl. He was a much abler man than his chief and Hitler, alone with him at the pre-Conference briefings, occasionally discussed alternative decisions. He was, nevertheless, unable to stop Hitler from giving completely unsound orders and bore as great a responsibility as Keitel for not putting his views forcefully. On the other hand it is only fair to point out that open opposition to Hitler always resulted in the dismissal of the officer concerned—no matter who he was.

Jodl also did not come from the traditional military caste whom Hitler disliked and distrusted. He was from a family of Munich intellectuals and was undoubtedly the first intelligence in the High Command. He allowed the almost unlimited prospects for him personally which would follow in a German victory to keep his eyes from the more terrible acts of the régime, and he too finished his life on the gallows at Nuremberg.

The third and most junior of Hitler's close associates was a completely different type. General Walter Warlimont, a handsome, polished Rhinelander, had brought himself to the notice of Hitler when in 1937, as a forty-three-year-old Colonel in the War Ministry, he had submitted, unknown to his superiors, a plan for a High Command under one Supreme Commmander. Up until this reorganization it had always been assumed that overall direction in war would come from the High Command of the Army (OKH) who would give orders to the Navy and the Air Force. Now a High Command of the Armed Forces (OKW) was set up which would control all three forces as well as the police and civilian authorities. The Führer liked the idea, put it into operation and, of course, himself became Supreme Commander. General Jodl was made Chief of Operations Staff and Warlimont became his Deputy and a general. He was present at almost all the great decisions, the attacks on Poland, on France and on Russia, and he undoubtedly believed in Hitler's military genius—at least until the last year when almost no one but Hitler himself still did so. He was in the hut at the Wolfsschanze when the bomb intended to kill Hitler went off and his health had deteriorated as a result of its effects. A few months later the doctors decided that he was no longer fit for the long hours and hard work at Führer Headquarters and he was invalided out. He had served Hitler devotedly for five years and went to bid farewell with considerable emotion: all the Führer said was, 'Go and lie down for a bit.' But the result of Warlimont's not having any more to do with the direction of the war may well have saved his life for he was not tried until four and a half years after the end of the war, and then as a 'minor' war criminal. He was sentenced to life imprisonment but this was later commuted to eighteen years and he was in fact released in 1958.

It was to Keitel, Jodl and Warlimont as well as his Chief of Staff, General Buhle, and his Minister of Armaments and War Production, Albert Speer, that Hitler first spoke of his great idea for an offensive in the autumn: 'Main point: some twenty-five divisions must be moved to the West in the next one to two months.'

But how? Where, in the autumn of 1944, after gigantic losses on both fronts, could twenty-five divisions be found? And, if the men were somehow found, where would their arms and equipment come from? Of the 2,300 assault guns and tanks that had been in Normandy only some 130 had got back over the Seine and vast quantities of transport, ammunition and supplies had been abandoned. The armies on the Eastern Front had lost hundreds of thousands of men and thousands of tons of equipment. Both fronts were demanding more men, more guns, more ammunition, more tanks. Hitler's generals told him it would be a miracle if the Army could replace half its losses; to create a new army was an impossibility. But Hitler reminded them that they had told him that many times before, and once more he would show them how to achieve the 'impossible'.

Within a few days of deciding on a new, great offensive he sent for Dr Goebbels and gave him complete authority to take any action which would increase war production and release men for the Army.

Goebbels had been wanting these powers for a long time—'It takes a bomb under his backside to make the Führer see reason,' he commented. In the ten weeks since the invasion, events had moved very fast. Germany had not yet been put on a total war-footing and non-essential activities were still allowed: Goebbels went back to Berlin and produced an order which put a stop to all that. All theatres, music halls, cabaret shows and other entertainments were shut down; schools of music, acting, art and even trade schools of no direct importance to the war effort were closed. These students and those at the universities studying subjects unrelated to the war were directed into the armaments industry. All publishing except of scientific and technical subjects was stopped. A minimum sixty-hour work week came into effect: all holidays were cancelled. Suddenly the German people were faced with total war.

To replace some of the million men lost in France Hitler made Himmler—already head of the SS and national Chief of Police—Commander-in-Chief of the Home Army. He was ordered immediately to raise and train twenty-five new infantry divisions to be known as Volksgrenadiers (People's Infantry). Goebbels lowered the call-up age to sixteen and a drastic reshuffling of jobs took place. Every man who could be taught to fight was needed in the line and his job, if essential to the war, was taken over by someone less fit. This meant bringing in the very young, the old, the sick and the crippled in order to squeeze out every man able to fire a gun.

To fill gaps in the fighting line the young men who had been chosen as potential pilots, air gunners and other aircrew were taken away from the Luftwaffe and sent to the Army. Although completely untrained as infantry they were later to fight with great courage and zeal. They were the pick of Germany's youth. The German Navy too was forced to acknowledge that it no longer had a rôle of its own and had to provide manpower for the new divisions.

No one escaped the great scraping of the manpower barrel: non-essential workers, small shopkeepers, the police, postal officials, teachers, men from the Air Raid Precautions services and even those officials in the Civil Service who had up until now been able to convince the authorities that they were absolutely indispensable, were all sucked into the great maw.

From the prisons came convicts formed into penal battalions and offered a chance to regain their civil rights on the battlefield. Even men who had so far escaped military service because of severe stomach complaints were called up and formed into units equipped to supply them with their special diets. They were known as the Magen (stomach) Battalions and there were also the Ohren (ear) Battalions made up of men who were either deaf or had one or both ears missing or badly damaged. A deaf soldier, needless to say, is likely to be more of a menace to his fellows than to the enemy for, in the dark, he is apt to fire first and find out who went there later.

After the collapse of the German Army in France some 300,000 soldiers had avoided capture and made their way back. Many were in small groups in charge of an NCO but otherwise completely cut off from military authority. Hunger, exhaustion and the ceaseless air attacks had lowered their morale; most of them half-hoped that the war would soon be over. The commands of some regiments, knowing that they were not going to get reinforcements sent out officers to stop any German soldier who could not explain where he was going and shanghai him. Those who escaped this were herded into control areas and sent to the new divisions.

By these methods the losses in the west were nearly made up and in only six to eight weeks concentrated training had these men ready to go into the line. By the beginning of November, Hitler had, to the amazement of the generals, succeeded in replacing his lost mobile reserve and also had been able to send eighteen of the twenty-three new Volksgrenadier Divisions to the Rhine.

Albert Speer, one of the most able of the Nazis, squeezed still more out of the factories. Despite the heavy bombing, German production actually increased in August, September, October and November 1944. Light industries, which made munitions, small arms and components for tanks and guns, had been dispersed to small towns or moved to Eastern Germany, and the workers lived in bomb-proof shelters or away from the towns. Many Germans worked longer than the minimum sixty-hour week and foreign workers were driven to the point of exhaustion. The 'pipe-line' of raw materials was used up and production of civilian goods was cut to the irreducible minimum.

The results were spectacular. In September 1944 alone, 3,031 single-engine fighters were produced—an all-time record; in the four critical months nearly a million and a quarter tons of ammunition were manufactured (also a record), while no less than three quarters of a million rifles, one hundred thousand machine-guns, nine thousand mortars and nine thousand heavy artillery pieces came out of Germany's bomb-shattered war industry. But all-important tank production was down and, of those produced, only three-quarters actually got to the Wehrmacht; the rest were destroyed by the Allied Air Force on their way to the Army. The Eighth US Air Force, in a series of highly accurate raids on the Henschel works in Kassel, cut the production rate of Tiger tanks by two-thirds and only just over a hundred were delivered before the great Ardennes counter-attack. But the factories assembling the high-velocity seventy-five millimetre assault guns had earlier been moved to Czechoslovakia and their production shot up—more were produced in the four months than during the whole of 1943.

The High Command of the Wehrmacht naturally expected that most of the new men and war material would be sent to make up the losses in the field. Hitler would not hear of this. Those shattered, depleted units would be sent the minimum reinforcements to enable them to hold: everything else would go to the great offensive which was going to change the war. Thus when the High Command told their Führer that the Army had lost more than twenty-seven thousand machine guns in the month of September alone and asked how many of the same month's production—of almost that number—they could have, the answer was one thousand five hundred. The month's losses in mortars had been about two thousand; the month's production could have replaced these but only three hundred went to the desperately weakened units in the line. The difference, as well as all other weapons and ammunition, were to go to the new divisions.

While every possible man was being hastily trained, the workers driven to exhaustion and the precious reserve of raw materials used up, the war went from disaster to disaster. Within a month almost all of Germany's prizes were snatched from her: the great cities of Florence, Paris, Brussels, Antwerp and Athens fell; former allies of the Nazis—Bulgaria, Roumania, Finland and Hungary—were lost and the occupied countries which had supplied Germany with food and labour were freed of German troops—Greece, Yugoslavia, Poland, France and Belgium.

In a series of brilliantly executed attacks on the Eastern Front the Russians inflicted colossal casualties, killing and wounding many more Germans than they took prisoner. On the Western Front the American armies flooded over France to the very frontiers of Germany and the British and Canadian armies, in one of the longest unbroken advances of the war, swept from the Seine to the Dutch–Belgian frontier. Aachen, one of Germany's oldest cities, and Strasbourg both fell.

During all this time Hitler, in his underground bunker in the dark forest in East Prussia, was in sole complete command of all German forces everywhere. At his daily Führer Conference he would listen to the reports brought by the representatives of field commanders or even by the generals themselves, and make his decision. The officer concerned would leave immediately to see that it was carried out. No discussion was allowed and, no matter how good the reasons, no retreat was to take

28

place. Any general who tried to rescue his men from a hopeless position was instantly relieved of his command and in at least one case, cashiered.

Hitler's amazing memory for detail and ability to summon the most obscure information from the recesses of his mind constantly confounded high-ranking officers used to large-scale thinking. He had a complete set of maps of France—less than half a mile to the inch—which showed every German installation and he studied them daily. On one occasion while going over the routine reports he discovered that there were two less anti-aircraft guns defending the Channel Islands and ordered the officers responsible to be punished. It turned out to be a miscount but the story was told everywhere. From then on no one knew whether the report he was asked to make might not be seen by the Führer himself.

The captured telephone log of the German 7th Army reveals that at times Hitler personally directed the movement of single battalions and the defence of particular villages. In the end he ordered all commanders of anything larger than a brigade to let him know—in time for him to countermand it—about any forward or backward move larger than patrol activity. At that time there were some three hundred German divisions on all fronts. Never in history has any commander exercised such far-reaching control over so many men as this ex-Corporal did in the last months of the war.

This last burst of daemonic activity stemmed from the failure of the bomb plot. Its effects, both physical and psychological, were profound.

Up until the serious fighting in World War II he had enjoyed remarkably good health, suffering no illness of any importance except for a growth on his vocal cords, which was removed, but as soon as the war started to go badly for Germany in 1943 his health began to deteriorate. It started with an uncontrollable trembling, particularly bad on the left side, perhaps due to an injury to the brain following one of his violent hysterical outbursts. He became convinced that his heart was weak although his doctors could find no evidence of it, and he took no exercise beyond a gentle daily stroll. He often complained of severe stomach cramps which his reputable doctors believed to be of psychosomatic origin, although Hitler's favourite medical attendant, Dr Morrell, was a notorious quack who filled Hitler with a variety of drugs including pills containing strychnine and belladonna which, no doubt, were responsible for the rapid deterioration of his health, a deterioration which, in some strange way, the explosion of the bomb in the assassination attempt, seemed to halt.

At the moment when the bomb exploded under the long table around which Hitler and twenty-three other people were standing, he was leaning right across to look at the top left-hand corner of a map of the Eastern Front. This meant that the heavy table screened most of his body, probably saving him from serious injury. The bomb had been put under the far right end of the table and the force of the explosion blew out the top there. Of the seven men standing around that end, four died and two were seriously injured.

The flash set Hitler's clothing and hair alight, tearing off his trousers and burning his right leg. The lath and plaster ceiling came down, bringing with it part of a roof beam which hit Hitler so hard across the buttocks that his backside was, in his own words, 'like a baboon's'. Another bit of flying debris struck him on the arm, causing bleeding under the skin and extensive bruises, but the most serious and lasting damage was to his eardrums. He was always afterwards partially deaf.

But the immediate effects of the shock and of having survived (as he thought miraculously) were a tremendous physical stimulus.

He had his burns dressed, he bathed and had his singed hair trimmed, his right arm bandaged and put in a sling, and dressed in a new uniform drove to the secret railway station of 'Gorlitz' to meet Mussolini. He greeted the Duce warmly and took him back to the ruined hut pointing out the accidental circumstances which had saved his life: the fact that, because the usual concrete bunker was being repaired, the conference had been held in a flimsy hut above ground (for within the deep shelter all would undoubtedly have been killed), the fact that it was a hot day and the windows were open, thus lessening the effects of blast. He was sure that the hand of Providence had saved him and that 'the great destiny which I serve will transcend its present perils and that all will be brought to a triumphant conclusion'.

But his euphoria lasted only for a few hours to be followed by one of those uncontrolled black moods which his closest associates had learned to fear. Later that afternoon when it had become known that the bomb was not an isolated incident but part of a nationwide plot, and someone was unwise enough to mention the terrible Blood Purge of June 30, 1934, the 'Night of the Long Knives', Hitler leapt to his feet and paced the room in a screaming frenzy, foaming at the mouth. Only sheer physical exhaustion finally made him drop into a chair and uncontrolled rage gave way to maudlin self-pity while

Mussolini, Field Marshal Goering, Admiral Dönitz, General Keitel and Foreign Minister Ribbentrop assured him of their loyalty.

From then on he was suspicious of almost everyone—even those who like General Warlimont had been close to him for years—if Rommel could have joined in the plot to kill him then anyone could be suspect.

Now he became convinced that he and only he could save Germany. His military decisions had always been right and those of the generals wrong and now they had lost their nerve. They were not only inept but cowardly and he would have to tell them what to do down to the smallest detail, and he would have to screw up their courage for them. The enemies of the Third Reich might be attacking it both from without and within, but he would hold it together alone and in one great unexpected blow change the whole situation.

Colonel-General Guderian, whose varied career included a spell as acting Chief of Staff, has described Hitler at this time: 'He was convinced that he alone knew what to do. He shut himself up in his bunker, engaged in no further private talks and ordered every word he uttered to be recorded. He lost himself more and more in a world of theories which had no basis in reality.'

But he was not so lost to reality as to believe that Germany could now defeat the combined Russian, American and British forces, remorselessly closing in on Germany. The sheer weight of numbers, a weight which would increase as more divisions crossed the Atlantic and as Frenchmen were armed, made a German victory impossible. But Germany's enemies, Hitler believed, were uneasy bed-partners, disliking and distrusting each other, and his one hope was to exploit these differences. Later he explained some of his thinking to the generals chosen to lead the last great offensive.

'In the whole of world history there has never been a coalition which consisted of such heterogeneous elements with such diametrically opposed objectives,' he told them. 'Ultra-capitalist states on the one hand; ultra-Marxist states on the other. On one side a dying world-empire temporarily supported by one of its ex-colonies anxious to take over the inheritance. The United States is determined to take over Britain's place in the world and the Soviet Union is anxious to get hold of the Balkans, the Dardanelles and Persia. These three states are already at loggerheads with one another and a great victory on the Western Front will bring down this artificial coalition with a crash.'

31

To others in his confidence he revealed more of his political aims. America and Britain would each blame the other if there was a great German victory; Canada was already disillusioned and would withdraw her troops from Europe. When the Western Allies realized that their plans for conquering Germany had been thwarted they would listen to proposals for a separate peace and give up their ridiculous demands for 'unconditional surrender'. Then he would conclude armistice terms with them and quickly switch the bulk of his forces to the Eastern Front. Russia, already weakened by casualties ten times greater than those suffered by the Western Powers, would also be glad to conclude a separate peace.

Germany would, of course, have lost all her gains but the Fatherland would remain intact. It would only be a matter of time before the Allies came to realize that they needed Germany if Europe was to be saved from the 'Asiatic hordes'.

One of Hitler's weaknesses was his complete lack of understanding of the make-up and psychology of both the British and the Americans. He had no conception of, and would not have believed in, the warmth of feeling for the Russian Army and people, that existed in England and the United States at that time. His intelligence reports had kept him fully informed of the criticisms that Patton and Montgomery made of each other, of friction in high places and, because he wanted to believe so, he was sure the Alliance was on the verge of breaking. He knew that the Canadians, who had been given some of the dirtiest, most uncomfortable and hardest fighting (about which very little had been heard) were bitter and angry, but he so misunderstood their actual feelings as to predict that when the great offensive started they would withdraw and go back to Canada.

Differences between the Allies there certainly had been, but there was complete agreement on one thing: the absolute necessity to carry the war into the heart of Germany and to destroy completely her armed forces and ability to make war again. In the British and American commands there had been differing views, strongly expressed, about how best to accomplish this but no one, certainly not Field Marshal Montgomery, had any doubts about who would make the final decision —the Supreme Commander, General Eisenhower.

By launching a great offensive in the west Hitler would be taking the one certain way of stopping the bickering among the Allies and uniting them in defence. Militarily such an offensive could only be mounted at the expense of the Wehrmacht fighting for their lives against superior forces. Either of these factors should have made him pause but he did not believe in the first and chose to ignore the second.

Patiently some of his generals tried to make Hitler realize the real situation but he brushed them aside. The disasters in France, he was now convinced, had been entirely due to his commanders not obeying his orders. He had removed the Commander-in-Chief West, Field Marshal von Rundstedt, but his successor, Field Marshal von Kluge, had begged permission to withdraw to defensive positions and had also been removed from command. To stop the rot in the West and gain time to mount the great offensive Hitler moved some commanders from the Eastern Front who had proved they knew how to fight. The first of these was Field Marshal Walter Model, called by Goebbels' press 'the saviour of the Eastern Front'; Model liked to refer to himself as 'the Führer's fireman'.

He had prevented total defeat three times: first when as commander of Army Group North he had brought the great Russian offensive against the Baltic States to a halt; next when Marshal Zhukov had smashed into Poland, Model had been switched to Army Group South and the situation had again been restored. Finally he had been moved to the command of Army Group Centre and had stopped the offensive against Warsaw. He was a master of improvisation and defensive strategy and if anyone could stabilize the crumbling Western Front, Hitler was sure Field Marshal Model was the man, and he ordered him to fly to Normandy.

Although he owed his meteoric rise to the Führer, Model was one of the very few who ever stood up to him. His method was to act first and ask permission afterwards and because he got results he got away with this. He understood the workings of Hitler's mind as well as anyone and handled him with con-summate skill, always avoiding situations in which the Führer could take up an uncompromising stand, for once he had done so nothing could shift him.

As soon as Model took command of the Western Front he ordered a general retreat without consulting Hitler. But it was very nearly too late, for the Falaise pocket had closed and the large German forces trapped within—'sacked' in the American phrase—were about to be destroyed piece-meal. Model ordered a breakout which cost many more casualties but also allowed thousands of German soldiers, including almost all the senior officers, to escape. Three weeks later the German Army had re-formed and order had been restored.

During this time the Allied front had continued to expand along its entire length. This had so strained the supply services, still denied the Channel ports by German garrisons obeying Hitler's orders to hold out, that no one sector had been made strong enough to deliver a decisive blow. The great Allied offensive virtually came to a halt, giving Hitler just the breathing space he needed to mount his counter-attack. All his military experts had told him that such a halt would never occur and the Allies would not allow him time to regain his balance. Once again they had been proved wrong and he right. There was no reason why the success of 1940 could not be repeated.

The problem of where to counter-attack the Allies occupied a lot of his time. Would it be the junction of the American and British armies by an attack launched from Venlo in Holland almost due west to Antwerp? This would cut the British Second Army and First Canadian Army from the Americans: the low-lying country was criss-crossed with canals and streams, hopeless for tanks and it would be difficult to achieve surprise. Regretfully he discarded this plan as too risky.

The junction of the forces that had come up from the Mediterranean landings, General Patch's United States Seventh Army, with General Patton's Third Army was a second possibility, but this section of the front was too fluid and a successful counter-offensive here could not have a decisive effect on the war for there was no foreseeable strategic objective.

One area in particular had long attracted him. This was the heavily wooded hills of the Ardennes where Luxembourg, Germany and Belgium meet, an historic invasion route through which the German army had triumphantly marched in 1870, 1914 and 1940 and the more he looked at it the more he liked it. The decision was taken: it would be the Ardennes again.

Miraculously it was the weakest part of the whole four hundred and fifty miles of the British–American front. At all costs it must remain so. Allied Intelligence must not be allowed to have the slightest suspicion that the new forces Germany was raising were going to attack through the Ardennes. As it was impossible to conceal the existence of his newly-created mobile reserve, the Sixth SS Panzer Army, it was moved to the logical position from which it could move against the flanks of the expected Allied thrust toward the Ruhr. As this is how his generals would have used the new army had it been left to them, both they and Allied Intelligence were completely deceived.

Hitler had decreed that no one, not even the generals commanding the Army Groups on either side of the Ardennes

34

sector, was to know about the coming offensive except those directly involved and they must sign solemn pledges not to discuss it with anyone and to be prepared to face a court-martial if they did. He knew by now that there was somewhere a serious security leak in the German High Command but he was determined that this time he would achieve complete surprise.

2

THE GERMAN PLAN

> *It must be remembered that the Ardennes Offensive
> was planned in all its details including formations
> involved, time schedules, objectives and so on by the
> Führer.*
>
> FIELD MARSHAL GERD VON RUNDSTEDT

The attack would be made by an entirely new Army Group of
whose very existence the Allies must be kept in ignorance. Its
two panzer armies would smash through the thin defences of
the Ardennes and keep moving north-west, splitting the Allies
apart. It would be a blitzkrieg on the classic pattern of the
invasion of Russia only this time the objective was comparatively near—the Channel coast.

To make certain of success Hitler would plan everything
himself, every detail, and would move his HQ from the dark
forest in East Prussia to the Western Front. From there he
would personally direct every phase of the offensive: he would
show his defeatist generals how wars are won by great decisions boldly carried out.

For the sake of appearances and because it would be good
for the soldiers' morale, the old, but much respected Field
Marshal von Rundstedt must be persuaded to come out of
retirement and assume nominal command: in fact he would
have very little to do with the actual battle.* Command of the
Army Group would be given to Hitler's current favourite,
Field Marshal Model, and the Sixth Panzer Army which would
spearhead the great offensive would be made up of the Führer's beloved SS Divisions and commanded by one of his
oldest comrades, Josef 'Sepp' Dietrich.

The core of the Waffen SS were seven crack divisions and
the rivalry among them was intense. By the end of 1944 these
were all panzer divisions and were always re-equipped with the
latest tanks.† Four of these seven crack divisions were chosen
to spearhead the attack in the Ardennes: the Leibstandarte,

---

* After the war von Rundstedt told Basil Liddell Hart that in the
Ardennes offensive 'the only troops I was allowed to move were the
guards in front of my own headquarters'.

† In December 1942, when technically the Leibstandarte was not
a tank division at all, they got two companies from the first small
production of the new Tiger tanks.

36

Das Reich, Hitler Jugend and Hohenstauffen. The average age, including officers, was eighteen.

Early in 1944 'Sepp' Dietrich was recalled from the Eastern Front and given the First SS Panzer Corps in the West to await the Anglo-American invasion. On June 7 he was ordered to drive the Allied forces back into the sea, but with only two divisions he failed and in trying to obey Hitler's orders not to retreat his First SS Panzer Corps were practically destroyed in the subsequent Normandy fighting. Dietrich, who by this time had a lot of experience of armoured warfare, lost his respect for Hitler as a great commander. 'There is only one person to blame for that stupid, impossible operation—that madman Adolf Hitler,' he said about the Falaise disaster—but not until after the war.

Nor, for that matter did Hitler have any illusions about Dietrich's ability as a general. The Goebbels propaganda machine had built him up into a legendary figure rivalling the great Rommel himself, but Hitler would probably have agreed with Goering's assessment—that at most Dietrich might command a division. He now took the precaution of appointing as Dietrich's Chief of Staff one of the most capable soldiers on the German General Staff, Major-General Fritz Kraemer. Although he had transferred to the Waffen SS, Kraemer was the complete professional soldier and would keep Dietrich from making too great mistakes.

It was important that the great offensive which was going to change the whole course of the war would be seen by the German people to have been carried out by loyal Nazis so that the rumours about the numbers of Germans involved in the assassination attempt could be countered. Everything therefore would take second place to equipping the new Sixth SS Panzer Army.*

The task of covering the flanks and rear of the Sixth SS and later to exploit the breakthrough would be given to the re-formed Fifth Panzer Army of seven mixed 'Volksgrenadier' and experienced panzer divisions made up of survivors of the old Fifth Panzer Army which had been chewed up in Normandy and whose commander had been captured.

To replace him Hitler sent for another of his Eastern Front 'fighting generals'—one of the best tank tacticians of the war, General Hasso von Manteuffel, who had just capped a brilliant

* Although usually referred to by this title the 6th Panzer Army was only given the honorific 'SS' by Hitler after the Ardennes Offensive.

37

career by a successful counter-attack against the Russians in Latvia.

This aristocratic regular Prussian officer was one of the very few whom Hitler would listen to, because, unlike so many of his fellow regulars, he had learned the new lessons of armoured warfare and had exploited them brilliantly. He was also one of the few who were not hypnotized by Hitler and would quietly express his own point of view.

But, unfortunately, the reconstructed Fifth Panzer Army had to be used as soon as it was ready, unlike the Sixth SS Panzer which was to be kept in reserve. General von Manteuffel had no sooner taken command than he was ordered to mount a counter-attack in Lorraine to try to stop General Patton.

The Fifth Panzer Army was given four hundred new Panthers and Mark Fours to equip new Panzer Brigades to be launched against Patton's southern flank, but before Manteuffel could gain the initiative General Patton unexpectedly renewed his advance. Three of Manteuffel's new divisions were pinned down and it was a week before he was able to put in the attack Hitler had ordered. When he did so his armour ran head on into the tough US 4th Armored Division and in the furious four-day battle that followed Manteuffel lost one hundred and fifty of his new tanks. As he had previously lost nearly a hundred to the Second French Armoured Division and twenty to thirty more in other actions, the new, 'reconstructed' Fifth Panzer Army had to be pulled out and reconstructed again before it could be used in the counter-offensive.

The third force selected for the attack, the Seventh German Army, had the same name as the army which had been holding that part of Normandy where the British had landed. This army had been almost totally destroyed in the long series of defeats and withdrawals. Now it, too, was rebuilt with divisions of the new Volksgrenadiers and Paratroopers trained as infantry. Its rôle was to throw up a protective wall along the outside flank of the 'left hook' to be delivered by the two panzer armies. Its commander was a thoroughly trained textbook soldier, General Erich Brandenberger, who, although unlikely to achieve anything spectacular, could be depended upon to perform the task given to him if the forces allocated were adequate and he did not encounter difficulties not covered by the book.

Hitler's plan called for these three armies to attack simultaneously along an eighty-mile sector of the front held by only five American divisions, four of infantry and one of tanks. It could not fail so long as Allied intelligence did not find out about it and reinforce the Ardennes and if, somehow, the rest of the Western Front could be stabilized for at least two months so that the Germans could get everything ready.

There were many other important factors: men, arms, tanks, guns, ammunition and fuel in large quantities must not only be found but secretly delivered to the right places. Lastly the weather at the critical moment must ground the dreaded Allied Air Force. Hitler, confident of his destiny, had no doubts about the weather or any of the other things he could not control.

When, inevitably, the weather did clear, then the Luftwaffe, who had been almost chased out of the air, must once again dominate the skies over the battlefield. Field Marshal Goering promised that at least two thousand of the new rocket planes would be ready to support the great offensive.

Also, for the first time in a very long while, the Parachute Corps would be used again, dropping behind the American lines to seize vital bridges and road junctions and hold them until the fast-moving SS Panzer divisions got there. Admittedly this once-great force had been almost annihilated by heavy casualties and now consisted of infantrymen, very few of whom had ever jumped, but somehow at least a battalion must be found.

Finally Hitler had one of his famous unorthodox ideas: one of the advantages the attackers would have would be the chaos, terror and disorganization the sudden appearance of German tanks, guns and soldiers far behind the American lines would cause. If this could be increased to absolute panic the defenders would be unable to stand their ground. Hitler thought he knew how this might be accomplished. He sent for another favourite—Otto Skorzeny.

Some eighteen months before a thirty-five-year-old Austrian engineer, who had been invalided home from the Russian front after a couple of years' hard fighting with the SS was called to the telephone in Berlin and told to go immediately to where an aeroplane was waiting to take him to Supreme Headquarters.

As he was only a captain and had never met any of the great ones he was surprised, but he had no false modesty and knew himself to be an exceptionally able man. It looked very much like opportunity knocking at the door and he answered eagerly.

His name was Otto Skorzeny and as a young man of twenty-four in his native Vienna he had gone to a political meeting addressed by Josef Goebbels who told his Austrian audience excitedly all about the new creed of National Socialism. Like many other young men he had been converted by the fiery little propagandist and had joined the new Austrian Nazi party. When this was banned a few years later he had joined the undercover equivalent, the 'German Gymnastic Association' which organized so-called defence units. These had been ordered into action when Germany marched into Austria.

Skorzeny first came to the notice of the powers in the Nazi party when, armed only with verbal authority, he walked alone into the Presidential Palace in Vienna and prevented a clash between the Old Guard and the new SS. He was a big, handsome man with an air of authority and a suggestion of reckless fearlessness which made most people think twice before challenging him.

He joined the Waffen SS at the outbreak of war and tried hard to get into the fighting but so quick were Germany's victories that the only enemy he saw were the long files of weary prisoners. It was not until the invasion of Yugoslavia in 1941 that, as a very new Second Lieutenant, he at last got into action. Much to his disgust the actual fighting lasted about two hours. From then on it was an unbroken German advance, until Yugoslavia surrendered. The German Army had achieved another lightning victory.

A few weeks later he took part in the invasion of Russia and once again it all seemed too easy—the main problem was to keep contact with the swift advance of the leading troops. It looked as though Russia, too, was going to succumb to the smashing blitzkrieg.

But slowly the situation changed and the Russians began hitting back with massed artillery, determined infantry attacks and tanks bigger and better than any the Germans had. For the first time Germany faced an enemy with a superior weapon. Their anti-tank projectiles ricocheted off the sloping frontal armour of the Russian T34s which were thus able to come on, supported by massed infantry. If the Russian Army had had large numbers of these tanks Germany might have been defeated before the end of 1941.

Skorzeny distinguished himself in the grim fighting and won the Iron Cross. He got to within sight of Moscow but was saved from the terrible hardships of the subsequent retreat by illness.

His recovery took some months but as soon as he thought he was fit (the doctors did not agree) he once more tried to get back into action. Instead Waffen SS headquarters offered him a job in Section Six of the Secret Service—a specialist formation trained in sabotage and espionage. It was Skorzeny's experience in these fields that led to his unexpected summons to the Wolf's Lair in July 1943.

Hitler's object in sending for Skorzeny was to choose a daring and resourceful man to entrust with the difficult task of rescuing Mussolini who, only the day before at a meeting of the Fascist Grand Council, had been forced to resign as Dictator and placed under arrest. He had been spirited away but Hitler was determined to find him and bring him to Germany. After talking to the six possible German officers he chose Otto Skorzeny who then and there fell under his spell completely.

A few weeks later he took an SS Commando unit up in gliders and crash-landed in the rocky grounds of the hotel six thousand five hundred feet up in the Abruzzi mountains where the Duce was kept prisoner. The guards were overwhelmed without a shot being fired and Skorzeny personally conducted Mussolini to Adolf Hitler and was decorated and promoted. From then on he was one of the Führer's favourites, often chosen for unusual daring missions, including the successful kidnapping of the Hungarian leader Admiral Horthy in September 1944.

This was the man Hitler sent for once again in October and Skorzeny was to be the first, apart from the actual planners, to know about the Ardennes Offensive. Hitler had another job for him—perhaps the most unusual yet.

He was ordered to go to the now-familiar Wolf's Den and he found Hitler in a happy, relaxed mood. Skorzeny was asked all about his latest exploit, the kidnapping of Admiral Horthy in Hungary, and was promoted to Lieutenant-Colonel and awarded the German Cross in gold. Hitler's mood then changed and he became serious; Skorzeny thought that the time had come for him to go but Hitler stopped him.

'I have perhaps the most important job in your life for you,' he said. 'In November Germany will start a great offensive which may well decide her fate and you have a great part to play in it.'

Hitler liked explaining his plans to an admiring listener and in a dazzling *tour de force* he now ranged over the whole Western Front explaining alternative attacks that had been considered and the reasons for the choice of the Ardennes and why he expected the offensive to have a decisive effect. Skorzeny, the simple man of action, was bewildered but completely convinced as was almost everyone whom Hitler ever tried to persuade.

'One of the most important tasks in this offensive I am entrusting to you, Skorzeny,' he said, and then explained his plan. Special units wearing American and British uniforms and travelling in captured Allied tanks and other vehicles were to go ahead of the advance to the first big obstacle, the river Meuse, and seize one or more of the bridges. Just as important, they were to cause as much chaos behind the Allied lines as possible by giving false orders, upsetting communications and attacking morale with wild rumours of German successes.

The mere presence of German troops disguised as British or Americans would cause universal distrust and seriously slow up the movement of reinforcements.

Skorzeny hurried off to try to organize the necessary specialist units in the short time allotted. A few days later he was handed a printed notice that was being distributed to all Wehrmacht units in Germany and at the front. At the top were the words: 'SECRET COMMANDO OPERATIONS' and the notice asked for the names of all English-speaking officers and men who were prepared to volunteer to serve in the formation commanded by Colonel Skorzeny for 'a special operation'.

Skorzeny was amazed and furious for he knew that his name and reputation for leading raids behind the enemy lines must be well-known to Allied Intelligence. This notice must reach them and its meaning could surely not be in doubt. He protested to Hitler that such a leak meant that the whole idea must be abandoned.

Hitler would not hear of it. He agreed that the order had been idiotic but insisted that Skorzeny's operation, now given the code name 'Greif'—a mythical animal—go ahead and he gave him sweeping powers to requisition anything he needed.

Skorzeny was worried about the status of any of his men who might be captured in enemy uniform and consulted an expert on international law who persuaded him that as long as his men didn't use arms while in Allied uniform they would be all right. It was decided that the special unit would wear German uniform with American or British uniform on top which they would take off before actually opening fire. It was just as well because when it actually came down to it very few Allied uniforms could be found.

First they were sent a mixed batch of parts of British uniforms, probably taken from the dead, and then greatcoats which Skorzeny knew were not worn by Allied troops in battle. He demanded battle dress and was sent a supply of American olive-drab combat jackets which were very fine except that they all had brightly coloured POW patches on the back. The only article of clothing the German army could find large enough to fit Skorzeny was an American Army pullover.

The 'English-speaking' volunteers came in from everywhere and language experts tried to sort them out. After a couple of weeks, Skorzeny says, the results were terrifying. Only ten men, ex-merchant sailors, could speak American perfectly and had a working knowledge of slang. Thirty-five could speak American or English well but knew no slang, three hundred and fifty could understand and probably get by if they were not required to say too much and the rest, the great majority, could say 'yes' and 'no'. These Skorzeny ordered to pretend to be too flurried and terrified to speak and to mix with the retreating Americans.

The muddle and inefficiency with which this special force was hurriedly got ready was typical of the rot spreading through the Wehrmacht command at this stage of the war when most senior officers realized that defeat was inevitable. A year or two earlier any idea of Hitler's would have been enthusiastically implemented. He had shown that unorthodox methods worked, but no one any longer believed in his magic except some of the younger, fanatical SS officers. Skorzeny was beginning to be disillusioned himself. When he had been called to the Wolf's Lair in September 1944 for briefing about his mission to Hungary he had been shocked by the difference in Hitler in the year since he had last seen him.

But when he saw him again to get orders for his rôle in the Ardennes offensive he was surprised at how much better Hitler seemed to be. He was alert and full of energy; it was obvious that the planning of the surprise offensive and the prospect of new, great successes had rejuvenated him. But this optimism did not spread to the High Command and Skorzeny found it impossible to obtain what he needed.

It had been intended to use two companies of American tanks but all Skorzeny got were two Shermans one of which developed transmission trouble and had to be left behind. Twelve Panthers were then disguised with wood and canvas to look like Shermans. They might, Skorzeny says, have deceived very young American troops seeing them very far away—at night.

Six captured British scout cars all broke down before the attack, leaving Skorzeny only four American scout cars, thirty jeeps and fifteen American Ford trucks. The deficiencies were made up by German vehicles painted in American green.

There were plenty of American anti-tank guns and mortars but almost no ammunition for them, and in the end it was possible to supply only one commando company.

All this was most discouraging, and Skorzeny, a practical

43

man, soon realized that he had neither the time nor the material necessary to achieve all that Hitler wanted. He would have to improvise desperately and limit the objectives to what was feasible.

In the first place it was not possible to take a heterogeneous mass of volunteers drawn from all branches of the service with different training and different skills and turn them into a well-trained, cohesive attack formation in four or five weeks. He demanded some regular units for stiffening and got two of the new parachute infantry battalions, a company from a regular tank battalion and an experienced signals company. In addition he already had his own specialist unit of two commando companies and a paratroop unit. These were the men he had used on some of his special missions and they were all highly trained: each man had had training as an infantryman and a sapper first and then had been taught to handle mortars, light field artillery and tank guns. Every man knew how to drive almost any powered vehicle from a motor-bicycle to a tank, not excluding boats and railway engines. They were also trained to use unorthodox weapons and explosives. This unit was to be the élite core of the three thousand five hundred strong 'Armoured Brigade 150' so confidently expected to sow havoc behind the American lines.

After the initial attack by massed infantry, Skorzeny would launch three separate battle groups, each aimed at one of the bridges over the Meuse. They would attack and destroy any weaker force they met and either avoid or bluff their way through a stronger. Their task was to dash for the Meuse in twenty-four hours, seize the bridges and hold them until the spearheads of the advancing panzer armies caught up with them.

From these bridgeheads the second and conclusive stage of the offensive would be launched: west of the river Meuse the country opens out and there is an excellent network of roads over which the tanks, self-propelled guns and carrier-borne infantry would move too fast for an organized defence line to be formed. Skorzeny's unorthodox operation, if successful, might well ensure the success of the whole offensive.

Hitler had learned about the immense value of even a few active men behind the enemy's lines from Franco's Fifth Column in Madrid during the Spanish Civil War and he had used the principle in the invasions of Holland and Greece. The suspected presence of German soldiers in disguise or Nazi civilian sympathizers had meant that all movement in the attacked area was seriously hampered by the need to guard every bridge and crossroads and to check everyone's credentials.

The Ardennes offered just such another opportunity for part of this frontier area had been taken away from Germany and given to Belgium as reparations after World War I. Many of the people are German-speaking and in 1944 most of these were Nazi sympathizers. With the area overrun with German soldiers and Skorzeny's men in Allied uniform the resulting confusion would cause everyone to distrust everyone else.

If this chaos could be encouraged it could well delay the arrival of American reinforcements and the whole of the Ardennes right up to the line of the Meuse could be quickly seized. This would net great supplies of war material, cause thousands of Allied casualties and cut the main supply line to the American forces north of the Ardennes poised to attack the Ruhr. These things alone would make the whole offensive worth while.

3

ALLIES AND RIVALS

*Marshal Foch said after the first World War that it
had caused him to lose much of his veneration for
Napoleon for he had only to fight coalitions and any
reasonably efficient general could defeat a coalition.*
JOHN WINANT: *A Letter from Grosvenor Square*

There was a certain amount of truth in Hitler's assessment of
relations between the British and American Commands at the
end of 1944. After the great successes of the summer the
autumn stalemate had been a disappointment and each was
inclined to blame the other. General Montgomery had commanded all the forces which assaulted the beaches—forces
which were equally divided between British and American—
and he had continued as overall ground commander in Europe
up to and including the breakout. But as the weeks went by
and American forces continued to arrive on the continent the
time came when they greatly outnumbered the British. American war correspondents scenting a good story made great
play of the fact that technically at least General Omar Bradley
had to go through General Montgomery to the Supreme
Commander General Eisenhower in London.

General Montgomery wanted above all else to keep control
of all Allied Forces in Europe, not so much for reasons of
personal ambition, although he had his fair share of that, but
because he passionately believed that a quick victory depended
upon there being a single ground commander. For this reason
he tried as hard as he knew to be tactful, not an easy matter
for one of his temperament, and in some measure succeeded.
He granted the Americans the latitude to operate as freely and
as independently as they chose and General Bradley said of
him at that time, 'At no time did he probe into First Army
with the indulgent manner he sometimes displayed among
those subordinates who were also his countrymen. I could not
have wanted a more tolerant or judicious commander. Not
once did he confront us with an arbitrary directive and not
once did he reject any plan that we had devised.'

The strategy of the breakout had been decided in advance
and the different rôles assigned to the British and American
troops had been determined by their different characteristics as
soldiers. It was commonly accepted that the Americans would

exploit a breakthrough with dash and daring and that the British would hold their ground and take punishment in a slugging match.

It was decided therefore that the British would make what looked like the main attempt to break out at Caen hoping to draw against them the bulk of the German armour in the west. While this armour was fully engaged the real breakout would occur from the American sector where, it was hoped, the enemy would be fairly thin on the ground.

General Bradley in his memoirs does not mince words about this: 'For three weeks Montgomery rammed his troops against those panzer divisions he had deliberately drawn towards Caen as part of our Allied strategy of diversion.... Monty's primary task was to attract German troops to the British front that we might more easily secure Cherbourg and get into position for the breakout.

'For another four weeks it fell to the British to pin down superior enemy forces in that sector while we manoeuvred into position for the US breakout. With the Allied world crying for Blitzkrieg the first week after we landed, the British endured their passive rôle with patience and forbearing. Eventually, however, the frustration they experienced here at Caen produced an extreme sensitivity to Patton's speedy advance across France. In setting the stage for our breakout, the British were forced to endure the barbs of critics who shamed them for failing to push out vigorously as the Americans did. The intense rivalry that afterwards strained relations between the British and American commands might be said to have sunk its psychological roots into that passive mission of the British on the beachhead.'

When the Allied Forces, having destroyed the German Seventh Army, reached the Seine, General Eisenhower came to France and assumed over-all command himself. General Montgomery was promoted to Field Marshal and became one of three commanders of Army Groups in France. The other two were General Bradley who now commanded the rest of the Allied Forces in northern France and General Devers, whose Sixth United States Army had successfully landed on the French Mediterranean coast.

Certain things inevitably grew out of this decision: following the American practice each army group commander became the independent commander-in-chief for his particular area. Naturally each wanted his particular front to be the scene of the main effort not only because as a professional soldier it was all-important to him personally but because he knew a great deal more about his own front and honestly believed that an all-out effort on it would bring total victory.

The invasion of France and defeat of Germany had been planned in England giving due accord to the strength of the defences and assuming, even if things went according to plan, that the German High Command would fight a textbook war drawing back to prepared positions when forced to do so and, by presenting the attackers with a coherent contracting front, make them fight for every mile of France and every yard of Germany. No one could have guessed what the full extent of the Russian successes on the Eastern Front was to be or that the Luftwaffe would be driven out of the skies or that the German Staff would allow their forces to be enveloped and destroyed. Even when this had happened the full extent of Germany's weakness in the west was not appreciated by Allied Intelligence. The original plan for pushing the Germans methodically out of France and the Low Countries before mounting an attack on Germany herself was adhered to although both General Bradley and General Montgomery wanted an all-out attack from their own sectors.

With pressure from his 'independent' commanders-in-chief, General Eisenhower decided that he had no choice but to try to advance everywhere along his broad front. This, Field Marshal Montgomery thought, was a great mistake for, he told Eisenhower, the Allies did not have the resources to maintain two Army Groups—his British Twenty-first and Bradley's American Twelfth—at full pressure. The only policy, he insisted, was to stop one in a defensive rôle and strike hard with the other. He offered to serve under General Bradley if Eisenhower would make him C-in-C Land Forces for 'single control and direction of the land operations is vital for success. This is a whole-time job for one man.' The great victory in France so far had been won by personal command and only that way would future victories be won.

Eisenhower refused to consider this proposal because he felt that the British public would never stand for Bradley now being appointed over Montgomery's head. He was also not willing to change the American method so that a single commander would exercise control.

Montgomery's plan to end the war, which was to use the Second British Army and the First US Army in a forty-division powerful thrust right to the industrial complex of the Ruhr, would have meant that Patton's Third Army would be held back in defence. 'That,' Eisenhower said, 'the American public would never stand for and public opinion wins wars.'

So, instead, the entire long front was expanded uniformly and by September this policy seemed to have been triumphantly vindicated for although the attacking Allied line was thinly manned the Germans continued to retreat in disorder. Thousands of their perfectly fit and well-armed soldiers had been glad to surrender without a fight in the pursuit across France and Belgium and it was known that in Holland there were only German garrison troops.

On September 4 the British captured Antwerp and it seemed reasonable to suppose that, by using this great port to supply fuel and ammunition, a powerful thrust due east across southern Holland for another hundred miles would smash into the Ruhr, thus cutting off half of Germany's coal and steel.

To the German commanders on the Western Front the position seemed almost hopeless and some of them were not afraid to tell Hitler so. On September 4 Field Marshal Model, the miracle worker, solemnly reported to the Führer Conference, as perhaps only he would have dared to do, that, 'The unequal struggle cannot long continue.' He added that Germany could not now hope to prevent the Allies from invading the Reich itself.

Field Marshal von Rundstedt, whose blunt advice to his fellow generals after the debacle of Normandy—'Make peace, you fools!' had cost him his command and whom Hitler persuaded once again, by a mixture of cajolery and flattery, to take over as Commander-in-Chief West, didn't mince matters in his first report either. 'All our troops are committed, are being heavily attacked, are becoming exhausted and there are *no* reserves. The enemy is advancing with two thousand tanks: we have one hundred fit for action. We need six weeks to make the West Wall fit for defence and we do not have sufficient strength to gain that time.'

On the same day that von Rundstedt made this defeatist, though realistic appraisal, the Allied forces coming up from the Mediterranean beaches joined with those from the Normandy landings and the Allies had an unbroken front from Switzerland to Antwerp on the North Sea.

In the original Allied 'long-term strategic concept' it had been assumed that by September the German armies in France would have been driven back to the Seine. Instead, practically all of France and Belgium had been cleared and it is not surprising that a jubilant General Eisenhower wrote to Field Marshal Montgomery at this time: 'We shall soon have captured the Ruhr and the Saar and the Frankfurt area, and I would like your views as to what we should do next.'

What then happened to prove wrong the best military brains on both sides? The answer, surprisingly, was 'that madman' Adolf Hitler to whom great setbacks acted as stimulants. He heard all the disastrous reports apparently without concern and confidently gave orders to restore the situation. The Allies must not be allowed to use the port of Antwerp; they must be held in Holland and they must be thrown off balance by a strong counter-attack and so be made to lose the initiative. All very fine in theory but apparently impossible of execution, as Germany had neither the men nor the material.

It was at this critical moment that Field Marshal Goering, who had long been out of favour, dramatically revealed that he had no less than thirty thousand fresh, tough young soldiers up his sleeve. These were men of the I Parachute Corps and Luftwaffe air crews and the man to command them, the famous commander of the I Parachute Corps, slow-speaking, fast-acting General Kurt Student, was in Berlin waiting for orders.

Hitler personally telephoned Student and told him to assume full responsibility for the defence of Holland. He was to take his own Parachute Corps plus Goering's Luftwaffe troops and form the First Parachute Army. His first task was to close the gap in northern Belgium between the troops which had been occupying Holland—the German Fifteenth Army isolated in the lowlands of Flanders—and the shattered remnants of the once great German Seventh Army being driven eastwards at the end of their long retreat from Normandy. Once this gap had been closed all three armies would form Army Group H whose task would be to deny the Allies the use of the port of Antwerp and to hold a line across southern Holland.

Although the gap between the two German armies was widening rapidly—it became fifty miles in three days—Student succeeded in bridging it and restoring order. He then set about accomplishing his next tasks.

The north and south shores of the mouth of the Scheldt were thinly held. To his soldiers Hitler sent one of his 'die where you stand' orders. Everyone, from the highest ranking officers to the humblest soldiers, had to take an oath not to surrender under any circumstances whatsoever.

The mouth of this estuary leading to Antwerp was heavily mined and the land around the defender's positions flooded so that the Canadians, who were given the task of freeing the approaches to Antwerp, had to fight waist-deep in water and were unable to use either tanks or any other vehicles.

The result of all this was that it was not until after much

THE BATTLE OF THE ARDENNES, DECEMBER 1944.

The Chains of Command

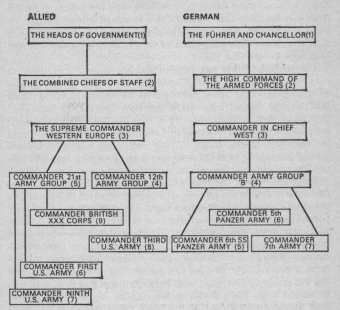

ALLIED

THE HEADS OF GOVERNMENT(1)

THE COMBINED CHIEFS OF STAFF (2)

THE SUPREME COMMANDER WESTERN EUROPE (3)

COMMANDER 21st ARMY GROUP (5)

COMMANDER 12th ARMY GROUP (4)

COMMANDER BRITISH XXX CORPS (9)

COMMANDER THIRD U.S. ARMY (8)

COMMANDER FIRST U.S. ARMY (6)

COMMANDER NINTH U.S. ARMY (7)

GERMAN

THE FÜHRER AND CHANCELLOR(1)

THE HIGH COMMAND OF THE ARMED FORCES (2)

COMMANDER IN CHIEF WEST (3)

COMMANDER ARMY GROUP 'B' (4)

COMMANDER 5th PANZER ARMY (6)

COMMANDER 6th SS PANZER ARMY (5)

COMMANDER 7th ARMY (7)

Notes

(1) Roosevelt and Churchill. As Commander-in-Chief of the Armed Forces the President had created the American Joint Chiefs of Staff who were therefore responsible directly to him. As the Prime Minister was also Minister of Defence the British Chiefs of Staff were responsible to him.

(2) The combination was of the American Joint Chiefs of Staff, Chairman Fleet Admiral Leahy, Chief of Staff of the US Army General Marshall, and the British Chiefs of Staff. Chairman Sir Alan Brooke. Meeting in Washington the Combined Chiefs of Staff exercised 'a grand strategic jurisdiction over all theatres of operations'.

(3) SHAEF. General Eisenhower.
(4) General Omar Bradley.
(5) Field Marshal Montgomery.
(6) Lt-General Courtney Hodges.
(7) Lt-General William Simpson.
(8) Lt-General George Patton.
(9) Lt-General Brian Horrocks.

Notes

(1) By this time Adolf Hitler was also Supreme Commander, Minister of War and Commander-in-Chief, Army.

(2) The OKW. Though nominally commanded by Field Marshal Keitel in practice, Hitler exercised command through Colonel-General Alfred Jodl, the Chief of Armed Forces Operations Staff.

(3) Field Marshal Gerd von Rundstedt. At first he was largely bypassed by Hitler working directly with Model. When the battle was seen to have failed von Rundstedt was called upon again.

(4) Field Marshal Walter Model, the real commander of the offensive.

(5) Colonel-General Josef 'Sepp' Dietrich. This army's honorific 'SS' was not actually given until after the Ardennes Offensive but Dietrich's force was generally known as 'the SS army'.

(6) General Hasso-Eccard von Manteuffel whom circumstances made the principal field commander.

(7) General Erich Brandenberger.

bitter fighting that the comparatively few German soldiers were overcome. The Royal Navy, with unarmoured vessels and light guns sailed in against heavy guns in concrete emplacements to land soldiers on the islands. They suffered many casualties and even when the stubborn defenders were defeated it took more than three weeks for a hundred mine-sweepers to clear the seventy-mile channel. It was not until November 28 that the first Allied ship docked in Antwerp—precious weeks had been bought for Hitler.

General Student also accomplished his second objective—to hold Holland—by throwing up a defensive wall along the line of the canal that runs right across southern Holland from Antwerp to Maastricht. Here the new 'paratroop infantry', described in the official history of one of the British divisions who fought against them here as 'magnificent soldiers', upset all attempts to put them to rout including both the biggest Allied parachute operation of the war, Arnhem, and the all-out onslaught on the Aachen area which saw some of the fiercest fighting of the war. On November 16 Student's troops had nearly ten thousand tons of bombs from two thousand five hundred bombers dropped on them but still came out of their fox-holes and blocked the follow-up attack.

In the grim fighting during October and November when positions changed hands scores of times, casualties were exceptionally heavy on both sides. Two American divisions in particular were badly mauled: the 28th Infantry Division and the 4th Infantry Division, who between them lost nearly fifteen thousand men. Both divisions were taken out of the line and sent to the quietest part of the front for a rest—the forest of the Ardennes.

Three things brought the Allied advance to a halt: the unexpectedly stubborn resistance of the German troops in Holland; the new spirit of German soldiers when fighting on their own soil; the lengthening of Allied supply lines—brought about by the rapidity and extent of the advance—to the point where it was impossible to keep the continually expanding front supplied. Now the Channel ports, still held by isolated groups of German troops, would have to be cleared and the great port of Antwerp opened up before the decisive attack on Germany could take place.

Hitler, just as he had assured his generals, had been granted the breathing spell he needed to mount the counter-offensive which would turn the tables.

At the beginning of November he sent Colonel-General Jodl to Field Marshal Model's Army Group B HQ with the complete, detailed plan for 'Wacht am Rhein' (Watch on the Rhine), the code name for: ORDER FOR ASSEMBLY AND CONCENTRATION FOR ATTACK (ARDENNES OFFENSIVE). It was the first intimation anyone outside the Führer's immediate entourage, other than Otto Skorzeny, had of the biggest German effort on the Western Front since May 1940 and the proposed date was November 25—barely three weeks away.

Three of the five commanders involved were told. Field Marshal von Rundstedt, newly reinstated as C-in-C West, Field Marshal Model, commanding Army Group B which had been formed for this offensive, and General Hasso von Manteuffel, commander of one of the armies to be used, the Fifth Panzer Army. The commanders of the other two armies, 'Sepp' Dietrich of the Sixth Panzer and General Brandenberger of the Seventh Army, were not present. Dietrich's name was magic with the German people and for many reasons Hitler wanted the SS to lead the offensive and to get the credit for the resulting victory but 'Sepp' Dietrich would have no part in the planning. He would be told exactly what to do and his very able Chief of Staff, Kraemer, would see that he did it and stop him from doing anything foolish. Brandenberger, a textbook soldier, could not help in the planning and anyway his rôle, to protect the left flank from attacks from the south, was a minor one.

Jodl then described the grandiose plan to his amazed listeners. An eighty-mile section of the front, beginning at a point about fifteen miles south of Aachen and running a few miles south of where the frontiers of Belgium, Luxembourg and Germany meet, was to be breached by a concentrated attack along its entire length by two panzer armies totalling sixteen divisions. The main thrust was to be on the right from the northern third of the line with a rapid advance due west for some sixty to eighty miles through the forests and hills of the Ardennes to the river Meuse between Liège and Namur. This was to be carried out by the Sixth SS Panzer Army with nine divisions including four armoured. The remaining two-thirds of the eighty-mile front was to be rolled up by the seven-division Fifth Panzer Army advancing north-west some seventy to eighty miles in a supporting left hook to the Meuse. Once across this river barrier the second phase of the attack would begin.

This was a double-pronged drive north-west another sixty miles to the port of Antwerp with Sixth SS Panzer Army making for the line of the Albert Canal between Antwerp and Maastricht to meet up with General Student's forces attacking south-west from Holland. Fifth Panzer Army would move parallel with Sixth SS Panzer, by-passing Brussels and cutting off Antwerp from the south by reaching the coast.

The overall objective was to cut off three armies, the Ninth US, the Second British and the First Canadian from the rest of the Allied Forces and then to destroy them.

As one man the three commanders protested that the far-reaching objectives were completely beyond their powers. Old, blunt von Rundstedt was scathing, 'Antwerp? If we reach the Meuse we should go down on our knees and thank God—let alone trying to reach Antwerp!'

What about their flanks, Model asked; what would the Third US Army in the south and the Ninth US Army in the north be doing all this time?

As the movement was essentially a left hook the forces enveloped inside would be cut like weeds before a scythe, Jodl said, but agreed that the long outside flank would have to be protected. This would be done by General Brandenberger's Seventh Army, throwing up a defence wall and holding off attacks from the south until the new front from Luxembourg to Antwerp could be stabilized. Admittedly the Seventh Army only had four divisions but the American Third Army, from which a relieving attack might be expected, would be kept busy by a diversionary offensive from General Blankowitz's Army Group G in the Saar.

Field Marshal Model agreed with von Rundstedt that Antwerp was too far away even to be considered at that stage. The newly created mobile reserve, the Sixth SS Panzer Army, should be used to wipe out the American troops round Aachen where the real threat to Germany was developing.

General von Manteuffel, whose Fifth Panzer Army had been in continual action since he had come from the Eastern Front, made several points quietly but firmly: there was not time to get the men and materials needed ready; the attack could not hope to be successful unless the Luftwaffe dominated the air and, even if everything was in their favour, at that time of year and in that terrain it would take the tanks four, not two days to reach the Meuse. Allied mobility was such that in that time they could move powerful forces at least to hold the line of the Meuse.

When they had all had their say Jodl told them simply that the plan was fixed and unalterable in even the smallest particular. It was Hitler's own plan and the Führer was not interested in criticism, advice or comment—they were to obey orders, nothing more.

'It is, I agree, an operation of the most extreme daring,' Jodl told them, 'but Germany is in a desperate situation and a desperate remedy is needed. We cannot escape our fate by remaining on the defensive. Such an unexpected bold attack may turn the tables. At the worst we shall cause the enemy to postpone his assault on us. Anyway, gentlemen, there can be no arguments—it is the Führer's orders!'

He did not tell them that the Operations Staff of OKW plan as submitted to Hitler had called for no more than a strike for the Meuse by two Panzer Armies and that Hilter alone had expanded the offensive.

This was the first time that a large-scale attack had been planned without reference to the High Command of the Army (OKH). Because of Hitler's obsession with treachery among the generals and because he had lost faith in their military ability following the long series of defeats he decided to plan and put into operation this decisive counter-offensive without their help or indeed without letting them know about it. It was an extraordinary decision.

Instead he had asked the so-called Combined Forces High Command (OKW)—in practice his puppets—to study the situation and recommend a plan. But as they were expressly forbidden to consult even those generals whose forces were to be used and had to work in the unreal atmosphere of the Wolf's Lair, they had an almost impossible task. Nevertheless they managed to produce a plan that was militarily feasible but Hitler's expansion of it so ignored the facts that none of the principal commanders in the field, who knew the real strength of the Allies, believed it could succeed.

In an attempted modification of Hitler's scheme Field Marshal Model worked out an alternative plan with objectives that would stretch his forces to the utmost, knowing that there was no hope that Hitler would consent to anything less. This, the 'modified solution', was to break through the American front lines, penetrate some thirty or forty miles and then turn the flanks inward, trapping a large number of American forces, capturing the supply dumps east of the Meuse, cutting the main Allied supply line to Aachen and using the Meuse to defend their new line. Even this, Model said, could only hope to be accomplished if the Luftwaffe could give temporary air superiority over the battle area. This should be combined with a supporting attack from the German Fifteenth Army on the right. If all this succeeded then a second offensive could be quickly mounted with Antwerp as the objective.

Hitler completely rejected this alternative. None of the

55

points brought up in the hours and hours of discussion caused him to change his plans by one soldier. If he was presented with unpalatable facts he ignored them—it was pointed out to him that the forces he had promised had just not materialized: neither the men, the tanks, the guns, the ammunition, the fuel nor the aircraft. If the original forces promised had not been powerful enough to achieve the objective how could it possibly be done with less? To this there was no reply except that the attack would take place and the timetable of the advance would be strictly adhered to.

When 'Sepp' Dietrich finally heard about the plan he protested louder than any of the others. 'All Hitler wants me to do is to cross a river, capture Brussels and then go on and take Antwerp!' he shouted. 'And all this in the worst time of the year through the Ardennes where the snow is waist deep and there isn't enough room to deploy four tanks abreast let alone armoured divisions! Where it doesn't get light until eight and it's dark again at four and with re-formed divisions made up chiefly of kids and sick old men—and at Christmas!'

Dietrich personally went to Hitler's HQ to say that his orders were impossible but got the same reply—'It is the Führer's orders—they must be obeyed.'

Time had been lost by the protests of the Generals. The original date of the offensive, November 25, soon became impossible and Hitler granted them another two weeks to December 10. The code name was changed from 'Watch on the Rhine' to 'Herbstnebel' (Autumn Mist) while the preparations went on frenziedly.

4

THE OPPOSING FORCES

A line cannot be strong everywhere.

MILITARY AXIOM

The Allies had reached the Ardennes in September when the broken German armies from Normandy retreated across Belgium seeking the protection of the massive defences of their famed West Wall. On September 11 men of a reconnaissance troop* probing ahead of their armoured division waded across the narrow river Our and so became the first Allied soldiers to step on German soil.

This first penetration of Hitler's Third Reich from the west took place along the edge of a rugged area of high, broken forest known as the Eifel. Beginning in the north near the German frontier town of Monschau it tumbles south for some seventy miles until cut by the valley of the Moselle. It consists mainly of two parallel ridges: the High Eifel on the west facing Belgium and the somewhat lower Volcanic Eifel on the east which slopes away to the Rhine. With its dense pine forests, deeply cut ravines, steep cliff-like ridges, narrow roads and many fast-running streams it is a natural obstacle, easy to defend and murderous to attack.

Almost in the centre there is a 2,286-feet high north–south ridge called the Schnee Eifel which, with the continuous river barrier formed by the Our, the Sauer and the Moselle running along the western and southern edges of the Eifel, effectively bars the way to Germany. The West Wall had been carried along the top of the High Eifel, including the Schnee Eifel, and the whole seemed to be an impregnable position.

The continuation of this kind of country westwards into Belgium and Luxembourg is called the Ardennes. It was from the Eifel and through the Ardennes that German invading armies had come in 1870, 1914 and 1940. But in September 1944 it looked as though the tables might be turned on the Germans for they did not, at that time, have either the men or the weapons to defend it properly. Also, because of the rugged terrain, they had built fewer pill-boxes and dragons' teeth in the Eifel than anywhere else along their West Wall defences.

*Of the Eighty-fifth Cavalry Reconnaissance Squadron, Fifth US Armoured Division of V Corps, US First Army.

57

In September the Allies were advancing fast in a mood of high optimism for there had been success along the whole line: on the left the British Twenty-first Army Group had reached the Dutch frontier two hundred and fifty miles from their start line on the Seine; the First US Army in the centre had now arrived at the Belgian–Dutch frontier after a two-hundred-mile advance; on the right the Third US Army, after clearing Brittany and being held up by a shortage of fuel, had advanced one hundred and seventy miles from the south-west of Paris and liberated Luxembourg. The Allies had reached a line in early September which, in the planning of D-day, had been scheduled as the objective for about May 1, 1945.

This great advance had been achieved with many fewer casualties than had been allowed for. Two million men had been landed in Normandy and casualties from all causes totalled only a little more than ten per cent. The Germans, on the other hand, had lost a million men and vast quantities of material in France and their retreat looked like turning into a rout.

It was expected that once behind their West Wall they would turn and stand but Allied superiority in numbers of men, guns, tanks and aeroplanes made it seem most unlikely that this resistance could hold.

Meanwhile it was most important to keep up the pressure relentlessly so that the retreating Germans would not be able to regain their balance. The pursuit must continue, even if it meant denying the pursuers themselves more than absolute minimum rest, relying on the Allied air force and artillery to ensure that the retreating armies were given no respite at all. If the pursuing troops drove themselves to the point of exhaustion, the retreating troops must collapse—at least that was the theory.

Therefore First Army's V Corps moved swiftly across Belgium on the heels of the German rearguards, only stopping a few miles short of the first barrier to the Reich, the famed West Wall.

This fortified belt, known to the Allies as the Siegfried Line, ran the entire length of Germany's frontier from Holland to Switzerland. It consisted of minefields and anti-tank obstacles backed up by gun emplacements and thousands of huge, reinforced concrete pill-boxes, each a miniature fort. Although by September 1944 it had been stripped of many of its guns, sent to reinforce the ill-fated Atlantic Wall, and was thought by the German General Staff to be obsolete* the German people still

* Rundstedt infuriated Hitler by dismissing the West Wall as a 'mousetrap'. (von Mellenthin: *Panzer Battles.*)

thought of it as an impregnable barrier. In the three disastrous months since the Allied invasion the German army had been desperately trying to make the neglected West Wall useful again, not as an impregnable barrier, for they were no believers in the Maginot Line philosophy, but as a delaying position to halt the Allies until mobile reserves, which the German plans called for, could be brought up to cut off any penetration.

But in September 1944 there were no mobile reserves in Germany.

Only two days after arriving at the Eifel, V Corps attacked the West Wall with two infantry divisions. The intention was to smash through, before it could be reinforced, and drive on to the Rhine at Coblenz seventy miles further east.

The 28th Infantry Division attacked through a narrow corridor just south of the Schnee Eifel and the 4th Infantry Division, one of the most experienced in the American Army, stormed the steep slopes of the Schnee Eifel itself. All information showed that the Eifel defences were hopelessly weak—in fact there were even fewer troops holding them than Allied Intelligence reported.

On paper the Eifel was held by the left wing of Army Group B and the right wing of Army Group G but the German troops on the ground, although named as two armoured corps, actually consisted of the 2nd Panzer Division which had been made up of the remnants of three panzer divisions smashed in the Normandy fighting and which had exactly three tanks, and the 2nd SS Panzer Division, similarly battered, which had another three. To back up these six tanks there were fewer than fifty guns of all types and almost no ammunition. The infantry consisted of the 5th Parachute, a division in name only of some headquarters troops, one composite company from the reconnaissance battalion, a security regiment, a motorized infantry regiment and miscellaneous soldiers who had been roped in to make up another company. The 5th Parachute Division had neither support tanks nor artillery.

On the face of it the Allied assault should have been a quick, easy victory, but it was not. For one thing the long chase had been almost as hard on the pursuers as the pursued. The American soldiers had had little sleep or hot food. What rations they did get were much less than they had been used to, for supply lines were by now so stretched from the Normandy beaches that only absolute essentials—fuel, ammunition and basic rations—were getting up. Ammunition, which earlier had been used carelessly, was now strictly rationed. In the attack on the Eifel positions the supporting artillery were limited to twenty-five rounds per gun per day.

Also the Siegfried Line had long been a bogey to the Allied troops actually engaged in the fighting. Having learned to respect the fighting quality of the Germans they distrusted their long retreat, believing that they would choose a good defensive position and then turn and fight as fiercely as ever. When the Allies reached the Siegfried Line they could not believe that these tremendous fortifications were only lightly held and were apprehensive about what seemed to be a hastily planned assault against long-prepared defences.

The German soldiers, on the other hand, few as they were, had reached a strongly fortified line which they had been told was practically impregnable and, even more important, had the great stimulus of defending their homeland.

Attacking south of the Schnee Eifel with towed anti-tank guns the 28th Division soon lost most of them in the unsuitable terrain and, on approaching the West Wall, were beaten back by rifle and machine-gun fire even though some of the huge pill-boxes contained only three or four Germans and others were unmanned.

After two days of fighting the tired 28th Division's soldiers had only succeeded in forcing two small breaches through the West Wall. When the Germans counter-attacked, the exhaustion of the long pursuit took its toll and men who had formerly fought bravely and well fell back in panic before fairly light attacks. There were ominous signs of falling morale—non-battle casualties mounted steeply and the commanding officer of one infantry regiment was relieved.

In one of the West Wall breaches the invading American troops occupied the pill-boxes but a reckless attack at midnight by only about seventy-five Germans, using a flame-thrower they had improvised from a half-track, overran and destroyed an entire American infantry company. After five days' fighting and one thousand five hundred casualties, it was apparent that 28th Infantry Division's advance had been halted. The two pencil-like penetrations of the West Wall were consolidated but the attack was called off.

Further north the regular army 4th Infantry Division had been given what looked like a more difficult task—to attack up the steep wooded slopes of the Schnee Eifel itself towards the West Wall fortifications on the top. The right wing attack advanced up to the ridge, went through the West Wall, which was virtually undefended, and occupied a dominating hill. The left wing also made good headway at first until a single 88-mm gun knocked out a supporting tank and the remaining tanks all tried to find cover. The infantry, thinking their armour was deserting them, began to panic but were rallied by their officers and then, ashamed of their momentary weakness, charged forward at a run and carried an important crest. At the end of the first day the 4th Infantry Division had ripped a two-mile-wide hole in the West Wall.

But by a tremendous effort the Germans found men, many of them rear-echelon or non-fighting soldiers seeing action for the first time, and got them into the line. On the second day the leading American battalion met stiff resistance and quickly lost thirty-five men wounded and eight killed including their commanding officer. As with the 28th Division on their right, exhaustion now began to tell and when they were shelled heavily the nerve of several officers broke and they had to be evacuated for combat exhaustion. One of these was the officer commanding the leading company and when the lieutenant who took over command was himself wounded the men decided they had had enough. The remaining officers lost control and the soldiers broke and retreated without orders, only half of them succeeding in getting back safely. The attack on this part of the West Wall had to be called off as well.

The success of comparatively few German soldiers in holding the Eifel defences against an American two-division attack in September was to have far-reaching effects. After the war, General Westphal, von Rundstedt's Chief of Staff, admitted that a stronger effort would have broken through and might well have brought about the collapse of the whole West Front.

But men are not machines and even the best of soldiers find their efficiency and aggressiveness seriously affected by exhaustion. Morale is a delicate balance depending basically upon confidence in leadership at all levels and acceptance of the odds—which means the enemy should not for long have an unreasonable superiority in numbers of men, quality of weapons or advantage of ground. A change in these factors can lower the morale and hence the fighting quality of a unit in a matter of days.

Most of the American soldiers who landed in Europe were supremely confident that man for man they were better soldiers than the Germans and that certainly they had more and better weapons. In combat they quickly learned to respect the fighting qualities of their enemy and discovered, with some bitterness, that though they had more weapons these were, in some cases, inferior. The German machine guns and machine pistols had a higher rate of fire, their multiple-barrel mortars were more effective than the Allies single weapons, their self-propelled anti-tank guns were better, while in tanks there was an enormous difference. The third-ranking German tank was at least the equal of the Allies' best and the best German tank, the Tiger with its 88-mm high-velocity cannon, was so immeasurably superior that a single one could, and sometimes did, hold up a dozen Shermans. The 57-mm anti-tank gun of which the Americans had many thousands had almost no effect on either Tigers or Panthers and infantry who had seen a Tiger trundle out in plain sight at point-blank range and methodically destroy a whole column of transport while the Sherman's short-barrelled 75-mm shells bounced harmlessly off it, had their morale badly shaken.

Nevertheless despite these things the great German Army was defeated in France, just as had been promised and the whole Allied front moved forward triumphantly. But, as has been seen, in the long pursuit the leading units were pushed to the point of exhaustion and efficiency began to suffer.* When, added to this, the resistance; which had been weak and ineffective, stiffened and they themselves were counter-attacked and some of their officers were unable to carry on, morale fell and their effectiveness rapidly decreased.

In circumstances where soldiers are being asked to go without sufficient rest, as in a pursuit or a continuing attack, the greater the responsibility any individual bears the less rest he will get: a private can drop in his tracks and sleep the whole two hours, a corporal or sergeant sees to his men first while an officer probably has to go to a conference for his next orders—and the higher his rank the longer the journey. Also the officer's tradition is to suffer all the discomforts of his men in battle and a bit more, and many did so. All this works all right until circumstances require, as General Montgomery said at this time in an Order of the Day, that men will be asked to perform not the impossible but the nearly impossible; then the most conscientious are the most tired and therefore the most likely to break.

Broadly this is what happened to the 4th and 28th Infantry Divisions in September who, after being more or less continually in action for a hundred days and after a long, exhausting pursuit, had torn holes in the famous Siegfried Line at a cost of more than two thousand three hundred casualties. Then resistance against them stiffened, they were counter-

* Not only the Americans, of course. The British failure in September to push on beyond Antwerp and trap the German Fifteenth Army was mainly due to exhaustion, after a two hundred and fifty mile advance.

attacked vigorously, their casualties mounted, some leadership failed and they ceased to be able to continue the attack.

The attempt to carry the Siegfried Line had been a gamble that the deteriorating supply position would probably have stopped anyway for at this time ninety per cent of the Allied material landed in France was still on the Normandy beaches.

But this setback marked the beginning of the steep rise in 'combat fatigue' which later, as the proportion of non-combat casualties rose to twenty-five per cent, caused considerable alarm to commanders—who swore at the psychiatrists.*

When the American advance was stopped on September 16, the front line in the Ardennes remained more or less the same until Hitler launched his counter-offensive, three months later to the day.

After the attack on the West Wall the 4th and 28th Infantry Divisions were rested for three weeks and then, re-equipped and reinforced, were sent north for the attack on Aachen. Here, in the drive through the Hurtgen forest in the Battle for Schmidt they were practically destroyed in the costliest divisional action of any American troops in World War II. Shattered, they were sent back to the quiet of the Ardennes to recover.

Meanwhile responsibility for the Ardennes had been handed over to VIII Corps who needed somewhere to rest after the Brittany Campaign. In the three months up to the German attack in December the Ardennes became a combination of nursery and old folks' home. Here new divisions were sent to be blooded without danger of being destroyed and old, tired divisions sent to lick their wounds and regain their strength.

In the American Army at this time the Ardennes was commonly regarded as a rest camp. There were luxuries like hot showers, real beds, films, USO entertainments, doughnuts and coffee and free cigarettes for combat troops. The rest centres were well beyond German artillery range and the food was better cooked and more varied than at the front. Combat soldiers were sent back from their foxholes in the cold and wet for forty-eight hours of near-normal life.

But when they returned to their units at the 'quiet front' they found that the war hadn't stopped. The Germans, once they had realized that the Allied attack was not going to come through the Eifel, had withdrawn their crack panzer troops and replaced them with lower-grade infantry, green units sent for training and, like the Americans, units needing rest and

* The British Army found that simply by calling 'shell shock' or 'battle fatigue', 'nervous hysteria' the number of cases dropped.

63

refitting. Nevertheless they patrolled aggressively and kept up a certain amount of discouraging artillery fire. The US 83rd Infantry Division, for instance, in their month's 'rest' in the Ardennes had twenty-six men killed, one hundred and seventy-six wounded and no less than five hundred and fifty non-battle casualties.

Later General Bradley, the Army Group Commander, realizing the weakness of this front, gave Troy Middleton, VIII Corps Commander, an Armored Division, the 9th, which had not yet been in action and a Cavalry Group, the Fourteenth, of two Squadrons. General Middleton held the tanks as his corps reserve and used the cavalry on his left to plug the gap between V Corps in the north and his own corps.

VIII Corps front finally extended for eighty-eight miles from south of Monschau down the length of Luxembourg. This long front, still extending into the West Wall positions in two places in the Ardennes, was held by three infantry divisions—the veteran 2nd holding the salient in the German defences in the Schnee Eifel, and the 8th and 83rd.

These troops stayed in the Ardennes for October and much of November and came to know their long, complicated front well. They worked out both counter-attack and withdrawal plans in detail and their artillery registered hundreds of points on which to bring down fire in the unlikely event of a German attack in force. Had they been there when the counter-offensive began it is certain that the first few days would have been very different. But they were not.

Between the middle of November and December 15, all three of these infantry divisions and a combat command from the armoured division were moved north for the fighting around Aachen. Their places in VIII Corps were taken by the two infantry divisions who had attacked the West Wall in September, the 4th and the 28th, returning to the Ardennes greatly under strength, and a newly-arrived division containing many of the first American eighteen-year-old draftees, the 106th Infantry who took over the experienced 2nd Division's positions in the high Schnee Eifel salient.

All these changes meant that in December the long rambling Ardennes front was held by part of a green armoured division and four infantry divisions almost completely unfamiliar with it. Two, the 4th and 28th, badly needed rest, re-equipping and reinforcements and the other two, the 106th, and one in the north in V Corps, the 99th, had yet to fight their first battle.

The 99th Infantry division, which had arrived on the continent in November had been sent to First Army's left wing,

V Corps, whose commander, Major-General Gerow, had put them on his extreme right, the quietest sector of his front, to shake down and get some experience.

Here in the forest south of Monschau, the northernmost part of the Ardennes, they had time to become reasonably familiar with their front and to practise the various counters to attack that a defensive rôle demands. Because the weather was so bad, the worst for fifty years, they covered the roofs of their dugouts with heavy logs and soil to keep the warmth in. Later this reinforcing was to save many lives.

So, although they hadn't yet experienced a full-scale attack the men of the Checkerboard Division had been shelled and their patrols had had a few short, vicious encounters. They knew their own front as well as it is possible to know a dense forest in winter and were confident of being able to deal with anything it seemed likely the Germans would be able to do.

For the men of the 106th Division, on the other hand, everything went wrong from the very start of what was to prove a disastrous campaign. Fortune is one of the great imponderables of war and the commander on whom it does not smile fights with a heavy handicap. At the beginning of the Ardennes Offensive luck was most conspicuously denied to the young men of the 106th Infantry Division.

They were to have landed at Le Havre on December 2 and have been quickly trucked to St Vith taking over the 2nd Division's positions.

Three weeks were to have been allowed for them to become acclimatized and used to the terrain and to complete their training. Aggressive patrolling, firing their weapons at the enemy and being fired on themselves, would give them experience and confidence and by early January they would be ready to support the attack towards the Ruhr.

Instead the weather in the English Channel was so bad they could not dock and had to ride it out for four seasick days. The trucks were needed elsewhere, for supply services were still stretched to breaking point, so when they finally disembarked in bitter cold and driving rain nothing was ready for them. All that night, the next day and night, they waited in the mud and rain until, when they were finally loaded into trucks, few of them had any dry clothing at all. The long journey across France and Belgium took another two days and a night and at the end of it they had to bivouac in the snow. Through some mistake one infantry regiment, the 422nd, had no overshoes so their feet stayed wet and cold. The young soldiers had been cynically told by the veterans to expect a Snafu but this had gone from Fumtu to Tarfu.*

They stayed in the wet snow for another day and a half while arrangements were completed to move the 2nd Division out and then the cold, wet and miserable young soldiers were trucked the last fifteen miles—the journey took four hours—and moved into the Second's dugouts to find that those experienced GIs had taken their stoves with them so there was still no way to get warm and dry their clothes.

But as the veterans of the 2nd Infantry Division on their way north to the shooting war told them—'You guys are lucky. This front is a rest camp.'

In these circumstances, their commander, Major-General Alan Jones was glad that there would be time to get his green troops acclimatized and forged into a battle-ready formation before they had to fight.

They had been ordered to move into the 2nd Division's positions exactly as they found them and to make no change. They were to get hold of the long-worked-out counter-attack plans but this was postponed as was much other military activity in order to get stoves into dugouts, dry clothing and, most of all, hot food. The exposure and extraordinary cold and damp had caused an unusual number of cases of trench foot in the new division. Worst hit was the 422nd Infantry Regiment who had no overshoes and within a few days seventy-five men had been evacuated with this condition. It was later estimated that when the attack came at least twenty per cent of the men in the front line were in some way affected.

Assuming, as they had every right to do, that the possibility of a German attack was remote, it is understandable that the first two or three days were spent in trying to make conditions liveable rather than extensively reconnoitring their positions or sending out many patrols. But, the Army being what it is, daily reports had to be made at all levels and these naturally said what was expected, so that the disorganization and unpreparedness along this front was not generally known.

To add to their troubles there was a critical shortage of ammunition and they discovered that the supply points were forty miles away over torn up, crowded roads. There was a shortage of ammunition for the carbines and of both anti-tank grenades and the tank destroying bazookas, the rifleman's most effective answer, in the absence of anti-tanks guns, to an arm-

* The American soldier's comparison of 'fouled up' is: Situation normal—all fouled up. Fouled up more than usual. Things are *really* fouled up!

oured attack. They had their complement of machine guns but many of them were without ground mountings.

All that was needed to correct these things was time, but that they never got. The three infantry regiments of the division moved, during the evening of December 11, into the salient high on the Schnee Eifel still jamming into the German lines where the US 4th Infantry Division had been stopped three months before. Then there had been a handful of Germans. Now a great force was secretly building up, for it was from either side of the Schnee Eifel that the Germans had decided to make their main effort.

By Mid-December the Ardennes front extended from the snow-covered forest south of Monschau and, following roughly the Belgian/German frontier through rugged forested country, ran across a fairly flat east–west entry known as the Losheim Gap and thence continued around the western edge of the Schnee Eifel (except for the salient on its top) and south along the river Our, which is the frontier between Luxembourg and Germany, into the High Ardennes (called Little Switzerland) finishing at the ancient Luxembourg frontier town of Echternach on the main road from Luxembourg City to Cologne. The distance along the twisting front was about one hundred miles and it was held by four and two-thirds American divisions. They tallied about eighty-three thousand men and they had 242 tanks, 182 self-propelled anti-tank guns and 394 heavy guns. Behind this thinly held front lay vast dumps of American stores of ammunition, fuel and food, a Corps, an Army and an Army Group HQ and the main supply route to the American Ninth Army in the North. It was no wonder that it seemed a glittering prize to Adolf Hitler.

The US 99th Infantry Division held the extreme left wing in the Monschau Forest with a series of strong points of battalion and company strength spread over twelve miles. On December 13 one of their three regiments attacked with the 2nd Infantry Division towards the Roer Dams and this attack, supported by considerable artillery, was still in progress when the German counter-offensive began. The unexpected presence of these forces at the northern shoulder of the German attack was to prove most important.

South of the 99th Division positions there was, unbelievably, a two-mile sector of the front undefended. Unbelievably, because this was the Losheim Gap, historic German invasion route from the Schnee Eifel into Belgium. A further weakness was that the boundary between VIII Corps and V

Corps occurred here and it is axiomatic that seams between units are usually weak points.

After these two undefended miles the next five miles of the front was lightly held by a screen from one of the two reconnaissance squadrons of the Fourteenth Cavalry Group (the Eighteenth) occupying eight garrison points based on six small villages. They were the extreme left-hand troops of VIII Corps and every two hours they sent a small party across the two-mile gap to meet a patrol from V Corps' 99th Infantry.

South of the Eighteenth Cavalry, on their right, after another undefended gap of a mile and a half in the line, the positions of the newly-arrived 106th Infantry Division began. German intelligence had immediately spotted them as green troops and this combined with the other factors—the undefended Losheim Gap, the weakness of the Eighteenth Cavalry positions and the tactical importance of the high ground a few miles north-west for a blocking position against possible reinforcements from V's Ninth Army—made them decide that this was the place to rip open a hole through which to pour their armour.

The 106th positions in the Schnee Eifel and south of it covered the next fifteen miles of the front to where the frontiers of Germany, Luxembourg and Belgium meet. From here along the river Our the 28th Division had been made responsible for eighteen miles of front, the quietest sector of the Ardennes, for this division most needed a rest, having lost 6,184 men in the Hurtgen Forest fighting. In December it was in the process of building anew from the ground up.

Between the 28th Division and the right wing of the Ardennes was one armoured infantry battalion of the green 9th Armored Division responsible for about four miles of the line.

Lastly, the extreme right wing was held by one of the most experienced infantry divisions in the American Army, the 4th, who had assaulted Utah Beach on D-day and fought throughout the campaign in every action since. But it too had been badly mauled in the vicious battle in the Hurtgen Forest, losing some five thousand men in battle and another two thousand five hundred 'non-battle' casualties—including an unhealthy number of 'combat fatigue' cases. It was time for this great division to have a rest and to be built up to strength again. It moved south into the Duchy of Luxembourg in the area known as 'Little Switzerland', completing its concentration only three days before the attack.

Refitting these two divisions was slow and reinforcements

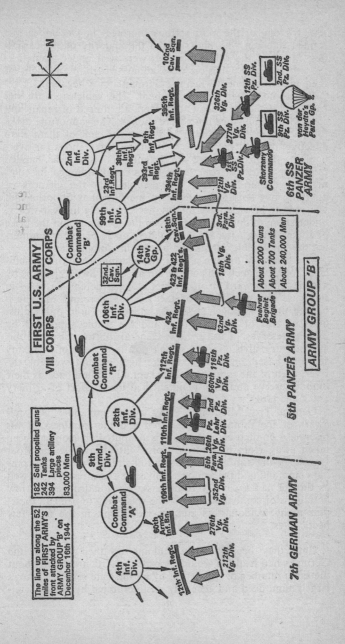

FIRST U.S. ARMY

V CORPS

VIII CORPS

The line up along the 52 miles of FIRST ARMY'S front attacked by ARMY GROUP 'B' on December 16th 1944

182 Self propelled guns
242 Tanks
394 Large artillery pieces
83,000 Men

N

102nd Cav. Sqn.

2nd. SS Pz. Div.

12th SS Pz. Div.

326th Vg. Div.

277th Vg. Div.

9th SS Pz. Div.

von der Heydte's Para. Gp.

395th Inf. Regt.

2nd Inf. Div.

9th Inf. Regt.

38th Inf. Regt.

23rd Inf. Regt.

393rd Inf. Regt.

394th Inf. Regt.

99th Inf. Div.

Combat Command 'B'

1st SS Pz.Div.

12th Vg. Div.

Skorzeny Commando

6th SS PANZER ARMY

3rd. Para. Div.

18th Cav. Sqn.

14th Cav. Gp.

32nd Cav. Sqn.

423 & 422 Inf. Regt's.

106th Inf. Div.

18th Vg. Div.

424 Inf. Regt.

Fuehrer Begleit Brigade.

62nd Vg. Div.

About 2000 Guns
About 700 Tanks
About 240,000 Men

5th PANZER ARMY

Combat Command 'R'

112th Inf. Regt.

560th Vg. Div.

116th Pz. Div.

28th Inf. Div.

110th Inf. Regt.

26th Pz. Lehr. Div.

2nd Pz. Div.

9th Armd. Div.

109th Inf. Regt.

5th Para. Div.

352nd Vg. Div.

Combat Command 'A'

60th Armd. Inf. Bn.

276th Vg. Div.

ARMY GROUP 'B'

4th Inf. Div.

12th Inf. Regt.

212th Vg. Div.

7th GERMAN ARMY

few, for one of the most serious shortages in December was trained riflemen who had suffered the majority of the casualties. Many of the rifle companies were well under strength—the 4th Infantry Division were about two thousand light of their full complement when the German attack began.

It was no better with equipment. The vehicles, worn out from continual use since D-day, were all in need of repair and soon the maintenance units were choked. The supporting tanks too needed attention and only twenty per cent of them were effective; most of the radios were in the repair shops for overhauling. In this state the 4th Infantry Division was handed thirty-five miles of front to look after and although its commander, General Barton, was assured that the chances of anything but nuisance raids from the Germans opposite him was remote he was, nevertheless, nervous. Only his war-weary, under-strength division lay between the Germans and the prize of Luxembourg City. He immediately made plans for countering the 'impossible' attack and briefed his commanders.

The best way to man a long meandering front with insufficient forces in such difficult terrain as 'Little Switzerland' is by a series of forward strong points along a defensible line—in this case the west bank of the rivers Sauer and Moselle—backed up by stronger positions, intended to hold out against odds of two or three to one, and the whole supported by mobile reserves. This is how General Barton disposed his 4th Infantry division: the strong positions were of company strength based on villages in the high ground west of the river; each of the three regiments kept a battalion back as their mobile reserve and each regiment had the support of artillery and some tanks.

General Troy Middleton, VIII Corps Commander, was well aware of the thinness of his front and the smallness of his reserve. A combat command of his armoured division had been taken away from him for V Corps' attack against the Roer Dams, leaving him only one other full-strength armoured combat command and the armoured division's own reserve. As well as this he had a cavalry reconnaissance squadron and a few battalions of combat engineers—he was going to need all these, plus many headquarters and service troops, in the next few hectic days.

Until they began quietly building up their strength the Germans had held the sector opposite the Ardennes with about the same number of troops but by an intricate series of moves largely unnoticed and generally misinterpreted by Allied Intel-

70

ligence the whole picture was most dramatically changed and by the night before the battle the eighty-three thousand unsuspecting Americans in the Ardennes had opposite them more than two hundred thousand combat troops with about five hundred tanks and nearly two thousand guns. How had this come about without Allied Intelligence warning SHAEF?

The answer would seem to be that Allied Intelligence fell into the error of assuming the enemy would make the militarily most correct moves and that the Germans assisted this thinking in every way. Also full credit must be given to the German skill in concealing their large-scale troop and material movement by confining most of it to the hours of darkness and during impossible flying weather, and to the most skilful use of camouflage.

The wrong guess about German intentions had several causes but the most important were the re-appointment of von Rundstedt as C-in-C West and the serious under-estimation of the resources still available to the Germans.

Field Marshal Gerd von Rundstedt was greatly respected by the Allies who considered him to be one of the best soldiers in the world and when it was known that he had once again assumed command on the Western Front it was thought that he would not have done so unless he had been assured, this time, of being in complete command. If he were, then he would use his strategic reserve—and the existence of the new, fresh Sixth SS Panzer Army was known to the Allies—in a determined effort to stop an Allied tank breakout from the Roer river crossing to the Rhine and the Ruhr resulting in a repeat of the tank race across France and Belgium. He would also most likely shore up his defences in the Saar opposite Patton's Third Army: what he certainly would not do was to attack through the Eifel and the Ardennes, even though it was only lightly held.

There were many reasons why such an offensive was not considered feasible: the terrain and the weather seemed to make large-scale armoured movement impossible: such an advance between heavy Allied concentrations in the north and the south would leave a vacuum behind it which these forces could rapidly fill, and lastly all intelligence reports indicated that Germany did not have the tanks, guns, planes, ammunition or men for anything but limited attacks.

This assessment was more or less agreed by everyone. In a directive published at his 21st Army Group HQ on the day the attack was launched (and written the day before) Field Marshal Montgomery said 'The enemy is at present fighting a

71

defensive campaign on all fronts; his situation is such that he cannot stage major offensive operations.' An intelligence summary of US 12th Army Group on December 12 summed up the position thus: 'It is now certain that attrition is steadily sapping the strength of German forces on the Western Front and that the crust of defences is thinner, more brittle and more vulnerable than it appears on our G-2 maps or to the troops in the line.'

Even General Patton, who usually assumed that his army was Germany's main concern, was of the opinion that the German Strategic Reserve would be committed to a spoiling attack in the Aachen–Düren area.

Allied air reconnaissance continued during the first two weeks of December even though the weather was often very bad and with the benefit of hindsight we can now see that they collected a good deal of evidence about the coming offensive, reporting large-scale movement at night in the area east of the Eifel, concentrations of searchlights, flatcars loaded with Tiger tanks moving west, many hospital trains waiting—always a sign of an impending offensive—and greatly increased rail activity.

But because of the generally held conviction that von Rundstedt was getting ready for a spoiling attack in the north all this activity was so interpreted. The main railway lines in the area west of the Rhine do run north and south, and would be used to carry reinforcements for the forces in the north. The fact that from these lines run branch lines into the Eifel was not seriously considered.

The Germans, of course, did all they could to encourage the idea that their attack was to be in the north. Troop movements towards that sector were not very carefully concealed and the troops south of there, which were in fact to spearhead the Ardennes attack, were arranged to appear to be the second wave of an attack north. Meanwhile every possible method of concealing the build-up was used.

The heavily wooded terrain east of the breakthrough sector offered ideal cover. Small villages were used to hide quite large formations and camouflage—an art of which necessity had made the Germans masters—was very strictly applied. Full trains were stored in tunnels during the day and unloaded only at night.

Security precautions covered every aspect: only the guns that had been in the line for a long time were allowed to fire and even they on a reduced scale to lend credence to the idea that the Germans were very low on ammunition. Radio communication was kept going at exactly the same rate as over the last month and patrolling kept down to a minimum. At the same time further north, where the attack was supposed to be going in, artillery fire and wireless communications was greatly stepped up, civilians were openly evacuated and a 'ghost army', the Twenty-fifth, was created with radio traffic, movements orders and all the paraphernalia of a new army. Some of the divisions which actually belonged to Sixth SS Panzer Army were nominally attached to this non-existent army.

These subterfuges succeeded mainly because they supported theories already decided upon: evidence for a strongly held opinion is seldom closely examined. When, for instance, the Fifth Panzer Army disappeared from the Roer front it was assumed that, as their casualties had been heavy, they were being pulled out for refitting and rest.

Part of the activity of front-line troops in a defensive rôle is I & R (Intelligence and Reconnaissance), and patrols are sent forward to probe the enemy positions, report any changes and, if possible, capture prisoners for identification purposes. By December 15 there were seventeen German infantry and armoured divisions opposite the Ardennes front. Only seven had been identified.

The success of the Germans in concealing the presence of this great force for so long was due to a combination of rigid discipline, and their own reconnaissance being limited to a few high-ranking officers, special precautions being taken against possible deserters (in fact there were only five on the whole Western Front in the first two weeks of December) and the strictest security regulations of the entire war.

All this succeeded brilliantly and the Allies were completely unprepared for the attack. After every possible excuse is made—and there are many—the conclusion must be reached that there was a gross failure of Allied Intelligence.

The Germans' success in keeping their plans for the great offensive secret was hardly more remarkable than the logistic feats they accomplished in the days and weeks of the build-up. The problems were immense: guns, tanks and men had to be brought to the Eifel from everywhere—literally from Norway to Austria. In addition certain units had to be extricated from the fighting on the Western Front, conveyed back over the Rhine, refitted and reinforced and sent back again over the Rhine to the Eifel. Vast quantities of fuel and ammunition had to be found and moved up to the attack area.

As early as September Hitler had ordered the Chief of Transportation to reinforce the Rhine railway bridges, so that one bomb could not drop any of them into the river, to modify ferries so that they could carry trains, and to prepare highway bridges for railway tracks if necessary. Finally, heavy spans of military bridging equipment were towed into place along the banks and camouflaged.

Trains were armoured and equipped with anti-aircraft guns to keep Allied fighter-bombers high, and miles of sidings were built to take full train loads. By these methods the German railways moved sixty-six divisions, as well as huge quantities of supplies, in the shuffle to build up forces for the offensive. By this time the German repair gangs had become so efficient that even after a heavy air raid they could quickly get the trains rolling again. For instance the vital marshalling yards of Coblenz, five days before the offensive, were bombed in broad daylight and over a hundred direct hits scored. All lines were in operation the next day. Of the five hundred trains used to transport men and supplies only fifteen carloads were destroyed by bombing.

The result of all this was that as well as the men, their tanks and guns, there was delivered to Army Group B before the attack over fifteen thousand tons of ammunition (estimated consumption was reckoned at one thousand two hundred tons a day) and more than four and a half million gallons of petrol—although more than two million was still west of the Rhine when the attack began.

So, although the final strength was less than Hitler had originally promised both in men and material it was a good deal more than his generals had either thought possible or dared hope for and the commanders in the field had switched from deep pessimism to mild optimism. In their three armies there were twenty divisions, seven of which were armoured and these, the real punch of the attack, were concentrated on a short sixty-mile front.

On the right, in the north, opposite the position of the inexperienced US 99th Infantry Division was one of 'Sepp' Dietrich's three corps, the LXVII Artillery of two volksgrenadier divisions. But also in the Monschau Forest, it will be remembered, was the 2nd Infantry Division, attacking through the Ninety-ninths lines and supported by much of V Corps artillery. The Germans would not, therefore, have the preponderance considered necessary for an attacker in this all-important 'shoulder' of their offensive.

Next, opposite the most thinly held section of the Allied Line, the Losheim Gap, where one squadron of the Fourteenth Cavalry occupied a few tiny villages with no support on their flanks, was the heaviest concentration; Dietrich's crack I SS Panzer Corps of two panzer divisions, two volksgrenadier divisions and a division of Parachute infantry, the 3rd. Waiting behind I SS Panzer Corps was II SS Panzer Corps with two more divisions.

Next came von Manteuffel's Fifth Panzer Army and his right wing, LXVI Corps, consisting of two volksgrenadier divisions facing a single troop of the Eighteenth Cavalry Squadron and the young soldiers of the 106th Infantry Division still trying to dry out and get warm after their nightmare journey from Le Havre. They had not yet properly tied in with the troops on their flanks.

The centre of General von Manteuffel's army was the LVIII Panzer Corps of a volksgrenadier division and a panzer division. These two were to rip open the seam between the newly-arrived 106th and the exhausted 28th Division.

But the Fifth Panzer Army's heaviest punch was to be from its left wing where the XLVII Panzer Corps of two armoured divisions and one infantry had only the 110th Infantry Regiment of 28th Division in their way.

Finally, on the extreme left of Army Group B's offensive came old General Brandenberger's Seventh Army. His right wing consisted of LXXXV Corps of a parachute and a volksgrenadier division who were facing the 109th Infantry Regiment of the 28th Division. His left wing had LXXX Corps of two volksgrenadier divisions: one was opposed by the Sixtieth Armored Infantry Battalion (part of US 9th Armored Division) and the other, the last German infantry division in the line, was to attack the Twelfth Infantry Regiment of the 4th Infantry Division.

German commanders at all levels had every reason to be confident: listening in to the security-careless American communications had told them that nothing was suspected and no reinforcements were on the way. Hitler's pre-battle command, 'Forward, to and over the Meuse!' was given to the waiting attackers and the general mood was of confidence and jubilation at the prospect of revenge on the invaders of Germany.

5

THE NORTHERN ATTACK PLAN

The defensive is easier than the offensive for all time
not turned to any account falls into the scale in favour
of the defence.

CLAUSEWITZ

Although on December 16 the overall objectives of the
Ardennes counter-offensive were still nominally those laid
down by Adolf Hitler in October—to surround and destroy all
the British and American forces north of a line running from
about the centre of the German/Luxembourg frontier to Antwerp, an enterprise which the bridge-playing German General
Staff ironically named 'The Grand Slam'—there is a good deal
of evidence that Field Marshal Model and his three army
commanders set their sights no further than the Meuse. If they
could seize crossings and establish bridgeheads over that river,
and if their flank protection still held, then they could consider
the next phase.

Field Marshal Model early saw that one of the dangers was
that reinforcements from the Ninth US Army in the north
would move down into the Ardennes before his panzers got
going for the Meuse and another was that Third US Army's
attack in the south would be called off so that General Patton
could attack the German left flank. Such reactions would be
the logical Allied answer to a German breakthrough in the
Ardennes.

One of the best ways to cover the exposed flanks of an
advance is to assign that responsibility to formations following
close behing the attacking force. This is Napoleon's famous
carré of two formations up and two behind who roll out flank
defence lines.

But the Ardennes front was too long and the forces finally
available too few to use this method. Instead, on the left the
German Seventh Army was given the sole task of protecting
that flank and on the right 'Sepp' Dietrich was told that his
Sixth SS Panzer Army would have to provide their own flank
defence.

Dietrich decided, or rather Kraemer his Chief of Staff did,
for Dietrich, like Patton, tended not to worry about his flanks,
to use two of his five infantry divisions to attack on either side

of Monschau and seize the high ground to the northwest as a hard shoulder from which to build a flank defence as far as Eupen. His other three infantry divisions would first be used to punch a hole in the thin American defences, through which his armour would pour, and then they too would wheel right and continue the defence wall from Eupen to the Meuse at Liège.

Realizing how important it would be to set up this flank defence quickly Field Marshal Model suggested a parachute drop in the vicinity of Krinkelt. This was the eastern edge of the Elsenborn Ridge, a few miles ahead of Dietrich's forward infantry and the parachutists were to hold the roads and high ground for the twelve hours or so before the infantry could get through. He put this idea to Hitler who immediately adopted it as his own and very much enlarged the paratroopers' task.

Instead of dropping just ahead of the attack Hitler decided to seize the main north to south road, down which reinforcements from Ninth US Army would come, by dropping paratroops fifteen miles behind the American Lines on a high, marshy moor known as the Hohes Venn. He got into touch with General Student, ordering him to organize this operation, on December 8, which was two weeks *after* the counter-offensive had been due to begin and only eight days before it actually did. General Student, as well as being commander of the Parachute Corps, was also commanding Army Group H, responsible for the defence of Holland where he had saved the situation in September. Now, hearing about the great counter-offensive for the first time, he was angry at not having been given a rôle in it. He sent a strong message to Hitler pointing out that his own troops were only fifty miles from Antwerp.

'Give me ten infantry and four panzer divisions and I guarantee to take Antwerp,' he said. Hitler was not displeased at this show of proper aggression and decided to order Student to start an attack on Antwerp from across the Maas* with a strong mixed battle group as soon as it was apparent that the counter-offensive was going according to plan. Meanwhile, he ordered Student to get on with organizing a parachute drop in the old tradition.

Tough, slow-speaking Kurt Student, a favourite of Goering's, was the pioneer of assault from the air, having led the parachute attack on Rotterdam in 1940 and organized the paratroop operations against Greece, Crete and in Russia. But by December 1944 the once-great German Parachute Corps had been reduced, by staggering losses and shortage of aircraft, to fighting as infantry. Although he had some thirty-five

* As the Meuse is called in Holland.

thousand 'parachutists' very few of them had ever jumped. Now Hitler was asking him to get a battalion—one thousand two hundred men—ready at a moment's notice. He sent for one of his most experienced officers, the man who had commanded one of the Parachute Regiments in Crete and who was now unhappily turning paratroopers into infantry in a combat school in Germany. This was Colonel Friedrich von der Heydte, a much-decorated, resourceful officer of the old school.

When Student had explained the mission, von der Heydte complained that the force allocated to him was not large enough for its task which was to open the roads behind the American front line for the passage of the Hitler Youth 12th SS Panzer Division, and at the same time spread out—in what he termed an 'oil stain' operation—to slow down American reinforcements hurrying down from the north. There was also simply just not enough time to organize such an operation properly. To all of which General Student gave him the customary answer: it was the Führer's order and not to be questioned or changed.

Colonel von der Heydte then asked Hitler (through General Student) if he could use his own old regiment, the famous 6th Parachute who were part of the Wehrmacht strategic reserve. Hitler refused this request as he was not willing to lose this entire regiment. Instead he ordered the commanders of parachute regiments each to send one hundred of their best and most experienced men to Colonel von der Heydte. Any soldier could have told the Führer what the result of such an order would be and Colonel von der Heydte was not surprised at having dumped on him in almost every case the men whom their commanders most wanted to get rid of.

When this order became known in the 6th Parachute Regiment itself two hundred and fifty of the parachute veterans 'deserted' and reported to Colonel von der Heydte. Greatly moved by the desire of so many of them to drop with him again he managed to prevail upon the authorities to allow them to stay with him.

After four days of frenzied preparations he reported to the commander of Sixth SS Panzer Army, General 'Sepp' Dietrich for his tactical briefing. It would have been difficult to have found two men less alike and there was instant antipathy between them.

Dietrich was openly contemptuous of this scratch force of paratroopers and told von der Heydte he had not wanted to use them at all.

'A parachute drop is the one certain way of alerting the

Americans about our attack,' he complained and went on to insist, over von der Heydte's objections, on the drop being made at night. The experienced paratroop commander pointed out that it would be inefficient as well as suicidal to drop into such difficult terrain in the dark but he was overruled. Von der Heydte pointed out that it was almost certain that his radios would be damaged and asked if he could take carrier pigeons. 'I am not the director of a zoo!' was Dietrich's answer.

Talking about that meeting today Baron von der Heydte says that Dietrich was a very good sergeant and insists that he means it as a compliment. 'He had all the qualities of a first-class NCO of the old German Army; he was personally brave, tough and disciplined and he cared for his men as though they were children and he chastised them like a stern father. He was feared, respected and even loved, but he was certainly not a commander.'

At the time of the Ardennes Offensive, von der Heydte says, it was obvious that the famous SS Commander was at the end of his tether—his nerves were shot to pieces and he was drinking constantly. He was never drunk but he was almost always 'under the influence'.

Dietrich's Chief of Staff, Kraemer, explained that von der Heydte's task was to jump a few hours before the German assault and seize control of the roads in the Malmédy area for a few hours until a special task force of heavy armour got up to him. This consisted of twenty-one of the latest mobile anti-tank weapons, the Jagdtiger. This monster weighed seventy-two tons, and its extra four inches of frontal armour made it practically invulnerable to anything except a direct hit by a heavy artillery shell. Mounting a high-velocity 128-mm gun on a Tiger Mk II chassis, these extra-heavy weapons were to follow close behind the infantry in the initial breakthrough and then wheel right and rendezvous with the paratroopers and hold the Eupen to Malmédy road against any American units attempting to move south. Dietrich told von der Heydte not to worry for the main SS Panzer Division would be up to him within a few hours—he would only have to hold his ground for the first day.

Von der Heydte thought this exceedingly unlikely but he ceased to argue for he saw that it was useless. Dietrich terminated the interview with the injunction, 'No time is to be wasted in the matter of prisoners!' an order he gave to all his shock troop leaders. Some like von der Heydte took it to mean that generally prisoners should be left for the following-up troops and surrendering Americans merely disarmed and sent eastwards, but, unfortunately, some of the young, fierce SS officers interpreted Dietrich's words as permission to kill and this resulted in some of the ugliest scenes in the ensuing battle.

The Paratroop Commander left Sixth SS Panzer Army headquarters determined, of course, to obey his orders as well as he could but feeling in his heart that this was probably the end of the German Parachute Corps whose exploits had won the admiration of soldiers everywhere.

He discovered that his transporters were old Ju 52s of the 'Stalingrad Squadron', so called in honour of their having kept supplies going to the German armies trapped in Stalingrad two years before. Now the planes were war-weary; half the pilots had never flown in combat and there had been no joint training with the jump masters. A few pilots were from the old parachute corps and the commander himself had flown von der Heydte in the attack on Crete.

Concealing his misgivings from his men he pushed ahead with training his inexperienced parachutists and arranged for three hundred dummy figures to be dropped to draw away ground defences. If the armour actually could get through to them in the first day there was a chance that they would succeed. At any rate Colonel von der Heydte was determined to have a damned good try.

As far as Dietrich knew the only troops in the Monschau sector were part of the green US 99th Infantry Division and it did not seem likely that they would be able to stand a two-division infantry attack followed by an armoured punch. Once the ridge north-west of Monschau was securely held the American First Army would be split and the Ninth Army could be prevented from coming south for the critical period his tanks needed to advance and seize the Meuse crossings.

Eighty miles to the south at the other end of the projected German assault line, opposite Echternach, General Brandenberger had been given only four infantry divisions and no armoured support at all. Their job was to throw up a protective screen for the long flank Manteuffel's Fifth Panzer Army's advance would create.

General Brandenberger allocated two divisions to the task of crossing the Sauer river in front of Echternach, breaching the American forward posts and seizing the one-thousand-foot high Schlamm Bach ridge about seven miles south of Echternach. This ridge was behind the American 4th Infantry Division's artillery covering the Echternach sector and possession of it would nullify those guns. This was essential; it would prevent the shelling of the supporting infantry and it would allow the engineers to get temporary bridges across the river undisturbed by shelling. Once these bridges were in, the anti-tank guns, howitzers and heavy field pieces that an effective defence screen needs would be moved up.

From the Schlamm Bach his next move was to be a drive south-west across the main road from Luxembourg, thus isolating Echternach, and then west to cut the busy Luxembourg to Aachen highway, principal lifeline of the Ninth Army in the north and known to the soldiers in the Ardennes as 'Skyline Drive'. Luxembourg itself, where General Bradley's 12th Army Group headquarters were, was not a target because Brandenberger's forces were not powerful enough to seize and hold it, but, naturally enough, when the offensive began Luxembourg was thought to be Seventh Army's objective, just as in the north Liège was thought to be 'Sepp' Dietrich's. (In fact, Hitler had expressly ordered Sixth SS Panzer Army to ignore Liège, passing to the south of it.)

This line—from Echternach through the Schlamm Bach and thence to Junglinster and a point north of Mersch, some twelve miles north of Luxembourg City—was to be the southern hard shoulder from which Seventh Army's own flank would be protected, after the moving screen shielding Fifth Panzer Army's advance had moved west.

This screen was to be formed by General Brandenberger's other corps, of a paratroop infantry division and a volks-grenadier division. Although they had almost no transport they were expected, after crossing the river Our just above where it joins the Sauer, to advance, trying somehow to keep up with Manteuffel's tanks and protecting them from attacks from the south.

So much for securing both flanks of the offensive which would use up nine of the thirteen infantry divisions. The remaining four, with four of the panzer divisions which were to be used in the first assault, were given the main task of reaching and crossing the Meuse.

In this the most important rôle had been given to 'Sepp' Dietrich. After three infantry divisions had ripped a hole in the thin American front the élite I SS Panzer Corps would pour through. Dietrich planned to unleash both the 1st SS Panzer Division, 'Hitler's Bodyguard' and their rivals, 12th SS Panzer Division, 'Hitler Youth'. The plan, in his own words, was 'to hold the reins loose and let the armies race'.

Confident of the might of his crack SS panzers he wanted to let them make the actual breakthrough of the Allied line themselves but he was overruled by Model, who had had unpleasant experiences on the Eastern Front of advancing armour without infantry protection.

Dietrich's tanks were to get to the Meuse south of Liège according to a strict timetable. They had to reach the high marshy moor behind Malmédy, the Hohes Venn, on the first day and get over it on the second, before the Allies could make it into a strong defence position: on the third day maximum ground was to be gained—over forty miles by road, to the Meuse and crossings had to be made and bridgeheads secured the same night.

If this timetable was kept and the rest of the offensive went according to plan then Dietrich's other armour, II SS Panzer Corps, would close up and continue the advance west from the Meuse.

On Dietrich's left, General von Manteuffel, with less strength than Hitler had allocated to his favourite SS, had been given two difficult tasks and a greater distance to cover. He was to outflank the Schnee Eifel and seize St Vith and also push his tanks to the Meuse taking Bastogne on the way.

His plan for seizing the important road and rail centre of St Vith about twelve miles behind the forward American positions in the Schnee Eifel was to send two-thirds of a volks-grenadier division around the northern flank, through the Losheim Gap and the other third through a narrow corridor to the south of the Schnee Eifel through which a main road from Germany entered Belgium. These two prongs would then close, trapping large American forces inside them.

In his centre Manteuffel planned for LVIII Panzer corps, which consisted of a division of tanks supported by one of infantry, to get across the Our on improvised bridges, over-run the lightly-held American advance posts, get up on to the 'Skyline Drive', two or three miles west of the river, within five or six hours and then go as fast as possible for the Meuse.

His main punch would be delivered by his other armoured corps on his left. This XLVII Panzer, would also get bridges across the Our before dawn and get through the forward positions and up on to 'Skyline Drive' by noon. From there an all-out thrust was to take them twenty-five miles to the communications centre of Bastogne, key to the Ardennes road network and a target laid down personally by Hitler who saw that if it remained in Allied hands the Allies could pour reinforcements into it from the south.

At the last moment the Führer, perhaps conscious that the disparity between Fifth Panzer Army and Sixth SS Panzer

Army was not going to help the offensive to succeed, produced, rather like a magician, some extra tank units for General Manteuffel.

One was the élite Panzer Lehr* Division which had been almost completely destroyed under the concentrated air bombardment which had preceded the First Army breakout in Normandy, and had been part of the composite division which, with only half a dozen tanks, had stopped the American advance through the Eifel in September. Panzer Lehr had then been re-equipped and brought up to strength and assigned to the Ardennes offensive. This automatically meant that it became one of the units which could not be committed to battle before the offensive without the Führer's personal permission. In flat disobedience to this order Field Marshal von Runstedt had thrown Panzer Lehr against Patton's attack in Lorraine and, once again, this division had been virtually destroyed. Somehow in just over two weeks it had been built up a third time, not to full strength, but still commanded by Fritz Bayerlein, a tank man who had fought with Rommel in Africa and in Normandy, and whose aggressiveness, dash and courage were well known to the Allies.

The other unit found by Hitler for Manteuffel was made up from one battalion of tanks taken away from the Eastern Front, three battalions of panzer grenadiers (armoured infantry) and the artillery that had guarded the Wolf's Lair, which Hitler gave up in November. Formed by expanding Hitler's own escort battalion, the Führer Begleit Brigade, it would fight under that name. Its commander, Colonel Remer, was the man who had been in command of the Berlin Guard Battalion when the assassination attempt on Hitler had been made and who had not obeyed the conspirators' order to arrest Goebbels but had reported to him instead. Now the Führer gave him an armoured brigade to command in battle.

Fifth Panzer Army's commander kept these two units back, intending to use them to reinforce the more successful of his two armoured corps. Manteuffel, a brilliant tank tactician, did not have so rigid a plan as Dietrich nor so precise a timetable. He was prepared to reinforce success by switching his forces at any time. He was aware that the counter-offensive had been arranged as a contest between the SS Panzers and regular army tank divisions and that the odds had been fixed but he was contemptuous of Dietrich's pretensions to command an army and sure that greater skill would make up for the difference in

* Literally, 'apprentice armour'—so called because it had originally been formed from a tank-training unit.

83

numbers.

These then were the initial five objectives: (1) the setting up of a hard shoulder on the high ground north-west of Monschau and (2) the seizure of a ridge south of Echternach at the other end of the front for the same purpose. These two operations, together with Seventh Army's moving screen, would secure the flanks and make sure that the attack could not be quickly pinched out. Then (3) 'Sepp' Dietrich's tanks would steamroller over the lightly held American line and race for the Meuse and Manteuffel, in the centre would (4) strike for the Meuse with half his tanks, bypassing strong points while (5) his remaining tanks would seize Bastogne before going on to the Meuse.

Let us see how well these plans succeeded.

In order to understand why, on December 16, the apparently simple task of setting up a flank defence along the high ground north-west of Monschau was to give Sixth SS Panzer Army so much trouble we must go back three days and follow the US 2nd Infantry Division whom we last saw handing over their positions in the Schnee Eifel to the newly-arrived 'Hungry and Sick'—the 106th Division.

The veteran 2nd Infantry had been transferred to V Corps to become the spearhead of the southern wing of a double attack on the great dams on the upper reaches of the Roer river. As long as the Germans controlled these dams the Allies dare not cross the Roer and start to advance over the low ground towards the industrial Ruhr for the whole area could be flooded by opening the sluice gates. Indeed, the Allied air force had tried to breach the dams and release the water in several bombing attacks but without success, so on December 7 General Courtney Hodges, the First US Army commander ordered General Gerow's V Corps to attack and seize them.

A double thrust from north and south was planned. We are only concerned here with the southern one, originating in the north of the Ardennes front, to be made by the 2nd Infantry Division attacking in a corridor through the 99th Infantry Division.

The point in the German West Wall defences selected for the breakthrough was a heavily defended crossroads deep in the Monschau Forest and the only approach to it from the west was from the twin Belgian villages of Rocherath–Krinkelt on the edge of the forest. From here a secondary road ran six miles north-west through the forest to the main road at Wahlerscheid which led straight to the Roer Dams area.

The thickness of the forest of great pine trees and the lack

84

of tracks meant that the division's vehicles, both wheeled and tracked, would have to keep to the road which was known to be mined. The infantry would be forced to plough through the underbrush and snowdrifts on either side of the road while the engineers found and lifted the mines. The narrowness of the only possible line of approach to this fortified crossroads meant that Major-General Walter M. Robertson had to advance his division by regiments in column, not the most satisfactory formation.

9th Infantry Regiment's task was to spearhead the attack and seize the crossroads in a frontal assault. 38th Infantry Regiment, following up behind, would then pass through and make the attack towards the dams.

At the outset 2nd Infantry's third regiment, the 23rd would be held in reserve near Camp Elsenborn about seven miles to the rear of the jump-off point, Rocherath–Krinkelt. Also in reserve for the moment was the supporting armour, Combat Command B of Armored Division who had come from VIII Corps at the same time as Infantry Division.

Finally, in support of this attack, a good deal of artillery had been concentrated including many 155-mm howitzers and larger field pieces, self-propelled guns, a battalion of 4·5 rockets as well as the division's own artillery and that of the combat command.

In Dietrich's original plan three volksgrenadier divisions had been assigned to this part of the American front thought to be held by only part of the 99th Infantry Division and a few hundred of the Fourteenth Cavalry Group in the northern half of the Losheim Gap. The unexpected presence of the 2nd Infantry Division and the unusually heavy concentration of artillery were to upset his plans.

Routing 2nd Infantry Division's attack through the middle of 99th Infantry Division's sector was most unusual. It had been decided upon because of 99th Infantry's comparative inexperience. However they were ordered to cover 2nd Division's flank with an attack of their own on the right, along a minor road through the forest. This took two of their 395 Infantry Regiment's three battalions away, leaving only one up in the north on the Manschau–Höfen front. Here 99th Division's northern boundary ran through the southern part of Monschau, the rest of the town and the positions north which would come under attack were held by the Thirty-eighth Cavalry Squadron.

The Wahlerscheid crossroads assault started from Rocherath–Krinkelt at 9.0 am on December 13. The infantrymen

carried enough rations, ammunition and anti-tank mines to
last them for at least twenty-four hours because of lessons
learned in the earlier Hurtgen Forest fighting of the difficulty
in getting supplies up to troops fighting in heavily wooded
country.

The objective was a complex of pill-boxes, concrete bunk-
houses and supporting gun positions which had been held for
some time by volksgrenadiers from 277 Division. But this
division had now been chosen as one of the three to smash a
hole in the American line for the SS Panzers in the coming
offensive. Consequently the volksgrenadiers holding the
Wahlerscheid crossroads had just been ordered to move south
to get into their attack position.

As soon as they moved out the crossroads defence would be
temporarily entrusted to a battalion from 326 Volksgrenadier
Division who were moving north for the attack on Monschau.
When they, in their turn, moved out replacement troops would
occupy the crossroads which, if the Ardennes Offensive succeeded, would soon be far behind the German front line.

So, while the American 2nd Division and 99th Division
were slogging north through the slush and snow of the Monschau Forest to attack the Wahlerscheid crossroads, completely ignorant of the coming German attack, the 277th
Volksgrenadier Division, guarding the crossroads, was getting
ready to move south to take part in that attack and the 326th
Volksgrenadier Division was about to occupy the crossroads
temporarily. Equally the Germans, of course, did not know
that they were to be one of the first objectives in V Corps offensive against the Roer Dams. Actual warfare is seldom as tidy
as sand-table exercises.

It was all a matter of timing: The German counter-offensive
would put paid to V Corp's Roer Dams attack, but, as this had
started three days before, it could in its turn—if it had proved
successful—probably have caused the Ardennes Offensive to be
postponed. But it was not successful, or rather the capture of
the Wahlerscheid crossroads took too long.

It was a most formidable obstacle: a small fortress of four
pill boxes, six concrete bunkers and two other reinforced buildings in a clearing surrounded by anti-personnel mines, concealed by the snow. The central buildings were protected from
surprise by up to ten rows of barbed wire entanglements and a
moat made by connecting natural ravines. All this was expertly
covered by mortar, machine-gun and rifle positions.

2nd Division's tough, experienced riflemen suffered heavy
casualties in their attempt to carry this miniature fortress.

Although the 155-mm self-propelled guns inched slowly up the road and fired 287 rounds at point blank range it was found out' later that not one shot had penetrated the thick concrete fortifications.

At the end of the second day, December 14, it was no longer practicable to use 9th Armored Division's Combat Command B on this front and General Hodges ordered it to be returned to VIII Corps the following day. Naturally this did not seem to be a very important move at the time and Combat Command B's hundred tanks and supporting thousand infantry did not get their orders until the next day, December 16. Had they moved to St Vith on the 15th it is possible that the disaster in the Schnee Eifel might have been avoided. But, in all fairness, war is full of such might-have-beens and it is an axiom that in the long run luck is evenly distributed, like weather.

By the evening of December 15, after three days of determined attack during which 2nd Division's 9th Infantry Regiment lost 737 men from all causes, the volksgrenadiers were still holding the Wahlerscheid crossroads. But that night a way was found under the wire and for hours riflemen wriggled forward one by one until at midnight they had surrounded the pill boxes and bunkers. Doors were blown in by beehive charges and all the defenders were either killed or captured by dawn.

But it was dawn on December 16.

BLITZKRIEG

We have in German a fine proverb:
'The Gods love and bless those who
seem to strive for the impossible.'
That is a divinity in which I believe.

ADOLF HITLER
(in a letter to Lord
Rothermere May 3, 1935)

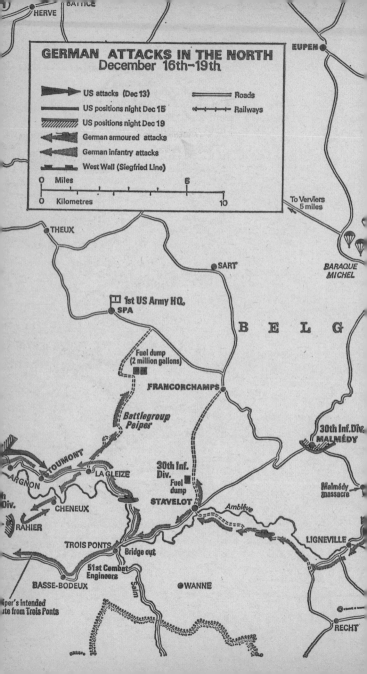

GERMAN ATTACKS IN THE NORTH
December 16th–19th

➤ US attacks (Dec 13)	══ Roads
▬ US positions night Dec 15	┼┼┼ Railways
▨ US positions night Dec 19	
◄ German armoured attacks	
◄ German infantry attacks	
▦ West Wall (Siegfried Line)	

```
0    Miles              5
0    Kilometres              10
```

HERVE

BATTICE

EUPEN

THEUX

SART

BELG

BARAQUE MICHEL

To Verviers
5 miles

⚑ 1st US Army HQ.
SPA

Fuel dump
(2 million gallons)

FRANCORCHAMPS

Battlegroup Peiper

30th Inf. Div.
MALMÉDY

TOURMONT

LA GLEIZE

ARGNON

30th Inf. Div.
Fuel dump

Malmédy
massacre

Div.

CHENEUX

STAVELOT

Amblève

RAHIER

LIGNEVILLE

TROIS PONTS

Bridge out

51st Combat Engineers

BASSE-BODEUX

⬤ WANNE

Salm

Recht

per's intended
ute from Trois Ponts

RECHT

LAMMERSDORF

KESTERNICH

SIMMERATH

KONZEN

102nd Cav. Gp.

IMGENBROICH

Part of 326th Vg.Div.

6th SS. PZ. ARMY (Dietrich)

MÜTZENICH

MONSCHAU

ROHREN

GERMANY

99th Inf. Div.

HÖFEN

LXVII Corps

326th Vg. Div.

Wahlerscheid cross roads

-RBRODT

2nd Inf.Div. attack

99th Inf.Div. In support

I SS. Panzer Cor

277th Vg.Div

12th SS.Pz. Div.

ELSENBORN

ELSENBORN RIDGE

BÜTGENBACH

1st Inf.Div.

ROCHERATH

KRINKELT

WIRTZFELD

99th Inf. Div.

277th Vg.Div

BULLINGEN

12th Vg.Div.

NES

Battlegroup Peiper

HONSFELD

LOSHEIMERGRABEN

Buckholz Sta.

Road bridge out

The Losheim Gap

1st SS.Pz. Div.

LOSHEIM

AMBLÈVE

V Corps

LANZERATH

3rd Para.Div.

HOLZHEIM

14th Cav. Gp.

BERTERATH

AFST

VIII CORPS

GERMAN ATTACKS IN THE SOUTH
December 16th-19th

German armoured attacks	=== Road
German infantry attacks	+—+ Railw
US positions night Dec 15	
US positions night Dec 19	
US counterattacks	
West Wall (Siegfried Line)	

0   Miles   5
0   Kilometres   5

116th Pz. Div.
DASBURG
2nd Pz. Div.

Part of Pz. Lehr

5 PANZER ARMY (Manteuffel)

26th Vg. Div.

XLVII Pz Corps

Part of Pz. Lehr

EMÜND

5th Para. Div.

LXXXV Corps

VIANDE

G E R M A N Y

WALSDORF
FOUHREN
109th Inf. Regt.

352nd Vg. Div.

7th ARMY (Brandenberger)

WALLENDORF

REISDORF
276th Vg. Div.

DIEKIRCH
BIGELBACH

LXXX Corps

EPPELDORF   DILLINGEN

212th Vg. D

BEAUFORT

LBRUCK

STEGEN   ERMSDORF   HALLER   ERDORF   ECHTERN

12th Inf. Regt

R   G

MEDERNACH

60th Armd. Inf. Bns.
(part of 9th Armd. Div.)

WALDBILLIG

LAUTERBORN

CHRISTNACH   MULLERTHAL   SCHEIDGEN   OSWEILER

LAROCHETTE   BREIDWEILER   CONSDORF   22nd Inf.
Regt.   DICK

GEYERSHOF

CC'A'
10th Armd.
Div.

MOMP

BECH   HERBC

4th Inf. Div.

8th Inf.

22nd Inf. Regt.

SCH

JUNGLINSTER   HQ.12th Inf. Regt.

To Luxembourg City 5 miles

6

THE INITIAL ASSAULT

> *It is a delusion to imagine that a plan of campaign can
> be laid down far ahead and fulfilled with exactitude.
> The first collision with the enemy creates a new situa-
> tion in accordance with the result. Some things in-
> tended will have become impracticable. Others which
> originally seemed impossible become feasible.*
>
> VON MOLTKE

Most of the more than two hundred thousand German troops
now poised for the great counter-offensive had only reached
their attack positions in the last few days of a movement
operation that was worked out almost to the minute. Naturally
everything everywhere did not go without a hitch: some units
were not able to reach their areas in time; there were mistakes
in the calibre of ammunition and the allocation of fuel;
formations took wrong roads and became entangled with
others. But ninety-five per cent of men, guns, vehicles, ammunition and fuel were delivered to the right place in time—
and all this took place without alerting Allied Intelligence. It
was one of the outstanding feats of military organization of
the war.

The artillery concentration finally achieved was remarkable
considering the length of front in the east and west that Germany was defending and her recent enormous losses. General
Stadtinger, who commanded the artillery of Sixth SS Panzer
Army, described the guns on his front in an interview after
the war. 'Besides the divisional artillery of both corps we had
one battalion of three batteries. Each with nine guns ranging
from 150 mm to 210 mm. In army artillery we had two Nebel-
werfer* brigades plus three brigades of heavy artillery—200
mm, 240 mm and 350 mm. We also had two or three volks-
artillerie corps of six battalions each.'

'Sepp' Dietrich favoured a very heavy opening barrage before
launching his infantry attack while von Manteuffel wanted to
attack the American forward positions first, to gain surprise
and then use his artillery to nullify the opposing artillery,

* Nebelwerfers are nine-barrelled mortars. Whistles attached to
their vanes produced a nerve-chilling noise and gave them their
nickname 'screaming meemies'.

knock out communications, delay reinforcements and destroy command posts. General Stadtinger had described the Sixth SS Panzer Army's tactics. 'We planned the following three types of fire for the first day: one, fire on the main line of resistance starting at about 5.0 am. Two, fire on the command posts, road crossings, villages in the neighbourhood of the front line and other strongpoints thus cutting your lines of communications. Three, fire on the more distant villages and strongpoints—especially roads on which we thought reserves would be brought up.'

Also General Stadtinger wanted to concentrate on the Elsenborn ridge which runs from Rocherath–Krinkelt to Camp Elsenborn because he thought the opposition would be heaviest there but he was overruled. Had he had his way and had the parachutists landed at Krinkelt as Model had asked, it is probable that the situation in the north would have been very different. Instead the artillery was distributed evenly along the whole twenty-five miles of Sixth SS Panzer Army's front and a rather higher proportion than is usual was wasted because of the thinness of the American line.

At midnight Colonel von der Heydte had his one thousand two hundred and fifty paratroops lined up and ready for the fleet of trucks which were to transport them the twenty-five miles to the airfield where the old Ju 52s were waiting. The hours went by but there was no sign of their transport. Finally, in a rage, von der Heydte got through to the officer commanding the transport and discovered that they had no fuel for the trucks—the dump had been emptied by one of the armoured units moving up for the counter-offensive. The parachute drop was postponed for twenty-four hours when, if Dietrich's optimism was justified, it would no longer be needed. The paratroopers were told to get some rest.

At 5.30 the whole Ardennes front erupted (except for one part of Manteuffel's sector—opposite the northern wing of 28th Infantry Division) and shells screamed over the heads of the waiting German infantry almost non-stop for an hour and a half. These volksgrenadiers, many going into battle for the first time, had been thrilled by stirring Orders of the Day from old Field Marshal von Runstedt and from the Führer himself. Many believed that they were about to take part in a great offensive that would somehow, miraculously, sweep the invaders out of the Fatherland. As they heard their own tremendous barrage and then saw the searchlights reflect down on their objectives they surged forward confidently.

In the north on Sixth SS Panzer Army's front the armoured infantry of the panzer columns were behind the volksgrenadiers closely followed by the tanks of the crack SS Panzer Divisions—the 12th Hitler Jugend on the right and their great rivals, the First, Hitler's Bodyguard on the left. Immediately behind the armour were Otto Skorzeny's saboteurs in American uniforms and riding in American jeeps impatiently waiting for the promised holes in the American line.

The final strength of Skorzeny's 150 Brigade was about three thousand three hundred which he divided into three battle groups each assigned to one of Dietrich's armoured columns. Overrunning weaker forces, bypassing stronger, they were to go ahead of the tanks as fast as possible and hold open a bridge for the following panzers. These three bridges—Engis, Amay and Huy—crossed the Meuse between Liège and Namur and aerial reconnaissance had shown them to be unguarded. As soon as the American 99th Infantry Division's front line had been breached a fast-moving reconnaissance party of Skorzeny's men would be passed through to dash for the bridges and report back on their condition and the arrival of any American forces. Their secondary tasks were to increase panic and confusion by false reports, to disturb communications by removing signposts or giving wrong directions, to cut telephone lines and to blow up ammunition dumps.

Skorzeny, although confident, pointed out that his Operation Greif could only succeed if Sixth SS Panzer Army achieved their first day objectives, for if they did not there was unlikely to be the confusion and panic behind the American lines upon which his operation depended. Army Group B's Chief of Staff General Krebs personally assured Colonel Skorzeny that by nightfall of December 16 the whole American front line would have ceased to exist and the German armour would be moving ahead gathering irresistible momentum. With this assurance from so senior an officer Skorzeny was content.

With no more than twenty tanks and thirty scout cars he could probably seize the bridges but could not hope to hold them for longer than twenty-four hours. Two days before the offensive he briefed his commanders who learned for the first time about the great offensive and their rôle. The next day they moved up to their positions on the tail of the leading SS Panzer battlegroup.

Skorzeny set up his own headquarters next to I SS Panzer Corps battle HQ at Schmittheim some nine or ten miles behind the start line and waited for word that the American line had been breached and his men launched on their dash for the bridges.

When the German barrage opened up the first reactions of the 99th Infantry in forward positions were that the shells were their own, 'outgoing mail' to support the attack on the Wahlerscheid crossroads on the way to the Roer Dams.

As soon as they discovered their mistake they dived into their bunkers and it was then that the stout log and mud roofs which they had put on for warmth saved many lives. The bombardment was long and heavy and came as a considerable surprise particularly on one section of the front where the last intelligence report had said that the Germans had only two horse-drawn guns opposite. After an hour's non-stop shelling the battalion executive office reported, 'They sure worked those horses to death.'

The shelling was assumed to be the German reply to the attack on the crossroads and even when the searchlights flicked on and the German infantry came forward out of the mist it was still thought to be a feint to draw off the troops from the thrust north. However, it was not long before it became apparent that the whole of the nineteen-mile Divisional front was under attack.

Of 99th Infantry Division's nine battalions, one was right up on the northern boundary holding Höfen, south of Monschau. Three more were attacking north as right flank protection for 2nd Division's attack; one was in reserve near the division's southern boundary some three miles back in the gap between V Corps and VIII Corps and the other four, on the right of the 2nd Division attack, were holding a six-mile north to south line along the eastern edge of the forest as far as the Intercorps gap. 99th Division's main line of resistance ran just east of the International Highway which was on the German side of the frontier and from a hundred yards to over a mile from the West Wall fortifications.

The northern half of this line, held by two battalions of the 393rd Infantry Regiment, was due to be assaulted by 277 Volksgrenadier Division. Their objective was to gain the northernmost of the three east/west roads in this sector and by capturing Rocherath–Krinkelt, Wirtzfeld and Elsenborn, block off the roads coming down from Ninth Army in the north.

The last three miles of 99th Division's long front, down to the corps boundary, was held by two battalions of 394 Infantry Regiment who were stretched across the projected path of the 12th Volksgrenadier Division. Dietrich believed these to be his

97

best infantry and he had given them the task of opening the Losheimergraben to Bullingen road for the tanks of the crack 12th SS Panzer Division, the Hitler Jugend, whose main route west was along this road.

Just south of 394 Regiment's First Battalion, holding the division's extreme right-hand position, a branch railway line wandered from Germany into Belgium through the unguarded gap between the two American corps. During the autumn retreat the Germans had blown up the bridge which carried the International Highway over this railway. The heavily forested country confined tanks to roads so, before the Hitler Youth armoured division could get to Losheimergraben to start their dash for the Meuse, German infantry had to take and hold the railway track so that the highway bridge could be repaired. A regiment of fusiliers from 12th Volksgrenadier Division was assigned this objective.

Two miles from the German frontier the railway comes to the small station of Buckholz. This was the area where the Third Battalion of the 394th Infantry were in divisional reserve and, unexpectedly it was to be the scene of the first engagement on this part of the front.

One company were quartered in and around the station itself. They had taken shelter when the shelling began at 5.30 am and had suffered no casualties. It had stopped about 7.0 and just before 8.0 the men lined up for their breakfast. It was foggy and figures marching two abreast down the railroad track were almost on top of them before they were recognized as the enemy. Everyone dived for his weapon and opened fire; the leading German fusiliers threw themselves into the ditches alongside the track and returned the fire. Some took shelter in freight cars standing in a siding but an American tank destroyer put shell after shell into these and when the men inside tried to break out and reach cover they were shot down. Mortar crews plastered the ditches and the Americans, though outnumbered, by fighting fiercely for several hours were able to stop any further German advance. About noon another company from the reserve battalion came up as reinforcements and the Germans withdrew leaving behind about seventy-five dead. Total American casualties had been not more than thirty and the railway line was still in American hands. The highway bridge could not be repaired and the panzers could not yet get moving.

However, south of the railway line Dietrich's third infantry division, 3rd Parachute, had sent a column sweeping through the two-mile gap between V Corps and VIII Corps which had swallowed up the platoon patrolling across the gap and successfully severed contact between 99th Infantry Division and their neighbour to the south, 106th Infantry Division. A wedge was being driven between the two American corps which would open the way for a German armoured thrust.

99th Division's main line was hit hard, soon after the barrage stopped at half a dozen places. On the left, in the northernmost position, the Third Battalion of 393 Regiment were deployed along the eastern edge of the forest less than a hundred yards from the West Wall positions. A road led from the German fortifications straight into the American line while behind them a track ran four miles through the forest to the twin villages of Rocherath–Krinkelt from where the 2nd Division attack had begun and through which the division's main line of communication ran. It was also at the eastern end of a high ridge running west for nearly five miles to Camp Elsenborn. This, the Elsenborn ridge, was a natural defensive feature which the German High Command had assigned as one of the first objectives. It will be remembered that it was Rocherath–Krinkelt that Model had wanted von der Heydte's parachutists to seize before the infantry attack. The twin villages were a most important target and 277 Volksgrenadiers commander, Colonel Hans Viebig pointing out that the ground favoured the American defenders in the forest, had asked for more men. But this was a request which practically every German commander in the attack was making and it simply could not be met for there were no more troops available—the bottom of the barrel had been scraped clean. Instead Colonel Viebig was promised very heavy artillery support.

This promise was kept and the whole of 99th Division's main line of resistance suffered a tremendous pounding for an hour and a half. All the front-line communications were knocked out and on the left of 393's sector, where their Third Battalion were holding positions nearest to the West Wall, the searchlights flicked on in the last few minutes of the barrage and the first assault waves rushed the American line almost as soon as the last shell fell.

Most of the infantrymen in the forward positions were killed or captured and by 9.30 am the front line had been pushed a mile back into the forest, if indeed it could be called a front line, for the Germans had been able to continue west on either side of the battalion command post. The German infantry attempted to overwhelm this too but were discouraged by extremely heavy mortaring—over a thousand 81-mm shells were rained down on them.

By nightfall the survivors of the Third Battalion in a tight circle around the command post reported that they could hold on for the rest of the night although the Germans had cut them off from the First Battalion to the south and had infiltrated behind them and cut their supply road. Nevertheless the tactically important objective of Rocherath–Krinkelt had not fallen.

Further south, on their right, the First Battalion of 393 Regiment had been hit by another of 277 Volksgrenadier's regiments who had attacked across a half a mile of open country as soon as the barrage had lifted but had been stopped by concentrated machine-gun sweeps and, again, by almost non-stop mortaring. The German commander had immediately committed his reserves and weight of numbers pushed the Americans back into the woods all along the battalion front.

Both attackers and defenders fought fiercely and both suffered heavy casualties. By the end of the day 393 Regiment's First Battalion had been reduced to half its fighting strength; its Third Battalion had lost nearly three hundred men. Although somehow a front had been restored it was dangerously weak and all through the night the triumphant German volksgrenadiers moved around in the forest firing into foxholes, shooting off flares and trying to discover the whereabouts of small American parties by shouting out in English.

But reinforcements from 2nd Division's reserve, the 23rd Infantry, came up and although the American front was shaky it held, blocking 277 Volksgrenadier's left hook towards Rocherath–Krinkelt.

South of 393 Infantry the last three miles of 99th Division's front was held by two battalions of 394 Infantry. On the right the First Battalion in front of the critical crossroads of Losheimergraben were attacked by a regiment of Grenadiers from 12th Volksgrenadier Division, but as they had had to work their way through the forest to get to the American lines and the trails were blocked with fallen trees, barbed wire and mines they were not able to assault the American forward positions until the afternoon. The attack, when it came, was heavy and the forward outposts were driven in. For a time it looked as though the Germans might succeed in smashing through to the Losheimergraben crossroads, essential for their panzers, but once again the young soldiers of the green 99th Division fought back like veterans. The situation was saved when the mortars were fired at an angle of 89 degrees. This brought shells down almost on top of their own troops but successfully broke up the German attack.

On the left of 394's First Battalion, in the centre of the six-mile line, the Second Battalion were opposite a road coming west from the German village of Neuhof down which came a company of fusiliers from 277 Volksgrenadier Division attacking out of the mist about 8.0 am. They were beaten off by rifle fire and artillery support but returned to the assault again in the afternoon, this time bringing some of the Hitler Youth Division's tanks with them. Large calibre high explosive shells from the American artillery concentrations a few miles back stopped the tanks and the position was held.

By nightfall the centre of 99th Division's line was holding everywhere but the situation was precarious because of the superior numbers of attackers and the day's casualties. In many important places there were no more than twenty or thirty men available for combat the next day and the divisional reserve, 394 Infantry Regiment's Third Battalion, having come under attack itself could not be used elsewhere.

But the 99th Infantry Division, who had only been in the line a fews weeks and whose first action this was, fought with extraordinary ferocity. Platoons were overwhelmed but went down fighting and on at least one occasion a detachment of no more than forty made a bayonet charge through the German attackers to re-establish a new line of defence with a cut-off platoon. Before the battle was over two of the division's battalions were to win Presidential Citations and individual honours included seven DSCs and three of the rare Medal of Honor, America's highest decoration.

The situation was not all black for luckily the 2nd Division's 23rd Infantry Regiment had been left behind at Elsenborn during the Wahlerscheid crossroads attack and by nightfall all three of its battalions were moving in to back up the 90th Division's tenuous front. And up in the north, on VII Corps' front the famous regular army 1st Infantry Division were fortunately not then committed. At midnight their 26th Infantry Regiment piled into their trucks and started for Camp Elsenborn. It was to be a most important move.

Surprisingly, despite their numbers, the achievement of complete surprise and the undoubted qualities of their infantry the Germans had not achieved penetration or breakout on this part of the front by the end of the first day. Their failure meant that the SS tanks were blocked behind them unable to bring their fire power against the American positions except in isolated instances. And behind the tanks in their American vehicles sat the frustrated members of Skorzeny's 150 Brigade.

At his HQ in Schmittheim Skorzeny had heard the great

opening barrage and the early confident reports that began to come into I SS Panzer Corps battle headquarters, but it was not long before his high hopes began to dwindle as it became apparent that the attack was not going according to plan.

'Apparently the artillery bombardment had had no great effect on the enemy positions at Losheimergraben, the Americans were defending themselves particularly stoutly and the attack was progressing but slowly,' he writes in his memoirs. These were the green soldiers of the US Ninety-ninth Division who had been expected to yield under the weight of the artillery barrage and follow-up attack in overwhelming strength.

'Up to midday,' he continues, 'the only news was of violent fighting, without any considerable gain of ground. The intended collapse of the whole front had not been achieved.'

The Leibstandarte's ('Hitler's Bodyguard') tanks moved up to the infantry start line and Skorzeny's columns followed, along roads that were already becoming jammed. His most experienced commander, while trying to bypass one of these traffic jams, hit a mine and was killed.

Skorzeny drove forward to Losheim to try to see for himself what was happening. He only got through by walking ahead of his car and ordering anyone of lower rank to get out of his way. It was obvious that the first day's objectives were not going to be reached and that 'Operation Greif' ought to be called off, but Skorzeny decided that there was still a chance of success if the armoured columns could break through during the night. In that case, if Skorzeny's men could have seized the bridges for them, they could reach the Meuse by the 18th and the offensive could still succeed. He selected three teams of his best men, all of whom could pass themselves off as Americans, and sent them off to find a gap in the American defences and to reconnoitre the main approach roads to the Meuse the panzers planned to use. These men in American uniforms were in captured jeeps, four to each vehicle and, when it became apparent that Germans in American uniforms were working behind the lines this was one of the ways they were identified for the Americans seldom had more than three in a jeep. If it was necessary to send four men they took two jeeps. This abundance of transport was something Skorzeny had not allowed for.

One of his teams did, in fact, get all the way to the Meuse on the first day and settled down near the bridge at Huy. The commander, a German sailor with an idiomatic mastery of American English, doled out some terrifying rumours to certain American units moving along the main Liège to Namur road. At nightfall when it was apparent that the German tanks were not going to appear the team made their way back again, tearing up telephone cables and removing signposts as they went. They returned along the main road from Huy running south-east and re-entered their own lines on Fifth Panzer Army's northern front, identifying themselves, after bluffing their way past an American forward post, by firing Very lights.

Other teams were able to blow up an ammunition dump, tear up the main telephone cable between Omar Bradley's 12th Army Group HQ at Luxembourg and Hodge's First Army HQ at Spa, fell trees and lay mines on roads which the Americans were likely to use to bring up reinforcements and, wherever possible, sow panic with false rumours.

The front from Monschau to Losheim, V Corps' right flank, had been hit hard, ground had been yielded, many casualties suffered and the remaining defenders were everywhere outnumbered. Still the line was somehow held.

But as the great German offensive gathered momentum it became obvious that the Wahlerscheid crossroads which had cost so much to capture would have to be given up. With the front line already disintegrating behind them it might not be possible to turn the 2nd Infantry Division round in time. Early in the morning on the day after the German offensive opened General Robertson sent the order 'withdraw at once' to his 9th Infantry finally in possession of the bitterly contested position. In their disappointment the 2nd Division called it 'Heartbreak Crossroads'.

They could not then know how their unexpected drive into his front had upset 'Sepp' Dietrich's plans to set up the all-important right flank of the counter-offensive.

It had been planned to establish this defence line in two stages: the first depended on bypassing Monschau with two volksgrenadier divisions and occupying the thirteen miles of road running along a ridge from Monschau north-west to Eupen to make a hard shoulder; the second stage would extend this shoulder from Eupen to the Meuse with the three volksgrenadier divisions who had earlier breached the American line.

The two divisions to be used in the first stage made up the LXVII Artillery Corps ('Corps Monschau'). One, the 326th Volksgrenadiers, was to attack north of Monschau and seize the village of Mutzenich on the main Eupen road and the other, the 246th, was to attack south of Monschau and then swing north-west to come up alongside the 326th.

But the unallowed-for attack by V Corps towards the Roer Dams that started on December 13 upset this plan. The 246th Volksgrenadiers were in the north and so were pinned down by the left wing of V Corps attack and unable to get to Monschau by D-day. Furthermore the attack on the Wahlerscheid crossroads had prevented the last of 326th Volksgrenadiers' three infantry regiments from leaving that area and the general disorganization caused by this attack had stopped one of the battalions of another of 326's regiments from keeping to their movement timetable.

So, instead of the two infantry divisions, totalling six regiments or eighteen battalions, which Corps Monschau had depended upon to set up the right flank hard shoulder, they were reduced to less than four battalions. General Hirtzfeld, the corps commander, was not too pleased but consoled himself with the thought that his very heavy artillery support, being further back, was still intact. His volksgrenadiers would have no less than ten battalions of artillery to blast open a way for them. There was one snag, though, even to that—Field Marshal Model had absolutely forbidden any shelling whatsoever of the beautiful historic little town of Monschau. The guns would have to fire to the north and south of it.

If the Germans had less than four battalions for the attack on Monschau the Americans had little more than one with which to defend it. The only troops north of the town were a cavalry reconnaissance squadron, while two miles or so south of Monschau the Third Battalion of the 395th Infantry Regiment of 99th Division occupied a line of foxholes outside the village of Höfen. This position was on the Allies' extreme left of the Ardennes front and was to prove critical.

Höfen was a good defensive position for it lay on high ground overlooking Monschau and blocked the south-eastern approach to the Monschau to Eupen road. The Third Battalion had spent six weeks preparing their positions. Their forward foxholes were well backed up by dugout positions and, not far behind them, a battalion of 105-mm howitzers.

Also during the night of December 14, a battalion of 3-inch anti-tank guns had been towed into forward positions just here in order to be able to support the second phase of 2nd Division's attack towards the Roer Dams. The sight of these was very good for the morale of the Third Battalion, waiting to fight their first battle and wondering privately, as soldiers always do, how they would acquit themselves.

North of Monschau, roughly for a mile along a railroad track, the Thirty-eighth Cavalry squadron had placed fifty machine-gun positions behind mines, barbed wire and trip flares covering the approach from the east. They were supported by assault guns sited in the village of Mutzenich and, on their left flank, a platoon of self-propelled anti-tank guns and a battalion of artillery. The Monschau position was held by few troops but the defences had been well planned and coordinated.

At 5.25 in the morning of December 16 a tremendous artillery barrage opened up from behind the West Wall in front of Monschau and rolled over the American lines. Many buildings in Höfen were set blazing and others were knocked flat, the supporting artillery positions were obviously all well-known to the Germans for the fire was deadly accurate. Telephone wires were cut and, as the shells burst and the howitzers screamed, the green troops of the Third Battalion felt their hearts pounding and their palms begin to sweat as they strained their eyes for the first movement out of the darkness ahead of them.

After twenty minutes the barrage stopped and at the same time hundreds of searchlights reflected off the low cloud over the American lines, creating 'artificial moonlight'. The wire to the supporting artillery had been knocked out and even radio communication wasn't working. The infantrymen clutched their rifles and the anti-tank gunners loaded and waited.

They didn't have long to wait, for ten minutes after the searchlights went on, assault companies of the 326th Volksgrenadier Division advanced steadily out of the mist right on to the Third Battalion's positions. They were without cover and at point-blank range. The result was not a battle but a slaughter.

The anti-tank guns fired into their ranks; the infantry pumped bullets into them. Like the men whom they were attacking they lacked experience; like them they did not lack courage. Despite the murderous fire they kept on coming—in at least three verified instances their bodies actually fell into the foxholes from which the bullets had come, an event which, however often it may happen in the films, is extremely rare in battle.

Some even got through the American lines and into Höfen but their support troops, two companies, were smashed and stopped by artillery fire from the American howitzers and mortars, who had quickly recovered from the German barrage and brought their guns to bear.

Within two hours the German attack was broken off. About noon an unenthusiastic attempt to get it rolling again was made but the Third Battalion, their spirits high, repelled it vigorously. At the end of the first day they had yielded no

105

ground, inflicted very heavy casualties on their attackers and had only four killed, seven wounded and four missing themselves. For a first battle, they told each other, it wasn't bad.

The German barrage on the cavalry positions to the north of Monschau had begun at the same time—about three hours before dawn. As the shelling began to slacken off the waiting cavalry, who had gone to ground and suffered few casualties, manned their weapons and waited. The other battalion of the unlucky 326th Volksgrenadiers came down the road leading straight into the prepared defences. When they reached the barbed wire roadblock the American artillery fired star shells above them and in the bright light the cavalry opened up with every weapon they possessed including shells from their light tanks. The attackers faltered and then fell back. At dawn they tried to filter around the northern end of the defences but were again stopped. By nightfall the Thirty-eighth Cavalry Squadron positions were intact and their losses had also been light. During the day, in both places, the 326th Volksgrenadiers had lost twenty per cent of their troops. The attempt to set up a hard shoulder north of Monschau had failed completely and it was a failure that was to become increasingly serious for the Germans.

7

THE SOUTHERN ATTACK

Cut from its promised eight divisions to four and with no tanks at all the German Seventh Army was the cinderella of Army Group B: all was sacrificed to give the two Panzer Armies every chance of success although General Manteuffel, not liking the idea of his left flank being uncovered should Seventh Army's attack not succeed, had begged for at least a few tanks to be allocated to General Brandenberger. But this request, like almost every other, was turned down at Führer Headquarters. Brandenberger was given only thirty self-propelled guns for his entire army and half of these had to go to the division of parachute infantry on his right wing whose rôle was to advance with General Manteuffel's left hook to Bastogne and beyond.

In the end Hitler was prevailed upon to allow Seventh Army a few of the new, long-range 120-mm guns and these together with more than a hundred rocket projectors and, as all along the attack front, heavy artillery support, were thought to be enough to ensure that the thinly held American front in 'Little Switzerland' was quickly overrun.

Seventh Army's four divisions were in two corps; the LXXXV on the right consisting of the 5th Parachute, who were to move west on the left of General Manteuffel's powerful armoured thrust and the 352nd Volksgrenadier Division. This was composed mainly of ex-Luftwaffe and ex-Navy men and, together with two divisions of the other Corps, LXXX, were to cross the Our, destroy the American front line and swing left to set up the southern hard shoulder.

The corps attack front was about ten miles wide and four principal areas of concentration were chosen for 5th Parachute Division and 352nd Volksgrenadier Division to launch their spearheads. There were about twenty-five thousand men in the two divisions opposing two battalions of 28th Infantry Division's right-hand regiment, the 109th. There was also a third American battalion in reserve and 109th regimental front covering the high ground west of the Our was backed up by two battalions of field artillery—excluding the gunners the Americans had about three thousand riflemen stretched along this ten miles.

On Seventh German Army's left, on the extreme southern end of the attack front, LXXX Corps' two divisions of volks-

107

grenadiers on the eve of the offensive were covering fifteen miles of the winding Sauer river from where it is joined by the Our to the region of Echternach. Their task was to establish crossings and bridgeheads, particularly opposite Echternach, advance westwards, pivot to the south and establish a strong defensive screen against any attempt by the Third US Army to move north and interfere with the westward thrust of General Manteuffel's panzer columns.

In the original plan General Brandenberger's army had been given a more grandiose objective by Hitler—no less than to set up a fortress wall all the way from Echternach to Charleville on the Meuse, a distance of eighty air-flight miles. But this was never taken seriously by the planners who knew the real forces available. After the war Jodl admitted that he would have been quite satisfied if Seventh Germany Army could have held a hard shoulder for twelve to fifteen miles from Echternach towards Luxembourg City.

These two new divisions, the 276th and the 212th Volks-grenadier, totalling another twenty-five thousand, had in front of them only the Sixtieth Armored Infantry Battalion (from Ninth Armored Division) on their right and US 4th Infantry Division's left-hand regiment, the 12th on the German left. These totalled only about three thousand four hundred but there was most of an armoured combat command in reserve and, once again, artillery support.

12th Infantry Regiment had taken over ten miles of front only three days before when after their terrible mauling in the Hurtgen Forest fighting, they had been pulled out and sent to this 'quiet paradise for weary troops' as this part of Luxembourg had been called. They were five or six hundred riflemen under strength despite continual reinforcements, for the 4th Infantry Division had lost over five thousand battle casualties and a further two thousand five hundred from trench foot, exposure and combat fatigue. Many rifle companies were at half strength.

Also, the division, having been in continual action since Normandy, had much of its equipment worn and faulty. Many of its support tanks had not been able to complete the move to Luxembourg under their own power and by December 16 forty-three of its complement of fifty-four were undergoing repair and hence out of action. Guns and radio sets had been sent to workshops but it was expected that all equipment would be made serviceable quickly, now that the division had been taken out of the fighting and sent to a quiet area.

Fairly extensive leave was granted, particularly to the

veterans, who went to Paris, England and a few to USA. Those soldiers not entitled to a long leave were allowed back to Luxembourg City on a rotation system and if the refreshment and entertainment might have been better it seemed pretty good to men coming from the grim fighting in the north. They drank weak beer and relaxed with the pretty girls while German agents worked overtime and to good effect, for when the attack came the volksgrenadiers had all the 12th Infantry Regiment's outposts pinpointed on their maps as well as the exact location of 4th Infantry Division's supporting artillery. This was most important, for these guns would have to be quickly silenced if the Germans were to get their transport and assault guns safely across the pontoon bridges they hoped to construct in the first few hours of the offensive.

General Brandenberger's plan was for 212th Volksgrenadier Division to cross the Sauer on either side of Echternach, in which there was a small American infantry unit* and from which all civilians had been evacuated, and for the columns to join up two miles behind the town. This would cut off Echternach, trap any American troops inside the net and establish a wide bridgehead from which the hard shoulder which would then be set up could be supported. He rated the 212th Volksgrenadier as the best of his four divisions even though, because of the scraping of the manpower barrel, it contained many seventeen-year-olds and had been withdrawn for rest and refitting after being shattered on the Eastern Front. But this had been in September, so they had had time to complete their training and feel they were a unit. Morale was high and the division was up to full strength in men but low on transport and communications, and had only four assault guns.

The main American artillery protecting 12th Infantry's front was on a plateau a few miles south-east of Echternach on the forward slopes of the one-thousand-foot Schlamm Bach ridge. This was 212th's objective and if they attained it, the next was to thrust south-west to the small town of Junglinster just over half way to Luxembourg City from Echternach.

Because of the length of front the 12th Regiment had to hold and the lie of the land—wooded heights, steep cliffs, gorges and crevasses—a minimum of troops were placed out in front and maximum reserves held back. Five villages practically in the line were each lightly held by a company HQ and a few men, while these companies' main fire power, the rifle platoons and weapon sections, were dispersed in outposts overlooking the river which divided them from the Germans.

* A company command post with its guard.

The river runs fast here and the assault companies trying to cross in rubber boats in the dark had considerable difficulties. The regiment west of Echternach* managed it but its running-mate in the east, on the extreme left of the German line, had to give up the attempt at the chosen site and move away further east to find a better place. This delay upset the German timetable.

No one in the American lines spotted the pre-dawn crossing of the Sauer west of Echternach and the first intimation of an imminent attack came, as at the northern end of the Ardennes front, with a heavy, accurate artillery barrage at 5.30 am. First targets were the battalion and company command posts in the villages and when dawn broke all wire communications had been cut and the full extent of the damage was unknown.

The German assault troops did not close with the defenders until about an hour after dawn and by that time reports of fighting to the north of 4th Infantry Division were coming in and at 9.30 the Division's commander, General Barton,† warned his regiments that attacks could be expected. About a quarter of an hour later the company command post at the village of Berdorf, three miles west of Echternach and two miles south of the river, saw a fifteen-man German patrol approaching, which seemed to mean that the four company outposts overlooking the river had been overrun before they could give the alarm. The company commander reported the patrol (this was the first intimation that 4th Division had that the Germans were across the Sauer) and decided to make a three-story reinforced concrete tourist hotel into a strong-point and hold out as long as possible. But with only sixty men, one machine gun and one automatic to add to the ordinary rifles, the situation did not look too good.

The attack on Berdorf came soon afterwards. It was made by the First Battalion of the 423rd Volksgrenadier Regiment who had already overrun three of the four American outposts capturing all the company's mortars, machine guns and anti-tank guns. Only one position had not been overrun: a platoon of twenty-one men and two artillery observers who were in a thick stone farmhouse from which they fought off all attacks for four days. Their radio, however, had broken down and they had not been able to warn their company HQ.

The Germans moved into Berdorf and advanced towards the Parc Hotel (*tout confort moderne; cuisine soignée,* the sign said) where, behind hastily sandbagged windows, the sixty de-

* The Sauer runs almost east and west at Echternach.
† Major-General Raymond O. Barton.

110

fenders let them approach. As the leading volksgrenadiers ran forward they were met with machine-gun, automatic rifle and scattered rifle fire. Discouraged, they went to ground. The situation was stalemate but it looked as though as soon as the Germans got a bridge over the river heavy weapons would be brought up and the hotel soon reduced to rubble.

Another column from 423 Volksgrenadiers attacking west of Echternach also overran the American forward positions and then moved quickly forward to cut the main Echternach to Luxembourg road at Lauterborn surrounding an American company there before they could get a messenger out.

Much of the difficulty and confusion on 4th Infantry Division's front that first day was due to the breakdown of normal communications due to the large number of radio sets undergoing repair, the cutting of telephone wires in the initial barrage and the nature of the terrain in 'Little Switzerland' which made radio communication difficult at any time.

Early in the afternoon General Barton committed some reserves in a number of operations to stabilize his hard-hit front. A company of infantry and a platoon of light tanks were sent to Lauterborn and the volksgrenadiers in possession, with no anti-tank guns, were forced to withdraw. The small town was retaken, the road to Echternach opened again and twenty-five American infantry, captured a few hours before, were released.

Also a task force of ten tanks with infantry support was sent to break through to Berdorf and rescue the sixty men besieged in the Parc Hotel but the Germans had expected this and had occupied houses on the outskirts of the village so the tanks were met with bazooka fire and the infantry stopped by rifle fire from concealed positions. The tanks fell back and the American infantry dug in for the night.

The Germans had succeeded in overrunning the forward positions in this sector and in bottling up a company HQ but were themselves prevented from moving on by the relieving American infantry. The First Battalion of the 423rd Volksgrenadier Regiment were behind their timetable.

The left wing of the German southern attack which went in east of Echternach was much less successful than the right. It was made, it will be remembered, by the 320th Volksgrenadier Regiment who had been unable to get their rubber rafts across the swiftly flowing Sauer and had been forced to travel three miles downstream before they could cross. This delay cost them the advantage of surprise and when they started to move towards their objectives they were stopped at the first village, Dickweiler, upon which the American outposts, warned in time, had been able to fall back. Here a German attack in two-company strength was beaten off and the volksgrenadiers took refuge in some woods half a mile from the village.

In this rugged, difficult country, it was essential for the defence to keep possession of the roads and this was accomplished by the determined resistance in the villages near the river by small bodies of American soldiers.

The regimental reserve was fully committed by midday and the divisional commander, General Barton, sending off tank/infantry teams to the worst trouble spots, soon practically stripped himself of spare tanks.

The divisional artillery on the Schlamm Bach ridge were heavily shelled in the opening barrage resulting in a complete breakdown of communications. Their spotter plane, which could have given them an idea of what was happening on their front, was shot down almost immediately. They asked for permission to withdraw but General Barton refused and by afternoon with the help of a second spotter plane—the amazed pilot reported that the ground beneath was 'as full of targets as a pin-ball machine'—they were able to get on target. They brought heavy fire down on the German forward infantry position and on the columns moving up and, even more important, were able to knock out the bridges Seventh Army's engineers were trying to erect so that no self-propelled guns or heavy mortars got over the river, leaving the volksgrenadiers at the mercy of the few American tanks.

By nightfall on the 16th much of the chaos and confusion of the morning had disappeared and the complete collapse of 12th Infantry Regiment, which at one time had seemed quite possible, had been avoided.

On Army Group B's left at the end of the first day although Seventh German Army had achieved complete surprise with a three to one superiority against a unit who only nine days before had been officially rated as 'a badly decimated and weary regiment' they had accomplished only part of their objectives. Echternach had not been cut off; the all-important Schlamm Bach ridge was still intact and, most serious of all, the way was still open for American reinforcements from the south.

12th Infantry Regiment's northern neighbours were the Sixtieth Armored Infantry Battalion, part of the 9th Armored Division, who, six days before the German attack had been assigned three miles of the front between the 28th Infantry Division and the Fourth Infantry Division so that the green troops could get some experience of shooting at a live enemy and being shot at themselves before going into action with 9th Armored tanks. If possible soldiers were always given this 'combat indoctrination' before being seriously committed and the battalion commander, Colonel Collins, became quite worried because the sector of front he was occupying was so quiet his men were getting no experience. It was a lack that was shortly to be righted.

The dividing line between the armoured infantry and the southernmost troops of 28th Infantry Division, a company from the Third Battalion of the 109th Regiment, was the valley of the river Sauer which is joined by the Our at Wallendorf and then continues south-east to and beyond Echternach, marking the boundary between Luxembourg and Germany and, at this time, the front line. On the armoured infantry's right, between them and the northernmost troops of 4th Division's 12th Infantry Regiment, there was a deep, tortuous gorge called the Schwarz Erntz which was a natural entry through and behind the American defences. Between the Sauer on their left and the Schwarz Erntz on their right was a distance of four miles, but Sixtieth Battalion, about eight hundred strong, were deployed in front of the small town of Beaufort along a two-mile forward curve on the high ground above the Sauer, which after flowing towards the east on their left flank turned south-east at Wellendorf across their front. Three miles behind them was their artillery support, a battalion of field guns near the village of Haller.

When they moved into the line on December 10 the sector opposite to them was very lightly held by some of 212 Volksgrenadiers, but in the intervening days 212 had been gathered in to concentrate opposite Echternach and a newly formed division, 276 Volksgrenadiers, had been moved from Poland and in two night marches had quietly concentrated along four miles of the West Wall almost exactly opposite Sixtieth Armored Infantry Battalion.

The 276 Volksgrenadiers was one of the divisions which had been practically destroyed in Normandy and had been re-formed in Poland mostly from wounded veterans who had been patched up and returned to duty. It was at full strength of about ten thousand but because of Seventh Army's shortage of self-propelled guns had been assigned none—its own artillery, of two howitzer battalions, was horse-drawn. Its task was to cross the Sauer at four places, outflank and overrun the Sixtieth Armored Infantry, eliminate the artillery position near Haller and then, swinging south, to join up with 212 Volksgrenadiers to form the centre of Seventh Army's defensive

113

screen. Considering that they were only opposed by about eight hundred American infantry who had never been in action their task did not seem a particularly difficult one.

But an armoured infantry battalion was equipped to protect its division's tanks and had nine 57-mm anti-tank guns and three 75-mm howitzers. These anti-tank guns were useless against all but the lightest German tanks but 276 Volksgrenadiers had no tanks and the American guns could wreak terrible damage to their soft-shell vehicles and horse-drawn artillery. Also the guns and howitzers of the artillery at Haller would be able to lay down a carpet of murderous shellfire on troops advancing across difficult ground. Despite their superiority in numbers it would not all be plain sailing for 276 Volksgrenadiers.

As elsewhere the first intimation of the attack was a heavy prolonged artillery bombardment. Most of the shells on the Sixtieth Battalion front went over their heads landing in Beaufort, the town two miles behind them where their 'B' company were in reserve, and in and around the artillery near Haller in an unsuccessful attempt to put the American guns out of action. About a thousand shells fell in this pre-dawn bombardment; at the same time the volksgrenadiers moved down to the river and launched their rubber assault boats.

The fog which in varying degrees lay all along the Ardennes front on this December morning was exceptionally thick here. It delayed the river crossing for an hour or so and the first German infantry did not move against the American outposts until about 7.0 am.

Shock troops from one battalion of 276 Volksgrenadiers pushed through a gap on Sixtieth Armored Infantry's left, between them and Third Battalion of 109th Infantry, aiming for a one-thousand-three-hundred-foot-high hill a mile behind the American armoured infantry's left flank from which the whole area could be dominated. A squad from one of Sixtieth Battalion's companies had been keeping the valley leading to this hill under observation but the sudden attack out of the thick fog overwhelmed them and they were wiped out.

But the experienced men of 28th Division's 109th Infantry Regiment on the heights to the north brought mortar fire down on the volksgrenadiers and, when they went to cover, kept them pinned down with machine-gun fire for most of the day. Later in the afternoon the German infantry got moving forward again by skilful use of the pines as cover and got in close to the village of Reisdorf. If they could seize this place they would be able to use a road from it to get behind the left flank of the armoured infantry's position, but the danger was realized and a company

114

of light tanks from 9th Armored's reserves was sent to a ridge from which this road could be dominated.

The other half of 276 Division's right-wing attack crossed the Sauer in the fog without incident and moved quickly up the slope for half a mile to the village of Bigelbach, about a thousand yards north of the left flank of Sixtieth Armored Infantry's ridge line and not including part of their defences. Nevertheless the volksgrenadiers radioed back that they had 'taken' Bigelbach and later that they were 'holding' it against attack. In fact the American reaction had been merely to shell the village but no attempt was made to drive the Germans out. They, for their part, seemed satisfied to remain where they were for the rest of the day.

These two columns, constituting the right wing of 276 Volksgrenadier Division's attack, had made very little progress and had suffered fairly heavy casualties from 109th Infantry Regiment on the heights to their north, from Sixtieth Armored Infantry's guns and from the heavy American artillery near Haller which kept the river crossing points, over which the Germans kept moving all day, under constant fire.

The most successful attack against the armoured infantry defence line was directed at their centre through the thick pine forest that lay between the American line and the river and by midday German infantry had penetrated at several points between the American positions. For a short time it looked as though the armoured infantry were going to be overwhelmed. Then their reserve company from Beaufort came up and steadied the line but, with the overwhelming German numbers, it could only be a matter of time before the position was overrun.

General Leonard,* 9th Armored Division's commander, now committed some of his reserves to protect the armoured infantry battalion's flanks. It will be remembered that the deep gorge of the Schwarz Erntz lay to the south-east of Sixtieth Armored Infantry, in 4th Armored Division's sector. The nearest troops of 12th Infantry Regiment were in the village of Berdorf a mile behind their own company's forward line on a ridge overlooking the Sauer. 12th Infantry's extreme left-hand troops were a mile south-east of the gorge; Sixtieth Armored's extreme right-hand troops were nearly the same distance north-west of it. Once again there was an undefended gap between two American divisions through which, this time, there ran a perfect natural entry.

* Major-General John W. Leonard.

This was the route chosen for the third of 276 Volksgrenadier's infantry regiments. The fog and the swift running of the Sauer on their front delayed the shock troops of this regiment too and when they finally crossed the river both the Sixtieth Armored to the right of them and the 12th Infantry to their left were under attack and the volksgrenadiers were able to pick their way along the tortuous gorge without opposition during the few hours of daylight left to them.

Although the presence of this force was not known the Schwarz Erntz was an obvious danger, with three deep cuts running from it into the area behind Sixtieth Armored Infantry's positions, and during the afternoon General Leonard covered these with tanks or tank destroyers from his reserve. He also sent a troop of armoured cars to guard the roads around Beaufort. By nightfall his narrow sector of the Ardennes front was still fairly intact although obviously endangered.

Seventh German Army's centre thrust by 276 Volksgrenadier Division had failed to achieve its first day's targets. 276's commander blamed lack of artillery support and the difficulty of radio communication caused by the number of steep, rock-strewn hills, but there is no doubt that the stubborn unwillingness of the untried American armoured infantry to give ground even in the face of considerable odds also had a lot to do with it. Perhaps 276 Division's untypical caution was due to the high proportion of wounded returned to duty in their ranks. Whatever the reasons General Brandenberger was displeased with their performance and ordered the divisional commander to continue his attack through the night in order to make up for his failure.

The northernmost of those Seventh Army divisions whose task was to set up the southern hard shoulder was the 352 Volksgrenadiers, about ten thousand strong and made up almost entirely of ex-Luftwaffe and Navy. Their attack sector was a couple of miles of the Our just north of Wallendorf where it joins the Sauer and they were opposed by the Third Battalion of 28th Division's 109th Infantry Regiment, holding the division's southern flank which extended south of the Sauer. It was from one of their positions on the high ground above the river that fire had been brought down on 276 Volksgrenadiers attacking the Sixtieth Armored Infantry.

The 109th Infantry were responsible for some nine to ten miles of front and their commander, Lieutenant-Colonel James Rudder, who had taken over command only a week

116

before the German attack, had put two of his battalions in the line and kept the third back in reserve. He considered that the prime objective of a possible German attack on his front was the town of Ettelbruck about seven miles west of the Our and behind his right flank. Its capture would cut the main north–south railway line, seize a bridge over the river Clerf and capture a good road running north-west to Wiltz, headquarters of the 28th Infantry Division.

Therefore he concentrated his right flank defences along a three-thousand-yard line on top of the high ground just west of the Our. From here the main road from Wallendorf west could be denied to the Germans as could another from Fouhren. His reserve battalion were stationed at Diekirch four miles behind this defence line where there were also two battalions of field artillery. In order to hold this sector so strongly the rest of his front to the north had to be thin on the ground (they would be hit by Brandenberger's 5th Parachute Division as part of the attack against Bastogne). His strong right wing lay across 352 Volksgrenadiers' projected line of advance.

Their task was to cross the Our at dawn on either side of Wellendorf, bypass the American forward positions and seize the heights above the Sauer and drive quickly west to Ettelbruck and then strike south-west to form the westernmost section of the southern hard shoulder. The assault would be made by a regiment of volksgrenadiers at each crossing with a third regiment in reserve. The opening German barrage on this front concentrated on the rear areas to knock out the artillery command posts and inflict as much damage as possible on the reserves at Diekirch. In fact on this part of the American front the German pre-attack shelling did least damage, not even knocking out wire communications between forward positions.

But the crossing of the Our, only fifty feet or so wide here, was quickly accomplished and the leading shock troops moved forward at first light. 352's left-hand column attacked the American outposts on the right flank of the strong three-thousand-yard defence lines, and were stopped.

The right-hand column of 352 had more success, moving fast through the gap between the northern end of the defence line and the nearest troops of 109th's Second Battalion holding the long regimental left flank. By 10.0 am this column had moved about two miles west and were attacking one of the artillery positions near Diekirch: by the afternoon they were behind 109th's forward defence line, within a mile of the main road from the Our to Ettelbruck.

Colonel Rudder then committed a platoon of tanks from his

117

small armoured reserve in an attack from Diekirch to stop this penetration and later reinforced this with the last of his reserve battalion (the rest had earlier been sent north against Fifth Parachute). After three or four hours of hard fighting the volksgrenadiers were checked and then slowly forced back, but they continued to probe further west during the night and by dawn of the 17th were established on the high ground north of Bastendorf nearly four miles from their start line. This was Seventh Army's maximum first-day penetration and General Brandenberger was satisfied with his ex-sailors.

But the ex-Luftwaffe who comprised the left-hand column of 352's attack had run head on to the well dug-in defences of 109th Regiment's southern flank with the natural defence line of the river Sauer on their right. The artillery near Diekirch had been able to keep the Germans pinned down for most of the day ten miles from their objective, the bridges at Ettel-bruck.

Nowhere on Seventh Army's front had the attack gone according to plan or had objectives been reached. General Brandenberger urged his divisional commanders to push on through the night so that they could be in a position the following day to make up for this failure, but time itself, once lost, can never be regained, and although the position of the hard-pressed American troops at the southern end of the Ardennes front was serious and would become more so, the German timetable for the setting-up of a hard shoulder on the left flank of their offensive had not been kept. Like the failure on their right flank in the north it was to have far-reaching effects on the battle.

8

'DEFEND IN PLACE'

*The side attacked always overestimates the strength
of the attacker.*

GNEISENAU

The Germans' first major task, the setting up of strong flank
protection had not been achieved. Another important require-
ment was for them quickly to gain control of the road network
for the difficult terrain and the weather conditions decreed that
only on hard-surface roads could tracked or wheeled vehicles
keep rolling fast enough to exploit a breakthrough fully.

There were many minor roads and forest tracks well known
to the Germans in this favourite of their invasion grounds, but
in the years since the blitz of 1940 tanks had become much
wider and heavier with ensuing advantages but with the disadvantage of being limited to hard roads or ground. The German tank man's favourite was the Mk V, the Panther which
weighed forty-five tons and was ten feet wide. The Mk VI, the
Tiger, fifty-six tons and twelve feet three inches wide, could
not cross soft ground, nor, of course, use narrow forest tracks.
It was often scornfully called a 'furniture van' by the experienced German tank crews from the eastern front. Also in
the Ardennes campaign were a few of the monster Tiger II
tanks weighing sixty-seven tons and therefore confined to main
roads or hard frozen ground.

If any of these tanks broke down on one of the narrow roads
of the Ardennes it effectively blocked all other vehicles for the
snow and slush of the verges lay on top of mud into which
wheels and tracks rapidly sank.

Therefore the few good roads would have to be seized as
soon as possible, not only for the use of the invaders themselves but to stop American reinforcements pouring into the
area from north and south—which is the direction most of the
good roads run. In order to control this network four communications centres would have to be captured and held:
Malmédy, St Vith, Houffalize and Bastogne, and to keep to
the timetable all four would have to fall on the first or second
day.

From the northernmost of these, Malmédy, three important
roads radiated; one went north, over the Hohes Venn through
Eupen to Aachen and another south-east to St Vith—both of

these were part of 'Red Ball Highway', main supply route to Ninth US Army. The third road ran south-west through Stavelot and then to Trois Ponts from where a good road runs along the valley of the Amblève river all the way to Liège. The three bridges, which give Trois Ponts its name, carry traffic on a south-east/north-west axis and obviously its capture was essential for the success of Dietrich's armoured thrust.

From Stavelot, an ordnance depot with two and a half million maps (the prodigal scale of American supplies amazed both her allies and her enemies), a road ran north through the largest fuel dump in Europe—nearly three million gallons—to Spa, headquarters of General Hodges' First Army* and the centre of a vast supply area. The ten-mile line, Malmédy–Stavelot–Trois Ponts, lay across 'Sepp' Dietrich's projected advance like a wall, but roads from Germany ran to all three towns and, after the volksgrenadiers had breached the thin front line, it would not take the SS Panzers long to reach them.

Malmédy itself was a service centre with engineering maintenance workshops, ordnance, medical supplies, military police and an evacuation hospital—on December 16 full of wounded from the Wahlerscheid crossroads fighting. From Malmédy the road towards Germany ran to the twin villages of Rocherath –Krinkelt from where the US 2nd Division attack had jumped off on December 13.

The road going north from Malmédy to Eupen climbs up to the highest part of the Hohes Venn and here, at a crossroads about eight miles from Malmédy, was where von der Heydte's paratroopers were scheduled to drop just before dawn on the first day of the attack.

Thirteen miles south-east of Malmédy sprawls the ugly crossroads town of St Vith, handed over to Belgium after World War I. Many of its inhabitants had welcomed the soldiers of the Wehrmacht in 1940 and at least half the population in December 1944—the German-speaking half— would stand in the streets and cheer when they returned. As far as the Germans were concerned it was the most important communications centre, focal point of five main highways and three rail lines. Without it they would have great difficulty in moving through the Ardennes. St Vith must be in German hands at the very latest by the end of the second day.

* In World War I this pleasant watering-place had been the Kaiser's headquarters.

Five or six miles east of St Vith the rugged, snow-covered Schnee Eifel effectively blocked a direct attack from Germany but good roads run around the high ridge both on the north and the south converging on St Vith and both were to be main lines of advance for General von Manteuffel's right wing.

The newly-arrived 106th Infantry Division's headquarters were in St Vith; the approach to it from the north-east was guarded by scattered outposts of their attached Fourteenth Cavalry Group; that from the south-east by some of their own green, young soldiers. In the Schnee Eifel itself, east of the ridge line, were two of the division's regiments, still, on December 16, suffering from the effects of cold and exposure in their long move across France and Belgium. The left-hand regiment had not yet tied in with the troops on their left, four platoons of the Fourteenth Cavalry Group occupying a line of villages across the road entering Belgium north of the Schnee Eifel. When the heavy German attack came through here the disparity in numbers would be greater than anywhere else on the long Ardennes front—with predictable results.

Houffalize, about twenty-five miles south-west of St Vith by road, lies in a narrow valley on both sides of the Ourthe river. The approach from the east is along narrow roads but westwards from Houffalize a good road runs along the river valley to La Roche from which a network of roads leads directly towards the Meuse bridges. This was to be the target for General Manteuffel's centre thrust and it was hoped that the attacks on St Vith to the north and Bastogne to the south would leave Houffalize comparatively unguarded.

Eleven miles further south brings us to the last and most important of the target communications centres, Bastogne, headquarters of VIII Corps. It was further from the German start line than any of the others and two rivers and high, difficult ground lay between, but on Hitler's master plan Bastogne was to be captured by the second day at the latest. It was then to be held against any counter-attack, for its importance lay not only in that it was the key to the east–west road network, vital to the left wing of the proposed advance, but in that if the Americans could hang on, Bastogne would obviously become the road and railhead into which reinforcements from Patton's Third Army in the south would pour. Hitler had seen clearly that Bastogne could become the springboard for an Allied counter-attack and he had made its capture an 'at all costs' objective. General Manteuffel entrusted this all-important task to the best of his corps, the XLVII Panzer, consisting of a regular army infantry division and two regular army tank divisions. They faced a single regiment of the US 28th Infantry Division and it did not look as though Bastogne would be any more difficult to capture than the other three. Early possession of all four would mean that the Americans, not being able to use the roads, would have to fall back to the Meuse.

After the roads, the next important features in the Ardennes were the watercourses.

Rivers have always played a big part in war, for as obstacles they are far superior to almost anything that man can construct himself. The same river names occur again and again in Europe's war-filled history. One of these is the Meuse, a classic obstacle to attackers from either east or west. As a major defence line its importance was well realized by the Allies in their over-all planning.*

But, because of the geological structure of the Ardennes and the Eifel, there are many other rivers. Springs find their way to the surface high in the hills and twist and tumble through deep cuts to join watershed courses, growing into streams and rivers. In so doing, natural defensive positions are created and some of these were to become the scene of small, bitterly fought actions. Where the rivers were deep and fast enough to be major obstacles, the difficulty of forcing them was to influence the whole course of the offensive.

In the early stages of the battle the most important rivers were the Our and the Sauer, which separated the two sides for nearly three-quarters of the front. Both General von Manteuffel and General Brandenberger would have to get not only their infantry but their transport, heavy artillery and tanks over them if they were to take St Vith and Bastogne and thus gain the Meuse crossings more than a hundred miles to the west.

From Bastogne the Wiltz river flows towards Germany for nearly twenty miles where it joins the Clerf, a north–south flowing river, parallel to and a few miles west of the Our. Both of these offered possible defence lines.

From six or seven miles north of Bastogne the Ourthe, the longest river in the Ardennes, flowed all the way to Liège. Troops falling back to the Meuse would obviously try to make a stand on this river.

The other rivers which were to be of tactical importance are

* In November, General Bradley asked the VIII Corps' Commander about his plans, should a big attack hit his lightly-held front. 'We can fall back and fight a delaying action to the Meuse,' Troy Middleton replied.

in the north, in the Malmédy area. One, the Warche, rises in the Hohes Venn, flows to Malmédy and then turns south to join the Amblève (which in turn joins the Salm at Trois Ponts). These rivers, though narrow in the Malmédy–Stavelot–Trois Ponts area, are swift-running in December and excellent for defence. Their bridges however were intact and the surprised Allies were not going to have much time to destroy them.

It is not difficult to get infantry over rivers, except where the flow is exceptionally fast. Small parties of specially trained troops can be put across in inflatable boats in the dark to knock out outposts and seize a bridgehead. Pontoon bridges can then be quickly put in place and over these the main body of troops, with much of their light equipment, can cross. But getting trucks, guns and tanks over is another matter entirely and in modern war infantry without this support are at the mercy of defenders who have it.

There were no bridges over either the Sauer or the lower reaches of the Our for the Germans had themselves destroyed them in their September retreat. We have already seen how the Sauer opposite Echternach flowed too fast for the left wing of Seventh Army's attack. The time that was lost in finding a crossing-place further downstream contributed to the failure to set up the southern flank on schedule. We have also seen how the artillery of the US 4th Infantry Division was able to prevent the building of bridges at Echternach strong enough to take big guns and so the German infantry, who had been able to get across, could not deal with the American artillery and tanks. The Sauer had proved to be a difficult obstacle.

Further north the Our rises in the north of the Schnee Eifel and pursues a snakelike course south to Wallendorf where it joins the Sauer. This sixty-mile curve formed the front line, except in two places: the salients in the Schnee Eifel, eight miles east of the river, and in an area south of the Schnee Eifel, where the West Wall east of the Our had been breached in September.

On the German side of the Our all of General Manteuffel's Fifth Panzer Army and half of General Brandenberger's Seventh Army had concentrated for the coming attack. On the Allied side, just under three American infantry divisions were stretched out in a series of defensive positions behind a line of forward posts, many of which were unoccupied at night.

On his right, Manteuffel planned to launch his LXVI Army Corps against St Vith; from his centre, for the long advance to the Meuse, his LVIII Panzer Corps was aimed through Houffa-lize while his XLVII Panzer Corps, on his left, was first to take

Bastogne and then continue on to the Meuse. At the same time General Brandenberger would also send part of his LXXXV Army Corps, on his right and next to Manteuffel's XLVII Panzer Corps, against Bastogne. All four of these corps would have to cross the Our.

Manteuffel's attack on St Vith properly belongs to operations on the right wing of the German offensive, for his LXVI Army Corps and some of Dietrich's SS Panzers were to be occupied with St Vith exclusively for some time. Its defence was to be as important as the much better known defence of Bastogne.

General Manteuffel had high hopes that his LVIII Panzer Corps in his centre, of a division of volksgrenadiers and one of panzers would be able to race through the vacuum in the area between St Vith and Bastogne, but first it was essential to seize crossings over the Our, capable of taking tanks and self-propelled guns. Fortunately for him there were intact bridges on this front used to supply the American troops of 28th Division in their salient east of the Our. He knew that they would almost certainly have been strengthened and would be well-maintained —ideal, in fact, to carry the tanks of the 116th Panzer Division. If these bridges could be taken intact in a surprise attack then the transport, guns and tanks to LVIII Panzer Corps could get off to the flying start necessary to take them all the way to the Meuse. To make sure of surprise the Americans here must not be alerted and Manteuffel ordered that along this section of the front the massed artillery of LVIII Panzer Corps would not join in the pre-dawn opening barrage.

Two of the intact bridges were at the pleasant village of Ouren which lies inside a horseshoe bend of the Our; there was a third bridge still in position a couple of miles north of Ouren just behind American artillery positions on the east bank. This salient had been gouged out of the West Wall defences by the American 28th Division in September and, coincidentally, troops from this same division were once again holding a line along a ridge a mile or so east of the Our.

Despite this being a sector in which the opposing soldiers were nearer to each other than anywhere else along the Ardennes front, usually nothing more than occasional shelling took place and for a long time the Germans had shown no signs of wanting to disturb the comparative quiet. It was for this reason that the men of the 28th Infantry Division had been sent there—to rest and refit after their recent terrible losses.

The soldiers of the 112th Infantry Regiment, occupying the old German pill-boxes and a line of foxholes in these forward positions, could see their German opposite numbers moving about quite openly but since shelling had little effect except to provoke a reply and it was obvious that neither side intended to gain ground, there was an understandable, if unmilitary, tendency to live and let live—for the time being.

Because of their nearness to the German lines, supplies could only come up at night but food was adequate and there was a fairly generous leave roster. All the survivors of the Hurtgen Forest Battle (the 112th had suffered about two thousand casualties out of a strength of just over three thousand) had been back at least to the rear area rest centres. Platoons had been built up again to their full numbers with newcomers from the States. The veterans thought that they would probably be kept in this quiet sector for another two or three weeks and then sent north back to Ninth Army for the coming attack across the Rhine. They had had more than their share of bad luck in the battles in November: they felt that it was unlikely that such a thing could happen to them again.

Opposite them, they knew, were the 26th Volksgrenadiers, an experienced division from the Eastern front who, like themselves, had been pulled out for rest and refitting and also, like themselves, were not eager to start the shooting war again.

The quiet on their front was disturbed during the nights of December 14 and 15 by the sounds of many iron-rimmed wheels of horse-drawn vehicles and the deep throbbing of engines labouring in low gear. This was reported back with the suggestion that this front was being reinforced before an attack, but the same sort of noises had occurred a few weeks earlier and had turned out to be just a routine change of units in the German front line. It was assumed that this had happened again.

A change had in fact taken place, but it was not a routine one. The 26th, Manteuffel's best infantry, were being moved south to spearhead the attack on Bastogne.

Their place, opposite the two forward battalions of the 112th Regiment, had been taken by a scratch lot of ex-garrison troops from Norway and Denmark formed into the 560th Volksgrenadier Division, almost none of whom had yet been in action. Part of Hitler's desperate attempt to find soldiers for his great offensive, this makeshift division was only about two-third strength, less than seven thousand men. They were, however, supported by a full-strength tank division, the 116th, refitted, after being practically destroyed in France, with 139 medium and light tanks. General Krueger's LVIII Panzer Corps, like many other units in the Wehrmacht at this time, was a corps in name only, for it had little more than half as many tanks as an American armoured division, or infantry as an American infantry division. On the other hand on the immediate corps attack front were only two battalions (about two thousand men) of one regiment of the American 28th Division, with another battalion in reserve who were mostly west of the Our. There were no American tanks in the immediate vicinity but one of 28th Division's artillery battalions were in position on the east bank of the Our a mile or so behind the advanced infantry positions.

The German artillery, which had been brought into position to support the offensive, consisted of a large number of howitzers and cannon of many different calibres and one of the German problems was going to be to get the right ammunition to the right place. Wrong calibre shells were often going to be delivered to German gun positions evoking the same sort of comments from the sweating gunners that were being uttered on the other side. Mistakes, like luck, are fairly evenly distributed in a battle.

Krueger had been told that there would be no artillery barrage on his front in the hope that the Americans there would think that they had been left out of the attack. Therefore, when the men of the Third Battalion of the 112th Infantry Regiment occupying the forward posts heard the rumble of heavy guns well off to the south at about 5.30 am on December 16 and turned out, nothing was stirring in the front of them. The sky a few miles south was lit up by flashes like summer lightning and later there was a glow as of a distant city as the searchlights went on. It was obvious that their own 110th Infantry were being attacked.

'Poor bastards,' somebody said, 'rather them than us.' At that moment white-clad men of the well-trained but inexperienced 560th Volksgrenadiers were working their way quietly around the American forward positions and reassembling in the woods behind them, searching out the gaps in the American wire.

At 6.30 am with an hour and a half to go before 'first light',* LVIII Panzer Corps cannons and howitzers suddenly came to life laying down a pattern of shells first on the American artillery positions to silence them, then on the rearward positions and finally, a quarter of an hour before first light, all along the carefully mapped forward positions. As the shells and mortars burst around them the searchlights suddenly flicked on,

* About half an hour before sunrise: traditionally the earliest time that infantry warfare is feasible.

126

reflecting off the low cloud, and the volksgrenadiers advanced.

The shock companies, many of whom had already penetrated the American forward line, now moved through the gaps which the Americans had left in the long, deep barbed-wire defences to facilitate the movement of supplies at night. These were to have been closed as soon as a German attack began, but surprise had been achieved and compact shock troops of volksgrenadiers moved quickly through them and into the unprepared rear areas. In one case they burst into a clearing in the woods just as a platoon were having breakfast. The sudden fire of machine pistols, grenades and rifles killed a number of 112th Infantry, including the platoon commander, and the rest broke. The volksgrenadiers moved swiftly on towards the two bridges over the Our.

But there is no substitute for experience in war: the best of training does no more than teach a man his job so well that he will react instinctively when under fire and frightened. Only actual battle experience will teach him, for example, to distinguish immediately between situations which require defensive and those requiring offensive actions—situations which can succeed each other with confusing speed. The green 560th Volksgrenadiers, flushed with their early success, advanced openly in front of defended pill-boxes and foxholes and the more experienced men of the 112th Infantry Regiment recovered from their first surprise and set about picking the invaders off with rifle fire, spraying them with machine gun and, when they retreated into gullies, plastering them with mortar. German casualties were heavy.

A regiment of these volksgrenadiers, who had been given the task of seizing the bridge to the north of Ouren, had particularly bad luck. They had maps showing the exact location of every American machine gun and had worked out their attack lines accordingly. But all these positions had been changed only the day before, so that when they put in their set-piece attack they were cut to pieces by enfilading fire from the new positions. What happened next was something which was often typical of German troops: apparently unable to believe that their maps were wrong or to adjust quickly to the changed circumstances they reformed and, with stubborn courage, attacked twice more in the same formation over the same ground. They were wiped out almost to a man.

At the bridge, south of Ouren, the volksgrenadiers got nearly to the river but were stopped and scattered by machine-gun fire from the protecting positions. When the 112th Regiment's

TROIS
PONTS

Battlegroup
Peiper

LIGNEVILLE — Amblève

WANNE   Part of
1st SS Pz.Div.

99th Inf.Div.(V Corps)

GRAND HALLEUX

PETIT THIER

POTEAU
CCA
7th Armd.Div.

EMMELS   NIEDER
OBER

CCR
7th Armd.Div.

SART LEZ-ST-VITH

S

HINDERHAUSEN

CCB
7th Armd.Div.

SALMCHATEAU

B E L G I U M

COMMANSTER

CROMBACH

HQ.
106th Inf

CIERREUX

ROGERY

BRAUNLAUF

9

BOVIGNY

BEHO

REULAN

CHERAIN

HULDANGE

alize

OUREN

112th
Inf.Regt.

TROIS VIERGES

116th Pz.Div.

L U X.

110th
Inf.Regt.

HEINERSCHEID

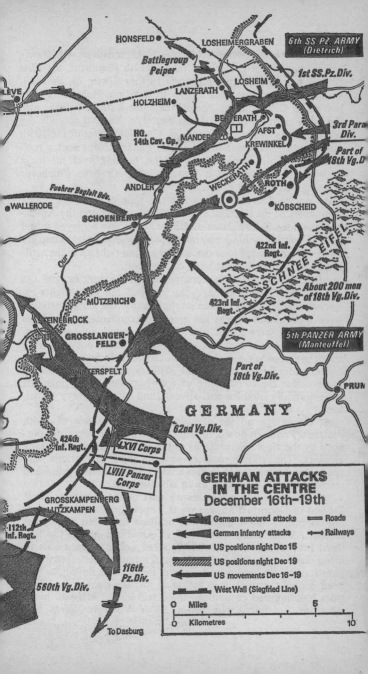

HONSFELD ●

LOSHEIMERGRABEN

6th SS PZ. ARMY
(Dietrich)

Battlegroup
Peiper

1st SS Pz. Div.

LOSHEIM

LEVE

LANZERATH

HOLZHEIM ●

BERTERATH

AFST

3rd Para
Div.

HQ.
14th Cav. Gp. MANDERFELD

KREWINKEL

Part of
18th Vg. D

ANDLER

WECKERATH

ROTH

KÖBSCHEID

Fuehrer Begleit Bde.

● WALLERODE

SCHOENBERG

Our

422nd Inf.
Regt.

SCHNEE EIFEL

About 200 men
of 18th Vg. Div.

MÜTZENICH ●

423rd Inf.
Regt.

5th PANZER ARMY
(Manteuffel)

STEINEBRÜCK

● GROSSLANGEN-
FELD

WINTERSPELT

Part of
18th Vg. Div.

PRUN

G E R M A N Y

62nd Vg. Div.

424th
Inf. Regt.

LXVI Corps

LVIII Panzer
Corps

GROSSKAMPENBERG

LUTZKAMPEN

-112th
Inf. Regt.

560th Vg. Div.

116th
Pz. Div.

To Dasburg

GERMAN ATTACKS
IN THE CENTRE
December 16th–19th

German armoured attacks	Roads
German infantry attacks	Railways
US positions night Dec 15	
US positions night Dec 19	
US movements Dec 16–19	
West Wall (Siegfried Line)	

0   Miles   5

0   Kilometres   10

reserve attacked over the bridge the volksgrenadiers withdrew.

The other front-line troops of the 112th Regiment, the First Battalion, held forward positions further north, on the divisional boundary line with the 106th Division. Here there were two more Our bridges: one in the First Battalion's area and the other right on the divisional boundary line but actually the responsibility of the newly-arrived 424th Regiment of the 106th Division. The commander of LVIII Panzer Corps sent a regiment of infantry against each bridge, holding back his main body of tanks, the 116th Panzers, to push over whichever crossing was secured first.

As on the Third Battalion front, a mile or so south, shock companies of the volksgrenadiers infiltrated around the American positions before dawn and here also some achieved initial success, getting behind command posts, shooting up company kitchens, ambushing lone trucks and getting right up to the artillery positions on the east bank of the river.

All this, however, was accomplished in the dark or with the aid of 'artificial moonlight'—the glow of the searchlights reflected off the clouds. When daylight came the First Battalion were waiting and caught the green volksgrenadiers out in the open. Many were killed and wounded, many others surrendered—so many in fact that some of the advance posts reported that they couldn't handle them all. The volksgrenadiers who had confidently approached the artillery positions in the dark came under the terrible fire of four-barrelled heavy machine guns normally used for anti-aircraft, and suffered heavy casualties.

At the bridge on the divisional boundary a few of 116th Panzer's Panthers nosed forward hopefully but were discouraged by the vigorous reactions of the 106th Infantry's anti-tank gunners. The volksgrenadiers sent to seize this bridge succeeded no better, for they came under heavy flanking fire and were practically destroyed as an effective unit.

All along the 112th Regiment's part of the Our river front the rest of December 16 was spent mopping up and consolidating operations. By nightfall the position had been largely restored. All the bridges were still in American hands, the forward artillery, far from being knocked out, had been able to bring down heavy fire on the German infantry sheltering in the pine forests; the regimental reserve, the Second Battalion, had been brought smartly into action at just the right place. Both sides had suffered casualties—the attackers, as is usual, more than the defenders, the green 560th Volksgrenadiers had apparently lost a thousand men* and the 116th Panzers six tanks—but, so far at least, morale was good on both sides.

Nevertheless General Manteuffel well realized at the end of the first day that his centre attack with LVIII Panzer Corps had failed almost completely to accomplish its objectives. Only at one point had troops of this corps been able to cross the Our.

Further south one volksgrenadier regiment had been able to march, almost without hindrance, straight to the river and to put infantry across to seize a bridgehead. This was at the site of a destroyed bridge which lay on the boundary between the 112th and 110th regiments and each had apparently assumed that its defence was the responsibility of the other. However, the approaches to the river from the east were mined and blocked with felled trees: it would take the German engineers at least a day's hard effort to get a bridge in. LVIII Panzer Corps was badly behind schedule. To try to catch up the next day the 116th Panzer Division were ordered to send a battalion of light tanks out of the corps area five or six miles south, to cross the river over a bridge, which had been established by the élite XLVII Panzer Corps, and then to turn north and come back along the American side of the Our to take the bridges opposite LVIII Panzer Corps from the rear.

As night fell on the 112th Regiment's front there was a general feeling of satisfaction. The new men, numbering two out of three, had, on the whole, done quite well after recovering from their initial surprise and the veterans did not tell them how much worse things might become. The two forward battalions had, after all, successfully broken up an attack by superior numbers, killed a good many and captured some and, although they had also suffered casualties they had yielded very little ground. They did not yet realize that what they had beaten off had merely been the opening moves in a major German offensive nor that the units on their right and left had not fared so well as they. Nor did they know that fairly large numbers of the volksgrenadiers had gone to ground between them and the river behind or that all during the night other German soldiers were worming quietly past them and that observers were methodically mapping and reporting back to the German artillery the exact location of every American position.

They knew that in all probability the Germans would come on again in force at dawn but they were confident that Allied

* But not actually, for one company had merely got lost in the woods.

131

tanks and infantry and air support must be coming to their aid.

There had been no hot food served all day and at night, when the temperature fell and the damp mist crept in, they shivered in their foxholes as they strained their eyes in the dark trying to distinguish shadow from substance. Few slept at all that night.

THE APPROACH TO BASTOGNE

*Our strategy is to pit one against ten and our tactics
are to pit ten against one.*

MAO TSE-TUNG

General von Manteuffel's attempt to push an armoured
column from the centre of his front through the gap between
the attacks on St Vith and Bastogne had failed and at the end
of the first day all of 116th Panzer Division's tanks were still
east of the Our and his infantry had only succeeded in establishing a bridgehead at one place.

This was disappointing but not critical for Fifth Panzer
Army's main blow was to be from their left where, following a
two-divisional infantry assault to establish four crossings, tanks
from two regular army divisions would converge on Bastogne,
seize and hold it with infantry and then crash through the
disorganized American rear areas to the Meuse crossing south
of Givet. Then, if all had gone well, the armour would keep
moving north-west, by passing Charleroi and Brussels, to
Antwerp.

These four German divisions, two volksgrenadier and two
panzer, were opposed by two American infantry regiments,
supported by a few batteries of field artillery, holding 28th
Infantry Division's centre and right flank. This sector of front
along the river Our from Dasburg to Vianden was nine or ten
miles measured in a straight line—air-flight miles—but as the
forward posts followed the winding river the distance was much
greater. Bastogne lay about twenty air-flight miles from the
northern end of this line and twenty-five miles from the
southern.

On the American left 28th Division's 110 Infantry Regiment
held rather more than half of this sector with two of their battalions in the line supported by two battalions of artillery. Their
third battalion constituted the division's only infantry reserve.
The American right was held by 28th's 109th Infantry Regiment.

The three main tactical features of the area between the
German start line and the approaches to Bastogne were first,
the river Our, second the main north and south highway, Skyline Drive, running on top of a ridge parallel to and some two

to three miles west of the Our which roughly marked the main line of resistance and third, two or three miles further west still, the river Clerf with three bridges from which roads led to Bastogne.

The American command here appreciated that a serious German attack would cross the Our because the defensive forces were too few to be able to stop it. Counter-attack plans were to harry and delay such an attempt and to try to hold the main line of resistance along Skyline Drive until reinforcements could be got up but, in any case, to hold the Clerf river crossings at all costs.

Both of 28th Infantry Division's regiments had disposed their forces in a line of strongpoints based on Skyline Drive in the north (in the 110th sector) and well forward of the highway overlooking the river Our in the south (in the 109th sector). Forward of these strongpoints, along the bank of the river, a number of outposts were held during daylight hours only. Most of the heavily wooded, ridged ground between the river and the highway was considered as no man's land for neither side were in complete control of it: at night German soldiers slipped across the river, which at places is no more than fifty to sixty feet wide, and moved about in the woods or, against orders, visited friends in the small towns along the river. Sometimes patrols from each side stalked each other in the dark. The Germans maintained camouflaged observation posts from which almost all the American defensive positions were marked on large-scale maps and sent back to divisional operations planning section.

In 110th Infantry Regiment's sector there were two good bridges over the Clerf and one narrow stone bridge. All three would be key targets in any German attack. One was at Drauffelt in the regiment's centre; another was at the old and beautiful small city of Clervaux where regimental headquarters had been set up and where men from the line went back for short leaves and rest. The third bridge was further south, on the regiment's right.

In order to control the road approaches from the east to these bridges the 110th had set up six defensive positions: two small towns astride Skyline Drive, Marnach and Hosingen, and four villages. Three of these village strongpoints were back, between Skyline Drive and the river Clerf; the fourth was forward, on the regiment's right flank, between the highway and the river Our.

Marnach and Hosingen were most strongly held, for their importance was obvious: from Marnach a good hard road led

134

west for a couple of miles to the main bridge at Clervaux and from Hosingen a road led to the Drauffelt bridge. From each of these bridges roads went to Bastogne.

Marnach and Hosingen were three miles apart along Skyline Drive and both were easily approached from the east. Marnach was only four miles up a good road from the Our crossing at Dasburg and Hosingen was even nearer to the river and accessible along good secondary roads. 110th Infantry occupied each in reinforced company strength and each was one of General von Manteuffel's earliest objectives.

Although the likelihood of an attack was considered remote the 28th Infantry Division's commander, Major-General 'Dutch' Cota and the 110th Regiment's commander, Colonel Hurley Fuller, were both well aware of the importance of Marnach and Hosingen and had disposed strong forces to support them. Between Marnach and the bridge at Clervaux one battery of artillery had been sited on high ground dominating the approach road, while south-west of Hosingen the other battery had been placed near Bockholt along a ridge from which it could either fire on troops approaching the Drauffelt crossing from Hosingen or, alternatively, on another east–west road a couple of miles further south.

This was the third of the roads which led up from the Our, across the highway and continued, by a narrow stone bridge, over the Clerf towards Bastogne. Three more of 110th Regiment's strongpoints lay on it; the most forward and most lightly held was Wahlhausen, which was only an observation post held by a platoon from the company stationed in Weiler, the regiment's right flank position. West of Skyline Drive was the next strongpoint, the village of Holzthum and another mile west the third, Consthum. Holzthum was held by a company of infantry; there was another company in Consthum and the battalion headquarters company.

From Marnach, as well as the main road west to Clervaux another road ran south-west four miles to the bridge at Drauffelt. To block this approach another of 110th Infantry's companies had been placed in and around Munshausen, a village on this road about two miles from Marnach.

Thus the 110th Infantry Regiment had disposed six of its eight available companies so as to block all the roads leading west through their centre.* Two batteries of artillery supported them. Four more companies, comprising their Second Battalion, were in reserve west of the Clerf together with a tank

* Their other two companies were north of Marnach and not in the path of XLVII Panzer Corps' attack.

135

battalion but these two battalions were 28th Infantry Division's entire reserve.

The division's right flank was held by their 109th Infantry Regiment with two battalions in the line and the third in reserve. The Our runs south-east along here and the distance between it and the ridge highway increases to five miles and more with intervening higher ground. 109th Infantry's forward positions were much nearer to the Our than 110th's and consisted of strongpoints which looked across the river and which were backed up by four well-defended company positions a mile or so behind.

As we have seen, 109th's regimental commander, Lieutenant-Colonel James Rudder, had concentrated two of his battalions and most of his supporting artillery on his right in order to protect the vital road and rail centre of Ettelbruck. This disposition had succeeded in stopping 352nd Volksgrenadier Division's initial assault while the troops from 109th Infantry Regiment on the extreme right had been able to direct enfilading fire on the German infantry from 276th Volksgrenadier Division who had attacked 60th Armoured Infantry Battalion's left flank.

Thus 109th Infantry regiment's concentration of strength on 28th Infantry Division's right wing had proved most valuable in blocking a German breakthrough there but 'a line cannot be strong everywhere' and the regiment's centre and left flank was necessarily thinly manned. This five miles north to 110th Infantry's sector was held by 109th's 2nd Battalion.

Two strongpoints, each of company strength, two miles apart and a mile or so west of the river supported a series of seven outposts along the river bank. A third company was in reserve two miles behind with a battery of howitzers in support.

The sector was weakly held but there was even less evidence of aggression on the German side here than in other places along the Our. On the morning of December 14 a strong American combat patrol crossed the Our at Vianden to test German reactions. Coincidentally, thirty-six hours earlier the volksgrenadiers who had long thinly held that section of the German front had been pulled out and moved south to concentrate for the coming attack and the parachute division who were to attack from Vianden on the 16th had not yet arrived. For a few hours Vianden was unoccupied. The combat patrol returned and reported that there were no German troops opposite 109th Infantry's left flank.

Most of the enlisted men of the 28th Infantry were raw

troops who had come as replacements (now, by order, referred to as 'reinforcements') for the heavy losses sustained in the Hurtgen Forest fighting. A small percentage were RTDs ('returned to duty') who had seen action, as had most of the officers and NCOs, but the great majority of the men had not. They were about to be attacked in overwhelming force and it would not have been surprising if they had been swept out of the way without seriously delaying the attackers.

The company entrusted with the defence of Hosingen, Company K of the Third Battalion of the 110th Infantry Regiment, was typical and a closer look at them will give the picture of the make-up of the other strongpoints. They were one hundred and sixty strong, almost all of whom were replacements, for Company K had been trapped near Schmidt for three days in November and practically annihilated. Hosingen, on Skyline Drive, was built on a ridge about four miles from the Our and the ground between consisted of heavily wooded country with a succession of north–south ridges cut by east–west ravines. Company K had taken over in mid-November from 8th Infantry Division troops and had spent the intervening month in improving the defences (soldiers are almost always highly critical of the defensive arrangements of units they replace) and in training the new men in scouting and patrolling, sniping and observation and giving them as much practical experience as was possible. This, unfortunately, was very little, for ammunition shortage had resulted in an order that no rifles or machine guns, mortars or artillery, were to be fired except at Germans actually seen west of the Our. This prohibition prevented the registration of guns on the ravines which ran towards the American lines from the river or the confirmation that mortars intended to bring shells down on dead spots (small areas concealed from observation by the lie of the ground) would actually do so.

It was permitted to fire weapons across the Our at the German positions and this gave an opportunity to test-fire new mortars and light machine guns. Reconnaissance patrols, usually consisting of an officer and six or seven men, made their way down through the woods to the river bank, often encountering German patrols when there would be a brief exchange of fire before both hurriedly withdrew, neither knowing whether the other had support. On one occasion an American patrol stumbled across a German observation post and killed one and wounded one before withdrawing. When this was reported to Battalion HQ orders came to return the following night with a 60-mm mortar and wipe out the observation post.

137

As might have been expected this patrol was itself ambushed and the new mortar captured. This sort of hide-and-seek went on intermittently during the month before the attack.

There was a great shortage of equipment (on one occasion training in map reading and reconnaissance depended on borrowing the commanding officer's compass) and ammunition. Despite strongly worded requests only one day's ammunition was kept and whatever was used was replaced daily. If the supply sergeant had not been an old soldier who had 'picked up' extra ammunition from time to time, ammunition would have been exhausted in the first few hours of the German attack.

The company were responsible for a two-mile sector of the highways extending from north of Hosingen to an east–west road which crossed Skyline Drive about half a mile south of the town. The defence line was an arc of foxholes which covered the high ground and possible approach routes from the east with rifle and light machine-gun positions. An observation post in a high water tower could give ample warning of any movement from the east.

At dawn on December 16 the eleven or twelve miles of American front based on Skyline Drive from Marnach to a point roughly opposite the Our crossing at Vianden was held by eight companies of infantry with another six in reserve, that is, fourteen companies (of about one hundred and sixty combat troops each) out of a divisional total of thirty-six. Behind them were a number of artillery and howitzer positions, too few to stop an attack in force: the division also had one battalion of tanks. Total strength was about four thousand men.

Opposite this part of 28th Division's front the Germans had quietly built up a force of at least fifty thousand men although, of course, only a small proportion of these could be brought to bear against the American positions at the outset of the attack, but the three to one superiority which an attacker is commonly accepted to need would certainly be exceeded.

Two armoured divisions and a division of volksgrenadiers came from one of General Manteuffel's armoured corps; the other division of parachute infantry was from General Brandenberger's Seventh Army.

The armoured corps, Manteuffel's main punch, was the Wehrmacht's 'Number One Reserve' on the Western Front, the élite XLVII Panzer. It was commanded by General Heinrich von Luettwitz, one of the most experienced of Germany's armoured commanders and one whom the Allies knew well. It was he who, with very few men, had stopped the

American attack in the Eifel in September. Since then his corps had been thrown in whenever something spectacular was needed.

In October, in southern Holland, he had so successfully attacked the US 7th Armored Division that Field Marshal Model had wanted to try to exploit the situation into a major offensive but had been stopped by Field Marshal von Rundstedt, no man to plunge his head into a noose. (One of the results of that attack, however, had been that General Bradley had relieved the commander of the 7th Armored Division and had given it instead to one of the more aggressive combat command leaders, Brigadier-General Hasbrouck, who was soon to be called to the Ardennes.)

Short, plump and monocled, Heinrich Freiherr von Luettwitz looked like a musical comedy German general but in reality he was physically tough, had undoubted personal courage and was a superb handler of armour. One of the old school of career officers from famous military families, he was a strict disciplinarian and drove his men hard. In the tradition of the old, regular army he also looked after them like a parent. Most of them feared, respected and liked him.

For the Ardennes Offensive his XLVII Panzer Corps consisted of a first-class infantry division, the 'old Twenty-sixth' from the Eastern Front and the famous 2nd Panzers, a regular army armoured division who had fought the Allies with spirit and courage all the way from Normandy to Germany, arriving at the Eifel in September with only three tanks. The rest had been lost in the fighting and the long retreat but many of the surviving crews had found their way back on foot and so formed the nucleus of the newly-formed 2nd Panzer Division. The replacements to full strength of fourteen thousand had mostly come from the division's home station, Vienna, and had been hand-picked to maintain an unusually high *esprit de corps*. They got priority in weapons too: forty-eight new self-propelled anti-tank guns and twenty-seven new Mark IV tanks—this was an old model but had proved itself to be thoroughly reliable. They were also sent, as their main punching power, fifty-eight of the latest type of Panther tank, some of which mounted one of Hitler's few, genuine 'secret weapons'. This was an infra-red searchlight which shone its beam of black light quite unbeknown to the enemy. It was mounted coaxially with the tank's cannon, making for bewilderingly accurate fire at night.

XLVII Panzer Corps was General von Manteuffel's main hope of reaching the Meuse. In reserve to 2nd Panzer Division he had another crack unit, Panzer Lehr Division who, after the infantry had forced the river crossings and 2nd Panzer were rolling, would be thrown in to add weight at the *Schwerpunkt*.*

The corps' infantry, the 26th Volksgrenadiers, were given a particularly difficult rôle: they had to force the Our, advance seven or eight miles and force the Clerf, hold both these rivers open for the armour to cross, then follow the tanks on foot another fifteen miles to Bastogne, which it was then their job to take, single-handed if necessary. And, as if this were not enough, they were then to protect the corps' flank to the Meuse. It was a formidable programme calling for infantrymen of unusual quality—which the 'old Twenty-sixth' were.

This regular army division had been in the van of the invasion of Russia in July 1941 and had fought, almost without rest, up until September 1944, when their losses had finally been so severe that Hitler had consented to their being withdrawn for complete re-equipping and rebuilding into a fresh fighting unit. To the surprise of the surviving veterans who, like veterans in all armies, had acquired a cynical disbelief in promises from above, they quickly got a full complement of weapons including forty-two of the new self-propelled anti-tank guns. Their numbers were made up to the exceptionally high figure of seventeen thousand. Most of these replacements were specially selected from the Navy and were of a much higher quality than the average intake at that time. Before being sent to the Western Front to join Manteuffel's Fifth Panzer Army they were re-named (to the disgust of the original members of the 'old Twenty-sixth') the 26th Volksgrenadiers.

Their commander, Major-General Heinz Kokott, an old tank man himself, knew how mutually dependent tanks and infantry are in an armoured advance—each is at a great disadvantage without the support of the other. Knowing that the troops immediately opposite his front were only about two thousand of the weary US 28th Infantry Division he did not think that he would have much difficulty in getting bridges first across the Our and then the Clerf. What worried him was his shortage of transport, for if his foot soldiers kept up with the tanks as far as Bastogne they would by then be too exhausted to put in an attack. His division did have some five

* Literally 'the centre of gravity' but a term much used by German military theorists for the place on an attack line which becomes the point of main effort.

thousand horses, many of which had been brought back from the eastern front (and so found the conditions in the Eifel in December almost mild) but these carried equipment, not men.

He decided, and both Luettwitz, the Corps' Commander, and von Manteuffel, the Army commander, agreed, that his division had been asked to do more than was militarily feasible but to requests for more men, guns and tanks Hitler was deaf—for the very good reason that he didn't have them. The 26th Volksgrenadiers would be able to perform its tasks providing that everything went according to plan and this meant particularly that Brandenberger's Seventh Army succeeded in blocking any American attacks from the south.

Early realizing that the success of his offensive very much depended on this hard shoulder, von Manteuffel had personally pleaded with Hitler for General Brandenberger to be allotted at least a few tanks to back up his depleted forces. In the original plan the German Seventh Army was to have consisted of eight divisions but necessity had cut it to only four and these were generally thought to be third-rate infantry—not exactly the troops to hold off General Patton's Third Army.

But this too Hitler refused, giving the tanks instead to his Sixth SS Panzer Army and gambling that they would achieve such overwhelming success on the right wing that the southern left hook would be carried on their momentum.

The Fifth Parachute Division, from Brandenberger's Seventh Army, were also to take part in Manteuffel's attack. Their task was to cross the Our on 26th Volksgrenadier's left, against the most thinly held part of 109th Infantry Regiment's sector, and move alongside XLVII Panzer Corps as far as Bastogne. When this important communications centre was captured 5th Parachute were to hold it against possible American counter-attacks. They were also expected to continue a flank defence line from Bastogne to the Meuse crossings.

5th Parachute Division were in a poor state not only because of their severe losses and half-trained replacements but because they had been one of Goering's and Student's special units and many of the surviving officers felt that they owed their loyalty to the Parachute Army and not to the regular army. This had resulted in rival factions and at the time of the Ardennes Offensive a clique of old paratroop officers had succeeded in getting rid of their commanding officer. He had been replaced at short notice by a tough regular army officer, Colonel Heilman, who expressed himself forcefully about his new command, describing them to Field Marshal Model, who had personally appointed him, as a 'grade four outfit'.

141

He pointed out that he couldn't keep up with the tanks of 2nd Panzer Division without motorized infantry. Also Fifth Parachute, when moving to the Ardennes, had been carelessly caught out in the open by the Allied air force and had lost most of its anti-tank guns and mortars and none had been replaced.

Field Marshal Model was well aware of these shortcomings, which by that time were common throughout the German army. He probably also realized that, like his own orders to take Army Group B to Antwerp, the tasks assigned to Colonel Heilman and General Brandenberger, Seventh Army's Commander, were impossible to carry out.

'You will have to make do with horses, at least at first,' he said. 'Soon there will be plenty of captured American transport to move your guns. Success will be won by the paratroopers' usual audacity.' He well knew that 5th Parachute Regiment contained only a handful of actual paratroopers but, initially at least, they would assault less than two companies of American infantry: such odds compensate for many deficiencies.

5th Parachute's own engineers would have to ferry their single brigade of motorized assault guns over the Our and then gather up their ferrying equipment and take it quickly six or seven miles to the next river, the Wiltz. Here they would once more ferry the assault guns across to join XLVII Panzer Corps' attack on Bastogne. 5th Parachute's assault front was a three straight-line mile section of the Our; along it four crossing places were chosen, two for each attack column.

The northernmost column would hit the seam between the 109th and 110th Infantry Regiments but, angling north-west, would soon be wholly in the 110th's sector. 5th Parachute's left-hand column would hit the centre of 109th Infantry, crossing the Our at Vianden and then move rapidly west eight or nine miles and cross the Clerf by a narrow stone bridge before angling north-west to Wiltz, 28th Infantry Division's HQ.

For the crossing at Dasburg, Manteuffel insisted on getting heavy bridging equipment, pointing out that otherwise he could not get his tanks across and that his mission was impossible without armour. He got his way and two huge sixty-ton pontoon bridges were sent to him. He assigned one to Dasburg and sent the other to Gemund so that the 26th Volksgrenadiers could get their vehicles and self-propelled anti-tank guns across the Our.

But the narrow roads leading to the river twist and drop steeply and the long trailers had great difficulty in getting the bridges down them at all. Nevertheless, relying on certain sur-

142

prise and the thinness of the strung-out American defences, General Manteuffel anticipated little difficulty in getting his forces over the Our, Skyline Drive and across the Clerf in the first few hours. He and his corps commander, General Luett-witz, gave most of their attention to the problem of getting the panzers and their supporting volksgrenadiers from west of the Clerf into and beyond Bastogne.

So that the Americans would not be alerted von Manteuffel forbade any of his tanks to move before dark or any of the infantry to cross the Our before the pre-dawn opening barrage, but General Kokott, the opportunistic commander of the 26th Volksgrenadiers, pointed out that his forward troops had been in the habit of putting men over the river at night and holding a line of outposts on the American side until dawn. If this didn't take place as usual it would arouse suspicion.

General Manteuffel agreed and Kokott took advantage of this concession to slip two of his three regiments over the Our during the hours of darkness. He ordered them to move quietly up through the woods into a line of departure just east of Sky-line Drive. As soon as the artillery barrage began, the right-hand regiment was to bypass Hosingen to the north and quickly seize the Clerf crossing at Drauffelt. The left-hand regiment was to advance along the third east–west road through Holz-thum and Consthum to another crossing of the Clerf and on to Wiltz. The capture of these two bridges would open routes for the tanks and self-propelled guns to attack Bastogne.

The tank commanders obeyed orders, keeping their panzers well back until after dark on December 15. Even then, because the engineers were still struggling to get the bridging equip-ment into position, the armour did not move but only its supporting grenadier infantry. When the 2nd Panzer Divi-sion's new* commander, Colonel Meinrad von Lauchert, real-ized that he was not going to be able to get his tanks across for several hours after the offensive began, he got permission to send his panzer grenadiers across in rubber boats to move quickly up through the woods and seize Marnach so that when the tanks did get across they would not be delayed there.

On XLVII Corps' left 5th Parachute's commander, Colonel Heilman, knowing that the 109th Regiment's forward observa-tion posts kept a continual watch across the Our on the West Wall positions, gave strict orders that no unusual activity was to take place before the attack. The bulk of the parachute infantry were ordered to lie low in the woods behind the

* The former commander had not been enthusiastic enough about the chances of success and had been replaced at the last moment.

dragons' teeth and pill boxes.

As most of his men had been continuously on the move for two or three days and nights and had been undergoing intensive crash training before that, they were glad of a chance to rest. Many took the opportunity to write letters home; some were later taken from prisoners or found on dead bodies and it is proof of Hitler's extraordinary powers of persuasion that so many of these young men even at this late stage of the war, actually started the battle exultantly believing in a great German victory. For a large number it was to be their first and last action.

10

THE OUR IS CROSSED

... thirdly, on the day of the battle to direct, by means of tactical manoeuvre, the main body to the decisive point upon the battlefield or that part of the enemy's front which it is desired to crush.

GENERAL JOMINI: *Précis de L'Art de la Guerre*

All along the east bank of the Our German assault troops began to collect before midnight and, in the early hours of a cold, foggy morning—the kind of weather Hitler had promised —moved down to their attack positions. Already, across the river, the two regiments from the 26th Volksgrenadiers who had stolen a march on the troops on either side of them, had moved up through the woods towards the highway on the ridge, Skyline Drive.

The timetable called for all the Clerf crossings five or six miles west of the start line to be held firmly by nightfall, less than twelve hours after the opening barrage. The American strongpoints would have to be captured quickly or bypassed. In either case it would be a tight schedule and unit commanders were impatient to get started.

Exactly at 5.30 am, three hours before sunrise, gunnery officers all long the line of massed guns gave the order and the quiet front erupted. These were the guns which had awakened the men of the 12th Infantry Regiment a few miles north. The first warning that many of the 110th Regiment got, sleeping soundly miles behind the line, was the crash of shells exploding all around them. They scrambled out of sleeping bags, into shelters and foxholes, and tried to see through the cold, swirling fog.

Local commanders could not discover the full extent of the attack for the guns of Manteuffel's XLVII Panzer Corps had succeeded within a few minutes in cutting field telephone communications between all the American strongpoints, thus adding considerably to the confusion. The heavy barrage stopped after half an hour; nothing more seemed to be happening.

Not a great deal of damage, beyond the knocking out of wire on the 110th Infantry front, seemed to have been done, for it would appear that in many cases—particularly from

General Brandenberger's three hundred guns opposite the northernmost companies of 109th Infantry—the Germans fired by the map, putting down heavy concentrations on deserted crossroads and laying a pattern of shells along Skyline Drive which was, at that hour, practically deserted.

Half an hour after the barrage stopped the forward outpost at Holzthum, behind Skyline Drive and a long way from the front line, spotted figures moving about in the gloom of their front. They held their fire thinking it unlikely that these could be Germans. In fact they were shock troops of 26th Volksgrenadiers' left-hand regiment, who had worked their way up nearly to Skyline Drive before the barrage began and had come on again as soon as it had stopped. The problem of identity was quickly solved when they opened fire on the American defences and attacked in force.

They were beaten off and, by using the radios of the artillery observation post, the defenders of Holzthum were able to flash a warning of the unexpected presence of German infantry in strength four miles west of the Our to 110th Infantry Regiment's HQ at Clervaux, by 6.15 am. This was the first intimation that the barrage was, in fact, a prelude to a real attack.

If it had not been for the artillery's efficient radio set it would not have been possible for Colonel Hurley Fuller to have maintained a coherent defence on December 16 at all, for his field telephone wires were all out and his strongpoints completely cut off from each other. Because their big howitzers and heavy guns are necessarily a considerable distance behind the front line the artillery must have quick, efficient communication with their forward observers; in modern warfare, which depends very much on radio, it is essential that it works well. That it did was to prove very important in the first few critical hours of the German attack.

Failing to take Holzthum by assault the volksgrenadiers tried to work around the north of it but this brought them under fire from the artillery battalion positions south-west of Bockholt, causing casualties and forcing them to go to ground. Annoyed, the German commander ordered a company to deploy for an attack against the guns, which had no infantry protection. This company marched up a narrow, secondary road to get into position. Seeing a half-track at a crossroads ahead of them they hesitated but were not fired upon. Instead, one of the crew of the half-track stood up and waved them forward in a friendly fashion. The volksgrenadiers resumed their march and before they got near enough to be able to identify it, the American four-barrel, fifty-calibre machine

146

guns opened fire killing at least a hundred and scattering the rest, successfully putting this entire company out of action.

Again and again the volksgrenadiers attacked the two villages of Holzthum and Consthum but were unable either to get possession of them or to get past and seize the narrow stone bridge over the Clerf only a couple of miles further west. At one moment they actually succeeded in capturing Consthum but were almost immediately driven out by a determined counter-attack. Later the German attackers cut the road between Holzthum and Consthum but a quickly formed force of twenty headquarters troops sallied out of Consthum and opened the road again, inflicting heavy casualties.

It was a most unexpectedly stubborn defence and it cost these volksgrenadiers, who had hoped to be the first German troops across the Clerf, all the time advantage they had gained by their night crossing of the Our. Desperately their commander flung his troops against the American artillery positions but the gunners put their shells on one-second fuses and fired over open sights. Some of the fuses were so short that parts of the shell blew back on the gun position. Although the battery commander and fifteen of his gun crews became casualties, the position was clung to until a platoon of tanks from 28th Division's slender reserve got through to them about twelve o'clock and made the battery comparatively safe: the German timetable was beginning to slip on this front too.

Meanwhile attacks were developing elsewhere on the long 110th Infantry Front. On the American right at Wahlhausen, the most forward of the strongpoints held through the night, the platoon at the observation post were able to see more of the volksgrenadiers openly assembling on their front as the light improved and were able to direct artillery fire on to them. The rest of this American company were in the village of Weiler, a mile and a half south and technically in 5th Parachute's zone, but because the parachutists had had to wait for the barrage before crossing the Our they had not yet appeared. The commander of the volksgrenadiers could not ignore either the artillery observation post at Wahlhausen which was directing fire on to his troops nor the strongly held position on his flank. He ordered two or three battalions to eliminate both Wahlhausen and Weiler.

In Weiler the infantry company had both mortars and anti-tank guns as well as their own automatic weapons and they beat off successive waves of attacking volksgrenadiers all morning inflicting very heavy casualties on the brave, but largely inexperienced young troops. The Germans twice asked for and were given permission to send stretcher bearers forward under a white flag to remove their wounded. At half past one in the afternoon they sent a third emissary forward, this time with an offer to Weiler's dwindling defenders, all of whose mortar and anti-tank ammunition was gone, of an 'honourable surrender'. This was refused. The attack resumed with a strong volksgrenadier force moving south and east to surround the small town.

At Wahlhausen the ammunition had soon begun to run out as the single platoon beat off attack after attack. They called for more ammunition and were told that tanks were on their way. But these never arrived.

They held on all day but after dark the volksgrenadiers came in again, this time supported by quick-firing light anti-aircraft guns and the position became hopeless. The last message from the survivors of the platoon at Wahlhausen who had put up so magnificent a fight was to call down artillery fire on their own position. Only one man survived.

At the same time the volksgrenadiers succeeded in surrounding Weiler where the Americans were down to their last few rounds of ammunition and it was obvious that no more would get through to them. The company commander divided his remaining men into two groups and ordered them to break out of the German ring during the night. A captain and twenty-five men succeeded in rejoining the regiment by the following night—the rest were all killed or captured.

By nightfall both the observation post at Wahlhausen and the strongpoint at Weiler—the two positions furthest east—had been eliminated, but it had taken much longer than had been planned. By then the Germans should have been across the Clerf.

At Hosingen the soldier on duty on the top of the water tower was one of the new men who had not yet experienced battle. At 5.30 am while he was actually making his periodic report by telephone to company HQ he broke off to say that the entire German line across the Our had suddenly become 'pin points of light'. While he was still puzzling this phenomenon the first shells started crashing into Hosingen and all wire communications were soon severed.

Several houses began to burn, lighting up the town: everyone stood to and after forty-five minutes the barrage stopped. Soon afterwards American outposts north of Hosingen heard infantry moving along one of the ravines to their front and

148

continuing on towards the west. Nothing could be done about this until it was light enough to see them, about 7.45, when the defenders opened up with their new light machine guns and these, with assistance from three mortars, slowed up the German advance. The volksgrenadiers found other routes further north and were able to cut Skyline Drive between Hosingen and Marnach at dawn and move rapidly towards the Drauffelt bridge four miles further west. This was 26th Volksgrenadiers' right-hand column which was then stopped by the field artillery near Bockholt, the same guns which also broke up the attack from the Wahlhausen to Holzthum road. The German infantry went to ground.

South of Hosingen another column from this right-hand regiment came down the road from the east and were engaged by a platoon of infantry and one of anti-tank gunners south of the crossroads. In the fight the Germans flowed north and so became involved in house-to-house fighting in the southern outskirts of Hosingen, something which they had been expressly ordered to avoid. But south of Hosingen the two American platoons were overwhelmed, all being killed, wounded or captured, and the east–west road became 26th Volksgrenadiers' main supply route.

The defenders in Hosingen called for reinforcements, ammunition and for artillery fire on this supply route, but the artillery were too busy stopping Germans moving immediately north and south of them and beating off attacks on their own position to be able to comply and Hosingen received no artillery support all day. About four o'clock in the afternoon five Sherman tanks were able to get through to Hosingen, for the attacking volksgrenadiers did not yet have the weapons to stop tanks. Three tanks were sent to the high ground south-east of the town to help slow the German advance, but within an hour they were driven back by self-propelled guns which the Germans were slowly managing to get across the river.

The rear had been endangered by the penetration north and south of Hosingen and a new defence line was established facing west so that the town was now surrounded by a perimeter defence reinforced by the five Sherman tanks. All through the night sporadic small arms and automatic fire was directed into the town from the north, west and south but no attempt was made to break through the defences.

Now General Kokott had to have Hosingen, for as long as the Americans were able to hold it his exit road from the bridge at Gemund was completely blocked. Although he had earlier thrown in his replacement battalion, who had managed to get a hold in the northern outskirts, and had elements bottled up in houses south of the town, the centre still held out.

But Company K's ammunition was nearly all used up; desperately they radioed for more.

Twenty-eight Infantry Division HQ was at Wiltz, ten miles south-east of Bastogne and on the boundary of its 110th and 109th Infantry Regiments. The divisional commander, General Cota, got reports of a heavy pre-dawn barrage all along his front and then confused messages of attacks everywhere. The first clear idea of what was actually happening came from Colonel Hurley Fuller, the 110th Regiment's commander in Clervaux who got through to General Cota about 9.0 am with details of the attacks on Consthum and Holzthum, from which it was apparent that the German assault was aimed at the Clerf river crossings.

From then on reports came crowding into 28th Divisional headquarters from both above and below and it was soon realized that this was no local attack but an all-out effort by the Germans along the whole of VIII Corps' front. All requests for assistance and reinforcement could not possibly be met and for the time being at least 28th Infantry Division would have to make do with what reserves it had: one battalion of infantry, the 110th's Second Battalion, and one of tanks, the 707th.

General Cota decided to continue to hold the Second Battalion in reserve until he could see where it would be needed most but to use his tanks where the danger was greatest—on his centre, where the 110th Infantry Regiment were everywhere being attacked.

This was almost certainly the right decision but General Cota split his reinforcements into too small units. He committed a platoon of tanks here and another there and sent even smaller numbers to try to deliver ammunition or to drive the Germans off side roads. One such group of tanks on their way with ammunition for the besieged American troops in Weiler and Wahlhausen, ran into German infantry too numerous to break through and so both those places went down. The five tanks who courageously fought their way through other German infantry into Hosingen brought no desperately needed rifle ammunition.

Also, with all the confusion and breakdown in communications, mistakes were inevitably made. A platoon of tanks sent to help the hard-pressed defenders of Holzthum and Consthum were warned that the road between these two places was in German hands. It had in fact been retaken by American troops who had set up an anti-tank gun which the relieving tanks promptly knocked out. The American infantry and tanks then fired on each other until they realized their mistake.

Because of this piecemeal commitment of his reserve tank force General Cota lost the advantage which the German failure to get bridges in during the night of December 15/16 had given him; the advantage of having tanks before the attackers had either tanks or self-propelled guns. It was an advantage which only lasted briefly, for by four o'clock in the afternoon the German engineers at last managed to get the huge pontoon bridge in at Dasburg and the tanks of the 2nd Panzer Division started to funnel into the 110th Infantry sector.

The road that led up through the woods from this bridge to Marnach, had, three months before, been the line of retreat of the Germans and they had most efficiently blocked it in depth by felling trees across it. In the intervening time the Americans had not cleared the road, since their main line of resistance lay to the west of it. Although the Germans now tried to clear a way as fast as possible, the tanks only made very slow progress. Meanwhile the traffic behind them snarled up and for some hours the bridge was of no use.

The panzergrenadiers who had crossed at Dasburg in rubber boats as soon as the barrage began and had started confidently up the road to take Marnach in a dawn attack were delayed when they ran into an American minefield but still got to the town on Skyline Drive by first light. The German artillery across the Our brought heavy fire down on Marnach to help this attack but the positions were well protected and the American infantry company had a platoon from a tank destroyer battalion to back them up while the attacking German panzergrenadiers had no heavy weapons at all yet. Not succeeding in a frontal assault, the panzergrenadiers infiltrated around Marnach on both north and south and so were able to block attempts to relieve the town. One of these came from the two companies of the 110th, who were holding strongpoints further north along Skyline Drive, and whose patrols ran into heavy fire and had to withdraw. Another attempt to help Marnach was made from the company who had been holding the position at Munshausen two miles south-west along the road to the Drauffelt bridge. Colonel Fuller, in Clervaux, ordered them to move up this road into Marnach, but they found the road impassable because of heavy, persistent small-arms fire from the panzergrenadiers who had bypassed Marnach on the south. They then tried to move across country but were soon pinned down. Meanwhile the garrison in Marnach fought on against mounting odds, suffering casualties at an increasing rate. Finally two platoons of American tanks rolled up the Munshausen road, past the American infantry which they were supposed to pick up, through the panzergrenadiers, who did not yet have the weapons to stop them, and right into Marnach itself. One platoon of tanks stayed in Marnach to bolster up the defence; the other returned to reinforce the position blocking the approach to the Drauffelt bridge, picking up the infantry who had earlier gone to ground.

By dusk the advance troops of 2nd Panzer Division's supporting infantry had pushed past Marnach and were approaching Clervaux* and at the same time German half-tracks, which had been able to get around the felled trees on the Dasburg to Marnach road, closed in on Marnach. Most of these mounted multiple machine guns and some had 20-mm cannon and their firepower, together with fresh troops, proved too much for the defenders who had been fighting all day. Their commander had been knocked out earlier and the battalion Executive Officer had taken over. His report of half-tracks, all guns firing, breaking through his outer defences was the last to come out of Marnach. It is now known that some defenders continued to hold out until about midnight when the German tanks and self-propelled guns at last got up the road from Dasburg and broke into the town.

Having taken Marnach, only a battery of American field artillery lay between the Germans and the all-important bridge at Clervaux. Colonel Fuller had gathered up a mixed batch of men who had been on pass in the town and sent them to form a protective screen in front of the guns sited on high ground half way along the road from Marnach to Clervaux. Not knowing that the Germans had succeeded in putting in heavy bridges over the Our or that the 2nd Panzer Division's tanks were already in Marnach, Colonel Fuller ordered a dawn attack.

The reports of attacks on every one of his strongpoints had been coming in all day and Colonel Fuller had first begged and then practically demanded that General Cota release the 110th's Second Battalion to him. But the divisional commander had held it in reserve all day, waiting to see which of his three regiments would need reinforcements most. By 9.0 pm

* All mines and booby traps had been moved from the Marnach/Clervaux area a few days before in order to enable the reserve battalion to practise moving across wooded country.

when most of the activity along his front seemed to have died down it was apparent that it was the 110th Infantry Regiment in his centre who had borne most of the weight of the German attack. He ordered one company of the reserve battalion to come to Wiltz to defend the divisional command post and released the rest to Colonel Fuller.

The 110th's commander immediately ordered the Second Battalion to attack at first light and restore the position at Marnach. They would be supported by a company of light tanks moving down from the north and the platoon of medium tanks which had earlier in the day arrived at the blocking position at Munshausen, two miles south-west of Marnach.

If this action could have been taken earlier in the day before the German armour got across the Our, it might well have saved Marnach and Clervaux at least for another critical day. This could have had far-reaching results but the big German tanks and the self-propelled guns were already moving around Marnach towards Clervaux and the position of the 110th Infantry Regiment would soon become hopeless. General Cota had waited too long before committing his infantry reserve and had weakened his armoured reserve by using it piecemeal.

Fifth Parachute Division who attacked 109th Infantry Regiment's northernmost battalion made remarkably little progress. Their right-hand column got rubber boats and portable infantry bridges across the narrow Our while the opening barrage was in progress. A specially trained assault party got into the western half of Vianden before dawn and in a sudden rush overwhelmed the American forward position in the ruined château before they could fire warning flares or make radio contact. They succeeded in crossing the Our at both their chosen places almost without opposition and moved west alongside 26th Volksgrenadier's left-hand column which had become involved in the heavy fighting against the defenders of Weiler. Although this place was in their zone 5th Parachute took no part in attacking it and by night-fall had got no further west than Skyline Drive south of Hoscheid in which Twenty-eighth Division's anti-tank company was stationed. Thus, although they had not yet accomplished much they were in a good position from which to attack on the next day.

5th Parachute's second column also showed little desire to push deep into American-held territory. After an easy crossing of the Our they moved unopposed through the gap between the two American strong company positions and into the unoccupied village of Walsdorf, two miles west of the Our.

For the rest of the first day two German regiments and three American companies circled each other warily like wrestlers waiting to get a hold. By nightfall 5th Parachute had penetrated no more than three miles.

Not surprisingly General von Luettwitz was not at all pleased at dusk on December 16 with the progress of his XLVII Corps or their supporting flank protection, 5th Parachute. Not one of his attack columns had reached their objective.

Worst of all and most unexpectedly, none of the American strongpoints had fallen except Marnach and even there there were still some troops holding out. The fact that Hosingen was still in American hands was most serious for it meant that the road from the crossing at Gemund was blocked and his crack Panzer Lehr Division. instead of racing across country towards the Meuse, was still east of the Our.

His assault infantry had suffered very heavy casualties in a number of comparatively minor actions and two small American field artillery positions had broken up attack after attack and were still holding on. Unless there were dramatic changes the next day the success of the whole offensive would be put in jeopardy.

On the other hand two heavy bridges, able to take Tiger tanks and siege guns, were in and some tanks and self-propelled guns were already moving towards Clervaux. All through the night more tanks, guns and flame throwers crossed the Our and moved up to be ready to smash the stubborn defence at Hosingen first thing on December 17.

If the hope of a quick, easy breakthrough on this front had been lost it was obvious that the defences were weakening, that they had been caught completely by surprise and that there were no reserves of any importance the Americans could call upon.

An all-out assault on the second day could regain most of the lost time and get the offensive rolling towards the Meuse.

11

THE TRAP IS SET...

> *Deceit in the conduct of war outweighs valour and is worthy of merit.*
>
> MACHIAVELLI

Because their tanks had to keep to the roads there were only a few places along the Ardennes front through which the Germans could launch an armoured attack. If any further evidence is needed of just how unlikely Allied Intelligence considered such an offensive on this front it can be found in the disposition of their forces near these danger points.

One historic invasion route from Germany into Belgium, from the Eifel into the Ardennes, is through the Losheim Gap. This is a narrow valley slicing south-west from north of the Schnee Eifel and forming its western edge. Two or three miles further west the Our winds over the valley floor; further west still the ground rises sharply again, quickly becoming heavily wooded. This is the Manderfeld Ridge, a natural defensive feature.

The only Allied Forces defending the centre of the four-mile-wide north-eastern entrance to this valley on December 16, 1944, were two troops of a mechanized cavalry squadron, a tank destroyer company with a few of their own reconnaissance troops and various service and headquarters staff—less than a thousand men in all.

They were part of the Fourteenth Cavalry Group which until a week or so before had been a skeleton HQ in bivouacs near Luxembourg City and which had been activated by the attachment of two cavalry squadrons. One, the Eighteenth, already in the Losheim Gap and the other, the Thirty-second, Chicago's famous 'Black Horse Troop', in reserve. These light reconnaissance units were fattened out by the attachment of part of a tank destroyer battalion and one of field artillery.

Fourteenth Cavalry Group's commander was ordered to secure the Losheim Gap and to coordinate his line of defence with that of the newly-arrived 106th Infantry Division to whom he was attached. About half his forces were already in position, these were the Eighteenth Cavalry Squadron who had moved into the Losheim Gap in October to secure the left flank of the 2nd Infantry Division, then holding the Schnee

Eifel salient.

A plan had been worked out should a German attack in strength try to come through the gap to split the American front: the Eighteenth cavalry would fall back across the Our to prepared positions along the Manderfeld Ridge and the 2nd Infantry would attack from the western slope of the Schnee Eifel against the flank of any force moving south-east down the valley.

Major-General Robertson, the experienced commander of the Second Infantry Division, had approved but had pointed out more than once that a single motorized cavalry squadron could be quickly overwhelmed in this wide, inviting entry. When his division were moved north for the Roer Dams attack and their position in the Schnee Eifel taken over by the green troops of the 106th Infantry his warning was heeded and the single squadron was increased to a full cavalry group.

This very considerably strengthened the Losheim Gap defences—or would have done when all the force was in position. Unfortunately the other squadron, the Thirty-second, had moved up only as far as Vielsalm, about twenty-five miles back, when the German assault hit the Losheim Gap. Also one of the three troops of cavalry already in the gap had been moved south of the Schnee Eifel and attached to 106 Division's right-wing regiment—thus only two troops were left, occupying six small villages across the centre of the gap.

Worse still, their flanks were wide open, for on their left, between them and the nearest soldiers of the next corps, there was an undefended gap of two miles, while on their right, between them and the nearest soldiers of 106th Infantry Division, was a mile-and-a-half-wide gap.

Opposite them were the wings of two panzer armies concentrating assault troops for a breakthrough. It was an extremely vulnerable position at a tactically important place and the Germans, who would have had to come through the Losheim Gap in any case, were delighted to find how unbelievably weak the American defences were.

On December 12 Colonel Mark Devine arrived at Eighteenth Cavalry Squadron's Headquarters at Manderfeld, a mile west of the Our, which then became Fourteenth Cavalry Group's Command Post. A strict disciplinarian of the spit-and-polish school noted for his insistence on physical fitness, he was critical of a certain staleness among men who had been so long undisturbed and shocked at the inadequacy of the defences. He reconnoitred the whole line of positions and ordered aggressive patrolling to the front as a result of which

156

three 18th Volksgrenadiers were captured. Intelligence got nothing from them for in all probability they did not know, even at that late date, of the impending great offensive.

Colonel Devine and his staff knew of the earlier counter to a German attack in strength worked out with the 2nd Infantry Division and tried to find out from the new 106th whether it was still in force but this was in the first hectic days of the 106th moving into the Schnee Eifel and no one at divisional Headquarters in St Vith seemed to have time to discuss what action should be taken if a German attack hit their weak left flank.

The Fourteenth Cavalry Group's commander knew that he could not possibly hope to hold up an attack in strength—such a defence-in-depth role is completely foreign to the training of mechanized cavalry—and that the most his troopers could do was to harass and delay a German advance.

One way of doing this was with minefields and he discovered from the staff of the Eighteenth Cavalry that these already existed—the Germans had laid great numbers in their September retreat and the Allied troops who had first occupied these positions had laid others—but now, it seemed, no one knew exactly where these mines were. Colonel Devine asked for engineers, for more mines and for marked maps to be distributed. He drove his staff mercilessly for three days and in the last hours before the German offensive they worked out a detailed plan for a fighting withdrawal independently of the 106th Division. This was to be a temporary measure until they could coordinate their plan of defence with the infantry division, which they anticipated doing as soon as the newcomers had settled in. There was, after all, no sign of any German activity and the front was seemingly dead. In fact, when a keen young intelligence officer of the 106th Division had reported the sound of enemy movement* he had been rebuked for being an alarmist.

Therefore when the Fourteenth Cavalry Group's plan for leap-frogging successive defence lines with supporting crossfire was finally finished late at night, orders were given for it to be circulated the next day.

But the next day was December 16.

The boundary line going west between the projected advances of the Sixth SS Panzer Army and the Fifth Panzer Army ran through the Losheim Gap and 'Sepp' Dietrich had

* It was Second Panzer Division's tanks moving south to attack the 110th Infantry.

put a parachute infantry division and a volksgrenadier division side by side to punch a hole for the westward dash of the SS Leibstandarte Division, poised immediately behind.

On the left of the SS, up against the northern slope of the Schnee Eifel, General von Manteuffel had stacked two regiments of volksgrenadiers, a battalion of tank destroyers and forty self-propelled assault guns. This force was to roll over the small groups of cavalry in the three villages in front of them and then race down the valley and strike for the Our Bridge at Schönberg. This would be the northern pincer of the plan to trap the American infantry regiments on the high ridge of the Schnee Eifel.

These were two of 106th Infantry Division's three regiments; the 422nd and the 423rd, holding a six-mile line on the east slope of the mountain, forward of the old West Wall defences and with a clear view of the German rear area. This position ran from about the middle of the Schnee Eifel down to the southern slope, including the road which entered Belgium from Germany here.

General von Manteuffel had placed the third regiment of his volksgrenadier division supported by a battalion of self-propelled guns, just south of this six-mile American-held line. They were to be the southern pincer with the task of outflanking the American position and then striking five miles northwest to Schönberg to close the trap.

Finally, on the St Vith Front, opposite 28th Division's right wing, held by its 424th Regiment, General von Manteuffel at the last moment moved a new volksgrenadier division into the West Wall positions at Habscheid on another main road from Germany to St Vith. Their target was the bridge over the Our at Steinebruck six miles from their start line. This town was only five miles south-east of St Vith along a good hard road and two regiments of volksgrenadiers were given the task of broaching the American line and seizing it. They were opposed by a single battalion of green American infantry plus a few units from divisional service and engineer formations.

Field Marshal Model approved these plans, particularly stressing the importance of speed. 'Quick exploitation of the success of the first day of the attack is decisive. The first objective is to achieve liberty of movement for the mobile forces,' he told his army commanders.

The German–Belgian frontier also runs through the Losheim Gap which meant that Dietrich's infantry would attack the Americans holding Belgian villages while Manteuffel's right-hand regiment would hit the Belgian village of Wecke-rath and his left the German village of Roth, two thousand yards south-east. Four or five nights before the offensive, patrols from the 18th Volksgrenadiers had discovered that this two thousand yards was completely unguarded and at the last minute the German army commander decided to send a strong force through it to seize the important crossroads town of Auw, two miles further back. Here there was only a company of American combat engineers. The volksgrenadiers expected to overwhelm them, then flood over and silence the artillery positions west and south of Auw and go on to capture the Our river crossing at Andler. From there the crossing at Schönberg, two miles down river, would soon be reached and as soon as the other 18th Volksgrenadier Regiment, which had come from south of the Schnee Eifel, arrived, the American forces in the pocket, which would include part of the Fourteenth Cavalry Group, a couple of field artillery battalions and two infantry regiments—some eight or nine thousand men—would be either captured or destroyed. It was a bold, ambitious plan.

The commander of this threatened division, General Alan Jones, was not at all pleased with the length of front his inexperienced soldiers were taking over, nor did he approve of the disposition of the supporting units of Fourteenth Cavalry Group. He asked permission to make alterations but nothing had been decided when the German attack came a few days later. This was one of the reasons why there was so little cooperation between the Fourteenth Cavalry Group and the 106th Division at the critical time.

Another reason would seem to be that neither the 106th Infantry commander nor his staff were familiar with the plans for withdrawal and mutual support that had been carefully worked out, although these had been handed over. But there is an enormous amount of administrative detail involved in changing over fourteen thousand men and all their vehicles and equipment and although it is easy today to say that priority should have been given to deciding on reactions to a German attack, the situation at the time—the cold, wet and miserable condition of the men after their gruelling journey, the shortage of ammunition and weapons and, above all, the fact that there had been almost no German activity on this front for three months, explains why the most pressing problems seemed to be to get stoves into the bunkers, dry clothes, dry boots and hot food for the men. Next priority was ammunition, for although the 106th had given their new weapons to the 2nd Division veterans and taken over the ones already emplaced—in order to conceal the relief from the Germans—the 2nd Division men, knowing that they were soon to be in action, had taken most of their ammunition with them, leaving only a standard allotment behind. The nearest supply points were forty miles away.

Lastly, the 2nd like every other experienced infantry division had managed to equip themselves with about fifty per cent more automatic rifles and light machine guns than was authorized—a precaution that was necessary on so thinly held a front. The new 106th, of course, had only the regulation issue.

The 422nd Infantry Regiment were the left-hand troops of the 106th Division and it was their duty to patrol the gap between them and the nearest Fourteenth Cavalry Group strongpoint a mile and a half north. But this was the regiment whose overshoes had, by an oversight, been left behind in the move from Cherbourg and continually wet feet in freezing weather had caused a large number of trench-foot cases. In the few days they had been in the line seventy-five men had been evacuated and at least one in five of the remainder were affected. What patrolling of the gap on their flank that was done was largely ineffective and the platoon of mechanized cavalry in the little village of Kobscheid were left with their right flank uncovered.

The position on the cavalry's left flank was just as unsatisfactory. Fourteenth Cavalry Group were occupying VIII Corps' northern boundary—their northernmost troops were a reconnaissance platoon from their attached tank destroyer battalion in the village of Lanzerath. Their neighbours to the north, the right-hand troops of V Corps, were some of the 99th Infantry Division, a thirty-man strong platoon in the village of Losheimergraben, connected with Lanzerath by the International Highway which crossed a railway about a mile and a half from Losheimergraben. The Germans had blown the road bridge in their September retreat and it had not been repaired.

From near this blown bridge a patrol from 99th Division travelled south every two hours to meet a patrol from Lanzerath. This fragile link was the only live connection between General Hodges' V Corps on First Army's left and General Troy Middleton's VIII Corps in its centre.

The purpose of the two-hourly rendezvous was presumably to make sure that the Germans had not tried to move through the gap and it took place punctually until the sudden attack

160

when both patrols were swallowed up and contact between the two corps at the front line broken. It was to be where the Germans would make their greatest initial penetration.

The centre of the long Ardennes front included the Losheim Gap in the north, the Schnee Eifel and the entry into Belgium south of it. A dozen miles to the rear was the prime objective of St Vith.

The line-up on this sector, from north to south, started with the two-mile gap between the American corps. Next came the five-mile-wide mouth of the Losheim Gap guarded by nine hundred cavalry. On their right there was another gap of a mile and a half. The next six miles, along the ridge of the Schnee Eifel down to its southern slopes was held by two of 106 Division's three infantry regiments. The next four critical miles of front, through which ran two good roads from Germany into Belgium, was held by reconnaissance troops and various divisional units amounting in all to about a thousand men. The final five miles of the long 106th Infantry Division's front was held by their third regiment, the 424th. It was anti-tank gunners from their regiments, between 106 Division and the 28th Infantry Division, who became involved with the attack by the German LVIII Corps on the 112th Infantry.*

The German line-up, in the same north to south order, started with 12th Volksgrenadier Division poised opposite the open gap between the two American corps. Next, opposite about half of the reconnaissance cavalry in the Losheim Gap, was the 3rd Parachute Infantry Division. Behind these two infantry divisions, ready to plunge through the hole they were to tear in the American line, were the leading tanks of the crack 1st SS Panzers, the Leibstandarte. These three divisions comprised 'Sepp' Dietrich's powerful left hook.

Opposite the other half of the cavalry in the Losheim Gap General Manteuffel had put two-thirds of his Volksgrenadier Division reinforced by a company of tank destroyers and one of assault guns.

The next part of the German line was their weakest, dangerously so, for out in front of the seven thousand American infantry in the Schnee Eifel positions were a token force of two hundred volksgrenadiers. All they could do when the great offensive began was to try to give an impression of a strong defence in order to discourage the Americans from moving forward.

Opposite the southern end of the Schnee Eifel, where the road ran from Germany to Schönberg, was the remaining third

* See page 131.

of 18th Volksgrenadier Division reinforced by a battalion of assault guns. In their way were the right-hand troops of 423rd Infantry Regiment, the attached troop from Eighteenth Cavalry Squadron and a company of tank destroyers.

Lastly, covering the rest of the gap between the 423rd Infantry and the northernmost troops of the 424th, was the 62nd Volksgrenadier Division. Newly-raised and without any battle experience they only managed to get up to their jump-off positions the night before the attack.

On the whole the German commanders were well satisfied with their prospects in the centre of the Ardennes front. They had the odds necessary for a quick victory—particularly north of the Schnee Eifel where the attackers would outnumber the defenders by ten to one—and, apparently, all their preparations had gone unnoticed. The American troops they were planning to entrap were obviously inexperienced and there seemed to be gaping holes in the American line.

But they did have one or two worries. The main one was the Allied air force. Although Field Marshal Goering had assured them that the skies over the battlefield would be full of the new Luftwaffe planes they had learned not to believe him. In the retreat across France they had seen what the rocket-firing Typhoons could do to road-confined vehicles and the terrible effect of attacks by fighter-bombers. If the Führer's promised period of bad flying weather didn't materialize all their superiority in numbers would mean little.

Then there was the glaring weak spot of their own centre—the two hundred volksgrenadiers spread out in front of the two American infantry regiments already on the eastern slopes of the Schnee Eifel. If American reaction to attacks on their flanks was to advance there would be no chance of stopping them. The important road and rail centre of Prüm was only five miles from the American line and its loss would endanger the whole offensive.

But nothing could be done, for the attacking forces were already many divisions fewer than necessary and no troops could be spared in a purely defensive rôle. The risk had to be taken that Allied Intelligence didn't know how few troops there were in front of the Schnee Eifel. Anyway, General Manteuffel and his LXVI Corps commander, General Lucht, decided that it was extremely unlikely that green American troops would be ordered to attack, particularly as it seemed that there was no reserve available to follow up.

The last German worry was due to the one precaution the American command had taken to make up for their weakness in this sector. Almost all of VIII Corps' artillery, eight battalions, had been cited to support the division in the Schnee Eifel salient. (When this had been held by the 2nd Infantry their own divisional artillery had carefully worked out a series of concentrations by which heavy fire could quickly be brought down on practically every crossroads in the Losheim Gap. But the 106th Division's artillery had not taken over these fireplans which would not have been of any use to them anyway for their guns were in different positions.)

The Germans were well aware of the very heavy concentration of American artillery opposite this portion of the front but all they could do was to have their own Corps artillery concentrate, at the beginning of the attack, on the American gun positions, to try to knock them out or at least silence them until the speed of the advance would enable the volksgrenadiers to overrun the guns. In order to make sure they knew exactly where these were, a special German field artillery observation battalion spent their full time marking every American gun and reporting even the slightest change of position.

On this front, as everywhere else, great care was taken not to do anything that would alert the Americans to the coming attack. Before any of the big guns were moved forward, their new positions were thoroughly camouflaged. These heavy guns were moved up in the dark and then not allowed to fire. The mobile assault guns would have to move through the West Wall defences which were not designed to allow that, of course. It would have been simple to blow up paths through the concrete Dragons' Teeth but this could hardly have failed to attract attention. Instead the Germans worked at night putting in underpinning supports to take inclined ramps. The night before the attack these were brought up and fitted into position, making roads through the West Wall. Behind them the assault guns on their tracks lined up, and between them the shock troops took their positions.

Everything was ready.

South of the Schnee Eifel there were two roads entering Belgium from Germany both of which went through the four-mile gap between the 423rd Infantry Regiment holding the southern half of the Schnee Eifel salient and the 424th Infantry Regiment, holding the southern half of the 106th Division.

The southernmost of these two roads had been widened and repaired by the Germans before the American autumn advance and was now twenty-two-feet-wide macadam. It ran from

Pronsfeld for some eighteen miles north-west to St Vith via the Steinebruck bridge. It was to be the centre line of the advance of the recently arrived 62nd Volksgrenadier Division. The Sixty-second was an untried division commanded by a general without combat experience. However, it was up to strength, completely outfitted with new equipment and opposed by only a few American troops.

The other road ran from Prüm west, skirted the southern slope of the Schnee Eifel, went to Bleialf, key to the road system here, and then continued north for another four miles to Schönberg. This was the route chosen for the southern pincer, and shock troops were to start from West Wall positions south of the road, gain it and strike quickly for Bleialf. When that had been secured the road could be opened for the self-propelled guns and other vehicles for the drive to Schönberg, the joining up with the northern pincer, and closing of the trap.

All that lay out in front of the 18th Volksgrenadier Division and 62nd Volksgrenadier Division was a series of lightly held American positions. In Bleialf there was a company from the tank destroyer battalion attached to Fourteenth Cavalry Group; a mile south-west was the troop from Eighteenth Cavalry Squadron which had earlier been sent to 423 Regiment for reconnaissance duties. On the other side of the gap, next to the 424th Infantry Regiment, there were only the divisional reconnaissance troop and the cannon company. In between were other divisional troops from various units which in all brought up the strength guarding the inter-regimental gap to a provisional battalion. In the same areas two of 106 Division's own Field Artillery Battalions had been deployed.

The newly-arrived young soldiers had been told by the 2nd Infantry Division that as soon as the Germans opposite discovered a new division in place they would try to feel out the positions with strong patrols. The first German attacks were assumed to be these. A Pole from 18th Volksgrenadiers was captured by a 423rd Regiment patrol on the afternoon of December 15. He seemed pleased to be out of the war for, he said, a large-scale offensive was about to start. He told of extensive preparations including the placing of searchlights to reflect off the low cloud making artificial moonlight to enable a pre-dawn attack to be made. All this information got no further than 106 Divisional HQ at St Vith.

During the night before the attack the American soldiers in forward positions on the Schnee Eifel reported much vehicle movement in front of them and constant low flying by German aircraft whose engines drowned out the sounds of whatever was going on. At Divisional HQ and even more at Corps HQ these reports were largely discounted, being put down to the natural nervousness of green soldiers newly arrived in the line.

The night was cold and clear in the Schnee Eifel area, enabling the German initial attack formations to move up to the jump-off line without artificial lighting. They hoped that the usual early morning ground fog would conceal their advance on to the American outposts. It was in these last cold hours of waiting that many of the assault commanders heard about the coming offensive and their own rôle for the first time.

12

...AND SPRUNG!

There are no bad troops, only bad colonels.

NAPOLEON

Punctually at 5.30 am on December 16 the German artillery
north and south of the Schnee Eifel opened fire concentrating
at first on the cavalry in front of 'Sepp' Dietrich's left wing
and on the American infantry holding the centre and south
slope of the Schnee Eifel. A few shells fell in St Vith itself.

The opening barrage knocked out all wire communications
but radio continued to function and soon reports were flooding
in on 106th Division's headquarters of heavy shelling on forward positions and, in one or two places, of small-arms fire.
Signals were also received from VIII Corps HQ in Bastogne
that similar attacks were being made on the divisions on
106th's right and left. It was evident that a major offensive was
developing but the extent and location of the main effort was
far from clear.

106th Infantry's centre, the 423rd Infantry Regiment,
seemed to be the German's main target and its commander
Colonel Cavender reported before dawn that Bleialf, in his rear
and key to the road network there, was under attack by three
separate columns of volksgrenadiers. A little later the town fell,
a platoon of American anti-tank guns were destroyed and the
attached troop of Eighteenth Cavalry Squadron to the south-
west were isolated.

General Manteuffel's southern pincer seemed to have got off
to an early start and the road to the bridge at Schönberg lay
open. But as soon as it was light 423rd Infantry on the
southern slopes of the Schnee Eifel were able to bring heavy
accurate fire down on to the German support troops moving
up to Bleialf, thus stopping the mobile weapons the Germans
needed to continue their advance.

Colonel Cavender asked for the return of his Second Battalion who were north of St Vith in divisional reserve, but this
was refused. He then mustered a scratch force from a company of combat engineers, a cannon company and service and
headquarters troops and sent them against Bleialf. After hand-
to-hand fighting in the streets and houses this key town was
retaken and the situation was abruptly reversed—General

Manteuffel's advance had been stopped two miles from its start line.

Further south on this sector the attempt by 62nd Volksgrenadiers to drive through to the Steinebruck bridge also ran into trouble. The German artillery had waited until the leading shock troops got up to their jump-off positions before laying a softening-up barrage on the American defenders and this delay had allowed them to take up good defensive positions. After a short, sharp period of concentrated shelling the Third Battalion, holding the regiment's left, were hit in the predawn murkiness by young German soldiers advancing erect, shouting and screaming. For several hours the battle could have gone either way but the battalion reserve was thrown in, followed by a vigorous counter-attack and the German advance was halted and nearly two hundred prisoners taken. The green German division suffered severe casualties in this, their first action.

By midday the 106th Division's centre and right, although having been hit hard and suffered many casualties, had contained the attack and yielded little ground. Their left-hand regiment high in the north of the Schnee Eifel had not been attacked at all. On the whole 106th Infantry Division HQ in St Vith were not dissatisfied with the way they were handling their first battle, unexpected as it had been. But they completely underestimated the danger on their left flank, in the Losheim Gap.

By the evening of December 15 the cavalry here had had three days of intense activity following their having been absorbed into the Fourteenth Cavalry Group and the arrival of the new broom in the person of its commander Colonel Devine. Now that the ground work was completed and the new routine established they looked forward to renewing the comparative quiet this sector had enjoyed for the last three months.

Instead 'Sepp' Dietrich's screaming shells woke them rudely at 5.30 am the next morning. It was the beginning of a long nightmare which only ended some sixty hours and four commanding officers later when, twenty-five miles to the rear the survivors of the Fourteenth Cavalry Group were attached to a tank division hurrying down from the north to the defence of St Vith.

Once again the opening barrage knocked out almost all wire between forward strong points. Powerful German transmitters broadcasting jazz records at full volume succeeded in preventing almost any voice communication, but the cavalry head-

167

quarters at Manderfeld managed to get a warning through to their forward troops.

Although at first none of the shells fell anywhere near these forward positions the noise of the barrage awakened the cavalrymen who stood to, manning their guns and peering into the darkness.

Shock troops of the 18th Volksgrenadiers arrived before Weckerath while it was still dark. One platoon of American Cavalry lay between them and the village, while behind, west of the houses, there were about twenty men of troop headquarters. At Roth, two thousand yards south-east of here, the leading units of another 18th Volksgrenadier attack column waited for a promised artillery softening-up before trying to break through a screen of two platoons of troop A of the Eighteenth Cavalry Squadron. A mile further south the third platoon of this troop, the extreme right of the Eighteenth Cavalry's position, were holding the village of Kobscheid in platoon strength. These three villages, in the southern half of the Losheim Gap, lay in an arc across the assigned line of advance of General Manteuffel's northern pincer.

From the German town of Ormont, in the northern half of the Losheim Gap, the 3rd Parachute Division started their attack down the road which led to Manderfeld. Their way was blocked by a line of good defensive positions which the Americans had built in front of the small town of Krewinkel and which extended north for about a mile to the village of Afst. It was here that the first engagement on this part of the Ardennes front took place.

After the opening barrage died away the American troops in their well-concealed positions east of Krewinkel were amazed to see German infantry advancing towards them in column of fours—a suicidal approach. They held the marching volks-grenadiers dead in their sights until they had almost reached the barbed wire and then fired every weapon. The close-packed column flew apart as the survivors ran back leaving their dead and wounded in piles. Shortly afterwards the parachutists attacked again but this time in open formation and in successive waves. The weight of numbers forced the Americans out of their positions and back into Krewinkel. Firing was intense on both sides and the Germans fought recklessly. For a time it looked as though they would take the town but the cavalry had the advantage of prepared defences, well-sited and protected and finally, still before daylight, the parachutists broke off their attack again. One of them, evidently a jazz fan, shouted in English, 'Okay you guys—take ten.' The Cavalrymen's replies were pungent if not witty.

A heavy German artillery barrage then pounded Krewinkel and the next village of Afst, which had experienced similar bitter fighting also with singularly little effect. When the 3rd Parachute came on again, full of fight despite their losses which had been exceptionally heavy, they were once more beaten back. American losses had been extraordinarily light and morale was high but pressure was building up and the superior weight of the German attack was soon bound to tell. Still, for the time being, the road leading from Germany over the Our to Manderfeld, a very important road, was still blocked and the commander of the leading battle group of tanks from the Leibstandarte, Jochen Peiper, waiting a few miles behind for the promised breach in the American lines was fuming at the delay.

A little later, but still before dawn, the cavalrymen in front of Weckerath, about two miles south-west of Krewinkel, were attacked by shock troops from the Eighteenth Volks-grenadiers. Although this was a new, green division they had been in the area for some time and had been able to complete their training without interruption or casualties and, confident of their numbers, they came on determinedly. But once more the positions of the cavalry had been well-prepared and the Germans were stopped by the extensive barbed-wire and their attack broken up by mortar and machine-gun fire. Without wasting time they withdrew and began to infiltrate around the small American position to take it from the rear. Here they were held off by automatic rifle fire from no more than twenty men from troop headquarters until 9.30 am when a platoon of the cavalry's light tanks from Manderfeld, a mile away, got through to them and the crumbling defences of Weckerath were shored up—at least temporarily.

The sky was heavily overcast and there was a steady drizzle when, at 8.30 am, both Roth and Kobscheid, further south, received a full salvo from one of the German batteries. Immediately afterwards they too were attacked in strength by the 18th Volksgrenadiers.

In Roth the few cavalrymen fought desperately. They radioed that a tank* was firing over open sights at them from a range of seventy-five yards and called for supporting artillery fire. Nothing more was heard of them although much later it was discovered that the last of the defenders had not sur-

* It was in fact an assault gun.

169

rendered until 2.0 pm.

At Kobscheid the volksgrenadiers quickly penetrated the defences but a vigorous counter-attack drove them out and about forty of them were taken prisoner by the small garrison.

But later, in a cold, drizzling dawn, a second, heavier attack smashed the defences and the defence in Kobscheid also went down.* With Roth and Kobscheid captured, the 18th Volksgrenadiers, Manteuffel's northern pincer, had only the crossroads town of Auw containing a single company of combat engineers between it and the place chosen for the closing point of the pincer movement, the bridge at Schönberg. A mixed assault column was formed without delay and pushed forward.

From the high ground to the north-west the defenders at Weckerath saw these German tanks (actually assault guns) and infantry moving across country towards Auw and were able to call down artillery fire from the batteries west of that town but this shelling had very little effect. By mid-morning Auw too had fallen.

The extreme left-hand troops of Fourteenth Cavalry Group were men of a tank destroyer battalion attached to the cavalry and deployed in an arc from Lanzerath south-east to Berterath, a distance of about two and a half miles. These were also the left-hand troops of VIII Corps and it was this tank destroyer outfit in Lanzerath who sent out a small patrol every two hours to meet one from the 99th Infantry Division, the right-hand troops of V Corps.

The tank destroyer company had to depend upon towed three-inch guns. These had been sited so as to cover the approaches from the east but the gunners had no infantry screen. Without this necessary protection they were unable to withstand the strong attack by 3rd Parachute Division who had moved quickly through the gap between the two American corps. The towed guns were unable to displace in time and all but three had to be destroyed by their own crews. These three were towed back towards Manderfeld and placed in defensive positions north of the town. The rest of the tank destroyer company, on reaching cavalry headquarters, were ordered to continue to fight as infantry.

When the opening barrage knocked out his communications with the troops in the forward outposts Colonel Devine had

* Some managed to conceal themselves and at dusk sixty-one men slipped out and made their way across country in the snow, arriving at St Vith two and a half days later.

assumed, as did almost every other local commander along the whole Ardennes Front that this was a German attack against his sector. He got through to 106th Divisional HQ at St Vith and asked for wire teams to be sent to restore the lines. Half an hour later he asked for the rest of his group, the Thirty-second Cavalry Squadron to be sent immediately up to him from Vielsalm.

Having taken these steps it was necessary to know what was happening all along his nine thousand yards of front. He decided to go himself to find out exactly the strength and extent of the German attack. He soon realized that this was a major attack and that his small strongpoints were hopelessly outnumbered. The garrisons in the Afst/Krewinkel position and in Weckerath, who together formed one of Eighteenth Cavalry Squadron's three troops, were still holding, but the weight of attack must soon overwhelm them. He ordered them to fall back to Manderfeld. They did so just in time, for Weckerath was completely destroyed by massed German shells only a few minutes after the withdrawal. As they left Krewinkel the cavalry's rearguard saw hundreds of new German infantry swarming towards the town. These were some of the crack SS armoured Infantry attached to 1st SS Panzers, the Leibstandarte, whose commander had grown tired of waiting for 3rd Parachute to open a hole for his tanks.

Colonel Devine got back to Manderfeld just before eleven that morning to find his headquarters a shambles with his staff frantically packing up and trying to destroy maps, records and orders. Contact had been lost with the 99th Infantry Division on their left and there was no sign of their Thirty-second Cavalry Squadron, expected hours before. The 106th Infantry Division at St Vith had been asked to counter-attack 'to save us'. The reply had been that no infantry support could be given at this time. The cavalry had felt themselves abandoned and the result was an undisciplined scramble to get out.

Colonel Devine stopped the panic and restored some sort of order. He got through again to Divisional HQ, explained the position on his front and asked for permission to withdraw and form a new defence line. This would run from Manderfeld two and a half miles due south to Auw. The time was 11.15 am and Auw was even then being attacked by the German forces which had overrun Roth and Kobscheid and destroyed one of Eighteenth Cavalry Squadron's troops. With the abandonment of Krewinkel the road to Manderfeld lay open while the loss of the tank destroyer positions at Lanzerath and Berterath meant that his left flank protection was gone. The proposed new defence line was quite unreal and could not possibly be held without strong reinforcements.

At the same time, Colonel Devine told the staff at division, as soon as his Thirty-second Cavalry Squadron reached him he would use them to counter-attack and retake Krewinkel, Roth and Kobscheid. This was wildly optimistic for the German forces attacking Roth had been correctly estimated at an infantry regiment (at least three thousand men) reinforced by tanks—as the assault guns were still being incorrectly called—another infantry regiment was at Weckerath and even larger forces at Krewinkel.

At St Vith the commander of the 106th Infantry Division, Major-General Alan Jones, was more concerned with his two regiments stuck out on the Schnee Eifel and an attack on his right wing than with his attached mechanized cavalry who ought, after all, to be able to manoeuvre. The proposed new defence line from Manderfeld to Auw would block the Losheim Gap again and the Cavalry group commander's confident promise to counter-attack seemed to imply that matters were not, after all, so serious on his front. General Jones agreed to Colonel Devine's plans and left the cavalry to take care of themselves.

Thirty-second Cavalry Squadron, Chicago's famous Black Horse Troop, resting and refitting miles behind a quiet front, had been caught off balance by the order to move immediately to Manderfeld in support of the Eighteenth Cavalry Squadron. At Vielsalm some of the vehicles and light tanks were partially dismantled, radios were in the repair shops and many of the men were on leave or on instruction courses. Despite all this the leading platoons were on the road within two and a half hours and the last—who had to reassemble their vehicles—within four hours of the emergency order being flashed from division. The leading troop came into Manderfeld before midday and Colonel Devine immediately deployed them on the high ground north-west and south from where they were able to support the withdrawal of the survivors of the Eighteenth Cavalry Squadron.

As soon as the rest of the Black Horse Troop arrived Colonel Devine ordered them to attack north, retake Lanzerath and cover his open flank. Less than two miles north of Manderfeld this force ran head on to 3rd Parachute's right-hand column which had, until then, been having things very much their own way, having bypassed the fighting at Afst and Krewinkel. The Cavalry had a troop of self-propelled howitzers with them which they quickly got firing and which caused severe casualties among the German infantry. A short hard fight followed and for a time it looked as though the American cavalry might break through and regain Lanzerath but there were many more parachutists and they, too, had self-propelled guns. This weight soon told and the cavalry had to break off the action and fall back to cover the approaches to Manderfeld, allowing the parachute column to keep moving north-west.

As the attacking German columns penetrated on both sides of Manderfeld it became clear that the town would have to be yielded. Once more Colonel Devine got through to 106 Divisional headquarters at St Vith. This time he requested permission to pivot his defence line using the Andler bridge, five miles south-west of Manderfeld, as the hinge and moving his northern end back from Manderfeld four or five miles north-west to the village of Holzheim. This new line would then run five miles north and south along the Manderfeld Ridge and effectively bar a German advance towards St Vith from the north-east.

The Andler bridge, still in American hands, was on the main road from the north which continued another two miles to Schönberg and went on to St Vith. It was essential for the defence of St Vith that this road be blocked and Andler was an ideal place to do it; 106 Division's staff gave Colonel Devine permission to withdraw from Manderfeld north-west with Andler as his southern anchor.

Floods of refugees from the attack area poured into Manderfeld with conflicting reports of terrible disasters and great German successes. Their evident terror was unnerving and when the staff at Fourteenth Cavalry Group headquarters were told of the decision to withdraw immediately to Holzheim and at the same time heard of the failure of the attempt to retake Lanzerath north of them and reports of German infantry and tanks bypassing them on the south, panic swept through them once more. They piled into their vehicles with what personal possessions they could grab and in an attempt to destroy anything which might aid the Germans simply set fire to the whole town, destroying it completely.

By nightfall the new line had been established. The little town of Holzheim high on the Manderfeld Ridge was occupied by three troops of cavalry. This strong force was necessary if Holzheim was to be held as the north flank anchor. At Andler, south flank anchor, there was another troop of cavalry. The

173

rest of Fourteenth Cavalry Group were disposed in good defensive positions between Andler and Holzheim making a five-mile-long defence it would be difficult for the Germans to crack.

The cavalry's intact light tank company were guarding the vital Schönberg to St Vith road and their own supporting artillery battalion, after firing all morning, had been able to withdraw without loss. They were now moving into a support position behind the new line and their rearguards reported that there was no sign of German pursuit; the cavalry seemed to have lost contact.

What in fact was happening was that 3rd Parachute Division were slogging through the rough, deep forests on Fourteen Cavalry's left and then angling north-west to bring them against Malmédy, while on the cavalry's right 18th Volksgrenadiers were driving south-west to complete the encirclement of the Schnee Eifel salient. This meant that their new defence line would not come under pressure except at the two anchor positions, Andler and Holzheim, both of which lay on roads which the German armour would need on the second day of the offensive.

None of this was known to American Intelligence, for the day's actions had been so numerous and so complicated and the changes so great that it was difficult to get a clear picture of either the Germans' intentions or their exact whereabouts.

But Colonel Devine believed that despite the severe losses his Eighteenth Cavalry Squadron had suffered in the dawn attacks he would be able to hold the new line, at least until reinforcements arrived. Late that night, near exhaustion, he made his way to St Vith to explain the disposition of his Cavalry Group to 106th Infantry Division's staff. Although he waited all night he was unable to see anyone with any real authority and at dawn, angry and discouraged, he returned to his new headquarters at Holzheim to find that two of his troops had retreated again during the night and there were reports of German tanks and infantry having penetrated his centre. Even worse, just before dawn, at Andler, one of the cavalry's reconnaissance teams had stumbled across a number of Tiger tanks and supporting infantry. The panzers were, in fact, lost and after a brief contact lumbered off to the north-west where they belonged but the sight was enough to cause the troop who were supposed to hold Andler to retreat without orders and the anchor position was abandoned. The headquarters of 106th Division were not informed of this and their situation maps continued to show Andler and Holzheim firmly held. Unfortunately neither was.

Holzheim had been occupied by three troops of the cavalry: two had requested permission to withdraw a further three miles west about 6.30 on the evening of the 16th and the group commander had agreed. The remaining cavalry who belonged to Chicago's Black Horse Troop were thus left on their own with an exposed left flank and their commander asked for permission to move to Honsfeld two miles north to link up with some of 99th Infantry Division. Permission was neither granted nor denied by Fourteenth Cavalry Group headquarters and the move was then made on the troop commander's own responsibility. It was an unlucky decision for at four o'clock in the morning Honsfeld was hit by the leading units of Battle-group Peiper from the Leibstandarte and the Black Horse lost all their vehicles.

With Andler and Holzheim both abandoned the positions between them were in danger of being isolated and Colonel Devine gave the orders for another general withdrawal, this time to a line just in front of the main road from St Vith north, the American main supply route. It represented a general withdrawal by Fourteenth Cavalry Group of about ten miles since leaving Manderfeld and with only the troops on the right who had withdrawn from Andler through Schönberg actually making contact with the enemy. Nevertheless it could be a useful blocking position and Colonel Devine informed 106th headquarters that it would be a 'final delaying position' and furthermore he added, with inexplicable optimism, he would soon be ready to counter-attack. Divisional headquarters, busy with their own affairs, merely acknowledged the message from their attached cavalry group and reported it to corps without comment. The feeling seemed to be that although the Fourteenth Cavalry Group had carried out a series of withdrawals without permission the final result, a roadblock to the north of St Vith, was satisfactory.

By now General Jones, the commander of the 106th Division, was very worried about the plight of 422 and 423 Infantry Regiments out on the forward slopes of the Schnee Eifel. By the end of the day the Divisional Intelligence had been able to join up most of the pieces in the puzzle that the many German attacks had created and in their appreciation of the enemy's intentions correctly saw that his object was to pinch out the two regiments in the Schnee Eifel salient. Because of exaggerated reports they overestimated the strength of the German forces employed in the two pincers.

Two of 106th Infantry Division's nine infantry battalions

175

were in reserve on December 16. One was well back, five miles north of St Vith. This was 423 Regiment's Second Battalion which the regimental commander had asked for when he was attacked. General Jones, as we have seen, refused this request, keeping it until he could see where reinforcements would be needed most. The other reserve battalion was at the Our crossing of Steinebruck and this one General Jones early sent south to help 424th Infantry Regiment holding his right wing.

One of the most difficult decisions any commander, whose positions are being widely attacked, has to make is when and where to commit his reserves.

In the north of the Schnee Eifel the 422nd Infantry had been ignored by the German attack except that by their quick advance through the Losheim Gap the 18th Volksgrenadiers had broken into the regiment's rear areas. The regimental command post, two miles behind the forward positions, had found itself endangered and a regimental task force on its way to relieve Auw had had to be diverted to come to its defence. By nightfall the 422nd, although still intact, had had its flank and rear dangerously uncovered.

At St Vith it was at last seen that the gravest situation was the breakthrough at the Losheim Gap and General Jones decided to move his last reserves from behind St Vith to Schönberg. The move took some time over choked roads and the battalion did not get to the town until about five o'clock. They detrucked and waited to see where they would be used. Since they had been ordered forward the situation had worsened.

All of Fourteenth Cavalry had now pulled back over the Our* and the Germans had advanced beyond Auw. In the afternoon they had tried to overrun the artillery positions south-west of Auw and had almost succeeded. But the American gunners had replied with point-blank howitzer fire on the shortest possible fuses and had counter-attacked with bazooka detachments. Three of the German assault guns had been knocked out and the artillery had lost thirty-six men themselves. At nightfall the Germans had begun to attack again, determined to remove this obstacle to their next day's advance. At about 8.30 pm the waiting reserve battalion in Schönberg was ordered to advance towards Auw and engage the German volksgrenadiers and assault guns there in order to take the pressure off the artillery and to enable them to retire and get their guns away.

For some reason no route was indicated, perhaps because

* Although Troop B of 32 Cavalry Squadron were holding Schönberg on the river.

the road which runs first north along the Our to Andler and then east to Auw seemed to be the only way. But the distance across country to the artillery positions was little more than half the road distance and the commander of the reserve battalion chose the shorter way. The green troops got lost two or three times and did not get up to their artillery for several hours, thus losing the time advantage of the direct approach. However, once there, they covered the retreat of the two battalions of field artillery who were able to withdraw all their guns. The reserve had done their job but, unknown to 106 Division HQ, because they had marched across country, the road from Andler to Auw was wide open.

Down this road just before dawn rumbled the Tiger tanks whose sudden appearance had caused the cavalry to pull out of Andler. These were the leading units of the Leibstandarte's left-hand column whose objective was Vielsalm in the rear of St Vith. Unable to get moving along the jammed roads in Sixth Panzer Army's sector they had wandered south into Fifth Panzer Army's territory and got lost in the dark. At Andler they were able to get on a minor road which carried them north-west into their own area again. It was this column, moving behind Fourteenth Cavalry's second defence line, in the early morning of the 17th, which triggered the further retreat of Colonel Devine's group.

During the night both sides were able to assess the results and decide on the next day's tactics and both were fairly optimistic.

The German command were highly pleased that none of their fears had materialized: the two American infantry regiments on the forward slopes of the Schnee Eifel had not advanced against the weak defences in front of them—surprisingly they had not moved all day—and would surely soon be encircled. Nor, for reasons which the German command could not understand, had the heavy American artillery concentrations been brought to bear in the first critical hours of the attack. Finally the Allies' dreaded fighter-bombers had not been seen in this sector at all.*

Fifth Panzer Army's best results had been spectacular, and

* Two hundred and thirty-seven sorties by fighter-bombers of XIX Tactical Air Command strafed and bombed road and rail convoys moving up to the battle area on December 16, but the weather in the Eifel/Ardennes area was too bad—one hundred sorties came back with 'unobserved results'. The Luftwaffe sent about one hundred and fifty fighters over the attack area but on the first day neither side's air power made any appreciable impression.

even the most disappointing—the attacks south of the Schnee Eifel where the southern pincer had been stopped at Bleialf and the drive by 62nd Volksgrenadiers for the Steinebruck crossing had not even reached Winterspelt—could be corrected the next day with strong reinforcements.

General Manteuffel promised tank support for the 18th Volksgrenadiers at Auw to enable them to drive through Andler and capture Schönberg. On the left he ordered the troops before Bleialf to renew their attack in strength before dawn and take the town 'at all costs' and then to advance quickly to Schönberg to close the trap. General Lucht gave similar orders to 62nd Volksgrenadiers to 'smash through to the Our'.

North of the Losheim Gap, on 'Sepp' Dietrich's front, 3rd Parachute's right-hand column had bogged down at Lanzerath when its attempts to move north-west had run into 99th Division's flanking troops along the railway line. But at midnight Battlegroup Peiper from the Leibstandarte, unable to get past Losheimergraben because the blown overpass had not been repaired, came into Lanzerath and its tough young commander 'persuaded' 3rd Parachute regiment's colonel to give him a battalion of infantry for flank protection for his tanks in a night march through the woods to attack Honsfeld.

But none of this was known at 106th Infantry Division headquarters in St Vith where, that first night, it was felt that the situation on the division's front was not too bad. Although the Losheim Gap had been overrun and contact with 99th Division in the north lost, a new defence line had apparently been established to guard the left flank while on the right, south of the Schnee Eifel, most front line units had recovered from the onslaught and were now holding their ground. One of the prisoners, a battalion commander from 62nd Volksgrenadier Division, had expressed his surprise and admiration for the stiff resistance the green American troops had put up and this praise from the enemy was a much needed morale booster, as was the news that armoured reinforcements were on their way.

General Jones had committed his only reserve, two infantry battalions, by nightfall and had asked VIII Corps for help—preferably tanks. A week earlier General Troy Middleton had had most of an armoured division in reserve but one combat command had gone north with the 2nd Infantry Division for the Roer Dams attack leaving him with only Combat Command R of 9th Armored Division for corps reserve and when his entire front was assaulted at the same time he naturally waited to see where this reserve would be most needed.

Fortunately General Hodges, First Army commander, had decided on the evening of December 14 that the unexpectedly stiff resistance at the Wahlerscheid crossroads made it unlikely that the waiting armoured combat command would be used and had ordered that it was 'to be returned to parent organization'. But this was, of course, before there was any sign of a German attack on VIII Corps' front and there was no sense of urgency. Combat Command B from 9th Armored Division waiting twelve miles north of St Vith in V Corps' area, was not told it was being returned to VIII Corps until 10.25 am on the morning of December 16 some thirty-six hours after General Hodges had given the relevant order and five hours after the Ardennes offensive had started.

As soon as Troy Middleton knew that he was to have this full combat command returned he sent the weaker, Combat Command R to back up the hard-pressed 28th Infantry Division in front of Bastogne and gave Combat Command B to General Jones in St Vith.

Strangely, General Jones made no move to get these tanks on the road but merely ordered one platoon of tank destroyers to come to his headquarters in St Vith together with Combat Command B's commander, Brigadier-General Hoge and his staff. They arrived soon after dark and it was decided to use the tanks on the left, sending them first to Schönberg and then to support an attack to recapture Auw.

But no sooner had this decision been taken than 106th Division's commander was told that more armour was on its way to him. This was Combat Command B of the experienced 7th Armored Division who had been part of Ninth US Army's reserve. They were some sixty miles north and would have to move in the dark but General Jones was assured they would reach him by 7.30 am the next morning. This estimate was hopelessly optimistic and certain experienced staff officers at 106th Infantry's command headquarters knew it was but no one told the commander. Naturally he made his plans on the assumption that a new armoured combat command would be available the next morning. Therefore he changed his instructions to Brigadier General Hoge and ordered him to move as soon as possible to the divisional centre, Steinebruck, and attack south-east through Winterspelt to block any German attempt to cross the Our in that sector. When 7th Armored Division's Combat Command B arrived before dawn it would restore the position on the left at Schönberg and Andler.

These two strong armoured forces would be used to create armoured corridors both north and south of the Schnee Eifel through which the regiments of infantry in the salient could, if necessary, be pulled back.

With his front secure now, his left holding, and, as he thought, Fourteenth Cavalry Group maintaining a defensive screen across the approaches from the north-east and a new armoured combat command hurrying to his assistance, General Jones felt that although the day had been full of unpleasant shocks the situation was reasonably under control.

He could hardly have been more mistaken.

13

THE BREAKTHROUGH

Better rashness than inertia; better a mistake than hesitation.
Truppenführung (The German official military manual)

All along the assault front fighting continued through the night of December 16/17 as the German commanders, for the most part not satisfied with the rate of progress of their troops pushed them forward, searching for weak spots, prepared to take severe losses to gain an outlet leading west.

In his new Führer Headquarters at Ziegenburg, about sixty miles east of the Rhine, Adolf Hitler turned all his attention to this small part of Germany's long front. As the reports came in, most not unnaturally playing down objectives not achieved and putting forward their soldiers' best achievements, he felt once again that surge of confidence in his destiny that always came with a German lightning conquest. It was all going to turn out just as he had predicted to his doubting generals: the unhappy Allies, Britain and America, would split like a rotten tree struck hard by a sharp axe.

But if at FHQ there was optimism and jubilation these decreased down the chair of command: Field Marshals Model and von Rundstedt knew that the blitzkrieg was not going to plan, while the individual army commanders were even more disappointed.

At Seventh German Army HQ General Brandenberger now knew that he had been given a quite impossible task. His three divisions of volksgrenadiers had not managed quickly to push aside the few American infantry in front of them and he had little hope that they could establish an effective wall against the inevitable counter-attack from the south. Also his fourth assault division, the parachute infantry who were supposed to have advanced pace for pace with General von Manteuffel's left hook had trailed ignominiously behind all day, even though Fifth Panzer Army's soldiers themselves had moved forward less than half the distance expected.

Nor was General von Manteuffel satisfied with his army's progress, except on his extreme right where the two-thirds of 18th Volksgrenadiers Division he had committed had done almost all that was asked of them in the attempt to entrap the two American regiments in the Schnee Eifel. But both jaws of a trap must close together—one moving alone is vulnerable to flank attacks from both sides—and unless the troops of the left-hand pincer were able to push on quickly to Schönberg, the vulnerability of his two hundred replacements in front of the six or seven thousand American infantry on the eastern slope of the Schnee Eifel could well be exploited.

General Manteuffel was also disappointed by the failure of the 560th Volksgrenadiers to seize the Our river crossings in his centre to let the 116th Panzer Division through, for he was sure that here, between St Vith and Bastogne, lay the quickest and easiest route to the Meuse. But this panzer division would have to be pulled back, turned south and sent over the same pontoon bridge at Dasburg that 2nd Panzer Division had had to wait so long to use. Precious time was slipping through his fingers.

The next few hours must be used to try to regain some of this lost time to smash through the stubborn defence in front of the Clerf and reach Bastogne before it could be reinforced. He thought this quite possible but unless 'Sepp' Dietrich's SS on his right got moving forward too, Fifth Panzer Army's advance would have an open right flank. All in all General von Manteuffel was not happy.

But unhappiest of all was 'Sepp' Dietrich to whom everything had been given and from whose élite troops so much had been expected. The famous 12th SS Panzer Division, Hitler Jugend, were still in the forest just ahead of the start line, held up by green American infantry who were supported by a surprisingly heavy concentration of artillery and, apparently, quite unknown to his Intelligence,* there was another infantry division, this time an experienced one, in the same area. His right wing had been stopped all along his front.

Nor had 1st SS Panzer Division, Hitler's Bodyguard, on his left done much better than their rivals, having been held up all day by the failure of the German infantry and engineers to gain possession of and repair the blown highway bridges. His only bright spot, late that first night, was a report that Colonel Peiper was past the American front-line defences and advancing his battlegroup swiftly westwards through the forest. But there was no guarantee that this single penetration would not run head on to a strong American defence which they had now had time to prepare.

* For some reason, still unclear, Sixth SS Panzer Army were not informed of Second US Infantry Division's attack on the Wahlerscheid crossroads.

Dietrich once more reflected that the Führer seemed to have lost his touch—neither of his unorthodox ideas had worked: Skorzeny's commandos in American uniform were still behind the assault troops and von der Heydte's paratroops, who by now should be holding a vital crossroads deep in American territory, hadn't even taken off.

Among the advantages that belong to the attacker is that he knows what he is trying to achieve and the direction and extent of his main effort and so knows how well or ill he is succeeding. He can alter the disposition of his forces in order to 'maintain the objective' and keep the defender from knowing what this is. Unless the initial attack is a complete failure, which in the nature of things only happens rarely, the defenders at first can only react with locally available forces and it must take time for a coherent defence to be formed.

During this early disturbed and unclear period there is always a tendency to overestimate both the strength of the attacker and the casualties on both sides. It is a most dangerous time for the attacked side, for the morale of the defenders undergoes great strain when all seems muddle and confusion and there are rumours of overwhelming enemy victories and of great disasters on their own front.

By the end of the first day of the Ardennes Offensive no one on the American side had any idea either of its extent or its aims, for the failure of communications at the front, the large number of small actions, the fluidity of the fighting and the complete unpreparedness for an offensive of this magnitude, succeeded in causing confusion so great that many of the messages exchanged at division, corps and army level made little sense. Orders were given to 'hold at all costs' ground which had already been lost and nearly twice as many German divisions were identified as were being used. Yet, at the same time, so little was the extent of the great German Offensive appreciated that the request of 2nd Infantry Division's commander to break off the Roer Dams attack and pull his dangerously extended column back was refused.

It would be some days before a coherent picture emerged and all defensive action could be coordinated and it would not be until after the war that exactly what had happened all along the Ardennes front during the first critical hours was understood or the importance appreciated of the delay inflicted on the attackers by the stout defence of many small units some of whom were later almost completely destroyed.

This surprise and confusion were, of course, depended upon by the Germans and were one of the main objectives of both

Skorzeny's 'Operation Greif' and Colonel von der Heydte's parachute drop and both, if only in this, succeeded in the next few days.

The paratroopers, after a crash course of training, had screwed themselves up to the necessary tension for so dangerous an operation which had then been called off at the last moment. The anti-climax took the sharp edge off their preparedness as they waited for another twenty-four hours. Finally, late at night on the first day of the battle, their orders came: the jump would take place even though 'Sepp' Dietrich's tanks should have already reached the parachute drop zone in the Hohes Venn north of Malmédy. That they had not done so could only mean that the American line had not collapsed and if the SS Panzers had been held for one day there was no guarantee that they would be able to get through on the second. Also, as the offensive was now in full swing, the element of surprise essential for a small parachute operation had been lost and it seemed practically certain that the American forces in the north, which it was the paratroops' job to delay, were already moving through the area into which they were to jump. Finally the meteorological report was of high winds and considerable turbulence over the Ardennes.

It was a discouraging prospect, but Colonel von der Heydte, assuming a cheerful attitude he by no means felt, led his men to the war-weary Ju-52s on the airfield of Lippspringe. The rest of his 1,250-strong force were to take off from Paderborn and both flights were to converge over the Baraque Michel, a two-thousand-feet-high, thickly-forested area ten miles north of Malmédy through which the Americans needed to move their reinforcements into the battle area from the north and which the Hitler Youth tanks needed for their drive to the Meuse crossings.

Privately, Colonel von der Heydte was convinced that at this late hour in the offensive he could only hope to control the roads for a day at most. If a strong force of panzers and volksgrenadiers did not get up to him quickly the fate of his young, courageous volunteers was sealed.

Because many of the pilots had little or no experience of night flying the course was indicated to them by searchlights as far as the battle zone, from where they flew on in darkness. The strong cross winds caused by the mountainous, broken country beneath scattered the aircraft in the black night and when the radio order to jump came the paratroops were no longer a single force. One rifle company fell behind the German lines, others in remote parts of the Ardennes far from houses, roads or even paths. Many, jumping for the first time, broke arms or legs on landing. Some of these, the fortunate ones, were found and made prisoners; others lay in the snow and slowly died of exposure or starvation. Bodies were still being found the following spring.

Colonel von der Heydte's experienced pilot, the same one who had taken him to Crete in 1941, flew directly to the drop zone identified by ground flares dropped by an earlier Messerschmitt. Only ten or fifteen of the original hundred or so Junkers had reached the right place but Colonel von der Heydte did not know this. He gave the order and a few minutes later, followed the last man out. It was to be the last operation of the once great German Parachute Corps.

It was 3.30 in the morning of Sunday, December 17. Two or three hours later von der Heydte was horrified to discover there were less than a hundred of his men at the crossroads rendezvous. Small parties were detailed to scour the surrounding woods to find and bring in others and in the end the force totalled about three hundred and fifty, less than a third of the original number. It would be impossible either to open the road for the Hitler Jugend or to slow down American reinforcements coming down from the north.

His signal platoon had disappeared to a man—they had come down six or seven miles to the east, landing in front of the surprised German infantry in the front line south of Monschau. Colonel von der Heydte's own radio had been smashed in the descent as had several others and it would therefore be impossible even to do the one thing so small a force was capable of—to reconnoitre and report American dispositions and movement.

But although the situation was discouraging he was no defeatist. He had told the men sent to him for parachute training that they 'must learn to believe in victory even when at certain moments logical thinking scarcely makes a German victory seem possible'. Such a moment had now come for him and he thrust all thoughts of surrender out of his mind, determined to do what he could with his small force. They would conceal themselves in the woods, keeping a watch on the road, attack units not too strong for them, capture some vehicles, take prisoners and, above all, keep on the move, thus giving the impression of being a much larger force.

But with little food, no blankets and no weapons larger than mortars and machine pistols he knew that they could not hold out for long unless the American line, fifteen miles away, was shattered the second day.

Just after first light the noise of a truck convoy climbing up to them from the north was heard and they prepared an ambush, but it soon became apparent that the American force was too strong to attack. As truck after truck, all crammed with American infantry, rolled past the hidden Germans, Colonel von der Heydte recognized the unit as the 1st Infantry Division, the 'Big Red ONE', most experienced in the United States Army and well-known to him from the fighting in Tunisia. He reflected bitterly that he wished that 'Sepp' Dietrich *had* been the director of the zoo—they could certainly use a few carrier pigeons now.

A regular army division, 1st Infantry had taken part in almost every campaign since their landing at Oran at the beginning of the fighting in north-west Africa. When, after much hard fighting against some of the best of Germany's troops, they had returned to Oran for 'refreshment' they found that the base troops ensconced there had taken over the clubs and installations which were off limits to the rough men from the front. 1st Infantry thereupon 'liberated' Oran for the second time and the subsequent rioting almost got out of control.

Proud of their unrivalled battle record and contemptuous not only of rear-area soldiers (who outnumbered combat troops about fifteen to one in the American army) but apt to underrate other fine fighting divisions as well, they flouted rules and regulations, wore that they pleased and were the Military Police's nightmare.

Despite their heavy losses this great division was chosen to assault the Normandy beach, their third landing under fire, and were constantly in action for the next six months. Finally, after taking part in VII Corps' thirty-one-day fight for the Roer and sustaining another six thousand casualties, they were at last pulled out for rest and refitting early in December.

When the alert was flashed to them during the evening of December 16 most of their men were scattered on leave all over France and Belgium and much of their equipment was stripped down for maintenance and repair. Nevertheless at midnight their 26th Infantry Regiment moved out from VII Corps' reserve area, rolled through V Corps and, as we have seen, through the German parachute position, reaching Camp Elsenborn at nine o'clock on Sunday morning. First to arrive was the Second Battalion whose rifle companies, because of casualties, numbered only about one hundred each, of which nine-tenths were green replacements—only seven of the officers had been with the regiment at the start of the Roer River battle a few weeks before. They were immediately committed and this reinforcement for the hard-pressed 99th and 2nd Infantry Divisions, desperately holding on to the Elsenborn ridge, was to prove decisive.

Word that there had been a big German parachute drop spread quickly and although Operation Hohes Venn, as the drop into the area of that name had (with a singular disregard for security) been called, was not to be of any positive military significance its effects turned out to be far-reaching.

The scattering of the paratroop-carrying planes by the wind gave the impression that the operation was on a much larger scale than was the case. Over three hundred of von der Heydte's men were rounded up at many different points almost immediately and when three hundred dummies were detected in one area it was thought that this was a major airborne operation in the style of Holland and Crete.

The second day of the Ardennes Offensive was one likely to encourage this kind of assessment, for all that was known in the higher realms of the Allied command was that a large number of local actions all along VIII Corps' front were taking place, in some cases with disastrous results. Reports of German attacks in overwhelming strength, of small units going down in last ditch defences, of pockets holding out, of panic retreats, of roads blocked by fleeing civilians and men from rear area units, of German soldiers in American uniform, and now of large forces of paratroops reported from widely spaced areas all combined to produce a frightening picture of an unbelievably heavy German counter-offensive. In almost every report the same phrase occurred—'All hell's broken loose!'

When General Omar Bradley got back from his conference with General Eisenhower at Versailles to his 12th Army Group Headquarters in Luxembourg City on the night of December 17 and saw the war map showing fourteen attacking German divisions, half of them armoured, he was dismayed. 'Just where in the hell has this sonuvabitch got all his strength?' he asked.

It was a question that many on the Allied side were asking but no one knew the answer.

One of Otto Skorzeny's teams had been captured near Liege on the first day of the Offensive and in the commander's pocket was found the detailed instructions for the recognition signals to enable Germans dressed in American uniforms to return safely through their own lines. The officer, who knew that he was probably going to be shot, tried to save his life by telling the Americans everything he knew about Operation Greif, which was not a great deal, and also everything he suspected, which was. This included a rumour which had started among 150 Brigade's junior officers, and which was based on an idea thought up by a young, imaginative officer who presented it to Skorzeny. This was that his English-speaking Germans in American uniforms would pretend to be convoying German prisoners to Paris. There would be several such bogus convoys, some even including Jagdtiger tanks which, it would be explained to the curious, were to be put on show at Allied headquarters. Skorzeny listened to this wild story without smiling and then told its inventor to go away, work out the details and tell no one. Within days the rumour had spread throughout 150 Brigade. This was Skorzeny's intention—the more rumours the better.

When the captured German officer outlined this projected attack on Allied headquarters it was dismissed as fanciful but such was Skorzeny's reputation for daring and unorthodoxy that the idea that he might try to kidnap General Eisenhower as he had Mussolini was taken seriously. There was also the possibility of assassination to guard against. For the next week or two the Supreme Commander moved in a cluster of security officers and guards—to his intense irritation.

Neither Operation Greif nor von der Heydte's parachutists were to contribute much to the Ardennes Offensive in terms of their original intentions but by their mere presence and the reputation of the two commanders they caused to be set in motion elaborate counter measures which tied up many troops needed elsewhere and considerably slowed down Allied movement for miles behind the actual battle.

For instance, an entire combat command from one of the armoured divisions brought in as reinforcements spent the first week of the offensive in an anti-parachutist rôle. They saw no parachutists for there were none to see but were prevented from taking part in the fighting where they were badly needed.

Because of the possibility of disguised German troops wreaking havoc in the rear areas strict measures to check all identities, regardless of rank, were put in force. For a considerable period it was impossible for individuals or small groups to move about without being stopped every few miles by an MP shoving a tommy gun at them and growling out trick questions.

Most of these were based on the assumption that any real American would be familiar with the names of comic strip characters, baseball and the private lives of film stars and often the more senior officers found it difficult to supply the correct answers. General Bruce Clarke, commander of one of 7th Armored Division's Combat Commands was locked up when he put the Chicago Cubs in the American League. General Bradley himself, after having correctly named the capital of his state and located a football position was stumped for the name of Betty Grable's current husband* but the MP Sergeant was so delighted at catching out one of the top brass he let the man who was commanding three quarters of a million soldiers pass.

One story, probably apocryphal, was that the orders were to ask the suspect for the words of the third verse of the Star-Spangled Banner—if he knew them he was a German.

The standard question about the capital of the suspect's own State could be tricky for often the questioner, nervous finger on the trigger of the notoriously unsafe Tommy gun, would be wrong himself. A major from Corps HQ was driving himself back from a division when he was stopped at a road block.

'So you come from Missouri, huh? All right—what's the capital?'

'As a matter of fact it's Jefferson City, sergeant, but...' quickly, 'many people think it's St Louis...'

'St Lewis...!' Suspiciously the gun is gripped a little tighter.

'I know most people pronounce it St Looey,' said the major desperately, 'but in Missouri we say St Lewis.' Fortunately, a GI, also from the mid-West, was able to confirm this and the major was allowed to pass.

Many Americans, of all ranks, spent hours in custody though, for the whole business was further complicated by the suspicious accent of soldiers from German–American families and by the custom of Allied soldiers of wearing German jackboots and carrying odd bits of captured German equipment.

Operations Greif and Hohes Venn, by adding to the confusion, hindering movement and tying up men were saved from being the complete fiascos that circumstances nearly made them. But the men who took part in them, all volunteers and among Germany's bravest, paid dearly. Those wearing any item of Allied uniform, and others who were not, were shot and after the news of Peiper's massacre of unarmed American soldiers became known† many of the parachutists were not

* Eight years later in Korea this question was still being used for the same purpose—and it was still the same husband.

† So efficient was the 'latrine telegraph' that most of the front-line units knew within twenty-four hours.

allowed to surrender. For a little while the situation looked like getting out of hand. One divisional commander ordered that no SS or parachutists were to be taken prisoner, but after their first anger the American soldiers did not obey this order and as soon as it became known higher up it was rescinded.

Colonel von der Heydte soon captured a number of American soldiers unlucky enough to be moving in small parties and these became an embarrassment to him, but he was an honourable soldier who could not contemplate the shooting of prisoners. Every night they were set on a road two or three miles from an American position and told if they kept walking down the middle of the road nothing would happen to them. As they had no arms of course, there was little they could do but obey.

I asked Baron von der Heydte if he was not worried that these men would reveal how small his force was and its whereabouts. He replied that his group kept moving, prisoners were passed from one small unit to another so they had no clear idea of how many parachutists there were. 'Besides,' he said with a smile, 'I relied upon their pride to exaggerate our strength.'

Whatever the reason it is certain that the parachutist danger was greatly overestimated: they were reported everywhere as was the presence of German soldiers in American uniform and it was not until some time after the war that the true facts were understood about how small and ineffectual both these operations had been.

Hitler had placed great faith in them as diversions but he had always known that the success of the Ardennes Offensive would depend, more than anything else, on the ability of the panzer divisions in the north to reach and seize the Meuse crossings on the first, or at the latest, the second day. Fifth Panzer Army's attack was important, as was the flank defence in the south that the Seventh German Army was to set up, but the Führer's hopes rode with the tanks of 'Sepp' Dietrich's I SS Panzer Corps.

The commanders of the SS Panzer Divisions knew that their rôle was decisive and each tried for the best roads, the highest quality of reinforcements and the most material. If the Sixth SS Panzer Army was competing with the Fifth Panzer Army the crack SS Panzer Divisions, who had been chosen for the initial breakthrough, were competing equally fiercely with each other.

They were the two most famous SS armoured divisions: on 1st SS Panzer Corps' right the 12th, Hitler Jugend, and five miles south of them in the centre, the 1, the Leibstandarte. Both had long records and had collected battle honours and decorations galore; both had suffered enormous casualties time and time again. The 12th SS Panzer Division 'had been terribly battered by the British round Caen'* and completely built up again. Its commander, Major-General Kurt Meyer had become the youngest divisional commander in the German army at thirty-three. In the Normandy fighting he had seen his great division reduced to forty tanks (from 214) in two months and although unquestionably courageous and a fanatical Nazi (he ordered his men to strap explosives to their bodies and throw themselves on Allied tanks, and in prison camp at the end of the war he volunteered to raise an SS Division to fight Japan†) he was not a great general, having neither the intellect nor training required to employ large formations tactically. He owned his promotion to his zeal and loyalty to the party and the fact that 'Sepp' Dietrich always supported him.

For the Ardennes Offensive his Hitler Youth had been given the shortest route and the best roads to the Meuse and he was confident that they would beat their great rivals, the Leibstandarte, Hitler's Bodyguard.

This division too had been destroyed in Normandy and not for the first time: in 1943 its commander 'Sepp' Dietrich had boasted that only thirty of his original twenty-three thousand of 1940 were still alive and uncaptured. But in December 1944, neither of these two once crack formations were more than a brave copy of their former selves.

Nevertheless they were still the best of the Waffen SS and only a few of the crack regular army panzer divisions who had not lost quite so many men were their equals, or, in one or two cases, their superiors. Although the Waffen SS had long since been unable to depend entirely on volunteers or to demand their former exceptionally high standards, they still had the pick of what was available.

The younger commanding officers, dedicated Nazis to a man, had learned their job in the terrible, no-quarter battles of the Eastern Front where the slaughter on both sides and the acknowledged policy of taking few prisoners had made them callous as well as tough. Many of these young majors and colonels, with most of their friends dead or seriously wounded and faintly surprised to find themselves still alive, were bitter about the older staff officers and generals who had not actually

* General Jodl in a post-war interview.
† *Defeat in the West*: Milton Shulman, p. 314.

experienced the fierceness of modern tank battles on a vast scale. Combat soldiers in all armies soon learn to dislike intensely the men in the comparative safety of the rear areas who make the decisions which so often decide who is to die and who to live, even while understanding that such decisions have to be taken by someone.

It is commonly accepted that by the end of the war the quality of the officers and senior NCOs of the regiments that made up crack SS Panzer divisions was still high, that the mass of their men were brave but lacked training and that there had been a serious falling off in the ability and quality of the senior and staff officers.

Typical of the most able of the young commanders was twenty-eight-year-old Lieutenant-Colonel Jochen Peiper, tough, handsome, daring and completely ruthless, who had made a great reputation on the Eastern Front for leading fairly small numbers of tanks in sudden lightning attacks against Russian weak spots, shooting up rear areas, killing and destroying, yet somehow, always managing to extricate himself. His losses were often heavy for he demanded an almost suicidal devotion from his men and in order to move fast and save his armour as much as possible he made a practice of sending one or two half-tracks ahead of his point tank with orders to advance until they were fired upon. His men were in awe of him and he became a legend in the German Army, a fact which perhaps rather went to his head for he soon became known for correcting generals at conferences where he was the junior officer present.

'Sepp' Dietrich picked him to command the battle group which would lead the Leibstandarte to the Meuse, the decisive rôle in Sixth SS Panzer Army's offensive, the centre thrust. On the Leibstandarte's right, about five miles to the north, a battle group from the Hitler Jugend would also strike for the Meuse along a route some ten to fifteen miles shorter than that assigned to Peiper and over good hard-surfaced roads. Peiper's roads were narrow and often unsurfaced. When he had been handed his marked map at the pre-offensive briefing he had exploded. 'This route is not for tanks but for bicycles!' There was an embarrassed silence and then the Chief of Staff gave the familiar answer: it was the Führer's orders; he had personally chosen the route and it could not be altered or even questioned. Peiper then accepted it, announcing that 'of course' his battle group would be the first to reach the Meuse, notwithstanding Hitler Jugend's initial advantages.

On December 11, before he officially knew anything about

the coming offensive, Peiper had been asked how long it would take for a regiment of tanks to advance fifty miles at night. He said that he would be able to give an accurate answer the following day and that night moved a whole regiment, fully blacked-out and in battle state, fifty miles across the German rear areas, stopping other units moving up and considerably puzzling Movement Control.

'It can just be done in a night subject to mine-free roads and the avoidance of established anti-tank positions,' he reported. He was thanked for his information but told nothing: nevertheless he went back, looked at the situation map, and guessed the Ardennes Offensive.

Both crack SS Panzer divisions had been top priority for refitting and Colonel Peiper's own command, the 1st SS Panzer Regiment of the 1st SS Panzer Division, got the pick of reinforcements and new tanks straight from the assembly line. The division, the Leibstandarte, had been down to fifty tanks in mid-October but by the Ardennes Offensive had been built up to two hundred and fifty tanks and three thousand five hundred combat troops.

For his dash to the Meuse bridges Colonel Peiper decided to use a fifteen-mile-long attack column. Because the roads were too narrow for overtaking he placed all his combat elements up front. As on the Russian front, armoured half-tracks would lead until stopped when tanks would move up to deal with the obstruction. The leading battalion consisted of half Mk IVs and half Panthers, his favourite tank. Like most experienced tank men in the German army Peiper considered the Tiger too heavy and too under-powered.

Between the leading tank battalion and one of Tigers was a battalion of armoured infantry. To lend even more weight and fire power to this spearhead there were a few of the monster Jagdtigers, self-propelled 128-mm guns and some anti-aircraft units with their dual-purpose 88s.

The column also included an additional engineering battalion with equipment to repair bridges. Kampfgruppe Peiper was a formidable force and once the volksgrenadiers had pierced the American line it didn't seem likely that anything could stop the German armour until it reached the Meuse about seventy-five miles west.

As part of the tight security and in order to deceive the Allied Intelligence the SS panzers were kept back until just before the offensive. At seven in the evening of December 13, the head of the armoured column moved out over roads unmarked except for yellow arrows every few kilometres.

Blackout and radio silence was absolute and by ten o'clock the next morning they were all tucked away out of sight in the woods near Schmittheim, 1 SS Panzer Corps' battle HQ, about ten miles north-east of the attack point.

At a midday meeting of all commanders the 1st SS Division's General Mohnke announced the whole plan and marked maps were issued. Peiper's showed the location of American fuel dumps along his line of march and on both sides of it. These were accurate but strangely did not show the largest dumps of all, the three million gallons between Malmédy and Spa near the village of Francorchamps, enough to carry the whole army all the way to Antwerp.

Peiper said that if the 12th Volksgrenadiers achieved penetration of the American lines by 7.0 am and cleared the road from Losheim to Losheimergraben of mines and if the engineers succeeded in replacing the destroyed highway overpass there by noon, he would guarantee to reach the Meuse by midnight or the early hours of the 17th. In his turn the commanding officer of the 12th Volksgrenadiers, Major-General Engels, sure that the heavy artillery barrage would destroy the American front line, guaranteed that his troops would be in Losheim by 7 am.

At the last conference, held at eleven in the morning of December 15, eighteen hours before H-hour, the bad news that the promised train-loads of fuel had not arrived was announced. 'Sepp' Dietrich had asked for the attack to be postponed but Hitler had replied that generals are never ready and the offensive would go ahead as planned. The leading tank columns would have to capture fuel from the Americans.

Peiper then called a meeting of his own officers and passed on certain orders including Dietrich's that 'no time was to be wasted with prisoners'. He also told them not to fire into small groups of the enemy nor to delay for looting because they could not afford the time. There would be plenty of loot once they had seized the Meuse-crossings.

He did not like the idea of Operation Greif because he thought that trying to pass a 'Skorzeny Unit' of men, Shermans, German tanks disguised as American, trucks and jeeps through a battalion of armoured infantry and then one of tanks would slow up his own advance for an hour or so. But he had no choice, for the orders for Greif came from Führer Headquarters itself.

At the beginning of the offensive Colonel Peiper was at the battle headquarters of the 12th Volksgrenadiers Division waiting, as soon as word came through that the American lines had been pierced, to set his battlegroup moving through the gap. As we know the American line did not collapse. 'Numerous nests of American resistance caused considerable trouble to the infantry and to us,' he said in an interview after the war. 'And I was at Major-General Engels' headquarters until two-o'clock in the afternoon when I decided to go forward myself and try to see what was happening.'

He discovered, as had Skorzeny, that the roads leading to the front were clogged with traffic of all kinds. 'Some idiot had ordered the horse-drawn guns to move up,' he said in the same interview, 'I spent several hours at the first bridge over the railway at Losheim trying to restore some sort of order. At 4.0 pm I ordered my combat teams to start rolling anyway, to push through and run down anything in their way ruthlessly. By 7.30 pm the engineers had got a temporary structure over the first bridge which carried our tanks and we headed for Losheimergraben.'

Here he found that the next highway overpass, on the Lanzerath–Losheimergraben section of the road, had still not been repaired. Without hesitation he sent his panzers down the steep embankment and ordered them to continue south towards Lanzerath. This approach still had the mines laid by the Germans themselves in their autumn retreat and Kampfgruppe Peiper lost five tanks and five other vehicles in less than two miles.

Arriving at Lanzerath at midnight he found the 3rd Parachute Division stopped, after overrunning the Losheim Gap and Manderfeld, by fire from the north.* The parachute infantry commander told the fierce-looking young SS Panzer colonel that his men had been repulsed three times trying to capture Honsfeld. He estimated the American defenders to number about a thousand. Peiper was sceptical.

'I asked the 3rd Parachute commander for all the information that had been brought in about the immediate enemy situation,' he said. 'His answer was that the woods were heavily fortified and that scattered fire from pill-boxes plus mines were holding up his advance. It was therefore impossible to attack. I asked him if he had personally reconnoitred the American position in the woods and he replied that he had received the information from one of his battalion commanders. I asked the battalion commander: he said he had got the information from a captain. I asked the captain and *he* said that he had not personally seen the American

* This was probably from 99th Infantry Division's right flank along the railroad line leading to Buckholz station.

forces but they had been "reported to him". At this point I lost my temper and demanded that the parachute regiment give me a battalion and I would lead the breakthrough.'

Peiper had to have infantry because tanks advancing at night are practically blind and vulnerable to even small parties of soldiers with bazookas. After a conference at one in the morning the column formed up; two Panther tanks led, followed by a series of armoured half-tracks and then a mixture of Mk IVs and Panthers. Half of the parachute infantry rode on the tanks, the other half provided flank protection on either side of the road, changing places with riders every hour. The night was particularly black and the column moved at infantry pace—in front of each tank a guide walked holding a white handkerchief.

They expected to run into the reported American resistance every minute but nothing, except some shelling of the woods on their right, took place. The area was completely unoccupied and Kampfgruppe Peiper reached the outskirts of Honsfeld just before dawn without having fired a shot.

Honsfeld, a 99th Division rest area, was crammed with American soldiers and here, it will be remembered, one of Fourteenth Cavalry Group's troops had come in from Holzheim earlier in the night. Their commander had set up a roadblock south of the town. All night long American vehicles retreating from the breakthrough area moved bumper to bumper along the road.

Suddenly the sergeant from the Chicago Black Horse Troop in charge of this roadblock was amazed to see a black-jacketed soldier walking in front of a huge tank with sloping sides. Behind came another and both bore black swastikas; behind them were half-tracks crammed with men, each of whom seemed to have an automatic weapon. His orders were to fire but it would have been suicidal, and not surprisingly, he quietly slipped back to Honsfeld to warn the rest of the troop, enabling an officer and forty-three men to escape.

Within an hour Peiper had captured fifty reconnaissance vehicles including half-tracks, about eight trucks and sixteen anti-tank guns and a considerable number of prisoners. Nineteen unarmed American soldiers were killed by some of Peiper's SS—the first of a number of massacres perpetrated by this battlegroup which were to have ugly effects in the ensuing battle.

Peiper was elated at his easy success. Only one thing worried him—fuel. The mountainous terrain, the detours and the crawl through woods had used double the amount allowed to bring him this far. He consulted his map: two miles to the north at Bullingen a large American dump was marked but there was a snag—it was on Hitler Jugend Division's line of march. On the other hand from the sounds on his right it seemed pretty certain that Hitler Jugend were still held up.* Without hesitation he swung north, overran a small army spotter plane unit and seized the dump. Fifty American soldiers were forced to fill the tanks of the panzers and half-tracks and were then shot down in cold blood.

Wasting no time Battlegroup Peiper swung south to Moderscheid, surprising and overrunning a small American force, and were soon back on their assigned route with full fuel tanks and having expended very little ammunition. By mid-morning on Sunday, December 17, Lieutenant-Colonel Peiper was congratulating himself on having achieved a clean breakthrough.

Although the Meuse bridges still lay a long way west German Intelligence had assured the SS commander that no American forces strong enough to stop his armoured battlegroup were in between.

Of all Adolf Hitler's ambitious plans for the great Ardennes Offensive the only one which looked like succeeding quickly was this bold, unprotected thrust between US First Army's V Corps and VIII Corps, a wedge which could split the front in two.

* They had in fact got no further than Rocherath–Krinkelt.

14

BASTOGNE IS REACHED

Bastogne must be taken. Otherwise it will remain an abscess in our lines of communication. We must clean out Bastogne and then march on.

GENERAL VON LUTHWITZ

Just about the time that Peiper's battlegroup was slicing through American-held territory against practically no resistance the second German breakthrough twenty-five miles south, destined to be the most successful of all, was finding it unexpectedly difficult to gather momentum.

This was General von Manteuffel's élite XLVII Panzer Corps led by its Second Panzer Division whose new tanks had had to wait all day while the corps' engineers struggled to get the great pontoon bridge in at Dasburg. This was only accomplished as the short winter daylight was running out but 3rd Panzer Regiment, spearheading the attack, lost no time in putting its Mk IVs across the river and it was these tanks which, about midnight, crushed the last resistance of the garrison at Marnach.

But the regiment's panzer grenadiers had crossed the Our in rubber boats before dawn eight hours ahead of the tanks and advanced up through the woods to assault Marnach and cut Skyline Drive. Before they succeeded in eliminating this 28th Infantry Division strongpoint they suffered fairly heavy casualties from the platoon of tank destroyers and well-covered infantry positions in the town as well as from the shelling by the artillery at Urspelt and the Sherman tanks which came in from Munshausen. Despite their losses the German armoured infantry pressed their attack hard and the 110th Infantry's Company B went down. In the early hours of Sunday morning the panzer grenadiers had moved past Marnach along the main road leading west as far as the high ground above Clervaux. From here they were able to pour rifle and automatic fire into the château. This, however, made little impression on the great stone walls of the castle which had dominated the main bridge over the Clerf for eight centuries.

It was occupied by regimental headquarters troops but 110th Infantry's command post, controlling the sector's defence, was in the Claravallis Hotel at the northern end of the town where the railway crossed the river and the commanding officer, Colonel Hurley Fuller, was too preoccupied with plans for a counter-attack to retake Marnach to do much about the mixed group of administrative and service troops in the castle other than to tell them to return the fire. Help would be sent to them when possible.

When three of his four Second Battalion's companies had been released to him from divisional reserve the night before, the 110th Infantry commander had ordered a three-prong counter-attack at first light on December 17. The objective was first to retake Marnach and then to relieve his hard-pressed company in Hosingen.

Two of the newly-arrived infantry companies would advance from a ridge east of Clervaux and strike straight for Marnach. At the same time the platoon of Sherman tanks at Munshausen would support an attack on Marnach by C Company. The third assault against this important small town was to come from the north by a company of light tanks of the 707 Tank Battalion who were in 112th Infantry Regiment's areas but had been given to Colonel Fuller to make sure of recapturing Marnach to plug the German outlet from the Dasburg bridge. They moved during the night into Company A's position in the village of Heinerscheid three and a half miles north of Marnach along Skyline Drive with orders to move fast down the highway in a dawn attack.

It was a bold, aggressive plan and had Marnach still been held only by the panzer grenadiers it might have succeeded but, as we have seen, during the last hours of the night German tanks entered the scene, drastically changing the situation. One column of Mk IVs moved along the road to Clervaux joining the panzer grenadiers firing into the château and another struck north along Skyline Drive towards Heinerscheid intending to take a minor road from there and approach Clervaux from the north.

About an hour before first light on Sunday morning all three of Colonel Fuller's attacks towards Marnach jumped off. The two infantry companies advancing from the ridge across the river from Clervaux were stopped almost immediately by heavy fire from the panzer grenadiers who had moved up during the night. Half an hour later the Mk IVs from Marnach came up, thus stopping all hope of an American advance from Clervaux.

The second thrust north-east from Munshausen by the Shermans and riflemen made more headway at first but they found the German position around Marnach had become much too strong for them and were allowed to pull back to Munshausen where they learned of the critical situation in Clervaux. The tanks were ordered to fight their way west to help hold the vital river crossing and the infantry to hold Munshausen to deny the Germans the road from Marnach to the Drauffelt bridge.

The third attempt to retake Marnach by the light tanks from Heinerscheid south along the highway was a disaster, for a company of self-propelled guns, which had followed the second battalion of panzers across the pontoon bridge, were deployed on the high ground north of Marnach and east of Skyline Drive. When the eighteen American light tanks emerged from the village of Heinerscheid they were allowed to come on until they were lined up like clay pipes in a shooting gallery. Eleven were knocked out in ten minutes. Two managed to get back into Heinerscheid inside Company A's defences and the remaining five got off the road and made their way by cart tracks to the American artillery position near Urspelt.

Both this position and that of Company A, which had so far escaped attack, were hit later in the day and all seven of the remaining tanks were lost.

Not only had the 110th Infantry Regiment's counter-attack failed but the forces committed to it were soon under heavy attack themselves. Colonel Fuller sent his Company D, which had not yet been involved, to add weight to the two companies on the ridge across the river and ordered this force to attack towards the Marnach to Clervaux road. At the same time he asked for more self-propelled guns and tanks to slow up the German advance.

28th Infantry Division's other two regiments, the 112th on the left and the 109th on the right, had not been hit so hard on the first day as 110th in the centre through which the main weight of Fifth Panzer Army's punch had come but on the second day pressure against them also increased.

The 112th Infantry, it will be remembered, were holding the salient east of the Our based on Ouren and had successfully blocked all German attempts to overrun them and seize the bridges behind them on December 16. The reconnaissance battalion of the 116th Panzer Division had been diverted south during the night and joined the queue to cross the Dasburg bridge with orders to move up to Marnach and then north along Skyline Drive to take the 112th positions in the rear. The Panther battalion was ordered to launch an all-out attack on Ouren at first light on Sunday and the inexperienced and badly-shaken 560 Volksgrenadiers were ordered to destroy the forward American companies 'at all costs'.

To replace the light tank company from 707 Tank Battalion which was sent to attack Marnach the Corps Commander sent 112th Infantry four self-propelled tank destroyers from his only armoured reserve, Combat Command R of the 9th Armored Division. They were committed, almost as soon as they arrived, against the attack launched by eighteen Panthers at first light which roared through the American infantry positions. In the clash that followed four Panthers were destroyed and three American tank-destroyers lost. In the next few hours the fighting on this sector was as fierce as anywhere else along the assault front, involving air support by fighter-bombers and the closest cooperation of the artillery, often forced to sight through gun barrels and fire at minimum range. But the odds were too great and when darkness fell the 112th withdrew across the Our and the Germans had gained another bridgehead.

German casualties had again been heavy; American comparatively light. The 116th Panzer Division itself gave up the attempt to cross the Our at Ouren and moved south with its infantry regiments to Dasburg where it was delayed by shortage of fuel, for the concentrated use of this one bridge had seriously upset the Germans' supply plans. However, the crossing was made on Sunday night and by Monday morning the entire panzer division was assembled around Heinerscheid for the dash west through the gap between the attacks on St Vith and Bastogne. Their advance effectively cut the 112th off from the rest of 28th Infantry Division.

The regimental commander reported to the nearest higher formation, the 106th Infantry Division and its General Jones attached the 112th to his command to fill an under-manned part of the contracting St Vith perimeter.

28th Division's third regiment, the 109th Infantry on their right, had also held most of their positions initially as we have seen and, although the pressure had built up against them steadily, they were still more or less in place at the end of the second day. They had suffered many casualties, committed all their reserves, held the 352 Volksgrenadiers but had been unable to stop the 5th Parachute Division from finally working its way west between them and the 110th Infantry.

During Sunday night the Germans on this front at last managed to get bridges in on their part of the Our and push assault guns, anti-tank guns and artillery across. It was the beginning of the end for 109th Infantry; five hundred officers

201

and men were lost in the three days' almost continual fighting as well as much material but the 352nd Volksgrenadier Division had been prevented from crossing the Sauer to join the southern hard shoulder and was unable to resume the attack until December 20.

But, like the 112th, the 109th had been split off from the 28th Infantry Division and forced south where it became part of 9th Armored Division's mixed force fighting on the extreme right of the Ardennes front.

Although the odds were increasing against them hourly the defenders of Clervaux continued to strike back. As soon as the arrival of the Mk IVs at the higher ground above the main bridge was reported to him Colonel Fuller sent his remaining Shermans, the platoon from 707 Tank Battalion, which had remained behind protecting Clervaux, to engage them. Crossing the Clerf by this bridge about 9.0 am they had then to climb slowly up the tortuous road towards the Mk IV's who were waiting in hull down positions. Tanks are most vulnerable when cresting a hill but there was no other road and the Americans were lucky to lose no more than three tanks. They knocked out four Mk IVs.

Their attack, together with a move by the American infantry on the ridge towards the main Marnach to Clervaux road, evidently worried the German commander, for pressure eased noticeably. The Americans were further encouraged when the platoon of Shermans which had been summoned from Munshausen, having been warned about the presence of panzers on the main road, had taken a minor one, and now suddenly appeared from the south and knocked out the leading Mk IV, effectively blocking the approach to the bridge.

At Troy Middleton's VIII Corps Headquarters in Bastogne urgent requests for help and from his meagre reserve had come in from all three of his divisional commanders. But the Clerf crossings, now obviously in great danger, were a priority and he sent a company of tanks from 9th Armored Division's Combat Command R to Colonel Fuller's assistance. 110th Infantry's commander split this force into three; one platoon was sent to push back the panzer grenadiers who had broken into the southern end of Clervaux, one was sent to back up the position on the ridge east of the town and the third to Heinerscheid to reinforce Company A now under attack.

This was not the best way to use so small a force of tanks but Colonel Fuller was seriously handicapped by explicit orders from his commander, General Cota, not to yield a foot of ground anywhere. The logical action for 110th First and

Second Battalions to have taken on the second day when the great strength of the German attack had been appreciated, would have been the destruction of the Clerf bridges and a tactical withdrawal to the area of Esselborn on the high ground west of Clervaux from which the main roads from the east and the north-east, which were the German objectives, could have been denied to the panzers. This, in fact, was more or less what Colonel Fuller wanted to do but his suggestion that he pull back to a more easily defendable line had been turned down.

'Hold at all costs,' General Cota had said. 'No retreat. Nobody comes back.'

Obviously it is sometimes necessary in war to give such orders but, equally obviously, they should never be given unless absolutely necessary, for men should not be asked to die or to be captured unless some important advantage can be gained by their so doing.

At 9.15 am on December 16, before he had any conception of the extent of the German attack, VIII Corps' commander issued the following order to all units: 'Troops will be withdrawn from present positions only repeat only if positions become completely untenable.' This gave local commanders very little leeway to adjust their dispositions; they could not 'roll with the punch'. In order to make sure that he was not misunderstood General Troy Middleton then laid down a specified defence line to be 'held at all costs'.

Soldiers will obey this dread order if they believe that it is necessary and that it is possible. As a temporary measure it was almost certainly necessary if only to detect the points of main pressure and so get a picture of German intentions but the line soon proved unrealistic and was breached by midnight on the first day. The order, however, was not changed: all positions were still to be held 'at all costs'.

Late on Sunday afternoon about thirty-six hours after the great German barrage had blasted his sector of the front Colonel Fuller, in his headquarters in the Claravallis Hotel in Clervaux, grimly contemplated the desperate plight of his regiment. Three companies had already been overwhelmed: one each in Heinerscheid, Marnach and Weiler. Five more were surrounded, running out of ammunition and pressure against them increasing. These were the three out on the ridge east of Clervaux and the companies in Munshausen and Hosingen. The survivors of two other companies, L and M of the Third Battalion, together with the battalion headquarters company, were still holding the important Consthum position on his right—but only just. This accounted for ten of his twelve companies; of the other two, one was in Clervaux itself, the other was forming part of 28th Divisional Headquarters' defences, hurriedly being prepared at Wiltz.

The final assault on Clervaux with tanks and infantry came from two directions: along the main road from Marnach which entered the town in the south-east and down a road from the north leading through Urspelt. The first attack seized the main bridge after the arrival of the Panthers had made the garrison in the château helpless, and the second entered Clervaux over a bridge at the northern end of town and knocked out a Sherman tank guarding the regimental command post in the hotel opposite.

It was the end for the gallant 110th Infantry Regiment as the tanks, self-propelled guns and armoured infantry of the crack 2nd Panzer Division poured over the First and Second Battalion strongpoints in the north and at the same time the Twenty-sixth Volksgrenadiers, now supported by tanks from Panzer Lehr Division, crushed the Third Battalion in the south.

The American infantry here were commanded by 110th Regiment's executive officer, Colonel Strickland, who had been sent by Colonel Fuller to the 110th's right wing at the beginning of the German attack when the barrage knocked out line communication.

With the help of the artillery, three tanks and three armoured cars, Consthum was held for the whole of the second day thus preventing 26th Volksgrenadiers or Panzer Lehr from crossing the Clerf. But, as the pressure increased the numbers of the defenders were steadily whittled down and it became obvious that the position would have to be yielded.

It had been hoped that the garrison in Hosingen who had proved to be such a thorn in the German side on the first day might be able to fight their way west to join the defenders of Consthum but because of the 'no retreat' order they remained where they were. Reinforcements were promised but none arrived. Company K, with the five Sherman tanks which had got through to them on the first day, and the attached combat engineers slowly contracted in house-to-house fighting until they were in a tiny circle in the centre of the town. The observation post in the water tower from where the first German attackers had been seen remained in operation most of the day despite being shelled by high-velocity armour-piercing shells from tanks and anti-tank guns. The thick concrete walls and the inner steel shaft around the stairway protected the soldiers inside who continued to report on the

German dispositions. Two of the Sherman tanks were knocked out but by nightfall on the 17th the defenders in the centre of Hosingen had still not surrendered.

But a meeting of officers was called to discuss the situation: no mortar ammunition remained and rifle ammunition was down to a few rounds per man. Company K's commander got through to the Third Battalion and reported the situation: the final decision was left to him.

At first light on Monday the 18th the commanding officer himself went out with a white flag and white sheets were hung over the tanks. All German fire ceased immediately. Three hundred Americans were taken prisoner but the American casualties had been remarkably light: seven killed and ten wounded. The forty-eight-hour defence of Hosingen was one of the unexpected actions which were seriously to upset the German timetable.

The refusal to yield Consthum was another. Here, despite repeated attempts to break through the position during December 17, the 26th Volksgrenadiers were held all day and all that night. Half an hour before dawn on the 18th their artillery laid down a heavy barrage on Consthum and as soon as it lifted the tough 26th came on again, determined this time to sweep this stubborn defence out of their way. Wave after wave of attackers were beaten off by the combined fire of the infantry's rifles and automatic weapons, the high-explosive shells from the few tanks and the accurate shelling of the artillery on the attackers advancing across open fields. Then a pea-soup fog rolled in from the east forming a perfect natural screen for the attackers and the surviving defenders were at last forced to fall back. Anti-aircraft Bofors were left behind to fight the rearguard and their fast accurate fire stopped the German infantry from coming any further than Consthum, at least for the time being. Using narrow, twisting roads which drop steeply down to the crossings where the Clerf from the north and the Wiltz from the west join the Sure, the remnants of the Consthum garrison with their wounded moved four or five miles south-west to the small town of Nocher where they linked up with supporting artillery as part of the attempt to defend Wiltz, 28th Infantry Division HQ.

Both Panzer Lehr Division and the 26th Volksgrenadiers, Fifth Panzer Army's best infantry on whom General Manteuffel had put his highest hopes, had been held up for more than two days by a single American infantry battalion supported by a few tanks and some artillery. This was despite the volksgrenadiers having stolen a march on the rest of XLVII

Panzer Corps by crossing the Our on the night of December 15/16 in order to seize the vital Clerf bridges. That neither they nor 2nd Panzer Division on their right succeeded in forcing the Clerf in the first twenty-four hours meant that there was just time for Bastogne to be reinforced from the south.

The Clervaux position was finally lost at about the same time, dawn on the 18th, although Colonel Fuller's own command post in the Claravallis Hotel in the north end of the town had not been able to hold out after German tanks broke into the town on the 17th. Earlier a battery of self-propelled anti-tank guns from the green 9th Armored Division had arrived at Clervaux and Colonel Fuller had sent them across the river by the bridge opposite his headquarters to block any attempt by German tanks to get into Clervaux from the north but within an hour, when the Panthers did appear, they withdrew precipitately without orders, losing one of their guns by overturning it in their hurry to get to the rear.

When these German tanks and their supporting infantry reached Clervaux the single company of Second Battalion defending the town itself withdrew. It was intended that they go back no further than Esselborn, a small village on high ground west of Clervaux, where they were to join the last of the battalion's companies due to come in from divisional headquarters at Wiltz. However, there was no sign of any American defence line forming at Esselborn and the troops from Clervaux kept moving. Once the decision has been taken to retreat it becomes increasingly difficult to stand, turn and fight again and this company was next reported as having 'passed the command post at Donnange (two miles further west) headed for the rear'.

Here artillery of VIII Corps reserve were backing up two hastily formed roadblocks of 9th Armored Division's Combat Command R and the gunners were ordered to stop the retreating infantry by force if necessary. They were stopped and later took part, with other survivors of the smashed 110th Infantry Regiment, in the hard fighting in front of Bastogne.

Meanwhile, back in Clervaux, German tanks and infantry flowed in on both sides outflanking the three companies on the ridge east of the town and Colonel Fuller soon had panzers firing directly into the Claravallis Hotel at point-blank range. From one of the upper rooms he got through to 28th Division Headquarters at Wiltz and bluntly reported that both his First and Second Battalion command posts had been overrun; he was now cut off from his Headquarters Company, isolated in the château, and that he wanted permission to get as many of his staff as possible out and back to the newly-forming defence line at Esselborn.

Just as bluntly the divisional commander's Chief of Staff to whom Colonel Fuller was speaking reminded him that General Middleton's orders to hold 'at all costs' had not been altered. A high-explosive shell from one of the German tanks bursting in a nearby room interrupted the conversation and Colonel Fuller hung up angrily. Minutes later he climbed out of a back window to the cliff behind and with a few men tried to find his way across country to Esselborn.*

The wounded men he had been forced to leave behind lay everywhere in the hotel listening to the ripping noise of the German automatic weapons and the loud explosions of bursting shells. A few, still unhurt or only lightly wounded, tried to make a break for it but were cut down by the machine pistols of the panzer grenadiers or taken prisoner.

At the switchboard, which was still functioning, the signals sergeant stayed at his post until there was no one left but the wounded. He then got through to 28th Divisional headquarters at Wiltz and reported that the 110th Infantry command post had been evacuated, German tanks and infantry were running wild in Clervaux and he was the only able-bodied man left. It was 6.39 pm on the night of Sunday December 17 and the next voice that came over the telephone was German.

At the other end of Clervaux the 102 headquarters troops in the château, although surrounded and having rifle, machine-gun, mortar and tank fire poured into their fortress all day, held on to their positions, returning the fire every now and then and tying down many of the panzers' supporting infantry.

The three companies from 110th Infantry Regiment who were holding the ridge east of the town were surrounded during the night by tanks and infantry. Only sixty-two of the approximately seven hundred managed to slip through the German ring in the dark and rejoin the badly cut-up 28th Infantry Division. At Munshausen the small force of American tanks and infantry were split into separate groups by the German attacks but fought on during the night until daybreak when most were captured or killed.

The Germans increased the efforts to take the château and finally when the great walls were riddled by armour-piercing shells and the inside was burning the surviving headquarters troops surrendered. Their last message was timed at 5.28 am on Monday, December 18 and read: 'Position surrounded by

* The German advance was too swift and after thirty-six hours moving through heavy forest they were all captured.

207

armor and infantry. More armor and Infantry moving N through town.'

It was the last word from Clervaux and it came forty-eight hours after General von Manteuffel's heaviest armoured punch had struck at Dasburg less than seven miles due east. This was thirty to forty hours more than had been planned and the difference, priceless to the Allied defence, had been bought by the gallant stand of infantry, tanks and artillery. The 28th Infantry Division's centre had been smashed, casualties had been heavy and many tanks, guns and vehicles lost, but the delay imposed on the attackers undoubtedly made the successful defence of Bastogne possible and was probably responsible for the German failure to seize the southern crossing of the Meuse.

VIII Corps' only armoured reserve, Combat Command R of the green 9th Armored Division, consisted of a battalion each of tanks, armoured infantry and field artillery and attached headquarters units. CCR was directly under corps' control and in early December was placed at Trois Vierges from where it could quickly support either the corps centre or its right wing. On the second day of the German offensive General Middleton moved CCR ten miles south to Oberwampach behind 28th Infantry Division's crumbling front.

As soon as he learned that Clervaux had fallen and German tanks and infantry were across the Clerf he ordered CCR to set up two strong roadblocks to bar the way to Bastogne and the road-net west. The first and weaker of the two was at the junction of the road from Clervaux running west and the main road from Trois Vierges running south-west to Bastogne—part of the 'at all costs' line.

This position, Task Force Rose, was manned by a company of Sherman tanks supported by a company of armoured infantry and a platoon of armoured engineers. Also most of CCR's field artillery was placed so as to cover this roadblock and the second, stronger, one five miles south-west on the Bastogne road and only nine miles from that town. This, Task Force Harper, consisted of the rest of CCR's tank battalion and two companies of armoured infantry and was intended to be a most formidable obstacle.

Both roadblocks were manned by midnight, December 17, and the men in the tanks and at the guns waited for the approaching Germans. But as 2nd Panzer Division's armoured infantry were tied down in Clervaux by the refusal of the defenders in the château to surrender it was not until ten o'clock the following morning that the Americans on the ridge overlooking the road at the first roadblock saw armoured cars and half-tracks approaching from Clervaux and German infantry dismount and move into the woods next to the road. These belonged to 2nd Panzer's reconaissance battalion and the German tanks, now moving steadily through Clervaux, ignoring small-arms fire from the few remaining 110th Infantry there, were only four or five miles behind this advance guard.

Soon the reconnaissance troops probed forward to test the strength of the roadblock. They were hit by high-explosive shells from the Shermans, small-arms fire from the dug-in amoured infantry and then pounded by howitzers from the supporting artillery. They went to ground—first round to the defenders.

About an hour later the first German tanks appeared, Mk IVs from 3rd Panzer Regiment cock-a-hoop after their success at Marnach and Clervaux. Almost immediately they lobbed smoke shells in front of the roadblock and, under the resulting cover, advanced to a good position about half a mile north of the larger American tanks. Surprisingly nothing then happened and after a couple of hours of quiet Task Force Rose reported that the German advance had been halted.

No sooner had this optimistic report been made than the Panther battalion arrived and quickly took up a position south of the American tanks. Both groups of German tanks then directed their fire on to the protecting screen of armoured infantry who were forced to fall back. Next an attack by panzer grenadiers supported by tanks outflanked the supporting howitzer battery who were also forced to withdraw. These two actions left the outnumbered and outgunned Shermans exposed to fire from three sides—an impossible position which could only result in their destruction.

When this was known to CCR's commander, Colonel Gilbreth, he asked General Middleton for permission either to send reinforcements up to Task Force Rose (which would mean weakening Task Force Harper at the next roadblock) or to withdraw his exposed tanks. But VIII Corps' commander, still persisting with 'hold at all costs' order, would consent to neither alternative. Quickly the Germans knocked out seven Shermans and forced the remainder to pull back. After dark the remaining Shermans tried to escape across country to Houffalize only to be ambushed by 116 Panzer Division. A few vehicles broke out and charged down the road into the Bastogne perimeter.

It was 2.30 in the afternoon of Monday and one of XLVII Panzer Corps' spearheads had at last gained a major approach road fourteen miles from Bastogne, Although Task Force Rose at the first roadblock had only held them up for four or five hours it had taken the armoured spearhead a surprisingly long time after the fall of Clervaux on Sunday evening to advance the next undefended five and a half miles. The German commanders knew that at this stage of the Ardennes Offensive every hour was critical because of the Allies' superior mobility and 2nd Panzer Division was told to increase its pace. Even before the first roadblock was completely eliminated light elements of the German advance guard reached Task Force Harper at the second roadblock, but realizing that the position was too strong for them, waited for their armour to come up.

This strong American position, nine miles from Bastogne, blocked both the main road from the north-east and another good road leading south to Wiltz, command post of the shattered 28th Infantry Division. The force of tanks, guns and infantry forming Task Force Harper was the strongest XLVII Panzer Corps had yet faced in this offensive and 3rd Panzer Regiment's commander, who only arrived at the roadblock with his Mk IVs and Panthers after dark, did not at all like his orders to attack immediately. He did so and to their surprise the Germans found the resistance unexpectedly slight. They destroyed two platoons of American tanks (the official German report says that only three Shermans fought back), set fire to the vehicles and by the light of the flames raked the supporting armoured infantry with machine-gun fire. The American commander, Lieutenant-Colonel R. S. Harper was killed and the survivors of the smashed roadblock fell back to the village of Longvilly.

Here, only five miles from Bastogne, CCR had set up its new headquarters under orders from General Middleton that this was to be its last backward step. Longvilly must be held to the last man for between it and Bastogne there was as yet nothing that could stop a German armoured column.

At Longvilly and Bastogne as night fell on the third day of the offensive all the news seemed to be bad. Reports were coming in that another German combined infantry and tank column had crossed the Clerf south of Clervaux that morning and was climbing up the tortuous roads of the valley of the Wiltz against almost no resistance. As well as this threat to Bastogne from the east there seemed every possibility of a third attack from the north from the forces now reported to be pouring through the gap torn between the 106th and 28th Infantry Divisions.

To give warning of such an attack a third force was

squeezed out of what was left of CCR, Task Force Booth. It consisted of some light tanks, a few tank destroyers and headquarters troops and was placed north of the road from St Vith to Bastogne but it, too, was to suffer the same fate as other isolated small forces for the collapse of the second roadblock cut it off and nothing more was heard from Task Force Booth for six days when a party of survivors managed to get into Bastogne. They told of dodging the German columns until they ran into a strong force of Second Panzer tanks and infantry and were smashed to pieces.

At Longvilly on Monday night there was confusion and depression as defeated soldiers streamed back and stragglers from attacks elsewhere came in, bringing garbled accounts of American units being overwhelmed, of panic withdrawals and heavy casualties and rumours of the Germans in great strength at a dozen different places. Colonel Gilbreth, at CCR's new headquarters here, tried to organize the survivors of the roadblocks together with odd groups of infantrymen, artillery and headquarters troops into a cohesive defence but the knowledge that the 28th Infantry, which it had been CCR's job to back up, no longer existed as a division, that German armoured columns were approaching fast from two directions, that the armoured help from Third Army promised for that afternoon had not arrived and no one seemed to know where it was and that VIII Corps Headquarters had been ordered by General Hodges of First Army to withdraw from Bastogne all seemed to make his situation pretty hopeless. He would, of course, obey the 'hold at all costs' order but it looked as though his badly weakened force was about to be overwhelmed and Bastogne about to fall into the German grasp.

But at that critical and dramatic moment the precious hours which had been bought so dearly by the gallant stand of the infantry in front of the Clerf bridges paid off, for at CCR's headquarters there suddenly appeared a liaison officer from the 10th Armored Division to report that 'Team Cherry' leading CCB was approaching fast from Bastogne with orders to hold Longvilly.

15

DESTRUCTION OF A DIVISION

In war the moral is to the physical as three to one.
NAPOLEON

For the Headquarters of the 106th Infantry Division and its attached Fourteenth Cavalry Group, Sunday, December 17, was one long nightmare as their front crumbled and disaster followed disaster until St Vith itself seemed about to be lost.

As the German attack penetrated north and south of his two regiments, stuck out in the Schnee Eifel position, General Alan Jones was intensely aware of their peril and suggested to VIII Corps that he pull them back as soon as it was dark on Saturday. General Troy Middleton neither approved nor disapproved but left the decision to 'the man on the ground'.

It was a terrible quandary for a newly-arrived divisional commander yet to fight his first battle. If the German onslaught later proved not to be as powerful as it seemed, then withdrawal would not only have badly damaged the carefully built-up fighting spirit of his green young soldiers but would probably mean the end of his career. Reinforcement was on the way—two combat commands of tanks were hurrying to St Vith and both were promised for early next day. If this armour could drive a corridor through on either side of St Vith to the Schnee Eifel while at the same time his infantry there turned and attacked the rear and flanks of the penetrations the initial German success might be turned into a crushing defeat.

All his instincts were to save his men—indeed General Jones's own son was one of the officers on that cold, wind-swept ridge—but all his training and instilled tradition were against withdrawal under attack. The decisive factor was how soon the badly-needed armour would reach him and as he had been assured that their arrival was only a matter of hours he made his decision: the troops on the exposed Schnee Eifel would be left where they were—at least for the time being.

He could not know that the time in which they could escape encirclement was already running out.

During the long dark December night both sides brought reinforcements into the battle for St Vith, although those from the American were badly delayed by the clogged roads. The German commanders, knowing that every hour counted at this stage, went forward personally to push their assault troops on; Major-General Hoffman Schönborn came up to the leading unit of his 18th Volksgrenadier Division to lead them against Schönberg while to the south of St Vith, General Lucht, the LXVI Corps commander, joined the troops preparing to seize Winterspelt. Late on Saturday night Field Marshal Model, walking by himself near Schönberg, encountered General von Manteuffel and ordered him to commit the Fuehrer Begleit Brigade the following day to make sure of breaking through to St Vith.

Fighting went on all night. On the German left volksgrenadiers of the 62nd Division, stopped by the 424th Infantry Regiment on Saturday, got possession of half of Winterspelt in a night attack and succeeded in driving the Americans right out in a second assault at dawn. General Lucht then took over personal command and led the 62nd on to seize the bridge at Steinebruck. At the same time, on 62nd Volksgrenadier's right, a regiment from 18th Volksgrenadiers flung themselves once more at Bleialf before dawn and after an hour and a half of bitter fighting it too fell and they pushed on towards the projected meeting point with the rest of their division at Schönberg.

Here the attack, also led by the divisional commander, had driven Troop B of the Eighteenth Cavalry Squadron back and about 9.30 on Sunday morning, when the southern pincer driving up from Bleialf arrived, the jaws of the trap closed.

Quickly the triumphant volksgrenadiers pushed on along the road running along the north bank of the Our towards St Vith nine miles away. But Troop B's few armoured cars and mortar jeeps had taken up a good defensive position just over a mile west of Schönberg and were able to hold up the German advance for two more hours. They might well have delayed them even longer but they received orders from Colonel Devine to move north-west to Wallerode to form part of his 'final delaying line'.

After the cavalry had once more broken and withdrawn without orders from the second delaying line, the commander of Fourteenth Cavalry Group chose this last one. It ran in a north-east facing arc from Born, five miles north of St Vith to Wallerode, two and a half miles north-east. Through the centre of this defence line the main road from the north to St Vith ran, a logical attack axis from the left flank of any German column moving west between VIII Corps and V Corps.

Although General Jones in St Vith had not authorized this

line any more than either of the others, he apparently approved of it—at least his reply to Colonel Devine's request for information about the general plan was 'stay where you are'. Colonel Devine promised to get a counter-attack force ready, 'available to your orders', but morale once broken is not that easily regained and within a few hours the Fourteenth Cavalry Group commander ordered another unauthorized withdrawal abandoning the 'final delaying line', pouring his armoured cars on to the St Vith–Vielslam road, thus producing a long jam of vehicles and leaving the approach to St Vith from the north-east wide open. Down this road were already approaching the advance guard of 1st SS Panzer Division's southern column.

Because of the inexperience of the staff of 106th Infantry the Corps Commander had assigned his assistant intelligence officer, Colonel Slayden, to 'help the division get on its feet'. This move was due to a feeling at VIII Corps HQ that 106th Infantry Division's own G2 was a 'nervous Nellie' who spent his time fretting about petty problems.

Colonel Slayden, in an interview after the battle, said that no one at 106th Division could possibly have known what was about to hit them. 'The 2nd Division cleaned out everything from their positions when they left and told the 106 staff that there would be no trouble at all in the sector. Everybody in 106th looked forward to the brilliant opportunity to get a little battle indoctrination where it was quiet and comfortable.'

Colonel Slayden noted in his diary the day before the attack that there was very little patrol activity on 106 Division's front and intended to bring this to the notice of the commander. He described the German activity on the first day as a reconnaissance in force. This was typical of the reactions at divisional and corps level to the German attack. He soon realized that the main danger lay to the north due to the scattering and disrupting of the Fourteenth Cavalry Group whose withdrawal exposed the north flank of the division.

Colonel Slayden was at 106 HQ when Colonel Devine came in on Saturday night 'completely demoralized by events' and with 'little knowledge of the location of his troops'. Had General Jones been more experienced he would have relieved Colonel Devine of command then and there. Instead he was sent back to his badly shaken unit which continued to retreat until by Sunday afternoon Fourteenth Cavalry Group's command post, which had been at Manderfeld twelve miles east of St Vith, was at Recht seven miles north-west.

But even this was not to be the end of the cavalry's withdrawal: just after dark on Sunday Colonel Devine and most of his staff were in two jeeps east of Recht which came under fire from advance units of 1st SS Panzer Division's southern column. The jeeps were abandoned but all the Americans escaped on foot. Colonel Devine made his way across country in the dark, reaching his command post about 11.30 on Sunday night, in a state of collapse. He handed over command of the cavalry group to Lieutenant-Colonel Damon, Eighteenth Cavalry Squadron CO, and went to bed. A few hours later, on General Middleton's orders, he was evacuated to the rear as a non-battle casualty and relieved of command.

Sunday had been an anxious and frustrating day for General Jones in St Vith too as the hours went by and the combat command from 7th Armored Division didn't appear. When, on Saturday night, General Middleton himself on the phone had assured him that this strong force of tanks and armoured infantry would be in St Vith by 7.0 am the next morning, the possibility that the corps commander could be wrong hadn't crossed his mind.* From well before first light General Jones anxiously awaited the arrival of the two combat commands.

Just before dawn, after an all-night move from the Monschau area, CCB of 9th Armored came into St Vith and, as already decided General Jones sent them to the south-east to cross the Our at Steinebruck and re-take Winterspelt. The armoured infantry were passed through the tanks and went on to meet the advancing volksgrenadiers.

On the other flank, east of St Vith along the approach from Schönberg, the position was rapidly becoming critical. Hourly expecting CCB of 7th Armored to appear, General Jones got together some 500 engineers, a platoon of infantry and three tank destroyers and sent them to halt the 18th Volksgrenadier's spearhead. The engineers had been engaged in routine duties in the St Vith area and few had received any instruction in handling bazookas or machine guns. They were to fight with great bravery but this lack of knowledge cost the lives of many of them.

At half past nine on Sunday morning having heard that both Winterspelt and Schönberg were firmly in German hands and

* Colonel Slayden, the Staff Officer, from VIII Corps HQ had been with General Jones when this conversation took place and he knew that it was not possible for 7th Armored to move so far so quickly. 'I should have said so,' he now admits, 'but that would have meant that I should have to have called the corps commander a liar.' Colonels do not contradict their generals in any army.

still with no sign of the missing tank force General Jones sent the following message to the commanders of both his trapped regiments: REINFORCEMENTS DRIVING THROUGH THIS AFTERNOON WITHDRAW FROM PRESENT POSITIONS IF UNTENABLE. Normal communications had by now completely broken down and this urgent message had to go by the divisional artillery's radio network which was badly overloaded. The order did not get through to the troops on the Schnee Eifel for six critical hours.

The reinforcements mentioned depended upon the arrival of CCB of 7th Armored by midday at the latest. General Jones gambled on it not being more than five or six hours late.

7th Armored Division, in reserve seventy miles north of the Dutch/German frontier, had received a laconic telephone message at 5.30 pm on Saturday afternoon: 'Alert your division for immediate movement to Monarch (code name for VIII Corps)'. Five hours later particulars of two routes and a time schedule were sent from Ninth Army HQ. On the West Route the main strength of the division—two combat commands led by the Cavalry Reconnaissance Squadron—were to move to the Vielsalm area. The division's reserve combat command and supporting artillery were assigned to the East Route and were to move off eighteen hours after the combat commands because the artillery were in action supporting 84th Infantry Division's attack in the Geilenkirchen sector and needed time to hand over their positions.

No one at 7th Armored Division HQ had any clear idea of the reason for the sudden move. Something was said about a 'three or four division German attack' in VIII Corps' area but no indication of the seriousness of the situation was given because this was still not realized. Many of the men in the 7th Armored column, finding themselves travelling south-west away from the front, thought that the war was over.

The commander of CCB, Brigadier-General Bruce Clarke, went on ahead to Bastogne to get his orders from Major-General Troy Middleton. He arrived at VIII Corps HQ at 4.0 am on Sunday where he found the corps commander reading (General Middleton was a victim of bursitis and often was unable to sleep).

'Glad to see you, Clarke,' General Middleton said calmly, 'General Jones's division has been hit pretty hard and he's got two combat commands in danger of being cut off. I want you to go and help him out in the morning—meanwhile get some sleep.'

Judging from the corps commander's calmness that the situation wasn't too serious and knowing that his combat command could not possibly reach St Vith before mid-morning or noon Bruce Clarke slept for about three hours and arrived at General Jones's HQ in St Vith at 10.30 am on Sunday. There the atmosphere was very different.

'Thank God you've come—I've been expecting you since 7.0!' Jones told him. 'You've got to attack towards Schönberg immediately—I've got two regiments cut off . . .!'

'I've got just four men with me,' Bruce Clarke replied, 'and I don't know when my command will get here.'

In fact CCB, which was to have started south at 2.0 am, had been held back until 5.30 waiting for road clearance and when Bruce Clarke reported to St Vith its tanks were still many miles to the north, struggling not against the Germans but against muddy, rutted roads clogged with refugees and retreating American soldiers.

When General Jones and the staff of 106th Infantry realized that the armoured support upon which they had built their entire plan had not arrived the feeling of hopelessness and inevitable defeat, which had never been far below the surface since the first shattering blows, began to take control. News from every sector was bad; the Fourteenth Cavalry Group's 'final delaying line' had been abandoned without orders; there was no contact with 99th Infantry Division on the left and the situation on the right, in the south, was hazy.

Here their third regiment, the 424th Infantry, who had been holding the division's right flank next to the 112th Infantry Regiment of 28th Division, were now in danger as the Germans drove through on either side of them. With the fall of Winterspelt and the advance of 62nd Volksgrenadiers to the high ground overlooking Steinebruck the situation south of St Vith had deteriorated completely. General Jones sent orders to the 424th Infantry commander to withdraw his regiment immediately and, at the same time, Brigadier-General Hoge was ordered to pull the tanks and armoured infantry of CCB, 9th Armored, which had just got into position back behind the Our that night.

A post-war American report has described the situation in St Vith on Sunday, December 17:

'Combat Command B of 7th Armored Division established its command post in the same building as the command post of 106th Infantry Division. Staff members of CCB tried to get a relatively accurate picture of the situation from officers of the 106th Division but it was obvious that the shock of the initial

German blow, together with their lack of combat experience, had partially disrupted the staff functioning of the 106th. All kinds of rumours were being spread; men who had fled from the front, apparently seeking to justify their action, gave an exaggerated and inaccurate picture of what was taking place. The situation most certainly was bad, and the impression that officers of CCB got was that the 106th no longer existed as an effective division. As staff sections of CCB began to arrive, carrying their equipment into the building, they met men from the 106th Division Headquarters leaving with their equipment.'*

Reports came in that the small force of combat engineers sent towards Schönberg had been forced back and that the Germans were advancing rapidly. From the roof of the school building, in which the two headquarters were, General Jones and Brigadier-General Clarke could see the line of German infantry in the distance only about three thousand yards away. Small arms fire was now coming into the command area.

'Clarke,' said General Jones, 'Take over the defence of St Vith.'

It was about 2.30 on Sunday afternoon and all the forces that Brigadier-General Clarke had to hold St Vith were two headquarters companies of combat engineers and a single platoon of infantry which had been the Command Post guard. There was also one battalion of field artillery, the 275th, in position about a mile north-east of St Vith but with no infantry support. They had made roadblocks with their batteries and sited their guns for direct fire. This was the only immediate artillery support for St Vith until the arrival of the divisional artillery of 7th Armored Division. Bruce Clark sent the combat engineers and infantry platoon each towards the firing, telling them to keep moving until they met Germans and then dig in and hold. Somehow they must stop the German advance until the arrival of CCB's tanks and armoured infantry. But it was mid-afternoon—where were they?

Major Don Boyer who was in a staff car behind the leading tank battalion of 7th Armored Division's Combat Command B described the situation later in a report. He arrived at the road junction of Poteaux some three miles from St Vith; about an hour behind him were the badly needed 38th Armored Infantry Battalion.

'As we arrived at the road junction, we were hit by a sight that we could not comprehend; a constant stream of traffic

* *The Defense of St Vith.* Prepared by The Armored School.

hurtling to the rear; nothing going to the front. It was a case of "every dog for himself", it was a retreat, a rout.

'Here would come a 2½-ton with only a driver, then another with several men in it (most bareheaded and in various stages of undress), next perhaps an engineer crane truck or an armoured car, then several artillery prime movers—perhaps one of them towing a gun—command cars with officers in them, quarter-tonners—anything which would run and which would get the driver and a few others away from the front.

'About a mile farther up the road we ran into a hopeless mass of vehicles fleeing to the rear on a narrow road. Vehicles streaming back had attempted to pass each other in the intervals between tanks of the 31st Tank Battalion and now no one could move. Slowly we opened a path and tanks began to roll at a snail's pace.

'Several times we had to wave the lead tank forward at full speed when some vehicle refused to pull over—usually the sight of thirty tons of steel roaring down on him was all that was needed to get the driver to move over.

'Finally at 8.15 pm we entered St Vith—it had taken two and a half hours to move three miles and all because of vehicles fleeing with men who refused to pull over and let troops through, troops who would actually save them if they could reach the town before the Germans.'

The 7th Armored Division's commander, Brigadier-General Hasbrouck, reached Bastogne at midday on Sunday where he was briefed by General Middleton. He then set out for St Vith, stopping at Vielsalm to set up his Tactical Command Post, and arriving at General Alan Jones' Headquarters about 4.0 pm. The congestion on the roads caused, as he said, 'by units withdrawing in a state of disorder' made him realize that his tanks would not arrive in St Vith in time to attack before dark. By nightfall traffic jams were so bad that the entire column was brought to a standstill. Only three of 7th Armored Division's units had managed to get into St Vith: a cavalry reconnaissance troop, a company of medium tanks and one of armoured infantry.

The delay meant that the last chance to drive through to the trapped regiments was lost for now the armour would have to try to save St Vith itself. As the units arrived they were fed piecemeal into the defence, one on the right, the next on the left until a cohesive line was built up east and north of the town. All during the night of December 17/18 this thin line was slowly thickened, sometimes only half an hour or so

219

before being hit by a German attack. Somehow St Vith did not fall. Once again the Germans had failed by a matter of hours to seize one of their prime objectives.

Meanwhile the rest of 7th Armored Division slowly closed into the assembly area. Combat Command was sent to Beho well to the south-west of St Vith as divisional reserve while CCR came into Recht, seven miles north-west of St Vith, during Sunday night. CCR's Headquarters had passed through Ligneuville three miles north only a half an hour before that place had fallen to the spearhead of Battlegroup Peiper. 7th Armored Division's Chief of Staff, travelling behind the column, had been attacked and killed by fire from one of the German half-tracks.

The headquarters of Fourteenth Cavalry Group, now commanded by Colonel Damon, had fallen back once more from Recht to Poteaux. About midnight on Sunday General Jones ordered them to halt their retreat and advance again as far as Born, which had been the northern end of the final delaying line. Fourteenth Cavalry's new commander discussed this order with his staff and it was agreed that it was 'impossible to comply for at least twenty-four hours'. A liaison officer was sent to St Vith to explain this decision to General Jones, citing the dispersion of Fourteenth Cavalry Group, its combat losses, the terrific traffic congestion and shortage of ammunition, as reasons. General Jones summoned the officer commanding Fourteenth Cavalry to him. Lieutenant-Colonel Damon went to St Vith leaving command to Lieutenant-Colonel Ridge, CO of the Thirty-second Cavalry Squadron, who was himself relieved by the appearance of the Fourteenth Cavalry's Executive Officer who had been one of the passengers in the ambushed jeep and had made his way back to Recht. This was Lieutenant-Colonel Duggan who ordered two task forces formed and sent one off towards Born.

Meanwhile 7th Armored Division's Combat Command R's headquarters opened in Recht. They had tanks only as their supporting infantry had been diverted to St Vith. Learning that the Germans were in Ligneuville CCR's commanding officer, Lieutenant-Colonel Warren, asked General Jones for a company of infantry to protect his tanks but was told they could not be spared from St Vith. When, at 2 am, the 1st SS Panzers came in from two directions it was soon obvious that the American tanks, without infantry protection, would have to retreat.

They moved in the dark back to Poteaux becoming ensnarled with units of Fourteenth Cavalry Group. The Germans followed up their victory but cautiously because this had been their first brush with American tanks and CCR was able to stop any further German advance.

An hour or so before dawn on Monday the new Fourteenth Cavalry commander sent his task force towards Born as ordered but before they had gone two hundred yards the two leading vehicles were hit and went up in flames. In the light from the burning tank and armoured car German infantry were seen advancing over the snow. A short, fierce fight followed.

Elements of rear headquarters and other troops were still retreating along the Recht–Poteaux–Vielsalm road in confusion. During the short fight between the Fourteenth Cavalry's task force and German soldiers of the 1st Panzer Grenadiers, eight huge 8-inch howitzers were abandoned in perfect working order by their American crews. This was one of several such panic abandoning of guns in the first frightening days of the German attack, actions in almost unbelievable contrast to the magnificent stand of many more American artillery units who manned their guns to the last, often firing over open sights or putting their shells on split-second fuses. The difference sprang from example and leadership; the ferocity and weight of the German attack quickly brought out both the best and the worst of these.

Once more Fourteenth Cavalry pulled back without permission—this time all the way to Petit Thier, only three miles from Vielsalm. General Middleton now relieved Lieutenant-Colonel Duggan of command and the remnants of the tragic Fourteenth Cavalry Group were placed under 7th Armored Division.

On the other side of the St Vith perimeter, where early on Sunday CCB of 9th Armored had crossed the Our to attack towards Winterspelt and aid the 424th Infantry Regiment, the German forces proved too strong as the whole of the 62nd Volksgrenadier Division with supporting self-propelled guns advanced with new determination. During Sunday night both CCB's tanks and its armoured infantry, together with most of 424th Infantry Regiment, managed to get back across the Our although the 424th had to leave most of its equipment behind. These two units now became part of the southern perimeter defence of St Vith. Although 9th Armored's tanks had not been able to force the Germans back and open an escape corridor for the right-hand regiment in the Schnee Eifel as had been intended, their appearance and particularly their artillery

221

support* certainly stopped the Germans from driving into St Vith from the south-east.

But not all the American troops in this area, between the Schnee Eifel and the northern boundary of 28th Infantry Division at Lutzkampen, were able to get back across the Our. Although most of the Bleialf garrison, after that place was lost, succeeded in joining up with the 423rd Infantry, their escape was to be short-lived. South of Bleialf elements of the 81st Engineer Battalion who had fought most valiantly were finally overrun and the troop of reconnaissance cavalry which had earlier been sent from Fourteenth Cavalry Group to work with the right flank of 106th Infantry were isolated. They attempted to get back over the Our but ran into a German column with a Mark IV. Only one armoured car escaped. The rest of the troop destroyed their vehicles and, travelling in small groups, tried to get through into the St Vith lines. About fifty succeeded in doing so.

The Reconnaissance Troop of 106th Division had also been operating in this area. In the confused fighting on Sunday it had been split up and had become separated from 424th Infantry Regiment to which it was attached. Left without orders or information, bewildered by the speed and fury of the German attack and without combat experience, most of the officers and men surrendered on Monday morning without a fight.

By midnight on Sunday nine thousand American troops were inside the German sack. These included not only most of 106th Division's two regiments in the Schnee Eifel, but the best part of two field artillery battalions, a company each of engineers, tank destroyers and medics, an anti-aircraft battery and the two reconnaissance troops.

The Germans manning the walls of this containment were much too thin for the job and a determined attempt to break out would almost certainly have succeeded although probably not without heavy casualties. But the trapped units had little contact with each other, knew nothing of the German strength and had not been ordered to attack. On the contrary both regimental commanders were assured that a strong force from St Vith would break through to them and that they would be supplied from the air. Consequently Sunday night was spent creating their own perimeter defence and waiting for the relief. With every hour that passed their situation worsened.

At two o'clock in the morning of Monday, December 18,

* One battery of 8-inch howitzers fired 108 tons of shells in 30 hours.

222

General Jones finally sent definite orders to his two regiments to come out of the Schnee Eifel and attack the flank of the German advance towards St Vith from Schönberg—the old plan, in fact, which had been arranged for the 2nd Infantry Division in the event of a German attack through the Losheim Gap.

At the same time the trapped regiments were promised an air drop of much needed ammunition, water and food and told that there would be an armoured attack from St Vith against the front of the German thrust at the same time as they hit the flanks.

There was no sign of the promised air drop. Forty planes had been loaded up in England during the early hours of Monday morning and flown to Florennes in Belgium where the pilots expected to pick up their fighter escort, their map coordinates, and to be briefed. None of these things awaited them; instead they were diverted to an airfield in France but apparently no one there knew anything about the operation. The loaded aircraft stood by ready to take off for the next five days before the mission was cancelled.

In the Schnee Eifel the two regimental commanders decided to start their breakout at 10.0 am on Monday. Excess equipment and field kitchens were destroyed, the wounded were left in the collecting stations with medical aid men to look after them until the Germans arrived and the able-bodied formed up and started forward, regiments abreast and in columns of battalions. The only contact between the two regiments was by patrols which is most unsatisfactory when moving across country towards unknown enemy positions and it is not surprising that soon after moving off there was little or no communication between them.

The 422nd fired off their last smoke shells into Auw to cover their move, spiked their guns and advanced in two columns trying to navigate by the map. They encountered few Germans but got hopelessly lost, finishing up at dusk a mile and a half from where they thought they were which meant that their planned attack for the next morning would end in confusion.

Their sister regiment started off down a minor road leading west from the slopes of the Schnee Eifel and after about an hour and a half its Second Battalion encountered the Germans along the Bleialf to Schönberg road. With the help of mortar fire from their heavy weapons company they forced the Germans to give ground but the Second Battalion alone were not strong enough to carry the attack right into German-held territory and sent an urgent plea for help. The Third Battalion were ordered to move up to them but once more communications failed. The American attack slowed and the German resistance stiffened. At the same time new orders came from General Jones—the relief armoured attack had been called off and now the two regiments were to move to Schönberg. About dusk the First Battalion got up to the Second but the respite had given the Germans the opportunity to secure their defences and to bring up their artillery.

On Tuesday morning the 422nd Infantry Regiment moved out of their woods three battalions abreast believing they were about two thousand yards from Schönberg. They reached the Bleialf–Auw road and came under heavy tank and machine-gun fire. In the resulting confusion the troops on the left spotted men moving towards them and opened fire. They were the right wing of the 423rd Infantry who immediately fired back.

The explanation was that the 423rd had been heavily shelled about 9.0 on Tuesday morning and in trying to get away their 2nd Battalion had got separated and wandered over into 422nd Infantry's sector. The Third Battalion managed to get to the outskirts of Schönberg but there were stopped by anti-aircraft fire.

The *coup de grâce* to the 422nd Infantry was delivered by the tanks of the Fuehrer Begleit Brigade who accidentally came on the scene on their way to support the attack against St Vith. They rolled through the American infantry who were without anti-tank weapons or ammunition for their bazookas. At the same time the volksgrenadiers attacked from both sides. At 2.30 pm discussions with the German commander started and at 4.0 all the 422nd Infantry surrendered except some four hundred who were organized by the Second Battalion executive officer and who held out until Thursday morning. Only about one hundred and fifty men of the 422nd Infantry succeeded in regaining the American lines.

The 423rd Infantry, who had suffered many more casualties than the 422nd, losing some three hundred men, were broken up by the shelling and became disorganized. Ammunition had almost run out and there were no supporting weapons. This regiment too surrendered about 4.30 pm on Tuesday.

At 106 Division Headquarters news was anxiously awaited of the movement of their two regiments, thought to be attacking towards Schönberg. The last message from these regiments, which merely acknowledged the change of orders, was despatched on Monday afternoon but not received in St Vith until Tuesday morning. After that there was silence and as the

Germans kept streaming in from the east it was thought that the entire force of Americans forward of the Our had been overwhelmed and had gone down fighting.

In fact American casualties were slight—on Sunday night for example the 422nd reported only forty wounded for evacuation—at least up until the last day when the 423rd were hit hard by the German artillery. Both regiments also suffered casualties when they fired on each other but at least ninety per cent of their strength were captured unhurt.

The Germans surrounding them, actually ringing the pocket as opposed to those attacking westwards, were comparatively few: three or four thousand volksgrenadiers (including the two hundred or so in front of the Schnee Eifel who had advanced over the hills) and about another thousand fresh troops. The soldiers manning this thin wall expected an American breakout attempt during Sunday night but to their surprise no move was made. The inertia of the large body of well-trained, well-equipped American infantry for over two days puzzled the Germans but the final result was a tremendous boost to their morale and, of course, a serious blow to Allied prestige.

At least eight thousand and perhaps as many as nine thousand American soldiers started the long march from the Eifel to prisoner of war camps in Germany. For most of these very young infantrymen as yet unused to hardship, it was the end of two weeks of hell starting on a crowded troopship tossing about in the English Channel for days, then the long, cold wet journey across France and Belgium and, before they had time to recover and find their feet, the short, bewildering battle in which nothing they had been told would happen in action did. Lastly, to their stunned surprise, came the humiliating surrender.

There have been many long and searching post mortems on this severest of all American defeats in Europe but when all is said and done certain factors stand out. One that should not be forgotten is the part that cruel bad luck played in the time of the attack. The Germans did not choose to try and entrap a green division, newly-arrived, under-armed, with little ammunition and suffering badly from trench-foot and the cold. They planned to outflank the experienced 2nd Infantry Division in the Schnee Eifel and if their attack had started on the date assigned they would have attempted to do so with, it is practically certain, very different results. If, on the other hand, the German attack had come a week or two later, again the result might have been different. But these are among the many imponderables of the Ardennes Offensive and as always, it is fruitless to pursue them.

The fact remains that the 106th Division were caught completely unprepared, that the reaction of divisional headquarters staff was slow and lacking in aggression as well as inefficient. A kind of hypnotized paralysis seeped down from top to bottom of the command; of all the possible reactions to attack the worst is to do nothing. Except for the 423rd Infantry Regiment's right-hand battalion, who fought extremely well in the Bleialf area on the first morning, the two regiments holding the important Schnee Eifel positions simply failed to react to an all-out German assault on their flanks.

The panic withdrawal of some of the divisional headquarters staff and other rear-area troops is a black mark on America's proud military record although it is in part lessened by the magnificent stand of the divisions on either side of the 106th Infantry as well as the stout defence put up by its own 424th Infantry Regiment. This regiment must, of course, have been trained and equipped and made up of very much the same kind of men as the other two which indicated that in different circumstances they too would have given as good an account of themselves.

A unit's morale is built up from practical considerations such as weapons, ammunition, food, troop dispositions and the lie of the land and by variable factors like the balance of forces, the weather and the deterioration of efficiency due to exhaustion. But there are other things, equally important but not easily measured, which can affect morale—letters from home, stories in local newspapers, the responsibilities of friendships started in training and forged in action and that pride which is known as *ésprit de corps*. But the solid base on which this complicated structure stands is confidence, of which the most important is confidence in leadership at all levels. Lacking this, the best equipped unit will crumble when hit hard; possessing it, outnumbered troops have often upset the mathematics of war.

16

TWENTY-FIVE MILES IN TWO DAYS

A tactical success is only really decisive if it is gained at the strategically correct spot.

VON MOLTKE

By midday on Sunday, December 17, the artillery trains and Combat Command R of the US 7th Armored Division were on their way from Eupen to the divisional assembly area around St Vith, moving south along a route which should have been well behind the fighting. But at the same time Battlegroup Peiper's spearhead was moving west from Moderscheid towards Stavelot: the two columns were bound to cross.

The point at which this would happen was a crossroads just south of Malmédy. CCR's tanks got there first and lumbered on towards Ligneuville; fifteen minutes after the last American tank had disappeared over the rise the first of Peiper's armoured vehicles passed just east of these crossroads. 7th Armored Division's artillery trains should have been passing then for their convoy position was immediately behind the tanks but the long column had become strung out and a few trucks had taken advantage of the gap to squeeze into the armoured division's column. These contained some 125 men of Battery B of the 285th Field Artillery Observation Battalion, a name which would soon be known to almost every American fighting in the Ardennes.

The machine-guns in Peiper's half-tracks raked the trucks and the surprised Americans leapt out and flung themselves into the ditches. They were quickly rounded up, disarmed and told to wait in a field by the side of the road until German troops following up could take charge of them. Battlegroup Peiper's spearhead then moved on towards Ligneuville.

The captured Americans waited quietly, watching the half-tracks, motor-cycles, tanks and self-propelled guns stream towards the west. From time to time the column stopped and Americans and Germans stared at each other. After some two hours someone in a half-track fired his pistol almost casually into the mass of American prisoners.

'Stand fast!' an American officer shouted, 'Don't run ...'

But almost immediately another pistol fired and then automatic weapons were directed into the group of bewildered and defenceless men. Soon there was only a mass of bodies, some writhing in pain, others still. The wounded who tried to crawl away were shot through the head. At least 86 of the prisoners were killed, but some survived by feigning death and later escaped to testify, after the war, against the perpetrators of the Malmédy massacre.

In the hilly Ardennes the Germans, like the Americans, suffered from faulty radio communication and the difficulty which the rear commanders of the larger formations had in keeping contact with their forward elements often affected the course of the battle. By the time Peiper's point reached Ligneuville he, a mile or so behind, was already out of touch with Sixth SS Panzer Army's battle headquarters and even his own divisional control. Before the offensive Hitler had required his commanders to swear that they would not trespass on to the territory of the neighbouring units for which he had even prescribed the death penalty but Peiper had already done so in seizing the fuel dump at Bullingen* and would not hesitate to do so again if he thought he could reach the Meuse more quickly.

Such a decision had to be taken at Ligneuville from where the main road goes five miles north to Malmédy and then on a good hard surface another thirty-five miles north-west through Spa to the Meuse crossings near Liège. This route belonged to Hitler Jugend Division; Peiper had been assigned to narrow secondary roads for the next fifty miles to the Meuse crossing at Huy. The shorter, easier route through Malmédy was very tempting and if Peiper could have got through to I SS Panzer Corps HQ he would probably have been switched to it. But he was unable to make radio contact.

He had to guess how far Hitler Jugend had progressed. He was certain that they were not level with him, but he thought they could not be far behind, whereas, as we know, they had still not been able to break through the Rocherath–Krinkelt position more than ten miles behind his point. Without this knowledge Peiper did not dare cut in front of his running-mate; reluctantly he turned away from Malmédy and directed his spearhead on to the secondary road leading to Stavelot.

Malmédy, a prize of great tactical importance, was at that moment practically defenceless as a disorganized crowd of headquarters, supply, service and other rear-area troops, panicked

---

* Peiper's excuse for heading north from Honsfeld was that his assigned road was narrow and almost impassable but he admits that his real reason was to seize the fuel which made his dramatic advance possible.

by stories of a German attack in overwhelming strength, by rumours of paratroopers all around them and by the sight of others fleeing, trod on each other's heels in their anxiety to get to the rear. Peiper's decision was critical; had he taken the easier route he would have seized Malmédy and the two huge fuel dumps around Francorchamps, thus changing his whole offensive. But Sixth SS Panzer Army's HQ, whose knowledge of his whereabouts was obtained by listening in to the American radio which obligingly broadcast precise details in clear, could not make contact with him, and Malmédy was saved—at least for the time being.

Peiper's route led through Ligneuville's narrow streets and then almost due west for nearly eight miles to Stavelot and a narrow bridge over the Amblève. Then, because a one-thousand-five-hundred-foot-high ridge rises steeply west of Stavelot, his armour would have to follow the river winding nearly four miles south-west to Trois Ponts. Here they could get across the Salm and on to the main road leading west to Werbomont, Hamoir, across the Ourthe river and finally to their objective at Huy.

After an interval to eat the hot lunch which the Americans he had surprised had just prepared and to allow his fifteen-mile long tail to compress, Peiper ordered his spearhead to resume the advance. It was difficult for the panzer column to move quickly through the narrow, winding streets of Ligneuville and when the point did get through and come out into the open at the western edge it presented a fine target to a couple of Sherman tanks accompanying the rear elements of 9th Armoured Division's CCB hurrying to join in the fighting near Steinebruck. The Shermans quickly knocked out the two decoy half-tracks, a scout car and the leading Panther. Peiper dealt with the surprise quickly and efficiently, destroying both Shermans and taking prisoners, but his advance had been delayed for an hour and, even more important, this was the first real resistance his Battlegroup had encountered and it cooled the enthusiasm of some of the leading panzer crews.

The delay meant that the German advance guard got to the high ground overlooking the Amblève bridge at Stavelot just as the short December day was ending. The narrow fast running river could be crossed by suitably equipped infantry but in order to get the tanks and other vehicles across, the bridge had to be captured intact.

Most of Stavelot lies on the north bank of the Amblève and, looking across, the Germans saw the roads packed with American vehicles and jumped to the conclusion that they had at last reached a heavily defended position. In fact the only combat troops in Stavelot were a single battalion of engineers hastily constructing a road block; there were no American tanks or anti-tank guns at all. The vehicles were trucks trying to evacuate the enormous fuel dumps a few miles north and some of US 7th Armored Division's transport moving south. The bridge was not mined, the roadblock not yet complete; Stavelot would have fallen to one determined thrust.

What happened next is something of a mystery even today. Three panzers in staggered line came fast down the road to the bridge, all guns firing. When the leading tank hit one of the few mines which had just been laid and threw a track, the other two pulled back. The commanders of the spearhead talked things over; they had, after all, been on the move for thirty-six hours and may well have decided that they had pushed their luck far enough. A report went back to Peiper that Stavelot was 'very heavily defended and could not be taken without infantry support'.

Uncharacteristically Peiper did not come up to the point to see for himself but consented to a halt. After the war he said that he did so because he now considered that having made contact with American armour he needed his Tiger tanks and armoured infantry, who were far behind. Whatever the reason the stopping of 1st SS Division's only really successful thrust at Stavelot over forty road miles short of the Meuse on the second night of the battle was the turning point in Sixth SS Panzer Army's offensive, for the Germans could not afford to pause to allow the Americans time to use their mobility.

During the night of December 17/18 a battalion of Tiger tanks and the panzer grenadiers got up to the spearhead and Peiper planned a pre-dawn assault to seize the Stavelot bridge. In the small hours of Monday morning an American armoured infantry battalion, which had come into Malmédy, sent a company to Stavelot. Two platoons of infantry and two tanks destroyers crossed the bridge to cover the minefield at the southern approach but were hit by the German attack before they could get into position. The American anti-tank guns were captured and the armoured infantry driven back across the bridge which, for some reason, was not blown. A Panther dashed across just before dawn turning the odds in favour of the attackers. Soon German tanks followed and spread throughout the town's streets forcing the American infantry towards the high ground north.

Most fell back towards Malmédy but in the confusion one platoon became separated and was pursued by panzers along a narrow road going north towards Francorchamps. When the retreating Americans reached the million-gallon fuel dump guarded by Belgian soldiers,* their commander ordered barrels to be poured out on the road where the petrol ran down through a deep cut. This river was then set alight and the blaze, which was kept stoked with 124,000 gallons, made an impassable tank barrier. The pursuing panzers went back and Peiper's Battlegroup turned south for their next objective, the bridges over the Salm and the Amblève at Trois Ponts. This was the key to the march to the Meuse for as Peiper later said, 'Once we had secured the bridge at Trois Ponts and captured fuel, it would have been a simple matter to drive on to the Meuse that same day.'

Like Malmédy and Stavelot, Trois Ponts had been ready for the taking the night before and even now, on the third day, there was only a single company of combat engineers there to defend it. This was Company C of the ubiquitous 51st Engineer Combat Battalion who had been quietly cutting up trees in the forest nearby to supply timbers for bridges and logs for dug-out roofs. On the second day of the offensive orders came for them to move to Trois Ponts and construct roadblocks covering the approaches from the East. This was to be the northern end of a 16-mile long Salm river defence line that was being hurriedly constructed from Trois Ponts south through Viel-salm to Bovigny.

The 140 combat engineers got to Trois Ponts about midnight on Sunday and were put into position at roadblocks covering the Amblève bridge where the road from Stavelot passes under the railway. Except for ten machine-guns and eight bazookas the engineers were armed only with rifles. Their commanding officer, Major Yates, didn't relish trying to stop a German panzer column with just these weapons so when a 57-mm anti-tank gun and crew, which had become detached from its unit in the fighting around Stavelot, wandered into their area he commandeered them and placed the gun out along the Stavelot road, just past the highway underpass, to cover a mined section of the road.

The 57-mm anti-tank gun was quite useless against the frontal armour of a German tank as the crew well knew but nevertheless when they saw a German armoured column approaching they held their fire until the leading half-tracks were almost on top of them and then stopped the following Panther by breaking its track. Although all four of this deter-

* By the Third Company of the 5th Fusilier Battalion commanded by Captain B. E. M. Burniat.

mined crew were killed in the hail of fire that immediately poured down on them the noise alerted the combat engineers behind and Trois Ponts' three bridges were blown. Peiper had been denied his badly-needed way out of the valley of the Amblève.

All he could do now was to continue following the river as it wound north-west for nearly five miles to the small towns of La Gleize and Stoumont.

Using up their fast-diminishing fuel at a critical rate the long column of tanks, self-propelled guns, armoured infantry carriers and mobile anti-aircraft guns struggled around the sharp curves and reached La Gleize without meeting any opposition. There were only a couple of hours of daylight left and the column was still on the wrong side of the Amblève. From time to time one of the tiny American army liaison aeroplanes would scoot out of the low cloud, have a look at the German column snaking westwards and then get quickly back into the cloud out of sight. The next small town west, Stoumont, three miles from La Gleize, if not yet defended, was an obvious choice for an American stand so Peiper was delighted when one of his forward reconnaissance teams reported that they had found an intact bridge over the Amblève at the village of Cheneux a mile south of the La Gleize–Stoumont road. From here it would be possible to bypass Stoumont and move across country through tiny villages to regain the assigned route at Werbomont. Encouraged by this evidence that his well-known luck had not deserted him Peiper swung his Battlegroup south and urged the point forward—it might still be possible to reach the Meuse that night.

Up until then Hitler's promised 'no-flying weather' had held, but on Monday afternoon the visibility improved for an hour or two and the American Air Force got some of their waiting four thousand aircraft into the air. One flight of fighter-bombers spotted Peiper's point and attacked: ten of the leading vehicles including three tanks were knocked out blocking the narrow road completely. Minutes later a bridge over a narrow deep stream a half mile ahead of the panzer column was blown and once more Battlegroup Peiper was brought to a halt. There was no choice but to go back over the 'lucky' bridge and regain the road to Stoumont on the wrong side of the Amblève. This time his reconnaissance reported that Stoumont was strongly held; the unsuccessful detour meant that he would now have to fight for it.

His armoured infantry, the 2nd Panzer Grenadier Regiment,

whose half-tracks were able to continue past the blown bridge which had halted the panzers, pressed on through the dark, hoping to get on to a road just ahead which would lead them to Werbomont where they would wait for the Panthers and Tigers to join them after seizing Stoumont. But Peiper's luck was running out for this column stumbled on to a roadblock. Forty yards from a waiting American tank destroyer the leading panzer grenadier's half-track switched on its running lights to negotiate a sharp bend. Three half-tracks were blown to pieces and three others abandoned and the surviving armoured infantry pulled back to Cheneux to form a flank defence position.

The American troops who had stopped the 2nd Panzer Grenadiers from getting to Werbomont and the ones who were now hurriedly preparing to defend Stoumont were from one of the regiments of the US 30th Infantry Division coming into the Ardennes fighting at the end of a long move from General Simpson's Ninth Army in the north.

Hitler and the German High Command had banked upon there being considerable delay in moving reinforcements into First Army's sector from the armies on either side because of the well-known independence of American army commanders. What they did not allow for was the informality which accompanied this independence which could, when necessary, eliminate 'channels' in a way which was unknown to the Wehrmacht.

Patton, Hodges and Simpson, the three commanders concerned, had been in the same class at West Point. Patton and Hodges had both failed as plebes in 1905, and Simpson had finished low in his class; Hodges had then enlisted as a private while Patton and Simpson had persevered at the Point and had passed out as officers in 1909. All three had fought in France in World War I and had been close friends ever since. Therefore, when Hodges picked up his telephone on the first day of the German attack against his thin front and asked 'Big Simp' for help the response had been immediate and generous. As well as the 7th Armored Division, which SHAEF had already ordered south, General Simpson offered to send his 5th Armored and 30th Infantry Divisions to General Hodges without delay. And, as we shall see, as soon as he was convinced that the threat to Hodges' army was a real one General Patton too was unstinting in his help.

The rapidity with which First Army was reinforced was one of the major reasons for the failure of the last German blitzkrieg.

On Sunday, December 17, the most imperilled part of First Army's front seemed to be the heavy infantry and tank onslaught against V Corps which looked as though it were about to break through 99th Infantry Division's extended front and so cut off the salient created by 2nd Infantry Division's advance to the Wahlerscheid crossroads. To counter this, 30th Infantry were ordered to move to the Eupen area to prepare for a counter-attack from the north against the German flank. Peiper's breakthrough between V Corps and VIII Corps changed everything, but by that time most of 30th Infantry were on the road.

After training for over four years 30th Infantry, a National Guard Division, had landed in Normandy about a week after D-day. In the intervening six months they had taken part in much hard fighting, suffered heavy casualties and had become a tough, efficient, force with a reputation second to none. One of their bitterest experiences occurred in July when on two consecutive days the American Air Force bombed them by mistake inflicting 876 casualties of which 86 were killed. From that time there was a deep distrust of the Air Force in this division, a distrust which, unhappily, was to be reinforced again in the Ardennes.

When the Ardennes Offensive opened two of 30th Division's regiments were resting and the third was in a quiet part of the line north of Aachen. No one took a great deal of notice of reports of a German counter-attack to the south; most of the officers and men were concerned with preparations for Christmas and the chances of leave—the commanding officer of the 117th Infantry Regiment left for seven days leave in London on Saturday afternoon and Major-General Leland Hobbs, the divisional commander, had a plane laid on for ten o'clock the next morning to take him to London for a short leave.

On that Saturday night parties of men from the resting regiments were driven to the rear for a few hours relaxation and some of them saw a film, *Dragon Seed*, and jokes were made about the addition to the sound effects the Luftwaffe were making. Driving back to their units later that night they noticed many more rockets going over their heads* than had been usual and early the next morning, Sunday, there was a paratroop scare caused by some of Colonel von der Heydte's scattered force coming down thirty miles north of their drop zone, but these were the only signs of the big German counter-

* These were landing in Liège and Antwerp.

offensive to the south.

About 11.15 that morning General Hobbs got a call from the Chief of Staff at XIX Corps. It didn't seem to be particularly urgent: 'You're being taken away from us ... I don't know any details except that you're going south and it will only be a temporary move—about ten days. I guess you'd better pack up and get ready to move as soon as you can.'

The 30th prided themselves on moving fast and the first Regimental Combat Team were heading south by 4.30 pm on Sunday. This was from the 119th Infantry Regiment and it was followed by one from the 117th (led by the regiment's commanding officer who had not got far on his leave) and the regiment who were in the line, the 120th, who handed over their positions and moved off last.

By midnight the combat part of the division was on the road in battle order 'prepared to fight'. A reconnaissance troop led followed by a regimental combat team, then tanks and tank destroyers, a second regimental combat team, the rest of the division's tanks and tank destroyers and last, the third regimental combat team—in all a very considerable force.

Most of the men had no idea where they were going until they were told by their favourite German radio commentator, 'Axis Sal' that 'Roosevelt's fanatical 30th Infantry Division were being rushed south to try and save the US First Army.'

During the night more news came in to First Army that Peiper's spearhead, having broken through the American main line of resistance, had reached Stavelot and General Hodges decided to use 30th Infantry Division to bridge the widening split between V Corps and VIII Corps. He ordered General Hobbs to divert his leading regimental combat team to Malmédy and Stavelot and 'seize and defend' both.

By the time the change of orders reached 30th Infantry the 119th had bedded down for the night and so the next, the 117th Regimental Combat Team, was re-routed through Eupen to Spa. At this last place the roads to the west were jammed with vehicles full of headquarters troops—many driving with blazing headlights.

It was rumoured that Malmédy had already fallen but although it had been abandoned precipitately by almost all the soldiers stationed there the only Germans who had been near it were some of Colonel von der Heydte's paratroops on reconnaissance who had reported back to him that the town was practically undefended. First Army had scraped up a small force on Sunday and sent them to Malmédy as a stopgap and it was a company from this battalion who had tried to oppose Peiper's crossing of the Amblève and later created the blazing roadblock, but they were too few to defend Malmédy.

The American soldiers who came into Spa and Malmédy after they had been abandoned found not only personal effects but maps, secret documents and supplies of all kinds including revolvers and other weapons lying about. The effect on the stunned and frightened Belgian civilians of this panic withdrawal was to add private cars and farm wagons to the traffic jams. The crowded roads and many abandoned vehicles made it very difficult for 30th Division's Regimental Combat Team to move up towards the front and it was not until 9.0 am the next morning, Monday, after about fourteen hours on the road, that the 117th Infantry arrived in Malmédy.

It is not often that ordinary riflemen get an opportunity to share the luxuries of rear area headquarters. There were large supplies of these in Malmédy and even more in Spa where First Army Headquarters had made themselves very comfortable. For days some of 30th Division's soldiers lived on prime steak and other delicacies. In Malmédy a large quantity of medical alcohol was found and an interesting and powerful drink concocted by mixing it with snow flavoured with vanilla essence.

One battalion stayed in Malmédy, a second went off to Stavelot and the third were deployed to hold the ridge line between these places. The supporting artillery battalion hurried up moving their guns and howitzers into support positions.

The battalion sent to Stavelot reached the fuel dump and the still blazing roadblock. Here they detrucked, made contact with the defenders and moved off towards the town. Peiper had left a small covering force of armour and infantry to hold Stavelot until the 3rd Parachute Division came up.

With the help of a platoon of towed tank destroyers on the north slope the 30th Infantry men were able to push the Germans back, knocking out two panzers and a number of half-tracks and advancing up to the houses at the northern edge.

The outnumbered Germans fell back to the square and their commander sent a hurried call to Trois Ponts for assistance. Ten panzers at the back of Peiper's column were turned around and came racing back to Stavelot to deal with the American attack.

The odds were now in the German's favour and things might have gone very badly with the men from 30th Infantry here if the arrival of the German tanks had not coincided with one of the brief spells of good flying weather. At about 4.0 pm on Monday the German tank commanders spotted the dreaded 'Jabos'* swooping down on them and scattered for cover. The American infantry resumed their attack and by dark held half the town. By nightfall a platoon of 117th Infantry's supporting tanks had come up and the artillery were in position to bring heavy fire down on Stavelot.

With the setting up of 30th Division's Forward Command Post at Francorchamps the important Malmédy–Stavelot–Francorchamps line was now strongly held and 117th Infantry were ready to go over to the offensive. If Stavelot could be wrested from the Germans and its single bridge either held or destroyed then Peiper's line of communication would be cut and his Battle Group isolated.

The 120th Infantry Regiment, which had been struggling to move down chewed-up muddy roads jammed with retreating rear-area troops and refugees, came in on the left of the division's lines late on Monday, December 19, thus enabling the Third Battalion from 117th Infantry to leave Malmédy and join the force preparing to recapture Stavelot.

The third infantry regiment, the 119th, which had already stopped on Sunday night near Eupen before the change of sector, were delayed for most of Monday by conflicting orders. Army and Corps often issued orders independently of each other in the chaotic early days of the German attack. Finally, 30th Division's commander, General Hobbs, had to insist that he be given orders from one source. About midday on Monday First Army HQ ordered him to move his third regimental combat team back to the west and swing them in a semi-circle around Spa. He himself was summoned to a conference at which the rôle of his division would be made clear, including further orders for this team; before leaving General Hobbs arranged a rendezvous with 119th's commander five miles north of Spa for later that afternoon.

Among all the bad news that kept pouring into First Army's Headquarters the most serious situations on Monday afternoon were the threat to Bastogne from XLVII Panzer Corps, whose leading panzers had just overrun 9th Armoured Division's roadblock, and I SS Panzer Corps' breakthrough along the inter-corps boundary spotlighted by Battlegroup Peiper driving towards Stoumont. The full significance of the attack towards St Vith and the fate of 106 Division's two regiments in

* Jagdbomber—the fighter-bombers which had destroyed so much German armour in the retreat across France.

the Schnee Eifel was not yet realized at First Army.

When considering the counter moves that were taken at this time it must be remembered that the Americans did not know the German objectives: At SHAEF it was still thought that the German attack might be nothing more than an effort to pull forces away from the Allied offensives then being planned to go in north and south of the Ardennes. It was not for another twenty-four hours that the scope of the offensive began to be appreciated at SHAEF and General Eisenhower abandoned his earlier plan of replying to the Ardennes Offensive with immediate counter-attacks by 21st Army Group in the north and 6th Army Group in the south.

At First Army Headquarters the concern was naturally with their own front. The assumption was that the Germans were after Liège—at least that those in the north from Sixth SS Panzer Army were. If this were so then Peiper would strike north-west from Stoumont and lead 1st SS Panzer Division along the valley of the Amblève to Remouchamps and Aywaillie. From here the panzer column would get on to the main north–south highway which came up from France through Bastogne to Liège, thus cutting First Army in two.

On the other hand if Peiper was not after Liège but aiming at maximum penetration then he could turn south after Stoumont and strike for Werbomont from where a good road ran west. (This was, in fact, his plan.)

To counter either of these possibilities General Hodges decided to divert one of the two airborne divisions, which were hurrying to his aid from Reims, to Werbomont to block Peiper, if he came that way and to be in a position to attack the left flank of the panzer advance if it went for Liège.

But the 82nd Airborne Division had not been able to leave Reims until Monday morning and could not possibly get to Werbomont in strength until the next day. A stopgap would have to be found and it could only come from 30th Division's 119th Regimental Combat Team.

General Hobbs was ordered to despatch this to Remouchamps: there one battalion of infantry with a company of anti-tank guns would split away from the main force and move south to Werbomont to hold Peiper's advance, if it came that way, until relieved by 82nd Airborne's paratroopers. The rest of the Regimental Combat Team would move south from Remouchamps and engage Peiper at Stoumont.

The 30th Infantry Division commander took these orders to his rendezvous with the commander of his 119th Regiment and the smaller force hurried off to Werbomont and there set up the roadblock which, as we have seen, successfully smashed the advance of 2nd Panzer Grenadiers' half-tracks on Monday night.

The main force of the 119th Regimental Combat Team came into the Stoumont area after dark. A perimeter defence north, east and south of Stoumont was formed with one battalion of infantry in foxholes supported by a few guns: three 57-mm anti-tank guns, useless against Panthers or Tigers, eight 3-inch tank destroyers which, not being self-propelled, had to be towed into position and would not be able to move once the attack started and two 90-mm anti-aircraft guns which, though not designed for it, could be used against tanks. Patrols were then sent forward to get an estimate of the strength of the coming German attack.

Pleased with their comparatively light casualties for an advance of some forty miles the German tanks crews, gunners, armoured infantry and the company from 3rd Parachute Division who had been picked up at Honsfeld, took no trouble to conceal their presence at La Gleize. They talked loudly, laughed and even sang songs, completely disregarding the presence of the American defence building up at Stoumont. Because of the security carelessness of the cock-a-hoop Battlegroup and the noise they were making the American patrols were able to get close enough to count over thirty tanks: Mk IV's, Panthers and Tigers. When the strength of the German force was reported to 119th Regiment's commanding officer who was with the main force three miles north-west of Stoumont he ordered ten Shermans from his supporting tank company to advance at dawn on Tuesday and reinforce the defence line on the eastern edge of Stoumont. A battalion of field artillery was also ordered to move up in direct support of the defenders of Stoumont.

Peiper had been out of touch with his own headquarters all day but some time during the Monday evening a powerful Luftwaffe radio set was got up to him and he learned that strong American forces were already moving down from the north against his flank. Strangely, he was not told that 12th SS Panzer, Hitler Jugend, were still being held almost at their start line thus leaving his long right flank uncovered nor the even more vital information that the rest of 3rd Parachute Division had not secured Stavelot and the important Amblève bridge behind him but had been diverted to a blocking position near Waimes ten miles further back.

On both sides the soldiers ate their rations, checked their weapons and ammunition and then tried to get a few hours' sleep in the bitter cold before the dawn brought what they well knew was going to be a bloody battle.

THE SHOULDERS HOLD

> *Natural hazards, however formidable, are inherently less dangerous and less uncertain than fighting hazards. All conditions are more calculable, all obstacles more surmountable, than those of human resistance.*
>
> SIR BASIL LIDDELL HART

The 12th SS Panzer Division, 'Hitler Jugend', fully equipped with new tanks, started the Ardennes Offensive, in which they had been awarded one of the star rôles, confident that as soon as their supporting infantry, the 277th Volksgrenadier Division, had steam-rollered a path through the single American infantry regiment in front of them, their panzers would advance to the Meuse by the end of the second day at the latest. The Volksgrenadiers, re-formed from one of the infantry divisions smashed in the Falaise Gap, were also confident that they could capture the twin villages of Rocherath and Krinkelt, key to the road network, within hours of starting their assault.

In fact by the end of three days' bitter fighting the Americans still held the villages, blocking the way west. The volksgrenadiers supported by the panzers had advanced only a few miles from their start line. The failure was not due to lack of courage or effort for both these tough, determined divisions smashed themselves to pieces in repeated attacks against heavy American fire.

The tremendous shelling* they met surprised them no less than the tough, skilful fighting of the 99th Infantry Division, who, they had been assured, were green troops. German Intelligence, usually most reliable, had failed to follow 2nd Infantry Division's move from the Schnee Eifel positions through to the attack on the Wahlerscheid crossroads but had reported that this veteran division was in reserve at Camp Elsenborn. Sixth SS Panzer Army's planning staff assumed that it was the 99th Infantry who were attacking at Wahlerscheid and so greatly underestimated the numbers of that division left to hold the vital Rocherath–Krinkelt road complex.

* On Monday, December 18, *one* battalion of field artillery on the Elsenborn Ridge fired more than five thousand rounds.

When, after a whole day's heavy fighting the volksgrenadiers finally reached the two villages they were not pleased to encounter soldiers of the 2nd Infantry Division* dug in there as well as many more of the 99th whom they had been fighting since dawn.

As soon as 2nd Infantry's commander, General Roberts, got permission to break off the attack against the Wahlerscheid crossroads he started to peel off the five battalions committed there. The first of these began to come back about 9.30 on Sunday morning and set up a rearguard north of Rocherath through which, all day long, the rest of the division at Wahlerscheid pulled back. Two battalions moved to a line in front of Wirtzfeld to cover the general withdrawal of the 99th Infantry Division and its artillery to the Elsenborn Ridge: the other two built up a defence east and south of Rockerath–Krinkelt. It was these who stopped the reinforced volksgrenadier attack late on Sunday.

But this complicated withdrawal under fire through a crumbling front was not so simple as it may sound. Sometimes 2nd Division men withdrew through 99th's positions which then quickly came under heavy attack which forced them back on top of the withdrawing troops. Not surprisingly many things went wrong; orders were misunderstood and each command was apt to blame the other. In the tangled fighting it was often difficult to distinguish between friend and foe; sometimes Americans shot at each other while more than once the German tanks opened fire on their own men.

The fourth of 2nd Division's battalions to come back from the Wahlerscheid crossroads were unlucky; before they could dig in they were hit by a mixed group of panzer grenadiers and Hitler Jugend tanks. The battalion lost most of two companies.

In the 'wild night of fighting' which followed men were captured, released and recaptured; positions were overrun and retaken; the artillery sometimes shelled their own troops, for, as companies got split up, it became difficult to know who was on either side. One bold German—perhaps one of Skorzeny's men—shoved a pistol in an American soldier's back and forcing him to give the password, got past two outposts. The third sentry spotted the deception and killed both men with a burst from his automatic rifle. At another place a small party of Americans suddenly found themselves surrounded by advancing volksgrenadiers. Quickly one of the Americans, who spoke German, shouted that they were German commandos in disguise and demanded to be let through to the American lines.

* From the reserve battalion moved from Elsenborn.

Then, without waiting for a reply they dashed forward and escaped.

Although many times it seemed as though the Germans would seize Rocherath–Krinkelt in the confused fighting in the dark—one battalion commander reported that he had men from sixteen different companies fighting under his command —when Monday's dawn came the twin villages, key to any advance west from this sector, were still in American hands. The attackers had inflicted severe casualties, especially on the forward companies of the 99th Division, but they had also been weakened by most serious losses and had to be reinforced during Sunday night, December 17/18. Hitler Jugend Division impatient at not being able to get on to their roads west, had recklessly pushed their tanks forward only to be stopped by bazooka, anti-tank and artillery fire. After forty-eight hours of continual assault the attack had still not succeeded in getting rolling but 1 SS Panzer Corps, at last realizing the American strength here, brought up more forces, determined to smash through the hard crust of defence on the third day, Monday, December 18.

Their final strength for this assault were three battalions of volksgrenadiers, a regiment of panzer grenadiers, a battalion of assault guns and a battalion of tanks with a second tank battalion moving slowly up through the deep mud of the churned-up minor roads to exploit the expected breakthrough.

But the Americans also built up their strength during Sunday night, bringing in 2nd Infantry Division's reserve battalion to positions east and south of Krinkelt. This made a total of nearly four battalions defending the twin villages. The American infantry were supported by a battalion of tanks, about a battalion and a half of tank destroyers and, most important of all, the very heavy artillery concentration along the Elsenborn Ridge. Other 2nd and 99th Infantry covered the flanks and the approach to Wirtzfeld; further back the 26th Infantry Regiment from First Infantry Division had dug in along the ridge from Dom Butgenbach thus sealing the southern edge of the gap which Battlegroup Peiper had ripped open.

Despite this increased strength no one thought it was going to be easy to stop the full power of 1 SS Panzer Corps' right hook. Just before first light the fog came rolling in, deadening the sound of movement and providing perfect cover for the attackers.

First to be hit were the 2nd Division battalion who were deployed north of Rocherath. Hitler Jugend Division had quietly brought up a company of tanks close to the American

243

lines during the night and these, with their supporting panzer grenadiers, attacked out of the fog at dawn. The veteran 2nd Division men quietly let the tanks pass and then came out of their foxholes and fired bazookas into the thin rear armour plating of the panzers, knocking out several and scattering the rest. At the same time they engaged the Germany infantry in close fighting in the swirling fog using bayonets and sometimes knives. The German attack failed but as soon as the fog lifted and it got light the panzers and their infantry came on again in strength and with determination. The fury of this onslaught was too much for some of the American infantry who had been under attack and without rest for a long time and a number broke and ran. They did not get far for their company commander personally halted the retreat and sent them back. Another company commander, when he saw that the Germans could not be stopped, called for artillery fire on his own positions—only twelve of his company escaped; yet another company lost all but ten men.

After six hours two-thirds of the defending battalion were casualties, and despite the most heavy artillery fire, the Germans succeeded in forcing their way into Rocherath. But the delay had enabled the other two battalions east and south of Rocherath and Krinkelt to regroup and face this attack from the north as well as on their other two fronts. Fighting went on here all day as the panzers and volksgrenadiers hurled themselves time and again at Krinkelt but when night fell somehow the Americans were still in possession of the two villages and 11 SS Panzer Corps' northern attack, most optimistic of all, which by now should have been well across the Meuse, had not yet been able to get Hitler Jugend's tanks on to the roads a bare five miles from their start line. And it was now, at the end of the third day, as everyone but Hitler realized, too late to do so.

While this fierce fighting was raging in the woods and villages in front of the Elsenborn ridge the small force holding the Monschau position, hinge of the northern shoulder, beat off two determined German efforts, one on Sunday and the other on Monday. The results of both were important although at the time eclipsed by the high drama of the fight for the twin villages, Peiper's breakthrough and the tremendous battles to seize St Vith and Bastogne.

General Kaschner, whose depleted 326th Volksgrenadier Division had been stopped in their tracks on Saturday, decided the American position at Höfen was too tough to crack by frontal assault but that if he were to concentrate an attack north of Monschau, against the extended lines of the Thirty-eighth Cavalry Squadron, he should be able to break through to his objective, the high ground to the north-west and the road to Eupen.

About four o'clock on Sunday morning an assault force probed forward towards the cavalry outposts but were quickly brought to a halt by heavy, accurate American artillery fire. Here, as elsewhere along the assault front, although the Americans were thin on the ground they had strong supporting artillery.

The Germans then laid an artillery barrage of their own along the front held by the Thirty-eighth Cavalry Squadron which was based on the railway line to Muetzenich, a mile north of Monschau. The assault teams of volksgrenadiers advanced right up to the edge of their own shelling, incurring casualties from their own guns. As soon as the barrage stopped, they came on in successive waves undeterred by the punishing streams of bullets from the many machine-guns of the cavalry and only finally being stopped by concentrated fire from artillery, howitzer, tank guns and anti-tank guns firing straight into their midst. By this time the German attacking line extended for about three thousand yards. When the advance was renewed, supported by strafing from the air by a couple of squadrons from the Luftwaffe, the thin cavalry line was breached in several places.

But once again a heavy artillery barrage stopped any further German advance and the Allied Air Force, whose help had been requested early in the day, finally turned up with Lightnings and smashed up the main force of 326 Volksgrenadiers in a village a mile behind the attack front. At the same time reinforcements arrived to thicken the American defence. This was the leading regiment of the US 9th Infantry Division who had been out of action at Eupen only nine miles away and who now arrived at exactly the right moment to throw the 326th Volksgrenadiers back.

Unable to get through north of Monschau General Kaschner decided on the next day, Monday, to try to knock out the 99th Infantry position at Höfen once again. As the rest of his division had now joined him he was able to use a fresh battalion to lead this attack. The technique was exactly the same as he had used the day before against Thirty-eighth Cavalry: at about five o'clock in the morning assault groups moved towards the American line and were very heavily shelled by artillery and mortar, suffering severe casualties. Nevertheless about half the attackers got into Höfen village and some of the

American defenders were forced into house-to-house fighting so that when, about an hour after a now familiar concentrated German artillery, rocket and mortar barrage, a reinforced German infantry attack was launched, the defence of Höfen teetered on the brink.

The American anti-tank guns, frozen in place by the exceptional cold, broke up the advance of the supporting armoured cars and tanks and cut great swathes in the ranks of the volksgrenadiers. The panzers retreated behind a ridge but the volksgrenadiers doggedly persisted despite heavy losses and attacked the American command post. The officer commanding, Colonel Butler, called for artillery fire on his own position, which succeeded in stopping the volksgrenadiers' advance, and counter-attacked as soon as the shelling stopped. It was the turning point and slowly the Germans were driven back; by midday the original defence line had been restored. The 326th Volksgrenadiers fought recklessly and fiercely but they were not numerous enough nor well enough supported to accomplish their task. Many paid with their lives, many more were injured. Their record was as good as any of the German troops in the Ardennes.

Here at Höfen, 99th's young soldiers, the Third Battalion of the 395th Infantry Regiment, in their first action, did so well they were later awarded a Presidential Citation. They and the Thirty-eighth Cavalry Squadron held the Monschau hinge for the first two critical days. Later they were joined by the whole of the 47th Infantry Regiment of the 9th Infantry Division and on Wednesday, December 20, were relieved when the 9th Infantry Division took over the Monschau sector. The Germans' last chance of cracking the northern end of the Ardennes front disappeared: 'Sepp' Dietrich's SS Panzer Army was jammed along four-fifths of its front.

Right at the other end of the long attack front General Brandenberger's two-division assault against a single regiment of 4th Infantry Division and 9th Armored Division's Sixtieth Armored Infantry had failed, surprisingly, to roll quickly over the comparatively weak American defences. The volksgrenadiers had poured across the Sauer but the American artillery on the Schlamm Bach ridge, although forced to move several times, had fired their fifteen howitzers almost without stop, slowing down the German advance and preventing the putting in of the strong bridges needed to carry the heavy supporting weapons.

Obeying literally General Barton's 'no retrograde movement' order all five of 12th Infantry Regiment's forward company positions held out although by midnight on the first day four of them were surrounded. Only at Lauterborn, where a counter-attack had forced the Germans out, was there a coherent defence, formed by about a hundred American soldiers. At Berdorf the sixty men in the Parc Hotel waited hopefully for their tanks to try again to break through the German ring; a garrison in Echternach formed a hedgehog position, based on a hat factory, from which they harassed the volksgrenadiers trying to move through the town. Here too the Americans expected a relief attack from Lauterborn to get through to them the following day. On the right the two companies holding the positions at Osweiler and Dickweiler had beaten off attacks all day but the Germans had continued to feed troops across the Sauer and, despite losses, had succeeded in surrounding both places by Saturday night. A message reporting this got through to 12th Infantry's command post, adding the ominous words, 'situation desperate' and the last reserve company was sent to their aid.

Once again precious hours in which to steady the front and move in reinforcements had been wrested from the Germans. Only his left flank had been hit so far and it was still too early for the divisional commander, General Barton, to make major changes in the dispositions of his other two regiments holding a long front running from south of Echternach down to the boundary between First and Third US Armies. Like every other American commander in the Ardennes General Barton had to guess at German intentions on the first day. He had no way of knowing that the forces attacking his 12th Regiment were the extreme left wing of a big German offensive or that further south General Brandenberger had left only two fortress battalions opposite the rest of 4th Infantry Division's long front.

By nightfall on Saturday, December 17, all of 12th Infantry Regiment's twelve companies were committed as was all the available armour—eleven out of the fifty-four tanks of the division's supporting armoured battalion. The artillery obviously badly needed strengthening and three 155-mm battalions and two batteries of 104-mm howitzers were ordered to move north during Saturday night.

When the shattered 4th Infantry Division had moved into the Luxembourg end of the Ardennes sector its commander and his staff had realized that the main prize they had to protect was Luxembourg City itself which was not only the centre of all communications but also housed General Bradley's 12th Army Group Headquarters and the advance command post of the Ninth Air Force. When the Germans attacked in force against the defence screen guarding one of the main approaches from Germany to Luxembourg General Barton naturally assumed that the city was probably the German objective* and he made his counter moves accordingly.

During Saturday night he committed the rest of his divisional reserves taking the 22nd Infantry Regiment's Second Battalion from the right flank and sending them, with two platoons of tanks, to reinforce the 12th Infantry Regiment. They were ordered to move at first light to Junglinster 'ready to fight'. He created a mobile reserve by moving his combat engineer battalion and troop of reconnaissance cavalry up behind 12th Infantry's lines to be sent in where they were needed most.

4th Infantry Division's own armour, the 70th Tank Battalion, were desperately trying to get their stripped-down tanks out of the workshops and into battle. Meanwhile 9th Armored Division's CCA came to the rescue by sending a company of Shermans to General Barton's assistance: better still was the news that 10th Armored Division from US Third Army had started north and that at least their advance guard would be with him on Sunday. Finally the corps commander, General Middleton, had told him that he could also have the 159th Combat Engineer Battalion, who were working in his area, if he could find them. The thin defence line which ran for about four miles on either side of Echternach although stretched to breaking was still holding as a stronger line was steadily being built up a few miles behind.

While considering the overall situation on Saturday night General Barton realized that his northern flank could be turned by a German advance through the gorge of the Schwarz Ernst which separated his division from 9th Armored's CCA. Here was the place for the reserve he had earlier formed of combat engineers and reconnaissance cavalry. At five o'clock on Sunday morning they were ordered to move into the village of Breitweiler at the southern end of the gorge. No sooner had they dug in along a ridge overlooking the gorge than they saw far below the reconnaissance tip of a long German column.

General Brandenberger had ordered the 276th Volksgrenadier commander, General Moehring, to commit his reserve regiment late on Saturday in an attempt to penetrate to the

* General Barton telephoned Major General Leven Allen, 12th Army Group's Chief of Staff, on Sunday to say that if 10th Armored Division didn't arrive soon 'Army Group had better get set to barrel out'.

rear of both the Sixtieth Armoured Infantry and the 12th Infantry. Disappointed with the failure of 276th Volksgrenadier's other two regiments to seize the important heights north of the Sauer the Seventh Army Commander had ordered all three regiments to continue their attack through the night. It was the advance guard of the southernmost regiment that had now reached Breitweiler. By 11 o'clock on Sunday morning American observers had reported counting five companies—'and they're still coming!'

General Barton ordered every gun which could drop its shells into this part of the gorge to join in a shoot. Eight Shermans which had been rushed out of the division's workshops moved to positions from where they could add the high-explosive shells of their 75-mm guns to those of the engineers' tank destroyers, the lighter armament of the cavalry reconnaissance, mortars and all the guns of three battalions of field artillery. The result in the narrow gorge was terrifying and the volksgrenadiers' attempt to advance became almost more than flesh and blood could bear but after the first shock they drove on without faltering to the village of Müllerthal. Prisoners taken later in the day were in a badly shaken state and said that the shrapnel among the rocks sounded like falling apples and had caused very heavy casualties.

But Müllerthal was a most important objective for access roads ran from it to Waldbillig and Christnach behind the Sixtieth Armoured Infantry in the line, and in the other direction, a road climbed up to Consdorf, command post of the 12th Infantry Regiment's Second Battalion from where the road network of 4th Division's flank could be controlled. Müllerthal was worth the casualties to the Germans.

The Americans immediately moved to counter this threat: at Consdorf everyone who could fire a gun was roped in to form a defence supported by a single headquarters tank. General Barton formed Task Force Luckett from a battalion of infantry supported by two platoons of tanks, assault guns, mortars and a battery of 150-mm howitzers and sent them half a mile west of Breitweiler in a blocking position across the southern end of the Schwarz Ernst.

Over on CCA's side of the gorge General Leonard as a precaution had posted some 76-mm self-propelled anti-tank guns covering the narrow roads leading up towards Waldbillig and Christnach from Müllerthal. But as soon as he learned that elements from a new German regiment had advanced to that village he ordered an attack by a troop of cavalry reconnaissance supported by four tank destroyers.

Because the terrain was impossible for armoured cars the cavalry had to advance on foot, led by the self-propelled tank destroyers. As it descended into the gorge the narrow road was compressed by stone walls at times to little more than the width of a tank. From behind the shelter of huge boulders and trees the volksgrenadiers were able to pour accurate small-arms fire into the dismounted cavalrymen. The troop commander was killed, the men went to ground and when the leading tank destroyer, inching down the steep icy track, reached a curve around an outcrop of rock it was knocked out by a bazooka and completely blocked the road and the attack could not continue. A protective artillery barrage had to be laid down to enable the American force to withdraw.

But this prompt offensive action by 9th Armored Division's Combat Command made the Germans pause; despite their numbers and the comparative weakness of the American units on either side of them they made no further attempt to continue their advance here. The Americans were then able to hurry reinforcements to both sides of this deep thrust and a dangerous inter-divisional penetration, which might have trapped 12th Infantry Regiment was stopped. Once more the Germans had lost a valuable initiative.

Seventh Army's commander, General Brandenberger was most displeased with the performance of the 276th Volksgrenadier Division, even though their centre regiment succeeded finally on Sunday in pushing back the Sixtieth Armored Infantry's supporting artillery and capturing Beaufort, forcing the American headquarters to withdraw to Savelborn and thus cutting off the three companies in the line. Seventh German Army's commander considered that this should have been accomplished on the first day. In the north 276 Volksgrenadiers' right-hand regiment, attacking between CCA of 9th Armored and the 109th Infantry, a weak seam, made hardly any progress on Sunday. General Brandenberger relieved the division's commander who, in the few hours left to him, tried to retrieve his half-trained division's reputation by ordering the right-hand regiment to capture Medernach the following day, supported by an 'anti-tank' company equipped with only fifty-four bazookas. Hurrying to arrange a simultaneous attack from his left flank he was killed by a burst of machine-gun fire. Like other German commanders in the Ardennes, General Moehring had been asked to do too much with too little; to attack against artillery, self-propelled guns, tanks and armoured cars with none of these things.

But the emergency 'anti-tank' force he had formed of volksgrenadiers armed with bazookas were lying concealed on Monday morning when a task force from 9th Armored Division took a wrong turn and blundered on to them. Seven tanks were knocked out and the task force prevented from getting through to the cut-off armoured infantry still hanging on to their disintegrating line. They were now out of touch with each other as well as with their headquarters but their last orders had been classically simple—'hold your ground'—and this they continued to do.

On Seventh Army's left, in order to compensate for US 4th Infantry Division's build-up of strength, the commander of the 212th Volksgrenadier Division, General Franz Sensfuss, was enabled to increase his forces for the second day's effort. Although his third regiment had been kept back as Seventh Army's only reserve the news of the US 10th Armored Division's move to the 4th Infantry's assistance was enough to persuade General Brandenberger to let him have a company of special shock troops from this regiment. Their task would be to clear Echternach and open the way for a drive south. And in order to knock the equally troublesome defenders of Osweiler and Dickweiler out of the way Seventh Army's commander also gave General Sensfuss one of the fortress battalions to add weight to that attack. Lastly, 212th Volksgrenadier's fusilier battalion were to capture Lauterborn once more. These plans depended on getting bridges in during the hours of darkness and introducing heavy weapons into the battle. With both Echternach and Lauterborn in their hands the Germans would then make an all-out effort to seize the primary objective, the Schlamm Bach ridge and capture or drive off the artillery there. The Americans holding out in the Parc Hotel in Berdorf and the small force which had been sent to relieve them would be overwhelmed by a tremendous artillery concentration followed by a strong infantry attack. Thus all five of the American forward positions still holding out would be eliminated on the second day.

For the attack against Echternach searchlights were brought up in an attempt to get a bridge in over the Saar during the night but the American artillery kept up such accurate shelling that this failed. Without heavy weapons the volksgrenadiers could not take the Echternach defended position by frontal assault. They split into two—some moved west to add weight to the attack on the Berdorf position while the rest continued south towards Consdorf.

At Lauterborn where 212 Volksgrenadier's fusilier battalion were to attack at dawn on Sunday the Germans had the initiative snatched from them by an earlier attack from the American force there who sallied out, reinforced by five light tanks, in a bold attempt to drive north and relieve the company in Echternach. They soon ran into the larger German force and had to be content with stopping their advance and consolidating the Lauterborn defences.

Unable to capture Lauterborn the fusiliers bypassed it and seized the village of Scheidgen just over a mile behind. This was less than a mile from the Second Battalion command post at Consdorf who were already fearing a German thrust from Müllerthal in the opposite direction. German troops continued to move around Lauterborn and by nightfall on Sunday both Consdorf and the rear of the Lauterborn position were seriously threatened.

At Berdorf too the initiative was lost by the Germans when an American force struck first in an attack from the south. These were tanks from 70th Tank Battalion, with infantry aboard, who crashed into the town and opened fire on the Parc Hotel believing that it was now held by the Germans. Fortunately for the defenders one of them found an American flag which was hastily run up from the roof on a makeshift flagpole. The firing stopped and the tank–infantry teams moved forward to try to link up with the men inside the hotel who, at the same time, came out in a rush to meet them. But the nearby houses were full of German troops, who had kept quiet enjoying the spectacle of the Americans firing on their target for them, and who now opened up with bazookas and automatic weapons and prevented the relief from getting through. When darkness fell the men from the hotel drew back inside and the tanks withdrew to their earlier positions in the southern edge of the town.

The German artillery, which had been ready to support the attack planned earlier, then laid on their postponed barrage and plastered the Parc Hotel and its surrounds with everything they had—rockets, mortars and heavy artillery—but with remarkably little success, for only one man was wounded.

The Germans had failed to take Echternach, Lauterborn or Bersdorf on Sunday and their attempt to break the American hinge at Osweiler and Dickweiler hardly fared much better. Here two companies of 12th Infantry Regiment had been surrounded on Saturday night but the relieving columns had got through to them although not until Monday and not without trouble: one platoon unexpectedly ran into a large German force and all the Americans were killed or captured and, just before dark, an American column moving north was cut in two

252

by a German one moving west. In the confused fighting which followed the Americans dug in and the Germans moved on to reach Scheidgen and join up with the fusiliers who had come from the north. This completed the encirclement of Echternach and Lauterborn but it was the end of the second day and the German High Command was disappointed with the performance of their troops on this front.

On the American side although 4th Infantry Division had been hit very hard and their front had been penetrated for four miles in two places they had been able so far to preserve a more or less connected defence line and had strong forces securing the flanks of the attacked sector. The German build-up in their centre, around Scheidgen, was a threat, but the main worry was the possibility that CCA 9th Armored would be overwhelmed, thus allowing the full weight of another German division to come in from the west.

The greatest danger was the seam between 4th Infantry and 9th Armored Divisions, the gorge of the Schwarz Ernst down which one of 276 Volksgrenadier's regiments had already advanced. The answer was the 10th Armored Division from Third Army which had been ordered to move north on Saturday, December 16, and whose leading units came into 4th Infantry Division's area just before nightfall on Sunday.

Tenth Armored's commander, Major-General William Morris, had been ordered by General Middleton to send one combat command to Bastogne and to use the rest of his division to help 4th Infantry Division to attack and drive the Germans back across the Sauer. He and General Barton had conferred in Luxembourg City on Sunday afternoon and had decided to commit three task forces from 10th Armored's CCA on Monday to restore 4th Infantry's line. One would push the Germans back along the Schwarz Ernst; one would advance through Consdorf and relieve the infantry trapped in Berdorf; the third would defeat the Germans in Scheidgen, advance through Lauterborn and recapture Echternach, relieving the company holding out in the hat factory. It was an ambitious programme for a single armoured combat command: let us see how they fared.

The attack on the American left was to be made by Task Force Chamberlain from 10th Armored together with Task Force Luckett from 4th Infantry who were already blocking the southern end of the Schwarz Ernst. Early on Monday morning, before the fog had lifted, tank–infantry teams began to descend into the gorge.

Strewn with boulders, densely wooded, the deeply cut

253

Schwarz Ernst is as wild country as can be found in the Ardennes and the narrowness of the track soon forced the advance into single file. This reduced the fire-power to one tank and when it was knocked out much time was taken up either to clear it away or to manoeuvre around it. The well-concealed Germans pumped automatic weapon fire into the American column and plastered them with mortar. From time to time a tank would explode in a great whoosh of flame as a bazooka charge found the fuel or ammunition. By nightfall the counter-attack had only been able to secure the line of the Waldbillig–Müllerthal road. The volksgrenadiers had not been forced back along the gorge but at least the seam between 9th Armored and 4th Infantry had been stopped from tearing further.

Tenth Armored's Task Force Standish had the job of driving through to relieve the men trapped in the Parc Hotel in Bersdorf and at first it seemed as though this plan would succeed. The new tank–infantry teams made contact with the force of 70th Tank Battalion and 12th Infantry Regiment in the southern end of the town, who had been forced back the day before, and began to move forward.

Almost immediately smoke shells came from across the river and under this screen the volksgrenadiers already in Berdorf came out of their holes and launched a double attack—against the American armour and, once more, against the Parc Hotel. Fighting continued for some three hours; American tanks and half-tracks were disabled and the volksgrenadiers fought hard for every house. German volunteers ran through the small-arms fire with explosive charges fixed to long poles and blew great holes in the hotel's walls but although they had only one machine gun and one automatic to add to their rifles, the men inside beat off the follow-up attacks.

By nightfall on Monday the relieving force of tanks and infantry had advanced only seventy-five yards and it did not look as though the sixty men in the battered hotel—its roof and upper story smashed and with gaping holes in the walls—would be able to throw back many more attacks.

The third of 10th Armored Division's attacks on Monday, by Task Force Riley, had the most success. Surprisingly, Scheidgen, which had seemed to pose so serious a threat, fell easily, for the German forces there had moved south-west during the night towards the line of their objective—a move which took them deep into 4th Infantry's rear area and later threatened a battalion headquarters. A surprise assault was then launched from Scheidgen by the tank–infantry teams,

254

ong the whole of the Ardennes front.*

There was an unpleasant conviction at SHAEF that this was o local spoiling attack but that somehow, unbelievably, the ighty German war machine which had seemed to be breaking own was on the move again. Suddenly it was realized that rom the Ardennes, scene of the last great breakthrough to the nglish Channel, the whole Western Front was now threat- ned. General Eisenhower called his top commanders to a conference at Verdun on the morning of Tuesday, December 19.

The time had come for command decisions.

* General Eisenhower, for instance, in the first edition of *Crusade in Europe*, said that the 99th Infantry Division 'was rapidly forced back in confusion'. This was changed in subsequent editions.

---

supported by two companies from the 159th Engineer Combat Battalion, which went through Lauterborn into the outskirts of Echternach where contact was made with the company holding the hat factory position.

Having beaten off several German attacks these troops were in good spirits and claimed over a hundred dead volksgrenadiers. The tank force offered to cover their withdrawal back to Lauterborn but the officer in charge, Captain Paul Depuis, refused, evidently not satisfied that his original 'no withdrawal' orders had been revoked. At that the tanks and their infantry turned back promising to come up again the next day in strength.

The company surrounded in Osweiler had heard that their relief had been ambushed on Sunday night so that when their supporting tanks saw troops approaching from the south on Monday morning they opened fire and it was only after two hours and some casualties that identification was achieved. The right flank now seemed secure but this was an illusion for the 212th Volksgrenadier commander, General Sensfuss, had given up the plan to break through the Osweiler–Dickweiler line and had sent fresh forces to drive due south from the Echternach bridgehead along narrow, unguarded roads running between Osweiler and Scheidgen.

Making good progress this force reached the western edge of the Schlamm Bach ridge, their division's first objective, five miles from the Sauer before they ran into any American opposition.

This happened when the German advance guard reached the south-eastern edge of a large wood and unwisely opened fire on an American column of towed howitzers moving along a road. After the first confused diving into ditches and exchange of small-arms fire the gunners went back and, without having time to uncouple their guns from the trucks, opened fire on the volksgrenadiers at stone-throwing range. Gradually all howitzers were brought to bear and after three hours the Americans were able to withdraw and warn the headquarters of 12th Infantry's Third Battalion at Herborn, a mile and a half away, of this nearby force of German infantry.

At the same time as this action was taking place the fusiliers who had earlier moved south from Scheidgen surrounded the headquarters of 12th Infantry Regiment's Second Battalion but tank destroyers got through and covered a retreat back to the Herborn position. Although 212th Volksgrenadiers had not penetrated right into 4th Infantry's rear they were handicapped by lack of either tanks or self-propelled guns and so could be stopped by comparatively small numbers equipped with these weapons. The German High Command was paying dearly for the decision to concentrate four and a half panzer divisions on the northern shoulder and to allocate none to the southern—one battlegroup from either of the two SS Panzer Divisions still waiting to get engaged on 'Sepp' Dietrich's front would now have made all the difference on General Brandenberger's.

After three days of constant attack all five of the American forward strongpoints which the 212th Volksgrenadiers were scheduled to knock out on the first day were still holding out and none were now surrounded. Fourth Infantry Division had received almost enough reinforcements to wipe out the manpower superiority the Germans had to have if their offensive was to succeed and unless General Sensfuss could now be reinforced and get heavy support weapons his division could not hope to achieve their original objective.

Nor was the position of the next of Seventh Army's volksgrenadier divisions much better. 276th Volksgrenadiers' losses had been high in three days of almost continual assault and their new commander, Colonel Hugo Dempwolff, decided they had to rest for all of Tuesday to recover. Meanwhile, as the Germans had finally succeeded in getting bridges in, he brought up his artillery and rocket projectors for a coordinated attack on Wednesday.

Taking advantage of the lull the cut-off Sixtieth Armored Infantry still in their original line were ordered to withdraw to 9th Armored Division's new defence line and about half of the six hundred or so green troops who had been sent for 'battle indoctrination' to this quiet sector eventually did so.

The last of Seventh German Army's three divisions available for setting up of the southern hard shoulder (the fourth, 5th Parachute, had the task of moving on alongside the 5th Panzer Army attack) was the 352nd Volksgrenadiers who also got heavy support weapons across the river and pushed the 109th Infantry Regiment out of Diekirch back to Ettelbruck. At the same time CCA's light tanks had been pushed back to Ermsdorf by 276th Volksgrenadiers' right-hand regiment. The result of these two German successes was that a dangerous four-mile gap was opened between CCA and 109th Infantry.

At the end of three days—the critical period of a major offensive—both sides took stock of their position. At the highest levels in the German army, with the exception of the Führer himself, there was pessimism amounting almost to despair. The Ardennes Offensive was seriously behind schedule

everywhere and most seriously on 'Sepp' Dietric   a
where hopes had been highest. Their one advance, t   n
Panzer Division's battlegroup, could not be kept goin   n
as St Vith and Malmédy remained in American ha   d
greatest chance of success lay in exploiting the gap bet   f
Vith and Bastogne now that Houffalize had been sei   l
two of Manteuffel's panzer divisions were moving pa   e
togne but here again real success required the Germans   c
control of Bastogne's communications.

By Monday night the Commander-in-Chief West,
Marshall von Rundstedt, that most experienced of G
commanders, knew that the original objectives could n
achieved and that the forces committed should start to pr
to defend the ground they had won. General Jodl, chief o
Wehrmacht Operations Staff, also realized that the great o
sive had failed but thought that the Meuse could still be
reached and considerable gains consolidated—the difficulty
would be to persuade Hitler to accept an abandonment of the
original plan.

Although the Führer gave no sign of admitting that his
grandiose plan to seize Antwerp and split the Allies in two was
no longer possible he did acknowledge reality by cancelling the
subsidiary attack by Fifteenth Army in the north which had
been due to start the next day. Instead everything
used to get the panzers moving westward fast and
stedt's orders to his army commanders sarcastically
to see that the tanks kept up with the infantry.

Seventh German Army was urged to increase its
in particular to tie up as much American infantry, a
artillery as possible on their front in order to crea
dom of manoeuvre for Fifth Panzer Army. And on
order went out—Bastogne and St Vith must be sei
whatever the cost.

Pessimism and confusion reigned at SHAEF too
black days with news of the near-destruction of tv
divisions, of German armoured columns far beh
that no longer seemed to exist and of wild rumou
chutists and saboteurs everywhere. The German st
ticularly of tanks and self-propelled guns, was g
gerated as was the extent of their success. No one h
of how far short of their initial targets the German
nor of the critical significance of the delay imposed
the refusal of many small American units to yiel
superior forces. Instead it was generally believed t
mans had succeeded in breaking through the A

18

COMMAND DECISIONS

War is not so difficult as people think.
GENERAL GEORGE S. PATTON:
War As I Knew It

Early in the Normandy Campaign a British staff officer, sent as an observer to an American corps commander's conference, listened in amazement to the divisional commanders' uninhibited criticisms of their general's plan for the next attack. Two or three hours were spent discussing alternative suggestions until a plan was agreed to by all which seemed to the British observer to be more or less the one originally put forward by the corps commander and later he pointed this out to one of the American brigadiers.

'Sure it was but you don't think we're going to sit there like a lot of dummies and have him tell us what to do, do you? We've got a *right* to have our say—now it's *our* plan.'

This is one of the most important differences in the way in which wars are fought in the British and American armies: unless he were asked to do so a British commander would not normally criticize his superior's decisions. He would comment about ground conditions or the strength or disposition of the enemy if he thought these might not have been fully appreciated; he would point out, and perhaps protest, if he thought the task was greatly beyond his unit's strength. But he would accept his orders as being part of a larger plan of whose full implications he was not aware.

The British method has more than once resulted in blinders entailing needless sacrifice and the American method also has its disadvantages—chief of which is that the need to be democratically fair to everyone means that sometimes the best decision, in a purely military sense, cannot be taken. Both methods are 'right' inasmuch as they are determined by the temperament and make-up of the men who are to do the fighting which in turn are the result of their background and traditions.

The logical extension of these different attitudes is that in the American Army, once the decision has been taken, the local commander is left alone to get on with his task while in the British Army there is apt to be considerable interference all the way down the chain of command.

The American way is the traditional way; indeed communications on the battlefield before World War II were such that it was not often possible for a commander to interfere with the conduct of one of his formations. From this necessity the tradition evolved of leaving the *method* of carrying out an order to the commander on the spot and it was a tradition that was very jealously guarded. In 1939, for instance General Guderian, perhaps the greatest of Germany's armoured tacticians, was given a panzer corps for the invasion of Poland and in his eagerness to demonstrate the new tank warfare tried to direct one of his divisions during the attack. Its commander promptly told him to mind his own business and keep to the function of a corps commander.* It was an incident which could well have happened in the American Army but almost certainly not in the British.

It would be difficult to find a commander less likely to understand the American way of making war than Field Marshal Montgomery, who was apt to treat any formation he commanded as an orchestra of which he was the conductor. He made sure that all the performers knew exactly what they were to do and fully understood the piece to be played, but he kept close control of all sections firmly in his hands. He believed that having arrived at a plan by close consideration of all the factors which only he knew, and having made his decision, all subsequent actions must further his design.

Montgomery was completely dedicated to soldiering—the epitome of the professional military man to whom every other activity is subservient to good soldiering, and one of his maxims was that 'You cannot make a good soldier and a good husband.' The result of a lifetime of concentration by his fine cool mind was an astonishing ability to reduce complicated military problems to a number of clearly perceivable facts and to find an answer for the problems thus posed by giving an exact military value to each factor regardless of the emotions and personalities involved. Utterly convinced he was right, he was impatient of criticism or alternatives.

The caution for which he was so often criticized had its basis in purely military considerations: the husbanding of resources, particularly trained soldiers of which the British army was always short and, most important of all in his way of waging war—'no defeats'. Do not hazard a force today which is necessary for tomorrow's victory. If the enemy is equally strong do not engage in all-out battle but draw him on to attack so that

* Basil Liddell Hart: *The Other Side of the Hill.*

he becomes weaker while you are building up your strength. If possible choose the battlefield and when you are overwhelmingly stronger and victory is certain, attack and defeat him.

Major General de Guingand who, as Montgomery's Chief of Staff, was probably closer to him than anyone else in the war, says of him, 'He disliked conferences which meant a lot of argument across the table. He preferred to be the only speaker, and the object of the conference to be the giving out of policy or orders. He liked to discuss the particular problem quietly in his caravan or office with his staff and commanders, and then spend a period by himself making up his mind as to the right action to be pursued.'

In complete contrast an American commander, at almost any level, has to be a 'regular guy'. He should be able to down his liquor, enjoy mildly dirty jokes, barber-shop quartets and playing poker with the boys. He must demonstrate, from time to time, that he is a human being by little acts of affection, by slapping backs and allowing his own to be slapped and no matter how competent a professional he may be—and the best American commanders were the equal of any anywhere—he must never be only a soldier. No rank can be high enough for him to be able to behave as though he believed he was not as other men. This is democracy and any American ignores its rules at his peril, as General MacArthur with all his undoubted ability discovered.

Field Marshal Montgomery who didn't smoke or drink, who ate sparingly, who did not seem to enjoy the company of women, who lived aesthetically—even his occasional game of golf seemed to be taken like a prescription for necessary relaxation—and who seldom attended even the highest level conferences himself but sent a representative, was not likely to be popular with American generals. When discussing his plans even with his senior commanders there was always something of the headmaster in his attitude. If this was galling to many British generals it was absolutely infuriating to the Americans.

One of the results of this clash of personalities was that the Field Marshal's enemies at SHAEF were able to score by taking advantage of the difference in attitude between him and General Eisenhower about the conduct of the war and also of any tactlessness on Montgomery's part—examples of which were not rare. The 'anti-Monty' faction had first made trouble during the second month of the Normandy campaign by misrepresenting the rôle of the British Second Army on the eastern flank. That situation had been cleared up but it had spoiled the, up until then, very good relations between the Allies.

After Montgomery had failed to persuade the Supreme Commander at the end of August to appoint a single ground commander and to strike hard for the Ruhr with a forty-division force he, with characteristic stubbornness, did not give up the attempt, but urged it again and again. In his memoirs, while still insisting that the war could have been ended in 1944 if the Allies had stopped on the right and concentrated their strength in a hammer blow on the left, he takes care to point out that anyway the decision that was taken—to advance to the Rhine on a broad front—was not implemented. 'We advanced to the Rhine on several fronts which were un-coordinated. And what was the German answer? A single concentrated punch in the Ardennes when we had become unbalanced and unduly extended.'

Not that the Field Marshal foresaw this German move—at the time he wrote an estimate of German offensive capabilities which was published at 21st Army Group on the day the Ardennes attack began:

'The enemy is at present fighting a defensive campaign on all fronts; his situation is such that he cannot stage major offensive operations. Furthermore, at all costs he has to prevent the war from entering a mobile phase; he has not the transport or the petrol that would be necessary for mobile operations, nor could his tanks compete with ours in the mobile battle.'

This was the widely-held opinion. General Bradley in his book generously admits that had he been preparing an estimate on the same day it would have been identical to Montgomery's. The Field Marshal's constant urging of the appointment of a single ground commander was particularly irksome to General Bradley even though Montgomery had more than once said that he would serve under Bradley if he were Eisenhower's choice for the job. In view of what was to take place now in the Ardennes battle the last meeting before that attack, between Montgomery, Bradley and Eisenhower, which took place, at the British commander's suggestion, at Maastricht in Holland on December 7, is interesting.

General Eisenhower had spent a night at Field Marshal Montgomery's TAC Headquarters during the preceding week. Despite their very different natures the two men got on well together, particularly when alone, and their talk ranged over the whole war in Europe: Montgomery, never reluctant to give his opinion, said that he thought 12th Army Group was not well balanced tactically and that some divisions should be taken away from General Patton's army and moved north to add weight to the attack to the Ruhr. A corollary of this would be, of course, the cancelling of General Patton's attack towards the Saar.

Bradley was not pleased when Eisenhower told him of Montgomery's criticisms and suggestions but nevertheless he wrote a moderate, reasoned letter to the 21st Army Group commander explaining that Third Army had to be kept strong in order to be able to launch an attack in conjunction with 6th Army Group on their right. 6th Army Group were unexpectedly strong because German garrisons were still holding the Channel ports so that seven divisions which had been intended for 12th Army Group had been diverted to the Mediterranean ports and given to General Denvers. And once in that sector they must be used.

During his evening with Montgomery General Eisenhower realized that once again two of his army group commanders were in fundamental disagreement: General Bradley was generally satisfied with the way the war was going and convinced that the strategy of the double thrust was sound; Field Marshal Montgomery thought that the Allied situation was far from good and he reminded the Supreme Commander that the objectives laid down in his orders to them of a month earlier had not been achieved—neither the Ruhr nor the Saar had been secured. He then suggested the Maastricht meeting at which he, Bradley and Eisenhower could give their views and a new plan could be made.

Predictably Field Marshal Montgomery used this opportunity to make once more a strong case for concentrating in the north and committing his and Bradley's army groups to advance to battle west of the Rhine, draw in on them all the German strategic reserves, destroy them and then close up to the Rhine. Once again he stressed the importance of a single, overall ground commander for such an operation who must be either himself or Bradley. And once again he expressed his willingness to serve under Bradley.

General Eisenhower had come prepared for both of Field Marshal Montgomery's suggestions and had decided to agree to neither. The concept of the double thrust would be kept: 12th Army Group would strike hard on the right and advance first some eighty miles east to reach the Rhine at about Worms and, second, develop a strong northerly thrust another hundred and thirty miles through Frankfurt to the Kassel area. At the same time 21st Army Group, reinforced by Ninth US Army of ten divisions, would advance eastwards, cross the Rhine and outflank the Ruhr from the north. Between these two main thrusts 12th Army Group's left flank would contain as many German divisions as possible by a series of feints and thrusts in the Cologne–Bonn area. And this, despite Montgomery's strong fundamental disagreement, was the plan decided at the Maastricht meeting.

21st Army Group Commander accepted the new plan, asking only that he take charge of all troops north of the Ardennes and Bradley all troops south of it. As this would have meant taking at least eight of First Army's fourteen divisions away from Bradley, Eisenhower turned the suggestion down flat. Instead the thrust north of the Ruhr would be made by a force whose right wing would be commanded by 12th Army Group and whose left by 21st Army Group.

But all this was in the future. For the moment 21st Army Group, along whose front there was little activity, would regroup for the Rhineland Battle and Montgomery ordered General Brian Horrocks to disengage his XXX Corps as the first move. General Bradley continued with his plans for a double assault: to seize the Roer Dams north of the Ardennes and to advance to the Saar south of it.

Thus when the German counter-offensive came, the northern end of the four-hundred-mile-long Western Front was held by 21st Army Group's fifteen divisions, of which four were armoured; Ninth US Army's seven divisions, two armoured, and First US Army's eight infantry and two armoured divisions. The centre was held by the remaining four divisions of First Army and ten of Third Army and of this total four were armoured. The southern end of the Allied front belonged to General Devers' 6th Army Group of seventeen divisions.

Modern offensives are built around the striking power of armour and the Germans concentrated practically all the tanks they had in the West, about six hundred and fifty, along the Ardennes front. In the area about to be attacked First US Army had two hundred and forty-two tanks. But, and this was a factor very much in the mind of the German commanders although dismissed by Hitler, north of the Ardennes were over eleven hundred British and about one thousand American tanks while in the south General Patton had another eight hundred.

As soon as news of the big German attack on First Army's weakened front reached SHAEF—coincidentally when Bradley and Eisenhower were in conference—it was decided as a precautionary measure to send in one armoured division from each side of the attacked sector: by Monday over five hundred tanks had been added to VIII Corps' strength.

To redress the manpower imbalance (two hundred and forty thousand Germans attacking eighty-three thousand Americans) SHAEF committed its only strategic reserve, two airborne divisions, on the second day and ordered two new divisions, an airborne in England and an armoured just landing on the continent, to move to the Ardennes as quickly as possible. Also orders given lower down the chain of command, in the three days before the top level decisions of the Verdun meeting, quickly upset the local superiority the Germans had achieved. From north of the battle three infantry and a second armoured division were started on the road to the Ardennes. Of these one complete infantry division and a regiment from each of the other two were in action by Monday.

At General Middleton's urging one of the airborne divisions was sent to Bastogne and he ordered the armoured division sent to him from the south to send a combat command there too. The other airborne division was diverted north to block the fast-moving spearhead of I SS Panzer Corps. These early tactical moves were to be of the greatest importance.

After three days of unbroken assault all along First Army's front from Echternach north to Monschau the following situation had emerged: the American forces trying to hold the southern shoulder consisted of the 4th Infantry Division (minus two battalions who were holding further south), CCA of 9th Armored Division, the 109th Infantry Regiment, who had been split off from 28th Infantry Division and 10th Armored Division less the combat command sent to Bastogne. These forces were being attacked all along their front by three divisions of volksgrenadiers with artillery support but no tanks.

North-west of this flank battle, in the American right centre, the survivors of the 110th Infantry Regiment and CCR of 9th Armored Division had been forced back to the eastern outskirts of Bastogne where there was a thin screen of combat engineers and, just arriving, 10th Armored Division's CCB. Also, leading elements of 101st Airborne Division were coming into Bastogne from the west after a wild drive through the night from Reims. Approaching Bastogne from the east were two German armoured and two infantry divisions.

Between Bastogne and the St Vith perimeter there was a virtually undefended gap through which were racing 5th Panzer Army's centre thrust which had cut the Bastogne to Liège highway by capturing Houffalize.

In the American left centre the mixed force consisting of 7th Armored Division, the remains of 106th Infantry Division and Fourteenth Cavalry Group, the 112th Infantry Regiment and miscellaneous combat engineer and artillery units were trying to hold St Vith against two volksgrenadier divisions. The Germans were bringing in an armoured brigade and a mixed force of panzer grenadiers and self-propelled anti-tank guns from an SS Panzer division.

North of St Vith the 30th Infantry Division was stretched in a long line from Werbomont (where one battalion was waiting to be relieved by the 82nd Airborne Division coming from Reims) to Stoumont, Stavelot (where they were engaging Battlegroup Peiper) and on to Malmédy.

In the north from Malmédy through the Elsenborn Ridge and the Rocherath–Krinkelt position the American line was now manned by the 1st, 2nd and 99th Infantry divisions, although the last had been reduced by casualties to about half strength. Around Monschau a battalion from 99th Infantry and the 38th Cavalry Squadron had been joined by a regiment from 9th Infantry Division. Trying to smash through the American northern shoulder were three divisions of volksgrenadiers, an SS Panzer division and a special commando brigade.

No summary of the position at the end of the first three days, however brief, should leave out mention of the part played by small groups of combat engineers on the American side whose courageous intervention often saved the situation or of the artillery who, more than once, stayed with their guns, firing at point-blank range, until overwhelmed.* On the German side the efforts of Colonel von der Heydte's parachutists and Otto Skorzeny's unorthodox force, though of little significance in the actual battle, had important effects on tactical planning.

So far the weather had limited air activity although both sides had been able to use air observers to good effect and both had employed medium bombers a few times. However, now that the Ardennes was top priority the Allied Air Force had over four thousand aeroplanes standing by for the inevitable break in the weather which would enable them once more to wreak terrible havoc on the German ground forces. German commanders looked at the sky every day wondering how long 'Hitler's weather' would last.

By Tuesday morning the original American strength in the Ardennes of one armoured and five infantry divisions had been increased to three armoured and ten infantry with more of both on the way. Manpower had grown, after allowing for all casualties and troops not yet arrived at the battle, to about a

*As reported by German prisoners.

hundred and twenty thousand, an increase of fifty per cent. There were about six hundred tanks operational, over a hundred per cent increase.

The Germans had committed nearly seventeen divisions of which five were armoured and eleven infantry. Also Fuehrer Begleit Brigade and Skorzeny's 150 Brigade had together about half the tanks of an SS Panzer division and about the manpower of a volksgrenadier division. Total German strength committed by the close of the third day's fighting was about a hundred and seventy thousand men and five hundred and seventy-five tanks. They were light on field guns, which had not been able to move up, but well supplied with mortars and automatic weapons. They had large numbers of self-propelled anti-tank guns and half of their tanks were greatly superior to any of the Americans'.

Army Group B had two more SS Panzer divisions at full strength poised to strike and one panzer division and six volksgrenadier divisions in reserve. The Americans had one armoured division and the remaining two-thirds of two infantry divisions arriving on the scene. Three new divisions, one infantry just arriving on the continent, one armoured and one airborne were on their way from England but it must be a week or more before their fire power could be brought into the battle.

From all this it will be seen that by the end of the third day and before major decisions for dealing with the offensive as a whole were taken the initial three-to-one advantage of the attackers had been nearly wiped out. However, the initiative still remained firmly in German hands with four of the five attacking panzer divisions having broken through the defence. Two deep penetrations had been made and the Ardennes was in danger of being broken into three parts.

The opening of Germany's great offensive had caught 12th Army Group 'fully committed without a division in reserve'* and SHAEF's strategic reserve of the two airborne divisions were both now committed. Somewhere more divisions had to be found.

Both General Bradley and General Patton had thought at first that the Germans had attacked in the Ardennes because Third US Army was about to launch its big offensive towards the Saar. This was scheduled for December 19 and Patton had his 10th Armored Division in reserve to be used in the follow-up punch. When it was taken away from him by Bradley on

---

* Bradley: *A Soldier's Story*. General Bradley said this was not unusual in the circumstances for Germany seemed beaten and therefore all reserves should be used offensively.

December 16 he protested vigorously and in order not to lose his other uncommitted armoured division, the 4th, he ordered the corps commander concerned to 'get it engaged'.

By the end of the third day General Bradley knew that what the Germans were attempting was much more than trying to put General Patton off his stroke and he summoned the Third Army commander to 12th Army Group tactical headquarters and showed him on the situation maps that the German penetration was much greater than he had thought. Bradley then asked Patton what Third Army could do about it.

Now convinced, Patton said that he would halt the corps attack in which 4th Armored Division were to have become involved and concentrate them near Longwy starting at midnight. The 80th Infantry Division, now on its way into the line after resting and refitting, would turn round and start for Luxembourg in the morning. Finally the 26th Infantry Division whose four thousand green replacements were undergoing special 'Siegfried Line assault' training at Metz could be alerted to move in twenty-four hours.

Bradley was pleased and told Patton that he understood that Eisenhower was going to give VIII Corps to Third Army too. The attack from the south would be made by Patton's III Corps, a new and untested command, who were ordered to move their headquarters from Metz to Luxembourg City. Patton returned to his own headquarters at Nancy and about 11.0 that night Bradley telephoned and ordered Patton to come to the Verdun meeting the following morning at 11.0. Knowing what was going to happen Patton immediately called a Staff Meeting for 8.0 am the next day and his officers spent most of Monday night preparing three complete plans for a counter-attack from southern Luxembourg: if the swiftness of the German Fifth Panzer Army's advance continued, either capturing Bastogne or bypassing it with strong armoured forces, then Third Army would drive north from the Neufchâteau area—well to the west of the present fighting—and throw a screen in front of the Meuse crossings south of Namur; the second plan was to jump off from the Longwy area, relieving Bastogne and retaking Houffalize and eventually relieving St Vith; the third and most ambitious was a drive north from Luxembourg City along the axis of Red Ball Highway and Skyline Drive which would recapture Diekirch, Hosingen, Clervaux and reach St Vith, slicing through most of the German lines of communication, cutting off their advance units and practically restoring the original Ardennes defence line— General Patton never lacked confidence. Before he left his headquarters for the Verdun meeting he arranged a simple code by which a telephone call could instruct his Chief of Staff which of the three plans to set in motion.

All offensive action on Third Army's front was called off and the 35th Infantry and the new 87th Infantry, who had been advancing slowly, were stopped. By midnight a combat command from 4th Armored started the divisions one-hundred-and-sixty-mile move; at dawn 80th Infantry Division climbed into their trucks for a hundred-and-fifty-mile drive and the 26th Infantry Division, only sixty miles from Luxembourg, moved out on to the same crowded highway just after midnight the following day. Third US Army had started the gigantic 90° turn which was to change dramatically the whole picture in the southern half of the Ardennes Offensive.

Before the December 19 meeting at Verdun General Eisenhower had thought of replying to the German offensive by massive counter-attacks on either side of it for he believed that by coming out of the safety of the Siegfried Line into the open and by committing their armoured reserve the Germans had given the Allies back the opportunity they had lost after the collapse in France. His first intention had been to reply with offensives by all three of his Army Groups: 21st under Montgomery to attack south-east, driving down between the Meuse and the Rhine; 6th Army Group (with four divisions from Bradley's 12th) to move north into Third Army's sector and then drive north-east from Thionville along the Moselle Valley towards Coblenz and 12th Army Group, after checking the Ardennes counter-offensive, to launch an offensive towards the Rhine between Cologne and Bonn. Had this plan been adopted and had it succeeded then the allied front would have been transformed from an expanding wall to a flat-topped pyramid with the weight concentrating against about fifty miles of the Rhine, a situation from which Field Marshal Montgomery's 'powerful single thrust' could have followed.

But by the time of the Verdun meeting it had become apparent that the German assault was far too successful for this offensive action. All Allied military activity, for the time being at least, must be secondary to the task of stopping Army Group B's advance through the Ardennes. This would be accomplished by holding in place or by yielding as little ground as possible in the north, where the main German effort was being made, while at the same time attacking from the south against the German left flank as soon as possible. The only forces available for this attack were in General Patton's Third Army and if they were now going to swing from attacking east

269

to attacking north then General Devers' Seventh Army on
their right would have to move north and take over responsibility for Third Army's positions. That, in turn, meant that
First French Army, holding the extreme southern end of the
Allied line, would stretch to take over some of Seventh Army's
front: 6th Army Group would have to stop all offensive action
—Hitler's gamble in the Ardennes was already having far-
reaching effects.

But there were further complications: First French Army
alone could not hold the long line from the Swiss Frontier to
the edge of the Saar because of the existence of the Colmar
Pocket beween Strasbourg and Switzerland. This second German 'bulge' thrusting into the Allied line was a defensive position and it contained the remains of the Nineteenth German
Army who had been holding the Mediterranean coast of
France at the time of the Allied landings in August.

Hitler had immediately perceived the importance to his
Ardennes Offensive of pinning down large Allied forces at the
southern end of the front and had decreed that the Colmar
Pocket was to be held 'at all costs'. To make sure he had given
command of the sector to Heinrich Himmler.

Now on December 19, when considering his moves, General
Eisenhower had to allow for the effects of this pocket. Third
Army would have to leave one of its corps on the borders of
the Saar and strengthen Seventh Army with a division and artillery to enable it to hold a longer front. Realistically, Eisenhower was willing to let his forces fall back to carefully defined
limits while Patton's Third Army redeployed and gathered its
strength for the counter-attack. In the north these limits on
First Army's front would be the line of the Meuse and from
Sedan to Luxembourg City and at the southern end of the
Western Front the line of the Vosges mountains. General
Devers would be told to defend his line against any major
penetration but to be prepared to yield ground rather than
endanger the integrity of his forces.

This meant that if necessary the city of Strasbourg would be
given up and when, as it had to be, this decision was finally
told to the French the anger and dismay such a possibility
evoked at General De Gaulle's headquarters in Paris can well
be imagined. This hard decision was one of the most difficult
of the war for General Eisenhower, faced with a choice between the militarily desirable and the politically disastrous.
Before it was resolved both Churchill and Roosevelt were
dragged into the dispute, but on December 19 this was just
one of the many factors which General Eisenhower had to

consider when taking the decisions at Verdun.

The Supreme Commander opened the meeting in a huge, very cold room in the Verdun Barracks, by emphasizing that the situation had presented them with an opportunity of inflicting a great and perhaps decisive defeat on the German Army in the West and that it was certainly not a disaster. 'There will be only cheerful faces at this conference table,' he said.

'Hell, General Ike!' Patton burst out, 'let's have the guts to let the sons of bitches go all the way to Paris! Then we'll cut 'em off at the base and chew 'em up.' The laughter that followed this typical Georgie Patton reaction eased the tension.

General Strong, the SHAEF Chief of Intelligence, gave a picture of the situation showing clearly that the Germans had achieved four major penetrations on First Army's front and there was no coherent defence. Communications with First Army were very bad and General Hodges had reported, 'The enemy front cannot be defined as front is fluid and obscure.' Nothing had been heard from St Vith and it was not known if Bastogne had fallen; two American infantry divisions had been practically destroyed and all reserves were not committed. Fog was still checking air operations.

After this report Eisenhower told Patton that he wanted him to go to Luxembourg and take command of the battle and asked him when he could go.

'This afternoon,' said Patton promptly. He was then asked how soon he could launch an attack by at least six divisions. He replied that he could start one with three divisions on the 22nd, an estimate which caused a gasp of astonishment in the room,* and with six by Christmas Day, but if he waited he would lose the advantage of surprise.

General Eisenhower ordered a three-division attack to start from Arlon towards Bastogne not earlier than December 22 nor later than the 23rd but he warned Patton against starting too soon without sufficient forces, for he did not think that the Third Army commander even yet comprehended the great strength of the German offensive. Eisenhower also told Patton that he would take over Middleton's VIII Corps the following day—or what remained of it.

Patton telephoned his Chief of Staff and gave the code word to set the second of the three alternative plans into operation. He spent the night at the headquarters of his XX Corps who

* It was not realized that Bradley had told Patton what was going to happen and that two of Third Army's divisions were already on the road.

had already sent off their 10th Armored Division on the first day. Now Patton ordered their 5th Infantry Division to pull out of the line and start for Luxembourg and he arranged for yet another infantry division, the 35th which had been in the line for a hundred and sixty days without relief, to be pulled back and quickly made ready to fight in the Ardennes.

Now that he was to attack Patton was happy again and with his usual unquenchable optimism he told his staff that they were going to advance to Bastogne in thirty-six hours, would then push on through Houffalize to St Vith where they would wheel north-east, drive the Germans back over the Rhine and seize the crossings.

Eisenhower then turned his attention to the north flank—'obviously the dangerous one'*—where it seemed probable that the Germans would try to envelop the entire northern wing of the Ardennes defence with another attack from still further north. He ordered Bradley to use First and Ninth Army, first to check the German advance and then, in conjunction with Montgomery's forces, to launch a large-scale counter-attack as soon as possible. Montgomery was told to examine the possibility of giving up ground to shorten the line and so collect a strong reserve for this counter-attack.

When he returned to SHAEF at Versailles on Tuesday evening Eisenhower found that the situation in the Ardennes had worsened. Communications had been almost completely disrupted and there was no firm intelligence about either Bastogne or St Vith and the position along the rest of the front was unclear. The Supreme Commander decided that Bradley could not exercise effective control over the whole area of the battlefield from Luxembourg City which was now too close to the fighting and to one part of the attacked front. He wanted 12th Army Group TAC HQ to move back to Verdun. General Bradley refused on the grounds that such a move would alarm the command and cause such panic among the civilians that the roads essential for Patton's deployment would become jammed.

In the north Field Marshal Montgomery although not yet directly concerned had taken certain precautionary action in case, as he said, the Germans succeeded in 'bouncing the Meuse'. He had moved four divisions behind the Liège–Namur line to block the approaches to Antwerp and had despatched reconnaissance troops south to report on the state of defence of the Meuse bridges and he had found spare troops to assist in forming effective cover parties. Around Brussels where the

* Eisenhower: *Crusade in Europe*, p. 385.

people were aghast at the thought of the possible return of the Germans hastily formed roadblocks had been thrown up.

Attached to Montgomery's tactical headquarters were a group of hand-picked young officers who, every day, visited a different sector of the fighting and every night after dinner told him what they had seen and heard. This bypassing of normal intelligence channels enabled him to have an up-to-date picture of the whole battle front. His 'gallopers' had been particularly busy since the start of the Ardennes Offensive and as a result of their reports he was not at all happy about how the Americans were dealing with the assault against such a large section of their front.

It seemed to him that whereas the Germans were acting according to a carefully worked out over-all plan the Americans were replying with piecemeal and disconnected small attacks everywhere. What was obviously needed was for an over-all commander to get a firm grip on the situation and to deal with the battle as a whole. And he knew just who that should be.

At SHAEF two of the most important staff officers, Major-General Kenneth Strong, the chief of intelligence, and Major-General J. F. M. Whiteley, deputy chief of staff for operations, were both British but both were above the squabbles of national rivalries. Naturally Montgomery was in touch with them and had impressed upon Whiteley that the situation really required an over-all commander for the northern half of the Ardennes. He had made the same case to Field Marshal Alan Brooke, the CIGS, and had asked him to use his influence to get Eisenhower to appoint him. The Prime Minister too had been made aware of the proposal.

Late on Tuesday night Strong and Whiteley discussed the matter dispassionately and then, fortunately before any word came from London, went to see the Chief of Staff, Lieutenant-General Walter Bedell Smith, Eisenhower's Number One and SHAEF's chief tactician. Famous for his flaming temper the 'Beetle'* was not one of Field Marshal Montgomery's uncritical admirers and the suggestion he now heard—that the front should be divided and the northern half be handed to Montgomery—produced an explosive reaction. But he was too good a soldier not to realize the truth in the contention that the Germans had already split the American forces beyond possibility of control by a single field command and that the solution was the only logical one. He called General Bradley and discussed the possibility, pointing out that it would mean

* His juniors called him 'The Barker'.

that British reserves could be committed immediately and indicating that he was in favour.

Not surprisingly General Bradley was hardly overjoyed, although he admitted that if Montgomery were an American commander it would be the logical thing to do. But because he was British and because of the long wrangle about a deputy ground commander which had at last seemed to have been dealt with, Bradley was against the Field Marshal being given even temporary command of two American armies. He denied that his communications with Hodges were failing and insisted that he was perfectly able to direct the battle from Luxembourg City.

After this discussion Bedell Smith put the idea to General Eisenhower. Once more the Supreme Commander was given the choice between the militarily sound and the politically unsound decision and knowing what was at stake and having no doubt where his duty lay he telephoned Bradley with the unpalatable news. Neither has since revealed the conversation but at SHAEF Eisenhower was heard to end the call by saying, 'Well, Brad, those are my orders.'

Command decisions of great moment had been taken, now time was needed to implement them, time that could only be bought by the lives and blood of the men who were doing the actual fighting, men who in many cases had already done more than could reasonably be expected, like the men in the foxholes in front of Höfen and Rocherath still withstanding the furious attack of 'Sepp' Dietrich's SS divisions; the exhausted men manning the St Vith perimeter against ever increasing pressure; the defenders of Bastogne damming the rising tide from the east; the forward strongpoints holding out on the southern shoulder and stopping Seventh Army's attempt to set up a screen—all these were wresting precious hours from the attackers and everywhere fresh troops were arriving, not enough yet to ensure victory but perhaps enough to continue to buy time.

The Germans too, in many cases, had done more than any neutral observer would have thought possible, particularly at that stage of the war. That they had failed to achieve their initial objectives was, except in a very few cases, not the fault of the fighting men. Many of them, half trained, had been asked to attack strongly defended positions in insufficient numbers and without proper weapons. They did so and a great many died most courageously.

By Wednesday, December 20, the outcome of the great Ardennes Offensive was far from settled: pessimists on both sides predicted a colossal defeat; optimists a decisive victory. There were insufficient perceivable facts for the truth to be discernible—that Germany had attempted a hopeless task.

On December 19 Berlin announced with pride that Germany was at last attacking in the west and the Allies were retreating and, further, that the offensive was all Adolf Hitler's doing. He was personally in command and once again his military genius would triumph. The German commanders in the field were not so sure.

Which way the battle now went would depend upon the soundness of the tactical and strategical decisions taken at the highest levels, on the competence of the field commanders, on the efficiency of the supporting services and finally, as always, on the skill and fighting spirit of those soldiers—a comparatively small part of the whole—who were actually trying to kill each other on the battlefield.

19

BASTOGNE IN DANGER

*Few men are naturally courageous but training and
exercise make them into good soldiers.*

THE BYZANTINE EMPEROR MAURICE

In Bastogne General Troy Middleton had been forced to
commit all his formal reserve by Sunday afternoon (December
17) but in an emergency such as now faced him he had the right
to call on the 1128th Engineer Group who were working in the
southern half of VIII Corps area.

These engineers were widely dispersed in many small working parties; now all jobs were stopped and valuable machinery
moved west to safety while the men came in and drew
weapons, unused for many weeks. Headquarters staff, clerks,
cooks and soldiers who had never fought, clustered around
instructors to learn how to fire a bazooka, a trench mortar or
to set a mine.

General Middleton sent some of these combat engineers east
of Bastogne behind the artillery and roadblocks to form a
defensive screen which ran in a seven- to eight-mile-long arc
between the village of Foy, three and a half miles from Bastogne along the main north-east road, and Neffe, two and a half
miles from Bastogne on the Clervaux road.

This dealt as well as was then possible with the threat from
north-east to east: in order to attack Bastogne from the south-
east the Germans would have to advance up from the Clerf
through the complex of secondary roads which wound across
the Wiltz valley. Here the critical positions the Americans had
to hold were certain crossroads and the town of Wiltz, some
twelve miles east of Bastogne, lying within a bend of the river
Wiltz.

At Weidingen a bridge crossed this river into Wiltz and led
on to the main highway to Bastogne from the south-east, a
road which would certainly have to be used by the Germans in
any attempt to move west in force.

Also on Sunday Middleton sent the 44th Engineer Combat
Battalion, reinforced by the six remaining tanks and five
assault guns of the 707th Tank Destroyer Battalion, six 3-inch
towed anti-tank guns of the 630th Tank Destroyer Battalion
and some anti-aircraft guns and light armoured cars, to join

276

the 28th Infantry Division's headquarters troops in Wiltz. Wiltz must not be allowed to fall into German hands for this would expose Bastogne's weak southern flank.

Although at this stage there was no sign of German troops approaching from the south Wiltz was on the boundary line between XLVII Panzer Corps and General Brandenberger's LXXXV Corps and both the 26th Volksgrenadiers and the 5th Parachute Division were to become involved in the fight. In the case of the parachute infantry this was not intended, for Colonel Heilmann ordered his division to bypass Wiltz and strike straight for Bastogne. By Monday, however, communications were so bad he had lost control with his leading units who became drawn into the attack on Wiltz.

On Sunday night the 26th Volksgrenadiers had seized the Drauffelt bridge over the Clerf which somehow had not been prepared for destruction, and the leading units of Panzer Lehr Division passed through them and headed west for Bastogne. They were led by the Panzer Lehr Reconnaissance Regiment who were pulled away from the Consthum fight, and immediately crossed the Clerf supported by the 902nd Panzer Grenadier Regiment. By Monday morning this column had reached the Eschweiler crossroads and here the Reconnaissance Regiment turned left to attack Wiltz while the 902nd Panzer Grenadier Regiment, led by the divisional commander General Fritz Bayerlein himself, raced on towards Bastogne.

In Wiltz General Cota heard, about ten on Monday morning, that CCB of the 10th Armored Division was hurrying up from the south to his assistance and would probably arrive that afternoon. This was good news indeed, for although the 44th Combat Engineers had two companies out north-east and east, the town was dangerously exposed on the south and south-east.

The first German attack on Wiltz came at eleven on Monday morning when panzers and volksgrenadiers drove the 44th Combat Engineers back with heavy casualties. Stubbornly they continued to cover the important bridge at Weidingen from high ground west of Erpeldange but the German fire was so heavy it was evident that the bridge might be captured in an overwhelming rush, so orders were sent to destroy it. For some reason this was not done, but German pressure suddenly eased. The reason was that Panzer Lehr's Reconnaissance Regiment was now needed by Bayerlein for the capture of Bastogne and it was pulled away from Wiltz, leaving the task of seizing it to the 26th Volksgrenadiers who had slogged up from the Clerf on foot.

Late on Monday afternoon General Cota got reports that a column from 10th Armored Division's combat command had been seen moving towards Bastogne along the road from Arlon. He sent an immediate request to its commander to place his tanks and anti-tank guns south and south-east of Wiltz but Colonel Roberts replied that he was unable to do this because of prior orders from General Middleton. CCB continued north arriving at Bastogne about 4.0 pm on Monday afternoon where it was desperately needed.

This was a blow to the defenders of Wiltz and when, on Tuesday, December 19, the 5th Parachute began to attack from the south and, with the final fall of Consthum, the Germans from there came on, it became apparent that the attack would be very heavy. General Cota ordered 28th Divisional Headquarters to withdraw fourteen miles west to Sibret leaving behind a Provisional Battalion of headquarters staff to stand with the 44th Engineers and hold Wiltz as long as possible. In addition the two hundred or so survivors of the Consthum defence, then south of Wiltz, were ordered to come in. They arrived about noon on Tuesday and their commander, Lieutenant-Colonel Daniel Strickler, took over responsibility for Wiltz from Lieutenant-Colonel Kjeldseth's 44th Engineer Combat Battalion.

With the bridge at Weidingen still intact it was decided to concentrate the defence here. There were only four tanks left—the 707th Tank Battalion lost over sixty in the four days fighting—and all were unable to manoeuvre. They were towed into positions to act as stationary guns and the crews manning the platoon of assault guns, on the point of complete exhaustion after some eighty hours of firing with no more than an odd hour or two of sleep at a time, were sent to cover the bridge.

At two in the afternoon the 26th Volksgrenadiers launched a full-blooded attack from the north-east and 5th Parachute hit the southern perimeter. Although the American artillery knocked out the panzers supporting the German advance by direct fire the parachute infantry came on and got among the guns, forcing their withdrawal. Twenty-eighth Infantry Division at Sibret tried to send reinforcements to Wiltz but by now the Germans were blocking all roads into the town. More of 5th Parachute came up, eager to be on hand for the kill while on the north the 44th Engineers were forced back with 150 casualties.

The stationary tanks were out of ammunition; there were not enough machine guns for all-round defence; radio communication had failed; the defence perimeter was pierced at many points and, finally, the Weidingen bridge was blown; Wiltz was going down.

Now it became a question of saving as many men as possible but it was too late for an orderly withdrawal and only the dark prevented a massacre. A surprisingly large number of American soldiers managed to get back to Sibret to join what remained of the 28th Infantry Division's headquarters at 110th Regiment.

With Wiltz captured the roads to Bastogne from the south lay open and the 5th Parachute and the 26th Volksgrenadiers hurried on to be in on the capture of that important target about to fall, as they believed, to the tanks and guns of Panzer Lehr Division.

Panzer Lehr's commander, General Bayerlein, had led the advance guard of fifteen tanks and four companies of panzer grenadiers from the Drauffelt bridge to the village of Nieder-Wampach only six miles east of Bastogne, arriving there about half past six on Monday evening. On his right, a few miles north, gunfire flamed in the sky as the 2nd Panzer Division engaged the 9th Armored Division's CCR's last roadblock.

From Neider–Wampach the tanks of Panzer Lehr could take a fairly good secondary road south-east for about three and a half miles and then gain the good, hard-surfaced main road, seven and a half miles from Bastogne, or Bayerlein could take a chance and move west for three miles along a narrow, muddy track to the village of Mageret, only three miles from Bastogne. As his orders were to capture Bastogne as quickly as possible he chose the shorter way guessing that it probably would not be guarded. For the first fifteen hundred yards the road was paved, at the edge of the village it became a dirt road which the tanks churned to deep mud, a thousand yards further on even this petered out. Now there was only a footpath from Luxembourg into Belgium which led to the village of Benonchamps just over a mile from Mageret. It would have created chaos to turn the tanks and the rest of the column around in the dark, so Bayerlein pushed on, getting to the outskirts of Mageret just before midnight.

His leading units were engaged by a detachment of combat engineers* blocking this approach to Bastogne, but by one o'clock on Tuesday morning Panzer Lehr's advance force had seized the village thus cutting the road from Clervaux only three miles from Bastogne. But here General Bayerlein heard

* Part of the defence screen General Middleton had created. See page 276.

279

some disquieting news: only a few hours before, a pro-German civilian told him, a great armoured column of fifty tanks and their supporting infantry carriers had roared through Mageret moving from Bastogne towards the sound of battle and, the civilian assured him, it was led by an American major-general.

Now a major-general would not command any unit smaller than a division and although it hardly seemed possible that the Americans could have moved a division into Bastogne so quickly, General Bayerlein hesitated. At that time an American armoured division consisted of two hundred and sixty-three tanks: Panzer Lehr had fifty-seven and only twelve of those were with him.

The sound of guns and the flashes in the sky over to the north-east seemed to be growing in intensity—was 2nd Panzer, perhaps, already being destroyed? He could hear tank tracks and they seemed quite near (they were from the rear of his own column closing up on Mageret) and the noise of a large number of vehicles moving along the Bastogne–Longvilly road (they were Americans retreating in panic). The night was full of strange noises and Fritz Bayerlein discovered as many lesser men have done that man's spirit is at its lowest in the dark hours before the dawn. He decided to wait and see, to set up roadblocks north and south of Mageret to cover his retreat if he were suddenly attacked by a greatly superior force.

In fact the American tanks reported by the imaginative civilian—thirty not fifty and led by a captain and not a major-general—were the advance guard of Team Cherry from 10th Armored Division's CCB moving from Bastogne with orders to hold Longvilly where, it will be remembered, the weakened and badly shaken CCR of 9th Armored were expecting to be hit by the full force of 2nd Panzer Division.

10th Armored's CCB had driven from Thionville in France straight to Bastogne. The commander, Colonel William Roberts, drove on ahead and arrived at General Middleton's headquarters about four o'clock on Monday afternoon. VIII Corps' commander and a small staff were trying to exercise control over a fast-crumbling front; the rest of his headquarters had already moved eighteen miles south-west to Neufchâteau.

General Middleton had now used all his engineer combat battalions to form the defence screen from north to south-east of Bastogne and a continuous, albeit weak, line of dug-in positions ran from Noville five miles north on the road to Houffalize, to Mageret, Marvie and a roadblock about a mile south of

Bastogne on the road to Arlon. By the time Colonel Roberts reported to him there was no reasonable expectation that his screen could hold: Task Force Rose on the Clervaux road had been overrun and the German armoured column was approaching Task Force Harper, less than nine miles from Bastogne; Wiltz was under heavy attack and a reconnaissance which had been sent to the east to see if it were possible to erect a continuous defence line from 9th Armored Division's tank force at Longvilly to Wiltz, had reported that more German tanks and infantry were already west of such a line and were winding their way up the narrow roads of the Wiltz Valley heading for Bastogne; lastly, and perhaps most serious for the larger picture, the Germans had torn a hole in the north between Bastogne and St Vith by pushing back the 112th Infantry Regiment and had moved so fast west that reinforcements could not now get to Houffalize in time to hold it. Houffalize was abandoned; the next place to stop the German penetration would have to be along the Ourthe river line five to ten miles further west. The loss of Houffalize meant that the German tanks would soon be on the good main road north of Bastogne where the only defence was the combat engineers at Noville.

General Middleton ordered Colonel Roberts to split his combat command into three teams and send one each to Noville, on the road north towards Houffalize, to Longvilly to support 9th Armored Division's CCR and along the main road to the south-east for three miles to the village of Wardin in order to block the approach from Wiltz.

Colonel Roberts was a veteran of World War I but was thoroughly modern in his ideas of the use of armour and did not want his coherent command split up and his tanks used as static defence positions but he also knew that this was not the time to protest. General Middleton, he reasoned, would not spread his armour thinly without very good reasons and Roberts formed and despatched the three teams as fast as his tanks arrived in Bastogne. In fact this decision of the VIII Corps' commander to be prepared to block threats from three directions instead of concentrating his tank reinforcements against the known attack coming in from the north-east was one of the factors which was to save Bastogne.

The leading team of CCB, of a tank battalion, an armoured infantry company and a platoon each of engineers and reconnaissance, came into Bastogne less than an hour after Colonel Roberts and were sent off to Longvilly with orders to join with CCR and the other troops there to hold that place if the Germans broke through the Task Force Harper roadblock a couple of miles further east.

Called Team Cherry after the commander of the tank battalion, Lieutenant-Colonel Henry Cherry, it was led by an advance guard of a company of tanks, some armoured infantry and the platoon of cavalry reconnaissance who halted west of Longvilly about half past seven on Sunday night. The road was jammed with vehicles full of badly shaken men anxious to get to safety. Colonel Cherry went ahead to CCR's headquarters to try to sort out the situation and discover their intentions but the series of hard blows, heavy losses and the destruction of both their roadblocks had badly lowered morale and Colonel Gilbreth was finding it difficult to keep the survivors reacting aggressively. Many were on the point of exhaustion and felt that they had done all and more than was expected of them in three days of continual fighting and that someone else should now take over. All that lay between Longvilly and the rampaging force of German tanks, guns and infantry who had just smashed Task Force Harper were some batteries of the 73rd Armored Field Artillery, some survivors of the 28th Infantry Division, including the reserve company from Wiltz, and four tank destroyers—not enough to stop the powerful German force which had swept through Clervaux and both roadblocks. Colonel Gilbreth had decided to withdraw through Mageret towards Bastogne.

Colonel Cherry went back to his team and ordered the advance guard, under Lieutenant Hyduke, to put out a screen west of Longvilly; the main body would stay about half a mile back until it became clear what CCR were going to do. He then drove back to Bastogne to tell Colonel Roberts at first hand about the situation in Longvilly as he saw it—a withdrawal in danger of becoming a rout. CCB's commander told him to go back and hold Longvilly with whatever support he could lay his hands on; he had permission to attach any man, vehicle or gun which came into his area but, if the worst came to the worst, Team Cherry would hold Longvilly alone.

Colonel Roberts had sent off his second team, which had come into Bastogne hard on the heels of the first, east of Bastogne to Wardin to stop the rumoured approach of German tanks along the main road to Bastogne that ran south of Wiltz, the road along which Bayerlein would have brought his Panzer Lehr advance guard had he not chosen to go across country to Mageret on Monday night. This second force from CCB, named Team O'Hara after Lieutenant-Colonel James O'Hara, commander of the armoured infantry battalion which led it, found the situation quiet at Wardin through which stragglers from the 28th Infantry passed all night long, mostly exhausted and badly shocked and with little idea of what had happened on their front.

The third team from CCB didn't get into Bastogne until after dark. It was led by Major William Desobry, youngest of the three commanders, who was told by Colonel Roberts to take fifteen Sherman tanks and a platoon of tank destroyers north to Noville and hold it.

'You're young,' said Colonel Roberts to Major Desobry, 'and by tomorrow morning you'll probably be nervous and you might think that it would be a good idea to withdraw from Noville. When you begin thinking that remember that I told you it would be best not to withdraw until I order you to do so.'

Colonel William Roberts was one of the oldest officers actually engaged in tank fighting and his skill and steadiness had completely won the confidence of the younger officers under him. Major Desobry had known him for years and accepted his word as gospel—it would not be many hours before that trust would be tested severely.

Now, knowing that the dark would slow his column down to about five miles an hour and warned that it would be a close race to get to Noville before the Germans, Desobry sent a cavalry platoon ahead to reconnoitre Noville and to choose positions for the tanks to occupy for the rest of the night. There were no maps, so an VIII Corps military policeman was put on the leading vehicle to point out the way to the road north: the lead tanks moved out with armoured infantry on their backs. Team Desobry arrived at Noville at 2.30 am on Tuesday morning to find everything quiet—it would not remain so for long for 2nd Panzer Division had not tried to continue into Bastogne through Longvilly for the city was not in their sector—although of course this was not known to anyone on the American side. Instead this armoured column, LXVII Panzer Corps' right hook, was intended now to move through Bourcy, Noville and to cross the next river, the Ourthe, just beyond Bertogne. Consequently, after passing through Allerborn, only two miles east of Longvilly, 2nd Panzer's advance guard turned abruptly right and headed north-west towards Bourcy. At about the same time the advance guard of Team Cherry was taking up positions to their right to cover the east and south-east approaches to Longvilly. An imaginary observer in a balloon above the battlefield would have seen two powerful columns of tanks, armoured infantry and guns moving towards each other from thirty miles apart on Monday only, when a mile separated them, to sheer right away from each other.

When 2nd Panzer turned right their commander pushed a small mixed force forward to test the strength of the American position at Longvilly and to discourage their advancing. Just before midnight CCR's artillery were firing over open sights on these Germans at two hundred yards' range. Colonel Gilbreth then ordered the remnants of CCR to withdraw to Bastogne through Mageret and Longvilly became the sole responsibility of Team Cherry.

In Noville Team Desobry's fifteen Shermans and supporting armoured infantry had come in about midnight. All exits were covered and forward outposts established. One of these was half a mile east of Noville at Bourcy towards which 2nd Panzer's advance guard was moving.

Shortly after he had given CCB's commander, Colonel Roberts, orders to send tank teams to the north and east, Middleton had another visitor. This was Brigadier-General Anthony McAuliffe in temporary command of the 101st Airborne Division on their way north to Werbomont. Because his car was well ahead of the rest of the division McAuliffe had decided to make a detour through Bastogne in order to find out the latest situation from General Middleton. Delighted, the VIII Corps commander told him to bring his division into the town as soon as possible and this change of destination was confirmed by higher authority.

A similar lucky chance had even more important effects: the leading 101st unit was part of the divisional artillery which arrived at a crossroads some seven miles west of Bastogne about eight o'clock on Monday evening to find the rear vehicles of the 82nd Airborne Division at that moment crawling—the rear of a convoy always seems either to be travelling at breakneck speed to close up or crawling—ahead of them and blocking the road. The officer in command, Colonel Sherburne, looked at the map and decided that it might be quicker in the long run to go to Werbomont by a detour through Bastogne. The MP Sergeant on traffic control duty told him that General McAuliffe had taken the Bastogne road a little earlier so Colonel Sherburne assumed that he had come to the same conclusion and he told the MP to divert all 101st Airborne traffic coming up behind along the same route.

This was done* and so, by a series of accidents, some of the 101st Airborne got into position at Bastogne hours earlier than they would otherwise have done—at a time when hours were of the greatest importance.

But at the time no one in the division was aware of this. For the paratroopers packed in the trucks, Bastogne was just a rear area town housing a corps headquarters where they would probably get their orders. None could have guessed that it was a name that was about to become part of their division's and their country's history. The acting commander, Brigadier-General McAuliffe, busy arranging his dispositions, could never have conceived in his wildest imaginings that some day his children's children would visit this small town in southern Belgium to stand in the Grand Place which would then be named 'Place Macauliffe' [sic].

General Middleton was only able to give McAuliffe a rough idea of the situation and spoke of a 'major penetration' and 'broken units'. It was not known where the Germans were— reports from men streaming back from overrun positions placed them everywhere in great strength—nor what had happened to 9th Armored Division's roadblocks. Nor was much known of 10th Armored Division's three teams from CCB beyond the fact that they were moving into position. It seemed at least probable that the Germans were well past Bastogne on the north and this could mean that the 101st's column might be attacked on the road in the dark when it was most vulnerable.

As soon as he knew that the 101st would be fighting in Bastogne General McAuliffe and his operations officer, Lieutenant-Colonel Kinnard, hurriedly made a reconnaissance to the west to choose an assembly area while it was still light. This action placed the division in a sheltered forward assembly area until it was needed—a fact which would greatly influence the coming battle.

The task of getting 101st Airborne's long convoy into Bastogne was made difficult by the tide of traffic flowing west of vehicles of all types, some evacuating rear headquarters and some containing fighting troops who had started to retreat and now did not want to stop. The centre of Bastogne looked like a vast car park but, nevertheless, the leading combat unit, the 501st Parachute Infantry Regiment, came into the assembly

* It was not, of course, quite so simple and straightforward as this. For instance Colonel Sherburne later found two military policemen, two hundred yards from each other, directing 101st trucks in quite different directions.

285

area about midnight on Monday, having covered the 107 miles from near Reims in rain and snow in eight hours. By nine o'clock on Tuesday morning, December 19, the division's other three regiments had all arrived in Bastogne.

Three other units were to contribute greatly to the coming defence of Bastogne: two battalions of field artillery equipped with 155-mm howitzers capable of reaching any point on the defence perimeter and a battalion of tank destroyers with the high-velocity 76-mm self-propelled guns, a great improvement on the short-barrelled 75-mm guns to the Shermans.

One of the artillery battalions, the 969th Field Artillery, had been firing in support of 28th Division until the German advance had threatened to cut them off. While displacing through Bastogne further west they were ordered to lay down a barrage north of Noville and in this way became part of the Bastogne defence. The other artillery unit, the 755th Armored Field Artillery Battalion were moved to Bastogne from Ninth Army in the north and arrived on Monday evening. Both joined the 420th Armored Field Artillery of 10th Armored Division's CCB on high ground about three miles south-west of Bastogne. Concentrated fire from these guns was to be responsible for tipping the balance against several German attacks.

The tank destroyer battalion, the 705th, without whose guns the Bastogne defenders could probably not have stopped the German armour, also came from Ninth Army in the north via Liège and their route took them through La Roche and Bertogne, both of obvious tactical importance. General Middleton radioed instructions for them to erect roadblocks at both places —another decision which was to have far-reaching effects.

While 2nd Panzer Division was fighting its way west through the 110th Infantry Regiment and VIII Corps' roadblocks the 116th Panzer Division on its right, after the initial delay at Ouren caused by the 112th Infantry's resistance and the subsequent detour south across the Dasburg pontoon bridge, moved west against very little resistance towards Houffalize. The division's reconnaissance troops swung south of this town, not realizing that it had been abandoned, and moved along the south side of the Ourthe river looking for a crossing. The obvious one was from Bertogne, about eight miles south-west of Houffalize and the same distance north-east of Bastogne, from where a secondary road crossed the Ourthe and led to La Roche and another important bridge.

At La Roche were the supply trains of the 7th Armored

Division in contact with the St Vith defence and although there had been no reports of German troops anywhere in the vicinity the officer in charge of 7th Armored's rations, fuel and ammunition had put out protective units to his south and east. One of these was on the opposite bank of the Ourthe bridge between Bertogne and La Roche and consisted of half-tracks with 37-mm anti-aircraft guns and a company of ordnance maintenance troops. When they arrived at their position they reported that someone had blown the bridge already.

The forward reconnaissance of 116 Panzer Division came up the road from Bertogne and stopped around the bend short of the bridge which they expected to be guarded. A patrol went forward and reported the position of the American half-tracks across the river and a self-propelled gun was brought up which destroyed both with four quick shots.

The American soldiers withdrew to a ridge from which small-arms fire could be directed at the crossing place thus preventing the Germans from repairing the broken span. Some hours later five more American anti-aircraft half-tracks came up and two of 705 Tank Destroyer Battalion's guns.

116th Panzer then pushed further reconnaissance down the road north-west from Bertogne to the main Bastogne–Namur highway. Here they turned right and discovered to their surprise that a good Bailey bridge was still standing at Ortheuville. As soon as this news reached 116th Panzer Division's commander, Major-General Siegfried von Waldenburg, he ordered his advance guard to move quickly to capture this important crossing.

This was the evening of Tuesday, December 19 and 116th Panzer were further west than any other German troops in the Ardennes. Once across the Ourthe nothing but small bodies of combat engineers lay between them and the Meuse crossing at Dinant (although strong forces were already on their way from the north) and the Ortheuville bridge was guarded by no more than a platoon of combat engineers who had been sent to prepare it for destruction. This they had not yet been able to do and it is likely that a reckless dash across the bridge by the Germans would have delivered it into their hands. But they reported back and waited for orders and during the delay a battalion of combat engineers, who had been relieved by 101st Airborne troops and were moving back, were ordered to Ortheuville. A little later the 705th Tank Destroyer Battalion, who had not been able to move through Bertogne because of the blown bridge, also came in and the opportunity for a *coup de main* was gone.

The advance guard of 116th Panzer had reached Salle, a mile and a half short of the main Bastogne highway to the west, when the commander of LVIII Panzer Corps, General Walter Krueger, decided that the Ortheuville bridge would undoubtedly be blown in 116th Panzer's face, that the crossing would then be covered so that it would be impossible to put in another bridge—and anyway his corps had no bridging equipment with it—and, that, in short, despite the apparent success of his panzer division's advance guard there was no future in their continuing in the direction they had chosen.

On the other hand their rear guard had occupied Houffalize without opposition and patrols had reported a complete absence of American troops to the north or north-west. A rapid advance to Samrée on the La Roche to Salmchâteau road and then across the Ourthe at La Roche would put him well on the way to the Meuse.

He ordered General von Waldenburg to turn his long divisional column round in its tracks (and it was now pitch dark) and to bring them all the way back through Houffalize.

This change of direction was to send 116th Panzer Division straight into First Army's newly-formed right flank and although at first it was to meet with considerable success the final result would be to put paid to 116th Panzer's chances of reaching the Meuse.

20

HIGH WATER MARK FOR BATTLEGROUP PEIPER

In a tank battle if you stand still you are lost.
GENERAL VON MANTEUFFEL (in an interview with
Basil Liddell Hart)

Battlegroup Peiper, the fast-moving, heavily armoured spearhead of 1st SS Panzer Division, had been diverted at Trois Ponts by the last-minute destruction of the river bridges there by a single company of combat engineers and had turned north in search of an alternative way across the Amblève so as to be able to regain their assigned route—the road through Werbomont to the bridge over the Meuse at Huy. By Monday night, it will be remembered, after an attempt to move south through Cheneux was foiled by the blowing of the bridge there by yet another of the small groups of engineers whose determined actions altered the course of the whole offensive, Battlegroup Peiper stopped at La Gleize, only three and a half miles north of Trois Ponts but less than eight miles from First US Army Headquarters at Spa.

A mile or so in front of the confident SS some of 30th Infantry Division's 119th Regiment had arrived after dark on Monday, December 18, and hastily thrown up a foxhole perimeter defence on three sides of the next town, Stoumont. Mines were laid, the eight available 3-inch towed tank destroyers were moved into position and three 57-mm anti-tank and two 90-mm anti-aircraft guns sited in support. Forward defence was supplied by 119th's Third Battalion; the First Battalion with tanks and artillery were lying three miles back on high ground near where the valley road forked south-west and north-west. Their job was to stop the Germans from taking either if they succeeded in breaking through the Stoumont position; the Second Battalion had been diverted south to Werbomont to block the way west through there until the arrival of the 82nd Airborne Division hurrying up from Reims.

First Army were still convinced that Liège was 1st SS Panzer's target and most of 119th Infantry Regiment's strength was concentrated on guarding the fork leading to the north-west but, in fact, Peiper intended to take the south-west one which led to a still unblown bridge across the Amblève and, after six or seven winding miles, on to his original route three miles east of Werbomont.

The main weakness of the forward Stoumont defence was the lack of artillery or tanks and the American commander had ordered both to move up from the main force at first light on Tuesday. But Colonel Peiper had no intention of allowing any more time for the Americans to strengthen their defences than he could help; during the last hour or so of darkness assault parties of Panzer Grenadiers moved up to the edge of fields which ran from woodland right to Stoumont, and parachute infantry* infiltrated to positions on high ground overlooking the town. The panzers, now including a battalion of Tigers, manoeuvred into positions from where they could support the infantry attack and then advance themselves—a few worked their way to the outskirts of the town. Finally a battery of 105-mm self-propelled guns backed up this assault and everything was ready for the kind of overwhelming, stunning attack for which 'Hitler's Bodyguard' had made themselves famous.

Along the western side of the fields the 30th Infantry's riflemen, many of whom were green replacements, waited in their foxholes. Behind them the gunners manning their now immovable 3-inch tank destroyers peered through the dark and prayed that when dawn came fog would not render them helpless.

While these preparations for battle were being made, another of 30th Infantry Division's regiments, the 117th, were waiting for first light to attack Battlegroup Peiper's tail and so cut his lifeline at Stavelot. Both these battles would go on all day; both would be critical.

As soon as visibility permitted, the German armoured infantry advanced boldly across the open fields but heavy smallarms fire, chopping holes in their ranks, checked them. Peiper immediately ordered the panzers to advance in two columns with the infantry following close behind. The early morning mist and winter dark screened the approach of the German tanks until they were almost on top of the American foxholes and no time was left for the anti-tank gunners, whose desperate call for illuminating flares was ignored, to engage them. As the great tanks loomed over them the American riflemen fled their foxholes for the houses behind; the towed tank destroyers were overrun, all eight being lost.

Sensing a quick victory the Germans surged forward, but at this critical moment ten Sherman tanks from the main force appeared and it was the German infantry's turn to seek cover. Peiper then ordered one of his favourite tactics—a flat-out

* From 3rd Parachute Division who had joined Peiper at Lanzerath.

charge by groups of two or three heavy tanks straight down the road supported by fire from other tanks and self-propelled guns. Although he lost six tanks—two to anti-aircraft gunners firing bazookas which they had only just been shown how to use—by half past ten on Tuesday morning, Battlegroup Peiper had seized Stoumont and inflicted heavy casualties on the Third Battalion who lost 267 men, 13 heavy guns, 10 vehicles and almost all their machine guns. Of the company holding the foxhole line east of the town only those who managed to scramble up on to the Shermans, which quickly withdrew without loss, escaped. The company south of the town was cut off and captured. Only the company holding the northern perimeter was able to withdraw under a smoke screen.

The comparative ease with which Stoumont was captured was due to the early loss of the eight 3-inch tank destroyers and the lack of artillery support, for the guns ordered forward at first light were not able to get up in time. The German strength had been appreciated on Monday night and the necessary guns and tanks ordered to support the Stoumont position, but the mistake was to delay the move until first light, for this was very often the time when the Germans attacked. It was also unfortunate, although it could not have been foreseen, that the divisional cannon company whose rôle was to defend the riflemen against tanks was with the Second Battalion at Werbomont.

The Shermans, which had managed to get up to the fighting at a critical moment, were left without infantry support and fell back precipitately but this disorganized withdrawal was stopped when infantry reinforcements advancing eastwards from the main body of the regiment encountered the tanks. Protected from bazookas the Shermans then withdrew properly, covering each other and so were able to slow up the German pursuit. This allowed time for a 90-mm anti-aircraft gun to be sited in an unusual ground-laying rôle at a road bend from where its crew were able to knock out the two leading panzers. The further delay this caused was enough for a strong roadblock to be established where the narrow road cut between a steep hill and the river. Tanks, artillery and infantry quickly turned this into a most formidable barrier but, unfortunately for the Americans, not across Peiper's route for the position was beyond the turnoff to the south-west.

All the Germans had to do now was to push a small force forward to keep the American defence busy while their main force crossed the Amblève and regained their assigned route— the road from Trois Ponts to Werbomont from where they could reach the Meuse that night—another triumphant advance for the famous SS 'Leibstandarte Adolf Hitler' Division.

But it was not to be, for the German tanks, assault guns, armoured cars and half-tracks were brought to a halt not by men and guns but by lack of fuel. Their tanks were dry and there was no sign of the promised replenishment.

The reason lay at Stavelot which Peiper thought was firmly held by 3rd Paratroop Division. Instead, that division had been diverted north to dam the tide of American reinforcements flowing towards the battle and 30th Infantry's counter-attack the day before had been able to seize two-thirds of the town back from the rear elements of his column. And while Peiper was fighting for Stoumont and the road west, a battalion from the 117th Infantry Regiment, supported by tanks and very heavy artillery fire, had attacked, and by midday Tuesday controlled all Stavelot north of the river. However, the Germans hung grimly on to the vital Amblève bridge, even trying to move panzer reinforcements across it but in the face of artillery and tank fire this attempt failed. Finally, after dark, an American demolition team loaded one thousand pounds of TNT into a truck and covered by smoke shells fired on to the opposite bank, dashed down to the river and completely demolished Stavelot bridge, thus pinching off Battlegroup Peiper's vital flow of fuel and ammunition. Now, unless the rest of 1st SS Panzer Division could break through or the Luftwaffe keep them supplied, they could go no further. What little fuel remained had to be husbanded carefully so that the panzers and assault guns would at least be able to manoeuvre when the inevitable American armoured attack came.

One of the strange blank spots in the German Intelligence briefing of I SS Panzer Corps was their ignorance of the enormous quantities of fuel and lubricants stored in this area—'sufficient to send all the German motorized columns to Antwerp with full tanks.'* One of these dumps, with just under a million gallons of fuel, was on the road from Stavelot to Francorchamps and had been the source of the blazing roadblock which had stopped the German probe in that direction on Monday. This dump was completely evacuated by midday on Tuesday but another, four miles north of La Gleize on the road to Spa with more than two million gallons of fuel, was hurriedly protected by a scratch force built round a headquarters company and various troops in the area. They scraped together a few assault guns, multiple mount heavy machine guns and a couple of anti-aircraft guns, and when all

* V Corps' G-3 Journal: December 19, 1944.

these opened up on a small German force reconnoitring the area, it withdrew. This was on Monday, the day before the battle at Stoumont and Peiper was not, of course, interested in turning north, but had he known of the existence of this vast supply of fuel he would certainly have seized it.

Now practically immobile, Battlegroup Peiper had to yield the initiative and prepare to defend themselves. Leaving a thin screen in front of the American position the main force pulled back in a tight ring round Stoumont. Puzzled by the sudden lull the Americans sent a probing force forward just after dusk. After knocking out three panzers they reported that the powerful German armoured column had apparently withdrawn. Once again when least expected the Americans had been given the advantage of time: once again the whole picture changed in a matter of hours.

The threat posed by Battlegroup Peiper, apparently aimed at Liège, had caused General Hodges to divert the 82nd Airborne from Bastogne to Werbomont and the eleven thousand troops of this élite division came into their new area during Monday night, after a breakneck drive from Reims, and at first light on Tuesday two regiments of parachute infantry marched from Werbomont eastwards along the main road towards Trois Ponts to make contact with either American or German troops —they did not know which, for, as yet, they had little information of the whereabouts of either. Two battalions turned north and relieved the roadblock from 119th Infantry who had smashed up Peiper's columns of panzer grenadiers the night before; the rest continued on, expecting to hit German forces at every ridge but to their surprise encountered none and by midnight were occupying two small villages only three miles from Trois Ponts where, quite unknown to them, the combat engineers were still guarding the blown crossing points.

Not knowing the whereabouts of either American or German troops in his area, the commander of the 82nd Airborne Division, Major-General Gavin, pushed forces north, east and south from Werbomont to form a shield. On the division's left, between Werbomont and Stoumont, parachute infantry moved on to the village of Rahier; two miles further on, unknown to them, the panzer grenadiers with tanks and self-propelled guns were prepared to defend the blown bridge at Cheneux. To the east of Werbomont the road to Trois Ponts was covered by the force which had moved to within three miles of that place: a company of parachute infantry was sent five miles south-east of Werbomont to the village of Bras.

The rest of 82nd Airborne Division were to remain in reserve around Werbomont but truck drivers bringing up supplies from the south reported that the Germans had cut the main Bastogne to Liège highway at Houffalize and had already sent reconnaissance nearly fifteen miles further west. The point of a panzer division seemed to be heading for the bridge at Hotton over the river Ourthe—last barrier before the Meuse.

Part of the American 3rd Armored Division was moving towards this area from the north but a block had to be thrown up in front of the panzers until the American tanks arrived and a battalion of glider infantry and a platoon of tank destroyers were sent hurriedly fifteen miles back along Airborne Division's line of march. By nightfall on Tuesday this small force was in position near Hotton wondering which would get to them first—the tanks of 3rd Armored Division or those of 116th Panzer Division.

Finally, to complete the shield, a company of glider infantry was sent seven miles due south of Werbomont to the crossroads of Manhay, blocking another approach to Hotton. Werbomont was not strongly protected and the troops from 30th Infantry Division who had been holding it were able to rejoin their regiment, the 110th at Stoumont, bringing with them their attached tanks and artillery—a most welcome reinforcement for the attack to be launched against Peiper from there the following day.

With the arrival of the 82nd Airborne Division on First Army's right, its parent organization, the XVIII Airborne Corps under Major-General Matthew Ridgway, who had been dramatically flown to the Ardennes Battle from England, was given responsibility for sealing the twenty-mile gap between V Corps and the remainder of VIII Corps in the south.

As well as his own airborne division General Ridgway was to have the 30th Infantry Division and the 3rd Armored Division (minus its CCA which was in a defensive rôle in the Eupen area) and any other troops in the area. At St Vith, unknown to either Ridgway or First Army, there was the mixed force built around 7th Armored Division and at several places there were the important small groups of combat engineers. Ridgway also got other troops which First Army scraped up, such as the 740th Tank Battalion who had only just arrived in Belgium and were drawing tanks at Sprimont, half way between Werbomont and Liège. XVIII Airborne Corps' initial task was uncomplicated—to stop any German advance from anywhere along a line extending from Battlegroup Peiper to as far south as La Roche, fifteen miles northwest of Bastogne.

Although, in this large area, the situation was extremely obscure there was an evident first priority: Battlegroup Peiper, who seemed to the American command to be poised to strike hard for Liège. It was known that their main line of communications had been cut at Stavelot but it was not appreciated yet that the doughty C Company, 51st Combat Engineers, were stopping them from receiving supplies via Trois Ponts either.

First Army Headquarters at Spa had been made uncomfortably aware of how near the advancing German armour was to them when, on Monday, a few panzers had explored the secondary road from Stoumont which ran through the woods to Spa. By Tuesday all of First Army Headquarters had moved fifteen miles back to Chaudfontaine, five miles east of Liège, but they were still anxious, for all that lay between Battlegroup Peiper's strong force and the prize of Liège, stuffed with supplies of all kinds, were the depleted 119th Infantry Regiment and a handful of Sherman tanks running short of ammunition. A large combat command from 3rd Armored Division was on the way but no one knew where it was. Also Bradley ordered the 84th Infantry Division in the Geilenkirchen area to hand over to the 102nd Infantry and move south to reinforce First Army. At Chaudfontaine the 84th's Planning Officer was told to assemble his division in the Marche area.

After three bewildering days of constant attack, retreat and shattered communications no one at First Army Headquarters really knew where anyone was any more. Reinforcements, like the 30th Infantry Division, had to be used immediately on arrival to dam the German tide or, like the 7th Armored, entered the area and were swallowed up in the fog of war. First news of the whereabouts of this division came on Tuesday, December 19, at the new First Army Headquarters in Chaudfontaine when an Intelligence Captain noticed two GIs wearing 7th Armored shoulder patches. He asked them where they had come from and what they were doing at Army Headquarters and they replied that they had driven over that morning from their divisional headquarters at Vielsalm to try to find a truck full of Christmas parcels they had been forced to abandon on the move south. They were startled to find themselves moved rapidly up the chain of command to the Chief of Staff himself, Major-General William Kean, who questioned them closely about the route they had taken and the troops they had come through. The two privates knew nothing of the fighting their division were engaged in nor much about anything except the location of 7th Armored Headquarters but as they were dismissed they heard General Kean say to an aide,

'This is the most information I've had all day.'

'Man,' said one of them, shaking his head, 'this shouldn't *happen* to a private!'

At First Army Headquarters there was only the sketchiest knowledge of the overall situation: little was known of the fierce fighting in front of the Elsenborn ridge or the mounting threat to Bastogne, and nothing of the defence of St Vith or the attempt to roll up First Army's right flank by the Seventh German Army at Echternach. Their whole attention had to be concentrated on stitching up the rent torn across their centre by the German armoured spearheads. Somehow a defence line had to be thrown across but this could not be done until fresh divisions arrived to fatten out XVIII Airborne Corps.

First of these to reach the area was 3rd Armored whose reserve combat command, led by the divisional commander, Major-General Maurice Rose, reached the Hotten–Soy road on Wednesday morning and were ordered to push out reconnaissance immediately. Unknown to them the advance guard of 116th Panzer Division were now also moving towards Hotton from the Houffalize to Liège road. 3rd Armored Division's CCB came into Theux, five miles north of Spa: First Army's new headquarters were now protected and order began to emerge from the chaos caused by widespread retreats and wild rumours.

By December 20 three American divisions, an infantry, an armoured* and an airborne were stretched in a long line from Malmédy south-west to Hotton and a fourth infantry division, the 84th, was moving to take up position on their right in the Marche area. In the next few days another armoured and another infantry division would fill in between Marche and the Meuse bridge at Dinant, but on Wednesday, before Montgomery's conference at Chaudfontaine, these decisions were not known.

If this newly-formed Ourthe river defence line could be held and if Bastogne did not fall then Fifth Panzer Army's advance could be funnelled through the gap between La Roche and Bastogne and led towards the Meuse crossings between Namur and Givet to which Montgomery was hurrying some hundred and sixty tanks and strong artillery support. Such a narrow German penetration would be vulnerable to Allied attacks

---

* 3rd Armored Division was still on the 'old tables' and therefore had three hundred and ninety tanks instead of the two hundred and sixty-three of the other American armoured divisions. Its CCB together with the headquarters and attached units were about equal to a normal armoured division.

from north and south—and these were already being planned.

But on Wednesday morning, December 20, this all-important defence line was only just forming and at any moment a strong German armoured thrust could shatter it. 2nd Panzer were on the point of crossing the Ourthe only fifteen miles south-east of Marche where as yet there were only token American forces and there was Battlegroup Peiper to worry about on the other flank. The 84th Infantry and 3rd Armored's reserve were hurried to the Marche–Hotton–Soy line while plans were made to hit Peiper's dangerous armoured concentration with simultaneous attacks from three sides.

Thanks to a powerful Luftwaffe radio which had been brought up to him Colonel Peiper was now able to talk with General Mohnke, 1st SS Panzer Division's commander and make clear his desperate shortage of fuel, and to a lesser extent of ammunition. In turn he was warned of the movement of the combat command from 3rd Armored Division towards his northern flank but as German Intelligence had not yet learned of 82nd Airborne Division's forced march Peiper did not realize that his southern flank was also threatened.

The only hope of getting fuel through to La Gleize was either to get a pontoon bridge across the Amblève by recapturing either Stavelot or Trois Ponts or for the Luftwaffe to do it by a parachute drop. 30th Infantry Division had built up a good defensive position at Stavelot with troops dug in the town, covered by tanks and artillery on the high ground behind, and it would take several days for even a strong German attack to re-establish a bridge here. In that time the stranded battlegroup itself would undoubtedly be attacked in force. Peiper therefore had to be supplied at once; it would have to be the Luftwaffe.

Sixth Panzer Army HQ were persuaded of this and asked the Luftwaffe for an immediate emergency supplies drop but command rivalries and politics in high places delayed the attempt for three days. By then Battlegroup Peiper, under great pressure, were just hanging on and most of the drop fell in the Stoumont area which was then in American hands. Peiper's men got only enough fuel to run the battery recharging motors for the radios and to move some of the panzers and assault guns to better positions. The Luftwaffe got such a warm reception from the anti-aircraft defences that they refused all further requests to drop supplies in the Ardennes.

Although 1st SS Panzer Division had concentrated its main weight in Battlegroup Peiper it did have three other columns following behind the battlegroup's thin penetration to enlarge it, to secure the line of communications, to replace casualties and finally, when the Huy bridge was seized, to keep the bridgehead open for I Panzer Corps to exploit.

Two of 1st SS Panzer Division's follow-up columns had tried to keep close behind Peiper's tail and it was the leading units from one of these who had attempted to rush the Stavelot bridge before it was blown. The fourth column, a much stronger force than either of the other two, had been assigned a parallel route further south. Held up at the outset of the offensive by newly-laid minefields on Fourteenth Cavalry Group's front they did not start moving west until Monday and were diverted south by jammed roads into Fifth Panzer Army's sector. About two o'clock on Tuesday morning this force hit 7th US Armored Division's CCR at Recht and were forced to stop. Since then the Fuehrer Begleit Brigade and the 9th SS Panzer Division had been moved to assault St Vith, thus allowing 1st SS Panzer's fourth column to break off and move north and join the rest of the division in an attempt to break through to Battlegroup Peiper. But this attempt would not be ready until Thursday, December 21 and on Wednesday Peiper's position deteriorated badly.

Although XVIII Airborne Corps commander had pushed troops eastwards from Werbomont on Tuesday to within a couple of miles of Trois Ponts he had obtained very little knowledge either of the location of any German forces, except Battlegroup Peiper's head at Stoumont, or of any V or VIII Corps troops in his zone. Nevertheless General Ridgway planned to use his Corps in a triple attack to start on Wednesday to encircle all German forces north of the Amblève. From the north 3rd Armored Division's CCB would attack towards La Gleize and Stavelot; from the west the 119th Infantry would attack to drive Peiper out of Stoumont and back to La Gleize. The troops of 82nd Airborne, on Peiper's left, would attack north through Cheneux to push the Germans there back into the La Gleize area and on to the guns of the force from 3rd Armored Division coming in from Stavelot. At the same time other airborne troops would move on to Trois Ponts to secure the bridges there and cut off Peiper's line of retreat.

On Wednesday reconnaissance paratroops reached Trois Ponts without encountering any resistance and found, to their surprise, that it was occupied by Company C of the 51st Engineers and that the three important bridges had been destroyed.

'I bet you guys are glad we're here,' was the greeting of the engineers' commander to the paratroops commander. They were—and so were the division, corps and army commanders when the information reached them—but the best news the airborne patrols sent back on December 20 was that they had made contact with the westernmost positions of the Seventh Armored Division in the village of Fosse just over a mile south of the airborne position at Basse Bodeux. With this connection another line had been threaded across the rent in First Army's front.

The airborne moved in to Trois Ponts and one battalion was put across the Salm to form a bridgehead. Now, it was thought, Peiper's destruction was certain, for there seemed to be no way out.

Also on Wednesday the concentric attacks against the trapped battlegroup began. 3rd Armored Division's CCB launched three task forces from the north. The most powerful, Task Force Lovelady, with fifty-eight medium tanks, nine self-propelled 105-mm guns and a company of armoured infantry, moved from east of Spa down through the woods and seized the road from La Gleize to Trois Ponts behind Peiper.

A second tank–infantry column struck towards La Gleize from just west of Spa but Peiper had anticipated this move and stopped the tanks with a well-placed roadblock. The American infantry then tried to make their way around this defence but a sharp counter-attack by panzer grenadiers from La Gleize drove them back to their tanks. Nightfall on the 20th found this second column in a small village a mile or so north of La Gleize.

The third task force from Third Armored moved from an area about three miles west of Spa towards Stoumont. The intention was that this attack would coincide with the one from 119th Infantry but once more Peiper had skilfully covered himself. Panzers in hull-down positions knocked out the leading Third Armored tanks and confined the rest to a road through woods too thick for tank movement. This force was also stopped well short of their target.

Nor did the attack from 119th Infantry against Peiper's front succeed in dislodging the Germans from Stoumont for they had laid minefields in front of them, covered by fire from panzer grenadiers dug in on high ground. Although the American infantry and supporting tanks pushed doggedly on, the going was slow and by Wednesday night they were still half a mile from the western edge of Stoumont. Only two tanks had been lost in crossing the five minefields, but rooting out the panzer grenadiers had caused much delay. With darkness thick fog rolled in and the 119th prepared to stand to all

299

night in case of a German counter-attack.

A cause for concern was a strong German infantry position in a large building on high ground nearby. This was a sanatorium dominating the road along which the Americans would have to spend the night, and so, of course, would have to be captured. An attack was laid on, the building was shelled and two companies of infantry climbed up in the fog and after a short fight in the swirling fog the panzer grenadiers were driven out and four 20-mm guns captured. The Americans turned the sanatorium into a fortress position with a line of foxholes surrounding it and sand-bagged emplacements inside. Four Shermans moved up the road to be able to add their fire in case the Germans attacked, for the 2nd SS Panzer Grenadier Regiment had dug in only some three hundred yards off.

In the sanatorium's deep underground rooms two hundred sick children and old people took refuge with the medical staff while 119th Infantry's riflemen occupied the ground-floor rooms behind sandbagged windows. The early part of the evening passed quietly, but about eleven o'clock shells burst inside the building. They had been fired from panzers which had somehow got up on the high ground behind in the dark.

A few minutes later the SS troops erupted from their cover and charged towards the sanatorium shouting 'Heil Hitler!' They were soon inside the building and engaged in grim room-to-room fighting with hand grenades and machine pistols.

The Shermans down on the road tried to get up to help but the slope was too steep. One was set alight by a bazooka and then the German tanks, firing by the light of the flames, destroyed two more. By four o'clock on Thursday morning the panzer grenadiers had regained the main building and taken thirty prisoners.

When Thursday's dawn came the 119th Infantry Regiment found that another of its battalions had been practically destroyed. This time it was the First and they had lost most of two companies in the night's grim fighting.

Encouraged by their success in driving the Americans out of the sanatorium the Germans decided that here was the weak link in the chain—if hit hard enough it would break. Early in the morning Colonel Peiper tried to burst free of Stoumont by an assault against the crippled 119th Infantry Regiment straight down the road but a heavy, accurate barrage from the artillery once more saved the day and when more American tanks arrived the roadblock was secured.

Behind, on their left, Battlegroup Peiper had left a strong

outpost at Cheneux to hold the light bridge over the Amblève. On Wednesday two companies of 82nd Airborne's parachute infantry tried to take this position but the Germans—more of the 2nd SS Panzer Grenadier Regiment—had mortars, heavy machine guns, light anti-aircraft and self-propelled guns and this weight of fire smashed up the American advance.

As they were without artillery support the airborne infantry took cover in a nearby wood and signalled for some heavy guns. Finally two self-propelled tank destroyers came up to them about dusk and it was decided to try to take Cheneux in a night attack supported by these. The parachutists formed up in four lines and tried to rush across four hundred yards of open ground in waves fifty yards apart against the dug-in panzer grenadiers. The first two waves were shot to pieces, the third brought to a halt by barbed wire. The tank destroyers then got to positions where they could fire directly at the German guns and the surviving parachutists rushed the German defences once more. 'A few men lived to reach the outlying houses.'*

Outnumbered, out of fuel, surrounded and with food and ammunition running low Battlegroup Peiper was still as dangerous as a wounded tiger, but as Wednesday night ticked away it could be seen that its position was hopeless. A screen of American tanks and tank destroyers lay across its right and rear; to its front the 119th Infantry's roadblock prevented tactical manoeuvring westward and, most serious of all, its route south was now blocked by the 82nd Airborne Division. The concentrated armour of the Leibstandarte, after being delayed at the start line for one all-important day, had used up two more days to advance, against very little opposition, sixty-five miles west, from Honsfeld to La Gleize. Although this deepest of all German penetrations in the first three days of the Ardennes Offensive was very worrying to the Americans it could not compare, as a blitzkrieg, with past German performances. The accumulated delay, which began with the failure of the German infantry to open a way for 1st SS Panzer Division on the first day and was steadily increased by the unnecessary stop before Stavelot, gave time for the bridges of Trois Ponts to be blown thus forcing Battlegroup Peiper into the steep and narrow roads of the valley of the Amblève. This in turn gave the Americans just enough time to bring in three divisions in a horseshoe around the heavy point of the German advance,

* Cole: *The Ardennes. Battle of the Bulge*, p. 352—combat between American airborne troops and German SS Panzer Grenadiers was always particularly bitter.

even though two of those divisions were not ordered to move to the area until the third day of the offensive. As General Bradley says,* mobility was the 'secret weapon' which the Allies used to defeat the Germans in the Ardennes.

By Wednesday night the rampaging tanks and infantry of Battlegroup Peiper seemed caged at Stoumont and La Gleize, with rivers on their left and rear whose crossings were in American hands, an armoured division spread across their right flank and a strong roadblock of infantry, tanks and artillery to their front. Being a sensible soldier Colonel Peiper knew that his attack had failed and the time had come to get back to his own lines. But Sixth SS Panzer Army Headquarters did not agree—'Sepp' Dietrich was not going to give up his one success and orders were sent to General Mohnke, 1st SS Panzer Division's commander, to launch attacks across the Amblève and re-establish contact with Battlegroup Peiper, supply them with fuel and ammunition and join them in a new thrust to the Meuse side by side with the II SS Panzer Corps, for on Thursday, December 21, the German High Command still believed that the rest of Sixth SS Panzer Army's panzer divisions were about to break through and advance to the Meuse.

In compliance with these orders General Mohnke and his staff planned a double attack. Some armoured infantry with assault guns would ford the river between Stavelot and Trois Ponts, get temporary bridges across and hold the ground on the far side until the guns could be got over and then attack the American troops which had got between Battlegroup Peiper and Trois Ponts. At the same time a second attack, which was to be the main effort, would advance west to cross the Salm river south of Trois Ponts and then, swinging north, swiftly move in to reinforce Peiper's left flank.

To coincide with this all-out effort by 1st SS Panzer Division the American left flank at Malmédy would be hit by an attack from Ligneuville by Otto Skorzeny's disappointed and frustrated Panzer Brigade 150, anxious to earn some glory. Their objectives were the roads from Malmédy to Stavelot, the American artillery positions on the high ground above this road and the key communications centre of Malmédy itself.

If these German attacks succeeded the situation north of the Amblève would be dramatically reversed and the Leibstandarte would be on the move again.

But the Allies had plans for Battlegroup Peiper too.

The 'nutcracker' operation which had begun its squeeze

* Bradley: *A Soldier's Story.*

on Wednesday would continue: 3rd Armored's Task Force Lovelady, now behind Peiper on the Trois Ponts to La Gleize road, would attack northwards against the encircled force while the 119th Infantry Regiment, together with another force of 3rd Armored tanks, would come in from the opposite side. The 82nd Airborne would continue to push against the German's left flank and, at the same time as these attacks, the 117th Infantry with tanks and self-propelled guns, would move from Stavelot along the north bank of the Amblève to Trois Ponts.

Then, after Battlegroup Peiper had been destroyed, 30th Infantry Division and 82nd Airborne Division would join and, with the tanks of the 3rd Armored Division, drive the Germans back beyond St Vith.

Thus, in the triangle Trois Ponts–Stoumont–Malmédy both the Germans and the Allies planned four attacks each for Thursday, December 21, and both sides were confident of a decisive victory.

Both sides were wrong.

21

ST VITH FALLS—BASTOGNE HOLDS

> *In war between partially mechanized armies the armoured attack must fail many times. Its supreme value lies in mobility which enables it to withdraw from a bad situation and retrieve it by striking successfully in a more favourable quarter. A governing principle therefore is the avoidance of a situation which commits tanks to attack along one line until they prevail or are defeated.*
>
> S. L. A. MARSHALL: Armies on Wheels

The failure to seize St Vith by Sunday was a severe blow to Fifth Panzer Army's plans for, since all main roads north and west ran through this communications centre, its possession by the Americans meant that Manteuffel's right wing could not give Sixth Panzer Army's only successful penetration—by 1st SS Panzer Division—the flank protection it needed.

The timely arrival of tanks, tank destroyers and armoured infantry in the St Vith area from the combat commands of the American 7th and 9th Armored Divisions had strengthened St Vith's defences just enough to hold the German attacks. On Monday, the remainder of 7th Armored Division closed on the area; one of 106th Infantry's regiments, the 424th, was able to get back and form part of the perimeter defence and on the next day, just when it was most desperately needed, the 112th Infantry Regiment was found by a 7th Armored patrol at Huldange, 9 miles south-east of St Vith. This was the regiment which had been holding 28th Infantry Division's left and had blocked the attempt of the 116th Panzer and 560th Volksgrenadier Divisions to drive straight west during the first two days of the battle. Eventually outflanked by the collapse of the 110th Infantry Regiment in their divisional centre the 112th had been forced back losing most of their vehicles and heavy weapons but suffering few casualties. Colonel Nelson, the commanding officer, reported to General Hasbrouck at Vielsalm about 11 on Tuesday morning that his men were in good fettle, although needing a hot meal and rest, and were ready to fight. Hasbrouck suggested to General Jones, whose headquarters were also now in Vielsalm, that he attach this regiment to his 106th Division. This was done and Colonel Nelson

304

was ordered to move towards St Vith and tie in with the right flank of the other surviving regiment of a destroyed division, the 424th, thus filling a dangerous hole in the horseshoe-shaped defence of St Vith.

The Germans launched attacks at many places along this perimeter on Monday: The earliest, which succeeded in pushing 7th Armored Division's CCR out of Recht, kept up the pressure and by midday Poteaux too had fallen, thus cutting divisional headquarters at Vielsalm off from CCB defending the town of St Vith.

At the small town of Petit Thier, half way between Poteaux and Vielsalm, a young armoured infantry officer who had become separated from his column during one of the brushes with the Germans on the way south, heard the firing only two miles to the east and rounded up other strays including odd tanks, half-tracks, some combat engineers and infantry and formed a roadblock. Named Task Force Navaho, after its commander (who had worked his way through college selling Indian blankets), this tiny force grew by grabbing passing stragglers, lost detachments and the headquarters of CCR, who came in from Poteaux, until it became a formidable position protecting Vielsalm. However, 1st SS Panzer Division's southern column, whose troops had seized Poteaux, were now ordered to move to Stavelot to reinforce Battlegroup Peiper so the hastily formed defence was not tested.

The Germans had to be pushed out of Poteaux. If they were able to consolidate there, 7th Armored Division would be cut in two and, as other German troops were already massing north, east and south of St Vith, the town would soon fall. Hasbrouck ordered his reserve, CCA, to come back from Beho south-west of St Vith and move north-west of it to recapture Poteaux.

First attempt to do so was made at 1.20 pm on Monday but the forces left behind by the Leibstandarte had dug in well around the important crossroads and their concentrated fire broke up the American assault. CCA reported that they had been forced back to cover south of Poteaux. General Hasbrouck's reply was brief and uncompromising: IMPERATIVE YOU SEIZE POTEAUX AND HOLD IT.

Just as the light was fading CCA launched another assault with a strong force of tanks and armoured infantry. The Shermans pumped shells directly into the small crossroads village while the infantry advanced in the teeth of heavy German shelling and, with automatic weapons fire and by storming the houses, finished the attack in room-to-room fighting. By nightfall on Monday Poteaux was once more in American hands and the road from Vielsalm to St Vith secured.

Also on Monday the Germans came from the north down the main road from Ligneuville towards St Vith and seized another small crossroads village, Hunningen, only a mile from the town's outskirts. Quickly the defenders sent three companies of Shermans and one of self-propelled guns which knocked out seven panzers, killed about a hundred panzer grenadiers and re-took this crossroads too.

At the same time as this strike from the north towards St Vith another came from the north-east, from the vicinity of Wallerode, towards Hunningen. Here the only American troops in the way were some of 7th Armored Division's cavalry reconnaissance and a few anti-aircraft half-tracks but they were able to delay the Germans until the arrival of tanks and tank destroyers hastily summoned from 9th Armored Division's CCB on the other side of the perimeter. Once again a half dozen panzers were destroyed and the German thrust held.

Still searching for a weak spot in the St Vith defence the Germans tried again, this time from the east down the Schönberg road advancing behind a creeping barrage laid down from the heavy German guns which had now moved up. The American artillery, the 275th Armored Field Artillery Battalion, whose guns had only stopped firing for short intervals since the attack began, poured nearly a thousand rounds on to the Schönberg road and the armoured infantry and combat engineers, after yielding initially, rallied, and by dark the Germans had lost their gains in this area too.

7th Armored Division's own artillery had been delayed by Battlegroup Peiper's piercing of their route at Stavelot, but on Monday afternoon just before dark the 434th Field Artillery Battalion came in and were quickly sent south-west of St Vith; a little later two batteries of another battalion arrived and were sent further south, and this much-needed additional fire power in an arc south-west of St Vith greatly increased the defensive strength.

During Monday the Steinebruck bridge, which had been preserved in hope that some of the troops out on the Schnee Eifel would be able to get back over it, had finally been blown at the last possible moment when German troops were already on the opposite bank.

But although the Germans had not succeeded in breaking the wall of defence and had lost men and tanks at several places it was obvious that they were hourly growing stronger: all through Monday night the sound of trucks and tracks warned the Americans that the assault would soon be renewed and that it would be even heavier. Mortar, 88-mm high explosive and artillery fire in battalion strength hammered road junctions and known American positions all night while several attempted probes in the dark had to be beaten back.

Once all hope had been abandoned of driving through to the regiments on the Schnee Eifel (whose fate was not known), the outlying armour and infantry had come in towards St Vith. Somehow, by improvising, by quick reactions, by replying aggressively to every attack, the scattered defence had coalesced into a horseshoe from a heterogenous mass of small units, almost always committed as soon as they arrived. The open end faced west and south-west where there was a gap to the Bastogne garrison, a gap through which Fifth Panzer Army's tank-and-infantry columns were swiftly moving west without, unfortunately for the St Vith defenders, any thought for the fighting on their right.

On Tuesday the Americans holding Poteaux were hit by panzer grenadiers from the newly-committed 9th SS Panzer Division, part of the second armoured wave, who had come into Recht as the southern column of the 1st SS Panzer Division hurried north-west to Stavelot. Traffic conditions were so bad that the 9th SS Panzer took nearly two days to move into position around Recht, a distance of about twenty miles. These fresh German SS troops attacked with ferocity and determination but the tanks and dug-in infantry of CCA were able to hold the vital crossroads and by nightfall patrols had established contact with their division's reserve combat command to the west.

German pressure was maintained against the St Vith perimeter all during Tuesday, December 19, with probing attacks from the north, east and south, all of which were beaten off. In fact the German command had decided to push troops past St Vith on both north and south, completing its encirclement and maintaining the objective of the offensive, the capture of crossings over the Meuse, leaving St Vith to be taken by fresh forces.

9th Armored Division's CCB, well to the south-east of St Vith, would be in a most dangerous position if, as must be considered likely, St Vith was lost, for there were no roads leading west except back through the town. It was therefore decided to pull CCB back after dark on Tuesday west of the railway which runs north and south behind St Vith and, despite a small German attack, this was accomplished. By dawn on Wednesday the horseshoe at St Vith had closed to form an island defence—'with a German tide rushing past on the north and south and rising against its eastern face'.*

American withdrawals and the elimination of the two 106th Infantry Regiments in the Schnee Eifel enabled the 62nd and 18th Volksgrenadier Divisions to join their flanks and close up, to press against the St Vith defence perimeter from the east. Also during Tuesday night 62nd Volksgrenadier's engineers got a bridge in across the Our to replace the blown Steinebruck bridge and heavy artillery began to move across it. To this new threat for St Vith was added another—an armored punch to be delivered by the Fuehrer Begleit Brigade who were waiting in Germany forty miles east of St Vith for their chance of glory.

Their commander, Colonel Otto Remer, had been a major in command of the Wacht (Guard) Battalion around Hitler's Headquarters in Berlin at the time of the July *Putsch*. He had disobeyed his superior, one of the conspirators, and reported to Goebbels who had allowed him to talk on the telephone with Hitler at Rastenburg. The Führer had promoted him to colonel on the spot and entrusted him with the safety of Berlin. Afterwards, when the Führer offered to reward him, Remer asked for a field command and was told to organize Brigade Remer whose main task would be to prevent a rumoured attempt by Allied paratroops to kidnap Hitler.

In November, when Hitler abandoned the Wolf's Lair and moved to Berlin, Brigade Remer was re-formed into the Fuehrer Begleit (Escort) Brigade with an HQ staff of a division (to which it was intended to enlarge it). About a week before the start of the Ardennes Offensive Colonel Remer was put in the picture and his force was assigned to Army Group B reserve. He was told that he would fight with Fifth Panzer Army and he spent the first two days of the attack at General von Manteuffel's headquarters.

Brigade was an elastic term in December 1944 when so many Wehrmacht Divisions existed largely on paper and the Fuehrer Begleit was a comparatively strong force. Its main punch came from forty-five Mk IVs, thirty-five assault guns mounted on Mk III chassis and ten self-propelled anti-tank guns. Support troops included a battalion of motorized infantry, an armoured car battalion—most of whose cars were equipped with anti-aircraft guns—a bicycle battalion and a company of combat engineers. There was good artillery sup-

* Cole: op. cit.

port: a battalion of twelve 104-mm and four 155-mm guns and the greater part of an anti-aircraft regiment with twenty-four of the deadly 88s, a battery of 20-mm and one of 37-mm guns and a battery of 4-barrelled machine guns. The brigade carried its own signal, medical and ordnance companies. Two companies of supply troops, to replace casualties, travelled with the rear echelon. Fuehrer Begleit was, in fact, a miniature armoured division.

General Lucht, the commander of LXVI Corps, one of whose tasks was to capture St Vith, had been demanding more armour since the end of the first day but Manteuffel could not release the Fuehrer Begleit Brigade to him until he had in turn persuaded the Army Group Commander who, always well aware that he was attempting too much with too little, husbanded his reserves.

Permission came late on Monday and Colonel Remer got his brigade moving from Daun to Prüm and thence south of the Schnee Eifel over the new Steinebruck bridge through Bleialf towards St Vith. He himself reported to General Lucht and was told to take part in the final assault on St Vith but was not to get entangled in the fighting there, for his main rôle was to drive hard and fast for the Meuse.

One of the main German bugbears in the Ardennes was shortage of fuel and this began to have effect very early in the offensive. Fuehrer Begleit Brigade was heavily mechanized and needed large quantities, particularly since the roads were clogged with slow-moving traffic. They started with 1·4 fuel units instead of the promised three and this shortage seriously limited their capabilities in the ensuing fighting.

Tuesday morning found Remer's brigade strung out in a long line with the head about three miles east of St Vith and the tail between Schönberg and Bleialf.* It took twelve hours for an assault force to move north of St Vith into woods between Born and Nieder Emmels and forty-eight hours before the whole brigade had made the shift. At dawn on Wednesday Remer struck with his available forces—two barriers of assault guns and a battalion of infantry—and took Nieder Emmels and Ober Emmels, a mile and a half north-west of St Vith.

On this morning, December 20, the Vielsalm defenders were by far the easternmost American position in the Ardennes 'a thumb protruding into the enemy's mouth—and one that could easily be bitten off.'† Although the Germans had not yet closed

* Having delivered the final blow to 106th Division's 422nd Infantry Regiment on the way. See Chapter 15, p. 212.
† Bruce Clarke: *The Defense of St Vith.* The Armored School.

behind St Vith, communications between 7th Armored rear headquarters and the St Vith command post were hourly getting more difficult and it was no longer possible for St Vith to have any direct communication with VIII Corps headquarters which had moved, eighteen miles further away, from Bastogne to Neufchâteau.

Because of this break in the chain of command General Hasbrouck sent a liaison officer to First Army at Spa with a letter to the Chief of Staff, Major-General William Kean, explaining the extent of the St Vith defence line held by his own division, 7th Armored, and their attached units—'My right flank is wide open except for some reconnaissance elements, tank destroyers and stragglers we have collected and organized ... I can delay [the Germans] the rest of today *maybe* but will be cut off tomorrow ...' At this time General Hasbrouck was most worried about the strong German forces south of him who were flowing west but likely to turn towards St Vith. His letter went on: 'VIII Corps has ordered me to hold and I will do so but need help. An attack from Bastogne to the NE will relieve the situation and in turn cut the bastards off in the rear. I also need plenty of air support ... Understand 82nd Airborne is coming up on my north and the north flank is not critical.'

This letter gave First Army its first clear picture of what had been happening at St Vith since 7th Armored Division, coming from the north, had disappeared in that direction. General Hodges' answering letter in turn told the St Vith garrison what was going on in their rear and, incidentally, cleared up the tricky command position: all forces in the St Vith area were put under Brigadier-General Hasbrouck's command and he, in turn, was to be under Major-General Matthew Ridgway, the XVIIIth Airborne Corps commander, as soon as contact was established between 82nd Airborne Division and 7th Armored Division. This took place about dusk on Wednesday, December 20, when patrols from the 505th Parachute Infantry met a reconnaissance party from 7th Armored in the village of Fosse, five miles north-west of Vielsalm.

The sector of XVIIIth Airborne now stretched for about sixty-five miles and faced the forward elements of I SS Panzer Corps on its left and Fifth Panzer Army's LXVI Corps in the centre and LVIII Corps on the right. More strength of all arms was on the way but for the present this part of the American front had to remain largely on the defensive and there was no hope of closing the thirteen-mile gap between the defenders of

St Vith and of Bastogne. Through this gap were moving the 116th Panzer Division and the 560th Volksgrenadier Division driving on Hotton and La Roche to cross the Ourthe.

The existence of these German forces threatened the right flank of the combined force holding St Vith against attacks from the east and north and, on December 20, General Hasbrouck despatched a mixed task force, commanded by Lieutenant-Colonel Robert Jones, twelve miles south-west to establish a seven mile east–west blocking line. It was not strong enough to stop a really determined German flanking movement but it could block key road junctions and send back warnings of any such attempt.

Created by stripping forces from the north and using almost all the reserve, Task Force Jones contained men from eight different battalions and included tanks, tank destroyers, armoured infantry, armoured engineers, armoured field artillery and what remained of the Fourteenth Cavalry Group. There was known to be a small force already in Gouvy and Colonel Jones decided to send a detachment to reinforce them and other detachments to villages east and west of Gouvy: Deiffelt and Chérain.

The story of the group holding Gouvy is one of little sagas of the Ardennes: on Monday an anti-aircraft battalion's headquarters battery had been sent to Gouvy, a railhead supplies dump. They had arrived just as three of 116th Panzer's tanks were reconnoitring north of their division's axis. The tanks fired off all their ammunition and retired to the south and the commander of the 440th Anti-aircraft Battalion, Lieutenant-Colonel Robert Stone, moved on into the village to discover that the few depot guards and MPs were holding 350 German prisoners of war and had, when the panzers approached, set fire to a store of eighty thousand rations. The fire was put out and over fifty thousand rations sent to St Vith where they were badly needed.

Colonel Stone was then sent a platoon of light tanks by General Hasbrouck and told that he must hang on to Gouvy, although he had no trained infantrymen at all. The next day, Tuesday, a nearby artillery battalion was persuaded to train a battery of its 155-mm howitzers on Gouvy in support. All day the tanks of 116th Panzer and the men of 560th Volksgrenadiers kept moving west a few miles south of Gouvy but made no effort to capture it. At night the rear guard of LVIII Panzer Corps, the 1130th Regiment of 560 Volksgrenadiers who had taken very heavy casualties in trying to break through 112th Infantry on the Our river line in the first two days of the

311

offensive, bivouacked in and around Gouvy. Colonel Stone concentrated his small force around the station, half·a mile north-east, to guard the stores, including a vehicle dump with earth-moving machinery badly needed further west, and the German prisoners.

The night passed quietly but about mid-morning on Wednesday the volksgrenadiers were observed forming up in attack formation near Gouvy church evidently intending to advance on the station. The promised artillery support was now called for and in a few minutes the big shells burst among the German infantry, scattering them. Before they could form up and get their attack started the detachment sent from Task Force Jones arrived and drove them out of Gouvy. Colonel Stone's small force was absorbed into the larger after handing over, with pardonable pride, the three hundred and fifty prisoners.

Colonel Jones had also sent small detachments into Deiffelt, east of Gouvy and two miles north of the right end of the horseshoe defence, and into Chérain, some four miles west of Gouvy. Although these strongpoints were not connected they covered all roads leading north to Vielsalm from the German-held Houffalize corridor.

General Hasbrouck's policy of an immediate, powerful reply to any German probe against his perimeter, coupled with his keeping back the minimum reserve and the heavy fire from the eight American artillery battalions inside the St Vith defence, caused the Germans to exaggerate the American strength greatly. For their part the Americans also overestimated the strength of the attackers at four panzer and three infantry divisions instead of one panzer division, the newly-arrived 9th SS at Poteaux, one armoured brigade, Remer's, and two infantry divisions, the 18th and 62nd.

As German successes made lines of battle hard to draw and lines of communication were ruptured, confusion in the higher realms of command increased. On December 20 VIII Corps passed from First Army to Third Army in the division of the Ardennes battlefield into two. General Middleton was told to get CCB of 9th Armored Division back before General Montgomery could claim it as his own. Brigadier-General Hoge was ordered to disengage at St Vith and move fifty miles south-west behind Bastogne to help block Panzer Lehr's advance. Had such a move been attempted CCB would have become involved long before reaching the destination and the Germans in front of St Vith could hardly have ignored the invitation that such a weakening of the perimeter would have offered.

But at General Hoge's request, General Hasbrouck persuaded the VIII Corps commander to cancel the order and 9th Armored Division's CCB remained in First Army.

Dawn on Thursday, five days after the advance towards St Vith had begun, found the Americans still in possession, the Germans jammed along the approach roads from the east unable to use the St Vith road net to push flank support forward for the armoured thrusts on the north and south. General Lucht, the LXVI Corps commander, was ordered to make an all-out attack and take St Vith—no excuses would be accepted. If the Fuehrer Begleit Brigade were not yet ready then the attack would be made without them but it would be made and it would succeed.

The forces available for this were the two volksgrenadier divisions, 18th and 62nd, and the Fuehrer Begleit Brigade. The bulk of the German attackers were concentrated in the north-east quadrant—all three of 18th Division's regiments, supported on their left by one of 62nd Division. Entry into St Vith from this quarter could be gained from the north along the axis of the road from Amblève, from the north-east along the Schönberg road, scene of the main German efforts so far and joined outside St Vith by the main road from the south-east. Four of the six volksgrenadier regiments were lined up to attack towards St Vith in this sector; the other two were to attack due west from some four to five miles south of the town to gain the main road from Luxembourg.

Fuehrer Begleit Brigade, it will be remembered, were in the Nieder-Emmels–Ober-Emmels area north-west of St Vith and most of the mixed force had now closed up. Lastly LXVI Corps artillery had finally managed to get through the traffic jams to positions from where fire could be brought down on St Vith, but this was only accomplished by midday on Thursday.

General Lucht planned a double assault: Fuehrer Begleit were ordered to attack straight south from Nieder-Emmels into St Vith at the same time as two of 18th Volksgrenadiers, regiments made the main effort along the axis of the Schönberg road. On the right of this attack the third of 18th Division's regiments was to attack south from the direction of Wallerode while on the left one of 62nd Division's regiments was to attack westwards.

Colonel Remer, trusting on his standing with the Führer, flatly disobeyed orders and, instead of advancing towards St Vith struck south-west towards Rodt on the St Vith–Vielsalm road, an action which was to have important results in the end but which did nothing towards capturing St Vith.

First indication that this was to be the Germans' all-out effort came on Thursday at 2.0 pm with a tremendous artillery barrage. Eighteenth Division's right-hand regiment then started to move south from the Wallerode area but were stopped by 7th Armored's supporting artillery.

The first German bombardment was succeeded by a second in which every gun was brought to bear on CCB's troops in the north-east sector. This continued for fifteen minutes and caused many casualties. The tank men and armoured infantry who had been holding here for nearly four days began to give way under the relentless pressure. The volksgrenadiers followed up the barrage with leap-frogging attacks in two-platoon strength moving along both sides of the Schönberg road and a strong attack south of that road. The regiment on the German right, which had tried earlier and been stopped, launched another attack south but once more were cut down and forced back.

Now it was evident to the Germans that the defence of the Schönberg approach was beginning to give way and, obeying the sound military rule of exploiting success, General Lucht moved his tanks and assault guns behind the volksgrenadiers, backed them up with the regiment which had been attacking on their left, and at 8.0 pm, once more struck hard at the Schönberg road defenders.

Earlier, when three tanks lost their commanders to small-arms fire here, the rest had withdrawn leaving the depleted infantry unprotected against armour. Now there were only three Shermans between the advancing German force of Tigers, assault guns and infantry. They were in staggered line on the main road with their guns trained on the ridge where the German armour would appear but, of course, it was pitch dark and first intimation of the presence of German tanks came with the firing of flares which blinded the crews and silhouetted the tanks. All three were knocked out in a matter of minutes and the volksgrenadiers surged forward. Some of the exhausted American armoured infantry stayed and tried to fight; most of these were killed or captured. Some broke in panic and fled through the woods towards the west.

Coinciding with this attack came one from the south-east which hit the seam between CCB 7th Armored and CCB 9th Armored, split them apart and reached St Vith shortly after the double column of volksgrenadiers who came in along the Schönberg road.

7th Armored Division had lost four companies of armoured infantry and not more than two hundred men escaped capture.

At 9.30 pm General Clarke ordered what was left of his combat command to fall back and form a new line north-west of the city. CCB of 9th Armored Division also pulled back a mile or more to tie in with this new defence line and at 2.0 am on Friday, December 22, when the situation had been reported to General Ridgway, the decision was taken to bring back the 424th Infantry Regiment and the 112th Infantry Regiment, still holding their part of the perimeter in the south, to try to form a defensive ring west of St Vith which would still delay the German advance.

During the night of December 18/19 two German panzer divisions and one volksgrenadier division had arrived at the edge of Bastogne: on the American side an armoured combat command had arrived, an airborne division was coming in and other smaller forces of artillery and tank destroyers were on their way.

The most serious threat appeared to be in the north-east from where the 2nd Panzer Division was apparently striking for Bastogne. The American attempt to block this was at Longvilly and consisted of the remnants of 9th Armored Division's CCR, with some artillery and infantry who had survived earlier attacks, and Task Force Cherry from 10th Armored Division's CCB strung out along the road.

Second Panzer, it will be remembered, had turned away from Longvilly and was heading towards Bourcy and Noville; Colonel Gilbreth had then ordered the remnants of CCR to withdraw to Bastogne through Mageret and so Longvilly had become the sole responsibility of Team Cherry.

This was now in three parts: Lieutenant Hyduke's advance guard deployed defensively outside Longvilly, Captain Ryerson with the main body some three-quarters of a mile back, and Colonel Cherry with a small headquarters force in a command post set up in Neffe Château about two miles west of Mageret.

At two o'clock on Tuesday morning Colonel Cherry learned that German tanks and armoured infantry had captured Mageret. This was, of course, General Bayerlein with the advance guard of Panzer Lehr and Colonel Cherry and his headquarters were thus cut off from his main force and the advance guard. Patrols determined that the German strength was too great for an attack to force them out and it was decided after consultation with CCB's commander, Colonel Roberts, that Longvilly would have to be given up.

Captain Ryerson was ordered to bring the main force back, breaking through the Germans in Mageret to join up with

Colonel Cherry's headquarters. Lieutenant Hyduke's advance guard would stay and block any German pursuit from the east—the advance guard had become a rear guard.

With Mageret in German hands CCR's escape route was cut and as there were signs of panic Colonel Gilbreth froze all vehicles until it was light. The narrow road was badly jammed and it took Captain Ryerson's main force from Team Cherry over an hour to move about a mile to the edge of Mageret. Here the leading Sherman was knocked out and two of 9th Armored's half-tracks, which tried to rush past, also went up in flames. The road was then hopelessly plugged and later attempts to outflank Mageret failed. From the blazing American vehicles all the way back to Longvilly the road was packed with transport full of men uncomfortably aware of their exposed position.

Nothing much apart from heavy shelling took place at Longvilly during Tuesday morning but about two in the afternoon Lieutenant Hyduke's force was suddenly hit by the greatest concentration of fire power the Germans had yet used in this sector, although the timing was largely accidental.

Two regiments from 26th Volksgrenadiers had come up by forced marches to Oberwampach, a remarkably good performance, and were ordered by General von Luettwitz to attack Longvilly. At the same time, but unknown to Luettwitz, General Bayerlein had decided to attack Longvilly too with a regiment of panzergrenadiers, a battalion of artillery and about twenty self-propelled anti-tank guns and this force moved off from Benonchamps about the same time as 26th Volksgrenadiers moved from Oberwampach. Finally, to add to the misfortune of the rearguard at Longvilly, the 2nd Panzer Division, moving north-west towards Noville, was shelled from the Longvilly area (by one of the 9th Armored Division's batteries) and the commander, General von Lauchert, sent six of the deadly, self-propelled 88-mm guns off to Chilfontaine to deal with this nuisance. None of the three German forces closing on Longvilly knew about either of the others; none knew that there was a considerable force of American tanks there.

Bayerlein's tank destroyers crested a hill south-west of the Longvilly–Mageret road just after two o'clock in the afternoon and saw before them a long line of American vehicles of all kinds on which they immediately opened fire with devastating effect and soon all twenty anti-tank guns were in operation. Coincidentally the force from 26th Volksgrenadiers, also with anti-tank guns, arrived on high ground a thousand yards southeast of Longvilly and together with the 88s from 2nd Panzer

Division, who were emplaced another thousand yards north-east of Longvilly, joined in the shoot.

The result can be imagined: the unprotected vehicles were driven off the road, the traffic jam became impossible to control and within an hour all the American tanks had been destroyed. Lieutenant Hyduke organized the survivors of his force and took them back on foot to join Captain Ryerson outside Mageret.*

Bayerlein had started to move towards Bastogne from Mageret about half past five on Tuesday morning and with eleven panzers reached Neffe railroad station about seven, unaware that there were American troops in the vicinity. Panzer Lehr's advance guard then inexplicably stopped for nearly an hour and in that hour the first of 101st Airborne's troops moved from Bastogne towards them. This was a combat team from the 501st Parachute Infantry Regiment of a battalion of infantry and a battery of anti-aircraft guns led by a reconnaissance platoon which drew German machine-gun fire about a half a mile west of Neffe. Fortunately for the parachutists the gun was firing low and they had time to hit the dirt as the bullets ricocheted over their heads. The road here runs dead straight into Neffe and only moments later shells came screaming down it but the Americans had taken cover in the rising ground on their left and quickly returned the German fire.

Once again the Germans and Americans overestimated each other's strength. Colonel Ewell, the 501st commander, decided to halt his First Battalion where they were, call on his artillery support and bring his other two battalions up on either side. Once all three battalions were in position the regiment would advance in trident—from Bixory on his left into Mageret, thus cutting off Neffe, from Mont on his right south-east to a road which led into Neffe and from the centre, an attack down the main road.

Neither side had suffered any serious casualties in this first exchange of fire but a battery of the airborne division's supporting artillery had moved forward smartly in response to the call for help and by ten o'clock in the morning were in position only a thousand yards behind the forward parachutists.† They immediately shelled the Germans causing about eighty casualties in an hour.

General Bayerlein mistook the sharp crack of the airborne artillery's special 105-mm gun for a tank's and assumed that

* Lieutenant Hyduke was later killed in Bastogne.
† A position they maintained throughout the siege without ever attracting counterfire.

317

he was now being opposed by armour moving out against him from Bastogne. He was also worried about small-arms fire coming in on his left, although this was only from Team Cherry's small force in the château, and estimated that he was being attacked by two battalions of infantry and a squadron of tanks. He gave up all ideas of reaching Bastogne for the present and, instead, pulled back to Mageret.

The other two battalions of 501st were held up by the spate of VIII Corps' evacuation but both got into their indicated zones by about midday and launched their attacks. On the left the Second Battalion were stopped by dug-in reconnaissance troops of Panzer Lehr earlier sent from Mageret whose aggressive reaction caused the American commander to report that for the time being he could not think of taking Mageret.

In Neffe Château Colonel Cherry and his headquarters force beat off repeated attacks all day. In mid-afternoon they were reinforced by a platoon from the Third Battalion Parachute Infantry at Mont but by nightfall the great wooden roof of the château was burning and there were half a dozen other fires inside the building. Colonel Cherry withdrew his own men and the relieving parachutists back to Mont to join the 501st right flank position.

The commander of the Third Battalion, 501st Parachute Infantry, found that he could not advance towards Neffe because open ground covered by concealed panzers and German infantry lay between. Also worried about his open right flank he despatched a company to check that there were no Germans between him and Wardin. This, it will be remembered, was where Colonel Roberts had despatched CCB's second force, Team O'Hara, the night before.

A steady stream of stragglers, mostly from 28th Infantry Division, had passed through O'Hara's tanks all night long but this stopped abruptly on Tuesday morning, a warning that the Germans were not far behind. A reconnaissance platoon was sent forward and, after knocking out a Volkswagen, came quickly back to report two German tanks approaching. Artillery fire on Bras, the next village east, was called for and an observer came up to the crest on which O'Hara's tanks were waiting for the panzers to appear. Suddenly an 88 opened up from woods south of the Wiltz–Bastogne road knocking out the artillery observer's tank and one of Team O'Hara's—the other four moved quickly to safety.

Now German shells began to fall and small groups of German infantry were seen. It was a dangerous situation for the unprotected tanks and when the commanders saw men in green uniforms moving towards them from behind, power turrets were rapidly swivelled to fire on them. One of the advancing men's shouts in English stopped them.

These were the company of 501st Airborne company sent from Mont, whose jump suits were green. Having reported back that the area between Neffe and Wardin was clear they had been told to carry on south and make contact with 'a friendly armoured roadblock'.

Not used to working in close cooperation with armour the airborne troops practically ignored Team O'Hara and continued through the tank position into Wardin where, after ambushing a twenty-five-man German patrol they were themselves attacked by seven panzers and a battalion of panzer grenadiers, losing fifty men. All the officers were hit, the company commander killed and the rest scattered.

For some reason this strong German force missed Team O'Hara but later that evening Panzer Lehr seized Wardin and, under cover of a concentrated artillery barrage, the American tanks and the surviving parachute infantry fell back to high ground north of Marvie. At the same time the other two battalions from 501 Parachute Infantry at Neffe and Bixory broke contact and fell back to a general line just west of those villages.

At three o'clock on Wednesday morning Colonel Roberts decided that the remnants of Team Cherry, who had hung all day to the eastern edge of Mageret against increasing pressure which cost them three more tanks, should come back across country and join 501st's left-hand position around Bixory. This move was completed just before dawn.

Most of these 10th Armored soldiers had been forty-eight hours without sleep or hot food and had been in continuous contact with the Germans for about thirty hours. They had taken severe casualties and had lost most of their tanks but, like the 110th Infantry in front of the Clerf river, they had bought precious hours for the defence of Bastogne. In the stern accounting of war their casualties had been worth sustaining.

The defence line which had thus more or less accidentally formed north of Bixory down to Marvie held for the whole of the siege of Bastogne. Both sides had overestimated the strength of the other when they bumped on the south-eastern quarter of Bastogne; both hesitated but the pause had more serious consequences for the Germans than for the Americans for it cost the attackers their best chance of breaking right through into the city while success for the Americans would only have meant that the main thrust would have come from

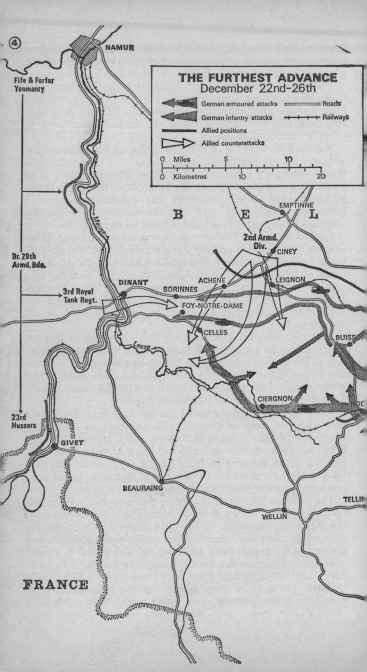

④

THE FURTHEST ADVANCE
December 22nd-26th

German armoured attacks ═══ Roads
German infantry attacks ┼┼┼┼ Railways
Allied positions
Allied counterattacks

0 Miles 5 10
0 Kilometres 10 20

NAMUR

Fife & Forfar
Yeomanry

Meuse

Br. 29th
Armd. Bde.

3rd Royal
Tank Regt.

DINANT

SORINNES

ACHENE

FOY-NOTRE-DAME

CELLES

Lesse

23rd
Hussars

GIVET

BEAURAING

B   E   L

EMPTINNE

2nd Armd.
Div.   CINEY

LEIGNON

BUISSON

CIERGNON   ROC

WELLIN   TELLIN

FRANCE

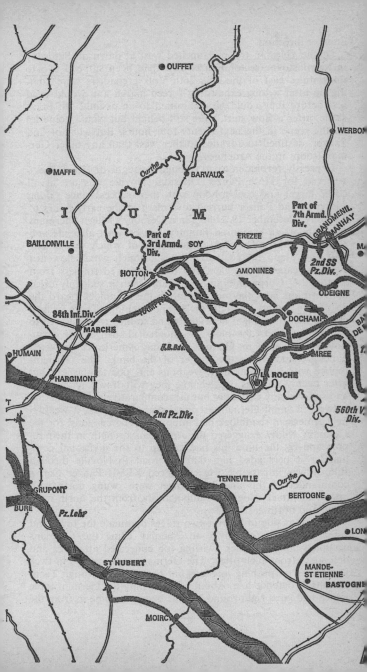

another direction.

Of the German troops launched west at dawn on Saturday in the Bastogne sector Panzer Lehr had been stopped two to three miles east of the city, 26th Volksgrenadiers were coming up after a long exhausting forced march and would need rest before they could be committed to an assault, 5th Parachute, after a slow start, were still behind but would come up on the scene in the next twenty-four hours. But what of 2nd Panzer, destined to advance further west than any other German troops in the Ardennes?

Expressly forbidden to go through Bastogne or Houffalize— reserved for 116th Panzer Division—Noville was an 'at all costs' target and cock-a-hoop with their success since taking Clervaux 2nd Panzer hurried towards it in the early hours of Tuesday, December 19. Here Team Desobry's fifteen Shermans and supporting armoured infantry had covered all exits and established three forward outposts one of which was a half mile east along the road to Bourcy through which flowed a steady stream of stragglers and badly shocked soldiers from shattered V Corps units until 4.30 am when it suddenly dried up. An hour later the men mounting the roadblock heard the distinctive sound of half-tracks approaching. There was a chance that they might be friendly and so they were allowed to come right up to the block. A shouted challenge was incautiously answered in German and the Americans showered hand grenades from the shelter of the bank. The Germans replied with their automatic weapons and 'potato mashers' but after twenty minutes of exchange they withdrew. Neither side had suffered any casualties but this comparatively minor action between a small German reconnaissance team and a weakly-held American roadblock had important repercussions, for the Germans wildly exaggerated the American strength in their report and by the time this had got up to the divisional commander it persuaded him that the road to Noville through Bourcy was impassable. He convinced XLVII Panzer Corp's commander of this and 2nd Panzer were swung north with orders to attack Noville simultaneously from the north-west, north and north-east at dawn.

From that side of Noville two ridges dominate the town and when the hour for dawn on Tuesday came the Germans occupied both but thick swirling fog concealed attackers and defenders from each other. The Germans sent panzers in twos and threes on probing missions but none broke through Team Desobry's defence line. About mid-morning the German force which had gone right round Noville began to come in from the west and the rest of 2nd Panzer also began to move forward so that the Americans heard tank engines and clanking tracks around half their perimeter although they could see nothing. Then suddenly the fog lifted revealing rows of Tigers and Panthers—the nearest only two hundred yards off. Both sides opened up and during the next hour the fog came down and lifted two or three times—on one occasion a sudden clearance revealed a row of panzers sharply outlined against the skyline and nine were hit in as many minutes. The action was fierce with losses on both sides but finally the Germans withdrew to hull-down positions on the ridges and settled down to methodical, concentrated shelling.

It could only be a matter of hours before every building, every wall in Noville would be levelled and Major Desobry decided that it was time for him to pull his forces back to high ground near Foy, a mile or so nearer to Bastogne. He called CCB's commander for permission to do but Colonel Roberts was convinced that the Germans must not be allowed to start down the main highway from the north towards Bastogne before the 101st Airborne could get firmly into position and, without answering Desobry went in search of the paratroopers. Luckily he ran into Brigadier-General Higgins, the assistant division commander, who, when he heard of the plight of the small force of tanks in Noville, despatched a newly-arrived paratroop battalion to their aid.

Hearing this Major Desobry decided to hang on and attack with the airborne reinforcements and capture the two ridges. The First Battalion of the 506th Parachute Infantry, under their commander Lieutenant-Colonel La Prade, marched into Noville about 1.30 on Tuesday afternoon but it was another hour before the combined attack could jump off, during which the Germans sent twenty to thirty shells into the small area punctually every ten minutes.

The plan was ambitious and aggressive, but it could not allow for the strength of the attackers because this was not known. In fact a force of thirteen medium tanks, half a dozen tank destroyers and perhaps a thousand infantry had no chance at all of driving the 2nd Panzer Division off commanding heights and the American tanks were stopped within five hundred yards. Some of the paratroop infantry reached the lower slopes of the ridges where they were pinned down.

In mid-afternoon the Germans launched their own big effort with two columns of sixteen tanks each and a battalion of panzer grenadiers. The paratroopers, despite their heavy casualties, replied vigorously, screened by the smoke of burning vehicles and the fog, which came down once more. The German tanks hung back afraid of bazookas and the panzer grenadiers and paratroopers slogged it out without armoured support.

At dark both sides pulled back: the Germans to the ridge again and the paratroopers into Noville. Both sides claimed that they had stopped an enemy counter-attack and both were right. The shelling continued all night long as the Germans, aware that their schedule was going down the drain, kept up the pressure with forays by panzers supported by infantry trying to find a way into Noville. In the foggy darkness both sides fired towards the gun flashes of the other. One 88-mm shell burst outside the window of the combined command post killing the paratroop commander, Lieutenant-Colonel La Prade and seriously wounding Major Desobry.*

During the long nightmare of Tuesday night the surviving paratroopers occupied a tight perimeter outside the village and the eight remaining Shermans stayed in the centre as a mobile striking force ready to plug any breach. Dawn on Wednesday found the perimeter still intact and revealed two knocked-out panzers at its edge.

It was apparent that Noville was in too exposed a position to be held and General McAuliffe called General Middleton and proposed that the surviving paratroopers and tank men be withdrawn to Foy. 'No,' said the VIII Corps commander 'If we are to hold Bastogne we cannot keep falling back.'

2nd Panzer Division's artillery, which had been toiling far behind, now came up and added their shells to those of the German tanks and mixed panzer and panzer grenadier teams attacked south cutting off Noville. A message from Noville was passed to the command post in Bastogne by the artillery radio, ALL RESERVES COMMITTED SITUATION CRITICAL. General McAuliffe then decided that trying to hold Noville for a few more hours—and no more was possible—was not worth the heavy casualties of a last-ditch stand. Instead an attack from two sides to clear the Germans out of Foy was ordered and the Noville survivors ordered to retire straight down the main road into the Bastogne defence perimeter.

There were still plenty of 81-mm shells in Noville which had to be blown up by a delayed action charge and more than fifty wounded had to be moved out of aid posts and got ready to move away. So many men had been lost that there were more than enough vehicles to carry all the survivors out. The elusive

* Major Desobry was evacuated but the hospital was overrun and he was captured.

fog had disappeared by mid-morning on Wednesday but it came down again a few minutes before the time of departure, screening the column perfectly and they encountered nothing more serious than occasional small-arms fire except for a brush with German tanks which knocked out three more Shermans. There was a great deal of confusion but by nightfall they passed through the paratroop line south of Foy and into the Bastogne defence.

Team Desobry had suffered very heavy casualties in tanks and men and the First Battalion of the 506th Parachute Infantry had lost two hundred and twelve men in twenty-four hours. Both forces had lost their commanding officers but the great 2nd Panzer Division had been held up for another forty-eight hours, had lost twenty tanks, had a further twenty-five damaged and had lost the equivalent of a battalion of panzer grenadiers. At dusk on Wednesday, December 20, when they finally occupied Noville the commander asked for permission to attack south and capture Bastogne.

'Forget Bastogne and head for the Meuse!' was the angry answer.

It was the end of the fifth day of the offensive and von Luettwitz XLVII Panzer Corps, the star of Fifth Panzer Army, was now three days behind schedule and the failure to capture Bastogne was a severe blow to Manteuffel's hopes of crossing the Meuse. It was, he said after the war, 'all the more critical because the forces available for driving to the Meuse and protecting the long southern flank while also cutting off Bastogne were not regarded as adequate even before the attack began. What was feared before the offensive began had not happened: the defence at Bastogne encouraged the enemy to turn this sector into a springboard for a decisive counter-attack.'

On the American side the mixed force which would defend Bastogne for the rest of the siege was completed with the arrival of the 705th Tank Destroyer Battalion from Kohlscheid in Germany, supplying some badly needed direct fire power.

The defence perimeter was holding everywhere, but the bit of news that most raised morale was that Georgie Patton's crack 4th Armored Division was on the road and would arrive soon.

22

THE DEFENCE HARDENS

*I think it would be better to order up some artillery
and defend the present location.*

ULYSSES S. GRANT to his staff, when
advised to withdraw his headquarters.

After three days of the most savage fighting on the northern
shoulder of the breakthrough both the American and the German commands decided on major tactical changes. General
Gerow, V Corps commander, had earlier ordered that the
Rocherath–Krinkelt–Wirtzfeld line be held so that the five
battalions of 2nd Infantry attacking at Wahlerscheid could be
brought back and the survivors of 99th Infantry's forward
companies could withdraw to the Elsenborn ridge. The last of
these tired, battered soldiers passed through 2nd Infantry
Division's positions during Monday night and then, despite the
increasing pressure on his front Major-General Robertson, 2nd
Infantry's commander, took the remaining 99th Infantry who
were fighting alongside his own men, out of the line too and
sent them back to man the Elsenborn defence.

The 99th had done well—better than anyone at the time
realized—but their casualties had been heavy, amounting to
nearly three thousand of which only about fifteen per cent
were non-battle casualties.* Considering the appalling weather
conditions, the lack of hot food, dry clothes, sleep or indeed
any reasonable rest, the proportion was low. The battlescarred
survivors who had crammed weeks of battle experience into
less than a hundred hours became the basis of a new 99th
Infantry Division which, by the end of the war, was considered
one of the best.

The 2nd Infantry Division, some of whose troops had been
fighting continuously from December 13 when they launched
their attack on the Wahlerscheid crossroads, had the difficult
task on Tuesday of disengaging from the Rocherath–Krinkelt–
Wirtzfeld line, where they were under considerable pressure, to
the new defence line of the Elsenborn ridge without allowing
the Germans to break through. A withdrawal under such conditions is one of the most difficult of battle manoeuvres,
necessitating as it does the abandoning of prepared positions

* Half of these were trench-foot cases.

and, usually, the occupation, however brief, of exposed or untenable ground. And because such a move almost always takes place in the face of superior power and after a period of incurring casualties and lack of rest, the morale, even of first-class troops, is under great strain.

But the Germans had also decided to withdraw their tanks from the area and to give up trying to ram 12th SS Panzer Division through Rocherath and Krinkelt. 'Sepp' Dietrich ordered this armour to disengage, pull back and go south through Losheimergraben and then strike west through Hunningen, Bullingen and Butgenbach gaining the original intended route at this last place. During Monday night the Hitler Jugend tanks withdrew from the front line and their place was taken by the 3rd Panzer Grenadier Division from Sixth SS Panzer Army's reserves.

The plan for Tuesday called for a fresh assault against Rocherath–Krinkelt to be made by the tired 277th Volksgrenadiers and the new 3rd Panzer Grenadiers attacking west, while at the same time the 12th Volksgrenadier Division's reserve regiment attacked north.

This double assault, however, would have to be made without the help of the Hitler Youth Division for these were to pierce V Corps' flank position at Butgenbach.

On Tuesday morning the German infantry once more tried to break through the Rocherath–Krinkelt position but without tanks they were unable to force the Americans out and when the artillery batteries on the Elsenborn ridge laid down a heavy barrage the German attack was stopped.

By evening arrangements were complete for an American withdrawal to a better defence line. As soon as German pressure eased orders were issued for this* to begin at 5.30 pm on Tuesday. Weapons and equipment which could not be moved were destroyed and troops not actually in contact moved back first. Then each forward position leap-frogged through the one behind it while the division's tanks and tank destroyers formed a covering force to discourage pursuit. By three o'clock next morning V Corps had abandoned Rocherath, Krinkelt and Wirtzfeld and were firm on the Elsenborn ridge. The new line ran north from just west of Bullingen to link up with the Monschau position and west to line up with 30th Infantry east of Malmédy.

12th SS Panzer Division, 'Hitler Jugend', had started their move from Rocherath–Krinkelt on Monday night and by the

* It was not called a 'withdrawal' but a 'move to new positions' or, as the GIs put it—'Walk, do not run, to the nearest Exit.'

early hours of Tuesday morning a dozen or so panzers and about a battalion of panzer grenadiers had arrived at Bullingen for the attack against Butgenbach. The deep mud of the churned-up roads delayed the rest of the panzers for another day.

Butgenbach, it will be remembered, was protected on the east and south by the 26th Infantry Regiment of the 1st Infantry Division which had come in on Sunday morning to protect V Corps' flank. Left virtually undisturbed while the fighting for Rocherath–Krinkelt had been going on the veteran infantrymen had been able to prepare an excellent coordinated defence.

About three o'clock on Tuesday morning American patrols near Bullingen–Butgenbach road reported the advance of German tanks and infantry. Immediately the division's own artillery fired star shells by whose light their observers were able to direct high explosive on the attackers.

This first effort was made with about twelve 'Hitler Youth' tanks and some three hundred infantry from 12th Volksgrenadier Division. Two or three tanks bogged down at the start, some would not face the bazookas and anti-tank guns that opened up on them and the few that did get through were abandoned when the big shells of the American 'Long Toms' began exploding all around them.

The next attempt, which began in mid-morning when the fog had cleared, was a series of exploratory thrusts all along the mile of front held by 26th Infantry Regiment's Second Battalion. All were beaten off by combined infantry, anti-tank and artillery fire; Hitler Jugend lost several tanks and 12th Volksgrenadier Division added to their growing casualty list.

1st Infantry Division's second regiment, the 16th Infantry, had joined the 26th on Tuesday, December 19 (taking position west of it around Waimes), just in time to beat off attacks by 3rd Parachute Division.

Realizing that the Americans were in Butgenbach in strength the Germans waited until all of 12th Panzer had arrived as well as the rest of 12th Volksgrenadier Division before trying twice again before dawn on Wednesday with determined advances by tanks and infantry. Many casualties were inflicted on the American defenders but the Germans were beaten off again: slowly their tank strength was being whittled away.

Finally 'Sepp' Dietrich decided to commit all the artillery which had been used against the Rocherath–Krinkelt positions to support another attack on Butgenbach with two more fresh battalions of infantry. A tremendous three-hour barrage against the American foxhole line on Thursday knocked out many American weapons, killed and wounded many rifle-men—even some who were in foxholes—and tore holes in the main line of resistance. As soon as the barrage stopped the German infantry and tanks came across the fields in assault formation under orders to keep going until they had broken through or were destroyed.

Now it was the turn of the American artillery and at least ten battalions of field guns who had been waiting for the word opened up. Shells poured down on the advancing Germans but despite terrible losses they kept coming. American crews manning the useless 57-mm anti-tank guns* were shot down; along one hedgerow a number of machine-gun positions were over-run and the position wiped out to a man. This opened a gaping hole in the line through which the panzers roared and it seemed that, at last, Hitler Jugend Division had broken through the American defence. But the next ridge was covered by a well-concealed 90-mm tank destroyer which knocked out seven panzers in quick succession. Another five were destroyed by other means and the volksgrenadiers, hammered by ten thousand shells, faltered and then broke off the attack. 12th Volksgrenadier's commander reported that his broken division could not continue fighting unless they got more tanks or self-propelled guns. Later an American patrol counted three hundred dead Germans in a wood in front of their position.

But the 1st Infantry had suffered casualties too and as the fighting took its toll they laid many mines in front of their lines and plans were made to withdraw a half a mile or so to shorten the line. The last reserves were committed. On Friday the Germans tried again with more forces and from a new direction and succeeded in penetrating an inter-company gap with about twenty Panthers and self-propelled guns but 1st Infantry employed a force of self-propelled 90-mm anti-tank guns with devastating effect and once again the artillery joined in. The vital Butgenbach position held and on Saturday, December 23, the shattered 12th SS Panzer Division was no longer a serious threat and its remnants were withdrawn. In a week of effort it had advanced no more than seven miles from its start line to a position which it had been expected to reach in the first few hours.

During this same period Sixth SS Panzer Army tried again to break through from Rocherath–Krinkelt towards Elsenborn and in the north from Höfen (which the Americans had given up in favour of a better position a couple of miles west) but neither of these attacks had succeeded. A week after the

* Useless against the frontal armour of Panthers, that is.

offensive had begun it was the Americans who were holding a hard shoulder against the Germans. This ran from behind Höfen south for nine miles to the Bullingen–Butgenbach road about two miles south-east of Butgenbach. From this corner it then continued west, covering the main road, for another seven miles to Waimes. The eastward-facing front was manned by the US 9th, 99th and 2nd Infantry Divisions; the corner and the southern-facing front from Bullingen to Waimes was held by the 1st Infantry Division. Behind this sixteen-mile long shoulder were a large number of field guns and howitzer batteries and either end was firmly tied in with the rest of the First Army's new defence line.

The Germans had five infantry divisions pressing against this shoulder but four of them were divisions in name only because they had lost so many men in the week of attack. These were the 12th Volksgrenadier, 3rd Parachute and the 277th and 326th Volksgrenadiers who were to have opened the way for the SS Panzer divisions and then swung north to hold off American reinforcements but had, instead, been practically destroyed. The only fresh division was 3rd Panzer Grenadiers thrown in from the reserve in a last attempt. Soon they would be moved to another part of the front.

Hitler's Sixth SS Panzer Army on whom he had placed such high hopes on December 16 was seen, a week later, to have failed completely. The greater part of this most powerful German concentration on the Western Front in World War II had been stopped a few miles from its start line, nor had it been possible to sustain and reinforce its one successful penetration. The SS Panzer divisions would be used with effect at other places in the Ardennes but the original main thrust from the north was now given up. It was decided to use these forces to exploit 5th Panzer Army's success. Once again the right decision was taken too late.

On the southern flank three of General Brandenberger's four volksgrenadier divisions, whose task had been to pivot a defence line west from Echternach through Mersch to stop reinforcements from Third US Army reaching the Ardennes, were a long way from achieving this after three days of fighting. On the German right the 352nd Volksgrenadier Division had, it is true, forced 28th Infantry Division's 109th Regiment back to Diekirch with severe losses* but their first day's target had been to seize the bridge over the Sauer at Ettelbruck three miles

* Five hundred casualties and most of the mortars, heavy machine guns and anti-tank guns.

further west so they were well behind schedule. In the German centre the 276th Volksgrenadier's mission had been to knock out the American armoured infantry and their supporting artillery on the high ground across the Sauer and then move south-west to form the middle of the projected south-facing blocking line. After three days 276 Volksgrenadier's right had pushed 60th Armored Infantry Battalion's left six miles back opening a three-mile-wide gap between 9th Armored Division and the 109th Infantry Regiment in Diekirch. The rest of the volksgrenadier division had succeeded in driving the armoured infantry's centre and right with its supporting artillery off the dominating heights back four miles and had pushed down the Schwarz Ernst as far as Müllerthal, thus threatening to split 9th Armored Division off from 4th Infantry Division. Although this was considerable success it will be seen that there was a gap on both of 276 Volksgrenadier's flanks caused by the failure of 352 Volksgrenadiers in the north and 212 Volksgrenadiers in the south. This division's task had been to drive 4th Infantry out of their forward positions facing the Sauer, to gain control of the road network between the river and Luxembourg City and to pivot south-west in unison with 276 Volksgrenadier Division. They failed to accomplish any of these objectives in the first critical two days when everything was in their favour and later the arrival of 10th Armored Division's combat command greatly increased their difficulties. By Monday night all of the American forward positions were still holding out.

On Tuesday 276 Volksgrenadiers in the centre paused for much-needed rest and food while the new commander, Colonel Dempwolff, moved up artillery and rocket projectors and consolidated his troops for an attempt to break through 9th Armored Division's right wing, scheduled for the following day.

The other two Volksgrenadier divisions tried once more to get their attacks rolling. In the north 352 Volksgrenadiers, whose artillery had at last got across the river, shelled the 109th Infantry in Diekirch and followed this up with several attacks. The divisional commander, General Schmidt, led one of these personally until he was seriously wounded.

The weary and depleted 109th Infantry yielded to this pressure and after blowing the Sauer bridges at Diekirch* fell back

* One bridge, however, was not cleanly broken and 352nd Volksgrenadier managed to get a regiment and its heavy weapons over it to attack Ettelbruck from behind.

331

to Ettelbruck during Tuesday night and on Wednesday morning destroyed the bridges there and fell back across the Sauer to form a north-facing defence running from south-west of Ettelbruck for seven miles west to Grosbous. With both flanks wide open they were still in an extremely dangerous position.

On the German left the 212th Volksgrenadiers were determined on Tuesday to clear the stubborn small forces of Americans out of the Parc Hotel in Berdorf and the hat factory in Echternach in order to be able to move forward and join up with the 276 Volksgrenadiers' left flank which had penetrated three miles down the Schwarz Ernst.

Task Force Riley from 10th Armored Division, who had pushed through to the Echternach garrison on Monday, went back on Tuesday morning as they had promised and covered the withdrawal of other American troops in the town into the hat factory position. Once more they offered to cover the whole force if it would fall back to Consdorf but the offer was again refused and the tanks withdrew as the light was failing.

Very soon afterwards 212th Volksgrenadiers attacked in Echternach in two separate columns and, with the aid of bazookas, demolition charges and an assault gun split the American force in two. Two volunteers took a jeep and careered down the road to the south to ask for the armour to return but 10th Armored Division's commander would not allow his tanks to try to move among buildings in the dark. Word was sent to the Echternach force to try to fight their way out during Tuesday night.

At Berdorf, where, on Monday, Task Force Standish, also from 10th Armored Division, had only been able to advance seventy-five yards towards the 4th Infantry besieged in the badly damaged Parc Hotel, the day was spent by the relieving column in slowly forcing the Germans out of the intervening houses. They could not get through to the hotel and, after dark 212 Volksgrenadiers were able to strengthen their position in the town.

This was about the extent of Seventh German Army's activity on Tuesday for no serious attempt was made to drive the Americans from the Osweiler–Dickweiler position, the threat in the deep centre seemed to have evaporated and the general impression was of a lull in the offensive.

In fact, on this southern flank, the Germans had, unknown to the Americans, decided to consolidate their blocking line more or less along the positions they had attained—running roughly from Dickweiler to Ettelbruck. To do this the gap between 276 and 352 Volksgrenadiers would have to be closed and all the American strongpoints in 212 Volksgrenadiers' rear wiped out in order for Seventh German Army to be able to present a coordinated defence against the inevitable American counter-attack.

For their part the American mixed force—the 109th Infantry Regiment, 9th Armored Division's CCA, 4th Infantry Division and 10th Armored Division, less its combat command in Bastogne—were expecting further heavier German attacks and their mission was to hold their ground while General Patton moved his Third Army divisions in for a powerful drive north through the Germans' extended left flank.

Although both sides were going over to the defensive on Wednesday the fighting that day was particularly fierce as the Germans used all available strength to reduce the Echternach garrison and to take Berdorf. A strong German attack was launched against the Parc Hotel before dawn on Wednesday with demolition charges blowing more holes in the wall and reckless attacks by volksgrenadiers which only failed when hand grenades burst among them. As soon as it was light another German assault drove the relieving force of 10th Armored's tanks right out of the small town. It had been decided to try to withdraw the men in the hotel as part of the general plan to form a coherent defence line further south but this could only be accomplished after dark on Wednesday when an artillery barrage drove the Germans to cover and a force of eleven tanks and six half-tracks forced their way to the hotel and got the exhausted defenders out past the burning buildings and back to the new line at Consdorf.

At Echternach the defenders of the hat factory found at dawn on Wednesday that they were surrounded by 'tanks' (these were probably some of the few self-propelled guns assigned to Seventh German Army and now brought in to erase this stubborn American position) and flashed a cry for help to Task Force Riley, waiting outside Lauterborn. The tanks tried with some of 12th Infantry's men later in the day to get through but without success.

General Sensfuss, in the desperate way of the German Army at this stage of the war, led the final assault in person. He was wounded but took a hundred and thirty-two American prisoners and, with the fall on the same day of twenty-three men who had held out in a stone farmhouse between Echternach and Berdorf since the earliest attacks, General Brandenberger's forces finally achieved most of their first day's targets.

The four volksgrenadier divisions of the left flank of the

Ardennes Offensive had been a great disappointment. So far 5th Parachute had been of very little help in Fifth Panzer Army's attack on Bastogne (although that was about to change) and the other three divisions obviously now had no chance of reaching the original screening line from Echternach west through Mersch—the best that could be achieved was a defence running from Echternach north-west to tie in with 5th Parachute near Wiltz.

Once more, as in the north, it was the Americans who were holding a hard shoulder and, once more, great new forces were on the move to drive into the Germans' exposed flank. The American troops who had upset this important part of the German plan had suffered about two thousand casualties, not an unusually high proportion considering the strength and fierceness of the attack. The Germans had lost about two thousand five hundred including some eight hundred prisoners and a large number of trench-foot and exposure cases. Most of them had fought bravely but many lacked experience and being forced to face tanks without any of their own or adequate anti-tank weapons was very bad for morale. But the main reason for their failure to protect the left flank of Fifth Panzer Army was twofold: they had not been given sufficient strength to do so, either in men or material and the Americans they attacked had not reacted as they had been expected to do. Fourth Infantry Division's artillery had not been displaced from the Schlamm Bach ridge and their forward strongpoints had held out for days instead of hours thus denying General Brandenberger's troops free use of the roads. Finally, as elsewhere in the Ardennes, the Americans had moved in reinforcements with astonishing speed.

The result of all this was that the line-up on the morning of Thursday, December 21, when the American counter-attack began, marked the furthest German penetration on the southern flank of the Ardennes Offensive. Five days later most of the ground yielded had been recaptured leaving the way open for Third US Army to advance north.

As long as the Americans succeeded in holding the shoulders of the breach firm the attack sector could be limited, but if the Germans could find the increasing force needed to keep driving in their wedge they could still succeed in splitting the Allied front in two. They had, in fact, already accomplished this to a limited extent, as General Eisenhower's decision to divide the Ardennes into north and south commands had tacitly acknowledged. By Tuesday night the only organized

American opposition from Bullingen south to Diekirch were the garrisons in St Vith and Bastogne and four panzer divisions had broken through of which only one, 1st SS, had been stopped. The other three from north to south were Manteuffel's 116th Panzer, 2nd Panzer and Panzer Lehr: all were still moving west.

As the strategy agreed at SHAEF was for General Patton's forces to launch an attack north against the extended German left flank the responsibility for stopping the point of the German armoured thrust now belonged entirely to Field Marshal Montgomery's northern half of the Ardennes.*

General Bradley had made an early move to throw a wall up in front of the German advance on Tuesday night by ordering the 84th Infantry Division to move from Ninth Army seventy-five miles to First Army's rear. The leading Regimental Combat Team, the 334th, was ordered to assemble in Marche-en-Famenne, the central road junction between the rivers Ourthe and Meuse, 'ready to attack north-east or east'. They closed on Marche about ten o'clock on Wednesday night reinforcing the 51st Engineer Combat Battalion (minus their C company in Trois Ponts) who had put out small forces at roadblocks from the east round to the south-east. One of these was three miles north of the bridge at Ortheuville on the main road to the west from Bastogne which 2nd Panzer Division had taken after capturing Noville.

This was the bridge which General Krueger, the 116th Panzer Division commander, had decided was not worth trying for because it was certainly prepared for destruction. 2nd Panzer Division had no alternative—if the bridge was blown they would have to put in one of their own and so their reconnaissance battalion, with artillery and engineer units, got to the east bank about ten o'clock on Wednesday night and after two hours of firing at the Americans on the opposite bank with everything they had, forded the river and also rushed the bridge. The American engineers pressed down the detonator—and nothing happened. The defenders retreated south-west to St Hubert and 2nd Panzer's advance guard pushed on and made contact with the 51st Engineer roadblock eleven miles south-east of Marche in the early hours of Thursday, December 21, but did not attack.

Field Marshal Montgomery had also made some early

* General Eisenhower radioed Montgomery on December 19: 'Our weakest spot is in the direction of Namur. The general plan is to *plug the holes in the north* and launch coordinated attacks from the south.' (Author's italics.)

moves to counter the threat to Brussels and Antwerp implicit in the German breakthrough. At this time 21st Army Group's only uncommitted forces were XXX Corps who had been pulled out of the line in great secrecy on December 13 to prepare for the next great offensive. Before he knew that he was to command the northern half of the Ardennes Battle Montgomery had stopped these preparations and sent three infantry and one armoured division* to form a secondary defence line between Brussels and Maastricht—across the approaches to Antwerp. This would deal with any German thrust north-west across the Meuse between Liège and Namur. The bridges across the section of the Meuse which ran south from Namur to Givet in France were also an obvious danger. As an emergency move a scratch force of troops in reinforcement centres, engineers and artillery personnel, rear area tank officers considered too old for front-line service and some Special Air Service men were hurried down to hold these bridges if possible; to destroy them if not.

In the Ypres area three regiments of the British 29th Armoured Brigade who had recently handed in their tanks, worn out after six months continual use, were waiting to be equipped with new Comets from England. At two o'clock on Wednesday morning the 29th Armoured Brigade's duty officer was telephoned direct from 21st Army Group HQ with orders for the regiments to pick up their discarded tanks, put back wireless sets, get engines running, draw fuel, rations and ammunition and move as fast as possible to battle positions along the Meuse. Their task was to 'deny the enemy the river crossings' from Namur southwards to Givet—about thirty miles.

The 29th Armoured's motor battalion, the 8th Rifle Brigade, which had only just pulled out of the mud and cold of the front line in Holland were sent on ahead to hold the bridges until the tanks arrived. They had a company on the bridges at Namur, Dinant and Givet by one o'clock on Thursday afternoon, December 21; by four-thirty a squadron of tanks had arrived at each bridge and by eight that night 29th Armoured Brigade reported that they were complete on the river line.

After taking these cautionary measures Montgomery watched the situation develop with increasing anxiety and waited for the call. On Tuesday night he telegraphed to Sir Alan Brooke, Chief of the Imperial General Staff, expressing his disquiet, 'There is a definite lack of grip and control of the situation; no one seems to have a clear picture. I have had no

* 43rd (Wessex), 51st (Highland), 53rd (Welsh) and Guards Armoured Divisions.

orders of any kind ...'* He reported too that he had privately approached Major-General J. F. M. Whiteley, the British deputy chief of staff for operations at SHAEF and insisted that he (Montgomery) be given the First and Ninth US Armies.

Early the next morning Eisenhower telephoned his decision and the Field Marshal was filled with an unholy joy. He immediately cabled Brooke again, 'I am to assume command of the northern front. That was all I wanted to know.'

It was indeed, for he knew what he was going to do: he had already decided that the Germans were aiming for the Meuse crossings between Liège and Namur and not, as First Army assumed, for Liège, and his counter plans were to be made accordingly. For the moment he arranged to visit, first, General Simpson at Ninth Army headquarters in Maastricht and then, about lunch time, General Hodges' First Army in Chaudfontaine.

News of the British moves to back up his battered line was brought to General Hodges in the middle of Tuesday night by one of Montgomery's liaison officers and in the morning Omar Bradley telephoned to tell him that First Army would pass to the Field Marshal at noon. Hodges visited V Corps and XVIIIth Airborne Corps headquarters to tell them of the command change and to learn the latest situation. He confirmed that V Corps were to hold on the left at all costs and that XVIIIth Airborne were to prepare to attack south-east towards Vielsalm.

Montgomery's Chief of Staff, skilled at smoothing down American feelings ruffled by his difficult Chief, arrived at Chaudfontaine, after a difficult flight from England below a thick belt of fog, in mid-morning and joined forces with his opposite number on First Army, General Kean. Old friend from the Normandy days when First Army had also been under Montgomery's command, they worked well together.

Hodges, like most of his staff, had had little sleep for the past hundred hours and arrived back, very tired, about noon. An hour or so later Montgomery's staff car was driven up. He had just visited General Simpson's Ninth Army Headquarters at Maastricht and was pleased with the general feeling there. He jumped out, waved at the sentries' salutes and walked briskly into the First Army conference room. He was wearing the red beret and camouflage jacket of the British Parachute Regiment and moved with a new jauntiness, obviously eager to get to grips with a difficult military problem.

While General Hodges was explaining the situation from

* Nobécourt: *Le Dernier Coup de Dés d'Hitler.*

337

Monschau to Marche in all its complexities Montgomery's driver brought in a wicker basket from which the Field Marshal ate a sparse lunch of fruit and sandwiches. He gave an impression of listening attentively but of already having made his decisions. He seemed supremely confident and, at least to some of First Army, unwarrantedly cheerful. They had, after all, heard nothing but news of disaster since the offensive started and had seen their units taking the full force of unceasing German attacks for four days, gaps torn on both flanks, their centre driven in and the approach of SS Panzers forcing their headquarters to move back fifteen miles. The road to Bastogne had been cut, there were reports of more German armoured columns moving between XVIIIth Airborne Corps and Bastogne and of a disaster in front of St Vith.

Montgomery on the other hand was only unhappy when he was not allowed to run things his own way, the only proper, workmanlike way. The present situation was just his 'cup of tea'—things had gone wrong, everything was in a muddle, the lines were untidy. But now things would be put right, the muddle cleared up, the front made tidy and, when everything was quite ready, the enemy defeated. Although so different he was in his way quite as confident as General Patton, who was preparing the German's downfall on his part of the front.

When Hodges had finished Montgomery excused himself and went into another room where his 'gallopers', his young liaison officers who had been sent to all parts of the front except St Vith, were waiting with the latest actual situation reports. Many of them had been stopped because of the Skorzeny scare and although their knowledge of the capitals of American states or of the positions on an American football team was hardly encyclopaedic, initiative was one of the qualities for which they had been chosen and each had talked his way out of the guard room. With his map now more up to date than First Army's own, Montgomery returned to the conference room.

He agreed that the defence shoulder from Monschau through Bullingen to Malmédy must be held firm at all costs, that 1st SS Panzer's force at Stoumont must be trapped and then destroyed and that Ridgway's XVIII Airborne Corps should drive through to make contact with the St Vith defenders. Then, having formed a really firm front the next thing was to collect a reserve for a counterstroke and, while this was being done, covering the open flank between 82nd Airborne Division and the Meuse.

3rd Armored Division were coming in and, as we have

seen, 84th Infantry, too, were on their way from Geilen-kirchen. The new 75th Infantry Division had just arrived on the continent from the United States and was moving up to join First Army as soon as possible. These would close the gap.

Montgomery said that he wanted the most aggressive American corps commander to take charge here and sufficient troops for him to launch a counter-attack to blunt the nose of the German advance. He already knew whom he wanted, Major-General J. Lawton Collins, 'Lightning Joe', whose VII Corps had been attacking towards the Roer Dams until the Ardennes Offensive stopped it. Hodges agreed and it was arranged for Collins to come to Chaudfontaine early the next morning.

Eisenhower was under no illusions about the weight of the German attack that was falling on the northern half of the Ardennes while Patton was pivoting his divisions to attack the southern half's flank. He sent the following message to Mont-gomery on the day command passed to him: 'Please let me have your personal appreciation of the situation on the north flank with reference to the possibility of giving up, if necessary, some ground in order to shorten our line and collect a strong reserve for the purpose of destroying the enemy in Belgium.'*

Montgomery replied, on his return from visiting Simpson and Hodges—'I am hopeful that the situation can be restored and I see no reason at the moment to give up any of the ground that has been gained in the last few days by such hard fighting.' He indicated that physical exhaustion might make some changes in command necessary: Hodges was 'a bit shaken, very tired and in need of moral support.' He added that he was unwilling to relieve American commanders per-sonally.

American confidence had been hit hard by this first and completely unexpected large-scale reverse and there were many recriminations, much bitter criticism—usually of the next higher command—and an inclination to look for scape-goats. One of the ways of rapidly building up an *esprit de corps* in the American Army—most of whose divisions were new—was to encourage the idea that other units were inferior and while this, when all is going well, hastens the advance by encouraging competition, the opposite reaction occurs when things are going badly, for then lack of confidence in the flank-ing unit is an added reason to pull back.

After six days of disaster Allied morale needed a boost:

* Eisenhower: *Crusade in Europe*, p. 383.

Eisenhower issued one of his rare Orders of the Day couched in optimistic terms which pointed out that 'By rushing out of his fixed defences the enemy may give us the chance to turn his great gamble into his worst defeat,' and, in rousing language, encouraging his commanders and soldiers: 'United in this determination and with unshakable faith in the cause for which we fight, we will, with God's help, go forward to our greatest victory.'

He also recommended to Washington that General Bradley be promoted and he sent messages of encouragement to Generals Hodges and Simpson. At the same time he let Montgomery know privately that if any command changes were necessary he himself would make them.

In turn General Eisenhower was assured by General Marshall that he had the complete confidence of the Joint Chiefs of Staff and that he would be left free to give his entire attention to the fighting. Churchill too realized that encouragement was needed and cabled Eisenhower that 'as a mark of confidence' Britain would somehow find a further quarter of a million men to put at his disposal.

For the Allies the next two or three days were the darkest hours since the invasion, but in fact no army or corps commanders were relieved and three weeks later Field Marshal Montgomery was to write in glowing terms to General Bradley about the quality of the American troops he had commanded and added: 'It has been a great pleasure to work with Hodges and Simpson; both have done very well. And Corps Commanders (Gerow, Collins, Ridgway) have been quite magnificent...'

But this is anticipating the outcome: at the time Montgomery took over, things looked very different.

23

CRITICAL HOURS FOR FIRST US ARMY

> *He who uses force unsparingly without reference to the bloodshed involved, must obtain a superiority if his adversary uses less vigour in its application.*
>
> CLAUSEWITZ *On War*

First Army's left flank, from Monschau to Malmédy, seemed to be firmly held. The main danger was in the centre from Kampfgruppe Peiper in the Stoumont–La Gleize areas, from the rest of I SS Panzer Corps, south of the Amblève and west of the Salm, and from Manteuffel's LXVI Corps attacking St Vith. Against these forces First Army had been able to place the 30th Infantry, part of 3rd Armored and the 82nd Airborne Divisions in the area between Malmédy and Werbomont while the force which had been built up around 7th Armored Division occupied an east–west oval whose extremities were St Vith and Vielsalm.

First Army's right flank, between the St Vith position and Bastogne, hardly existed after the first few days of the assault, after, that is, 116th Panzer Division had gone through Houffalize and 2nd Panzer had crossed the Ourthe, but if the Germans were going to be stopped, here was where it must be accomplished.

Major-General Matthew Ridgway, XVIIIth Airborne Corps commander, who had been fog-bound in England, got back and resumed command on Tuesday morning, December 19. His orders were to block any further German advance from La Roche, an Ourthe river crossing only twenty miles from Bastogne, to Stoumont, twenty-five miles from Liège.

For this large task Ridgway had on his left a mixed force made up of the 119th Infantry Regiment, from 30th Infantry Division; CCB of 3rd Armored Division; the 740th Tank Battalion and detachments of combat engineers. Corps centre was held by his own 82nd Airborne Division who were supporting the attack against Battlegroup Peiper, probing east and south to make contact with the St Vith defenders and pushing out a screen all around Werbomont. The south-western extremity of this screen was a small force of glider infantry and tank destroyers who were blocking the approaches to the Ourthe bridge at Hotton until 3rd Armored Division's reserve combat command came in to take over XVIIIth Airborne Corps' right wing.

The hole in the defence between 82nd Airborne at Werbomont and the Meuse bridge at Dinant was slowly being filled as more American troops were moved behind the front. 3rd Armored Division's CCR had reached the road between Hotton and Soy on Wednesday morning, December 20, and fanned out south and east pushing reconnaissance beyond La Roche on the right and to Manhay on the left and contacting the advancing Germans at Dochamps in the centre. The second regimental combat team of 84th Infantry closed on the Marche area late on Thursday afternoon, the third at midnight.

Also on Thursday decisions were taken at the second of the daily First Army conferences with Montgomery which brought about great changes on this part of the front. General Collins and his VII Corps staff handed over their existing divisions to XIX Corps north of Monschau and took over four other divisions on First Army's right to be used in a decisive counterattack against the nose of the German offensive represented by the 116th and 2nd Panzer Divisions.

This new VII Corps would consist of the 84th Infantry Division, the new 75th Infantry due to reach the area by midnight, 3rd Armored Division's CCR, already engaged in the Hotton–Soy sector, together with its CCA released from its defensive role in the Eupen area and, finally, in order to put some real weight into the punch, the whole of 2nd Armored Division from Ninth Army's reserve were ordered to move to the area. Strong artillery and fighter-bomber support would all add up to a most formidable force.

But while these movements were taking place the Germans had not let up on their efforts to exploit the gap to break through to the Meuse and the first conflict took place between 3rd Armored Division's columns moving out of the Hotton–Soy area and LVIIIth Panzer Corps, leading tanks and infantry.

When General Rose's small armoured reserve reached their designated area reports had been coming in that German tanks, after capturing Houffalize, were moving on towards Liège and Rose was ordered to probe forward to find, and if possible, stop them. But because most of his tanks were occupied elsewhere 3rd Armored's commander was only able to form three small teams. On Wednesday he sent one towards La Roche, one towards Samrée and one as far as the highway from Houffalize to Liège to occupy a tactically important section including the crossroads of Manhay and Baraque de Fraiture. This last place, one of the highest points in the Ardennes, was held on Tuesday night by three 105-mm howitzers, survivors of an artillery battalion which had been overrun in the Schnee Eifel, but was reinforced on Wednesday with four anti-aircraft half-tracks from 7th Armored Division mounting multiple machine guns.

General Rose kept back, south of Soy, a battalion of armoured infantry, three companies of tanks and one of engineers as a reserve. Nothing was known at this time of any American troops further south but in fact there were a number of roadblocks manned by small groups of soldiers, some by combat engineers and, in particular, at La Roche and Samrée, by units from the supply trains of the 7th Armored who had been moved away from the threat to St Vith and concentrated there.

The commander of this force, Colonel Andrew Adams, had learned on Tuesday that the head of a German panzer column had appeared at a blown bridge over the Ourthe only some seven miles to the south-east and, as a precaution, moved most of his supplies from La Roche five miles north-east to Samrée. This seemed to be a wise move but it will be remembered the 116th Panzer—whose advance guard these tanks had been— did not cross the Ourthe but were reversed in their tracks by General Krueger and sent back to Houffalize. Then, after moving north along the main highway, they had turned left to strike for Samrée.

Thus on Wednesday, December 20, columns from 3rd Armored and 116th Panzer were moving towards Samrée in complete ignorance of each other's presence. General Rose's right-hand column, Task Force Hogan, moved from Soy to La Roche where it made contact with 7th Armored's trains and then continued east for three miles until stopped by a German roadblock. The left-hand column, Task Force Kane, moved almost due east to Malempré, on high ground dominating Manhay, without opposition.

But the centre thrust, Task Force Tucker, striking for Samrée, was engaged by 116th Panzer's advance guard at Dochamps two miles north of Samrée and the American commander split his attack into three in an attempt to flow round. The left-hand splinter turned east and made contact with the column near Manhay; the centre fell back three miles to the reserve at Amonines and the right-hand force circled west and south to approach Samrée, where a small force from 7th Armored Division's trains were being attacked by LVIIIth

343

Corps' panzers and volksgrenadiers.

These infantry were some of 560th Volksgrenadier Division who had been able, by forced marches and by taking advantage of the time lost by 116th Panzer's about-turn near Ortheuville, to close up and support the attack on Samrée and the combined force was proving too much for the single light tank, a half-track, a few field artillery pieces, some quad-mount machine guns and less than a company of service troops. But the local commander, Lieutenant-Colonel Miller, had been told that help was on the way including tanks from 3rd Armored Division and so he gave orders that no supplies were to be destroyed.

The German assault, preceded by rocket fire, consisted of tanks and armoured infantry who soon overwhelmed the defenders. The splinter force which had circled Dochamps, led by two armoured cars, got into Samrée from the north but the six tanks following were quickly knocked out by German tanks. The surviving tank crews clambered on board the armoured cars and escaped south-west to La Roche as had most of the 7th Armored personnel in Samrée. The supplies had to be abandoned and General Krueger's LVIII Corps got twenty-five thousand gallons of fuel and some fifteen thousand rations.

The loss of Samrée was a severe blow and 3rd Armored Division's commander ordered an all-out attack the next day to retake it but General Krueger had no intention of losing momentum and ordered a battlegroup of panzers, self-propelled guns, mortars and armoured infantry to advance northwest during the night. This force moved along side roads between the Ourthe and the main Amonines–Dochamps road during Wednesday night, intending first to gain control of the road from Hotton to Soy and then to seize the Hotton bridge and quickly push all of LVIIIth Panzer Corps on to the western bank of the Ourthe before the Americans had time to form a blocking line.

At the same time as this German force was moving northwest two companies of armoured infantry from 3rd Armored Division's reserve and the remnants of the centre armoured column moved south-east and closed up to Dochamps. Thus, at dawn, they were behind the German battlegroup moving towards Hotton and Soy; the rest of 3rd Armored's reserve were around the latter place—General Krueger would not find Hotton quite so easy to take as Samrée. On the other hand General Rose's meagre resources were tightly stretched with his left column, Task Force Hogan, three miles south of La

Roche, his centre and reserve between Soy and Dochamps and Task Force Kane seven or eight miles to the east in the Manhay area.

The German commander learned on Wednesday that 2nd SS Panzer Division were on their way from 'Sepp' Dietrich's front to lend support to his open right flank. Pleased, he despatched an eighty-man patrol of 560 Volksgrenadiers to seize the Baraque de Fraiture and hold it open for the SS Panzer Division. Openly approaching the crossroads just before dawn the Germans were cut to pieces by the deadly quad-mounts on the anti-aircraft half-tracks. The survivors went to ground in the nearby woods and maintained a watch on the American position until 2nd SS Panzer could come up and take it.

Also on Thursday Task Force Hogan, south of La Roche, was engaged by more of General Krueger's infantry and about one o'clock in the afternoon was ordered to fall back and join the centre force near Amonines who, by then, had their hands full. It was, however, too late, for the Germans were in strength between the Ourthe and the Amonines–Dochamps road and night found Task Force Hogan cut off on a hill near Macouray.

First intimations of the presence of German troops near Hotton came just before dawn on Thursday when a patrol from the reserve at Soy were fired on. Shortly afterwards mortar and small-arms fire came down at the bridge position. Here some 200 American troops with one light and one medium tank were holding the eastern end and a platoon of combat engineers with three anti-tank guns and a Sherman the western end of the bridge. The only other force available to protect Hotton was 3rd Armored's reserve at Soy and once the German tanks and infantry had succeeded in getting on to the Hotton–Soy road it was comparatively easy, owing to the ground, for them to protect their rear.

At the eastern end of the bridge engineer trucks were used to block the roads but the trees growing down almost to the river's edge enabled the panzers and their support infantry to get up close for a sudden assault. Breaking out of the woods the German tanks advanced with all guns firing followed closely by the infantry firing their automatic weapons. The two American tanks were destroyed and then, miraculously it seemed, an American 90-mm self-propelled gun suddenly appeared 'from nowhere' and knocked out the leading German tanks.

The mixed bag of defenders on the opposite bank opened up with rifle, machine-gun and bazooka fire which checked the

Germans. Later in the morning they lost two or three more panzers to bazooka fire.

Part of 3rd Armored's reserve moved north-east from Soy and got round into Hotton to stiffen the defence there. An urgent request for help to beat off 'many German tanks attacking Hotton' was flashed to 84th Infantry Division's regimental combat team at Marche, only five miles away at nine in the morning, but for some reason this was not taken seriously and no troops arrived until late afternoon. The 82nd Airborne promised a battalion of parachute infantry but they did not arrive for another thirty-six hours.

Hotton was defended for the all-important first few hours by the few combat engineers from the ubiquitous 51st Battalion, some of 3rd Armored's reserve and small groups of signal, service and headquarters troops and the bridge was held, an event which had decisive effects on the entire Fifth Panzer Army attempt to drive its three armoured divisions through to the Meuse, for the 116th were kept on the wrong side of the Ourthe which left 2nd Panzer's right flank unprotected and forced its commander to peel off badly needed forces to cover it.

The defence of Hotton could not have succeeded if it had not been for attacks against 116th Panzer Division's flank from the 3rd Armored force left in Soy and from the force between Amonines and Dochamps which forced the German commander to turn much of his strength to face north-east and east.

It was this threat to his flank as well as the toughness of the defence of Hotton which caused General Krueger to make another of his radical changes—the 116th Panzer Division were ordered to disengage at Hotton and pull back as quickly as possible to Samrée and then to cross the Ourthe at La Roche, which the 7th Armored trains had abandoned. This move took another full day and it was not until the night of December 22/23 that the 116th crossed the Ourthe at La Roche and began to move north-west again towards the road between Hotton and Marche. By that time the position on the American side had strengthened considerably.

The CCA of 3rd Armored Division came in north of Manhay during Thursday night and on Friday 2nd Armored Division moved nearly one hundred miles in twenty-two hours and closed on the Liège area. With the arrival of the 75th Infantry Division in VII Corps' sector by midnight on Friday all the forces for the projected First Army counter-attack completed their moves but it was evident that another full day would be needed to move up to attack positions and to get the gun batteries sited, so the battle was postponed until Sunday, December 24.

On December 23 VII Corps officially assumed responsibility for some fifty winding miles of front from the junction of the rivers Lesse and Meuse south of Dinant to Manhay, on the Bastogne to Liège highway. The three experienced divisions— 2nd Armored, 84th Infantry and 3rd Armored were in the line and the untried 75th Infantry in reserve. The corps' right flank was covered by the British 29th Armoured Brigade who now had a regiment covering each of the bridges at Givet, Dinant and Namur* backed up by considerable artillery west of this section of the Meuse.

At the same time as these preparations were taking place 3rd Armored Division's CCR had been fully occupied on their important part of the front. Task Force Hogan trapped at Macouray had tried to break out on Friday but found the German grip was too strong. Running out of fuel, surgical supplies, ammunition and food they asked by radio for 'maximum support', having refused a German request for an 'honourable surrender'. By this time the Germans were attacking everywhere and 3rd Armored had no one to spare. An attempt to supply the trapped force by air was broken up by Krueger's anti-aircraft guns at La Roche. In the end Task Force Hogan destroyed their vehicles and weapons, left their wounded behind with volunteer medics, and slipped away in small groups during the night of December 24. All but one man regained the American lines by Christmas Day—the unlucky one was shot by a green sentry of the newly-arrived 75th Infantry Division.

The last of 3rd Armored Division's original three columns committed on December 20, Task Force Kane, who had occupied high ground dominating Manhay on the first day without trouble and had spent Thursday morning also without contact, sent a detachment of eleven tanks and a reconnaissance platoon south to reinforce the Baraque de Fraiture force which, that night, formed a ring of alternate tanks and armoured cars around the crossroads.

The rest of Task Force Kane was ordered to come back to the centre force around Dochamps on Thursday afternoon but moved only two miles before dark. The next day the move was continued as far as Lamormenil, less than two miles from Dochamps, but just outside that village the lead tanks were stopped by German anti-tank guns.

* 23rd Hussars at Givet; 3rd Royal Tank Regiment at Dinant; 2nd Fife and Forfar Yeomanry at Namur.

At the Baraque de Fraiture the American force was further built up by the arrival of a company of glider infantry from 82nd Airborne but Task Force Kane's eleven tanks were then withdrawn and a platoon of tank destroyers which were sent to take their place lost their way and were captured.

Task Force Kane tried again, this time with the help of some eighty parachute infantry, to take Dochamps but the 560th Volksgrenadier Division could not be knocked off the Samrée–Dochamps ridge and the American centre position began to deteriorate—particularly after what happened at the Baraque de Fraiture on Saturday, December 23.

There had been signs of increasing activity on the German side and just before dawn on Friday a German officer patrol had been captured and identified as 2nd SS Panzer Division. An attack was then expected but although shelling increased at daylight nothing else happened for 2nd SS Panzer, like every other German mechanized unit, was suffering from fuel starvation and it was not until four o'clock in the afternoon that two panzer companies got up to the position having had to wait for an emergency supply of fuel.

With an entire regiment of panzer grenadiers they smashed into the defence perimeter and two hours later it was all over. The American position had been wiped out although forty-four out of the hundred and sixteen men did manage to escape in the dark and general confusion.

Second SS Panzer were not in control of a vital communications control point from which they could strike north or west. Still mainly concerned with the threat to Liège the Americans had placed a detachment of parachute infantry, reinforced by odd tanks and tank destroyers, north of the Baraque de Fraiture to block the way to Manhay, the next important crossroads, but 2nd SS Panzer first moved infantry and self-propelled guns east and attacked Task Force Kane's outpost at Odeigne with panzer grenadiers and self-propelled 40-mm guns. Third Armoured's position was perilous as 560th Volksgrenadiers renewed their attack, the fresh 2nd SS Panzer moved in and other German troops were reported on the way.

During the night 560th Infantry penetrated Task Force Kane's position about a mile west of Dochamps and next day, Sunday, tried to seize both villages but were beaten back with heavy casualties. Task Force Kane was able to withdraw to the north.

Meanwhile, realizing that time was on the Allies side, the Germans continued to push hard to cover the last few miles to the Meuse. The leading units of 2nd Panzer Division having spent Thursday night in Tenneville, after seizing the Ortheuville bridge, pushed north-west towards Marche reaching the village of Bande at 2.0 pm on Friday, December 22. The point hit a roadblock formed by 84th's infantry and anti-tank guns and some 3rd Armored's vehicles and lost a Tiger or Panther. This resistance deflected the advance guard to the west and by six o'clock that evening the two leading panzers were moving along the Marche–Rochefort road where they were fired on by a reconnaissance company of 84th Infantry sallying out of Marche. Still trying to avoid delaying involvement the advance guard of 2nd Panzer moved away and at Hargimont took a minor north-easterly road to the village of Humain. Here, and on the high ground just beyond, most of the division closed up to spend the night. Second Panzer had advanced a further fifteen miles on December 22, and were less than twenty by road from Dinant bridge.

Second Panzer had lost forty-four tanks (including six Tigers) and about a battalion of Panzer Grenadiers but still had about forty-four tanks and twenty-five self-propelled tank destroyers. They were encouraged by the lack of resistance: 'Our parachutists and GREIF commandos have sown panic in the Allies' rear areas,' 2nd Panzer's commander reported on Friday night. 'Enemy morale seems strongly shaken. Since our fight at Noville we have encountered only weak resistance easily overcome—except south of Marche today. Enemy planes have been little active. The Luftwaffe has not yet intervened in the battle. Revictualling and re-fuelling is insufficient and irregular, strongly restraining the tactical mobility of the division. We will continue our advance along the axis Buissonville, Chapois, Conneux with our main force. We will put in a roadblock at Leignon (NW of Chapois) awaiting our promised flank guard. We will occupy the zone Celles, Conjoux and prepare to cross the Meuse at Anseremme.'

This last was a railway bridge a mile and a half south of the Dinant bridge which the Germans expected to be blown before they could seize it. Von Lauchert's plans for Saturday and Sunday were ambitious but he was encouraged by the apparent emptiness of the ground he was covering. He had no knowledge of the movement of the American 2nd Armored Division from the north who, the night that he wrote this report, were closing on the rear of the new VII Corps area south-west of Liège, nor of the presence of a British armoured regiment, the 3rd Royal Tanks, in and east of Dinant. Both these were to prove an unpleasant surprise to him.

During these days when Manteuffel's LVIIIth Panzer Corps had been trying hard to drive west through First Army's right flank the battle had flared up again on their left and centre with both German and American attacks.

For the Germans on this front the two main problems were Malmédy, a communications centre they must capture if Sixth SS Panzer Army's right wing were to have any chance of still getting to the Meuse, and the relief and reinforcement of I SS Panzer Corps' spearhead, Battlegroup Peiper.

The firm stand of the American troops along the Elsenborn Ridge had held the SS Panzer division in check and made it impossible for Skorzeny's 150 Panzer Brigade to carry out their original mission. Their commander asked 'Sepp' Dietrich to allow him to use his special commandos to capture Malmédy which would draw off troops from those facing I SS Panzer Corps and open a way west behind the American defence. Dietrich agreed and Skorzeny's tough, well-armed men, with added tanks and armoured cars, collected in Ligneuville during Wednesday afternoon and night. Before dawn on Thursday, December 21, they launched a double attack against Malmédy.

The right-hand assault, moving north along the Ligneuville–Malmédy road was engaged by first one and then two battalions of 30th Infantry Division's 120th Regiment and stopped. Badly hammered by a long concentrated artillery barrage the Germans withdrew. The left-hand group tried to come into Malmédy from the west by circling along secondary roads but were stopped by a minefield and then practically destroyed by shell fire, machine gun and grenades. Skorzeny's reserve then advanced in fog to the Malmédy–Stavelot road with infantry and tanks and achieved considerable initial success, driving the Americans back and forcing them to abandon four 3-inch Tank Destroyers. This fight took place along the seam between 30th Division's 120th Regiment, holding Malmédy and its 117th at Stavelot. Wild reports of a large German mixed tank and infantry force, 'north-west of Malmédy and advancing', caused great concern in First Army Headquarters, and enforced their belief that Liège was the German's main target.

There was little substance to the reports and this attack too was beaten off. Skorzeny lost most of his armour and his infantry suffered very heavy casualties from the American artillery, who were now using the new POZIT fuse,* and were

* This top secret weapon, hitherto used only at sea so that defective shells could not be examined, contained a radar device which exploded the shell a few feet from the target with devastating effect.

forced to withdraw. It was an ignominious end to the first and last German attempt to capture the northernmost of the four essential communications centres.

The failure also marked the end of Operation Greif on which Hitler had placed such high hopes. Although odd jeeps full of Skorzeny's commandos masquerading as Americans would appear from time to time elsewhere in the Ardennes, 150 Panzer Brigade had ceased to exist as a tactical force. Their most valuable contribution had been the effect on American morale—particularly in the rear areas—the hindering of free movement behind the line and to a much lesser degree their initial interference with communications. Had Sixth SS Panzer Army broken the American front line, as intended, Skorzeny's force would probably have been militarily worthwhile; as it happened the effort and matériel were largely wasted. Certainly those commandos who were captured, often without firing a shot, courtmartialled and executed must have thought so.

The rest of 1st SS Panzer Division were in the area south of the Amblève and east of the Salm, cut off from Battlegroup Peiper by the American possession of Stavelot and the blown bridges of Trois Ponts. On Thursday, December 21, General Mohnke the divisional commander made strenuous efforts to restore communications with his halted spearhead by attacking north across the Amblève between Stavelot and Trois Ponts and west across the Salm, between Trois Ponts and Grand Halleux.

The attack across the Amblève came in the early hours of Thursday morning when SS infantry waded the icy waters under cover of fire from tanks on the south bank and established a small bridgehead. But as soon as it was light the 117th Infantry, whose sector this was, were able to bring small-arms and mortar fire down on to the follow-up German troops catching them in mid-river and killing about eighty.

The German infantry assault coincided with another made by a company of panzer grenadiers and four tanks already north of the Amblève, who came from the west and pushed the Americans back about a hundred yards but once again as soon as it was light the American artillery were zeroed in and this attack too was smashed up. Fighting continued near here all day Thursday but the Germans were unable to make further progress and most withdrew before dawn on Friday. However, a force of panzers and self-propelled guns were left on the north bank of the Amblève dug in on high ground west of Stavelot but separated from Peiper by one of 3rd Armored

Division's columns.

The other attempt made to relieve Peiper by 1st SS Panzer Division on Thursday came when General Mohnke tried to push most of the rest of his force due west across the Salm (which runs south from Trois Ponts through Vielsalm) intending to swing north and come up on Peiper's left flank. The 82nd Airborne, who had pushed east to the Salm with their 505th Parachute Infantry, were holding the northernmost four to five miles of the river.

About noon German self-propelled guns, appearing out of the fog, were destroyed by a bazooka team from a small American bridgehead on the east bank and during the rest of the day there were a number of short sharp actions with first one side and then the other trying to establish bridgeheads. The bridge at La Neuville four miles south of Trois Ponts was blown in the Germans' faces and their attempt after dark to get across the broken span of the railway bridge at Trois Ponts was broken up by shellfire. Thursday night passed with the thinly stretched American forces on the west bank of the fordable river acutely aware that the Germans opposite were hourly increasing in strength.

On Thursday the Americans were able to prevent reinforcements reaching Peiper but although they attacked at four different places around the perimeter of the trapped German force they did not succeed in destroying it. Three attacks failed almost completely and the only one to succeed was most costly. It took place at Cheneux where Peiper had a mixed force holding open his only bridge over the Amblève and where two companies of 82nd Airborne's parachute infantry had fought their way into the village during Wednesday night by charging across open ground against 20-mm anti-aircraft guns. Before dawn on Thursday fresh parachute infantry came in with orders to wipe out the remaining Germans. Peiper withdrew most of his men here during Wednesday night—thus giving up his only ground south of the Amblève—but left behind a tough rearguard who were killed almost to a man before the airborne troops finally gained Cheneux. Of the two companies of parachute infantry who had launched the first attack one had eighteen men left by Thursday afternoon and no officers; the other had thirty-eight men and three officers. Although the Germans left behind many guns and vehicles they got all their tanks but one back to the main force.

The 30th Infantry planned to launch two attacks against Stoumont from the west: one reinforced battalion was to recapture the sanatorium and then drive on, the other was to circle north and by coming in behind stop the Stoumont force from getting back to La Gleize.

The assault on the sanatorium was scheduled to begin an hour before sunrise but Peiper struck first. He pushed three self-propelled guns supported by infantry out of Stoumont about five o'clock in the morning towards the American position. Four Shermans were knocked out followed by heavy mortar and automatic weapon fire. This short fierce action so thoroughly disorganized the Americans that they had to postpone their attack against the sanatorium until noon.

The battalion attempting to circle north found the going very confusing and the commander, Major McCown, himself went out on reconnaissance, was captured and taken to Colonel Peiper in Stoumont.

A determined assault by the American infantry succeeded in driving the Germans from the sanatorium: once more the Americans occupied the building. Down in the basement the patients and staff listened fearfully for the shooting to start again. Later, by keeping the sanatorium between it and the American tanks and guns down the road, a Tiger tank was able to come in close from the north and rapidly fired 88-mm high-explosive shells through the windows. The Americans were forced out and the sanatorium changed hands for the fourth time. After dark four Shermans managed to get round behind the sanatorium and their shells, fired through the windows, drove the Germans out for the last time. The Americans re-occupied the shattered building, discovering to their amazement that not one of the patients or staff had been killed or wounded.

A mixed force of 3rd Armored's tanks and 117th Regiment's infantry, who had been stopped on Wednesday night by a German roadblock north of La Gleize, tried again on Thursday morning to break through but the German position was too well covered and the Shermans were unable to get off the road. A headlong attack would have been suicidal so the task force withdrew and tried to approach from the east only to be halted by another well-dug-in German roadblock.

The fourth American attack against Peiper on Thursday was made by Task Force Lovelady who had reached the area north of Trois Ponts on Wednesday. They moved northwards, under cover of fog, to seize the high ridge from which La Gleize could be dominated, but Peiper had covered his back door with a minefield on which the two leading American tanks blew up. A few minutes later an anti-tank gun firing out of the mist

353

destroyed the last two tanks in the column and the road was completely blocked. Attempts by the infantry to move up on to the ledge were stopped by well-sited machine guns.

The attacks against Battlegroup Peiper by 30th Infantry Division and 3rd Armored Division's CCB on Thursday, December 21, were made by strong forces backed up by artillery. The Germans were unable to manoeuvre, were practically out of food and fuel and desperately low on ammunition yet the end of the day found them still intact while the Americans had suffered severe losses and were badly shaken. The main reasons were the superiority of the German tanks—particularly when in hull-down positions, screened by infantry and approachable only along straight roads—and the ferocity and tenacity of the Leibstandarte who, knowing they were trapped, could only hang on until reinforcements broke through to them.

It had been a disappointing day for those XVIII Airborne Corps units who had been given the job of wiping out the Germans north of the Amblève and the commander of the operation, General William Harrison, did not mince matters in his report on the 'real picture'. He said that two of his battalions had been cut down, were now demoralized and 'in pretty bad shape'. His tank support had not been able to help because the thick woods confined them to the roads which Peiper had well covered. The Germans were too strong and too well placed for his depleted force to be able to defeat them in position—if they were unwise enough to try to come out then the tables would be turned.

General Hobbs, the 30th Infantry Division commander, then asked General Ridgway if the 82nd Airborne Division on the south could help by attacking Peiper's flank on the high ground north of the Amblève. Such an attack would have been very costly but the question never arose because by this time XVIII Airborne Corps were fully occupied fending off attacks against their centre and right wing by 116th Panzer and 2nd Panzer Divisions. Also it seemed likely that the St Vith defenders would be pushed back on to 82nd Airborne's front. The paratroopers would hold the lines of the Amblève and the Salm, keeping Peiper bottled up, but that, for the time being at least, would be all they could do.

First Army turned to the Air Force, whose scheduled missions on Wednesday had once more been wiped out by fog, requesting their help against the still dangerous force of panzers, self-propelled guns and SS troops around Stoumont. The meteorological report was hopeful that Friday would bring flying weather: 30th Division's air support officer hastened to get the targets ready.

The Americans did not, of course, know that Peiper's fuel tanks were empty and that therefore he could not continue his advance even if they got out of his way. It was during Thursday night that the Luftwaffe made their one attempt to refuel 1st SS Panzer Division's point by air but most of the canisters fell outside Peiper's zone and he got only enough to run his battery charging motors and to move some of the tanks to better defensive positions.

It was going to take much longer than expected to eliminate the powerful force holed up in Stoumont and La Gleize and meanwhile Fifth Panzer Army continued to drive through the gap between XVIII Airborne Corps and Bastogne and the main danger seemed to be the Meuse crossings south of Namur.

24

MORE THAN MAN CAN BEAR

> *They grant us sudden days*
> *Snatched from their business of war.*
> *We are too close to appraise*
> *What manner of men they are.*
>
> RUDYARD KIPLING

As the airborne and armoured reinforcements came into Bastogne they had to be hurried to the north and the east where German pressure was greatest. The southern perimeter was manned at first by whatever other troops could be found: lone stragglers, detached parties of three or four and broken units falling back in disarray were funnelled into a net set up by Colonel Roberts' headquarters and steered into the centre of Bastogne where a special formation kept hot food and warm billets ready round the clock. Hungry and half-frozen, these exhausted soldiers' morale was, in many cases, dangerously low, but after a good meal, some hours of sleep and a wash and shave most of them were ready to fight again.

In this way Team SNAFU, numbering over 600, was formed to supply task forces to deal with sudden trouble spots as well as to send replacements for front line casualties.

The road running south-west from Bastogne to Neufchâteau, the link with VIII Corps' HQ, was cut some time during Wednesday night, probably by 5th Parachute's reconnaissance. It was a severe blow to the Americans and it should not have happened for earlier that day there had been adequate forces in the area to deal with such an obvious German move. But the confusion caused by the rapidly changing command situation had caused them to be withdrawn.

An advance party from the first of Third Army's units to be committed to the counter-attack, 4th Armored Division, arrived in Arlon on Tuesday, December 19. Because VIII Corps was then the only higher authority operating in the area Brigadier-General Holmes Dager, commanding CCB, reported to General Middleton. He was ordered to move his command north and close on villages half way between Neufchâteau and Bastogne and by midnight a powerful American armoured force had been placed in a most important tactical position.

General Dager had pointed out to General Middleton the importance of keeping CCB together as a mobile armoured force and the Corps commander had agreed that it would not be split up but during Tuesday night someone at VIII Corps HQ called on CCB for limited help in Bastogne. The reports from there were so alarming that night that it looked as though the defenders were about to be overwhelmed. General Dager was ordered to send a small team of tanks, self-propelled guns and supporting infantry north 'to aid CCB of 10th Armored'.

The commander, Captain Bert Ezell, drove on ahead to find out where his force was to be committed: Task Force Ezell moved out about ten-thirty on Wednesday morning. In Bastogne the young captain was passed from one commander to another: he reported to the Chief of Staff who sent him to the Operations Officer who sent him to the airborne divisional commander who sent him to Colonel Roberts who told him to assemble around Villeroux.

This village lay between Sibret, where the remnants of the 28th Infantry were trying to build a defence, and Senonchamps, the main artillery position which was also the new objective for 26th Volksgrenadiers whose Reconnaissance Battalion were about to start their advance from five miles to the east.

At noon VIII Corps passed to Third Army whose III Corps, charged with responsibility for the counter-attack against the German flank, had arrived in Luxembourg. The rest of 4th Armored Division came into the area and its CCB reverted to III Corps' control.

4th Armored had been in action for five months without a break, coming out of the line only a week before the start of the Ardennes Offensive. Its reputation as one of the star performers of the American armies in Europe had not been earned without paying a heavy price. Its brilliant commander, Major-General John Wood had driven himself to breaking point in the break-out from Normandy and the tough fighting in Lorraine. He had been returned to the USA for rest and recuperation. Patton had then given the command to his own Chief of Staff.

Now, unexpectedly committed to battle again, the division was badly under strength in men and tanks. Its new commander, Major-General Hugh Gaffey, commanding a division in action for the first time was angered to find that his leading combat command had been given orders by VIII Corps* which

* General Middleton had cleared this with General Bradley who told him that he could employ 4th Armored's combat command when it reached his area but only 'if necessary to hold his position'.

357

were already whittling away their strength. He ordered CCB to get back Task Force Ezell and the whole command to come all the way back to an area south-east of Neufchâteau.

Captain Ezell then withdrew from Villeroux without informing anyone in Bastogne, assuming that such major decisions would be communicated at a higher level of command, and, together with the rest of CCB, moved right back, nearly to Arlon, to become part of the left wing of III Corps' counterattack. These moves left the Neufchâteau to Bastogne road unguarded and the forward German column cut it thus allowing Bastogne to be encircled. When III Corps launched their attack it would take 4th Armored Division more than a day to move up to the villages their CCB had held during the night of December 19/20.

Patton had promised that his counter-attack would be launched on Friday, December 22, and it was hoped that Bastogne would be relieved the following day. This meant that the garrison would have to hang on for two more days after the first German assaults had been held.

There had been command difficulties in Bastogne at first when the relationship between 10th Armored's CCB and 101st Airborne Division had been the unsatisfactory one of voluntary collaboration but this was cleared up on Wednesday when General Middleton gave command of all American forces within the Bastogne perimeter to McAuliffe. From that time on Colonel Roberts operated from the 101st Command Post and General McAuliffe listened to his advice about the proper use of armour: tanks must not be used as roadblocks, they were to attack in maximum strength where needed and released after each engagement to maintain a powerful armoured reserve. At the end of the siege of Bastogne these tanks and airborne infantry were working so well together that they asked higher command 'whether it wouldn't be possible for them to be joined together in one large force.' They had come to believe that together they were irresistible.*

The German new moves began late on Wednesday when 26th Volksgrenadier advanced swiftly west, seized high ground near Assenois and launched the main punch, with the division's reconnaissance battalion reinforced by some twenty self-propelled guns, intended to capture Senonchamps less than five thousands yards west of Bastogne. Led by its commander, Major Kunkel, an officer with a reputation for daring combined with tactical skill, the seven-hundred strong 26th Reconnaissance Battalion moved west through the darkness and

* S. L. A. Marshall: *Bastogne. The First Eight Days.*

struck hard at Sibret at dawn on Thursday, December 21.

Here General Cota had organized what was left of the 110th Infantry and the divisional headquarters into a 'strongpoint'—but with only three howitzers, two bazookas and about two hundred men armed with rifles they could not hope to stop an armoured attack.

5th Parachute Division were also moving west parallel to 26th Volksgrenadiers. Its left-hand column marched on Martelange, where a bridge carried the main Arlon to Bastogne highway over the Sûre. Here its advance guard encountered one of VIII Corps' small detachments of determined combat engineers and was deflected to the north. The parachutists left a company behind to keep the Americans south of the river.

About three o'clock on Thursday morning a company of infantry from 5th Parachute forced their way into Sibret from the south and shortly afterwards Task Force Kunkel, with its self-propelled guns and some tanks lent by Panzer Lehr's reconnaissance battalion who were trying to find a way to the Meuse past Bastogne on the south, came in from the east. Sibret was captured about 9.0 am on Thursday morning.

But back at 26th Volksgrenadier Division's headquarters in the village of Bras General Kokott had been impatiently waiting to hear that his assault group had taken Senonchamps: instead first news was that they were heavily engaged against the 'strongly garrisoned' village of Sibret—once more the German timetable was slipping.

Task Force Kunkel of 26th Reconnaissance Battalion continued their advance, moving north-east from Sibret along the main Neufchâteau to Bastogne road intending to turn left at the Villeroux crossroads for Senonchamps. At the same time Panzer Lehr (less a battle group which had been left near Marvie to help 26th Volksgrenadiers capture Bastogne) passed through the infantry and reached Moircy on the Ourthe river by Thursday evening, the third of Fifth Panzer Army's armoured divisions to reach that last barrier before the Meuse.

Things started well for Major Kunkel's force when his advance guard overwhelmed the 771st Artillery Battalion, catching them on the move with guns hooked to prime movers. The gunners fled leaving their engines running and 26th Reconnaissance Battalion were able to add twenty 155-mm howitzers to their force. This was the end of their good fortune though, for the commander of the American artillery position at Senonchamps had asked for infantry protection when Sibret fell and Team Pyle of about two hundred infantry and fourteen medium tanks came from Bastogne and engaged the

Germans south of Senonchamps. Time was thus gained for two battalions of artillery in Villeroux to pull back and join another around Senonchamps and by nightfall a four-thousand-yard-long defence line had been thrown across this approach to Bastogne from the west and after one unsuccessful attempt to breach it Major Kunkel drew back into the shelter of the woods until 26th Volksgrenadiers' artillery could come up and help.

Although disappointed with the failure to capture Senonchamps the German command was not displeased with the larger picture at Bastogne on Thursday night. All roads on the north and south were now cut and, as panzer divisions had reached the Ourthe on both sides, Bastogne was virtually cut off. It was known that US Third Army were preparing a relieving attack from the Arlon area but General Brandenberger was able to report that Seventh Army's right wing had reached their assigned blocking line from the Our to the Neufchâteau road which meant that Fifth Panzer Army could concentrate on reaching the Meuse and capturing Bastogne without having to worry about their left flank.

But General von Luettwitz, whose XLVII Panzer Corps had been ordered to capture Bastogne, knew that he did not have sufficient forces to do so. The 26th Volksgrenadier Division had taken severe casualties and the regiment of panzer grenadiers and fifteen Panthers left behind by Panzer Lehr were hardly enough to tip the scales even when his corps' heavy field guns finally closed up, for the Americans had eighteen thousand troops, eleven battalions of artillery, a tank destroyer battalion and about forty medium tanks inside the perimeter. Again, never far from the German commanders' thoughts, there were the large numbers of fighter bombers waiting for the skies to clear. General von Manteuffel asked for and was promised fresh reinforcements from OKW reserve to enable him to achieve the superiority in numbers needed to capture Bastogne.

Nevertheless, either the Germans were confident that the town really could be completely destroyed by their heavy artillery or Luettwitz decided to try a bluff: at 11.30 am on December 22, the men at the roadblock west of Marvie saw four Germans walking slowly towards them carrying a large white flag. Three American soldiers went out to meet them, one of whom could speak German—it was not, however, necessary.

'We are parliamentaires,' a German captain announced.

Taken back, blindfolded, to the company command post

they handed over an envelope for the American commander in Bastogne. While they waited with the glider infantry the message was taken to the 101st's Chief of Staff, Lieutenant-Colonel Moore. Typed in English and German it asked for the 'encircled' town of Bastogne to be 'honorably surrendered'. If it was not, an entire artillery corps plus six anti-aircraft battalions would concentrate their fire and annihilate the US troops in and around Bastogne and, it was added, civilian losses would be bound to be heavy. The offer would remain open for two hours but the envoys would have to be released by two that afternoon. The German attack would not be resumed until three.

General McAuliffe, who had been trying to catch up some of his lost sleep, came in and asked what the message said. Colonel Moore told him.

'Oh shit!' McAuliffe said disgustedly. A message was sent back to the waiting envoys that the surrender terms were rejected but the senior, a major in the Panzer Lehr Division, protested that as he had brought a formal document he was entitled to a written reply.

Realizing the fairness of this General McAuliffe sat down and tried to frame a formal refusal to surrender but without success.

'I don't know what the hell to say to them,' he said.

'How about that first remark of yours?' Colonel Kinnard, his Planning Officer, suggested. 'That would be pretty hard to beat.'

The proposal was greeted with laughter and general approval but in the end McAuliffe wrote the one word 'NUTS' on a single sheet of paper which was sent back to the Germans. And so a piece of American folklore was born.*

On Friday the main German effort at Bastogne was made by Kunkel's force, now reinforced by self-propelled guns, who tried four times to break the Senonchamps position, heart of the American artillery defence. Built round CCB's 420th Armored Field Artillery and named Team Browne after the battalion's commander it comprised an anti-aircraft and three howitzer battalions protected by about three hundred infantry, seventeen Shermans and some light tanks. The volksgrenadiers tried hard but the American tanks fired into their midst, the

---

* This paper has never come to light. General Luettwitz only admitted sending the ultimatum, which Hitler had not authorized, fifteen years after the war and was non-committal about the whereabouts of the American reply. If it should ever be offered for sale it will undoubtedly fetch a very high price.

shells of the artillery burst among them and the quad-mount machine guns poured bullets into them. When Major Kunkel finally called off his last attack he had lost half of his self-propelled guns and about one-third of his men. He called for counter fire on the American positions from XLVII Panzer Corps' own artillery which had now moved up. This heavy shelling continued all night causing, Colonel Browne reported, 'terrible casualties'.

As night fell on the 22nd it was realized inside Bastogne that the besieging Germans were bound to make an all-out effort very soon to overwhelm the defence before reinforcements could arrive. It had not been possible to bring in enough supplies of ammunition and fuel, at first because the roads were clogged and then later because the German sweeps north and south had cut off most of the supply routes. Everything was desperately short: food, bandages, medicines, blankets for the wounded and fuel. Vehicles were kept with practically empty tanks until needed so that if they were knocked out the least fuel would be wasted and ammunition was rigorously rationed: after the last German attack on Friday the 420th Armoured Field Artillery ordered that no matter how tempting the target no more than five rounds could be fired at it and each gun was limited to that number per day. Everything depended upon the visibility improving enough to allow an air drop but so far the weather Hitler had promised his commanders had held with remarkable consistency. Anxiously the besieged troops waited for relief from the air—and from the ground.

In fact there was a large element of bluff in the German claim to have Bastogne surrounded on December 22. The road west, which went through Ortheuville, had been used by 2nd Panzer Division but they had not set up a block sealing off the exit from Bastogne, leaving that job to the 26th Volksgrenadier Division who had been unable to occupy the road because it could be brought under fire by the American artillery in the Senonchamps position. Furthermore much of the circle of Germans surrounding the city were no more than a thin line of strong points connected by patrols. This was particularly true for almost all of the northern half of the perimeter where two tired and badly weakened volksgrenadier regiments faced the larger part of three parachute infantry regiments for the whole siege. General Kokott had concentrated his strength on the south-east—the armoured battlegroup from Panzer Lehr were opposite Marvie—and the south-west where the 39th Grenadier Regiment had moved beyond and on the left of the 26th Reconnaissance Battalion, opposite Senonchamps. Thus it can now be seen that the number of Germans surrounding Bastogne on December 22 was probably less than the number of Americans inside and it is at least possible that one of the objects of the ultimatum was to conceal this weakness.

But even though this was so the airborne infantry and the tank crews who had been hit hard by the attack had no way of knowing that the 2nd Panzer Division they had engaged at Noville had moved on or that most of Panzer Lehr in the east and south-east had left the area. With their ammunition perilously low and German shelling continuing all night long, the American infantry stood by their foxholes waiting for the inevitable attack.

The temperature plummeted that night and just before Saturday's dawn the Luftwaffe dropped their first bombs, an ominous sign. Everywhere in Bastogne men shook hands with those near them knowing that in the next few hours their positions might well be overrun. The cold drove away the fog and clouds and the sun rose out of a clean-scrubbed, pale blue sky, its rays reflecting dazzlingly off the new-fallen snow.

'Visibility unlimited' reported the air control posts: it was what the pilots of the waiting aircraft had been waiting long days for and soon they began to take off from many airfields—carriers, bombers, fighter-bombers and fighters. It would be the Air Force's day and no one who was in the Ardennes on that Saturday, December 23, 1944, will ever forget the sight.

Friday and Saturday, the seventh and eighth days of the Ardennes Offensive, saw important changes in the northern half of the battlefield too. Renewed efforts were made to eliminate the danger from Battlegroup Peiper; two fresh SS Panzer Divisions came from the north against the Salm River line; Manteuffel's three panzer divisions continued their apparently irresistible advance to the Meuse south of Namur and the Germans finally eliminated the troublesome St Vith salient.

Late on Thursday night General Hasbrouck in Vielsalm learned of the disaster in St Vith, of heavy losses in men and matériel. Because of disturbing stories of uncontrolled withdrawals officers were placed at control points along roads leading west from St Vith and stragglers were collected and units assigned to positions in a new defence line based on the firm north flank which had not yet been heavily engaged. At the same time as this bad news came into Hasbrouck's HQ, Intelligence reported that two German officers captured earlier

363

in the evening on his weak southern flank belonged to the 2nd SS Panzer Division. He reported the situation to his new Corps commander, General Ridgway, who ordered the St Vith forces to hold a fortified oval with its long axis running from the Salm between Vielsalm and Salmchâteau east to the Rodt and Neundorf area and its short axis from Poteaux south to Beho. Holding this area would deny the Germans their way west from St Vith and the American troops inside it included 7th Armored Division's three combat commands, a regiment each from 28th and 106th Infantry Divisions, a combat command from 9th Armored Division, five battalions of field artillery plus attached tank destroyer, anti-aircraft and combat engineer units.

These were powerful forces but the forward infantry had been under great pressure for four days, the tanks had suffered many losses, German shelling was increasing as their big guns finally struggled up into position, ammunition was running low, many of the men were suffering from long exposure in the damp and penetrating cold, had been without food for over a day and were near to complete exhaustion. Half of the troops who had been overrun east of St Vith and who found their way back had to be evacuated.

To break off a losing battle and regroup almost immediately is one of the most difficult of battlefield moves, particularly when there are no reserves and the attacker continues to follow up his success. But during Thursday night the Germans had their difficulties too. The volksgrenadiers who had finally broken into St Vith had become disorganized in the fight and had to regroup. The narrow roads, jammed with traffic, made this impossible to do quickly.

There was a force available to continue the attack—Colonel Remer's Fuehrer Begleit Brigade which instead of attacking St Vith from the north as ordered had struck south-west towards Rodt. This key village was captured about two o'clock on Friday morning cutting the main line of retreat to Vielsalm and splitting the new American defence line along the boundary of 7th Armored Division's combat commands.

On the north CCA and CCR fell back to form a peninsular defence around the Vielsalm to Poteaux road; on the south CCB's line formed a shoulder north of Hinderhausen, east of Crombach down to Neubrück to link with 9th Armored's CCB. Hinderhausen, on the left flank, had to be held, for from it ran the only remaining line of retreat to Vielsalm.

Not long after Rodt fell an attack came in against Poteaux from the direction of Recht. It was beaten off and the Germans were identified as new ones in the area, the 9th SS Panzer Division, a cause for considerable dismay at this moment in the battle. The situation was not as bad as it appeared though for most of this division was strung out in a long line back to 'Sepp' Dietrich's front and the major part of the battlegroup which had arrived north of St Vith on Thursday, and which did not include the divisional tank regiment, had been sent north-west in an attempt to break through to Peiper. A small force had been left behind to prevent an American advance against the division's flank and it was some of these who had probed towards Poteaux.

7th Armored Division's staff had no way of knowing this, of course, and as 2nd SS Panzer had been identified on their right and Remer's brigade was mistakenly thought to be the crack Grossdeutschland Division, the appearance of yet another fresh armoured division on their left understandably caused them to recommend withdrawal from the fortified oval to General Hasbrouck.

Consequently, when one of Montgomery's liaison officers turned up at Vielsalm about eleven on Friday morning to ask about the American intentions, General Hasbrouck said that they would hold if it were considered vital to do so but his own recommendation was now withdrawal. Later he told General Ridgway the same thing when he suggested that the St Vith defenders, even if surrounded, could be kept supplied by air. The armoured commander pointed out that supply was not the vital factor but the smallness of the area which would make it impossible to manoeuvre his tanks. They could only be used as pill boxes which would be suicidal.

General Ridgway had placed the whole St Vith force under General Alan Jones' command on Thursday night because he outranked General Hasbrouck (a change which made no difference to the conduct of the battle) but on Friday when he visited Vielsalm and met the tired and badly shaken senior officer who had seen his fresh division practically destroyed in its first action, Ridgway designated General Jones as 'Assistant to the Corps Commander' and gave General Hasbrouck overall command.*

The question of whether to hold the surrounded oval area or to pull back was settled by Montgomery without hesitation: the St Vith defenders would withdraw. 'They can come back with all honour. They come back to more secure positions. They put up a wonderful show.'

* Just after midnight General Jones had a heart attack and was evacuated.

In St Vith Field Marshal Model arrived at noon, having had to walk the last mile or so because of the snarl-up of traffic, and urged the continuation of the attack. The volksgrenadiers who had pushed south of St Vith and had therefore not had to go through the town now moved forward advancing along the railway. At the underpass just north-west of Crombach they were held up by machine-gun and mortar fire—the 81-mm mortars on half-tracks fired over 600 rounds in twenty minutes tearing the guns from the mountings—but there were no mines or explosives to drop the bridge and Crombach fell. Some American infantry got out on tanks, some on other vehicles and some marched west all night.

Ammunition had been used at a tremendous rate during the desperate hours before St Vith fell and in covering the retreat to the new defence line and by Friday the supply position was acute, many of the 105-mm guns being down to a few rounds. Fuel was also very short and there is no doubt that the final withdrawal would have been much more costly in both men and material had not a 90-truck convoy, which had travelled along back roads with service troops sitting on tailboards with tommy guns, come through ambushes and arrived in mid-afternoon with small-arms ammunition, fuel and five thousand rounds of 105 mm.

On Friday night the southern part of the breached American line ran from north-east of Hinderhausen down between Crombach and Braunlauf to Grufflange then west to Beho and north-west along a minor road through Rogery and Cierreux to join the main road running north along the narrow valley of the Salm to Salmchâteau.

Holding this line from left to right were 7th Armored Division's CCB, whose 87th Cavalry Reconnaissance Squadron were assigned to hold Hinderhausen in a rearguard action until all the rest had got out, then 9th Armored's CCB who were to go out through Beho, then all that was left of the 106th Division, its 424th Infantry Regiment holding near Braunlauf, and lastly 28th Division's 112th Regiment and Task Force Jones, holding the southern flank.

North of the penetration at Rodt the American defence line was held by 7th Armored's CCA and CCR who beat off attempts to outflank them during Friday night. As long as they could hold on to Poteaux it should not be too difficult to fall back through Petit Thier to Vielsalm although, as they were now surrounded on three sides, they could expect to be attacked as soon as they attempted to withdraw.

There was no such easy route for any of the other forces,

for the German capture of Rodt and Crombach eliminated both of the main roads from St Vith to Vielsalm and plans now had to be made to bring the bulk of the infantry and tanks out along back roads from Hinderhausen and Commanster, narrow unsurfaced roads which would almost certainly mire the vehicles. Fourteen hours of darkness were allowed to pull all the troops back across the Salm but time was used up in drawing up the tight, complicated schedule and in despatching liaison officers to all units concerned. The plan was for Hoge's CCB to move back at 3.0 am picking up some of the 424th Regiment and going through Beho to the main road north to cross the Salm at Salmchâteau. At 6.0 am Clarke's CCB was to move out in two parts: the southern portion was to fall back through Crombach and Braunlauf and follow Hoge's tail; the northern portion, the bulk of the combat command, was to try to withdraw over an emergency route, a narrow, unsurfaced track which ran through the woods from Hinderhausen to Commanster where it joined a minor road to Vielsalm. The rest of 7th Armored Division near Poteaux were to start to pull back when all the forces south of Rodt, except the 112th Infantry who were to hold the rearguard, were across the Salm.

But the volksgrenadiers south of St Vith renewed their attack during Friday night involving both CCB of 7th Armored and CCB of 9th Armored and making it impossible for them to start their withdrawal. If Hoge tried to disengage he would uncover Clarke's flank and both commanders reported that the withdrawal would have to wait. In Vielsalm General Hasbrouck, surveying the whole picture which included the 9th SS Panzer on his left and the 2nd SS Panzer on his right, decided that Hoge and Clarke would have to come out 'ready or not'.

At 6.05 am on Saturday CCB of 9th Armored, first of the reinforcements to arrive in St Vith, began to slip away. A company of tanks took up defensive positions at Muldange, two miles east of Beho and blocked all German attempts to come on, finally falling back and joining the rest of the combat command with a loss of only two tanks. CCB crossed the river at Salmchâteau and moved quickly west for another six miles to take their place in the line next to 82nd Airborne.

Now it was the turn of the southern portion of CCB of 7th Armored but meanwhile the Germans had captured Crombach so the tanks and other vehicles had to go round it to Braunlauf. There they found some of 424th Infantry in a fire fight. Taking them on board they charged through the volksgrenadiers losing two tank commanders to snipers and moving through Beho. The 112th Infantry mounted the last rearguard in the villages of Rogery and Cierreux and CCB passed through them, crossed the Salm at Salmchâteau by midday and continued north-west for twenty-five miles to the new defence line.

At Hinderhausen the major part of 7th Armored's CCB, now called Task Force Lohse, got on to the 'emergency exit', the narrow road from Hinderhausen through the woods to Commanster. Only hours before the ground would have been too soft and the tanks and other vehicles would have been hopelessly mired but during Friday night the temperature plummeted, a freezing wind blew and by dawn the crust was firm enough to support the Shermans' thirty tons.

Leaving part of 87th Cavalry Reconnaissance Squadron to block pursuit through Hinderhausen the rest of Task Force Lohse of four companies of tanks, one of tank destroyers, two troops of cavalry reconnaissance and many hitch-hiking infantry moved steadily along praying that there would not be a sudden thaw or that a tank would not break down and plug the escape route. At Commanster there was a monumental traffic jam caused by most of nine battalions of artillery displacing west. As usual some people were more eager to get away than others and there might well have been chaos if discipline had not prevailed—the sight of General Clarke doing traffic duty himself at a main crossroads changed the mind of more than one officer who had decided to use his rank to jump the queue.

The Fuehrer Begleit Brigade had attacked Hinderhausen as soon as Task Force Lohse began to move but the cavalry rearguard held Remer up until the tail of the column was west of Commanster and then fell back themselves. The Germans did not try to follow but hurried south to join the volksgrenadiers moving through Beho, increasing the threat to the 112th Infantry. The 87th Cavalry caught up with Task Force Lohse and just after midday the last of 7th Armored's CCB was west of the Salm on the way to the new defence line.

In the north the rest of 7th Armored Division, CCA and CCB in the Poteaux area, surrounded on three sides, had been ordered to wait until the combat commands in the south were across the Salm before making their move. Two events which could not have been foreseen now helped the Americans. Some of the 18th Volksgrenadiers who had captured St Vith came up to seize Poteaux and, after passing through the Fuehrer Begleit Brigade at Rodt, moved rapidly on. But the 9th Panzer troops who had been left to screen Recht sent a force south towards this same road and mistaking the volksgrenadiers for Americans opened fire on them and delayed their advance. As this was happening more troops from 9th SS Panzer attacked Poteaux from Recht. They were beaten off by tank and artillery fire but were still dangerous—particularly if the Americans began to withdraw—but about an hour before the order to do so came from Hasbrouck, a flight of Lightning fighter-bombers who had lost contact with their ground control and were looking for 'targets of opportunity' found the 9th SS Panzer column on the road from Recht and shot it up.

All this enabled the Americans to start their withdrawal without hindrance. The armoured infantry scrambled out of their foxholes and piled on to the half-tracks which got on to the Vielsalm road. They were followed by the tanks—the last ones exchanging shots with German tanks—and then the artillery which retired battery by battery to give fire support. CCR followed leaving a small rearguard of tanks, tank destroyers and infantry whose orders were to fall back 'with maximum delay'. The American artillery continued to fire as long as possible and the last of CCR got over the Vielsalm bridge just as dusk was falling; the last of 7th Armored Division, the rear guard of the 87th Cavalry crossed at 7.0 pm under fire from the pursuing Germans. With everyone out the plunger was pushed to blow the bridge. Nothing happened.

This was the responsibility of the 82nd Airborne Division and one of their parachute infantry officers led a series of charges against the closing German infantry while the explosives were replaced and rewired. He then detonated them. By midnight most of the bridge was gone but one span did not fall completely and German infantry were able to work their way across.

The last of the St Vith defenders to come out of the oval were Task Force Jones who had assembled at Bovigny and the 112th Infantry east of the Salm whose job was to cover their withdrawal. These troops were hit by the Fuehrer Begleit Brigade and driven from Rogery to Cierreux in some confusion but a tank destroyer from Vielsalm turned up, hit the two leading panzers and drove the rest to cover.

As Task Force Jones was moving north towards Salmchâteau the reconnaissance battalion of the 2nd SS Panzer Division came in from the south-west and got into the town ahead of them. At the same time the Fuehrer Begleit Brigade followed the 112th Infantry from Cierreux on to the narrow valley road. In the failing light Remer tried to tack on to the end of the retreating column but he was spotted and engaged by some light tanks and towed tank destroyers which had been sent to reinforce the 112th Infantry. The bigger guns of the Fuehrer Begleit Brigade knocked out five of these and many Americans abandoned their vehicles and made their way on foot. The middle of the trapped column found a narrow trail leading west and most found their way into the 82nd Airborne Division's lines during Saturday night but much matériel was lost and many were taken prisoner.

But more than fifteen thousand men, about a hundred tanks and most of the nine battalions of field artillery had got back by Sunday morning to reinforce Ridgway's XVIII Airborne Corps line stretched dangerously thin in an east-facing 'U' from Werbomont to Trois Ponts to Salmchâteau to Fraiture, the village north of the Baraque de Fraiture crossroads seized by 2nd SS Panzer during Saturday night. There was little rest for the weary soldiers from the St Vith defence because the increasing pressure from newly-committed German troops would not allow it: some of 7th Armored Division and the 424th Infantry Regiment were sent to 82nd Airborne's shaky right flank, 9th Armored's CCB were sent to Malempré to help block the road to Liège from the Baraque de Fraiture and the survivors of the 112th Infantry became part of the reserve.

By Sunday morning the Germans had closed to the Salm river at Vielsalm and Salmchâteau from where they could gain the roads west but it was eight days after the attack, which was intended to capture it in two, had been launched. The delay, although bought at so heavy a cost,* had been every bit as significant as the one at Bastogne. After the war General Manteuffel freely admitted that the unexpected six-day defence of St Vith and the further two days it had taken to close up to the Salm was the principal reason for the failure of his army's right-wing attack. In a press interview in America in 1964 he said that on the evening of Sunday, December 24, he had personally recommended to Hitler's adjutant that the German forces in the Ardennes return to the West Wall, giv-

* The exact number is not known because the armour and infantry concerned were committed again the following day and final casualties could not be broken down as many records had been lost. A conservative estimate for the period from December 16 to December 23 in the St Vith area including the Schnee Eifel debacle would be about fourteen thousand casualties and over one hundred tanks, forty armoured cars, hundreds of other vehicles, many guns of all sizes and large quantities of other equipment lost.

ing as his reasons the delay caused by the American stands at St Vith and Bastogne, the supply position of his centre armoured thrust which had brought them to a halt and had given the Allies time to move powerful forces in front of them, the complete failure of Sixth SS Panzer Army to break through in the north and the failure to exploit Fifth Panzer Army's success by diverting Dietrich's reserves quickly to their front.

Both von Rundstedt and Model appreciated the importance of the capture of Vielsalm and Salmchâteau and the German overall plan was changed to fit into the new situation. On the Allied side the vulnerability now of the 82nd Airborne salient and the danger of a successful German drive between XVIII Airborne and VII Corps called for new dispositions. But before looking at the next and final phase of the battle in this sector we must go back to the beleagured Battlegroup Peiper whose determined resistance was pinning down tanks, artillery, infantry and airborne troops badly needed elsewhere.

First Army had decided that it was taking altogether too long to eliminate the bottled-up force from 1st Panzer Division and priority was given on Friday to smoking out this hornet's nest with a number of concentric attacks aided by heavy artillery bombardment and strikes by fighter bombers.

Before Battlegroup Peiper itself could be tackled it was necessary to deal with the relief detachment from 1st SS Panzer who had earlier crossed the Amblève and were dug in along a ridge west of Stavelot. Between this force of panzers, self-propelled guns and panzer grenadiers and Peiper lay 117th Infantry Regiment's 3rd Battalion while on the west, between these Germans and Trois Ponts, was Task Force Lovelady from 3rd Armored Division. After a preliminary softening up by Lightnings both these American forces were to attack, but once again fog back at the airbases kept the planes grounded and the assault had to be made uphill against well dug-in positions. Two rifle companies from the 3rd Battalion and one from Task Force Lovelady made the attempt but the Germans had a 270° field of fire and it was not until a fourth company of riflemen attacking from the east added their weight that the ridge position was taken. Even then there were pockets of German soldiers still in the woods.

The sanatorium, chief stumbling block to an attack against Stoumont from the west had, it will be remembered, finally fallen to the Americans on Thursday night. This enabled a two-prong assault from the west and north to be mounted on Friday morning. The Americans expected the same tough resistance that had marked the earlier fighting here but during

Thursday night Peiper had contracted his defence circle and was now concentrated in La Gleize. Stoumont fell without a shot being fired—the only soldiers found there were the wounded, both Americans and Germans.

On the German side on Friday, General Mohnke, the 1st SS Panzer Division commander, tried once more to drive west across the Salm between Trois Ponts and Vielsalm with a number of seemingly disconnected attacks all of which were beaten back. The bridge at Grand Halleux was the only one still standing and two companies of SS infantry attempted to seize it in a rush late in the evening. It was blown while the leading Germans were actually running across it and General Mohnke reported that he could not now continue west across the Salm. General Priess, I SS Panzer Corps commander, asked for 9th SS Panzer Division, now moving towards Vielsalm, to be diverted to capture Stavelot but this was refused.

During Friday night, in which there was a full moon, the Luftwaffe dropped fuel and ammunition in the Stoumont area not apparently having been told that Peiper had withdrawn to La Gleize. The main effect of this drop was a fresh batch of paratroop rumours which caused most of the infantry and all the anti-aircraft gunners to stand to all night.

On Saturday, December 23, the skies cleared and the Americans ringing La Gleize waited for the promised fighter bombers at last to pound Battlegroup Peiper's dug-in Tigers. In Malmédy, now safely in American hands, the inhabitants and the men of the 120th Infantry Regiment saw the flights of American bombers glinting in the bright sunlight. The next moment there was a frantic diving for shelter as the bombs rained down destroying practically every building and killing many civilians and soldiers. Unbelievably, exactly the same thing happened for the next three days.* The worst raid occurred on Sunday, December 24, in which at least thirty-seven American soldiers and a great number of civilians were killed. With no water pressure for the fire hoses the centre of Malmédy blazed and engineers had to use explosives to keep the fire within limits.

All during Saturday the American artillery poured shells into La Gleize forcing most of Battlegroup Peiper into the cellars. But every time the tanks and infantry tried to follow up the bombardment they were stopped by murderous fire from the dug-in panzers and anti-tank guns or ran on to mine fields and were raked by small-arms fire. An attempt to outflank the

* The 30th Infantry Division were bombed in error thirteen times between Normandy and the Ardennes.

German position by bringing in infantry from the woods to the north of La Gleize was broken by concentrated fire from 20-mm anti-aircraft guns and cross machine-gun fire. By nightfall Peiper was still in possession and General Rose, the rest of whose 3rd Armored Division were being attacked in the Hotton–Soy area, pressed for the return of his forces tied up at La Gleize. CCB were ordered to start to move south during Saturday night but without most of their tanks who would be left behind to take part the next day in one more all-out attempt to wipe out the stubborn SS.

Knowing that his situation was hopeless and could only end in the extermination of his men Colonel Peiper had been requesting permission to withdraw and finally on Saturday afternoon it came. He was to break out during the night, bringing all his wounded and all his vehicles with him. This was a completely unreal order and characteristically Peiper ignored the impossible conditions. He would go out on foot leaving his own wounded behind with the American wounded. All American prisoners would be released except Major McCown, the battalion commander from 30th Infantry who had been captured on Thursday, who would be taken with them.

About one o'clock on Sunday morning the unwounded survivors of Battlegroup Peiper began to move out quietly in single file going south through the woods. The men were very hungry and near to exhaustion but each carried a full pack, his personal weapon and ammunition, and although their mood was now very different from what it had been five nights before when they had joked and sung before the attack on Stoumont they were still a disciplined body of soldiers who were determined to get back to fight again. A small rearguard waited for an hour or so after the last man had slipped away and then destroyed the tanks, guns and other equipment and followed the rest through the woods. By daybreak on Sunday eight hundred survivors of Battlegroup Peiper had crossed the Amblève and were concealed in woods north of Trois Ponts. Here they lay up all day and started again after dark at first still moving south and then swinging left to ford the icy Salm. They saw no American troops, apart from some of 82nd Airborne's parachute infantry who were retreating in the opposite direction. There was a short, sharp encounter, which gave McCown his chance to escape, and which ended by mutual consent. On Christmas Day Peiper and eight hundred of his men rejoined the 1st SS Panzer Division.

When the Americans advanced towards La Gleize on Sunday expecting a grim fight from the desperate SS, they encountered no fire and found the position which had given them so much trouble abandoned. There were over three hundred wounded Germans as well as twenty-eight panzers, twenty-five guns and seventy half-tracks in La Gleize and these, added to the rest of Battlegroup Peiper's equipment which had been lost earlier, comprised a large part of 1st SS Panzer Division. Although the German ordnance worked feverishly over the next few days they were able to create only a single tank company out of the remnants. 1st SS Panzer was to appear therefore in the Ardennes as no more than a crippled shadow of a once crack SS Division.

PART THREE

THE ROLES ARE REVERSED

The whole art of war consists in a well-reasoned and extremely circumspect defensive, followed by rapid and audacious attack.

NAPOLEON

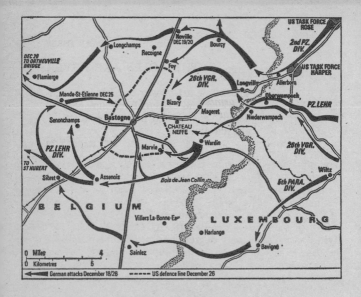

The Defence of Bastogne
(Reprinted from *Bastogne – the Road Block* by permission of
Ballantine Books)

25

TURN OF THE TIDE

The history of armoured warfare—and of cavalry warfare before that—shows that great prizes can be won by speed, daring and manoeuvre.

MELLENTHIN: *Panzer Battles*

General Patton's promised counter-attack northwards from the Arlon–Luxembourg City area jumped off right on time— 6.0 am Friday, December 22. The first phase of the offensive was made by one armoured and two infantry divisions under III Corps whose headquarters and staff were, as yet, untried.

Only alerted on December 18, III Corps had swung these divisions through ninety degrees and moved them swiftly from the Saar to close along a 35-mile-long line facing north about twenty miles from Bastogne. 80th Infantry Division were on the right; 26th Infantry in the centre and 4th Armored Division on the left.

Their objectives were ambitious even for America's most confident commander and included not only the quick relief of Bastogne but a broad front advance to St Vith followed by the driving back of the German invading armies for another sixty or seventy miles right across the Rhine.

First of Third Army forces to arrive in Luxembourg had been 4th Armored's Combat Command B which, as we have seen, while briefly under Middleton's VIII Corps had advanced to half way between Neufchâteau and Bastogne and had then sent a task force up to within four miles of Bastogne. The arrival of the rest of the division, and then III Corps, had resulted in all these troops coming back ten miles to take up their position on the left of the start line. Major-General Hugh Gaffey's 4th Armored Division were charged with the task of relieving Bastogne.

The attack from the centre was to be made by Major-General Willard Paul's 26th Infantry Division, a very large proportion of whom were recent replacements and were practically untrained. After a long weary move this division closed on its assembly area in thick fog and mist during the night of December 20/21, and took up positions along some six miles of the start line from 4th Armored's right wing, whose projected axis straddled the Arlon to Bastogne highway, to roughly half way between Arlon and Mersch. They learned the next day that the attack would begin in twenty-four hours and their objective was Wiltz, which had become the new headquarters of General Brandenberger's Seventh Army.

On the right wing of the offensive was 80th Infantry Division which, having been rested and replenished in preparation for Third Army's attack against the West Wall, was in first-class condition. Its part of the attack line ran from just behind 26th Division's right for five miles east to include the main road from Luxembourg City to the north (Red Ball Highway) which was intended to be the division's axis. Its commander, Major-General Horace McBride only learned on Thursday that his division was to attack at dawn the next day, maintaining contact with 26th Infantry on their left and the American forces holding the southern shoulder—now organized as Third Army's XII Corps—on the right. The mission was 'to advance north towards St Vith'.

The strength of III Corps was considerable: each infantry division, as well as a full complement of riflemen, had a tank battalion and one of self-propelled guns attached. 4th Armored Division arrived short by about seven-hundred-and-fifty men and fifty tanks but would still be able to put three powerful task forces in the field, one of which was equipped with some Shermans mounting a new, long-barrelled, high-velocity gun. Eleven battalions of field artillery had been found to support the corps' attack.

The Corps commander was Major-General John Milliken and his instructions from General Patton were simple and uncluttered with detail: attack would be made in depth and the corps would advance to St Vith, relieving Bastogne on the way. 'Drive like hell,' Patton added.

Milliken in turn issued his attack order to the divisions concerned: move to the north and north-east, find the Germans, fix their positions and destroy them.

III Corps had practically no knowledge of what German forces were likely to oppose them but in fact all that lay in front of these three reinforced divisions was the much-battered 5th Parachute Division, stretched thinly across the approaches to Bastogne, and the 352nd Volksgrenadier Division who had finally managed to move west as far as Ettelbruck. Acutely aware of the difficulty of trying to maintain a 25-mile-long blocking line against an inevitable American counter-attack, General Brandenberger had practically begged OKW to release some of its reserves to him. On December 21, an armoured brigade and a half-strength infantry division were started from

378

Germany to reinforce him but this tardy addition to the German strength still left Seventh Army's right wing far weaker than the American attack force even without American air superiority.

Theoretically Patton's counter-attack should have gone as he expected, or, at least, should have closed up to a line from Vianden through Wiltz to Bastogne fairly quickly. It was expected that 4th Armored Division's two combat commands driving in tandem would be in contact with the German troops on the south of Bastogne within twenty-four hours or so. Instead Third Army was to have two weeks of some of the most savage fighting of the war as it slogged its way slowly north against tired, hungry German soldiers not yet ready to acknowledge the defeat their leaders had already accepted.

The entire III Corps line started to move before dawn on Friday, December 22nd. The two regiments of 80th Infantry—318 on the right; 319 on the left—marched quickly north for five miles or more to hit and practically destroy a German column unsuspectingly moving west. This was part of the 352nd Volksgrenadier Division who, having captured Diekirch and Ettelbruck, believed that they had broken into the clear. The 80th Division attack columns hit the centre of this column outside Grosbous and the rear of it on the outskirts of Ettelbruck but the German advance guard was already west of 80th Division's zone—in that of the 26th Infantry.

Warned by reports of attacks in their rear the German forward patrols discovered the right wing of 26th Infantry Division's advance, the 104th Infantry Regiment, on the move and attacked them with great suddenness and ferocity, driving them back for about half a mile. But superior strength, particularly in artillery, finally told and the remnants of the 352nd Volksgrenadier column were driven back and Grosbous captured before dawn on Saturday.

The other attacking column of 26th Division, the 328th Regiment on the left, advanced without opposition for about six miles nearly to Arsdorf before being brought to a halt by fire from self-propelled guns north of the village. There were disturbing reports that the Germans were in strength in Rambrouch, two miles behind, but it was essential to gain bridgeheads over the Sûre river, which ran across the projected line of advance of both the 26th and 80th divisions, so 26th Infantry were ordered to continue their attack through the night. The 328th Regiment were pulled back to the road east from Martelange from which it is possible to get to a bridge over the Sûre at Heiderscheidergrund.

But they were stopped at the first village, Grevels, by small-arms fire and tank guns. Despite half an hour's intense bombardment by the artillery the small force of Germans refused to be budged. Dawn found the Americans still two miles south of Eschdorf whose capture was essential if the 26th Division were to get on the road to Wiltz. They flowed round this block and joined the 14th Regiment in moving slowly and cautiously forward for all of Saturday expecting to encounter the Germans in strength at every successive ridge.

By nightfall 26th Infantry had two companies pinned down by a pocket of two hundred volksgrenadiers south of Grosbous, others were surrounding Grevels and the advance had been so delayed that 80th Division on their right were well ahead of them while on their left a dangerous gap had opened between them and 4th Armored's CCA.

The armoured division had attacked with CCB on the left, CCA on the right and CCR in reserve. CCB had started while it was still dark and although delayed by VIII Corps' earlier demolitions had advanced nearly twelve miles to within sight of the hamlet of Burnon by midday. This place was less than nine miles from Bastogne but the tank column was stopped first by a blown bridge and then by a small German rearguard left in Burnon by 5th Parachute Division. This meant that the advance could not continue until after midnight.

The next village was Chaumont and orders came from General Patton for CCB to continue the advance in the dark to 'relieve Bastogne'. But an anti-tank gun in Chaumont knocked out one of the lead tanks and it was decided to wait until light only an hour or so away and then to lay on a massive set-piece attack starting with a heavy artillery barrage and followed up by twenty-two Sherman tanks and a battalion of armoured infantry going in against the village from three sides.

At this time all the Germans had in Chaumont was a single company of 5th Parachute Infantry supported by some artillery further north whose ammunition was running out but in the time it took to arrange the set-piece attack General Kokott was able to move a dozen self-propelled guns into Chaumont. Their presence decisively changed the situation.

4th Armored's right wing CCA, moved off at 6.0 am in two task forces moving abreast but the demolitions on side roads soon funnelled both forces on to the Arlon–Bastogne highway where they were brought to a complete halt by an enormous crater and so did not get to Martelange and the blown Sûre bridges until about 1.0 pm. Here some of VIII

Corps' doughty combat engineers were holding, while across the river a single rifle company, which had been left behind by 5th Parachute when their advance guard had hit the engineers two days before, had dug in. Their fire was good enough to hold the Americans down for the rest of the day and most of the night and only when inexplicably, they fell back about three o'clock on Saturday morning were the armoured infantry of CCA able to get across one of the broken spans and establish a bridgehead. But the engineers would have to come up and put in a ninety-foot-long Bailey bridge before the tanks and other vehicles could get across. It was not until 3.0 pm on Saturday that CCA were able to get moving again and, impatiently, General Patton ordered a single task force of medium tanks and armoured infantry to advance once again through the night to Bastogne, but at Warnach, two miles north of Martelange, they were fired upon losing four vehicles and became engaged in a fire fight that went on all night and half the next day—it was noon on Sunday before Warnach was cleared.

CCB's great attack on Chaumont on Saturday was made with the help of an entire battalion of field artillery, a strike by Lightning fighter bombers and a three-prong tank assault but the tanks bogged down in the thawing ground and Kokott's self-propelled guns knocked out eleven of them. Of the attacking armoured infantry sixty-five became casualties and every officer was killed.

These two severe setbacks were not the end of 4th Armored Division's misfortunes for the reserve had to be committed to seal the gap between them and 26th Infantry and were involved in a battle at Bigonville which went on until midday on Sunday.

All three of 4th Armored's Division's combat commands had been stopped by a few guns backing up single regiments or less of 5th Parachute Division, few of whom had ever had a parachute on their backs and who had been described by their commander as 'a Grade Four outfit'.

On the other side of III Corps' front the going had been equally hard. On Saturday all three of 8th Infantry Division's regiments made determined and valiant efforts to get on: on the right the 318th launched three separate attacks to clear the Germans out of Ettelbruck incurring heavy casualties, including a battalion commander and all his company leaders, but dusk found the Germans still holding on and the attack had to be called off. In the centre the reserve regiment, the 317th was thrown in late in the day in an attempt to seize Wahlscheid north of Ettelbruck but the dark-uniformed American infantry advancing across the snow in bright moonlight were an easy target for the waiting German machine gunners and this attack too had to be called off. On the left the 319th Regiment captured Heiderscheid, after some bitter fighting, and beat off German attempts to recapture it. A battalion moved north and captured the village of Kehmen, north of Wahlscheid, and another pushed forward, seized the hamlet of Tadler on the banks of the Sûre and sent a company west to overlook the important bridge at Heiderscheidergrund.

At the end of the second day the 80th Division, III Corps' left wing, held an arc facing north-east from the small detachment outposting the Heiderscheidergrund bridge round to Ettelbruck. Facing them on the right were what was left of 352nd Volksgrenadier Division hanging on round Ettelbruck; to their front on the high ground at Bourscheid, south of the Sûre, were part of the new-arrived 79th Volksgrenadier Division; on their left and also on 26th Infantry's right, were part of the Fuehrer Grenadier Brigade who had just come in too. Both these units had been wrung from OKW's reserve by General Brandenberger's pleas: both had been decimated in earlier fighting and were full of green replacements. Formerly entrusted with the outer guard at the Wolf's Lair, the Fuehrer Grenadier Brigade, six thousand strong, had forty panzers, a battalion of infantry carried on half-tracks and lorries, another which had to march, a battalion of self-propelled guns and a reconnaissance battalion. If all this could have been brought to bear on one part of the front they might have delivered a crushing blow but by now the Allied Air Force was operating and bomb damage along the grenadiers' route from Germany, particularly at the Our river crossing, had delayed them and caused them to be strung out so that they were committed piecemeal and practically destroyed—not before, however, they had been able to do a great deal of damage.

The 79th Volksgrenadier Division was at no more than half-strength, about six thousand, and had no anti-aircraft or self-propelled guns but these two forces were all that General Brandenberger had been able to get from OKW and he had to make do with them. There was little joy at Seventh Army headquarters as the American pattern became more and more apparent. In the south the left wing of two volksgrenadier divisions more than had their hands full trying to contain the increasing American XII Corps' strength on the southern shoulder and the Army's right wing was dangerously over-extended, with 5th Parachute's screen stretched across the southern approaches to Bastogne and the battered 352nd Volkgrenadier Division hanging on around Ettelbrück.

Nevertheless Seventh Army's blocking line was still holding after forty-eight hours of the American counter-attack and Fifth Panzer Army had been given time to make another attempt to capture Bastogne.

When Saturday dawned bright and clear there were few soldiers in besieged Bastogne who did not look anxiously towards the western horizon. About an hour after sunrise, while the Germans were making yet another attempt to break through, two aeroplanes came in low and a Pathfinder Team dropped neatly into the chosen drop zone.

This area was some large fields on a gentle slope west of the 101st command post and was rimmed with 5-ton trucks and men waiting to snatch up ammunition and rush it to the hungry guns. Quickly the specialists who had parachuted in set up radar sets to guide the C-47s of Troop Carrier Command to the precise spot.

About noon the welcome deep throbbing noise of many engines was heard and the first flight of the big aircraft flew steadily through the German flak to drop their loads. Flight after flight followed and the Germans put up all the shells they could. The men in Bastogne watched a number of C-47s crash in flames but they also saw the ones following hold rigidly to their flight path, an example of courage and devotion to duty which gave a boost to morale in the besieged town. Within four hours 1,446 bundles had been dropped by 241 aircraft and Bastogne's guns were firing some of the ammunition dropped while the last of the flights were coming in.

The carriers had been protected from attack by the Luftwaffe by an umbrella of Lightning fighter-bombers who, after the carriers had turned for home, having marked the German positions, came down in screaming dives with fragmentation bombs and napalm. As they pulled out they fired long bursts of machine gun. The Germans threw themselves under their vehicles or whatever other cover they could find and cursed Reichmarshall Goering of whose promised two thousand aircraft they had so far seen only a few bombers the night before.

General Kokott was particularly unhappy to see the dreaded Jabos enter the battle for he knew that he did not have enough forces to take Bastogne against the existing American strength. He was also worried about the pressure building up against 5th Parachute Division who were supposed to be screening his flank. 'It is an uncomfortable feeling to have someone launching a drive to your rear,' he said in a post-war interview, 'and I feared 4th Armored. I knew it was a "crack" division. I talked to General von Manteuffel on the telephone and told him that I could not watch two fronts. He told me to forget 4th Armored, that it was quiet for the moment. The only solution to the problem was to attack Bastogne. He directed that I stop worrying and devote all my efforts to the attack from the north-west.'

This conversation took place on Saturday night after General Kokott had tried and failed to break into Bastogne with three different attacks. At dawn Kunkel's Battlegroup had hit Team Browne's position after a particularly heavy opening barrage. Four successive waves of tanks and infantry, the grenadiers in white snow suits, the panzers whitewashed,* came on, but Team Browne held against these attacks and against another from the west made by Kokott's 39th Grenadier Regiment.

At the same time as these assaults were trying to overrun the guns around Senonchamps the 39th Grenadiers, who had moved right round to the west of Bastogne, tried to penetrate the defences on that part of the sector. They captured Flamierge, just over five miles WNW from Bastogne, but were driven back by a spirited counter-attack from the 327th Glider Infantry Regiment. Supporting panzers then shelled the airborne troops and the grenadiers moved in for the kill, but the guns at Senonchamps took time off from their own problems and stopped the attack with salvos of the newly-delivered 155-mm shells. Nevertheless the appearance of the Germans in strength on this new sector caused McAuliffe to pull his western perimeter in closer to Bastogne.

The battlegroup left behind by Panzer Lehr stayed hidden in woods opposite Marvie until the last of the Lightnings had gone. This force consisted of two companies of tanks and the 901st Panzer Grenadier Regiment. Just as daylight was fading they launched an attack against Team O'Hara on the American left and the 2nd Battalion of the 327th Glider Infantry on the right. The fighting went on all night and came within an inch of capturing Marvie. McAuliffe despatched the last of his reserves; the artillery at Senonchamps again turned their guns away from the Germans attacking them; three tank destroyers and two batteries of anti-aircraft guns were moved to reinforce the position; some of the combat engineers of VIII Corps who had originally held Marvie joined in and some of 501st Parachute Infantry from Mont on the left also came to the assistance of the hard-pressed Marvie defenders and Marvie was held.

* The Americans shrouded *their* tanks with bed linen stripped from the houses.

The Americans were hit hard, suffered severe casualties and gave ground, but by dawn on Sunday this critical portion of the Bastogne perimeter was somehow still holding. Saturday night had been Bastogne's darkest hour and 101st Airborne's Planning Officer got through to his opposite number at VIII Corps with an urgent request for help. 'Our situation is getting pretty sticky around here. The enemy has attacked all along the south and some Panthers and Tigers are running around in our area. Request you ask 4th Armored Division to put on all possible pressure.' Coming from the 101st Airborne Division, whose reputation had been made by their success in fighting when surrounded, this statement was taken very seriously, but there was little more that could be done, for 4th Armored were experiencing some of the hardest fighting of the war in their attempts to put on 'all possible pressure'.

In Bastogne half the defence perimeter had been badly dented by the German attacks and the whole was now far from being a tied-in defence line, supported by artillery and backed up by reserves, that a model deployment would have provided. On Sunday the defence perimeter was pulled in towards Bastogne on the south-western quarter and the artillery re-sited. The Germans also made new dispositions.

On Saturday the Führer received a report that 2nd Panzer Division's advance guard were less than five miles from the Meuse. It was the news he had been waiting for and he immediately released two fresh divisions to von Rundstedt and Model to exploit this success. But the trouble for the Germans was that reinforcements were desperately needed in several places—on Fifth Panzer Army's front to block Patton's drive to Bastogne, to capture that stubbornly-held fortress and to drive across the Meuse to establish and hold a bridgehead— and the two new divisions, 9th Panzer and 15th Panzer Grenadier, were only enough for one of these tasks.

Bastogne was not yet paramount in Hitler's mind but it was in Model's and early on Christmas Eve he sent an urgent order to Manteuffel 'to lance this boil on the southern flank'. To accomplish this a battlegroup was taken away from 15th Panzer Grenadier Division and sent to reinforce Kokott's 26th Volksgrenadier group and a battlegroup taken away from 9th Panzer and placed south-east of Bastogne to help 5th Parachute hold off Patton's counter-attack. The rest of the two divisions from OKW reserve would be rushed westward to add weight to the point of Fifth Panzer Army approaching Dinant, an arrowhead with 2nd Panzer forming the point, Panzer Lehr the left and 116th Panzer the right wings.

Kokott's reinforcements, 115th Kampfgruppe from 15th Panzer Grenadier Division, consisted of four battalions of infantry, two battalions of armoured field artillery, a company of self-propelled guns and seventeen panzers. Kokott moved his headquarters to Givry north-west of Bastogne and deployed these fresh troops between there and Flamierge. The divisional artillery were also massed in this area. The Luftwaffe promised a preliminary softening-up bombing.

This new attempt to capture Bastogne was timed to start at three o'clock in the morning on Christmas Day with an hourlong heavy artillery bombardment followed by a stunning blitz from 115th Kampfgruppe whose schedule called for the American perimeter to be broken by six o'clock in the morning and for the centre of Bastogne to be seized by nine o'clock at the latest—before the Jabos could arrive.

The Luftwaffe bombing was expected to disorganize the American command and supporting attacks by 26th Volksgrenadiers from Senonchamps, which had been abandoned when the perimeter was contracted, from Assenois in the south and from Champs in the north-west, would keep the front line troops fully occupied and give 115th Kampfgruppe the maximum chance of success.

In Bastogne the command was aware that the Germans were preparing another even heavier attack although they did not know of the concentration on the north-west. A message was sent to 4th Armored Division Headquarters: 'There is only one more shopping day before Christmas!'

Both the armoured combat commands driving for Bastogne had taken hard knocks: CCB had only two platoons of tanks left after the costly fight for Chaumont and CCA, who had also taken severe losses, were held up by German strength building up along a ridge just ahead of them. It was decided that the tanks needed more infantry support and two rifle battalions were taken away from 80th Infantry Division on the corps' right and one each sent to CCA and CCB. Both these battalions were considerably under strength after the fierce fighting around Ettelbruck.

But what would turn out to be the decisive tactical move occurred when CCR was moved from 4th Armored's right all the way behind the front and concentrated on the left. The area chosen was across the Neufchâteau–Bastogne road some nine miles north-east of Neufchâteau. It was practically the same location that CCB had occupied on the night of December 19 and CCR reached it at dawn on Christmas Day. Their orders were to attack towards Bastogne assisting CCB on their

386

right and covering the left flank of III Corps' advance. CCR were only five miles behind the 26th Volksgrenadier force about to attack Bastogne from Assenois, Colonel Kaufmann's 39th Grenadier Regiment.

The promised Luftwaffe bombing of Bastogne came early on Christmas Eve but although it was very heavy its military significance was slight. But the heavy artillery barrage which started at 2.45 am knocked out many front-line communications and pinned the defending troops down. Grenadiers in white snow suits had crept forward during the bombardment and the moment it stopped they rushed forward and were soon engaged in hand-to-hand fighting.

All seventeen of 115th Kampfgruppe's panzers struck from Flamizoulle and made such good progress that by a quarter to nine on Christmas morning they flashed back a message that they had reached the western edge of Bastogne. Less than a mile from 101st Airborne's command post half of these tanks in one column were delayed briefly by two guns of 705th Tank Destroyer Battalion and in the time it took the Germans to knock these out the airborne infantry took cover and turned a hail of small-arms fire on to the panzer grenadiers riding on the tanks. Two more of 705 Tank Destroyer's guns came up and quickly knocked out three panzers and the airborne infantry got another two with bazookas.

The other half of 115 Kampfgruppe's panzers, having broken through the American line, tried to seize the village of Hemroulle but were exposed to the waiting guns of tanks from CCB, four more of 705 Tank Destroyer's, a whole battalion of artillery and more bazookas. All the German tanks were destroyed and the broken American line closed again behind the smoking wrecks.

The panzer grenadier battalions fared as badly, after an initial success, being pounded by artillery and mortar and raked with machine-gun fire. By nightfall there was little left of 115 Kampfgruppe—one Battalion had lost every one of its staff and was commanded by a 19-year-old Lieutenant.

At the end of this most discouraging day General Kokott curtly refused the request from Colonel Kaufmann in Assenois for permission to move 39th Grenadier Regiment's command post because the 'situation was most dangerous'. Instead Kaufmann was ordered to keep facing Bastogne and not to form a front to the south until they were actually attacked.

Christmas Day, the fourth of Third Army's counter-attacks, had been discouraging for them too. Weakened by the loss of two battalions to 4th Armored, 80th Infantry were checked by well-directed fire from the new German forces and in an attempt to attack across open ground the assault battalions lost nearly two hundred men. The end of the day found them still on the wrong side of the Sûre. Most of the day 26th Infantry spent in a grim battle for possession of Eschdorf and Arsdorf which resulted in severe casualties and left them also on the wrong side of the river.

The 4th Armored Division tried to push all three of its combat commands on to Bastogne on Christmas Day. CCB, together with the infantry reinforcement from 80th Division, fought a long, difficult battle against the stubborn 5th Parachute soldiers who had dug themselves in inside the woods and met the mixed American force with small-arms fire—all they had left. The Germans fought grimly, in many cases only yielding to hand grenades and the bayonet. Over a hundred Americans were hit and it was well after dark when Chaumont and the woods to the south were finally cleared. CCB were still six miles short of Bastogne.

CCA found the going difficult on Christmas Day too and their infantry support, the other battalion from 80th Division, suffered heavy casualties and needed the help of eight Lightnings before the village of Tintage, blocking the tanks' route to Bastogne could be cleared. Nightfall found them held up at Hollange, more than seven miles from Bastogne.

Nor had CCR on the left any better success for they were held up all day at Remoiville by more of the determined 5th Parachute. Nightfall found them in possession of the village but delayed by a huge crater. They were also some seven miles from Bastogne.

Christmas had been a desperate day for the defenders of Bastogne and when they learned that night that 4th Armored had made little progress and the nearest combat command were still six miles away they were angry and disappointed. General McAuliffe, tired of the daily promises of relief by 4th Armored Division, telephoned General Middleton saying that his position was now critical and adding: 'We have been let down.'

The bitter disappointment of the bone-weary soldiers in Bastogne was understandable but they did not know how grievously 4th Armored division had been hurt in trying to obey General Patton's orders to 'Drive like hell'. Tanks and men had been lost at a rate which could not be afforded if there was to be any chance of breaking through the German's fiercely defended blocking line.

4th Armored Division's tactics were changed: every advance would now be made with ample infantry support and would be preceded by concentrated artillery fire. There must be air support on tap, flights of Lightnings on a few minutes' call and above all there would be no more costly night attacks. Pushing tanks in the dark through close country containing infantry armed with bazookas is tantamount to throwing away the advantage of armour and General Patton admitted after the war that he had been wrong to order it.

General Gaffey's three armoured columns would resume the attack towards Bastogne the following day, December 26, and would not stop until they had broken through the German ring—but no more signals announcing their imminent arrival would be sent.

Inside the perimeter, now contracted to sixteen miles, the troops manning the defences braced themselves for more, even stronger, German attempts. They could not know that they had won, that now the troops surrounding them were too weak to hope to succeed and that the German High Command had decided to throw everything into one last attempt to seize a Meuse crossing. If they could do so the Allies would have to fall back to the line of that river and then the troublesome Bastogne garrison could be dealt with at leisure.

The decision to persist with the offensive had been Hitler's alone. His commanders in the field, acknowledging harsh military truths, had advised that the Ardennes Offensive be called off and the troops pulled back to the West Wall. When that was rejected Field Marshal von Rundstedt had proposed that they settle for most of the gains they had won and hold a twenty-mile-wide bulge intruding into the centre of the Allied front. This projected line would run from the West Wall west to Malmédy then south along the bank of the Amblève and the Salm through Houffalize, along the Ourth to return east along Seventh Army's blocking line south of Bastogne.

This proposal the Führer also turned down and insisted upon offensive and not defensive strategy, pointing out that if Germany were to go over to the defensive in the west it could only mean postponing defeat because of the increased Allied superiority in men and weapons. General Manteuffel, who understood the workings of Hitler's mind at this time as well as anyone, next proposed that the direction of the offensive be changed from west to north towards the Liège to Eupen sector and that at the same time a new German attack from the Aix-la-Chapelle area should drive south-west to meet the Ardennes attack. This compromise was a disguised abandonment of the original plan and Hitler would have none of it.

Instead he ordered that all available forces be concentrated at the westernmost penetration, first to gain control of the Marche plateau and then to drive across the Meuse in the vicinity of Dinant. At the same time he ordered a great attack in Alsace which 'will compel Patton to withdraw the mass of his forces, which are now seeking to relieve Bastogne, in order to meet the offensive. With this the pressure on the south flank of the Ardennes Offensive will relax and we shall have a free hand for a drive northwards again.'* He also consented to take two more divisions away from 'Sepp' Dietrich's front to strengthen Fifth Panzer Army's punch—something for which Manteuffel had been asking for days.

The Fifth Panzer Army commander had, on Saturday, December 23, three panzer divisions ready to strike for the Meuse: on the left Panzer Lehr was about to attack Rochefort; in the centre 2nd Panzer, the point of the Ardennes Offensive, were strung out from Hargimont, south of Marche, to a crossroads on a ridge about five miles from Celles astride the road to the bridge at Dinant; on the right 116 Panzer, having crossed the Ourthe at La Roche, had advanced another nine miles and been stopped by 84th Infantry's blocking line running from Marche to Hotton.

When Panzer Lehr, minus the battlegroup left with General Kokott for the attack on Bastogne, had moved on to the west its advance had been slowed down by comparatively tiny forces of combat engineers or isolated artillery batteries. Eight howitzers from the 58th Armored Field Artillery Battalion had withdrawn from supporting the Longvilly defenders after that place fell and taken up position at Tillet eight miles west of Bastogne. They held off Panzer Lehr's attacks until only one gun was still firing and then escaped south. At Moircy, an Ourthe crossing, and at St Hubert, key communications centre fifteen miles west of Bastogne, the 35th Engineer Combat Battalion blocked the approaches so efficiently that Panzer Lehr lost another day. Impatiently the Fifth Panzer Army commander himself went forward and, on Saturday, December 23, led Bayerlein's division from St Hubert to the outskirts of Rochefort which had to be in German hands before the coordinated attack on Dinant could go ahead. There was no evidence that the town was strongly defended and Manteuffel ordered Bayerlein to capture it during the night and then left

* Quoted by Manteuffel in his account of the Battle of the Ardennes in *Decisive Battles of World War II: The German View*. Jacobsen & Rohwer, Editors.

himself for 116th Panzer, at this time still east of the Ourthe, in order to push them forward on the right.

At this time both Manteuffel and Luettwitz, the XLVII Panzer Corps commander, were becoming increasingly worried about their flanks, particularly the right of both corps and army for there was evidence that the Allies were building up their strength there. Although Luettwitz had been forced to strip troops from both Panzer Lehr and 2nd Panzer to cover the shoulders of the thrust to Dinant he had still been able to concentrate considerable forces for the two-prong drive on Dinant—through Rochefort and from Humain through Buissonville to Celles. On the right 116th Panzer, who had finally crossed the Ourthe and advanced towards 84th Infantry's Marche/Hotton line, were given the task of capturing Marche and driving forward to join up with 2nd Panzer. If all these plans succeeded Fifth Panzer Army would drive over the Meuse with a spearhead made up of the advance guards of three panzer divisions.

Both these armoured drives were launched during Saturday night. On the left Panzer Lehr attacked Rochefort about midnight advancing through a narrow defile dominated by two hills. Although his patrols had reported that the town was empty General Bayerlein was beset by doubts and fears as he had been before Bastogne and did not like the task he had been given. 'OK—shut your eyes and let's go in!'* was how he put the order to attack.

His misgivings were justified, for during the day 84th Infantry Division had put almost a battalion of infantry supported by tank destroyers and combat engineers in and around Rochefort and these topped the German onrush inflicting heavy casualties. Always at his best when dealing with a concrete problem Bayerlein now brought up his artillery to destroy the American positions on the hills and to keep the Americans inside the town occupied while he closed up for a concentrated assault. He also sent a force around Rochefort to take possession of the Dinant road.

Rochefort held out until Sunday afternoon by which time Panzer Lehr had gained control of the market place crossroads and linked up with their force on the Dinant road. After dark the remaining Americans broke out, some escaping in trucks to Givet, sixteen miles west, and the rest marching north towards the Allied blocking line. This action cost the 84th Infantry a badly needed battalion but by stopping Panzer Lehr for one more day it probably saved Dinant.

* 'Also los, Augen zu, und hinein!'

The reconnaissance regiment of 2nd Panzer Division pushed on during Saturday night for Celles, less than six miles by road from the bridge at Dinant. Behind them were a battalion of Panthers followed by a regiment of panzer grenadiers and then most of the division's artillery. The rest of 2nd Panzer stopped south of Marche to protect the corps' right flank and because there was only enough fuel for the spearhead to reach Dinant. The first vehicle, scouting ahead of the reconnaissance, was one of Skorzeny's commando teams in an American jeep.

Most of Dinant, a small town of narrow streets, is squeezed along a narrow strip of flat land on the east bank of the Meuse between the river and steep bluffs. The main approach road from the east enters Dinant by joining the road running alongside the river from the south, at one point passing through a narrow opening cut out of solid rock. Here some of the British 29th Armoured Brigade's motor battalion had set up a check point, and a little further on, had placed a necklace of Hawkins mines which could be pulled across the road should any vehicle refuse to stop. About midnight on Saturday a jeep with American markings crashed through the check point and was blown to bits on the mines. As the dead occupants wore American greatcoats it was at first feared that one of war's tragic errors had been made, but underneath they were found to be wearing SS uniform.

Captured German orders for the Ardennes Offensive had stressed the importance of night fighting so although the 3rd Royal Tank Regiment, charged with the responsibility of blowing the Dinant bridge when the Germans appeared on the other side in force, had concentrated their defence on the western side, they had put one squadron across the river on Friday night. These tanks had advanced to a ridge from Sorinne to Achênne some five miles east of Dinant and one tank was put out to cover each of the approach roads from the south.* Orders were that if the Germans appeared in strength the bridge at Dinant would be blown and the tanks on the wrong side of the river would hold up the advance as long as possible placed in such a position as to form a roadblock when they were knocked out. None was to come back.

This was ironically called a 'death or glory' operation but as is so often the case when the worst is expected nothing happened during the whole of the first night. Orders were unchanged for the second night, Saturday, December 23, but towards dawn lack of sleep began to tell so that when one of 2nd Panzer's reconnaissance columns, probing forward to find

* The author commanded one of these tanks.

resistance, came up a road towards a hull-down Sherman, its exhausted crew were all asleep.

They were awakened by the sound of straining engines and the clank of tank tracks and the horrified tank commander, suddenly seeing a long line of German vehicles approaching, shouted the order to fire. The equally bemused gunner aimed at the leading vehicle, an armoured car, but neglected to bring down the range on his sight set for a bend in the road some fifteen hundred yards off. This resulted in the high-explosive shell which had been in the breech hitting a truck well down the line which was evidently loaded with ammunition for it blew up with a tremendous roar and set fire to another behind carrying precious fuel. The road was completely blocked and the front of the column cut off.

Now a little better organized, the Sherman crew methodically worked down the line first knocking out a Mark IV, then a half-track and finally a scout car before a German self-propelled 88-mm determinedly pushed past the blazing wreckage and fired up at the Sherman which hastily pulled back behind the ridge.

A quarter of an hour later a second Mark IV was destroyed on another approach road to be followed by the knocking out of two Mark V Panthers moving along yet another back road. Radios crackled busily on both sides 'Heavy armoured resistance', reported the German commander: 'We tore him apart!' was the modest British claim.

The Germans now drew fire whenever they moved and the British artillery west of the Meuse fired at maximum range on concentrations of Panzer Lehr's troops concealed in copses or around farms. These positions were reported by the newly-revived Belgian underground led by Captain Jacques de Villenfagne, the owner of the château at Sorinne who had nearly got himself taken into custody when the British first arrived by demanding supplies of hand grenades and offering to lead officer patrols—the more senior the better—forward to find the enemy.

2nd Panzer Division's spearhead had been stopped five and a half miles from Dinant* not entirely, as the British tank crews not unnaturally believed, because they had lost four tanks but because they were practically out of fuel and were now under attack all along their right flank. Although orders came for them to leave their vehicles and advance to the Meuse on foot this was as far as they would go. They had

* The westernmost tank of the Ardennes offensive was knocked out in the curé's garden in Foy Notre Dame.

advanced further than anyone else in Army Group B, sixty miles in eight days, had nearly got to the Meuse—just as in 1940 they had nearly got to Dunkirk and nearly to Moscow in 1941—and had, except after crossing the Ourthe, never faltered in their advance. They had fought well but they had been badly delayed by the American infantry before Clervaux, the airborne troops at Noville and shortage of fuel. They had been diverted from Marche, which they badly needed, by the American troops rushed there from the north and finally their spearhead had splintered against a thin line of British tanks. Out of fuel and running low on ammunition and food 2nd Panzer stretched in a long line from Celles back to Hargimont, south of Marche, waited for the inevitable American assault from the north.

Moving down towards them were fresh task forces from one of the great American armoured divisions, the 2nd, 'Hell on Wheels', whose total strength consisted of some fourteen hundred men and three hundred and ninety tanks. 2nd Panzer who had crossed the Our with eighty-eight tanks and twenty-eight self-propelled guns were down to about half that number. The result of the coming action could not be in doubt.

26

THE ADVANCE IS CHECKED

*The strength of an army, like the momentum in
mechanics, is estimated by the weight plus the velocity.*

NAPOLEON

By now the German soldiers in the van of the attack were
getting very tired. For seven days and nights, in the wet and the
cold, they had pushed westward towards a promised great
victory, fighting hard to overcome resistance only to find, a
few miles further on, fresh, well-armed American troops waiting for them. The first heady optimism, nourished by the early
successes and apparent lack of resistance, began to wither as
the shortage of rations, the lack of sleep and the constant
shelling drained their energy and determination.

A devastating blow to their morale came with the clearing of
the skies on Saturday, December 23, and the consequent un-
leashing of the mighty Allied air power. In four days over
seven thousand sorties were flown. As long as light lasted the
Ardennes battlefield was hit hard at dozens of critical points;
after dark the bombers pounded the lines of communication all
the way back to the Rhine. On Sunday fourteen hundred
heavy bombers dropped over three thousand five hundred tons
of bombs on practically every Luftwaffe airfield, another six
hundred and thirty-four concentrated on fourteen key communication centres west of the Rhine and three hundred and
seventy-six medium bombers dropped seven hundred tons of
bombs in the Ardennes.

All this caused widespread cratering and cutting of roads,
the knocking out of bridges, blocking of choke points and
passes, the piling of rubble in the streets of villages forcing
detours along narrow, muddy roads and causing heavy destruction of all kinds of transport. 'The attacks from the air
were so powerful that even single vehicles could only get
through by going from cover to cover,' said Major-General
Richard Metz, the commander of Fifth Panzer Army's artillery
in a post-war interview. 'Sepp' Dietrich admitted losing nearly
a third of his vehicles.*

* 'And the worst of it is that those damned Jabos don't distinguish
between generals and anyone else—it was terrible!' 'Sepp' Dietrich,
ETHINT 15.

Bitterly charging the Luftwaffe with cowardice the German soldiers threw themselves into ditches or hastily-dug holes, helpless to prevent the splintering of their carefully constituted spearheads. Their accusations were hardly just, for there was little the now badly-depleted German Air Force could do against the massive strength the Allies were able to bring to bear. At most Germany could put up one thousand five hundred craft along the whole Western Front while the Allies had four thousand to commit against the Ardennes Offensive alone —including the heavy bombers which flew from England and smashed the sources of supply. The Luftwaffe fighter pilots did go up and many pressed home their attacks against stronger forces most courageously. Almost all were engaged before they reached the battle area and so were not seen by the German soldiers at its forward edge.

German air losses were appalling. Lieutenant-General Adolf Galland, the commander of Germany's fighter arm, said, after the war, that it was in the Ardennes that the Luftwaffe received its death blow.

Although the incessant Allied air attacks destroyed some tanks and guns and other equipment and lowered the fighting spirit of the German soldiers, it was the almost complete disruption of communications which did most to halt the Ardennes Offensive. The fast-moving forward units could not be continually supplied, as essential for blitzkrieg tactics. And of these supplies the most important shortage was fuel; man can advance with the minimum of food, tanks and guns can be used with the minimum of ammunition but without fuel a modern armoured attack stops dead.

A considerable measure of success was within the Germans' grasp after the first few days, before the skies cleared, but fuel shortage caused a drag even then as the roads became blocked by the mistake of trying to move too much forward too soon. Shortage of fuel robbed Battlegroup Peiper of choice of manoeuvre long enough for a block to be thrown up in front of them; shortage of fuel delayed the clearing of the area between St Vith and the Salm, just as, twenty-four hours earlier, it had prevented the 116th Panzer from crossing the Ourthe at La Roche. After the third day 2nd Panzer had been bedevilled by fuel shortage and we now know that this was the main reason for the fatal pause in front of Dinant. 2nd SS Panzer had been forced to delay their seizure of the key Baraque de Fraiture crossroads because their tanks were dry and 9th SS Panzer were not able to reinforce the subsequent attack in this sector for the same reason—and the heavily mechanized Fuehrer Begleit Brigade's lightning advance lost momentum four times as one engine after another was starved to a halt.

All these checks to the German armoured spearheads accumulated to bring about a critical pause, a breathing spell for the Allies to create a firm blocking line without which the offensive could not have been stopped east of the Meuse.

The German commanders—Model, Manteuffel and Luettwitz—were not as discouraged as their weary assault trops for it seemed from the vantage point of the high command that the conditions necessary for a successful breakthrough to the Meuse and seizure of a crossing had at last been achieved providing that Bastogne was captured, that Patton's counterattack was held and that fresh, battle-worthy units could be hurried up to the spearhead in time.

Von Rundstedt had been insisting for days that it was useless for five assault divisions to be kept in the Elsenborn sector and Hitler had finally listened to his most experienced commander and consented to give up Sixth SS Panzer Army's original mission and to man that front with second line troops so that the SS Panzer Division could be switched to exploit Fifth Panzer Army's success.

First to move had been II Panzer Corps' two armoured divisions and, as we have seen, the 2nd SS Panzer captured the Baraque de Fraiture crossroads and the 9th SS struck at the Salm river front in the area of Vielsalm after the American withdrawal from St Vith. The badly mauled 12th SS Panzer were ordered to disengage from the Elsenborn fighting and move south to the scene of the new effort. Also the Führer ordered the 9th Panzer Division to move from Holland to back up 2nd Panzer at the point and promised to send 3rd Panzer Grenadier Division as well.*

If Fifth Panzer Army could succeed in reaching the Meuse and establish a bridgehead the inevitable adjustment of the Allied line would allow Sixth SS Panzer Army to get moving again. In order to reinforce I SS Panzer Corps, which now consisted only of the greatly weakened Leibstandarte, Manteuffel's two volksgrenadier divisions, which had captured St Vith, were ordered to move north. With what remained of 1st SS Panzer Division they were to attack across the Salm and then push hard towards the north-west.

---

* 3rd Panzer Grenadier Division had been committed from the reserve on December 20 in an attempt to capture Elsenborn and had suffered such severe casualties from the US 99th Infantry and their supporting artillery that they were not, in fact, able to take part in the final attempt to reach the Meuse.

The Allied assessment was not much different from OKW's, for Field Marshal Montgomery had become convinced that the Germans were about to make their greatest effort and decided to postpone the attack by VII Corps against the German point and, instead, to create a firm shoulder to block their advance either to the north or north-west while allowing them to flow south-west where they could do little harm. This tactic would also enable him to withdraw certain divisions from contact and collect them into a strategic reserve for a later decisive counter-attack. One of the main differences between Montgomery's and Patton's way of fighting a battle was this one of reserves: Patton believed in using everything he could lay his hands on, gambling on a quick victory; Montgomery considered a battle won when he was able to withdraw units to form a reserve.

Now, in order to implement his plan, Montgomery ordered General Collins to draw back VII Corps' left wing to the natural defence of the high ground from Manhay to Hotton and stipulated that his three divisions were not to become involved in fighting—they were, in fact, 'released from all offensive action'. For the time being the Germans were to be contained but not attacked.

But the pressure of events was to prevent Montgomery from fighting the kind of battle at which he excelled—a carefully planned attack in overwhelming strength at a time and a place of his own choosing*—for, on Saturday, no less than six German panzer divisions were moving towards First US Army's front. Furthest south, as we have seen, Panzer Lehr was attacking 84th Infantry's force in Rochefort; 2nd Panzer's advance guard was approaching Dinant while the rest of that division was stretched all the way back to south of Marche with the double task of attacking west and of giving flank protection to XLVII Panzer Corps. Ninth Panzer were on their way from Holland to back up 2nd Panzer's drive to the Meuse; 116th Panzer crossed the Ourthe at La Roche and built up strength on the western bank for a thrust to break through 84th Infantry's position along the Hotton–Marche road which

* It is probable that the Field Marshal anticipated some difficulty in calling the tune for on December 22 he wrote to General Eisenhower: 'I am not optimistic that the attack of Third Army will be strong enough to do what is needed and I suggest 7th German Army will possibly hold off Patton from interfering with the progress westwards of 5th Panzer Army. In this case I will have to deal unaided with both 5th and 6th Panzer Armies ...' Pogue: *The Supreme Command.*

was to be followed by the capture of Marche. Finally, on the German right, the two SS divisions, 2nd SS Panzer and 9th SS Panzer, were preparing to strike through the Baraque de Fraiture and Manhay area.

As well as these armoured divisions the 560th Volksgrenadiers were assaulting the remains of 3rd Armored Division's task force in the Hotton–Soy area; the Fuehrer Begleit Brigade was moving from Salmchâteau, intended to reinforce II Panzer Corps and the 1st SS Panzer, although badly weakened by the destruction of Battlegroup Peiper, were still a force to be reckoned with in the Stavelot–Trois Ponts–Grand Halleux shoulder.

The withdrawal of the St Vith defenders had left 82nd Airborne Division dangerously exposed along a U-shaped front facing north, east and south opposed on all three by German armour. Unless considerable reinforcements, including artillery and tanks, could be brought inside the 'U', 82nd's line was untenable. To make matters worse the airborne's right flank which ended at the village of Fraiture, a mile north-east of the vital crossroads, was dangling in the air. This had been caused by the 560th Volksgrenadiers who, though near to exhaustion, had advanced ten miles in a remarkable burst of energy in another attempt to seize the crossing at Hotton.

Some of the troops which had just retreated from St Vith were hurried forward again to form a blocking position from Malempré to Manhay, the next crossroads north of the Baraque de Fraiture. 3rd Armored Division's CCB was started from the La Gleize area on Saturday night to reinforce their comrades hard beset around Soy but it would be many hours before they could arrive on the scene in strength.

The veteran 2nd Armored Division, which had been moved south in great secrecy in order to supply the armoured weight for VII Corps' projected counter-attack, were concentrated north of Marche on the axis of the main road to Huy. Patrols worked forward east of the Meuse and about 10.30 am on Saturday an armoured car from one of these was shot up near Ciney.* The reaction of General Ernest Harmon, 2nd Armoured's commander, was immediate and predictably aggressive—CCA was sent to the area to deal with the 'many German tanks' reported.

Although the only tanks found were British, there were

* It was never discovered who fired on this 2nd Armored patrol but it may well have been one of the British reconnaissance units working out of Ciney which was occupied by 'C' Squadron of 3rd Royal Tank Regiment on Friday, December 22.

confirmed reports from reconnaissance units of large German forces in the south moving steadily west. Harmon quickly moved two battalions of field artillery up to give CCA fire support and started his whole division moving south. He then got on the telephone to General Collins, the VII Corps' commander, and reported his actions. 'Joe,' he said, 'I'm committed!'

The fighting which was to see the end of German hopes to reach the Meuse would take place in three main areas: between Dinant and Marche as the two flanks, moving obliquely, became entangled and turned to face each other; between Marche and Hotton where the 116th Panzers tried to break through 84th Infantry Division's defence line and from the Baraque de Fraiture crossroads area where the newly arrived II SS Panzer Corps would try to drive north-west to the Manhay crossroads splitting the two American corps from each other.

An outstanding German success at any one of these would have signalled a switch of the main effort to a new *Schwerpunkt* which might well have changed the course of the battle and consequently of the offensive. We will look first at the attempt against the centre and then the German right, for the outcome of these decisively affected the more dramatic events at the spearhead of the offensive.

After his division had finally crossed the Ourthe at La Roche on Saturday, Major-General Siegfried von Waldenburg slipped two dismounted companies of 116th Panzer's reconnaissance, during the night, through 84th Infantry's Marche–Hotton line. By dawn they were hidden in woods along a ridge north of the village of Verdenne, some three miles east of Marche and about a mile south of the vital Hotton to Marche highway. More 116th troops, panzergrenadiers, went into position south-west of Verdenne and most of the rest of the supporting infantry were deployed on the right, maintaining pressure against the Hotton garrison in the area south of the town and west of the Ourthe.

The plan was for 116th to capture Verdenne on Sunday and then cut the main Hotton–Marche highway, seize Marche and move up on 2nd Panzer's right for the final push to the Meuse. The panzers should have attacked at dawn but once again the timetable was upset by shortage of fuel and the Americans, who learned of the presence of German troops in their rear from a cooperative prisoner, attacked first and routed the infantry concentration north-west of Verdenne which was forming up for assault.

But when 116th finally got their fuel and put in a strong armour–infantry attack, Verdenne fell and the 84th were driven back almost to the main Hotton–Marche road which it was imperative to hold. An American counter-attack later in the day had some success but nightfall found the Germans entrenched in Verdenne and building up a force to hit the American line the following day, Christmas Day.

Brigadier-General Alexander Bolling, commander of the 84th Infantry Division, lost no time in correcting this dangerous situation and regaining the initiative. After a massive artillery concentration had pounded the Germans in Verdenne during Sunday evening he launched a three-company-strong attack. About midnight one of the American columns bumped a force of 116th's tanks moving forward in the dark, thus accidentally discovering a new threat. The fighting that developed spread and continued all through Christmas Day until Verdenne was recaptured—with nearly three hundred German prisoners.

During the day the Fuehrer Begleit Brigade, who were switched all over the battlefield with the changing German plans, came in on 116th Panzer's right and were immediately given the task of watching Hotton thus freeing Waldenburg's armoured infantry from its flank guard rôle. He decided to use these to break through to his reconnaissance troops surrounded in the woods behind Verdenne by the American recapture of that village. At the same time a company of panzers was thrown against Verdenne itself. Both attacks failed although one mixed group of armoured infantry and tanks did manage to cut through to the trapped force.

The panzer attack ran on to the hull-down Shermans of the 771st Tank Battalion who knocked out all nine of them and the following day, December 26, after a costly assault by 84th Infantry had failed to shift the panzer force in the woods north of Verdenne, the Germans were hammered all the rest of the day by 8-inch howitzers and 155-mm 'Long Toms' followed by showers of incendiary shells from a chemical mortar company.

When the 84th Infantry moved forward on the 27th they found only abandoned equipment—including two disabled tanks. The rest had escaped during the night, for Waldenburg had been told that as he was losing the Fuehrer Begleit Brigade, who were now switched to Bastogne, 116th Panzer must go over to the defensive at once.

Before being hurried south Remer's force had been used in the last attempt to seize Hotton. The LVIII Panzer Corps'

401

commander, General Krueger, whose single infantry Division, the 560th Volksgrenadiers, had simply not been strong enough to overcome the American defence, decided to try to break through from the south by having the Fuehrer Begleit Brigade capture Hampteau while a force of 116th Panzer's tanks and armoured infantry seized the next village west, Ménil.

But by now the American artillery had concentrated behind this defence and the Feuhrer Begleit Brigade were first hit hard as they formed up and then smashed when they tried to come in. The attack was a complete failure and, as we have seen, orders then came which sent what remained of Remer's brigade off to help in the capture of Bastogne, now number one priority.

The attempt of 116th Panzer to seize Ménil was hit by the simultaneous fire of no less than three battalions of field artillery which knocked out six tanks. Bravely the German infantry tried to advance over open ground for a quarter of a mile: more than two thousand high-explosive shells were poured down on them and the attack collapsed.

The action between Marche and Hotton marked the end of 116th Panzer's courageous and determined effort to reach the Meuse. They had been asked to do too much with too little, as indeed had all of 5th Panzer Army. Their losses were very heavy, particularly at the end when their former high morale began to flag. This was seen in the number of prisoners—some 600 in the Verdenne action alone—and an increasing unwillingness to make reckless attacks. As the division pulled back and went over to the defensive and the survivors were put to work digging trenches and emplacements for the remaining tanks and guns they realized at last that Germany had lost the war. Many began to think of personal survival and although most of them were later extricated from the Ardennes by skilful German staff work the great 116th Panzer Division had been broken so thoroughly that it was never again an élite formation.

Their final opponents, the US 84th Infantry Division, had also suffered: moved suddenly on Thursday, December 21, some seventy-five miles from Geilenkirchen to man the Ourthe river line, they had been continuously in action almost from the moment of their arrival. Circumstances had forced them to try to hold too long a front and their right had been routed by Panzer Lehr division while their left had become involved, first with 560th Volksgrenadier Division and later briefly with the Feuhrer Begleit Brigade. As we have seen, their weakened centre withstood the full blast of 116th Panzer Division's attack. After five days' hard fighting they had lost some six hundred men of which 112 were dead.

On the morning of the sixth day, Wednesday, December 27, the 84th moved forward to resume the battle only to find that their front had suddenly become quiet for, unknown to them, the centre of the offensive had been shifted to the south. The 84th spent five more days holding their section of First Army's front during which they were able to rest, re-equip and replace their casualties. Then, on January 1, they moved north to combine with 2nd US Armored Division in the new Allied offensive which would finally erase the Ardennes Bulge.

During the days that the 116th Panzer had unsuccessfully tried to break through the 84th Infantry and capture Marche the Germans had launched two other strong efforts to keep the momentum of their assault going in order to carry it to the Meuse. One was at the point of Fifth Panzer Army's furthest penetration and the other was against VII Corps' left wing along its boundary with XVIIIth Airborne Corps. In the Hotton–Soy area, VII Corps' left was held by the survivors of 3rd Armored Division's Task Forces who had run into the 560th Volksgrenadiers and the 116th Panzer Division when attempting to strike south from Hotton. The right of XVIIIth Airborne Corps was, on Sunday, December 24, insecurely held by elements of three divisions badly mauled in the St Vith Defence—the 7th Armored, 9th Armored and 106th Infantry—who had been hurried into the line again after the 2nd SS Panzer had seized the Baraque de Fraiture crossroads. Communications between these forces and their higher commands or from one to the other were very bad, an important factor in what followed. The airborne corps centre was the U-shaped line of the 82nd Airborne Division whose dangling right wing at Fraiture was in danger of being outflanked.

The main threat was obviously from the Baraque de Fraiture crossroads where the Germans were building up their strength for a push north-west to the Manhay crossroads from where they could strike north for Liège or west to Hotton and the Meuse crossings. The 2nd SS Panzer were, in fact, waiting for fuel and supplies, delayed by the Allies' bombing, and for the Fuehrer Begleit Brigade who were to come up and reinforce the attack with a blow on the right at Fraiture.

Remer's brigade crossed the Salm at Salmchâteau, advanced five miles west to capture Regné, and moved quickly a mile and a half west to Fraiture, where a single battalion of glider infantry were prepared to try to block 2nd SS Panzer Division's advance. This new threat made the American position impossible and they fell back, abandoning Fraiture. The way north through Malempré to Manhay seemed open but the German command, desperately short of troops, now decided that Manteuffel's front should have priority and the Fuehrer Begleit Brigade was moved west to join 116th Panzer Division's attack on the 84th Infantry Division with the results we have just seen.

Although General Willi Bittrich, the commander of II SS Panzer Corps, had been promised two more divisions from 'Sepp' Dietrich's army to add weight to his attack, the Allied Air Force prevented them from arriving in time and he had to make his attempt with 2nd SS Panzer alone. They were helped, however, by the doughty 560th Volksgrenadiers who threw in one of their much reduced regiments against the remains of the 3rd Armored Division's troops in order to capture Odeigne. The volksgrenadiers force was practically destroyed but Odeigne, from which a narrow road ran to Manhay, was wrested from the Americans. This small village is two miles west of the Baraque de Fraiture and separated from the crossroads by thick forest. 2nd SS Panzer's engineers built a road for the panzers through the woods finishing it early on Christmas Eve.

The way was now open for 2nd SS Panzer to launch a two-prong attack against Manhay—from Odeigne and from Fraiture. Lieutenant-General Heinz Lammerding launched his attack about nine o'clock on Christmas Eve in the bright moonlight with a regiment of panzer grenadiers and a regiment of panzers moving out of Odeigne and a battalion of panzer grenadiers quietly moving through the woods from Fraiture towards Malempré. Because of the terrain and, perhaps even more, because of the shortage of fuel, the main body of panzers were kept back hidden in the woods east of the Baraque de Fraiture.

Unfortunately for the Americans this double advance towards Manhay coincided with a most complicated series of moves brought about by Montgomery's withdrawal orders. Most of the newly-committed 'troops in this sector were ordered to fall back to the new defence line as also were 82nd Airborne Division. The plan called for most of CCA of 7th Armored Division, some of CCB of 9th Armored and part of 3rd Armored Division, all to move back through Manhay during Christmas Eve night.

General Lammerding was aware of his inferior strength— what was to have been a two- or three-division strong assault would now be made by his armoured infantry with minimal tank support—but he thought that a bold thrust during the night against what his experienced assessment told him was a disorganized and disconnected defence would have a good chance of success. The attack from Odeigne was led by a captured Sherman tank on the assumption that it would be identified by the Americans from the sound of the engine and the colour of the exhaust. The panzer grenadiers moved through the woods on both sides of the tank column.

When the commander of a force of American tanks and armoured infantry in a blocking position north of Odeigne saw a tank column approaching him led by a Sherman he, understandably, assumed that they were probably from one of the other armoured divisions withdrawing through Manhay. Communications on this front at this time were in a hopeless state and there was no way of quickly determining who the approaching tanks were. Within minutes German bazookas started firing from the cover of the woods (the panzer grenadiers had moved up quietly ahead of the panzers) and the Americans quickly lost four tanks. The remainder turned and retreated north at full speed. The American armoured infantry, abandoned by their tanks, also broke and the triumphant 2nd SS Panzer column swept on to the next American blocking position who had not been warned by the first. Here the ruse of using a Sherman as point tank worked again and ten dug-in Shermans were hastily abandoned by their crews when the panzers opened fire. The supporting rifle company was over-run.

On the German right the small force of panzer grenadiers had been surprised by the ease with which Malempré fell to them for they did not, of course, know that the American withdrawal here had already begun. The last American tanks left the village only a few minutes before the German riflemen came in. Shortly afterwards the withdrawing Americans heard the sound of firing around Manhay, north of them. The force of Shermans and armoured infantry then circled Manhay and, getting on the road north, moved all the way back to Werbomont.

A task force from 3rd Armored Division, cut off by the advance from Odeigne, moved in to Malempré, believing it to be still in friendly hands. The lead tanks were knocked out by the Germans there and as there was only one road with Germans at either end the American commander ordered the vehicles to be abandoned and *sauve qui peut*—every man for himself. Most eventually regained their own lines.

The mixed armoured column attacking from Odeigne, after

overrunning the second American position, kept up their pressure and arrived in Manhay in time to wreak havoc on the rear of the headquarters column of CCA 7th Armored Division who were just pulling out of the village. By midnight this crucial road junction was in German hands.

The night had seen a brilliant German success and a dismal American failure—one that was to be subjected to long, searching enquiries—but, as had happened before in the Ardennes, the Germans did not exploit their success and the Americans quickly recovered from their failure.

For Manhay to be of any use to them, 2nd SS Panzer had to seize and hold the high ridge north-west of it, and this task had been given to the supporting infantry formations but during Christmas Eve night they advanced no further than Manhay itself and the woods south of it. The respite was all that the Americans needed and by dawn on Christmas Day the commanding high ground was held by a battalion of armoured infantry, a battalion from the 106th Infantry Division's surviving regiment, the 424th, and the tanks from the south who had found their way round Manhay during the night.

American artillery were able to shell the Germans in and around Manhay and during the morning Allied fighter-bombers sought out and destroyed a number of SS Panzer tanks. More forces were directed to the new blocking line which hourly grew stronger and 2nd SS Panzer's chance to secure their grip on Manhay disappeared.

It was not known, of course, what the Germans intended to do next but as they now had control of the main Bastogne to Liège highway and had a panzer division on it less than thirty miles from Liège with two or three others coming up behind, it seemed logical for their drive to strike north along the axis of the good road. From the beginning of the offensive First Army Headquarters had thought that Liège was the main target and the panzer division's drive from the Baraque de Fraiture north to the Liège highway seemed to confirm that assessment. Therefore most of the available force was deployed to block this way out of Manhay.

In fact the Germans wanted Manhay in order to get on to the good roads leading due west which would allow them to send their tanks smashing through VII Corps' left flank to gain the Meuse crossings. For this it was essential to seize a bridge over the Ourthe and because Hotton had obviously now been built up into an extremely well-defended position, the one at Durbuy, six miles north, had been chosen. The projected route lay through Grandménil and Erezee and all that lay in front of

2nd SS Panzer were a few of the badly-battered 3rd Armored task force and the leading units of the newly-arriving, green, 75th US Infantry Division.

The German advance west from Manhay, still led by the captured Sherman tank, met with early success, driving a small force of 3rd Armored's tanks out of Grandménil, a mile west, some hours before dawn on Christmas Day. The 2nd SS pushed on in pursuit of the retreating American mediums and ran into a battalion of 75th Infantry forming up for a dawn attack. After cutting the infantry line the panzers faced north and south alternately and blasted the inexperienced young soldiers out of their hastily dug foxholes.

In all probability the German armoured column would then have pushed on to Erezee from which there was easy access to Durbuy if it were not for one of the small but decisive acts which have so often upset great plans. A solitary 75th Infantry Division soldier—he is unknown and was probably killed soon afterwards—went forward and put a bazooka into a Mark V Panther at a point where the road ran between a high cliff and a sheer drop, thus completely blocking it. The panzers had long since outstripped their infantry support and tanks without infantry protection in close country at night are extremely vulnerable. The 2nd SS Panzer pulled back to Grandménil.

Encouraged, the 75th launched an attack against Grandménil at first light on Christmas Day but were repelled. More strength was necessary and it arrived in the afternoon in the shape of 3rd Armored Division's CCB which, it will be remembered, had been hurried down from the La Gleize area after the defeat of Battlegroup Peiper. A company of armoured infantry and a company of Shermans joined with the 75th Infantry for a strong thrust to capture Grandménil and then to attack Manhay.

They were assembling in the woods and getting into their attack formation when suddenly low over the trees came eleven Lightnings who plastered the area with their bombs killing forty Americans and completely disrupting the projected attack. It was one more in the series of mistakes by the Air Force which badly strained relations between ground and air in Europe during World War II. The tanks of 3rd Armored Division were displaying bright orange recognition panels and the assembly area was at the forward edge of the 'no bomb' zone but the Air Force said that ground control (of 7th Armored Division) had not told them of the presence of American tanks in the vicinity and pointed out that many German tanks now sported orange panels too.

The prime cause of this error, like the disorganization which led to the fall of Manhay, was the almost complete breakdown of communication in the fighting zone between commands—in this case between 7th Armored and 3rd Armored Divisions. Both these divisions had suffered severely in the recent fighting and each command felt that it had a legitimate grievance against the other. Then again Field Marshal Montgomery's order for a general withdrawal in the face of attack was completely against American military thinking. Opposition to it and support for it split the American command from First Army headquarters down to the units actually concerned and this, combined with the loss of St Vith and the apparent strength of the German armoured thrust, made Christmas Eve and Christmas Day the blackest forty-eight hours on First Army's front since the beginning of the offensive. With hindsight we can realize that the Germans, with their troops tiring, their communications hopelessly blocked and their mobile reserve either consumed or incapable of intervening in time, had no chance by Christmas Day of achieving their objectives but this did not seem to be the case at the time.

These were anxious hours for SHAEF who saw that the Germans were concentrating all their armour, six panzer divisions, against First Army while apparently being able to prevent Patton's Third Army from advancing without using a single panzer division against them. The most gloomy of the prophets at Supreme Headquarters were predicting that the Germans would be across the Meuse within forty-eight hours.

There was anxiety at the front too but certainly not despair for the defence line had been well chosen, the Air Force controlled the sky and Allied superiority in artillery was immense. All day 2nd SS Panzer Division's supporting infantry had tried to form up for the attack but every time were smashed by tremendous concentrations of shells.

By completely dominating the sky the Air Force kept the whole battlefield under constant surveillance and were able to strike immediately at anything that moved. The 9th Panzer, ordered to come quickly up to add weight to the attack from Manhay, could only move at a walking pace and 2nd SS Panzer, whose infantry were now badly weakened, were not reinforced.

The tank force of 3rd Armored, reformed after the bombing error, attacked and captured Grandménil during Christmas night but the Germans, knowing that they would have no room to manoeuvre if they were confined to Manhay, immediately counter-attacked and, though it was costly to them, regained Grandménil.

The loss of Manhay had been a severe blow to the American command and the danger its possession by the Germans posed was well understood. General Ridgway ordered the 7th Armored Division to attack immediately and 'recapture Manhay before dark'. This order was given on Christmas Day but by then nine days of almost continual battle, heavy casualties and physical near-exhaustion had temporarily taken the snap and aggression out of this great division. The attempt to capture Manhay was a half-hearted one and it failed as such attacks almost always do. The 424th Infantry Regiment, whose performance had regained the reputation of the 106th Infantry Division, sent a battalion against Manhay. One-third of them became casualties and the few hundred yards of ground wrung from the Germans at such cost had to be given back again when night fell.

On December 26 General Lammerding made a last desperate attempt to break 2nd SS Panzer Division out, sending one regiment of panzer grenadiers—or rather what remained of them—northward and the other from Grandménil west to seize Erezee. The northern thrust was stopped and routed by the glider infantry and the western, a two-pronged assault, on one road, ran into 3rd Armored's task force moving up for their own attack and along the other road were stopped by felled trees and artillery. Although the superior Mark V Panthers knocked out all but two of 3rd Armored's Shermans another sixteen were brought forward while three battalions of field artillery pounded the panzers and their supporting infantry. This was too much for the Germans, who pulled back yielding Grandménil to 3rd Armored's task force.

The 7th Armored were ordered to make one more try to recapture Manhay but in their exhausted and dispirited condition were again stopped by the dug-in panzers. That night, after no less than eight battalions of field artillery had poured their shells into Manhay, a battalion of parachute infantry, also released from the fight against Battlegroup Peiper, attacked and retook Manhay. In fact the German commander had concluded after the failure of both his panzer grenadier attacks that Manhay could become a trap and had pulled out in the night leaving his wounded behind.

On the 27th 2nd SS Panzer were ordered to move west and join the 12th SS Panzer, due from 'Sepp' Dietrich's front, in an attack towards Erezee from the south. Once again the Allied Air Force spoiled the German schedule and only a regiment of panzer grenadiers arrived from 12th SS Panzer to join 2nd SS

Panzer's available force—a battalion of self-propelled guns with two companies of supporting infantry. Fuel shortage prevented the tanks from taking part in the night attack.

Extremely confused fighting took place for the next thirty hours or so with both sides splitting into smaller bodies and without a coherent front but by dawn on Friday, December 29, the Germans had been stopped with heavy loss and the Allies had established a firm line from the Ourthe just south of Hotton to the Salm at Trois Ponts, a line from which they never again retreated.

It was the end of the attempt to reach the Meuse not only for 2nd SS Panzer Division but for 9th SS Panzer and 12th SS Panzer as well, three of the four élite divisions in Sixth SS Panzer Army on whom such high hopes had been placed. The fourth, 1st SS, the Leibstandarte had been reduced to the strength of a single company by the loss of Battlegroup Peiper's tanks and guns and had not been able to help in the Manhay Battle. On Tuesday, December 26, 1st SS Panzer were ordered to the Bastogne area which had now become, in Manteuffel's words, 'the central problem', but despite tremendous efforts by the German ordnance not more than fifty tanks could be created out of the mass of damaged armour. Ten days after the start of the offensive the four crack SS Panzer Divisions, which had been launched towards Antwerp, were still well east of the Meuse, with a combined strength equal to about one division, and were now to move south instead of west.

The Sixth SS Panzer Army had clearly failed but what of Fifth Panzer Army's point a few miles from the Dinant crossing? Here on Saturday night, December 23, Panzer Lehr had attacked Rochefort and 2nd Panzer division had pushed its reconnaissance regiment to Celles as the beginning of a double-pronged attempt to gain a Meuse bridgehead. But Panzer Lehr were delayed for a critical day by the resistance of a single battalion from 84th Infantry Division. The flank of 2nd Panzer became entangled around Leignon with the leading units of the US 2nd Armored Division's CCA during the night and the German point was stopped at dawn on Sunday five miles from Dinant by the British 3rd Royal Tank Regiment. All this brought about changes on both sides.

Because both the Allied and the German commands were now concerned for their unprotected right flanks moving obliquely towards each other, both made moves to cover them which necessarily weakened their attacking power. Charged with the primary aim of seizing the crossing near Dinant, 2nd

Panzer was ordered to supply flank guard facing north between Marche and Celles: on the Allied side orders were sent to 2nd Armored Division on Sunday to pull right back to Huy and Andenne in order to establish a hard flank but because the order was sent over the air in clear it was couched in ambiguous terms referring to the two towns by their initial letters without indicating that they lay to the rear. The 2nd Armored's aggressive command found two villages with the same initial letters in *front* of them and enthusiastically attacked. A second order 'to roll with the punch' quickly halted this advance but not before the presence of the 2nd Armored Division in strength had been revealed to the Germans.

After some discussion both VII Corps and 2nd Armored Division's commanders decided despite orders from First Army that they were to go over to the defensive, that they would attack on the next day, Christmas, with two reinforced combat commands. The command loophole which made this possible was that General Collins was not ordered to fall back but only authorized to do so on his own judgment, and his assessment of the situation, with which General Harmon entirely agreed, was that a withdrawal would practically hand the Dinant crossing over to the Germans on a platter. Furthermore they were certain that 2nd Panzer had been badly hurt during the fighting on Saturday, December 23.

One of the results of that fighting had been that 2nd Panzer's advance guard, of a battalion of tanks and a regiment of armoured infantry, had been cut off near Conneaux from the rest of the division. Colonel Lauchert asked to be relieved of his responsibility for guarding XLVII Corps' flank in order to push a strong force through Rochefort to relieve his trapped forces. Luettwitz, the corps commander, refused this request. He did not dare weaken his flank and he realized that the Allies now so dominated the air that to put a large force on the road in daylight was to invite destruction. He preferred to bring the advance guard back from their exposed position rather than to move up to them. When the Fifth Panzer Army commander visited XLVII Panzer Corps during Sunday afternoon Luettwitz put the situation to him and requested permission to bring back his point as soon as it was dark.

In fact Hitler had already made it quite clear that no withdrawal could take place anywhere without his express permission and Manteuffel knew that there was no hope of that. Luettwitz's request was refused. Instead he was told that he could use the advance units of 9th Panzer Division, who were just coming in from Holland, to take over flank protection and allow 2nd Panzer to push through to the Conneaux pocket. Lauchert formed a mixed force—a couple of battalions of tanks and one of artillery, including some anti-aircraft guns, a battalion of panzer grenadiers and some engineers to deal with obstacles—and moved west out of Rochefort and turned north-west at the village of Ciergnon to strike towards Celles. At the same time Panzer Lehr were ordered to attack through Humain and capture Buissonville in order to clear communications. Also, as we have seen, 116th Panzer were expected to advance through the 84th Infantry and come up to form the right shoulder of the expanding salient.

On the American side the plan for Christmas Day was for 2nd Armored to attack with two task forces. CCB, centred on Ciney, would strike south-west to hit the forward assault force of 2nd Panzer in the Foy Notre Dame–Conjoux area and CCA would drive south from Buissonville to Rochefort where, it was believed, a battalion of 84th Infantry were trapped. Thus CCA and Panzer Lehr moved towards each other on Christmas Day.

Between Buissonville and Rochefort lie the villages of Harenne and, a mile or so east, Humain. On Christmas Day the first was unoccupied but CCA had a troop of their reconnaissance, the Fourth Cavalry Group, outposting Humain.

From Rochefort two assault groups from Panzer Lehr started north before dawn on Christmas morning and from Buissonville CCA moved south. A platoon of panzers reinforced by a company of panzer grenadiers drove the small American detachment out of Humain at first light and a similar force went through Havrenne towards Buissonville but then met the main strength of CCA coming the other way and in the ensuing fight lost five Panthers and were forced out of Havrenne. By this time it was known that the 84th Infantry in Rochefort had escaped so CCA halted their advance.

Aided by a company of Shermans the Fourth Cavalry Group attempted to retake Humain but Panzer Lehr were too strongly entrenched and at midnight the Americans moved away to cover the approach to Marche from the west. During the night the veteran 9th Panzer Division finally arrived from Holland and relieved Panzer Lehr in Humain with orders to attack towards Buissonville at dawn on December 26.

The 2nd Armored Division's other Christmas Day attack succeeded better. CCB split its strength into two task forces, A and B. The first moved from Ciney south-west with its right flank screened by the division's reconnaissance battalion. The plan was to move through Achêne to clear a large wood, the

Bois de Geauvelant, lying between that village and Celles where the German point had been stopped the day before. Task Force B was to advance on the left of Task Force A through Conjoux and, with a left hook, hit Celles from the south-east.

This 2nd Armored Division attack against the westernmost elements of XLVII Panzer Division was to strike from the north while on the Meuse the small British combined tank and infantry force were to block any German attempt to continue west. Because of the increasing numbers of panzer grenadiers on his front and the strong rumours of German parachutists having dropped in the south the local British commander, Colonel A. W. Brown, pulled his tanks back in a tight ring east of Dinant bridge on the night of December 24th. His orders were that the bridge was not to be blown under any circumstances but that 3rd Royal Tank Regiment were to defend the crossing 'to the last round and the last man'. Later in the evening new orders came for an advance at dawn on Christmas Day, against the point of the German armoured thrust, to clear and hold Sorinne, Foy Notre Dame and Boiselles. These last two villages had been occupied by the Germans when the British tanks pulled back.

Both the British and the American attacks began at dawn: a squadron of 3rd RTR Tanks and a platoon of the Rifle Brigade each advanced along a road from Dinant eastward. The right-hand column drove the Germans from Boiselles and the left occupied Sorinne without opposition and linked up with the forward elements from 2nd Armored Division's reconnaissance battalion.

Task Force A of 2nd Armored Division, with Shermans leading, swept through the Bois de Geauvelant and came under fire from Foy Notre Dame but a 'cab rank' of Lightnings were called upon who flushed out four Panthers and strafed General von Lauchert's relief force, which had moved up from Rochefort during the night in an attempt to get through to the main German Force trapped at Conneaux. In their enthusiasm the Lightnings strafed the British tank column as well but this time caused only one casualty.

Foy Notre Dame fell to a combined British tank and American infantry attack and the survivors of 2nd Panzer Division's reconnaissance battalion surrendered. Task Force A's tanks swept down on Celles, across the front of the thin line of British tanks holding the high ground to the west, and joined up with Task Force B which, after a short exchange of fire near Conjoux had swung left to come up to Celles from the

413

south. The advance guard of 2nd Panzer Division were wiped out and the relief force for the trapped main forward force were ordered back to Rochefort. It was the beginning of the end for Fifth Panzer Army's most successful panzer division.

On the following day the pocket was hammered mercilessly by the artillery and the air force and the woods around slowly and methodically cleared by tanks and infantry. The trapped German force were ordered to destroy their vehicles and equipment and to try to break out during the night on foot leaving their wounded behind. The German commander managed to get six hundred of his men safely back to Rochefort but large quantities of desperately needed war matériel had to be left behind.

After the battle the indefatigable leader of the Belgian Resistance, Captain Jacques de Villenfagne, whose reconnaissance had been responsible for some deadly artillery concentrations, carefully went over the ground. 'It was a great cemetery of destroyed vehicles and abandoned equipment, half-buried in the snow. The Germans left behind 840 vehicles, including 40 tanks and we counted 900 dead Germans in the woods and fields to the north of Celles.'*

CCA of 2nd Armored Division, who had become involved with Panzer Lehr around Havrenne and Humain on Christmas Day and been forced back towards Marche, did not know that during the night the exhausted Germans had been replaced by a fresh division, 9th Panzer, who had orders to attack at dawn on December 26 from Humain and capture Buissonville.

The American reconnaissance, units of the Fourth Cavalry Group, had been ordered to withdraw from Humain during Christmas night but had set up observation posts on the high ground to the north and about 7.0 am these spotted a mixed tank and infantry force moving along the road towards Buissonville. To break them up a concentrated barrage from all the heavy guns within range was laid on Humain and although it fell behind the column of fifteen Mk Vs followed by half-tracks of panzer grenadiers and so did not stop their advance, the second wave, forming up in the village, was completely disrupted.

In Buissonville the Americans had deployed tanks covered by anti-tank guns and armoured infantry. The tanks of 9th Panzer stopped short of the village and shelled it briefly. This was followed by determined assaults by the panzer grenadiers which were thrown back three times with increasing loss.

* *The Battle of Celles*: A report by Captaine Jacques de Villenfagne de Sorinne.

Meanwhile the artillery kept pounding Humain while the light tanks of the cavalry reconnaissance on the high ground to the north had a field day firing at the half-tracks which were sent to reinforce the attempt to capture Buissonville. Nightfall brought a stalemate: the Americans still held Buissonville, the Germans Humain.

It was a situation which could not be allowed to continue, for Humain was a threat to 2nd Armored Division's left flank and the reserve, CCR, was now brought forward with orders to recapture it. During the night of December 26 the German tanks were withdrawn from Buissonville and Humain but 150 panzer grenadiers were left behind with orders to hold Humain to the last man and it took CCR with four separate columns of tanks and armoured infantry all day to defeat them. It was nearly midnight on December 27 when the last house in Humain was cleared and even then some of the most determined panzer grenadiers holed up in the old château and only surrendered when CCR called in British flame-throwing tanks.

The German failure at Humain, Buissonville and in front of Dinant marked the end of the attempt to cross the Meuse, although this acknowledgment of the hard military facts was concealed from Hitler by Model and Rundstedt. The XLVII Panzer Corps were ordered to make one more effort to take Bastogne and the crippled 2nd Panzer Division was brought back through Rochefort, Panzer Lehr moved south-east to Remagne, five miles north-west of the Neufchâteau–Bastogne highway, from where it could strike Third Army's left flank and the Fuehrer Begleit Brigade was ordered to break off the attack against Hotton and to move immediately south around Bastogne. In order to make sure this time that Bastogne would fall Manteuffel was also given the 3rd Panzer Grenadier Division, the Fuehrer Grenadier Brigade and what was left of the Leibstandarte.

First Army had succeeded in stopping the mass of German armour from Elsenborn to Dinant and had forced them to go over to the defensive. Although American casualties had been heavy at the beginning of the offensive the scale had dipped the other way at the end. At Dinant the British casualties were remarkably light and 2nd Armored Division lost only five Shermans and twenty-two light tanks while knocking out eighty-two German tanks and eighty-three guns. The 2nd Armored had about two hundred and fifty casualties, of which seventeen were killed, while inflicting heavy losses on 2nd Panzer, Panzer Lehr and 9th Panzer, including over one thousand two hundred prisoners.

After the end of the battle in the north both sides moved troops for a great set-piece battle in the south the result of which would determine whether the great Ardennes Offensive was to have some measure of success or be seen to have been a complete disaster.

Everything now depended upon Bastogne whose beleaguered garrison we last saw waiting angrily and anxiously for General Patton's promised relief, driving slowly up from the south.

27

COUNTER-OFFENSIVE

Adherence to dogmas has destroyed more armies and lost more battles and lives than any other cause in war. No man of fixed opinions can make a good general.

GENERAL J. F. C. FULLER

With its right wing held fast, its point broken and its left wing under increasing pressure the German Ardennes Offensive had arrived at a phase which required strategical and tactical re-thinking. The German ground commanders, practical men, trained soldiers, assessed the relative strengths, the available reinforcements, the questions of supply and the unchallengeable Allied air superiority and knew that at the best they would now have to settle for a great deal less than the original objectives.

Model and von Rundstedt, tacitly abandoning the idea of an advance beyond the Meuse, decided to shorten their line and regroup before returning to the attack with limited objectives. Adolf Hitler, whose complete authority was still unquestioned, ignored military facts and refused to sanction any retreat anywhere or any modification of his original plan. Instead Germany would start another offensive: the German First Army were ordered to come out of their West Wall positions and attack south towards the German Nineteenth Army trapped in the Colmar Pocket. These, with forces from north of Strasbourg, would launch an attack to meet the Nineteenth Army thus cutting off Allied troops in north-eastern Alsace. The new offensive was called 'Nordwind' and, Hitler told his generals, it 'will compel Patton to withdraw the mass of his forces which are now seeking to relieve Bastogne ... with this the pressure on the south flank of the Ardennes offensive will relax and we shall have a free hand for a drive northwards again.'

Nordwind was scheduled for December 31 but meanwhile what should be done in the Ardennes? General von Manteuffel the commander most closely involved wanted to bring back the divisions at the point and concentrate them against Bastogne, capture it and then close up to the Meuse between Namur and Givet but Hitler would have none of this. 'On the evening of

December 25th,' Manteuffel says bitterly,* 'typical orders arrived from Hitler instructing Fifth Panzer Army—without any consideration for the situation which had developed in the meantime—to use all available forces to seize the heights around Marche.'

But if the Führer could not be disobeyed he could be circumvented and Model and Rundstedt went quietly ahead with their plans, bringing the Fuehrer Begleit Brigade back across the Ourthe into the Bastogne area, ordering the 3rd Panzer Grenadier Division together with the remnants of the Leibstandarte to move towards Bastogne from the north and directing new divisions released from OKW reserve to the same area. In order to preserve the illusion of unremitting assault, 9th Panzer, 116th Panzer and 2nd SS Panzer were shown as attacking from the Ourthe sector although they were, in fact, going over to the defensive.

All these moves would bring about a new grouping of the German forces in the Ardennes in the shape of a broad arrow pointing west at Rochefort with the southern edge running through St Hubert, Wiltz and Ettelbruck to the Sauer river and the northern running north-east in front of the American Marche–Hotton–Soy line as far as Amonines and then east through the Baraque de Fraiture, Vielsalm and St Vith.

Bastogne, the 'running sore', was to be cleaned out by this concentration of forces, the southern flank strengthened to hold off Patton's counter-attack and then the whole front would move forward to the Meuse destroying the Allied forces east of that river.

It was time for the Allies too to reconsider strategy and tactics to deal with the new situation and on their side also the ground commanders disagreed with the higher command. Eisenhower and Montgomery, aware of the acute shortage of manpower, decided withdrawals were necessary in order to release the divisions needed for a great counter-attack.† Bradley and Patton, strongly opposing any withdrawal anywhere, advocated a coordinated attack from north and south of the bulge to start almost immediately. Most of the American commanders in First Army agreed with the Bradley–Patton plan and were very much against Montgomery's decision to erase salients, form a solid defence wall and withdraw divi-

* *Decisive Battles of World War II: The German View*, p. 409.

† As early as December 20 Eisenhower had directed Bradley 'to choose the line he could hold most cheaply and effectively no matter how far back he had to go to establish it.' Pogue: *The Supreme Command*.

sions into reserve.

General Bradley would have been less than human had he not, after losing an army to Montgomery, been ready to be disappointed with how it was used. Trained in the American school of constant attack and no retreat he found it very difficult to appreciate Montgomery's willingness to move forces to gain an advantage of terrain or manpower without regard to prestige. Always greatly influenced by General Patton—who had been his superior officer—he now agreed with his criticism that Montgomery was taking too long to make his move and on Christmas Day Bradley went to the Field Marshal's headquarters in Holland to urge coordinated attack from both sides of the Bulge. Patton's redeployment of three divisions from facing east to attacking north in only four days had been a dazzling performance, so dazzling that it had, perhaps, blinded Bradley to the fact that after four days of attack III Corps had taken heavy casualties and were bogged down along the whole line of their front. He assured Montgomery that although Bastogne had not yet been relieved Patton was certain that it soon would be and then Third Army would immediately launch a counter-attack north-east. If First Army would match it with one south-east the Bulge could be destroyed.

Montgomery pointed out that First Army, which had been some seven thousand men short when attacked by superior forces had taken severe losses in men and matériel. Although they had been reinforced by stripping Ninth Army and he had replaced two hundred and fifty-four of the two hundred and sixty-three tanks they had lost from the British pool in Normandy they were opposed by the entire weight of German armour.* Before a successful counter-attack could be mounted the Germans must be allowed to make one more attack in which they would be seriously weakened and he would have to create a new powerful reserve. This could only be found by withdrawals—not only in the Ardennes but on the Western Front as a whole by falling back to the line of the Saar–Vosges or to the Moselle.

Eisenhower had told Montgomery, on appointing him to the command of all forces north of the Bulge, 'to examine the situation on his northern flank with a view to giving up, if necessary, some ground in order to shorten our line and collect a strong reserve.' At that time the German offensive had made

* From north to south these were: 1st SS Panzer, 9th SS Panzer, Fuehrer Begleit Brigade, 116 Panzer, 2nd Panzer and Panzer Lehr. 9th Panzer were just arriving.

three deep penetrations and, unless there is a reserve available strong enough to exploit them, weakly-held salients invite destruction. Nevertheless Montgomery had replied that he saw no reason at that time to yield any of the ground which had been so dearly won. But after the loss of St Vith he ordered the 82nd Airborne Division to give up its untenable U-shaped salient and pull back to a natural defence ridge line. General Gavin protested that his division had never retreated in its combat history (which at this time was six months) and delayed the withdrawal, a delay which enabled the Germans to capture Grandménil. The other opposition with which Montgomery had to deal came from the commander of the 2nd Armored Division, General Harmon, who, privately encouraged by General Hodges, attacked 2nd Panzer when his orders were not to become involved in aggressive action. This involvement left Montgomery without a mobile armoured reserve—but it also resulted in the destruction of the 2nd Panzer Division.

In his account of the Battle of the Ardennes General von Manteuffel says this of Montgomery '... the operations of the US 1st Army had developed into a series of individual holding actions. Montgomery's contribution to restoring the situation was that he turned a series of isolated actions into a coherent battle fought according to a clear and definite plan. It was his refusal to engage in premature and piecemeal counter-attacks which enabled the Americans to gather their reserves and frustrate the German attempts to extend their break-through.' This is the generous tribute of one highly professional soldier to another but it is not the whole story. In their reconstruction of battles generals are inclined to give too much weight to the result of command decisions and too little to chance and accident and tend to forget that some decisions were forced on them by circumstances they had not brought about.

That is what happened to Montgomery when VII Corps became so involved it was impossible to withdraw them into reserve. This situation forced him to bring British XXX Corps across the Meuse to take up the positions held by First Army's right and to attack the German left flank. He had not wanted to do this for three main reasons: XXX Corps were deployed as a backstop in case the Germans did succeed in crossing the Meuse; to introduce them into the battle would necessitate moving them across the American lines of communication which could result in a disastrous tangle and, most important of all, XXX Corps were urgently needed for the next phase of 21st Army Group's advance into Germany. But the danger of a

German crossing of the Meuse had now receded; the XXX Corps divisions could be introduced by crossing the Meuse at Dinant and further south (over a bridge to be built at Chanly about fifteen miles east of Givet) so as to interfere with the American supply routes as little as possible and Montgomery was convinced that the Germans had shot their bolt in the Ardennes so that XXX Corps' commitment would be short. He was so sure of this that he sent the corps commander, General Horrocks, back to England on Christmas Night 'to have a rest before a big battle I've got in store for you as soon as we've cleared up this mess here'.*

This occurred on the same day as he told Bradley that he could not mount a counter-offensive without more troops and that these could only be found by withdrawing Allied forces from salients and holding shorter fronts.

Disappointed at what he considered to be Montgomery's timidity Bradley flew back to his own headquarters where he dined with Patton who joined him in condemning the way the American forces in the north were being used. Bradley telephoned to SHAEF and told the Chief of Staff that he would now consent to move 12th Army Group Headquarters back to Namur if First and Ninth Armies were returned to his command. From there he could coordinate all three armies in a massive counter-attack to wipe out the Bulge. He also asked that three fresh American divisions which had just arrived on the continent† be given to General Patton to take over Third Army's left flank and allow an attack north-east from the right. Bradley also wrote personally to General Hodges encouraging him to continue to oppose Montgomery's attempts to pull American troops back to form a reserve. 'Although you are no longer under my command I would view with serious misgivings the surrender of any more ground on your side of the Bulge,' he wrote.

In a report to SHAEF General Patton added his fire-power to this assault on Montgomery: 'Third Army troops know and understand the attack. They do not know or understand the retreat or general withdrawal.' He went on to say that III Corps were now threatening the German lines of communication through the salient, a claim which on December 26, was optimistically premature, and that with three new divisions he would be able to launch an attack through Echternach towards Bonn—a hundred miles or so north-east.

This attack would be made with Third Army's XII Corps

* *A Full Life.* Lieutenant-General Sir Brian Horrocks.
† 11th Armoured, 87th Infantry and 17th Airborne.

which had taken over from the mixture of VII Corps units who had stopped General Brandenberger's attempt to set up a hard shoulder—the 4th Infantry Division, CCA from 9th Armored Division and the 109th Infantry Regiment from 28th Division: to these had been added, first, CCA from Third Army's 10th Armored Division and, on December 22, more of XII Corps: the 5th Infantry Division, some fifteen battalions of Field Artillery and lightly armoured cavalry reconnaissance units.

The first of 5th Infantry's regiments to arrive launched a piecemeal attack on December 22 which took the pressure off the hard-pressed 4th Infantry facing its sixth day of battle but did not drive Brandenberger's volksgrenadiers back, for they were by then too well entrenched in familiar country for anything less than a full-scale assault to get them out. Such an assault was launched on December 24 when 5th Infantry Division complete and a combat command from both 10th Armored and 9th Armored Divisions supported by overwhelming superiority in artillery and air power began to drive the two tired and depleted German divisions back across the Sauer.

The difficult terrain—thick woods, steep gorges and a succession of ridges—was strange to the Americans but now well-known to the Germans who yielded ground only when it became impossible to hold and who flowed back as soon as opportunity offered. XII Corps put seven battalions of tanks and tank destroyers as well as the armoured combat commands alongside the fresh infantry division and supported their assault with twenty battalions of artillery, who fired over twenty-one thousand shells in the first day, and napalm and fragmentation bombs from the Lightnings.

Against this massive strength the Germans had two infantry divisions who had been fighting for eight days and whose rifle companies were down to about forty men apiece and who were supported by six battalions of artillery, two companies of anti-tank guns and some self-propelled 88-mm guns. They had no tanks and no support from the Luftwaffe.

It should have been an American walkover but the ground greatly favoured the defenders (as 4th Infantry had discovered when it was they who were defending) who also fought with skill and determination. On the first day the 212th Volksgrenadiers inflicted heavy casualties on the 5th Infantry Division killing and wounding over two hundred and yielding very little ground except at one place, the American left flank, where the 212th were split away from the 276th Volksgrenadier

Division on their right.

On XII Corps' left the strong armoured task forces pushed 276 Volksgrenadiers back into the area of the original bridgehead by Christmas Eve night. This was more or less the objective so that Christmas Day saw little activity on the armoured front. But 5th Infantry had another long hard day's fighting before bringing its centre and right up into line with its left and forcing the Germans back to the Sauer.* The second day's attack had been made with tank support and concentrated artillery bombardment and these were used again the following day, December 26, at the end of which most of the Germans had been pushed back across the Sauer and into the protection of the West Wall. The German retreat was not complete though and roving patrols continued to operate on the west side of the Sauer for more than a week.

The left wing attack of Seventh German Army had finally been defeated but the cost had been high: in the first five days of the German offensive the Americans had suffered over two thousand casualties; in the five days of the American counterattack they had lost about the same number and of these the 5th Infantry Division incurred nearly a thousand battle casualties. The two German divisions lost over six thousand men in ten days, perhaps half the number actively engaged in the battle.

It was the end of the Ardennes Offensive on the southern flank for the next major action here would be the Allied counter-offensive which began on January 18. The clearing of the Germans from the west bank of the Sauer enabled the American troops there to be returned to their higher commands: CCA of 9th Armored moved west to Arlon and III Corps; the 109th Infantry rejoined the 28th Division and VIII Corps on the left flank; 10th Armored Division were moved back to XX Corps at Metz.

Now 6th Armored Division came in from the Saar and took over the armoured rôle in this area while 80th Infantry were taken away from III Corps and given to XII Corps. Together with 4th Infantry Division in the centre and 5th Infantry on the right they held the southern hinge firm while strength was built up for a counter-attack.

Both sides had reason to be pleased with how their soldiers fought at the southern end of the Ardennes Offensive. When the Americans had been suddenly struck by a three to one assault they had refused to panic, and hit back hard and had

* In some cases, quite literally: on Christmas night many volksgrenadiers had to swim across the icy river to escape.

yielded ground only slowly. By hanging on to crossroads and communications centres they had completely upset the German timetable. When the time came for the Germans to withstand even greater odds they too contested every ridge and hollow.

Considering the immensity of its task and the paucity of its means the German Seventh Army's four infantry divisions accomplished a great deal more than cold military logic could reasonably have expected. The two divisions on the left wing did succeed in setting up a hard shoulder and were only forced back when Third US Army was able to commit a fresh corps against them; the right wing's two divisions held twenty-five miles of front alone against all the might of III Corps' counterattack for the first two days. OKW then committed another division of infantry and an armoured brigade to block the American 80th and 26th Infantry Divisions but 5th Parachute were left to hold 4th Armored Division off Bastogne by themselves. After two more days of bitter fighting the Third Army offensive, which had been intended to slice swiftly through the German flank, cutting their lines of communication, relieving Bastogne, was still slogging painfully forward.

On the right 80th Infantry, weakened by casualties and the loss of two battalions sent to reinforce 4th Armored's combat commands, had finally struggled to the near bank of the Sûre but had been unable to force a crossing. In the centre 26th Infantry's advance had been brought to a halt by tough pockets of resistance but the reserve regiment had attacked and got across the Sûre, establishing a bridgehead on the northern bank. Now, if 80th Division could move up on their right, the way lay open for them to advance to Wiltz, thus cutting the German's main line of communication south of Bastogne. But a gap had been opened up on 26th Division's left and 35th Infantry Division were moved up from Wiltz to fill it. Their orders were to attack northwards and seize the road from Clervaux to Bastogne. Their advance would also cover 4th Armored Division's right, CCA, which had advanced as far as Tintange some seven miles short of the Bastogne perimeter.

CCB of 4th Armored had got as far as Chaumont, six miles short by Christmas Night and was the favourite to break through to Bastogne, but on III Corps' left, in a flank protection rôle, the reserve combat command had reached Remoiville only five miles from the southernmost positions of the Bastogne defences.

On December 26 all three of 4th Armored's combat commands were ordered to move forward as swiftly as possible for it was realized that the troops inside the perimeter could not withstand another attack of the magnitude of the Christmas Day effort.

The Air Force continued to fly in supplies whenever the weather permitted—Christmas Day had been too overcast*— and when December 26 dawned with 'visibility unlimited' Troop Carrier Command got their C-47s off in a continuous stream, breaking all records with 289 flights. Once again the escorting Lightnings added their bombs and rockets to the tremendous weight of shells which III Corps artillery were pouring on to 5th Parachute Division's strung-out defence positions.

Not surprisingly this division, which had been fighting against increasing odds for ten days, now began to crumble, but for every young German who was ready to surrender there was another who seemed determined to die fighting. Armed now only with rifles and automatics they inflicted heavy casualties on the American infantry trying to force them out of dug-in positions and there were many scenes of last-ditch defences and examples of crossroads or groups of houses cleared by a costly attack which later were found to be occupied and so had to be stormed all over again. The Germans who did surrender complained that their artillery support had abandoned them, the Luftwaffe had not put in an appearance, their wounded were not cared for and they had not eaten for days.

These actions were time-consuming and the American tanks were further slowed by the large numbers of mines the Germans had been able to sow in an area which they had occupied for several days. By the end of the fifth day's fighting, December 26, CCA on the right had been able to move only another three miles north along the axis of the Arlon–Bastogne highway and CCB, the division's main hope of breaking through to Bastogne, had been able to get only as far as the woods outside Hompré which had been General Kokott's command post until December 24 when he moved west of Bastogne. He had left a 'few guards and had directed the placing of some anti-aircraft guns on the heights' and these lay between CCB's advance guard and the 101st soldiers manning the Bastogne perimeter two miles away.

At the rate of progress 4th Armored's two combat com-

* But eleven gliders had got through bringing, among other things, medical supplies and four surgeons desperately needed for emergency operations.

mands were making it would be at least another full day, perhaps two, before Bastogne could be relieved and General Maxwell Taylor, who had chosen to travel with CCB because they seemed most likely to reach his besieged division first, was disappointed with the speed of their advance.

But on the left the smallest of 4th Armored Division's combat commands, CCR, charged with giving CCB flank protection, had also moved off at dawn on December 26. The night before they had taken Remoiville but had been held up by a large crater at a point where a detour was impossible. This was filled during the night and the temperature dropped making the ground rock-hard and perfect for tanks. Colonel Wendell Blanchard, CCR's commander, worked out a plan for December 26: the armoured column would strike for Remichampagne, a mile and a half north, and then to Clochimont just over a mile north-east.

If Clochimont could be reached by early afternoon, with two or three hours light left, then the whole force would swing left and strike north-west for Sibret on the main Neufchâteau to Bastogne road. Sibret was reportedly held by a large German force and it was expected that the rest of December 26 would be consumed in its capture. Then at dawn the next day CCR would advance the last couple of miles to the defence perimeter, if CCB or CCA had not already relieved Bastogne.

CCR's support consisted of the 4th Armored Field Artillery Battalion with a battery of 155-mm howitzers and some self-propelled guns and they had also been promised help from the 362nd Fighter Group whose Lightnings would go in at crossroads and villages in front of the tanks. The combat command's own strength consisted of the 37th Tank Battalion now down to twenty Shermans and the 53rd Armored Infantry Battalion who were some two hundred and thirty men short. The infantry was commanded by Lieutenant-Colonel George Jacques and the tanks by Lieutenant-Colonel Creighton W. Abrams.*

December 26 started well when, unasked and unexpected, flights of Lightnings appeared overhead, peeled off and went in with bombs and machine gun which so blasted Remichampagne that the Germans there offered no resistance. Clochimont was approached warily by a flanking advance intended to draw fire but the Germans here had slipped quietly away and by three o'clock in the afternoon the tanks and half-tracks of armoured infantry were in possession.

* Who is at the time of writing the four-star general in command in Vietnam.

There was less than two hours light left and the attack plan now called for a swing to the north-west and the capture of Sibret two miles away. The two commanders examined the map and Colonel Abrams pointed to Assenois, a mile or so north on a direct secondary road to Bastogne.

'How about heading for Assenois and trying to dash straight through into Bastogne?' he asked Colonel Jaques.

The idea appealed to the infantry commander too for if Sibret were strongly held* he might lose too many men to be able to break through to Bastogne the following day. Anyway, why not take the shortest way to Bastogne in the Patton tradition?

Higher authority agreed and the reserve tank and armoured infantry team was brought forward to take over the lead. All possible artillery was ranged on Assenois and at 4.20 pm with the light already failing, Colonel Abrams gave the order to Captain William Dwight which started the dash for Bastogne. 'It's the push!'

A column of eight Shermans moved out of Clochimont followed by half-tracks carrying a company of armoured infantry. In the leading tank was a thirty-three-year-old veteran tank man, Lieutenant Charles Boggess. At 4.45 pm he called for the hastily arranged artillery bombardment of Assenois.

Colonel Abrams had checked with the waiting guns only a minute before and now he asked for a 'Concentration Number Nine' from all the artillery which had been tied in to support this unexpected attempt to break through to Bastogne. This calls for a complicated firing schedule designed to bring the shells from every gun on the target at the same time—a terrifying and devastating experience for the soldiers on the receiving end. Although it was not possible with the improvised communications quite to achieve this perfectly, in the next ninety seconds thirteen batteries fired ten rounds rapid on Assenois.

There Lieutenant-Colonel Kaufmann, the unhappy commander of the 26th Volksgrenadiers' 39th Regiment, was obeying General Kokott's orders and keeping his men and anti-tank guns facing Bastogne despite the growing evidence of activity in his rear. Suddenly the world erupted as hundreds of 155-mm shells exploded everywhere in the village. While the last shells were still falling the American tanks, all guns firing, came charging down the road followed by the half-tracks. The armoured infantry flung themselves out and ran for shelter of

* In fact there was only a small detachment of panzer grenadiers there.

427

wall or doorway as the last shells burst around them. One half-track was blown to bits by a direct hit.

Dust and smoke cut visibility to a few yards, tanks and half-tracks collided, then the shelling suddenly cut off. Almost immediately the Germans came out fighting. Guns, bayonets, knives and grenades were used as the German grenadiers and American armoured infantry became locked in a desperate fight for the village. Ignoring this, Lieutenant Boggess, followed by two Shermans, a half-track of armoured infantry which had accidentally got into the tank column, and two more Shermans, drove straight through the mêlée and out of the village to continue the dash for Bastogne.

The heavily-loaded half-track could not keep up with the Shermans bowling along at thirty miles an hour and a gap was created. A few Germans who had taken cover by the side of the road ran out and strewed Teller mines hoping to disable the next tank and block the road. The half-track hit one and was destroyed but the crews of the following Shermans carried the remaining mines out of the way and then leapt back into their tanks which hurried to catch up with the leaders.

The point where the road from Assenois entered the Bastogne defences was guarded by some of 101st Airborne's 326th Engineer battalion who had been warned that friendly tanks might appear on their front. At 4.40 pm, only five minutes or so after the artillery bombardment had begun, they heard tanks approaching and took cover but they had been seen by Lieutenant Boggess in the leading tank who thought he recognized the uniform. 'Come here—this is the 4th Armored,' he shouted.

After reporting that three tanks, believed to be friendly, had appeared on his front—news which was immediately flashed to 101st HQ where it caused great excitement—the airborne officer went forward to the first tank.

'Lieutenant Webster of the 326th Engineers, 101st Airborne,' he said, holding out his hand, 'and are we glad to see you!' Lieutenant Boggess leaned out of his tank and shook hands vigorously.

The siege of Bastogne was over.

Twenty minutes later Colonel Abrams and General McAuliffe were shaking hands at the 326th Engineers outpost and by one o'clock in the morning after fighting for Assenois had continued for hours* the highway to Bastogne was in American hands. The first convoy in consisted of seventy ambulances

* Five hundred German prisoners were taken in and around Assenois.

and it took thirty-six hours to evacuate nine hundred and sixty-four stretcher cases. During the siege the number of badly wounded men needing surgery had reached about two hundred and plans had been made to send surgeons in under a white flag, but on the last two days a liaison plane and gliders had come through the heavy anti-aircraft fire to land the desperately needed medical help.

Supplies were pumped along the one lifeline at maximum pressure, convoys following each other right round the clock. Trucks were unloaded fast and turned round for another load. Not all travelled back empty, for some seven hundred German prisoners who had confidently been waiting to be rescued when Bastogne fell started instead their long journey home by way of a prisoner of war camp.

Although the narrow corridor was important it was not enough to remove the threat to Bastogne which was now, more than ever, a key target for the Germans had to capture it if their offensive was to achieve even a limited success and the Americans must hold it securely before they could continue their drive north.

Both sides knew that the key to possession of Bastogne lay with the one, vulnerable entry now held by the Americans and both sides made their next moves accordingly. The Germans planned simultaneous attacks from north and south of the corridor to pinch it shut again; the Americans took steps first to harden the edges against such attacks and then to drive through to Bastogne on either side, opening both the Neufchâteau and the Arlon roads into the city.

Whoever succeeded would win the long, hard fight for Bastogne.

28

LAST DESPERATE GERMAN EFFORT

Better an end in horror than a horror without end.
GERMAN PROVERB

On the left the Assenois corridor was screened only by the remnants of Troy Middleton's shattered VIII Corps; on the right the main combat commands of 4th Armored Division were trying hard to close on Bastogne but their right flank was open because 26th Infantry Division had not been able to fill the gap. To seize the opportunity this vulnerability offered the Germans quickly prepared attacks from both sides: one from the south-east would be made by a new armoured corps, the XXXIX Panzer whose headquarters, sent from OKW reserve, took over a number of patched-up units either already in or coming into the Bastogne area, while the other, from the north-west, was entrusted to Luettwitz's XLVII Panzer Corps.

This attack would depend heavily on the Fuehrer Begleit Brigade who, it will be remembered, had been ordered on December 26 to break off their supporting action in the Hotton area and to move immediately towards Bastogne.

'I tried to change this order,' Remer says, 'because I didn't want to break up an attack during the day. Such a manoeuvre is exceedingly dangerous ... however, the corps commander ordered me to move immediately regardless of my present situation and I was obliged to discontinue at once. Tanks of 116 Panzer which had been pinched off in the Marenne area were left stranded by my withdrawal.'

Fuehrer Begleit crossed the Ourthe at La Roche and moved through Champlon intending to get into Sibret that night. This was the same time as 4th Armored's CCR was scheduled to seize Sibret and had both carried out their intentions a full-scale tank battle would have taken place which might well have changed the whole picture. But fuel shortage stopped Fuehrer Begleit and, as we have seen, the American armoured column went through Assenois into Bastogne instead.

By the time Remer had got hold of a small amount of fuel—many vehicles had to be towed—Sibret had been occupied by other American tanks. 'My plans were changed,' he said after the war. 'Instead we built up a flak line in case the Americans tried to move north.'

The attack had been turned into a defence thus completely upsetting the German plan and the tanks whose unexpected presence brought this important change about were from 9th Armored Division's CCA who, after a rather grimmer 'battle indoctrination' than they had bargained for in the Echternach sector, had been switched right across Third Army's rear and given the task of opening the Neufchâteau road into Bastogne.

CCA launched two task forces towards Bastogne at dawn on December 27 and, after some delay caused by having to find and pick up mines hastily laid behind VIII Corps' retreat, one column struck for Sibret, the other for Villeroux.

After a softening-up bombardment Villeroux was occupied without much trouble but as it was nearly dark and it could not be certain that there were no German infantry with bazookas concealed in the village the tanks were pulled out to nearby open ground.

Sibret was occupied by a small detachment of panzer grena-diers who were waiting for Fuehrer Begleit's tanks and guns. Despite an American assault by a whole company of Shermans firing high explosive and machine gun almost continuously, these German soldiers put up so spirited a fight it took all night to drive them out. Some of the survivors infiltrated into Villeroux, a mile to the east, and General Kokott scraped up a force from 26th Volksgrenadiers Pioneers and moved them into nearby woods with orders to recapture Sibret at dawn.

While this night fighting was going on Remer moved his main force into Chenogne, two miles north of Sibret, and waited for the 3rd Panzer Grenadier Division to come up into Senonchamps on his left. This should effectively prevent any further American advance west of Bastogne from this area and would make a good jumping-off place for a counter-attack.

Remer's anti-aircraft unit, the crack Hermann Goering Flak Regiment, were waiting when, because of the limitations of the Assenois corridor, the Air Force flew one more air lift into Bastogne. The C-47s came in low and straight and the German 88s shot down nine out of fourteen.

On December 28 CCA were determined to make sure of their two objectives: Villeroux was smashed by concentrated artillery fire followed by fighter-bomber strikes and then Sher-mans advancing in rows firing non-stop and the few Germans there were driven out; at Sibret General Kokott's brave but untrained Pioneers marched out of their woods at dawn and advanced in column towards the tanks and foxholes of the Americans. When they had recovered from their astonishment the 9th Armored raked them with automatic fire and later

431

over fifty dead Germans were counted lying in a well-disciplined line as though they had been stood against a wall and executed.

CCA now held Villeroux and Sibret but immediately ahead of them the Germans were building up a strong force. From 'Sepp' Dietrich's front the 3rd Panzer Grenadier Division had finally come in after a long, difficult march. They had filled in the large wooded area in between Chenogne and Senonchamps and absorbed the Fuehrer Begleit Brigade. On the right of this force were what remained of Bayerlein's Panzer Lehr, weakened but still dangerous and on the left the German line up to Bastogne was held by the survivors of the 26th Volksgrenadier and 15th Panzer Grenadier mixed force which had been shattered in the 'desperate effort' to break into Bastogne from the west on Christmas Day.

When CCA tried to resume their advance north-east towards the Marche–Bastogne highway on December 29 they ran head on into this new German line. Some tanks were knocked out but it was the supporting infantry who took the heaviest casualties, so heavy that morale was affected and, in some cases, the tanks were left to go on alone. Four Shermans which broke into Senonchamps had to fall back again because they had no infantry protection.

Ninth Armored's CCA had been badly hurt in their three-day fight—the infantry were down to one and a half companies and the armour to twenty-one Shermans—but on this front as on the Sauer river defence they had done their job well, once more buying the time which, with every day that passed, was increasingly on the side of the Allies. The Fuehrer Begleit Brigade had been prevented from driving across the corridor from the north and now fresh American divisions came up for a new counter-offensive west of Bastogne.

While this struggle for the initiative had been taking place north of the Assenois corridor the two main combat commands of 4th Armored Division had continued their slow, costly attempt to break into Bastogne from the south. On December 27, the morning after their reserve combat command had crashed through the German ring into Bastogne, 4th Armored's tanks moved off expecting the German resistance to be considerably weakened. To their dismay there was no sign of this: CCB on the left ran into new forces, some of 15th Panzer Grenadier Division, and took all day to push forward and make a tenuous contact with the Bastogne perimeter. On the right CCA, moving north along the Arlon highway, were held up by fierce resistance from the remaining

5th Parachute in the villages of Sainlez and Livarchamps. Before these places fell many more 4th Armored had become casualties and nightfall found the discouraged combat command still four miles short of Bastogne.

Another of the divisions initially committed in Third Army's attempt to drive north through Fifth Panzer Army's extended flank, the 26th Infantry, also fought itself out in the bitter fighting at the end of the year. After five costly days they put one battalion over the Sûre river and seized the village of Liefrange. This straddled an approach road to Wiltz, now a German keypoint, and on December 27 their attached combat engineers got a bridge in and a platoon of Shermans and a few tank destroyers were quickly moved up so that the advance would not lose momentum.

The first objective was one of the main German supply routes, the highway which ran south of Wiltz into Bastogne, but the ground between the Sûre and this road was ridged and broken, containing many natural positions from which the narrow roads could be dominated. Also, because the divisions on either side of the 26th had been held back, any further advance would have to provide flank cover, thus weakening its striking power.

Predictably the Germans reacted strongly to the breaching of their Sûre river line and part of the Fuehrer Grenadier Brigade was switched opposite the break where they struck hard, knocking out half the Shermans. The American reply was to use their superior fire power: twelve battalions of artillery followed by fighter-bomber strikes pounded the German positions. It still took two days to clear the small villages and hills but by the evening of December 28, the Yankee Division had pushed a two-regiment front three miles forward to cut the highway at Buberscheid, less than four miles from Wiltz, the next objective.

That night most of the American artillery poured their shells on Wiltz and the next day the infantry advanced towards it along a wide front. They were met by a devastating fire from 88s, multi-barrelled rocket launchers, mortars and dug-in panzers. Many of these American soldiers were new men who had been sent up to the front line by an order from General Patton for all rear area units to cut their establishment by ten per cent in order to replace the very heavy losses of riflemen in frontline companies and most of these replacements—or reinforcements as it had now been ordered to call them—had had very little training. Some learned fast and lived but others were wounded or killed on their first day in action. Some who were taken prisoner were in a state of shock or bewilderment; some had but little idea of where they were and in a few cases did not know which division they were in. If even the veterans of the tough Yankee Division found the fighting between the Sûre and Wiltz in fog and freezing slush the hardest of the war it is not surprising that it proved too much for some of the inexperienced new men to take.

But the attempt to capture Wiltz was renewed on December 30 and 31 with a last burst of effort. The Fuehrer Grenadier Brigade was drawn into reserve and their place taken by the 9th Volksgrenadier Division who, despite the discouraging experience of having had a battalion wiped out in its first action on this front, resisted the American attack with great determination and inflicted grievous casualties on the American infantry. The reduction in numbers and general exhaustion combined with the weather and the hardening of German resistance now brought 26th Infantry's advance to a halt.

The other two divisions who had launched III Corps attack on December 22nd, 80th Infantry and 4th Armored, also fought themselves out by the end of the year. General Earnest, commanding 4th Armored's CCA had to face the fact that his force had been badly depleted by battle casualties and, after six days of exposure to the worst winter in that area for over thirty years, by an increasing number of frost-bite cases. The infantry battalion borrowed from 80th Division were at the end of their tether and due to be returned. The new 35th Division who were supposed to move abreast of him had been slowed down by the difficult ground and appalling weather conditions and were three miles behind, thus leaving his right flank uncovered. He asked that their reserve, the 134th Infantry Regiment, be committed to capture the village of Lutrebois, three miles ahead on his right where the Germans had been reported in some strength. It would be folly for his weakened command to push on to Bastogne leaving this force poised behind their right wing.

His request was granted and the 134th relieved 80th Infantry's exhausted battalion during the night of December 28 and launched an attack the next day which put a battalion into Lutrebois by nightfall. As their sister regiment, the 137th, were already holding Villers-la-bonne-Eau, two miles south of Lutrebois, it looked like a model flanking screen but, unfortunately for the 35th Infantry Division, both these villages had been chosen as the first objectives of XXXIX Panzer Corps offensive to cut the Assenois Corridor from the east.

This new battlegroup had been formed out of the wreckage of the Leibstandarte, brought down from Sixth SS Panzer Army's front, and a division of infantry hurried from Hungary, the 167th Volksgrenadiers, a third of whom were hard-bitten veterans from the Eastern Front. To these were added the exhausted survivors of the original German troops who had tried to break into Bastogne from the east.

Three hours or so before dawn of December 30, General Karl Decker, the commander of the new Corps, launched two mixed assault forces from the Lutremange area. One soon turned right to strike for Lutrebois and the other left, for Villers-la-bonne-Eau.

Seven panzers, supported by armoured infantry, smashed into Villers-la-bonne-Eau overwhelming two companies of the 137th Infantry Regiment. Two hours before dawn more German tanks and armoured infantry hit Lutrebois from three directions but here the 134th Infantry had only seized the village themselves a few hours before and so were not caught napping. Fierce, confused fighting went on all day with the Americans calling in tanks, tank destroyers and fighter bombers as well as heavy artillery support. The Leibstandarte lost about thirty-five panzers and the panzer grenadiers took severe casualties but they pushed their assault forward and finally overwhelmed the 134th Infantry there, the third of 35th Division's companies to be lost, and recaptured Lutrebois. Both these villages were held against repeated American attacks until the general German withdrawal from the Ardennes.

4th Armored Division's CCA had inevitably been drawn into the heavy fighting on their right flank and their involvement had meant that CCB had had to side-step east to take over many CCA positions thus weakening the striking power of the division. 4th Armored had now been continually in action for nine days and had taken much punishment. The survivors were exhausted and there were only forty-two tanks left—it was obviously time for them to be relieved. 6th Armored Division, no longer needed on the Sauer river front, came in to take over the attempt to get into Bastogne from the south.

The three divisions of III Corps, launched confidently against 5th Panzer Army's left flank on December 22, had now fought themselves to a standstill and, except for a single, narrow corridor into Bastogne, were still south of a line through St Hubert–Bastogne–Wiltz–Diekirch–Wallendorf. This meant that most of the German lines of communication were open enabling them to build up and support, even at this late stage in their unsuccessful offensive, enough strength for one more major effort.

General Patton was noted for pushing his attacks forward without flank protection, a gamble which had often paid him well. In the past the German blitzkrieg tactics had also depended upon speed and depth of penetration to throw their enemy so off-balance he could not mount a counter-attack on the exposed flank and this had been tried again by Kampfgruppe Peiper whose ultimate defeat was due as much to having its rear cut by a flank attack as to the resistance encountered by its point. In Fifth Panzer Army's case although the forces allotted to protect the southern flank were woefully inadequate they had, by taking advantage of the ground and by fighting with great spirit, prevented the Third Army attack from reaching its objectives.

Now if General Manteuffel were not to have Bastogne but, on the contrary, were to be forced to give up ground then Third Army had to have fresh forces. SHAEF had two divisions in reserve on the continent, the 87th Infantry and the 11th Armored and a third, the 17th Airborne, on its way from England. Eisenhower was waiting to hear from Montgomery before committing them.

At his daily staff meeting on December 27 word came that the Field Marshal now had his counter-attack plan ready* and the Supreme Commander immediately went to Brussels to consider it. Montgomery had decided to commit British forces in some strength on First Army's right so that VII Corps could make the main thrust towards Vielsalm and Houffalize. For this attack General Simpson would have two armoured and three infantry divisions and his flanks would be protected by supporting attacks: on the south by British XXX Corps—a double advance, by paratroops and tanks on the right and an infantry division on the left—and on the north by the 82nd Airborne Division. The counter-attack was to jump off on January 3. Well pleased with the prospect of this powerful blow from First Army, Eisenhower telephoned Bradley releasing SHAEF's two reserve divisions to him.

Bradley immediately gave them to Patton but with the strict injunction that they were to be used only on his left. This was to ensure that the Third Army commander, with his fondness for the bold, dramatic gesture did not launch them towards the Rhine.

Both these divisions were newly arrived on the continent

* 'Praise God from Whom all blessings flow' was Eisenhower's immediate response.

although the 87th had been briefly blooded in the Saar before being pulled out on Christmas Eve and moved into reserve at Reims. The 11th Armored had no battle experience for their final training in England had been interrupted and they had been hurried to France to man the southern end of the Meuse.

Patton decided to attack immediately without waiting for First Army's coordinating attack from the north. He expected to have taken Houffalize before First Army's assault got really started. 11th Armored were ordered to move up immediately and they started an eighty-five mile move at two o'clock in the morning of Friday, December 29, and by four that afternoon had their advance guard in attack positions. The 87th Infantry were moved the one hundred miles from Reims on the same day and detrucked the following morning, December 30, moving off immediately to the attack.

Third Army's assault was to be made by Middleton's reconstructed VIII Corps, to which the new divisions had been given, as well as 9th Armored Division's CCA and the 101st Airborne with their attached troops in Bastogne. The tanks of 9th Armored, who had taken heavy losses in their drive towards Senonchamps, were to move on the right of the attack giving flank protection while the forces in Bastogne were to hold in position.

On the other side of the hill the Germans also planned an attack from west of Bastogne for December 30, which was once again designed to cut the Assenois Corridor by linking up with an attack from the south-east. This was to be followed up by the pushing back of the now evidently tiring III Corps divisions and, finally, the storming and capture of Bastogne.

The forces Manteuffel was able to scrape up for this blow consisted of the now weakened 3rd Panzer Grenadier Division with the Fuehrer Begleit Brigade attached. On the right of this attack the badly battered Panzer Lehr Division, down to about a dozen tanks, were to hold facing south and west while on the left the remnants of the shattered 26th Volksgrenadier Division and the battlegroup from 15th Panzer Grenadier Division, down to less than a battalion after their abortive attempt to break into Bastogne, were to close up on the retreating Americans.

The main punch of VIII Corps was to be made by a combat command of 11th Armored on the right, another in the centre and one regiment, the 345th, from 87th Infantry Division on the left. A second infantry regiment was to form a left wing blocking position around St Hubert while the third was held in reserve.

Once again the Americans enjoyed very strong artillery support—some ten battalions of field guns—and complete domination of the air. The attack started at dawn on December 30 with both the new divisions moving off into battle straight from their assembly areas. The infantry, 345th's First Battalion, arched along the axis of highway N26 towards the village of Pironpré on the St Hubert to Bastogne road. The advance guard drew light outpost fire from Moircy, about five miles from their start line, and the leading company bypassed this village leaving the following company to deal with it. But at Pironpré the Americans were met by heavy, accurate fire which halted them with many casualties and when the reserve company tried an outflanking movement they too were hit hard by tank guns and automatic fire. By dark the survivors of these two companies fell back to Moircy which had meanwhile been captured, but four or five hours after sunset a fierce German attack led by tanks firing tracers set many houses on fire and threw the green American infantry into confusion. Anti-tank guns were abandoned and because communications failed the order to pull out was received by only about half the men in Moircy.

But the Germans were not given the opportunity of capturing the infantry left behind for almost immediately 240-mm shells from the American artillery began bursting all around them and the panzers quickly pulled back. As soon as the bombardment stopped, the surviving First Battalion riflemen, who had been sheltering in the cellars, withdrew with their wounded. As the Germans had also taken theirs, only the dead from both sides were left in the broken and deserted village. For the 87th it had been a bitter, disappointing day which had cost them a hundred and thirty-two men for very little advance.

The 11th Armored, responding to the challenge of their first battle, launched their two combat commands towards the Germans without reconnaissance, choosing their routes from hastily issued maps. As these were without properly marked contour lines one task force selected a village in a hollow as their objective. The reinforced battalion of tanks, Task Force Poker, reached this without difficulty and, fortunately, the officer in command realized its complete unsuitability for tanks and pushed on to high ground near the village of Houmont. CCB's other attack was made by Task Force Pat, which consisted of armoured infantry in half-tracks led by a company of tanks. They also moved off as soon as they got to the start line but their leading reconnaissance had map-reading trouble and led the column in a circle back on to its own tail. By the time they had reorientated themselves and advanced again, their objective, Chenogne, had been covered from the west by Remer's panzers who knocked out seven of Task Force Pat's Shermans and stopped the advance.

As 11th Armored's CCA, attacking from the centre, had been stopped with over a hundred casualties by Panzer Lehr some four miles behind CCA's maximum penetration at Houmont, the end of the first day found 11th Armored Division with one battalion of tanks out in front without infantry protection and the rest of the division held not far from their start line.

But there were few illusions left on the German side despite their success in holding the American offensive west of Bastogne, for the writing on the wall was too clear to be misunderstood. Talking about this situation after the war Remer told Robert Merriam* 'The American forces were moving to the north of us, on the west and also on the east and I thought it was the end for my Fuehrer Begleit. I radioed Corps that we were fighting our last battle and they should send help.'

There was little that Luettwitz could do with his line stretched to breaking point. The Fuehrer Begleit Brigade were now under 3rd Panzer Grenadier Division who had been pinned down for most of the day by heavy, accurate artillery fire. Now in answer to Remer's cry for help, its commander, Major-General Denkert ordered troops to move into the ruins of Chenogne during the night in order to back up Fuehrer Begleit's panzers and stop 11th Armored's right-hand column, Task Force Pat, whose next objective he rightly guessed was Chenogne. At the same time he covered Remer's right flank from the threat of the tanks in Houmont (Task Force Poker) with 15th Panzer Grenadier's 115th Regiment, now only one-third strength.

On the American side, although the VIII Corps' attack had got off to a disappointing start General Middleton had no complaints about either the morale or fighting spirit of the new, untried divisions and he consented to a proposal that for the second day of the attack 11th Armored concentrate all three combat commands behind Task Force Poker at Houmont. This drawing in of the 11th Armored's right would add to 87th Infantry's task by giving them sole responsibility of breaking through Panzer Lehr but it offered the tanks the chance of exploiting their single penetration and advancing beyond the Bastogne–Marche highway to occupy the critical

* ETHINT 80.

439

positions of Mande St Etienne and Flamierge.

To help 87th Infantry's attack VIII Corps' artillery turned the full weight of its available batteries on Panzer Lehr but this crack formation, one of the best in the Ardennes, though now with only a handful of tanks, a shortage of ammunition and fuel, held steadily in position and not only stopped the strong infantry–tank attack which followed the bombardment but drove them back. The American 345th Infantry Regiment lost so many dead and wounded they had to be pulled out. The 347th then took over and grimly slogged forward for four days to seize Bonnerue and gain control of the St Hubert to Bastogne road.

The 11th Armored, too, had four days of fierce, costly fighting to push 3rd Panzer Grenadier Division and the Fuehrer Begleit Brigade back. Tremendous pounding by concentrated American artillery followed by fighter-bomber strikes were needed before the tanks could gain ground and even then the stubborn Germans broke up assault after assault and retook villages from which they had been ejected. In the end sheer numbers—of men, bullets, bombs and shells—told: on the fourth day twelve battalions of artillery fired three thousand eight hundred rounds on targets in front of 11th Armored's tanks—and Mande St Etienne was occupied and control of the Bastogne–Marche highway gained.

But it had been a terrible baptism for the young soldiers who had been snatched from their training in England and hurled straight into the fire of battle. They had acquitted themselves proudly and had gained six miles in four days, six very important miles at a critical moment in a great battle but the price they had paid had been a dear one: six hundred and sixty-one casualties and fifty-four tanks lost. Their place was taken over by yet another green division, the 17th Airborne, and they too were to count their dead and wounded in hundreds before the Germans gave up the ground they had seized.

As the last minutes of 1944 were ticking away and the fighting was blazing around Bastogne, Adolf Hitler, still believing that attack in the west would reap a great reward, increased his efforts by flinging most of what was left of the Luftwaffe in a reckless daylight strike at Allied airfields and launching Army Group G's First Army in a strong attack along some fifty miles of southern-facing front in Alsace. It was the opening of 'Nordwind' whose strategy was to maintain pressure against the western allies by keeping them off balance. Tactically First German Army was to drive hard south towards the Severne Gap to link up with attacks from the east by units from Army

Group Oberrhein thus cutting off American forces in Northern Alsace, endangering Strasbourg and routing the French forces surrounding the Colmar Pocket.

On New Year's Eve the crews of ten élite Luftwaffe formations were sworn to secrecy and told that they were to take off at dawn and, flying at ground level, attack a number of Allied airfields in northern France and Belgium with cannon, machine gun and light bombs. The intention was to put the Allied Air Force out of action for the few critical days of a renewed all-out attack at Bastogne and for 'Nordwind'.

Eleven hundred fighters—Focke-Wulf 190s and Messerschmitt 109s—were divided into three groups each of which was led by a navigating Junkers 188 to a different area. The targets were twenty-seven airfields crammed with rows of bombers and fighters and it was hoped that the pilots and ground staff would not be at their most alert at dawn after New Year's Eve.

Because so little had been seen of the Luftwaffe in recent days complete surprise was achieved in what the air force wryly named the Hangover Raid. In Holland the pilot of a tiny monoplane engaged in spotting for the artillery could hardly believe his eyes. 'At least two hundred Messerschmitts flying low on course 320 degrees!' he reported frantically. But before the startled operator at the receiving end could take action German planes were sweeping in low over the main airfield at Eindhoven and a Typhoon Wing and a Spitfire Wing were wiped out on the ground. At Brussels airport over a hundred aircraft were destroyed on the ground or while trying to take off. The Luftwaffe's total score on New Year's Day was over three hundred.*

It was a stunning blow and it did grant the Germans a brief respite from the attentions of the Allied Air Force but it was much briefer than they had expected. Three days later the OKW War Diary records one thousand US and four hundred and eighty British aircraft over Germany and this sort of figure was repeated on January 6 and 7. By then the Allies had replaced all their losses and the terrible, relentless bombing of Germany was stepped up to full scale again.

In exchange for a few days of decreased air activity the Luftwaffe had 'received its death blow'† for the raid had cost them over three hundred aircraft including the scarce nightfighters and the now ever scarcer trained pilots. If this sacrifice

* Including Montgomery's own Dakota which was immediately replaced by Eisenhower with the gift of his personal Flying Fortress.
† Lieutenant-General Adolf Galland.

had been made in order to bring back quickly as many men and as much matériel as possible from the Ardennes for the now inevitable battle for Germany itself it might have made some sort of sense but as Model and Manteuffel were ordered at the same time to go on attacking and to yield no ground Hitler's motive would seem to have been based on emotional rather than military reasons, something which was to become increasingly frequent in the final hours of the Nazi nightmare.

Operation Nordwind against General Devers' 6th Army Group came just as Eisenhower was trying once more to build up a Strategic Reserve, this time by withdrawing divisions from the comparatively quiet southern sector. At first he did not allow the German attack in Alsace to affect this decision and he ordered Devers to shorten his line by drawing his main forces back to the Vosges Mountains. This would mean giving up the city of Strasbourg and the decision was received with horror by the French—once again the Allied Supreme Commander had made the militarily correct but politically disastrous decision. Great pressure was brought to bear on him to change his orders and on January 3 he decided merely to swing 'Sixth Corps back from its sharp salient with its left resting in the Vosges and its right extending southward generally towards Strasbourg'.* The American forces were turned round in their tracks and sent back to Strasbourg which had been left practically undefended and General de Gaulle was content.†

Nordwind's right-hand thrust was stopped in two days but attacks on the German left were then stepped up and gains of twenty to thirty miles made in the next three weeks. It was not until SHAEF was able, after the Ardennes Battle, to release five divisions to 6th Army Group that this ground was won back again.

In the Ardennes three great attacks were launched on January 3: in the north Hodges' First Army attacked along a twenty-five-mile front; in the south Patton's Third Army tried once again to drive through to Houffalize and to clear Wiltz and the deadly hills from which the Germans had killed and wounded so many riflemen from the 80th and 26th Infantry Divisions; the third attack came from the Germans around Bastogne and it was the biggest and most determined attempt to capture the city and consolidate their gain.

The weather became even more appalling, with temperatures

* From a letter from Eisenhower to Marshall, January 6, 1945.
† The whole 'Strasbourg Affair' is dealt with in great detail in Jacques Nobécourt's *Le Dernier Coup de Dés d'Hitler*. Paris, 1962.

around zero Fahrenheit, ground fog, driving sleet and deep snow. For the first few days none of the attacks made anything but nominal progress and discouragement and pessimism spread through both sides and even the crack divisions faltered. On January 4 the US 6th Armored was routed in the worst day of the war for them and the green 17th Airborne Division, in their first action, advanced into a holocaust—some battalions incurred forty per cent casualties—and that night even the great-hearted Patton was moved to write in his diary, 'We can still lose this war.'

North of Bastogne First Army's main assault, made by VII Corps, had its flanks secured by coinciding attacks. On the right the British XXX Corps pushed forward two prongs, tanks and paratroops on the right and infantry on the left. The extreme right-hand probe was made by Brigadier Harvey's 29th Armoured Brigade of three regiments of tanks (some hundred and sixty) reinforced by two battalions of the 6th Airborne Division who had been alerted in England before Christmas and hurried to the Ardennes. Now they, together with the tanks of the Fife and Forfar Yeomanry, were to attack towards the German defence line facing north-west along a high ridge some eight miles from St Hubert.

The XXX Corps' other attack alongside VII Corps was to be made by the 53rd Welsh Division to secure crossings of the Ourthe and to cut the road from Rochefort to St Hubert which it was essential for the Germans to keep open in order to maintain the integrity of their shrinking front as forces were pulled in for the attack on Bastogne.

The left flank of VII Corps would be screened by an attack by 82nd Airborne Division towards Vielsalm and Salmchâteau. Later the rest of First Army as far as Malmédy would join in pressing back the bulge.

On First Army's right the Germans had built a defence line of dug-in tanks and guns supported by machine guns along high ground from Forriere to Bure. The only approach was along the valley of the Lesse and the German guns covered every road. A battalion of 6th Airborne supported by a squadron of Fife and Forfar's tanks were sent against Bure and a similar force against Wavreille, a fortified crossroads village south-west of the German right anchor position at Forriere.

It was a bitter, costly assault which went on for six days and cost thirteen tanks and a hundred and eighty-nine parachutists. One paratroop company was reduced to an officer and twenty men on the first day. Bure was declared 'clear of the enemy' three times but each time the Germans counter-attacked and regained part of it. On one occasion a British ambulance drove forward to tend to the many wounded lying in the snow and a German tank, probably a Mk V of Panzer Lehr, moved up alongside, its long gun looming over the driver. 'Take away your casualties this time, Tommy,' the commander said in English, 'but do not come forward again—it is not safe.' It was a gesture which once again underlined the difference between the Wehrmacht and the SS.

On 29th Armoured Brigade's left—between them and VII Corps—first the 53rd Welsh Division and later the 51st Highland Division attacked through the deep snow and, after a slow start, these veteran troops made dogged progress in the shocking conditions to capture La Roche and Mierchamps in eight days. On that same day, January 11, patrols from 6th Airborne made contact with 87th Infantry in St Hubert, the first link-up at the front line between 21st Army Group and 12th Army Group since the Ardennes Offensive had split them apart.

The main First Army attack by Collins' VII Corps was made at dawn on January 3, by 2nd Armored Division on the right and 3rd Armored on the left. Each carried a regiment of infantry on the tanks* with the rest of an infantry division following to exploit a breakthrough. The general objective was the sector of the German line from Vielsalm to Houffalize held by three panzer divisions and volksgrenadiers division who were dug in in good defensive positions and helped by the deep snow and icy roads. The going was extraordinarily difficult and after a week First Army had covered only half the distance to Houffalize. On the other side of the bulge Patton's Third Army had needed the same time to halt the last all-out German offensive against Bastogne.

The attack of 82nd Airborne Division on VII Corps' left reached the outskirts of Vielsalm and Salmchâteau at the end of five days fighting opening the way for the road back to St Vith. All these successes forced Hitler to realize something of the strength the Allies were now employing in the Ardennes and on January 8 he ordered the forward units to fall back to a line running south from Dochamps, in the Samree–Baraque de Fraiture area, to Longchamps, five miles north of Bastogne. Even more significant were OKW's orders for the SS Panzer Divisions who were still on the northern end of the Ardennes front to go over to the defensive. The Ardennes was quietly dropped by the German propaganda machine and new panzers

* The 345th Regiment (84th Division) rode with 2nd Armored and the 330th (83rd Division) with 3rd Armored.

coming off the assembly line were diverted to the Eastern Front.* These actions did not surprise the German commanders in the Ardennes who had known for some time that their offensive had failed. On January 3 Field Marshal von Rundstedt, as ever the realist, informed his commanders that there was no prospect for the success of the Ardennes attack as planned. The only sensible thing to do was to save what they could of the men and matériel still left—but that depended on Hitler.

It was during these first days of 1945 when the Allies were taking some of their severest casualties and progress seemed tragically slow that Churchill and Field Marshal Brooke, the Chief of the Imperial General Staff, visited the front. Not surprisingly they were shocked and disturbed by what they saw and heard. On January 6th Churchill wrote to Roosevelt plainly expressing his concern.

As well as the extra quarter of a million troops he had recently promised he now undertook to bring into or nearer the front line 'a number of infantry brigades including several from the Marines'. He reinforced SHAEF's pleas for replacements for the heavy losses incurred by the infantry divisions. 'I am deeply impressed with the need of sustaining the Foot, who bear two-third of the losses but are very often the last to receive reinforcements ... there is this brute fact, Mr President: we need more fighting troops to make things move. I have a feeling that this is a time for an intense new impulse, both of friendship and exertion, to be drawn from our bosoms and to the last scrap of our resources. Do not hesitate to tell me of anything you think we can do.'

The long run of Allied successes and the tremendous preponderance of American strength in Europe had tended to eclipse Churchill's personal participation in the war, a situation which he was not by nature equipped to accept with resignation, and the reverse in the Ardennes acted on him, as reverses always did, as a stimulant to action. Thinking, as he so often did, globally, he saw that a certain way to deal the knockout blow in the Ardennes was to force the Germans to turn their attention to the Eastern Front and he got Eisenhower's permission to write personally to Marshal Stalin.

This letter was written on the same day as the one to President Roosevelt and it reflected the same mood of pessimism. Its results on the post-war world were to be immense.

'The battle in the West is very heavy...' Churchill wrote, ... You know yourself from your own experience how very

* On January 9 Guderian warned Hitler that the Eastern Front 'is like a house of cards'.

anxious the position is when a very broad front has to be defended after the temporary loss of the initiative ... I shall be grateful if you can tell me whether we can count on a major Russian offensive during January. I regard the matter as urgent.'

Stalin replied immediately pointing out that their planned offensive had been held up by the weather—good visibility being essential—'nevertheless, taking into account the position of our Allies on the Western Front, GHQ of the Supreme Command has decided to accelerate the completion of our preparation and, regardless of the weather, to commence large-scale offensive operations against the Germans along the whole Central Front not later than the second half of January.'

Six days after this, fourteen Russian infantry divisions and two independent tank corps advanced across the Upper Vistula, the opening, eight days early, of the great offensive which was to put the Russians in so favourable a bargaining position at Yalta, invitations to which Stalin sent out three days after receiving Churchill's call for help.

The results of the offensive in the east were immediately felt in the west. Hitler had already withdrawn Sixth Panzer Army into reserve under his personal command and called the remnants of the Leibstandarte back from Bastogne. Both the First and Third Armies found there was a distinct falling off in the strength of the German resistance. Wiltz finally fell to the fresh troops of the 90th Infantry Division, who had relieved the badly damaged 26th, and right round the other side of the bulge, the surviving 106th Infantry regiment crossed the river at Stavelot and struck south at the same time as the 30th Infantry Division attacked from Malmédy. Middleton's VIII Corps and Simpson's VII Corps launched attacks designed to meet at Houffalize and by January 15 the 2nd Armored Division and its attached 84th Infantry reached Achouffe three-and-a-half miles north-west of the objective. The nearest 3rd Army were some of 11th Armored Division ten miles south but Patton was determined not to let Montgomery's troops beat him to Houffalize and, disregarding his resolve not to hazard armour at night again, he ordered a force of sixty vehicles of all types to push through the woods in the dark.

It was a reckless move and it was not made for sound military reasons but for prestige. The men in the column, well knowing they would be at the mercy of any determined Germans lying in wait with bazookas, cursed and repeated their often-heard complaint about their general—'Old Blood'n'Guts—yeah, our blood and his guts!' But yet again General Patton's remarkable luck held, for not a single German soldier was encountered. Dawn found the little force nine miles ahead of the rest of the Third Army and only a mile or so from Houffalize.

It was January 16, 1945, exactly a month after the quiet Ardennes front had burst into flames, and at nine o'clock that morning the 11th Armored patrol joined hands with 2nd Armored's infantry in Houffalize. From then on the Germans could no longer have any offensive intentions inside their bulge but would have to concentrate on saving what they could from the disaster.

As Hitler's 'Wacht am Rhein' moved towards its Götter-dämmerung-like ending in freezing, stormy weather there was a distinct change of mood on both sides. The German soldiers who had only recently been carried forward by the elation of renewed success and had allowed themselves to dream of victory now knew that it had only been a dream and that the nightmare was about to begin.

Some divisions had been reduced to twenty to thirty men per company; many guns were being sent back because there was no ammunition for them; there was a paralysing shortage of fuel, rations and medical supplies and the 'damned Jabos' seemed to be able to find and destroy every supply column that tried to bring some up. Hundreds of panzers, self-propelled guns, artillery pieces, mortars and multi-barrelled rocket launchers, soon to be desperately needed to defend the Fatherland, lay broken in the snow of the Ardennes.

Wearily the German soldiers realized that it was the end, and the enormity of their defeat added to their misery and despair.

On the American side the survivors of the positions on whom the storm had first burst, of the units thrown in to stem the German advance, of the forces sacrificed to buy time and of the divisions broken by the fierce fighting of the counter-offensive, paused and thought of those they had known so well—sometimes from enlistment—who were now missing or wounded or dead. They remembered the moments of shame—the equipment abandoned in panic, the unreasoning flight, the terror of bursting shells, screaming mortars and the cries of dying men, the nagging presence of unfamiliar defeat. But they remembered too the moments of defiance, of taking casualties and hitting back and the acts of heroism which had retrieved everybody's self-respect.

Now as their units were being re-equipped and brought up to strength and they looked at the unfamiliar faces of the new men steeling themselves for their first battle and they heard the almost continual sound of the big guns mercilessly shelling the Germans and saw the planes confidently dominating the sky they slowly realized that, after all, it was going to be all right. The Germans were going to be defeated and not only in their Ardennes adventure but in their whole mad attempt to dominate the world.

Few imagined that the victory would be quick or easy. The soldiers opposite them may be outnumbered, outgunned, without air support and short of all the matériel of war but they were not surrendering, not yet even retreating and when they attacked they struck hard. They had been misguided and misled but they were brave men who were about to fight in their native land and who were convinced that neither they nor their families would be shown any mercy by their conquerors —whether they came from the east or the west.

Germany had lost the war but many more lives were going to be lost, many young men maimed, before the German people would be forced to accept the hopelessness of 'unconditional surrender'.

29

A SUMMING UP

> *It would have been a brilliant brain-wave* if *Hitler had still possessed the forces and resources to give it a fair chance of success in the end.*
>
> SIR BASIL LIDDELL HART:
> *The Other Side of the Hill*

The great gamble to split the Western Allies by ramming two panzer armies through the Ardennes to Antwerp was Warlord Hitler's last great offensive for, after the loss of his mobile reserve, some hundreds of tanks and self-propelled guns and the virtual destruction of the Luftwaffe who lost more than a thousand aircraft, he was never again able to seize the initiative on a strategic level.

In the hundred days left between the failure of his offensive and his suicide amid the ruins of Berlin all Hitler's War Directives were concerned with defence and, although he kept the puppet-master's strings firmly in his grasp he confined himself to forbidding any retreat and to vetoing his generals' proposals for tactical regrouping, saying that he saw no point in transferring catastrophe from one place to another. The disastrous result of what he had expected to be a dazzling master-stroke drained his confidence and turned him from hunter to hunted —a fatal change for a would-be world conqueror.

By the end of January 1945 the Germans were back to where they had launched the attack six weeks earlier. On their left Nordwind's divisions had been brought to a stop everywhere and their commanders knew that it was only a matter of time before an Allied counter-attack would force them back into Germany. On both these fronts German casualties in men and matériel had been very heavy, as had Allied (at the time each side claimed to have inflicted about double its own casualties on the other; as far as can now be determined the score was about equal) but the Germans could no longer replace their losses while the Allies could and did.

The odds in the west swung even more in favour of the Allies when the Germans were forced to switch divisions back to the Eastern Front in a frantic effort to counter the tremendous blows from the roused and angry Russian giant.* Already

* For the attack on the middle Vistula sector in the Warsaw–Berlin direction the 1st Belorussian and 1st Ukrainian Fronts had

on the defensive all along the western front the Germans now hurriedly withdrew behind their West Wall.

All this meant that there was little chance of a major German offensive in the west* and SHAEF was able to give the go-ahead for the final campaign to clear the area west of the Rhine, to cross the Rhine and to advance eastward into Germany, without having to allow for the logical German riposte —a strong flank attack against the main penetration. Seventeen German divisions in Scandinavia were a background threat but there was no sign of their being brought into battle yet.

Bradley got back his First Army at midnight on January 17, and allowed Hodges to push for Cologne; Devers, reinforced with five divisions, regained the initiative in the south, though not without heavy casualties; in the 12th Army Group centre Patton started his Third Army crashing through the Eifel towards the Rhine and Montgomery, who had succeeded in keeping US Ninth Army,† launched the Battle of the Rhineland: it was the beginning of the end for the Germans on the Western Front.

The utter failure of Hitler's great offensive left Germany at the mercy of her attackers. Was Hitler's decision to hazard all on a surprise attack against a fundamentally stronger opponent justified? Did Germany gain any advantages for her costly sacrifice?

I think the answer to both these questions is a qualified 'yes' although it is hard when an enterprise has failed to assess with any degree of accuracy what it might have accomplished. However, we can make a reasonable guess at what might have been and we can look at the balance sheet to see whether the gamble brought any advantages to set against the ultimate loss.

In judging the merits of the decision to concentrate all available strength on a drive for Antwerp we should consider the

---

one hundred and sixty-three divisions, 32,143 guns and mortars and four thousand seven hundred and seventy-two aircraft. In manpower this was some fifty thousand more than the Allies had on the Western Front—and there were three more Russian armies waiting to join the offensive.

* 'G.I.G.S. does not think that Rundstedt is capable of mounting another counteroffensive on the scale of his December thrust. The chances of anything really worrying even on a smaller scale have grown much less as the result of the start of the Russian winter offensive.'

From a letter from the Director of Military Operations to Field Marshal Montgomery sent January 15, 1945.

† As had been agreed between him and Eisenhower before the Ardennes Offensive.

alternatives. The first choice was between attack and what Hitler called the 'barren rot of defence'. If all the German forces had been pulled back to form a 'national redoubt' in an easily defended part of the country the only result would have been to postpone defeat: the abandoned territory would have been quickly occupied and the combined Allied air forces would have been free to concentrate their bombs on the defended area. Supplies would have been cut off, stocks destroyed and many more Germans killed. The final result, though postponed and though with heavier Allied casualties, would still have been unconditional surrender. Although having a certain emotional appeal the alternative of a last-ditch stand with no hope of victory was never a practical proposition.

The second alternative of course was to acknowleege defeat and surrender and this is what the professional soldiers would have chosen had they been in control. Logically this was the best decision, for victory for Germany was impossible after September 1944. But Adolf Hitler was not logical and, as we have seen, his will still prevailed.

The third alternative was to launch an offensive elsewhere and this was seriously considered. The decision to attack in the west instead of the east was largely influenced by the estimated destructive power of the force it was possible to assemble which was thought to be, if everything went favourably, the elimination of some thirty divisions. Such a loss would have made little or no difference to the Russians but it represented one third of the Western Allies' invasion army.* There was also no strategic objective on the Eastern Front, no 'opposite pole', whereas the port of Antwerp was just such an objective. Finally Hitler underrated the Americans as soldiers, being convinced that they would crumble if hit hard enough.

Once the Eastern Front had been ruled out the only other place was Italy, but there the railway connections were quite inadequate to carry the five hundred train loads needed and Allied air reconnaissance would have detected road movements of such dimensions and the essential element of surprise would have been lost.

It had to be the Western Front then. But was the objective—the splitting of the Allies and the capture of Antwerp—too grandiose? Would Model's and Manteuffel's 'small solution' have been better? I think not, for an attack to wipe out the American Aachen salient would have run head on into maxi-

* As it turned out Army Group B destroyed two American divisions and badly damaged another fifteen.

451

mum Allied strength, could not have been a surprise and, had it succeeded, would have resulted in no more than a change in the shape of the front, a temporary setback to the Western Allies.

If, on the other hand, Sixth Panzer Army had succeeded in capturing Antwerp it could have changed the situation completely.

After the war Field Marshal Jodl was asked what Germany's future offensive plans would then have been. He replied: 'Because a larger force would have been necessary we would have taken more reserves from the entire front. We calculated that the Allies would be incapable of launching an attack in any other sector of the front. We would have moved troops from every Army sector and initiated concentric attacks against Aachen from Monschau, Maastricht and Holland. With their supply lines cut we would crush your forces in the Aachen pocket. This was the only method which seemed promising. We could defeat those strong forces only by cutting off their supplies.

'Had we taken Antwerp the situation would have been difficult for the Allies. It is hard to say whether we could have destroyed the forces in the pocket or whether you, using your entire air force, could have supplied them by air. In any event it would have made a terrific impression on political, military and public opinion.'

Given that there was no alternative to unconditional surrender and that this was not yet acceptable, then Hitler's decision to seize the initiative with a great offensive was the right one for Germany. The sector chosen was the right one and the objective, as difficult of achievement as it was, could not have been less and still have justified the hazarding of the forces collected with such difficulty. Hitler made many wrong military decisions, particularly during the last years of the war, but the Ardennes Offensive was not one of them.

Nevertheless the offensive failed and six weeks later Germany was once again awaiting the Allied onslaught in the west, but now was not only without reserves on that front but fully committed in a great battle on the Eastern Front as well. What then had the Ardennes Offensive accomplished—if anything?

First, on the German credit side, the initiative was wrested from the Allies whose long-planned final offensive had to be postponed for five weeks; second, serious damage was inflicted on the Allied war machine at a critical moment; third, Eisenhower's already unhappy command structure was further weakened, for even if Hitler's expectations of a rupture beween the British and American commands did not take place, the command changes, the quarrels and recriminations which came with the battle had lasting, adverse effects on SHAEF's efforts to prosecute the war with singleness of purpose.

On the other hand none of these German gains had a decisive effect: the time lost was largely made up by the subsequent German weakness; although the Allied war machine was damaged by heavy losses of men and matériel it was not put out of action or even seriously crippled; Allied supreme command continued to function.

But at the end of January 1945, although they knew that their great offensive had been a failure, the German High Command believed that it had brought them certain substantial advantages. 'From the information on hand it can be seen that the enemy has employed practically all troops available to him and that several could be regarded as unfit for battle for a long time,' was how the German War Diary put it. Other advantages were that two crack American airborne divisions had been used up as infantry, the Allies had been knocked off balance and had suffered such severe losses in men and matériel they would not be able to mount a major offensive for some considerable time.

Allied casualties were indeed grievously heavy. It is impossible now to give a statistically accurate figure because many records were lost or destroyed and only a few of those that did survive separate the period of the Ardennes fighting from what occurred before and after.

Contemporary records listed an exceptionally large number of men as missing. This was due to the early confusion and the fluidity of the battle and many of those so listed later rejoined their units or turned up in hospital. Others were confirmed as prisoners or as killed. The best estimates that can be made now from comparing the various official American figures for different formations over differing and sometimes overlapping dates indicate that the Americans lost not less than a hundred and forty thousand men from all causes and that some sixteen thousand of these were killed. These figures are from December 16, 1944, to January 25, 1945, and include the losses incurred in stopping Nordwind as well as in driving Army Group B back behind the West Wall. British casualties in the Ardennes were about one thousand five hundred of which two hundred were killed.*

* In the action before Dinant British casualties were remarkably light and the forces committed in First Army's counter-attack were withdrawn about January 13 for the opening of the Rhineland battle.

The Germans also virtually destroyed two American infantry divisions and badly mauled nine of the remaining fourteen involved in the Ardennes. All eight of the American armoured divisions which took part lost heavily and five of them were eliminated, at least temporarily, as attacking forces. All three airborne divisions could not be used in their proper rôle for some time afterwards.

The already acute shortage of infantrymen in the American army was made worse and losses of highly-trained specialists such as combat engineers, artillery technicians, army aircraft personnel, signals, medical, maintenance and supply men seriously lessened the ability of the Americans to mount a broad front advance into Germany at full strength. In terms of effective manpower the Ardennes Offensive reduced the Western Allies by ten per cent.

It was not enough.

But losses of arms and equipment were also very heavy: more than one thousand tanks. five hundred aircraft and thousands of rifles, machine guns, mortars and artillery pieces up to the largest calibre in the six weeks Ardennes and Alsace battles. Over a million and a quarter rounds of artillery and several million rounds of small-arms ammunition were fired off. Thousands of vehicles of all types were lost and enormous quantities of fuel consumed. Allied losses in tanks, guns and other war matériel were between fifteen and twenty-five per cent of what they had been holding in Europe on December 16.

This, too, was not enough.

By January 1945 the tremendous industrial complex of the United States was geared to war production and tanks, guns, aircraft and vehicles of all types came continuously off the conveyor belts matched by shells, bombs and bullets from the factories. It was production such as would not have been thought possible only a few years before. The tremendous problems of getting these enormous quantities to the scene of battle as quickly as possible were solved by a mixture of American experience in moving large, unwieldy goods over great distances and the acceptance of wastage on a scale which would have bankrupted any other economy.

Although the Americans fired four times as many shells and used six times the amount of fuel and lost more tanks, guns and vehicles than the total number the Germans had been able to collect for their offensive, they were able to make all this good within *two weeks*. The reserves piled for the Roer and Saar offensives were fed to the divisions in action and supply ships were hurried forward to fill the dumps again.

Shortly after receiving news of the big German offensive the Joint Chiefs of Staff moved up the sailing dates of seven divisions and diverted two more, not originally intended for the European theatre, to February sailings. This flood of men and matériel saw the Allies with more men, more tanks, more aircraft, more guns—in fact more of everything—two weeks after the offensive than when it began. The weight of the American supply tail, so often criticised by her Allies, paid off in the Ardennes.

The costly, hard-fought victory in one way strengthened the American divisions who fought the battle, for their losses were replaced and the survivors knew that they had withstood the most powerful assault the Germans could mount and in the end had been able to drive them back. Together with a healthy respect for their opponents came the knowledge that they could be and would be defeated.

For the Germans on the other hand the result of the battle was a disaster both in material terms and in its effect on morale. Their losses could not be made up and those Germans who had been deluded into believing in the possibility of victory now knew that defeat could only be delayed.

German losses in the west from December 16 to January 25 are even more difficult to ascertain—particularly for the last two weeks, after the opening of the Russian Offensive which inflicted casualties in numbers that dwarfed the losses in the west. Up to then and, therefore, not including the casualties incurred during the retreat from the Ardennes back behind the West Wall (a very well-conducted operation in which the Germans lost far fewer than might have been expected), Army Group B had at least thirteen thousand killed, forty thousand wounded and over thirty thousand taken prisoner. In the last two weeks the Germans lost about half as many again, most of whom fell in the Nordwind battle.

Although there are no reliable overall figures a number of divisional commanders have made their own estimates of their losses and these are from two to three thousand per division. 'Sepp' Dietrich said: 'I lost 37,000 men killed, wounded and frozen.' This is probably a fairly accurate estimate and does not include the heavy losses of the volksgrenadier divisions on his right who broke themselves on the Monschau–Höfen defences. Divisions who came into the battle later were often reduced by half within days. The 9th Panzer Division made its first attack on Christmas night when it had some ninety tanks and thirty-five self-propelled guns. Four days later its panzer

455

regiment was left with twenty tanks and the two panzer grenadier regiments each had about four hundred men. The average strength of the 212th Volksgrenadier's rifle companies falling back across the Sauer was twenty-five to thirty men. General Kraemer, 'Sepp' Dietrich's Chief of Staff, said that when the 560th Volksgrenadier Division was taken into Sixth SS Panzer Army after the fighting for Hotton and Marche 'it was reduced to almost nothing'. Many of the German divisions in the battle were so badly torn up they had to be almost completely rebuilt before they could be used again.

Total German casualties in the Ardennes and Nordwind Offensives were not less than one hundred and thirty thousand of which some nineteen thousand were killed. It was now no longer possible to make up losses of this order; 'Sepp' Dietrich, taking his army towards Budapest after the Ardennes, received twenty-two thousand replacements for the thirty-seven thousand he had lost—and his SS Panzer divisions still had priority over all others.

German losses of weapons and equipment were also very heavy. 'Sepp' Dietrich admitted losing three to four hundred tanks and twenty-five to thirty per cent of all his ammunition and fuel-carrying vehicles. On his way east he dropped off a thousand vehicles for repairs. The Fifth Panzer Army lost over two hundred tanks and much other equipment. German matériel losses, though not so heavy as Allied, were more serious because they were irreplaceable.

The third advantage gained by Germany from the offensive was the damage to the Allied command structure. Relations had already been strained between Eisenhower and Montgomery, Bradley and Montgomery, Eisenhower and Patton and between Third Army's staff and SHAEF. During the course of the Ardennes fighting certain events occurred which upset these relationships even more. Some just caused irritation but the one which nearly caused a major rupture was undoubtedly the press conference called by Montgomery on January 7, the day after the release of the story of Eisenhower having placed him in command of the northern half of the battle.

Montgomery's relations with the military correspondents were never very happy. One of the main reasons was that he underrated their abilities and the extent of their technical knowledge, assuming that because they wrote in a simplified way for non-military readers (for example the name they gave to the von Rundstedt Offensive, 'The Battle of the Bulge'—any partly successful offensive produces a salient and there were already two such 'bulges') that they themselves had to be spoken to in such terms. This oversimplification made accurate reporting most difficult.

Now, addressing a large number of press and radio correspondents at his headquarters, he wanted 'to explain how during the Battle of the Ardennes, the whole Allied team, throwing national considerations overboard, had rallied to the call and how Allied solidarity had saved the situation'.* This wholly admirable motive was defeated however when the Field Marshal found himself in one of his best-loved rôles—expounding in simple terms to a captive audience just how he had been able to win a difficult battle.

In his memoirs Montgomery gives the full text of the notes from which he spoke and there is nò denying that he called for full support for Eisenhower as the 'Captain of the Team' and paid handsome tribute to the fighting qualities of the American soldier, saying, 'I have tried to feel that I am almost an American soldier myself so that I might take no unsuitable action or offend them in any way.' He finished with an earnest plea for 'team-work'.

Nevertheless he did offend the American soldiers deeply by implying that he had practically single-handedly brought order out of chaos and that it had been British troops who had saved the situation. And unfortunately in putting the case for team-work he seemed to be saying that Eisenhower should be supported only because he *was* the 'captain of the team' and not because of the quality of his leadership—which may well have been what he felt but should not have revealed at so sensitive a time.

After describing how the Germans had split the American forces in two he told of his own actions before being given command: 'As soon as I saw what was happening I took certain steps myself to ensure that if the Germans got to the Meuse they would certainly not get over that river.'

Let us examine that claim.

Montgomery's first action was on December 19, the fourth day of the offensive, when the immediately available troops—Tank Replacement Centre personnel in Brussels, some headquarters staff and detachments of Special Air Service troops, were sent to the Meuse crossings between Namur and Givet. They arrived on December 20 and on that day, 29th Armoured Brigade, of three tank regiments (about one hundred and sixty tanks) and a motorized reconnaissance battalion, was moved

* Montgomery's words in a private telegram to Winston Churchill. (Quoted by Arthur Bryant in *Triumph in the West*.)

from north-west Belgium to take over from this scratch force the awesome task of holding twenty-five miles of the Meuse against a panzer army. The entire British force had rather fewer tanks and less artillery support than an American armoured division.

Montgomery covered the Meuse crossings from Namur to Liège by moving one armoured and three infantry divisions into a blocking position some twenty-five miles north-west. Both these forces were in position by the night of Thursday, December 21.

Thus, after six days' battle, a thin line of British tanks and guns held the Meuse crossings towards which Fifth Panzer Army's three armoured divisions were thrusting while the crossings which were the objective of Sixth SS Panzer Army's four armoured divisions were practically defenceless and the nearest serious opposition was the XXX Corps screen half way between the Meuse and Antwerp.

But on the German schedule two fresh SS Panzer Divisions should have been across the Meuse south of Liège at the latest during the night of December 19/20 with Fifth Panzer Army's tanks on their left already across the Sambre. Had the Americans not held the Elsenborn ridge and St Vith or had Battle-group Peiper been able to cross the Amblève or Fifth Panzer Army not been delayed at the Our and at the Clerf and around Bastogne, the problem of guarding the Meuse crossings would have been academic.

Montgomery's statement to the press continued: 'General Eisenhower placed me in command of the whole Northern Front. I employed the whole available power of the British Group of Armies ... and finally it was put into battle with a bang and today British divisions are fighting hard on the right flank of First US Army.'

The key phrase here is 'whole available power' which the reporters present naturally assumed to be a considerable force. At the time the Field Marshal was speaking, one British infantry division, two battalions of paratroops and two tank regiments* were fighting as flank guard of First Army's main attack and a second British infantry division and a third regiment of tanks were in reserve in the same area. All these troops fought well, suffered casualties and reached their objectives and were only withdrawn after ten days because the contraction of the German line squeezed them out. But the chief burden of the Allied counter-attack which pushed the

_____
* At that time a British tank regiment was about three-quarters the size of an American combat command.

German Offensive back was carried by two powerful American forces—four divisions from First US Army and five from Third US Army and these attacks were later joined by eleven more divisions at other places around the salient.

The difference in casualty figures is a fair indication of the relative strength involved: when Montgomery was talking to the press the American dead in the Ardennes were over eight thousand, the British less than two hundred. A few days later Churchill in the House of Commons tried to undo some of the damage that had been done to Anglo-American relations: 'Care must be taken in telling our proud tale not to claim for the British army an undue share of what is undoubtedly the greatest American battle of the war and will, I believe, be regarded as an ever-famous American victory.' His displeasure was made even more plain in a final, growled sentence: 'Let no one lend himself to the chatter of mischief-makers when issues of this momentous consequence are being successfully decided by the sword.'

To most of the reporters present the implications of Montgomery's remarks were that the Americans had been on the verge of defeat and had been saved by his superior generalship and large-scale intervention of British troops. British newspapers renewed demands that he be appointed over-all land forces commander and the Germans intercepted the BBC correspondent's despatch, doctored it skilfully and rebroadcast it as a BBC transmission. This clever bit of propaganda bait was swallowed whole at Bradley's and Patton's headquarters.

Not surprisingly, they and their staffs were furious that the news release which revealed that two American armies had been under Montgomery's command for seventeen critical days had been followed so quickly by a statement from him which obviously strengthened his claim to command their armies and which had not been cleared with SHAEF.

Bradley issued his own statement—also not cleared with SHAEF—angrily making it clear that the change had been purely temporary and Eisenhower once more found himself with a major command row on his hands. Only the week before the tense situation had come to a head when Eisenhower decided to make a resignation issue of Montgomery's demands for greater power. De Guingand had impressed Montgomery with the brutal fact that if the crunch came it would be he who would be forced to resign and the Field Marshal had sent a 'most immediate' signal unreservedly withdrawing all his demands. Eisenhower had thought that the land forces commander problem was solved but now the press had revived it.

He dealt sharply with Bradley's threatened resignation and confirmed that as soon as the northern and southern counter-attacks met, First Army would be returned to him. He made it quite clear that there was no question of his giving up any of his powers of Supreme Commander to anyone or of altering his broad front strategy.

But the damage was irreparable. Relations between Montgomery and Bradley were spoiled permanently and this in turn was responsible for a rivalry between their armies which had the effect of actually slowing down the advance into Germany in the closing phase of the war.

Montgomery's motive in setting the British press off on a line which could only worsen relations between him and the American generals will always remain an enigma. It has been said of him by no less an authority than General de Guingand, who served him with unswerving loyalty and admiration, that 'when he was convinced himself that a particular course is right he feels justified in bringing all influences to bear in order to win his point; in fact the end justifies *almost any means*'. (My italics.)

Here perhaps is the key not only to the press conference but to certain statements and actions of Montgomery's during the period of confusion which the success of the sudden German onslaught created. Eisenhower and Bradley, caught badly off balance, were temporarily unable to fix and control the fluid front, largely because of communications failure. At the best, dismay, and at the worst, panic, was found at all levels. German successes were overestimated and the full significance of the American defences which held for those all-important opening days was not appreciated.

At this moment when morale was at its lowest and the American command at the top might be thought to be vulnerable to pressure Montgomery brought all influences to bear to win his points—first, command of all forces north of the Ardennes and, later, to have Bradley's Army Group put under his command.

Convinced that only in this way could the war be won more quickly he painted the picture blacker than it was in order to enlist the wholehearted support of Field Marshal Brooke, the CIGS, and of Winston Churchill.

During the evening of December 19, before the telephone call from Eisenhower which told him that he had won his first point, Montgomery sent Brooke a long telegraphed situation report. This began: 'Situation in American area is not—repeat not—good . . .' and then went on to say that the Germans had captured Malmédy, Vielsalm, Hotton, Marche and La Roche and that 'in that part of First Army north of Line Udenbreth to Durbuy there is great confusion and all signs of a full-scale withdrawal ... Bradley is still at Luxembourg but I understand that he is moving as his Headquarters are in danger ... My own opinion is that ... The Germans can reach the Meuse at Namur without any opposition.'

There are a surprisingly large number of errors in this top-level report. At the time all five towns were in American hands; La Roche was abandoned two nights later as part of the withdrawal to create VII Corps' defence line and Vielsalm fell five nights later, after St Vith, but the other three towns were never captured by the Germans although as far as Malmédy is concerned it is only fair to point out that the British press reported its fall, the American army publication, *Stars and Stripes*, printed a map showing it in German hands and in Eisenhower's *Crusade in Europe* the Ardennes Battle map also awards it to the Germans.

The line north of which Montgomery saw a full-scale withdrawal taking place included the anchor position of Monschau and the Elsenborn ridge, the key communications network of St Vith; Stavelot which the Americans had just recaptured and which, with Trois Ponts and Stoumont, enclosed Battlegroup Peiper; and 82nd Airborne's sector.

Nearest German troops were fifteen miles from Luxembourg and Bradley had no intention of moving his headquarters.

Montgomery's opinion that the Germans could reach the Meuse at Namur 'without any opposition' could only have referred to the threat offered by the spearhead of 1st SS Panzer Division, Battlegroup Peiper, for the 116th Panzer, which would eventually attack Hotton, had just been turned back at the Bertogne bridge and were retracing their steps through Houffalize, twenty miles away and the other divisions heading for the Meuse, 2nd Panzer and Panzer Lehr, were still fighting near Bastogne.

Peiper's force had been diverted by the Americans holding Trois Ponts, had been cut off by the American recapture of Stavelot and had been stopped at Stoumont which was forty miles from Namur and over thirty from the Meuse crossing he was aiming for, Huy.

After this loud sounding of the alarm bell, Montgomery, like the tough fighter he is, went over to the attack: 'I have told Whiteley that Ike ought to place me in operational command of all troops on the northern half of the front. *I consider he should be given a direct order by some to do so.*' (My italics.)

This telegram produced the effect intended: the CIGS sent a copy to Churchill who telephoned to Eisenhower and put Montgomery's case only to be told that the decision he was urging had already been taken.

Major-General Kenneth Strong, SHAEF Chief of Intelligence makes it quite clear* that the recommendation for the command change came in the first place from him to General Bedell Smith, the Chief of Staff, and was made on purely military grounds independently of Montgomery's activities or considerations of national prestige.

By December 20 the strain of a hundred hours of unremitting attack against every portion of the line was beginning to tell at First Army Headquarters and morale had not been helped by their having suddenly to abandon their well-organized and comfortable headquarters in Spa the day before. The arrival at Chaudfontaine of Field Marshal Montgomery, cheerful, brimming with confidence and carrying the aura of his great reputation was tremendously reassuring, as those who were there have admitted. Montgomery's own comment in his next report to the CIGS, 'They seemed delighted to have someone to give them orders,' could not have been far short of the mark.

But considering the unexpectedness and strength of the German attack on their weakest sector First Army had dealt with the emergency well and no doubt Montgomery for his part was also delighted to find that the situation was nothing like so bad as he had thought.

On the extreme left of the attacked front the defence of the Monschau–Höfen position had held and was now being taken over by a fresh infantry division, the 9th; the 2nd and 99th Infantry Divisions holding the Elsenborn ridge against Sixth SS Panzer Army had been reinforced just in time by the 1st Infantry Division. Thus the all-important northern shoulder was secure. The sector from Waimes to Stavelot was held by the 30th Infantry Division who, as well as pinning down Dietrich's 3rd Parachute, were also attacking Battlegroup Peiper's front and rear. The 3rd Armored Division and the 82nd Airborne Division were attacking Peiper with part of their forces while the rest, together with the 84th Infantry Division, were extending First Army's defence screen all the way to Marche. Finally contact had been re-established with the mixed force of armour, infantry and artillery holding out in St Vith.

General Manteuffel in his account of the battle has described this situation as 'a series of isolated actions' and credits

* In *Intelligence at the Top*. Cassel/Giniger. London, 1968.

462

Montgomery with extending the defensive front from Stavelot to Marche. This judgment does less than justice to First Army's dispositions and decisions already taken by December 20: the isolated actions—which had resulted inevitably from the number of German attacks—had been knit, in the north, into a coherent defence line—Monschau–Butgenbach–Malmédy; in the centre the major penetrations were being contained; the right flank was being screened and two counter-attacks had been ordered.

Valid criticism of First Army is that first reactions were slow and valuable time was lost, communications broke down and were not quickly re-established and in their appreciation of German intentions they clung too long to the belief that Liège was the main objective. Tactically, the counter-attacks were ordered too soon, certain forward positions were held without sufficient military justification and no attempt was made to create a reserve.

Montgomery was sure that the panzer armies were heading for the Meuse crossings south of Liège in order to debouch on to the flat ground and race north-west for Antwerp. He had already taken steps to block such an advance and now he wanted to strengthen First Army's east–west defence line allowing the German armour to flow south-west extending their lines of communication without a compensating advantage, while he built up a powerful reserve on their flank which could be used to destroy them at the right moment.

One of the remarks at the press conference which angered the American generals on the other half of the battlefield was, 'The battle has been most interesting; I think possibly one of the most interesting and tricky battles I have ever handled. The battle has some similarity to the one that began on 31st August 1942 when Rommel was "seen off" by the Eighth Army.'

The battle he referred to was Alam Halfa when the Afrika Korps was encouraged to advance for several miles between two strong British positions and, as Montgomery described in his memoirs, 'the strictest orders were issued that the armour was not to be loosed against Rommel's forces; it was not to move; the enemy was to be allowed to beat up against it and to suffer heavy casualties.' This had, in fact, happened and the German main panzer force, caught in the crossfire of dug-in guns and hull-down tanks, had apparently been about to be destroyed. Then, to Rommel's amazement, Montgomery had allowed him to withdraw without attempting to follow.

There is not space here to go into the pros and cons of Montgomery's decision but the significance of Alam Halfa for the Ardennes was its effect on the German High Command's assessment of what Montgomery would do* and the clue it gives to Montgomery's intentions, for he planned to use the same tactics again.

This necessitated the creation of a strong reserve placed along a natural defensive feature. The reserve could only be formed by breaking off offensive action wherever possible and withdrawing from salients to form a flankless front and the position chosen could only be maintained intact if the units along it did not become engaged prematurely. Montgomery attempted to bring about both these conditions and had his orders been carried out then a battle might well have ensued which bore some similarity to Alam Halfa—but they were not carried out.

As each division arrived to form the reserve it became embroiled in battle, reacting to attack with counter-attack, thus making it impossible to lead the Germans neatly into a tidy position from which they could be attacked by a fresh, waiting force. Furthermore, Hodges, encouraged unofficially by Bradley, flatly refused to withdraw anywhere on his left or centre, pointing out that to do so would mean the abandonment of St Vith. Instead he insisted on Ridgway's XVIII Airborne Corps attacking to push the Germans right back to the line Malmédy–St Vith–Houffalize. Considering the known strength of the German divisions involved this was a quite unrealistic objective. Chester Wilmot's comment, 'The stubborn determination to stand their ground was a source of great defensive strength to the Americans but sometimes it resulted in a considerable sacrifice to tactical flexibility and strategic balance,' sums up the situation on First Army's front. Nevertheless, Montgomery, rather surprisingly, agreed to this use of XVIII Airborne Corps.

Had any attempt been made to 'tidy up' the front by, for instance, creating a more or less straight-line defence from Monschau to Malmédy, the jammed SS Panzer Divisions would have been released with results that are now undeterminable but which would almost certainly have included the overwhelming of St Vith and, probably, the relief and strong reinforcement of Peiper.

Because Sixth Panzer Army's main forces were held almost at their start line and because Fifth Panzer Army's right wing

* And not only the High Command—Bayerlein, Panzer Lehr's commander, had been a colonel at Alam Halfa and concurred with Rommel's opinion that Montgomery 'was a very cautious man who was not prepared to take any sort of risk'.

attack was held for a critical period by the defence of St Vith, Montgomery was granted the time needed to bring in a new corps. These delays on the right of the German offensive together with the delay on the left caused by the defence of Bastogne meant that those German forces which did meet XVIII Airborne Corps and VII Corps were not heavy enough to break through the comparatively thin Allied line.

Then when Allied air attacks damaged the forward German units still further and virtually stopped their supplies the initiative slipped from the Germans and at close of battle on December 26 the offensive against Montgomery's front was halted, thus allowing him time to collect forces for a counter-offensive and to move them into position. A week later when that offensive was launched the German High Command had already ordered a withdrawal to a series of three lines, the first of which was La Roche to Bastogne. Consequently Montgomery did not, as he had planned, launch a strong attack against the flank of an overextended, advancing German force but against one deployed defensively and under orders to retreat.

But apparently none of this was appreciated by him at the time for he gleefully told the reporters how he thought he had fought the battle: 'The first thing I did was to get the battle area tidy—getting it sorted out. I got reserves into the right place and got balanced. I reorganized the American and British armies. It [VII Corps] took a knock. I said, "Dear me, this can't go on. It's being swallowed up in battle." I set to work and formed the corps again and once more it began to disappear in a defensive battle and I formed again—you must have a well-balanced, tidy show when you are mixed up in a dog fight.'

In fact the main fighting that went on between Manhay and Celles from December 21 to 26 which decided the battle in the northern half of the Ardennes never was 'a tidy show'. It could hardly have been less like the kind of warfare at which Montgomery excels for it was not a chess game but a bar-room brawl. It was a disorganized series of frenzied, fierce fights almost unrelated to each other and marked by faulty communications and command disputes at almost every level.

Ridgway, for instance, wanted the 7th Armored Division to stand and fight east of the Salm. Hasbrouck, their commander, said that if they did so there would be no more 7th Armored Division and Montgomery backed him up. But later the fiery Ridgway objected to pulling 82nd Airborne Division back to a practically impregnable ridge south of Werbomont

465

and this time Hodges backed him up. Montgomery gave way and 82nd Airborne were nearly lost when the Germans launched a powerful attack which captured Grandménil.

Chance and luck, not military reasoning, ruled the battlefield and the fighting was only resolved in the Allies favour by the inability of the German command to keep their armour fuelled, to reinforce their exhausted attacking troops or to replace their losses, to defend themselves against the tremendous air attacks or to match the speed and weight of the Allied build-up. Finally, of course, a major factor in the German failure was the totally unexpected ability of the American soldiers to recover from an overwhelming attack which tore up their front and produced chaos and confusion and to stand and fight and then to attack themselves. It was a reaction which upset the fine timing on which the offensive depended.

One half of the Battle of the Ardennes was handed over to Montgomery after four days, four critical days in which most of the things which doomed the offensive to failure had already taken place. Chance and other factors over which he had no control decreed that he would not be able to exercise that absolute control which was essential to his kind of generalship.

Field Marshal Lord Montgomery of Alamein is one of the very few soldiers of World War II to attain 'Great Captain' stature and his reputation rests firmly on the twin pillars of the Battle of North Africa and of the Invasion of North-west Europe. Nothing can ever rob him of his place in history, but when the final assessment of his career is made the Battle of the Ardennes will, I believe, not be considered one of his triumphs.

In the southern half of the battlefield the suddenness, ferocity and strength of the German attack seems at first to have stunned the Supreme Command and there was a dangerous delay of at least thirty-six hours in replying strategically and tactically to a major offensive. It was only the German inability at the end of 1944 to exploit this period which prevented them from at least reaching the Meuse. Deficiencies in men and matériel together with unbalanced deployment contributed to the Germans' initial failure but certainly as important as these things were those American units who held their positions where cold military logic said they could not, and so upset the timetable that the projected blitzkreig was turned into a slogging match which the Germans could not possibly win.

SHAEF and 12th Army Group concentrated their attention on that part of the assault front which was nearest to them and left the First and Ninth US Armies to deal with the attacks in the north on their own. Hodges, who lost operational control of VIII Corps early in the battle, told Montgomery that he had not seen Bradley or Eisenhower since the attack against his army had begun. Fortunately he and General Simpson, Ninth Army's commander, were lifelong friends and the transfer of divisions from one to the other was arranged informally over the telephone without reference to SHAEF, an 'irregularity' never envisaged by the German planners.

Because of the breakdown in communications and 'the considerable confusion and disorganization in the rear of the American troops'* very little was known at SHAEF about what was happening at the fighting line until about the third day—which is why most accounts of the battle begin then. Later, when the great German offensive had been defeated, the rôle of the companies who had taken the first shock, had held for valuable hours or even days before being overwhelmed, was played down while, not unnaturally, the units which had taken part in the final victory were written up in heroic terms. Propaganda too is a weapon of war and the dead do not give interviews.

General Patton on the other hand always made time to talk to the correspondents and his colourful personality and picturesque language ensured that Third Army was seldom out of the newspapers. Although it was not until the Germans in the west had been greatly weakened by the near-annihilation of their forces trapped in the Falaise pocket that Third Army was committed, Patton, convinced that the war had not been moving quickly enough, thought he would show how it should have been done.

Ignoring Bradley's orders to establish a strong force across the 'neck' of Brittany in order to stave off a possible counterattack from the east, he sent his armour instead racing west towards Brest. As there were practically no German troops in Brittany except those guarding the ports, Third Army were able to move fast, aided by the fifty thousand or so French underground who were starting to take over.

The public badly needed a morale-lifting fanfare of trumpets at this time and Patton's 'end run' was seized by the newspapers and played up for all it was worth. Bradley was very angry, saying that Patton seemed more interested in making headlines than using his head on tactics. 'George was stimulated by headlines,' he wrote after the war. 'The blacker they were the more

* As reported at the time by General Whitely, acting chief of staff for operations at SHAEF.

recklessly he fought.' It was General Patton's great good fortune that his superiors understood him so well, knew both his undoubted qualities and his weaknesses.

No other general would have dared to have pushed across France as quickly and as heedlessly as he did, but he was extremely fortunate in the unusual circumstances, for at any previous moment in the war or on any other front at that time he would probably have lost an army. But Georgie Patton, with his ivory-handled revolvers, his blistering language and his contempt for caution, was a maverick, an animal always greatly admired by the American public. The soldiers whom he pushed on so remorselessly may have grumbled a bit but they enjoyed the prestige that went with being one of 'Patton's boys'.

Everyone told stories about him, and if Eisenhower complained that Georgie Patton caused him more grey hairs than the Germans and Bradley was often infuriated by him, they nevertheless held him in great affection. He was a thorn in their sides, he was Peck's Bad Boy, he threw away the book and he was always offending someone, but he got away with it and he got things done; every man who was not in the front line being shot at himself thought Patton's rumbustious ways were how to win wars.

In the Ardennes, as we have seen, tactical control of the southern half of the battle was exercised by Patton, who started with a bang. His feat in disengaging a large part of his army from action on one front and swinging it through ninety degrees to attack on another in four days* fully deserved Bradley's praise, 'one of the most astonishing feats of generalship of our campaign in the West'. But after this dramatic start Third Army made disappointingly slow progress. Although three divisions backed by great numbers of guns and with dominant air support attacked an outnumbered, outgunned, outarmoured German force holding a hopelessly overextended line they were continually stopped and took five days to advance one armoured column, the westernmost, into Bastogne, another week to push the Germans away from the southern perimeter and a further two weeks to drive through to Houffalize.

But Patton, like Montgomery, had not been able to fight the kind of battle he liked: instead of an all-out attack concentrated on a narrow front designed to cut through the base of

---

* Not three days as is usually said: Patton started 10th Armored Division for Luxembourg and cancelled an attack by 6th Armored on December 17 and on the 18 stopped XIIth Corps' attack and ordered 4th Armored and 80th Infantry to prepare to move to Luxembourg. His counter-offensive began on December 22.

the salient—in short to reply to the German blitzkrieg with one of his own—he had to try to push a twenty-five-mile-wide front some twenty miles through country which seemed to consist of a series of natural defensive features. His attacking forces wore themselves down against Seventh Army's tough and elusive defences before arriving where Fifth Panzer Army was strong and, because it was now pulling divisions back from the point and at last receiving some of Sixth SS Panzer Army's divisions, getting stronger. Patton got his reinforcements late and committed them too soon with the results we have seen. Third Army's final complete victory was largely due to the Germans pulling back behind the West Wall when the Russian offensive began.

Apart from the speed with which he moved into battle General Patton did not add to his reputation in the Ardennes. He frankly admitted some of his mistakes in his memoirs but not that in his eagerness to show up Montgomery's slowness he launched two green divisions into battle without proper reconnaissance or preparation or that because he started his counter-offensive from the Bastogne area too soon it became a number of individual actions rather than a battle fought to an overall design. On a lesser scale his advancing a comparatively small task force at night ten miles through country which might well have been strongly held, in order to be able to claim that Third Army got to Houffalize at the same time as First Army, was risking lives for prestige and not military reasons.

But 'Georgie' Patton would not have been the great, aggressive leader of men that he was if he had not had his particular faults, a fact which, fortunately for him, was well understood by his superiors. Any attacking army needs to have a few reckless commanders who ignore cold facts and take chances which horrify the sober, calculating military brains. Patton's personal motto, 'Do not take counsel of your fears', exactly sums up his attitude to war, and if he was also sometimes inclined not to take counsel of his intelligence reports about the strength of the enemy the wonder is that he got away with it so often. He was a firm believer in reincarnation, 'remembering' his rôle in other wars and other times—if he comes back again in our time let us hope it is on the right side.

General Bradley, thought by many to have been the best of the American high command in Europe, was particularly unlucky with both the timing and the location of the German offensive. Caught without a single division in reserve and with a shortage of front line infantry which had already become the major problem, he was hit on a sector against which an offensive, at least of the dimensions it was reasonable to suppose the Germans could mount, made no kind of military sense. By stripping a defensive front and concentrating on a well-chosen place it is almost always possible to break through an attacker's front but unless there is at least a tactical objective of great importance the disadvantages which must follow are obvious. General Bradley has said that holding the Ardennes so lightly was 'a calculated risk' but this is only true in the sense that a line cannot be strong everywhere and there must always be places where an attack is least likely and these must obviously be most lightly held. Another of the myths of the Ardennes is that Allied Intelligence gave warning of the coming German offensive and here the germ of truth is that if all the intelligence reports are now carefully read some will be found to refer to the possibility. Some will also be found referring to other, equally startling possibilities.

Bradley cannot be faulted for not having anticipated the Offensive or for the weakness of the Ardennes front at a time when major offensives against the Germans were being prepared on either side of VIII Corps' sector. Nor should it be forgotten that his prompt despatch of 7th Armored and 10th Armored Divisions to the threatened sector certainly saved St Vith and probably Bastogne from falling.

He perhaps should have returned to Luxembourg City from Versailles sooner than he did and he certainly should have moved 12th Army Group Headquarters back to where he could control First and Ninth Armies despite the effect this would have had on civilian morale. He was naturally bitterly disappointed to lose those two armies to Montgomery after only three days of dealing with the situation and to be left with only one army commanded by a general he had always difficulty in controlling. His encouraging—to put it no stronger—Hodges to resist Montgomery's wish to yield ground to create a tidy front, though firmly in the American tradition, certainly made Montgomery's task more difficult. His threat to resign, with Patton's support, added to Eisenhower's heavy burden.

All in all the Ardennes Offensive did not greatly enhance Bradley's reputation either.

Finally we come to the Supreme Commander himself: by mid-December 1944, having concluded that all the plans for the next phase of the war had been made and the necessary order given, General Eisenhower had allowed himself to relax and to enjoy life a little more. He had been under great emotional and physical strain and needed a rest. The furious German onslaught caught him at a bad time and he found it

470

difficult to respond to the immediacy of the emergency. For a brief period there was a hesitancy in control at the top and, although by the Verdun meeting General Eisenhower was again functioning in top gear the damage had been done and the physical split in the Allied armies, brought about by the German advance, had become a split in command thinking and in mental attitude as well, with lack of trust, suspicion and jealousy on either side. For a time it looked as if though one of Hitler's objectives—internal dissension among the Western Allies—would be attained.

Eisenhower saw clearly, as he said in his Order of the Day, that in the Ardennes the Germans 'by rushing out of their fixed defences' had in fact done the one thing which would make it possible to destroy them and to end the war sooner but at the time the Germans seemed to be having such success that his prediction seemed unlikely. His plan for dealing with the offensive outlined at the Verdun meeting on December 19, to plug the holes in the north and launch a coordinated attack from the south, was amended the following day, after Montgomery had taken over, to launching a counter-offensive from both sides of the salient. The Supreme Commander did not hesitate to take large measures—the stopping of all offensive operations elsewhere, the turning over of most of Third Army's sector to 6th Army Group and authorizing withdrawal 'as far as necessary' in order to gain time and save troops. His action in handing over command of two American armies to Montgomery demonstrated once again his high moral courage. Among the reasons put forward by several German commanders for the failure of their offensive was 'enemy reacted more rapidly than expected', 'fast regrouping of American forces' and surprise that Montgomery's appointment did not have to be cleared with London and Washington.

His British critics claimed that Eisenhower was not a brilliant strategist, that his chief gifts were those of an administrator, that he was too easily swayed by his close associates. These changes were not borne out in the Ardennes emergency for after a slow start—which could be explained, at least in part, by his having to consider that the attack might have been the spoiling operation General Patton believed it to be—he decided on his strategy, as just outlined, which was unpopular with de Gaulle and de Lattre de Tassigny to say nothing of Churchill, but which was undoubtedly correct, and his tactics to deal with the immediate threat of the breakthrough. These were first to prevent it becoming an 'expanding torrent' by shoring up the shoulders then to slow down the point by driving into the flanks, then to blunt the point and, finally, to cut through the salient as near the base as possible. It was necessary for him to step firmly on both Bradley's and Patton's toes for these tactics to be carried out and he did not hesitate: 'Tell Georgie, Ike's running this war!' when Patton protested and, 'Well those are my orders, Brad,' when Bradley did.

Eisenhower matured late—after passing out 61st at West Point he came first in his class at the Command and General Staff School eleven years later—and he had no personal combat experience. Both these points would have counted against him in the British Army; neither would in the German. Perhaps this is why he was rated higher by his enemies than his allies.

Once their offensive had failed there was little sense in the Germans trying to hold on in the salient for it merely meant defending a long arc instead of a straight line and there were no important military objectives inside to justify that. But Hitler insisted that the surviving units of Army Group B stay where they were, yielding no ground. Most were concentrated in the west near the forward edge of the salient and while they were no longer strong enough to attack, the Allies daily grew stronger. It was an extremely vulnerable position and by all the rules should have resulted in their near complete destruction. Instead they were eventually allowed to withdraw almost all the men and weapons they had left behind the West Wall.

It is difficult to discover now why this happened, why the attacks at the base of the salient were not reinforced or why, after the juncture at Houffalize, the combined First and Third US Armies were not able to destroy the crippled, retreating German divisions. One German general has suggested that it was because they had by then had plenty of practice in withdrawing in front of a superior enemy through snow and ice. Undoubtedly the hard battle had taken a lot out of the American divisions involved and the weather conditions were appalling but both Bradley and Montgomery could, had they wished, have taken fresh troops from the concentrations they were preparing for the next offensives. In Montgomery's case his action in rapidly pulling all British troops away from the Ardennes and moving them back to Holland for his next battle had been admiringly described as 'maintenance of the objective'.

If the objective was the defeat of Germany then the wiping out of Sixth SS Panzer Army and Fifth Panzer Army, the cream of the German forces in the west, might have attained it. If the objective was to drive through the Ruhr come what may then Montgomery was right. Anyway the opportunity that was offered required Montgomery and Bradley to put aside their pet projects and work in harmony together and that was no longer possible.

Some battles catch the imagination of those at home and are translated into legend and their myths are then preferred to history. 'The Battle of the Bulge' is one of these and has already taken its place with The Alamo and The Battle of the Little Big Horn. Nevertheless, the historian must try to resurrect the truth, 'War's first casualty', and destroy the myths* although he will be angrily contradicted by those who participated, even vicariously, in something which has become folklore. The great German offensive on the Western Front which came when the Allies' road to victory seemed clear was a traumatic experience not only for the soldiers but for the civilians supporting them. It was natural to ignore the highly complex nature of what was happening and to see things in black and white: cowardice or heroism, total defeat or total victory, and this simplification and the myths have persisted: that the surprise blitzkrieg succeeded in breaking through the entire American front in the Ardennes and the Germans 'very nearly won the war'; that British troops were hurried to the front and stopped the rot while a handful of American paratroopers in Bastogne beat off hordes of 'fanatical Nazis' and Tiger tanks attacking continuously all round the perimeter; that Old Blood'n'Guts smashed through to relieve Bastogne and win the battle or, alternatively, that Montgomery took over and turned defeat into victory with a meticulously worked out 'master plan'.

Among the lesser myths are that large numbers of German paratroopers (mostly dressed as nuns) were dropped behind the American lines and there were hundreds of German soldiers in American uniform and speaking faultless English operating far behind the front, some of whom were trying to kill or kidnap Eisenhower.

The facts are less colourful: as one might have expected some front line units gave way under the weight of the attack, there was some panic and breakdown of discipline but there was also much solid resistance and occasional epic heroism; far from nearly winning the war the Germans did not achieve their first main objective, the establishment of Meuse bridgeheads; the principal contribution of the British troops in the early part of the battle was 'to be there', thus relieving the

* Robert E. Merriam in *Dark December* (New York, Ziff-Davis Publishing Co. 1947) dealt with many of these myths and skilfully demolished them.

Americans of the need to create a second line of defence west of the Meuse, later they were committed for a comparatively short time in an important but not a major rôle.

The Siege of Bastogne was truly heroic and it does not diminish the achievement of the airborne infantry, tank and artillery soldiers who were surrounded and refused to surrender to point out that there was a large element of bluff in the German claim to have the city surrounded in great strength and under threat of annihilation by their artillery. After 2nd Panzer Division moved on from Noville the northern half of the perimeter was only held lightly and most of the large calibre field guns were unable to move up. From the German point of view the siege kept a strong American force bottled up at a critical point and did not prevent the panzer divisions from going on to the Meuse.* Field Marshal Jodl said afterwards that Bastogne only became important because it was a pocket in the German rear after it was apparent that they were not going to be able to cross the Meuse. The battle of Bastogne that came after the relief caused more casualties than the siege.

We have seen that the parachute operation was a dismal failure and that Skorzeny's disguised commandos actually performed about one per cent of the bizarre feats attributed to them. There was never any plan to kidnap or assassinate Eisenhower. The contribution these irregular operations made to the offensive was the large number of Allied troops who were tied up by rumours of their activities.

As for the question 'Who won the battle—Patton or Montgomery?' the short answer is, neither—the Germans lost it.

Apart from the few surviving records the most revealing German sources on the Ardennes Offensive are the series of interviews with many of the commanders concerned carried out during their captivity. General Jodl talked frankly and at length giving a picture both of the large-scale intentions and of the extent of the failure of the plan.

It is accepted that one of the prime German mistakes was in not committing their reserves or switching the focal point of the offensive to exploit success soon enough. About this Jodl maintained that the trouble never was lack of troops but the severity and terrible conditions of the roads which stopped them from using all the troops they did have.

On the other hand Manteuffel, the most successful German

* On the other hand Jodl maintained that St Vith was an *absoluter Schlüsselpunkt* (absolute keypoint) because it blocked the way west and could not be bypassed.

474

commander, said that there were not enough troops and Fifth Panzer Army did not get reinforcements in time because Hitler was too concerned with 'his Waffen SS'. As well as the unexpected quick reaction of the Americans and their command of the air, Manteuffel blames the failure of supply, saying that for camouflage reasons most supply dumps were east of the Rhine and there was fatal delay in bringing up even the most urgently needed ammunition and supplies for the fighting troops.

Other German commanders find other reasons: Dietrich said, '... it was mainly bad preparation, lack of fuel, supplies and training plus the time of year—in that order.' Kraemer, his Chief of Staff, gave as his reasons: quality of men and leaders at the late stage of the war; the German army was not as mobile as it had been; bad roads coupled with bad driving; the Allied Air Force. Buechs, one of Jodl's staff officers, says the decisive factor was the failure to secure the heights of Elsenborn. 'Jodl saw great danger from that direction (because I SS Panzer Corps' route lay south of the Elsenborn ridge) and said on December 19 that we would not succeed in breaking through and crossing the Meuse before you could bring reserves up to hold the Meuse line and make counter-attacks.'

On the American side Hugh M. Cole the author of the American army's fine account of the battle gives six reasons why the German armoured mass did not move forward as planned: unexpectedly tough American resistance; supply failure; Germans denied free use of the road net; the jamming of the shoulders; attack lacked depth due to slowness of the build-up; the quick American tactical reaction. It will be seen that both sides find considerable common ground.

Absolute truth will forever elude us: 'It is as impossible to describe a battle as a Ball,' was how Wellington put it. But we will always try, and although it is quite unreal—and unfair—to re-fight a battle on paper with the advantage of hindsight that too will always be done. Prefaced with that apology my own attempt after three years' close study (and six years in tanks in World War II) might be allowed.

I have already made it clear that I consider the delay imposed on the assault wave by the stand of some American troops at the shoulders and in the centre was the first and also one of the most important reasons for the German failure. The offensive had to achieve a tactical breakthrough within three days if it were to have any chance of complete success. Next the rapid Allied reshuffling and redeployment of large formations was vital to them and the contribution of the air force, once the weather cleared, was enormous. Later the determination and persistence with which the counter-attacks were prosecuted and the willingness of the divisions concerned to take casualties broke the back of the equally determined and persistent German attackers.

But could the Germans have succeeded or at least have accomplished more than they did?

Although the odds against a major German offensive wholly succeeding anywhere in December 1944 were undoubtedly very long there were no alternatives, so Hitler, having brought off daring gambles in the past, decided to stake everything on one great blow.

I think he decided on the right front and the best sector but I think the length of American front chosen for the breakthrough, even though undermanned, was too long and that the strategic objective, Antwerp, was too far away. Brussels, the capture of which would have meant a major change in the war in the west, was only forty to fifty miles from the Meuse crossings and was practically undefended, while there were strong British and Canadian forces in the vicinity of Antwerp. Also, had Brussels fallen Antwerp would have become untenable.

There is not space to go into a suggested shorter assault front in detail but briefly one that ran from Losheim to Roth would, I think, have offered a better chance of a quick breakthrough. In that case the northern hard shoulder would have run from the Elsenborn ridge along the high ground to Spa. The Elsenborn area would have been assaulted by a dawn paratroop drop and then attacked from the south by the first panzer and volksgrenadier forces through the Losheim Gap, the major entry point.

The southern hard shoulder might have been established from opposite Diekirch and through that place along the high ground north of the rivers to Wiltz and Bastogne.

The available armour, five panzer divisions (allowing one each for the setting up of the hard shoulders) might have taken three routes for the Meuse crossings between Huy and Dinant (including both). Two panzer divisions and supporting infantry through the Losheim Gap to Huy and Andenne; one panzer division and supporting infantry through the sector between Bleialf and Ouren and two panzer divisions and supporting infantry going through Dasburg and Clervaux towards Houffalize and then to Namur and Dinant.

Seventh Army, with a panzer division added, would have had the sole responsibility for the capture of Bastogne as well as protecting 5th Panzer Army's left flank. The strong forces flowing west from either side of the Schnee Eifel would have seized St Vith on the way.

Once across the Meuse, as has been indicated, the reserve panzer divisions would race for Brussels with the main force on the right and a smaller mixed force going east of Charleroi and west of Brussels to sweep round and, by joining the main force moving north-west, cutting off Brussels and severing Antwerp's routes south.

I think such a plan would have succeeded in establishing Meuse bridgeheads but, after all, XXX Corps (British) were out of battle and would undoubtedly have been committed before Brussels. Further, the American Divisions which in the event moved into St Vith and Bastogne and which formed the Ourthe river line would have been available to attack both flanks of the penetration. One has to conclude that it is extremely unlikely that the Germans could have reached Brussels for they were simply not strong enough to do so.

Today, a quarter of a century later, it is possible to find traces of the fierce fighting if you get off the roads and walk through the woods and rugged countryside. Along some of the smaller rivers the temporary bridges are still in place, in some market squares a huge Tiger or Panther quietly rusts away, at some crossroads there are the remains of the guns. The Ardennes has recovered from its awful punishment and the shattered villages and towns have been rebuilt. The older people remember the nightmare clearly; to the younger it is all part of many futile past wars and some of them who live in places which escaped destruction envy those in the villages which are almost all new buildings.

There are other reminders too—memorials and war cemeteries, in one of which one of the plain white crosses among thousands bears the army number 02605 and the name George S. Patton Jr., for he was buried in the Ardennes at his own request.

The twenty thousand Europeans who died in the Battle of the Ardennes would have been disagreeably surprised if they could have been vouchsafed a glimpse of what the final result of their fight was to be.

Historically speaking the major effect of Hitler's decision to launch his offensive on the western front was the effect it had on the final positions of the armies invading Germany, with consequent political results. The Western Allies' advance into Germany was postponed for five weeks while the Russians' final offensive was brought forward by eleven days. When Roosevelt and Churchill met Stalin at Yalta on February 4, 1945, the Russian leader was able to negotiate from strength. After reminding his allies that the offensive in January had been launched in reply to Churchill's appeal for help and had been a 'moral duty', quite unconnected with the obligations accepted by Russia at the last meeting in Teheran, he called upon General Antonov to give an account of what had been accomplished in just over three weeks.

Warsaw had been captured, Budapest was under siege and eleven panzer divisions were pinned down around it, the German forces in East Prussia had been fragmented and those in upper Silesia encircled. The foremost Russian troops were only forty miles from Berlin.

Against these impressive accomplishments all the Western Allies could throw on their side of the scales were paper plans.

Shrewdly Stalin asked for no advantage, being content to store up credits to be used in future bargaining and relying on Roosevelt's instinctive response to an unselfish action. But in the ensuing grave discussions which were largely to settle the fate of Europe for a generation or more the relative position of the Russian, American and British forces was one of the few concrete facts among all the surmise and speculation and it carried great weight. Other important factors at Yalta were Churchill's gratitude for the 'noble venture' of the premature Russian offensive and Roosevelt's complete trust in Stalin's good will.*

Some seven weeks later when the decision was taken by Eisenhower not to push his forces on to Berlin one of the reasons was American belief at the top that Russia was not pursuing political aims. 'Berlin,' Stalin wrote to Eisenhower, 'has lost its former strategic importance.' This statement was accepted by Eisenhower, Marshall and Roosevelt, despite Churchill's vehement protestations. Stalin cashed his Ardennes credit when it brought him maximum advantage.

Hitler's movement of large forces from east to west and the priorities granted to Army Group B, which took almost all of Germany's war production for a critical period, seriously weakened the Germans on the Eastern Front. Also, in early January the Allied counter-offensive was pinning down many divisions in the west and keeping the German High Command fully occupied. These factors were probably more important in

* 'Of one thing I am certain,' the President said, 'Stalin is not an imperialist.'

the Russian decision to bring their January offensive forward than Stalin's 'moral duty'.

Russian historians have never admitted this but have persisted in two incompatible claims—on the one hand insisting that the Ardennes Offensive was not a serious attack at all but only a sortie in force, while on the other maintaining that the Western Allies were only saved from a crushing defeat by the opening of the Russian Offensive on January 12. The numbers of troops and weight of war matériel involved are sufficient answer to the first claim—Field Marshal von Rundstedt described the Ardennes Offensive as 'Stalingrad No. 2'—and we have seen that all chances of a major German victory had disappeared by as early as December 26 when, as the German War Diary itself records, the original far-reaching strategic aim was abandoned and limited tactical ones substituted.

Hitler's real objective in mounting a last desperate Offensive against the Western Allies in December 1944 was not to win the war, for by then even he knew that was impossible, but to create a situation in which Germany, thought defeated, might remain whole.

He believed that if his panzer armies could split the Western Allies they would accept a stalemate on their front and allow him to switch his strength to the east. Then, he thought, the Russians in turn might offer terms which would more or less leave their armies where they were. These assumptions were, of course, completely mistaken, for nothing short of a German nuclear weapon could, by December 1944, have stopped the Western Allies and Russia from occupying all Germany. Hitler, who understood the psychology of the German people so well, was always mistaken when he tried to assess other nationalities.

It is one of the ironies of history that the long-term result of Hitler's attempt to keep Germany intact is that today East Germany's frontier lies about a hundred miles further west than it would have done had the Ardennes Offensive never been launched.

ORDER OF BATTLE

THE ARDENNES OFFENSIVE
December 16, 1944–January 2, 1945

GERMAN

1st SS Panzer Division
2nd SS Panzer Division
9th SS Panzer Division
12th SS Panzer Division

Panzer Lehr Division

2nd Panzer Division
9th Panzer Division
116th Panzer Division

3rd Parachute Division
5th Parachute Division

9th Volksgrenadier Division
12th Volksgrenadier Division
18th Volksgrenadier Division
26th Volksgrenadier Division
62nd Volksgrenadier Division
79th Volksgrenadier Division
167th Volksgrenadier Division
212th Volksgrenadier Division
246th Volksgrenadier Division
272nd Volksgrenadier Division
276th Volksgrenadier Division
277th Volksgrenadier Division
326th Volksgrenadier Division
340th Volksgrenadier Division
352nd Volksgrenadier Division
560th Volksgrenadier Division

3rd Panzer Grenadier Division
15th Panzer Grenadier Division

Fuehrer Begleit Brigade
Fuehrer-Grenadier Brigade
150 Brigade (Skorzeny)

US

2nd Armored Division
3rd Armored Division
4th Armored Division
6th Armored Division
7th Armored Division
9th Armored Division
10th Armored Division
11th Armored Division

17th Airborne Division
82nd Airborne Division
101st Airborne Division

1st US Infantry Division
2nd US Infantry Division
4th US Infantry Division
5th US Infantry Division
9th US Infantry Division
26th US Infantry Division
28th US Infantry Division
30th US Infantry Division
35th US Infantry Division
75th US Infantry Division
80th US Infantry Division
83rd US Infantry Division
84th US Infantry Division
87th US Infantry Division
99th US Infantry Division
106th US Infantry Division

BRITISH

51st (Highland) Division
53rd (Welsh) Division

29th Armoured Brigade (11th Armoured Division)

6th Airborne Division

A SELECTIVE BIBLIOGRAPHY

This is divided into three parts: the principal published works consulted; a list of secondary, but most useful, sources; general works, pamphlets and articles. Not all books read in the four years it took to write this book are listed and other main sources, unpublished, are described in the Foreword.

1. MAIN WORKS

Relevant volumes of the official American history, *The United States Army in World War II: The European Theatre of Operations* published by the Office of the Chief of Military History Department of the Army (hereafter referred to as OCMH) in Washington D.C. Various dates. The most important are:

Cole, H. M., *The Ardennes: The Battle of the Bulge*.

Pogue, F. C., *The Supreme Command*.

Bradley, Omar N., *A Soldier's Story*. Eyre & Spottiswoode, London, 1951. New York, 1951.

Bryant, Arthur, *Triumph in the West*. Collins, London, 1959.

Churchill, Winston, *Triumph and Tragedy*. Vol. VI of *The Second World War*. Cassell, London, 1954.

De Guingand, Francis, *Operation Victory*. Hodder & Stoughton, London, 1947.

Ehrman, John, *Grand Strategy* (Vols. V & VI). HMSO, London, 1956.

Eisenhower, Dwight D., *Crusade in Europe*. Heinemann, London, 1949. Doubleday, New York, 1945.

Ellis, L. F., *Victory in the West* (Vol. II), HMSO, London, 1969.

Horrocks, B. G., *A Full Life*. Collins, London, 1960.

Liddell Hart, Basil, *The Other Side of the Hill*. Cassell, London, 1948.

Luttichau, C. V. P. von, *The German Counteroffensive in the Ardennes*. In *Command Decisions*, OCMH, Washington, 1960.

Manteuffel, Hasso von, *The Battle of the Ardennes 1944–5*. (In *Decisive Battles of World War II: The German View* edited by Jacobsen and Rohwer.) André Deutsch, London, 1965.

Marshall, S. L. A., *Bastogne: The Story of the First Eight Days*. Infantry Journal Press, Washington, 1946.

Merriam, R. E., *Dark December*. Ziff Davis, Chicago, 1947.

Montgomery, Bernard L., *Normandy to the Baltic*. Hutchinson, London, 1947.

Nobécourt, Jacques, *Le Dernier Coup de Dés de Hitler*. Robert Laffont, Paris, 1962.

Patton, George S., *War As I Knew It*. W. H. Allen, London, 1947. Houghton Mifflin, Boston, 1947.

Shulman, Milton, *Defeat in the West*. Secker & Warburg, London, 1947. Dutton & Co., New York, 1948.

Skorzeny, Otto, *Skorzeny's Special Missions*. Robert Hale, London, 1947.

Strong, Kenneth, *Intelligence at the Top*. Cassell, London, 1948.

Wilmot, Chester, *The Struggle for Europe*. Collins, London, 1952.

2. SECONDARY SOURCES

Arend, Guy Franz, *The Battle of the Bulge*. Nuts Museum, Bastogne, n.d.

Bekker, Cajus, *The Luftwaffe War Diaries*. Macdonald, London, 1967.

Bernard, Henri, *La Résistance 1940–1945*. La Renaissance du Livre, Brussels, 1968.

Blond, Georges, *L'Agonie de L'Allemagne 1944–1945*. Librairie Arthème Fayard, Paris, 1952.

Buchanan, A. R., *The United States and World War II*. Harper & Row, New York, 1964.

Bullock, Alan, *Hitler, A Study in Tyranny*. Odhams, London, 1952.

Butcher, Harry C., *My Three Years With Eisenhower*. Heinemann, London, 1946. Simon & Schuster, New York, 1946.

Butler and Young, *Marshal Without Glory*. Hodder & Stoughton, London, 1951.

Cartier, Raymond, *Hitler et Ses Généraux*. Librairie Arthème Fayard, Paris, 1962.

Cole, Hugh M., *The Lorraine Campaign*. US Army in World War II, OCMH, Washington.

Critchell, Laurence, *Bastogne*. (In *Combat European Theater World War II*.) Dell, New York, 1958.

Crouquet. Roger, *La Bataille des Ardennes*. Editions Libération 44, Brussels, 1945.

D'Arcy-Dawson, John, *European Victory*. Macdonald, London, n.d.

Delaval, L. S. D., *La Bataille des Ardennes: G.I. Joe Plaide Non Coupable!* Imprimérie Médicale et Scientifique, Brussels, 1958.

Farago, Ladislas, *Patton: Ordeal and Triumph*. Arthur Barker, London. 1966.

Flower and Reeves (Eds), *The War 1939–1945*. Cassell, London, 1960.

Foley, John, *Mailed Fist*. Panther, London, 1957.

Freiden and Richardson (Eds), *The Fatal Decisions*. Michael Joseph, London, 1956. Morrow & Co., New York, 1956.

Fuller, J. F. C., *The Second World War 1939–45*. Eyre & Spottiswoode, London, 1948.

Gaulle, Charles de, *The War Memoirs* (Vol. III). Simon & Schuster, New York, 1955.

Gilbert, Felix, *Hitler Directs His War*. Oxford University Press, New York, 1950.

Goldston, Robert, *The Life and Death of Nazi Germany*. Phoenix House, London, 1968.

Gorlitz, Walter (Ed), *The Memoirs of Field-Marshal Keitel*. William Kimber. London, 1965.

Greenfield, Palmer and Wiley, *The Army Ground Forces. The Organisation of Ground Combat Troops*. US Army in World War II, OCMH, Washington. 1947.

Guderian, Heinz, *Panzer Leader*. E. P. Dutton, New York, 1952.

Heydte, F.-A. von, *Daedalus Returned*.

Kennedy, John, *The Business of War*. Hutchinson, London, 1957.

Killen, John. *The Luftwaffe: A History*. Frederick Muller, London, 1967.

Liddell Hart, Basil, *A History of the Second World War*. Cassell, London, 1969.

Liddell Hart, Basil, *Strategy—The Indirect Approach*. Faber, London, 1954.

Liddell Hart, Basil, *The Tanks: The History of the Royal Tank Regiment*. Cassell, London, 1959.

Macdonald, Charles B., *The Siegfried Line Campaign*. US Army in World War II. OCMH, Washington D.C., 1963.

Macksey, K. J., *Panzer Division: The Mailed Fist*. Ballantine Books. New York, 1968.

Macmillan, Norman, *The Royal Air Force in the World War*. Vol. IV.

Manstein, Erich von, *Lost Victories*. Henry Regnery, Chicago, 1958.

Mellenthin, F. W. von, *Panzer Battles*. University of Oklahoma Press, Norman, 1956.

Moorehead, Alan, *Montgomery: A Biography*. Hamish Hamilton, London, 1946.

O'Neill, R. J., *The German Army and the Nazi Party*.

Pitt, Barrie (Ed), *Purnell's History of the Second World War*. British Printing Corporation, London, 1960.

Ridgway, Matthew, *Soldier: Memoirs*. Harper, New York, 1956.

Ryan, Cornelius, *The Last Battle*. Simon & Schuster, New York, 1966.

Saunders, H. St George, *The Red Beret*. Michael Joseph, London, 1950.

Shirer, William L., *The Rise and Fall of the Third Reich*. Simon & Schuster, New York, 1959. Secker & Warburg, London, 1960.

Stacey, C. P., *The Victory Campaign*. Vol. III of the Official History of the Canadian Army in the Second World War. Department of National Defence, Ottawa, 1960.

Stein, George H., *The Waffen SS: Hitler's Elite Guard at War 1939–45*. Cornell University Press, New York, 1966.

Summersby, Kay, *Eisenhower Was My Boss*. Werner Laurie, London, 1949.

Thomas, Lowell, *History As You Heard It*. Doubleday, New York, 1957.

Thompson, R. W., *The Battle for the Rhineland*. Hutchinson, London, 1958.

Toland, John, *Battle: The Story of the Bulge*. Muller, London, 1960.

Trevor-Roper. H. R. (Ed), *Hitler's War Directives 1939–45*. Sidgwick & Jackson, London, 1964.

Warlimont, Walter, *Inside Hitler's Headquarters 1939–45*. Weidenfeld & Nicolson, London, 1946.

Williams, Mary H., *Chronology: 1941–45*. US Army in World War II, OCMH, Washington, 1960.

3. OTHER PUBLISHED SOURCES

Battle Babies: A History of the 99th Infantry Division.
Brest to Bastogne: The Story of the 6th Armored Division.
Conquer: The Story of the Ninth Army.
The 84th Infantry Division in the Battle for Germany.
The History of the 26th Yankee Division.
Lucky Forward: The History of Patton's Third U.S. Army.
Mission Accomplished: The Story of the Fighting Corps (the XVIIIth Airborne Corps).
Saga of the All American (82nd Airborne Division).
St. Vith: Lion in the Way (106th Infantry Division).
A Short History of the First U.S. Army in World War II.
Short History of the Seventh Armored Division June 1943–July 1945.
The Story of the 11th Armored Division (American).
Taurus Pursuant: A History of the 11th Armoured Division (British).
Victory Division in Europe: A History of the Fifth US Armored Division.
Work Horse of the Western Front: The Story of the 30th Infantry Division.

486

487

488

489

490

491

493

503

Pironpré: 438

Pogue. *See Supreme Command, The*

Police. *See* Military Police

Poteaux: 218, 221, 305–7, 312, 364, 366, 367, 368

POZIT fuse: 350, 350 n.

Presidential Citation. *See* Distinguished Unit Citation

Press. *See* Montgomery

Priess, General Hermann: 372

Prisoners: 73
  captured Allied: 196, 197, 205, 207, 222, 225, 227, 229, 300, 314, 333, 353, 369, 373, 453
  captured German: 167, 178, 185, 187, 249, 312, 401, 402, 415, 428 n.
  orders to shoot: 80, 190, 194, 227, 228

Pronsfeld: 164

Prüm: 162, 164, 309

Radios and Radar: 104, 110, 146, 166, 167, 172, 184, 229, 235, 239, 296, 336, 383, 393. *See also* Communications; Intelligence

Rahier: 293

Railroads: 73, 97, 136, 244

Rambrouch: 379

Rastenburg: 308

Rations. *See* Shortages; Supply

Recht: 215, 220, 221, 298, 305, 364, 369

Reconnaissance patrols: *See* Patrols

Reconnaissance troops: 161, 174, 209, 219, 235, 298, 401

'Red Ball Highway': 119, 268, 378

Regimental Combat Teams. *See* Teams

Regne: 403

Reims: 238, 265, 266, 286, 289, 293, 437

Reinforcements: 112, 137, 149, 174, 178, 179, 185, 187, 188, 205, 211, 212, 216, 239, 243, 250, 265, 268, 274, 292, 294, 303, 304, 318, 334, 347, 362, 419, 433

Reinforcements, German: 73,

125, 268, 292, 314, 320, 327, 378, 392, 436

Reisdorf: 114

Remagne: 415

Remer, Colonel Otto: 83, 307, 308, 313, 364, 368, 369, 401, 402, 430, 431, 439

Remichampagne: 426

Removille: 388, 424, 426

Remouchamps: 238

Rhineland Battle: 264, 450

Rhine River: 57, 59, 71, 72, 73, 74, 125, 181, 261–3, 269, 272, 395, 436, 450

Ribbentrop, Joachim von: 31

Ridge, Lt.-Col.: 220

Ridgway, Maj.-Gen. Matthew, B.: 294, 340, 409
  and command of XVIII Airborne Corps: 294, 298, 310, 338, 341, 354
  and St Vith withdrawal: 315, 364–5, 370, 464, 465

8th Rifle Brigade: 336, 413

River crossings. *See* Bridges; Bridging operations; Ferries; and rivers by name

Roadblocks: 105, 151, 176, 190, 196, 206, 209, 210, 218, 230, 231, 233, 236–9, 272, 276, 278, 280, 282, 284–7, 291, 293, 298, 300, 320, 335, 343, 358, 392

Road nets: 119, 121, 163, 177, 192, 193, 208, 241. *See also* Obstacles.

Roberts, Colonel William: 242, 278, 281–4, 315, 318, 319, 323, 356–8

Robertson, Maj.-Gen. Walter M.: 85, 103, 156, 326

Rochefort: 349, 391, 398, 410–15, 418, 443

Rocherath–Krinkelt: 77, 84, 85, 95, 97–100, 120, 197 n., 228, 241–4, 266, 274, 326–9

Rodt: 313, 364, 367, 368

Roer dams: 67, 70, 73, 104, 156, 178, 183, 264, 339

Roer River: 71, 73, 186

Rogery: 366, 368, 369

505

506

Tadler: 382
Tank Battalions
  31st: 219
  37th: 426
  70th: 248, 252, 254
  707th: 150, 199–202, 276, 278
  740th: 294, 341
  771st: 401
Tank Destroyer Battalions
  630th: 276
  705th: 286–7, 325, 387
Tank Destroyers: 294
  losses: 347, 350, 370
  self-propelled: 287, 301
  towed: 289–91, 370
Tanks
  Comet: 336
  Crocodile (flame-throwing): 415
  light: 158, 199, 345
  losses: 199–202, 204, 205, 210,
    222, 232, 254, 278, 287,
    290, 299, 315, 316, 323–
    5, 346, 353, 393, 401,
    405, 415, 433, 438, 441
  medium: 153, 219, 299, 345,
    381
  Sherman: 43, 62, 149, 194, 198,
    199, 202, 204, 209, 229,
    239, 248, 284, 290, 291,
    295, 300, 305, 314, 320,
    324, 345, 353, 378, 380,
    392, 401, 409, 412–13,
    428, 431–2
Tanks, German: 27, 36, 62, 125,
    154, 229
  losses: 196, 202, 230, 232, 233,
    237, 290, 305, 317, 318,
    325, 328, 346, 348, 393,
    396, 405, 406, 412, 415,
    430
  Mark IV: 38, 139, 193, 196,
    198, 199, 202, 209, 210,
    222, 239, 308
  Mark V (Panther): 38, 43, 62,
    119, 130, 139, 193, 196,
    200, 204, 206, 209, 210,
    229–33, 239, 323, 329,
    385, 407, 409, 414,
    444
  Mark VI (Tiger): 27, 36, 62, 72,
    119, 174, 177, 193, 230,
    233, 239, 290, 314, 323,
    353, 372, 385, 473
  T 34: 40

Tiger II (Jagdtiger): 79, 119,
    188, 193
Tank Replacement Centre (Brus-
    sels): 457
Task Forces: 111, 251. See also
    Teams
  A (CCB 2nd US Armored Divi-
    sion): 413
  B (CCB 2nd US Armored Divi-
    sion): 413
  Booth: 211
  Chamberlain: 253
  Ezell: 358
  Harper: 208, 209, 282
  Hogan: 344, 345, 347
  Jones: 311, 312, 366, 369
  Kane: 343, 345, 347, 348
  Lohse: 368
  Lovelady: 299, 303, 353, 371
  Luckett: 249, 253
  Navaho: 305
  Pat: 438, 439
  Poker: 438, 439
  Riley: 254, 332
  Rose: 208, 209, 281
  SNAFU: 356
  Standish: 254, 332
  Tucker: 343
Tassigny, de Lattre de: 471
Taylor, Maj.-Gen. Maxwell D.:
    426
Teams: See also Task Forces
  Browne: 361, 384
  Cherry: 211, 280, 282, 283,
    315–18, 319
  Desobry: 283, 320, 322
  O'Hara: 282, 318, 384
  Pyle: 359
  117th Regiment of 30th Divi-
    sion: 234, 235
  119th Regiment of 30th Divi-
    sion: 234, 238, 239
Telephone Communications: See
    Communications.
Teller mines: 428
Tenneville: 349
Theux: 296
Thionville: 269, 280
Tillet: 390
Tintange: 388, 424
Traffic control: 219, 221, 284,
    317, 368. See also Ob-
    stacles; Roads; With-
    drawal operations

508

About the Author

PETER ELSTOB, English-born, a graduate of the University of Michigan, lives in London. He served with the British unit in the Battle of the Bulge and is the author of several volumes, among them *Bastogne: The Road Block* and *Battle of the Reichswald,* both published by Ballantine Books.